Studies in the History of Medieval Religion
VOLUME LVIII

THE PASSION AND MIRACLES OF ST. THOMAS
BECKET BY BENEDICT OF PETERBOROUGH

Studies in the History of Medieval Religion

ISSN 0955-2480

Founding Editor
Christopher Harper-Bill

Series Editor
Frances Andrews

Previously published titles in the series are listed at the back of this volume

THE PASSION AND MIRACLES OF ST. THOMAS BECKET BY BENEDICT OF PETERBOROUGH

TRANSLATED BY
RACHEL KOOPMANS

THE BOYDELL PRESS

© Rachel Koopmans 2025

Some rights reserved. Without limiting the rights under copyright reserved above, any part of this book may be reproduced, stored in or introduced into a retrieval system, or transmitted, in any form or by any means (electronic, mechanical, photocopying, recording or otherwise)

The right of Rachel Koopmans to be identified as the author of this work has been asserted in accordance with sections 77 and 78 of the Copyright, Designs and Patents Act 1988

First published 2025

The Boydell Press, Woodbridge

ISBN 978 1 83765 264 8 (Hardback)
978 1 83765 271 6 (Paperback)

The Boydell Press is an imprint of Boydell & Brewer Ltd
PO Box 9, Woodbridge, Suffolk IP12 3DF, UKw
and of Boydell & Brewer Inc.
668 Mt Hope Avenue, Rochester, NY 14620-2731, USA
website: www.boydellandbrewer.com

Our Authorised Representative for product safety in the EU is Easy Access System Europe – Mustamäe tee 50, 10621 Tallinn, Estonia, gpsr.requests@easproject.com

A CIP catalogue record for this book is available from the British Library

Open Access Licence: CC–BY–NC–ND

The publisher has no responsibility for the continued existence or accuracy of URLs for external or third-party internet websites referred to in this book, and does not guarantee that any content on such websites is, or will remain, accurate or appropriate

Please be advised that this book contains discussions of violence which readers may find disturbing or shocking.

In memory of Kathleen McGarvey, Bridget Chérie Harper, and Nora Faires

Contents

Acknowledgements	viii
Note on the Translation	x
List of Abbreviations	xiv
Introduction	1
The Passion of St. Thomas Becket	60
The Miracles of St. Thomas Becket	76
Prologue	76
Book I	82
Book II	109
Book III	164
Book IV	216
Additions	296
Biographical Notes	305
Appendix: William of Canterbury, The Parallel Miracles	323
Select Bibliography	355
Index of Biblical Allusions	366
General Index	370

Acknowledgements

Any project such as this involves many debts. I am grateful to the Social Sciences Research Council of Canada for providing funding for my work on Benedict's *Passion and Miracles* and the Thomas Becket miracle windows of Canterbury Cathedral, and to Janet Friskney for helping me craft a successful SSHRC application. My colleagues in the history department of York University in Toronto, particularly Marlene Shore, Margaret Schotte, Jennifer Bonnell, Deborah Neill, Richard Hoffman, Tom and Libby Cohen, Joan Judge, Marlee Couling, Barry Torch, and Ludia Bae, have provided much support and encouragement. So have my colleagues at the Pontifical Institute for Medieval Studies, with special thanks to James Carley and Ann Hutchison, and to a former PIMS Mellon Fellow, now medieval and early modern librarian of the Wellcome Collection in London, Elma Brenner. Like all medievalists living in Toronto, I have been blessed to be able to draw on the extraordinary resources of the PIMS library: long may it flourish.

John Van Engen helped this project get off the ground and saw it through to completion. I am very grateful for his friendship and for his continuing mentorship of his long-graduated student. Shelagh Sneddon reviewed the entire translation for accuracy, provided numerous corrections, and also caught biblical echoes that I had missed. I am so thankful for her help. John Jenkins generously read and commented on the entire translation, saving me from errors and providing a great deal of practical aid and information. Anne Duggan has led the way in so much Becket scholarship. Her interest in my work, which began when I was just starting out as an assistant professor, has meant a great deal. This translation is indebted to her path-breaking publications on the manuscripts of Benedict's *Miracles*.

My work on Benedict's *Passion and Miracles* has progressed in tandem with a major project re-examining the glorious stained glass picturing Becket's miracles in Canterbury Cathedral. My colleagues at the cathedral, particularly Léonie Seliger and the glaziers of the stained glass conservation studio, Cressida Williams and the cathedral archivists, and Caroline Plaisted and the many wonderful Friends of Canterbury Cathedral, have cheered this translation on and patiently waited for its appearance. My academic colleagues in Canterbury, particularly Sheila Sweetinburgh and Emily Guerry, have gone above and beyond to support my work and make Canterbury feel like home, as have my generous hosts, Simon and Mary Brown.

Over the course of my career, I have tried out my ideas about Benedict's *Miracles* in numerous conference presentations, lectures, essays, and journal articles. The venues, audiences, editors, and reviewers are too numerous to name here, but I am very grateful for their input. The comments and suggestions of the anonymous reviewer at Boydell Press and the careful reading of Caroline Palmer have brought this work to publication.

Friends and family members have seen this project through over the past decade. I am especially thankful to Jeanne Petit, Linda and Rick Groen, and my brother Ryan Koopmans. My parents, Sherwin and Karen Koopmans, read and commented on the introduction and very generously provided more than two-thirds of the cost for this text to be made Open Access. They see this as "a gift to humanity." I am very grateful for that and for the innumerable gifts they have given to me.

I dedicate this translation to the memory of three dear and much-missed friends taken before their time: Kathleen McGarvey, Bridget Chérie Harper, and Nora Faires. I have thought of them often as I have translated these stories.

Note on the Translation

THIS translation is based on the edition of Benedict of Peterborough's *Passion and Miracles of St Thomas of Canterbury* published in 1876 by James Craigie Robertson for the Rolls Series.[1] I have changed the title "of St. Thomas of Canterbury" to "of St. Thomas Becket" for easier name recognition.[2] Some portions of the *Passion* were translated by Canon A. J. Mason in 1920 and by Michael Staunton in 2001. Translations of select miracles have appeared in a variety of publications, with the largest number to be found in Edwin Abbott's 1898 study *St Thomas of Canterbury: His Death and Miracles*.[3] This is the first full English translation of the *Passion and Miracles*.

The *Passion*, as the name implies, focuses just on Becket's last day and the aftermath of his death. It was not embraced by medieval readers, who preferred more expansive *Lives*. There is no manuscript that contains the *Miracles* that also includes the *Passion*, and in fact no complete copy of the *Passion* is known to survive.[4] Fortunately, the writer Elias of Evesham utilized large portions of the *Passion* in the late twelfth-century compilation now known as the *Quadrilogus*

---

[1] James Craigie Robertson, *Passio Sancti Thomae Cantuariensis*, in *Materials for the History of Thomas Becket, Archbishop of Canterbury*, Rolls Series 67, 7 vols. (London, 1875–85), vol. 2, pp. 1–19, and *Miracula Sancti Thomae Cantuariensis*, MTB, vol. 2, pp. 21–267.

[2] On the evolution of Thomas' name, see John Jenkins, "Who Put the 'a' in 'Thomas a Becket'? The History of a Name from the Angevins to the 18th Century," *Open Library of Humanities* 9:1 (2023), doi: https://doi.org/10.16995/olh.9353.

[3] See A. J. Mason, *What Became of the Bones of St Thomas?* (Cambridge, 1920), pp. 22–9; Michael Staunton, *The Lives of Thomas Becket* (Manchester, 2001), pp. 203–5; Edwin A. Abbott, *St Thomas of Canterbury: His Death and Miracles* (London, 1898), vol. 2, pp. 76–273. See also John Shinners, *Medieval Popular Religion, 1000–1500: A Reader* (Peterborough, ON, 1997), pp. 159–74.

[4] The known manuscripts of the *Miracles* utilize other works as an introductory text, such as John of Salisbury's *Life* of Becket, or simply present the *Miracles* alone. For a listing of manuscripts with descriptions of their contents, see Anne Duggan, "The Santa Cruz Transcription of Benedict of Peterborough's Liber Miraculorum Beati Thome: Porto, BPM, Cod. Santa Cruz 60," *Mediaevalia. Textos e estudos* 20 (2001): 27–55, at pp. 30–8, and Nicholas Vincent, "William of Canterbury and Benedict of Peterborough: The Manuscripts, Date and Context of the Becket Miracle Collections," in Edina Bozóky (ed.), *Hagiographie, idéologie et politique au Moyen Âge en Occident: Actes du colloque*

II. This compilation was intended to tell the story of Becket's life via four different author's accounts (like to the four Gospel writers), with a fifth, Benedict's *Passion*, supplying the majority of the description of Becket's last day and death.[5] Robertson believed that most of the *Passion* was preserved in the *Quadrilogus II*, and I have translated it as Robertson edited it, with each of the eleven "extracts" numbered I–XI. We have lost whatever prologue Benedict may have given the text, along with his description of the first blow struck by the knights, but otherwise the eleven extracts read as a remarkably coherent narrative.

For the text of the *Miracles*, Robertson relied on two medieval manuscripts (the two surviving in England) along with a partial collation of a third manuscript held in Paris.[6] Today, very largely due to the work of Anne Duggan, we have a much greater knowledge of the numbers and locations of manuscripts of the *Miracles*, and an editor might well choose different manuscripts as a basis for an edition. Still, the differences that Duggan has identified between the manuscripts have not been radical, and the text presented by Robertson provides a sound basis for a translation.[7] I have, however, made two changes to the numbering of chapters in Robertson's edition. The first is in Book II, where many manuscripts present the chapters Robertson ordered as number 61 and 62 in reverse order.[8] I have switched their positions in this translation. The second change I have made is at the end of the *Miracles*. Chapter 94 of Book IV was the original end of the collection, and some manuscripts go no further. Other manuscripts carry on with

---

international du Centre d'Études supérieures de Civilisatione médiévale de Poitiers 11–14 septembre 2008 (Turnhout, 2012), pp. 347–88, at pp. 367–72.

[5] The full text of the *Quadrilogus II* was edited by J. C. Robertson in *MTB*, vol. 4, pp. 266–405. On this interesting compilation, see Michael Staunton, *Thomas Becket and His Biographers* (Woodbridge, 2006), pp. 6–7 and Anne Duggan, "The Lyell Version of the Quadrilogus Life of St Thomas of Canterbury," *AB* 112 (1994): 105–38.

[6] The manuscripts are Cambridge, Trinity College MS B.14.37 and London, Lambeth Palace Library MS 135, with further collation from Paris, Bibl. Nationale Lat. MS 5320: see Robertson, *MTB*, vol. 2, pp. xxiv–xxvi.

[7] Duggan has published collations of a number of manuscripts in "The Lorvão Transcription of Benedict of Peterborough's *Liber Miraculorum Beati Thome*: Lisbon, Cod. Alcobaça CCXC/143," *Scriptorium* 51 (1997): 51–68, at pp. 64–8, and Duggan, "Santa Cruz," pp. 47–55. When I follow Duggan's collations rather than Robertson's edition, I have made note of the fact. Philipp Lenz has done a partial collation of another early manuscript, St. Gallen MS 580: see Lenz, "Construire un recueil de miracles: Les Miracula Sancti Thomae Cantuariensis de Benoît de Peterborough," unpublished PhD thesis, University of Geneva, 2003, pp. 128–30. The text's stemma has yet to be worked out.

[8] See Robertson, *MTB*, vol. 2, p. 106 nn. 1 and 5, and Anne Duggan, "Santa Cruz," p. 51. The St. Gall manuscript also has these chapters in reverse order, and the caption writer saw these chapters in reverse order as well.

xii NOTE ON THE TRANSLATION

two more stories, while others add on these two and then seven more. In some manuscripts, all nine of these additional chapters are included as part of Book IV, while in others, the final seven additions are made into a very short Book V.[9] For his edition, Robertson followed the sole manuscript that includes still more additions, four stories composed by an anonymous Christ Church monk after Benedict's death, and he split up the end of the *Miracles* into not just a Book V but a Book VI as well.[10] For this translation, I have placed Benedict's nine added stories after Book IV and numbered them Additions 1–9. I have not included the stories composed after Benedict's death.

Robertson tracked down and provided references for Benedict's citations from classical texts, work I have relied on below, but he decided not to identify the far greater number of biblical citations and allusions in either the *Passion* or the *Miracles*. He explained that he feared filling the margins with references, and also that "such references would usually be needless," because those who "had an ordinary degree of acquaintance" with the Bible would recognize them easily.[11] The level of familiarity with the Bible that Robertson could assume from his late nineteenth-century British audience is quite different from what is general today, and I have identified and indexed as many of these citations as possible. For the sake of consistency, I have utilized the verse and chapter numbering of the Douay–Rheims Bible (an English translation of the Vulgate Latin Bible utilized by medieval Christians) and Chicago-style short abbreviations for the names of the books of the Bible. Benedict felt free to play with biblical or liturgical passages, often inserting words or phrases that made them more relevant to whatever he was discussing. I have, therefore, translated his biblical echoes and citations as it seemed best within the context rather than trying to follow the Douay–Rheims translation. Despite my best efforts, I am sure that I have not caught all of these biblical echoes nor done Benedict's writings full justice in this regard. Still, a rough rule of thumb for the care Benedict took over the composition of a passage is the density of its allusions, and to miss this humming subtext is to miss a large part of what Benedict intended readers to find pleasurable and compelling in his writings. To give today's readers something of the same experience, I have italicized passages in which Benedict was echoing another text.

Benedict almost always provided a place of origin or family name for the subjects of the miracles. When I was able to identify these places of origin, I translated

---

[9] Anne Duggan did the foundational work with the manuscripts that revealed how these additions worked: see Duggan, "Lorvão Transcription" and Duggan, "Santa Cruz."

[10] Robertson unfortunately followed post-medieval handwriting in this manuscript (Lambeth Palace Library MS 135) as a basis for his creation of a Book VI. No medieval reader would have thought of the *Miracles* as having six books.

[11] Robertson, *MTB*, vol. 2, Note B, pp. xlix–l.

them into modern English (e.g., Ansfrid of Dover), but when I was defeated, I retained the Latin in italics (e.g., Ralph *de Tangis*). When Benedict was referring to a family name, or when an individual's name is conventionally spelled in this manner, I retained the Latin 'de' without italics (e.g., Ranulf de Broc).

For the reader's convenience, I have adopted the captions to the chapters that are found in most manuscript copies of the *Miracles*.[12] Medieval readers used them as means of navigation, and they can serve the same purpose for today's readers, though it pays to be wary. Benedict was all but certainly not their author. They look to have been written by someone who skimmed through a manuscript fairly quickly, was prone to picking up wrong names and places, and did not always grasp the most salient point of a chapter. When a caption contains an incorrect name, place, and/or illness, I have corrected it and made note of the fact by brackets and a footnote.

I am very grateful to Dr. Shelagh Sneddon for checking the entire translation for accuracy and making many suggestions that I have adopted here, though of course all errors that remain are my own. I have tried to strike the balance that all translators desire – to create a readable text in English while remaining faithful to Benedict's words. I hope that the result will bring more readers to his remarkable work.

---

[12] In the manuscripts, the captions are usually found either grouped together at the beginning of the manuscript (such as St. Gallen MS 580 and Cambridge, Trinity College MS B.14.37), or split up into books, such that the captions for Book I are found at the beginning of Book I, those for Book II at the beginning of Book II, and so forth (see British Library Egerton MS 2818; Porto, Bibl. Públ. Mun. MS 349; Lisbon, Bibl. nacional, cod. Alcobaça CCXC/143; and Lisbon, Bibl. nacional, cod. Alcobaça CCLXXXIX/172). Two manuscripts with no chapter headings are Heidelberg, Universitäts-Bibliothek, cod. Salem IX.30 and London, Lambeth Palace MS 135. Robertson printed the captions as a general table of contents: see *MTB*, vol. 2, pp. iii–xv.

List of Abbreviations

AB	*Analecta Bollandiana*
ANS	*Anglo-Norman Studies*
Bosham, *Vita*	Herbert Bosham, *Vita Sancti Thomae Cantuariensis Archiepiscopi et Martyris, MTB*, vol. 3, pp. 155–534
BR	Joan Greatrex, *Biographical Register of the English Cathedral Priories of the Province of Canterbury, c. 1066–1540* (Oxford, 1997)
Caviness, *Windows*	Madeline Caviness, *The Windows of Christ Church Cathedral, Canterbury*, Corpus Vitrearum Medii Aevi: Great Britain, Volume II (London, 1981)
Cantus ID	Identification number in Cantus: A Database for Latin Ecclesiastical Chant: https://cantusdatabase.org
CB	*Cartae Baronum*, ed. Neil Stacy, Pipe Roll Society n. s. vol. LXII (Woodbridge, 2019)
CTB	*The Correspondence of Thomas Becket, Archbishop of Canterbury*, ed. and trans. A. J. Duggan, OMT, 2 vols. (Oxford, 2000)
DD	K. S. B. Keats-Rohan, *Domesday Descendants: A Prosopography of Persons Occurring in English Documents 1066–1166, II: Pipe Rolls to* Cartae Baronum (Woodbridge, 2002)
DMLBS	Dictionary of Medieval Latin from British Sources, eds. R. E. Latham et al. (Oxford, 1975–2013)
DP	K. S. B. Keats-Rohan, *Domesday People: A Prosopography of Persons Occurring in English Documents 1066–1166, I. Domesday Book* (Woodbridge, 1999)

EC	*Epistolae Cantuarienses*, ed. William Stubbs, *Chronicles and Memorials of the Reign of Richard I*, RS vol. 38:2 (London, 1865)
EEA	*English Episcopal Acta* (London, 1980–)
EYC	*Early Yorkshire Charters*, ed. W. Farrer (Edinburgh 1914–16) and C. T. Clay (Yorkshire Archaeological Society record series e.s., 1935–65)
FitzStephen, *Vita*	William FitzStephen, *Vita Sancti Thomae Cantuariensis Archiepiscopi et Martyris, MTB*, vol. 3 (London, 1887), pp. 1–154
Gervase	*The Historical Works of Gervase of Canterbury*, ed. W. Stubbs, RS 73, 2 vols. (London, 1879–80)
Grim, *Vita*	Edward Grim, *Vita Sancti Thomae Cantuariensis Archiepiscopi et Martyris, MTB*, vol. 2, pp. 353–450
HRH	David Knowles, C. N. L. Brooke, and Vera C. M. London, *The Heads of Religious Houses: England and Wales, I: 940–1216*, 2nd edition (Cambridge, 2001)
LCGF	*The Letters and Charters of Gilbert Foliot*, ed. A. Morey and C. N. L. Brooke (Cambridge, 1967)
LCHII	*The Letters and Charters of Henry II, King of England 1154–1189*, ed. Nicholas Vincent, OMT, 7 vols. (Oxford, 2022)
LJS	*Letters of John of Salisbury II: The Later Letters (1163–1180)*, ed. W. J. Millor and C. N. L. Brooke (Oxford, 1979)
Monasticon	William Dugdale, *Monasticon Anglicanum*, ed. J. Caley, H. Ellis and B. Bandinel, 6 vols. in 8 (London, 1846)
MTB	*Materials for the History of Thomas Becket, Archbishop of Canterbury*, ed. J. C. Robertson and J. B. Sheppard, RS 67, 7 vols. (London, 1875–85)
ODNB	*Oxford Dictionary of National Biography*
OMT	Oxford Medieval Texts
PR	*The Great Rolls of the Pipe of the Reign of Henry the Second, 5th to 34th years*, 30 vols. (Pipe Roll Society, 1884–1925)

Reames, "Liturgical Offices"	Sherry Reames, ed. and trans., "Liturgical Offices for the Cult of St Thomas Becket," in Thomas Head (ed.), *Medieval Hagiography: An Anthology* (New York, 2001), pp. 561–94
RS	Rolls Series
Slocum, *Liturgies*	*Liturgies in Honour of Thomas Becket*, trans. Kay Brainerd Slocum (Toronto, 2004)
Swaffham	*The Chronicles of Peterborough Abbey, Volume Two: Robert of Swaffham and Walter of Whittlesey*, ed. and trans. Edward King (Northampton, 2022), pp. 64–107
Thómas Saga	*Thómas Saga Erkibyskups: A Life of Archbishop Thomas Becket, in Icelandic*, ed. and trans. Eiríkr Magnússon, RS 65 (London, 1883).
Urry, *CUAK*	William Urry, *Canterbury under the Angevin Kings* (London, 1967)
William of Canterbury, *Vita*	William of Canterbury, *Vita Sancti Thomae Cantuariensis Archiepiscopi et Martyris*, MTB, vol. 1, 1–136
William of Canterbury, *Miracula*	William of Canterbury, *Miracula S. Thomae Cantuariensis*, MTB, vol. 1, 137–546

Introduction

BENEDICT of Peterborough's *Passion and Miracles of St Thomas Becket* puts the reader in Canterbury on the day of one of the most famous murders of all time. It reveals how a monk thrust into the role of recorder sorted out and attempted to understand the beginnings of a pilgrimage that would draw hundreds of thousands of medieval pilgrims to Canterbury. It takes us into the homes of people suffering from a vast array of ailments and accidents and follows them on the road to Canterbury and a humble tomb in a cathedral's crypt. While medieval readers looked to Benedict's work for signs of Becket's sanctity, today it is the text's vignettes of hundreds of medieval lives that most appeal to the imagination. We can laugh along as Benedict tells stories in which the great saint turns his attention to minor matters – the lost cheese of a little girl named Beatrice, for instance – and feel the terror and hope of people desperately appealing to Becket, such as the unjustly accused Eilward of Westoning facing a sentence of blinding and castration, or the gravely ill Eremburga of London demanding at Becket's tomb that she either die or be made well enough to walk home.[1] Readable, relatable, and jam-packed with drama, Benedict's *Passion and Miracles* is one of the most extraordinary texts produced by a medieval British writer.

Benedict was a monk of Christ Church, the monastic community attached to Canterbury Cathedral that looked to the archbishop of Canterbury as its titular abbot. He was in Canterbury on December 29, 1170, when four of King Henry II's knights argued with the archbishop, left to arm themselves, and came back and killed him. The *Passion* is the best account we have of the trauma felt by those who witnessed this violence and saw the archbishop's dead body lying on the cathedral's floor. No complete copy of the *Passion* has survived to the present day. Fortunately, an author working at the end of the twelfth century, Elias of Evesham, decided to include extracts from the *Passion* as part of a compilation now known as the *Quadrilogus II*. These extracts are extensive, and it appears that Elias utilized a very significant portion of the text.[2] Translations of those extracts are placed here, as Benedict would have intended, to be read before the *Miracles*.

---

[1] See III.51, IV.2, and II.42.
[2] See the Note to the Translation above and Robertson's comment, *MTB*, vol. 2, pp. xx–xxi: "we may safely assume that the missing portions of [the *Passion*] cannot have been very considerable."

Benedict started collecting miracles in the late spring of 1171, after the Christ Church monks allowed pilgrims access to Becket's tomb. He worked assiduously, showing the drive and focus that would later make him a fine administrator. By the time the news arrived in Britain of Pope Alexander III's canonization of Becket on February 21, 1173, Benedict had finished the bulk of the *Miracles*. It began to circulate after he wrote the last chapter of Book IV, a miracle story that can be dated to late March/early April 1173. From mid to late 1173, he made two minor additions to the text, totaling nine more chapters. The entire work, including the *Passion* (most likely written in 1172), was completed by the first celebration of Becket's feast day on December 29, 1173. It had taken him less than three years to produce all of this text.[3]

The *Miracles* found eager readers across Europe. A monk of São Mamede in Portugal, some two thousand kilometers southeast of Canterbury, was so grateful for Benedict's *Miracles* that he offered a blessing at the end of his copy: "May he who brought the text of the book to this land be blessed by the living God and His saints and live a long life, honoured by his princes and kings, and by the bishops and the whole clergy of this and foreign lands."[4] Three thousand kilometers to the east of São Mamede, the cathedral chapter of Kraków owned a collection of Becket's miracles, very likely Benedict's, by the late twelfth or early thirteenth century.[5] The *Miracles* was easiest to find in monastic libraries in England and in France, but copies also found their way to St. Gall in Switzerland, Böddeken in Germany, Heiligenkreuz in Austria, Vallombrosa in Italy, and Tui in Spain.[6]

---

[3] Books I–III of the *Miracles* have been dated to c.1173–4 and Book IV to 1179 due to the mistaken estimation of Emmanuel Walberg, "Date de la composition des recueils de *Miracula Sancti Thomae Cantuariensis*," *Le Moyen Âge* 22 (1920): 259–74, at 261–4. For an analysis of where Walberg went wrong and a detailed argument for the dating of the *Passion and Miracles* to 1171–3, see Rachel Koopmans, "Benedict of Peterborough's Compositions for Thomas Becket: Passion, Miracles, Office," *Medium Ævum* 90:2 (2021): 247–74.

[4] For this colophon and its translation, see Anne J. Duggan, "Aspects of Anglo-Portuguese Relations in the Twelfth Century. Manuscripts, Relics, Decretals and the Cult of St. Thomas Becket at Lorvão, Alcobaça and Tomar," *Portuguese Studies* 14 (1998): 1–19, at pp. 1 and 19; see also her analysis of the manuscript in "Lorvão Transcription."

[5] Waclaw Uruszczak, "Répercussions de la mort de Thomas Becket en Pologne (XIIe-XIIIe siècles)," in Raymonde Foreville (ed.), *Thomas Becket: Actes du colloque international de Sédières 19–24 août 1973* (Paris, 1975), pp. 115–25, at p. 116.

[6] The shelfmarks of these manuscripts are St. Gallen, Stiftsbibliothek, Cod. Sang. MS 580; Paderborn, Erzbischöfliche Akademische Bibliothek Theodoriana Ba 2; Heiligenkreuz, Stiftsbibliothek Cod. Sancrucensis 209 and 213; Florence, Biblioteca Medicea Laurenziana, Conv. soppr. 230; and Tuy, Archivo de la Cathedral de Tuy MS 1. The most recent listing of the manuscripts of Benedict's miracle collection is found in Vincent, "William of Canterbury and Benedict of Peterborough," at pp. 367–72. For a mapping of references to manuscripts in English medieval library catalogues and other documents,

Further north, there are fragments of a copy in the Danish National Archives, and far to the northwest, in Iceland, a writer working at the turn of the fourteenth century had access to the stories Benedict had written in Canterbury many years before.[7] No other British collection of miracle stories was copied and read by people living so far from its point of origin, and few other texts composed in late twelfth-century Britain, of any type, traveled so far.[8] Another monk at Christ Church, William of Canterbury, wrote a full *Life of St Thomas* and an even longer collection of miracles. But it was Benedict's *Miracles* not William's that saw astonishing circulation for a miracle collection.[9]

The distances the *Miracles* traveled underline the breadth of the European fascination with Becket, but they are also a testament to the text's readability and excellence. Edward Grim, the writer of a widely read *Life* of Becket, praised its "elegant style."[10] The literary qualities of miracle collections tend to receive very little attention from scholars, but Grim's assessment was not misplaced. In the late twelfth century, an elegant style meant not only graceful writing, but also texts filled with allusions, echoes, comparisons, and parallels, in particular allusions to biblical figures, passages, and events.[11] Benedict's ability to sound such chords

---

see Rachel Koopmans, *Wonderful to Relate: Miracle Stories and Miracle Collecting in High Medieval England* (Philadelphia, 2011), Figure 7, p. 131.

[7] For the Danish fragments, see Synnøve Midtbø Myking, "Thomas Becket, Clairvaux, and Ringsted: Saintly Diversity and European Influences in a Twelfth-Century Fragmentary Legendary from Denmark," *Classica et Mediaevalia: Danish Journal of Philology and History* 72 (2023): 255–88. For the presence and use of Benedict's *Miracles* in Iceland, see *Thómas Saga Erkibyskups: A Life of Archbishop Thomas Becket, in Icelandic*, ed. and trans. Eiríkr Magnússon, RS 65 (London, 1883), pp. clv–clvi. As Anne Duggan has explained, the international interest in Thomas Becket's cult was in part a result of Becket's networks and friendships: see Anne Duggan, "Religious Networks in Action: The European Expansion of the Cult of St Thomas of Canterbury," in Jeremy Gregory and Hugh McLeod (eds.), *International Religious Networks* (Woodbridge, 2012), pp. 20–43.

[8] For studies focused on other contemporary British miracle collections, see Simon Yarrow, *Saints and Their Communities: Miracle Stories in Twelfth-Century England* (Oxford, 2005); Ruth J. Salter, *Saints, Cure-Seekers and Miraculous Healing in Twelfth-Century England* (York, 2021); Anne E. Bailey, "Reconsidering the Medieval Experience at the Shrine in High Medieval England," *Journal of Medieval History* 47:2 (2021): 203–29; and Tom Lynch, *Making Miracles in Medieval England* (London, 2023).

[9] William of Canterbury, *Miracula S. Thomae Cantuariensis*, MTB, vol. 1, 137–546. For the comparative circulation of the two collections, see Vincent, "William of Canterbury and Benedict of Peterborough," Tables 2 and 3, pp. 367–73.

[10] Edward Grim, *Vita Sancti Thomae Cantuariensis Archiepiscopi et Martyris*, MTB, vol. 2, pp. 353–450, at p. 448.

[11] For a description of this kind of connective, allusive, and episodic literary style, see Nancy Partner, *Serious Entertainments: The Writing of History in Twelfth-Century England* (Chicago, 1977), esp. pp. 197–222; for an example of a contemporary hagiographer writing

surely contributed to the Europe-wide readership of the *Miracles*, and also to his selection as the composer of Becket's liturgical Office, the music, lyrics, and readings that would be used throughout Latin Christendom to celebrate the feast day of St. Thomas of Canterbury on December 29.[12]

At the end of the translation, I have provided biographical notes for persons in the *Passion and Miracles* who can be found in other contemporary documents, such as witness lists to charters, rentals, and Pipe Roll accounts. Nearly all the people who can be identified held some wealth and position. Ordinary people, priests, and the poor left few or no traces in late twelfth-century records. Still, seeing names from the *Miracles* appear in other documents underlines the simple but important fact that Benedict met with and described the stories of real, living people. Of course, this does not mean that we hear the unfiltered voices of those people in the *Miracles*, nor that those speakers themselves, when they told their stories at Canterbury, did not dramatically edit, shape, and embellish their lived experiences. Nevertheless, behind this text are hundreds of encounters with living, breathing visitors who had stories to tell about themselves. Benedict did not see himself as writing fiction. Nor should we, however much we might interpret miracle stories and the history and meaning of Becket's early cult differently than he did.

I have also included, as an appendix, a translation of eighteen stories from William of Canterbury's collection of Becket's miracles. These are the "parallel miracles": stories that both Christ Church collectors, Benedict and William, decided to recount in their respective collections.[13] William started his collection in June 1172 while Benedict was still hard at work on his. William meant his text to be no mere continuation of Benedict's, but a free-standing, wholly independent collection.[14] As such, he decided to provide his own accounts of significant mira-

---

with such literary aims, see John of Forde, *The Life of Wulfric of Haselbury, Anchorite*, trans. Pauline Matarasso, Cistercian Fathers Series 79 (Collegeville, MN, 2011), and Matarasso's introduction, pp. 78–9, 82–3.

[12] The Becket Office is indexed in the Cantus Database (https://cantusdatabase.org) as Feast no. 14122900. For an edition of the monastic version of the Office, see *Liturgies in Honour of Thomas Becket*, trans. Kay Brainerd Slocum (Toronto, 2004), pp. 135–48. For the secular version, see Sherry Reames, ed. and trans., "Liturgical Offices for the Cult of St Thomas Becket," in Thomas Head (ed.), *Medieval Hagiography: An Anthology* (New York, 2001), pp. 561–94.

[13] The first person to focus on the "parallel miracles" (his phrase, adopted from the synoptic study of the Gospels) was Abbott, *St Thomas of Canterbury*, vol. 2, pp. 76–273.

[14] For the dating of William's *Miracles*, see Koopmans, *Wonderful to Relate*, pp. 139–58 and 181–200. For an updated listing of the manuscripts, see Vincent, "William of Canterbury and Benedict of Peterborough," Table 3, pp. 372–3. Many scholars have taken the opportunity to compare the two collections on specific themes. See, for instance, Didier

cles that he would have known Benedict had already described in his text. A year later, when Benedict was wrapping up his collection, this situation may well have been reversed. William might have written his accounts first, with Benedict deciding to add on stories he deemed important to his collection. The eighteen parallel miracles are valuable for dating evidence and for revealing places in which the collectors were utilizing letters, but they are most interesting for showing how two monks working in the same place and at essentially the same time could describe the same miracles very differently.

The introductory material that follows is divided into two parts. In the first part, I address the relationship of Benedict and the Christ Church monks to the living Thomas Becket, Benedict's account of the murder in the *Passion*, the atmosphere at Canterbury in the first months after Becket's death, and why and when Benedict began writing the *Miracles*. In the second part, I turn to the making of the *Miracles*. I discuss how Benedict gathered material, looking at how he categorized stories, whose stories he valued the most, and his use of notes and letters. I then focus on two defining features of his construction of the *Miracles*: his efforts to match similar miracles together and the many parallels he drew between Becket's miracles and biblical events and passages. I suggest that "connective" is a better term than "chronological" or "thematic" to describe the organizational style of his collection. Dated stories in the early parts of the *Miracles* are an aspect of Benedict's work that has especially enthused modern scholars. I list and analyze them, arguing that Benedict used them to draw still more parallels between Becket and Christ. After examining the circumstances in which Benedict brought the *Miracles* to completion, I conclude by considering the ways in which his later life and career continued to be shaped by Canterbury's new saint.

Some stories in the *Miracles* are almost startlingly contemporary, such as the experiences of a teenager who attempted to take her own life, a pregnant woman

---

Lett, "Deux hagiographes, un saint et un roi: conformisme et créativité dans les deux recueils de *Miracula* de Thomas Becket," in Michel Zimmermann (ed.), *Auctor et auctoritas: Invention and conformisme dans l'écriture médiévale, actes du colloque de Saint-Quentin-en-Yvelines (14–16 Juin 1999)* (Paris, 2001), pp. 201–16; Gesine Oppitz-Trotman, "Penance, Mercy, and Saintly Authority in the Miracles of St Thomas Becket," in Peter Clarke and Tony Claydon (eds.), *Saints and Sanctity* (Woodbridge, 2011), pp. 136–47; Hilary Powell, "The 'Miracle of Childbirth': The Portrayal of Parturient Women in Medieval Miracle Narratives," *Social History of Medicine* 25.4 (2012): 795–811; Franca Ela Consolino, "Gli spazi del meraviglioso nei miracoli di Tommaso Becket," in Franca Ela Consolino, Francesco Marzella, and Lucilla Spetia (eds.), *Aspetti del meraviglioso nelle letterature medievali* (Turnhout, 2016), pp. 47–58; and Rachel Koopmans, "The Smallest Matters: Vanishing Water, Missing Birds, Revived Animals, Recovered Coins, and Other Trifling Miracles in the Thomas Becket Collections," *Journal of Medieval History* 48:5 (2022): 587–606.

in terrible distress who could not give birth, a workman presumed killed in an accident on a construction site, a man who consulted with many doctors and still did not recover from his sleep disorder, and many other people and their families struggling to deal with the consequences of serious illness and disability.[15] Benedict did not shy away from describing intense emotions: the monks who could not stop crying after Becket's death, the father pleading for the revival of his dying daughter, the pilgrims rejoicing and dancing in the street when one of their traveling party became well, the amazement of a lord who found that his leprous shepherd boy, whose company everyone had shunned because he smelled so bad, came home from Canterbury perfectly healed, or the woman so happy with her recovery that she said she felt she could fly.[16] Benedict was a good observer as well as an elegant writer. We are fortunate that he was the one who wrote this text.

Part One

BENEDICT'S ORIGINS, THE MONASTERY OF CHRIST CHURCH, AND THOMAS BECKET

Little is known about Benedict's background aside from what can be inferred from passages in the *Miracles*. He was fluent in French, as we know from a story in which he describes how he saw the archbishop in a vision and asked him a question in that language (I.1). He would have been equally fluent in English, as he describes himself as having a heated argument with a poor woman from Woodstock (III.31). In a couple of stories, he talks about his relationships, mentioning that a knight named Robert Puintel was known to him (II.45), and that a clerk was his schoolfellow (III.20). Speaking French as well as English, knowing knights, going to school: these are all indicators that Benedict was born into a comfortably situated Anglo-Norman family. His name may indicate that he was destined for the monastery from his birth. St. Benedict was a founder of monasticism, and Benedict was not a common name for boys in Anglo-Norman England. Benedict's works certainly reveal a deep familiarity and facility with biblical and liturgical texts, strongly suggesting that he became a monk at a young age.

The choice of the monastery of Christ Church may well have been made for Benedict by his family. It was one of two celebrated monasteries in Canterbury. The other was the monastery of St. Augustine, located just outside the city walls. St. Augustine's had its own abbot, but Christ Church, as a so-called "monastic cathedral," claimed the Archbishop of Canterbury as its abbot. Because

---

[15] See Addition 8, IV.54, Addition 7, and I.13.
[16] See Prologue, IV.65, III.42, IV.76, and II.24.

archbishops were often elsewhere and had much to occupy their attention as the head of the English Church, the prior of Christ Church took on nearly all the day-to-day administration of the monastery and cathedral. It was a prestigious and powerful position that Benedict himself would hold. Nevertheless, monks who entered the community made their professions to the archbishop, not the prior, and the archbishop had the right to intervene in the monastery's affairs.

Benedict likely became a monk at Christ Church around the time that Theobald served as Archbishop of Canterbury (1139–61). The writer Gervase of Canterbury made his profession as a Christ Church monk to Becket in 1163, while the miracle collector William of Canterbury was ordained a deacon by Becket in 1170, facts they carefully noted in their writings.[17] Benedict made no such statement in his works, and there are other indications that he was older than either Gervase or William. Starting in 1173/74, Benedict was rapidly promoted. In the space of a few years, he became the chancellor of Becket's successor, Archbishop Richard of Dover, then the prior of Christ Church, and finally, in 1177, the Abbot of Peterborough, a position he held until his death in 1193. It does not seem likely that he was a young man when these promotions began. Perhaps he was in his thirties or early forties. King Richard I (b. 1157) would warmly refer to Benedict as his "father," adding weight to the idea that Benedict was in his thirties or early forties in the 1170s.[18] Benedict died on Michaelmas (September 29) 1193, perhaps, if these accountings are accurate, when he was in his fifties or sixties.[19] The Peterborough chronicler Robert of Swaffham wrote that Benedict was prevented by death from finishing a building project near Peterborough Abbey's brewhouse.[20] This, along with the fact Swaffham never describes him as elderly, suggests that he had not reached a great age.

We know much more about Thomas Becket's early life.[21] The son of a merchant named Gilbert Becket, he was born in London. The date of his birth is not

---

[17] See *The Historical Works of Gervase of Canterbury*, ed. W. Stubbs, RS 73 (London 1879–80) vol. 1, p. 231 and William of Canterbury, *Vita Sancti Thomae Cantuariensis Archiepiscopi et Martyris*, MTB, vol. 1, 1–136, p. 119.

[18] *The Chronicles of Peterborough Abbey, Volume Two: Robert of Swaffham and Walter of Whittlesey*, ed. and trans. Edward King (Northampton, 2022), pp. 64–107, at pp. 73 and 75.

[19] For the date, see Swaffham, p. 75. Michaelmas is also recorded as Benedict's death day in British Library Arundel MS 68 f.43v.

[20] Swaffham, p. 71.

[21] For scholarly biographies of Becket, see Frank Barlow, *Thomas Becket* (London, 1986), and Anne Duggan, *Thomas Becket* (London, 2004); for a work more aimed at a general audience, see John Guy, *Thomas Becket: Warrior, Priest, Rebel: A Nine-Hundred-Year-Old Story Retold* (New York, 2012).

certain, but is generally assumed to be c.1120.[22] He went to Paris for schooling, and joined Archbishop Theobald's household in Canterbury by 1146. He was then in his later twenties and was one of many clerks. At this point, monks of Christ Church (probably including the young Benedict) would have had only passing acquaintance with him, if any. Theobald made Becket the archdeacon of Canterbury in 1154. A short time later, in January 1155, Becket had a major career break – the newly crowned King Henry II chose him to be his chancellor.[23] The Christ Church monks must have been cognizant of Becket at this point, but they probably had next to no personal contact with him. Becket continued to hold the post of archdeacon while serving as the king's chancellor, but all the indications are that he held the role in absentia and spent very little time in Canterbury.[24]

When Theobald died, in 1161, Henry II was eager for Becket to be elected archbishop. Few Christ Church monks could have wanted him to receive this post.[25] Theobald had been a monk, as had all but one of the archbishops appointed since the Norman Conquest. Becket was a secular clerk, a man who enjoyed luxurious clothing, fine dining, hawking, and all the trappings of wealth and power. He was no scholar, and betrayed few signs of spiritual depth before he became archbishop;[26] but King Henry's will prevailed and Becket was consecrated Archbishop of Canterbury in 1162, so becoming the abbot of the Christ Church monks as well. Shortly after his consecration, Becket scandalized his monks by wearing secular clothing when he entered the choir of Canterbury Cathedral, the place where the monks sang their daily services. Such a sartorial gaffe suggested that Becket had no respect for his new position. Multiple chroniclers record that the Christ Church monks grumbled over this faux pas, and it is safe to assume that Benedict was one of them. The new archbishop did change his clothing – warned to do so, as some chroniclers had it, by the vision of a Christ Church monk.[27] He also changed his attitude towards Henry II. No longer the king's right-hand man, Becket began to tangle with him over various

---

[22] In the *Passion* (see Extract XI below), Benedict stated that Becket was fifty-three when he died, putting his birthdate c.1117.

[23] On Becket's early life up to his appointment as chancellor, see Barlow, *Thomas Becket*, pp. 24–40.

[24] See Barlow, *Thomas Becket*, p. 38.

[25] For analysis of the monks' attitude to Becket, see Michael Staunton, "The *Lives* of Thomas Becket and the Church of Canterbury," in Paul Dalton, Charles Insley, and Louise J. Wilkinson (eds.), *Cathedrals, Communities and Conflict in the Anglo-Norman World* (Woodbridge, 2011), 169–86, esp. 172–5.

[26] For discussions of Becket's character, see Michael Staunton, "Thomas Becket's Conversion," *ANS* 21 (1999): 193–211 and Hanna Vollrath, "Was Thomas Becket Chaste?" *ANS* 27 (2004): 198–209.

[27] On this incident, see Grim, *Vita*, p. 368; William of Canterbury, *Vita*, pp. 10–11; Anonymous I, *Vita S. Thomae*, in *MTB*, vol. 4, pp. 1–79, at p. 21; and Guernes de Pont-

matters of the rights and interests of the Church. Becket would spend little time at Canterbury before his dispute with the king became hot. In the fall of 1164, he fled England for France. Though many of his clerks and family members went into exile with him, not a single Christ Church monk did.[28]

During his long years of exile in France, Becket expressed the thought that his monks back in Canterbury were selfish, myopic, and possibly even traitorous. One of Becket's most important clerks, John of Salisbury, wrote letters in which he excoriated the Christ Church monks for failing to send funds to support the archbishop: "Where has your charity been, I ask you? Where your love and your affection for your father?"[29] Becket himself turned to threats. In a letter sent to the subprior of Canterbury in June 1169 (sent to the subprior because Becket refused to acknowledge the election of Prior Odo in 1168 because it had been done without his permission), Becket complained that "you have not so far made contact with us in our needs and those of Christ's poor, exiled in him with us." He urged the monks to support his campaign against his hated enemy, Gilbert Foliot, bishop of London, warning them to no longer "dissimulate" or "serve two masters," because "we shall certainly spare no one in the future, but full vengeance will be taken according to the nature of the fault."[30]

This frustration should be counterbalanced by a consideration of the difficult position of the Christ Church community. In Becket's absence, Henry II had put Ranulf de Broc in charge of Canterbury's estates, and Ranulf in turn entrusted some of the work to his nephew, Robert de Broc. The one thing about life at Canterbury during Becket's exile that Benedict makes very clear is how much he loathed and feared the de Brocs, whom he terms "sons of perdition" in both the *Passion* and in the *Miracles*.[31] A picture of the situation at Christ Church is found in Book I of the *Miracles*, where Benedict describes the de Brocs as "men who mocked the name of the exiled martyr, detested his works and hated his person," being so terrifying that "no one dared even to mutter against them. But they could speak, inflict harm on everything to do with us, and do nothing to promote the business of the lord of Canterbury" (I.18). In this "tempest," Benedict writes, a

---

Sainte-Maxence, *La Vie de saint Thomas Becket: A Life of Thomas Becket in Verse*, trans. Ian Short (Toronto, 2013), pp. 37–8.

[28] For Becket's early tenure as archbishop and the growing dispute with Henry II, see Duggan, *Thomas Becket*, pp. 33–83, and Guy, *Thomas Becket*, pp. 139–213.

[29] *Letters of John of Salisbury II: The Later Letters (1163–1180)*, ed. W. J. Millor and C. N. L. Brooke (Oxford, 1979), no. 300, p. 703. See also letters nos. 243–4, 292–5, and 299.

[30] *The Correspondence of Thomas Becket, Archbishop of Canterbury*, ed. and trans. A. J. Duggan, OMT (Oxford, 2000), vol. 2, no. 209, pp. 910–21, at pp. 911 and 917.

[31] See Biographical Notes, Ranulf de Broc and Robert de Broc; Extracts I and VIII of the *Passion*; and I.14, I.18, and III.17.

Christ Church monk named Ralph was sent out of Canterbury, to Colchester, because he "was zealous in his resistance to the enemies, even though his zeal profited neither himself, nor us, nor his father." When Benedict wrote this telling passage, he believed Becket to be a martyr and miracle-working saint, yet he still thought that Ralph's full-throated support of the exiled archbishop was wrong. It had put "us," the Christ Church monks, in too much danger.[32]

Whether Benedict blamed Becket, the king, the de Brocs, or all of the above for this perilous situation is hard to tell. By choosing to write a short *Passion* rather than a full *Life* of Becket, Benedict avoided many minefields. He did not have to describe Becket's life as a clerk or chancellor, delve into the ramifications of his dispute with Henry II, or discuss the venomous quarreling that came with it. He decided to describe just "the end and what happened after the end," as the compiler who extracted parts of Benedict's *Passion* put it.[33] This diplomatic decision may well have aided Benedict's later political fortunes, but it makes it difficult to know what he thought about Becket's actions during his lifetime. Writing in the 1180s, Gervase of Canterbury praised Becket in that he "did nothing in prejudice to the convent [of Christ Church] but showed them all favour and love." However, he also stated that Becket "promised he would do them greater honor than any of his predecessors. But he was prevented by martyrdom, and God absolved His glorious athlete of his promise."[34] The best Gervase could say, in sum, was that the balance was even. Becket did not actively work against the rights and interests of Christ Church when he was their abbot, but he did not do anything for them either, before his life was cut short. Benedict may well have agreed.

When the archbishop returned to England in late 1170, he was in Canterbury for less than a month before he was killed. In his *Life* of Becket, William of Canterbury described that month in some detail. Becket's reunion with his monks was not rapturous. Although he greeted the monks with tears and the kiss of peace, absolved monks who had had contact with men he had excommunicated, and also accepted new monks into the community (including William himself), he also initially excluded some monks who had entered the community without his permission during his exile.[35] There was very little time for the monks and the archbishop to get reacquainted or to sort out the mess caused by the de Brocs

---

[32] A later copyist, no doubt startled at the idea that anyone could display excessive zeal against Becket's enemies, would cut out this passage. See Robertson's comment in *MTB*, vol. 2, p. 51 n. 3.

[33] *MTB*, vol. 4, p. 425.

[34] *Gervase* vol. 1, p. 48. Translation from Staunton, "The *Lives* of Thomas Becket and the Church of Canterbury," pp. 172–3.

[35] William of Canterbury, *Vita*, pp. 102 and 119.

before four of the king's knights arrived in Canterbury and confronted Becket in the archbishop's palace. The date was Tuesday, December 29, 1170.

THE MURDER AND BENEDICT'S *PASSION*

Benedict's *Passion* is among the earliest and most vivid accounts of the events of December 29 that have come down to us.[36] Much of what he wrote has the ring of his own eyewitness. The compiler of *Quadrilogus II*, the text in which extracts from Benedict's *Passion* are embedded, writes that Benedict was there "on the day when the victorious martyr was killed," and "set down in order all of the things he saw and heard with faithful testimony and truthful style."[37] The "seeing and hearing" rhetoric is very similar to what one finds in Benedict's own description of his compilation of the *Miracles* (I.7), and the compiler may have had access to a now-missing prologue in which Benedict stated that he was present in Canterbury on the day of the murder.

The surviving extracts start with the rancorous conversation between Becket and the king's knights in the archbishop's chamber late in the afternoon of December 29 and the knights' departure to arm themselves (Extract I). Next comes Becket's reluctant retreat from the archbishop's palace into the cathedral, the arrival of the knights, an angry exchange of words, and then the blows that killed Becket (Extracts II–VI). Benedict provides an especially interesting and important account of the immediate aftermath of the murder, describing the knights' looting of the archbishop's palace, the appearance of Becket's dead body, the collection of his blood, and the stunning discovery of a hair shirt on the archbishop's corpse (Extracts VII–X). He concludes with a careful accounting of exactly when Becket died (Extract XI).

This basic chronology and structure of the events accord well with other contemporary descriptions of the murder, but there are some items and emphases that are unique to Benedict. First, while all of the chroniclers of Becket's martyrdom drew parallels with Christ's passion,[38] Benedict did so more than most, even proclaiming to his readers that "it would not be easy to find a passion of any other martyr that would seem to accord with such similarity to the Lord's passion"

---

[36] For translations of accounts of Becket's murder, see *The Lives of Thomas Becket*, trans. Michael Staunton (Manchester, 2001), pp. 182–203. See also Staunton's excellent analysis of the different accounts in *Thomas Becket and His Biographers*, pp. 184–215, and the article by Dawn Marie Hayes, "Body as Champion of Church Authority and Sacred Place: The Murder of Thomas Becket," in Mark D. Meyerson, Daniel Tiery, and Oren Falk (eds.), *A Great Effusion of Blood? Interpreting Medieval Violence* (Toronto, 2004), pp. 190–215.

[37] *MTB*, vol. 4, p. 371.

[38] See Staunton, *Thomas Becket*, p. 51.

(Extract X). He described Becket as "the lamb of God" and "the Lord's anointed" (terms used for Christ in the Bible), compared Christ's and Becket's attempts to protect their respective followers, and noted Christ's and Becket's foreknowledge of their deaths (Extracts II, III and X). He also drew parallels between what Christ and what Becket said to their persecutors (Extracts III and IV), the mocking words of the soldiers at Christ's crucifixion and those of Becket's killers (Extract V), and the seizure of Christ's clothing with the looting of the archbishop's palace (Extract VIII).

Benedict also emphasized the actions of Christ Church monks on that last day of Becket's life, describing how the knights attempted to sway the monks to their side until "the kind father responded for his sons," and how the monks forced open a door for Becket and "urged their unwilling father to be led away" (Extract I). Benedict named the monks Richard and William, the cellarers of Christ Church, as the ones who unbolted a door for Becket (other writers state that the bolted door opened miraculously), and it is "some monks" who left vespers that bring Becket into the cathedral itself (Extract II). Benedict was also the only chronicler who portrayed Becket as trying to save some of his monks and followers by pulling them through a door into the cathedral (Extract II).

Becket's fearless actions in his last hours made a strong impression on Benedict. His portrait of Becket is of a man who was aggrieved, weary, and despairing of justice for himself, a man who knew that death was coming even as he refused to register the physical danger he was in, a "father" who displayed concern for his "sons" just before his death. The only faintly critical note comes in Benedict's description of the angry interview at the archbishop's palace. He reported John of Salisbury's criticism of Becket's retorts to the knights: "Would it not have been better to take council with those present here, and to give them a more mild response?" In general, though, Benedict's archbishop is a second Christ on the way to his death.

Contemporary writers agree that, of Becket's company, only the clerk Edward Grim remained with him as the knights struck him down. That Benedict was probably in the near vicinity, though, is suggested by his description of what the murderers shouted as they left the monastery ("The king's knights, the king's!" (Extract V)), and his vivid description of the looting of the archbishop's palace and the theft of archives (Extract VII). He likely saw for himself the slaughtered archbishop sprawled on the cathedral's floor. In Extract VIII, he described the appearance of Becket's dead face, stating that he had blood around his head like a crown, but that his face was marked only by a single line of blood running across his face. He stated that a small iron hammer and an axe were found underneath Becket's body, and frankly confessed that for a time after the murder "everything was disordered and confused," so much so that "each person could do as he liked" and take away mementos stained with Becket's blood. The monks themselves collected this blood in a "most clean vessel," and gave away some of Becket's clothing to the poor on behalf of his soul, two decisions that would have long-term consequences.

Alone among the chroniclers, Benedict describes the trauma of the murder for those at Canterbury, writing that the night of the murder 'was passed in suffering, groans and sighs' (Extract IX). On the next day, the monks were forced to bury Becket immediately to preserve his corpse from mutilation and desecration. Herbert Bosham notes that "many of [the monks], just as the men of this world, had doubted the man's sanctity," but that their minds were changed by what they found: a hair shirt on the dead man's corpse.[39] Rough and coarse, a hair shirt – often made of goat's hair – caused irritation when worn next to the skin, and so was worn by the religious as a form of penance. It was not what one would expect to find on the body of a man known for his fine clothing and luxurious living. The monks, Benedict writes, were "stunned by the sight of such hidden religion beyond what would have been believed, and with their reasons for mourning so multiplied, their tears began again" (Extract X).

Very few people, including Becket's closest companions, had thought of Becket as a saint before his death. Minds had to be changed, and for the Christ Church monks, change happened much faster than for most. There is no reason to doubt that the violence within their beloved church traumatized the Christ Church monks, and that their discovery of the hair shirt on Becket's corpse came as another shock. Even after this, there was at least one monk at Christ Church who thought that Becket merited his exile and laughed at the idea that he would be performing miracles, as we know from an account in William of Canterbury's miracle collection.[40] The majority of the monks, though, no doubt reacted to the murder the way Benedict did: with tears, horror, and a new way of thinking about their now dead archbishop and abbot. In the next six months, they would take a series of actions – including the beginning of the *Miracles* – that would put Becket on course to being recognized as England's greatest saint.[41]

---

[39] Herbert Bosham, *Vita Sancti Thomae Cantuariensis Archiepiscopi et Martyris*, MTB, vol. 3, pp. 155–534, pp. 521–2. On the hairshirt, see Karen Bollermann and Cary J. Nederman, "Dirty Laundry: Thomas Becket's Hair Shirt and the Making of a Saint," in Clare Frances Monagle (ed.), *The Intellectual Dynamism of the High Middle Ages* (Amsterdam, 2022), pp. 131–46.

[40] William of Canterbury, *Miracula*, I.9, p. 148; see also Grim, *Vita*, p. 440.

[41] In some scholarship, there is a perception that Christ Church community was resistant to Becket's cult for months if not years after the murder, with Prior Odo in particular being against it: see R. W. Southern, *The Monks of Canterbury and the Murder of*

THE FIRST DAYS OF MIRACLES: A CLOUD OF PERSECUTION AND KEY DECISIONS REGARDING BECKET'S TOMB AND BLOOD

In the first awful months after the murder, the future for the church in general and Canterbury in particular felt very uncertain. The monks weeping at the close of the *Passion* carry on crying in the Prologue of the *Miracles*. "I speak in Christ before God," Benedict declares, "the sons of the church could not restrain their tears at table… eating they silently mourned, and mixed their drink with tears." Benedict did not want this to be read this as hyperbole, noting later that one monk was suffering so much from grief that he felt as if he were near death (I.6).

Becket's murder did not mean that the dispute with Henry II was resolved in his favor, or that he was straightaway hailed as a saint. Nearly all those in power took a wait-and-see approach, a potent symbol of which is the fact nothing was done to reconsecrate Canterbury Cathedral, defiled by Becket's death, for almost a year. Until December 21, 1171, when the building was finally reconsecrated, the liturgical round of services could not be performed. This deprived the Christ Church monks of their raison d'être, a suspension Benedict felt keenly. He brings up this enforced liturgical silence more than once in the early parts of the *Miracles*, arguing that it made the monks' mourning all the worse, as they alone had to suffer this consequence of the murder.[42]

Miracles would have made them feel better, but for months, as Benedict made clear, they were few and far between. He used the evocative phrase "the first days of miracles" – by which he meant days *without* many miracles – to describe this time, which stretched to from the murder into May 1171.[43] Gervase also referred to a "prelude" period in which the martyr "began to shine forth in minor miracles," while William of Canterbury spoke of the "first" or "primitive" light of miracles appearing around Easter week 1171.[44] Especially telling is the first story in

---

Archbishop Becket (Oxford, 1985); Barlow, *Thomas Becket*, p. 265; Peter Kidson, "Gervase, Becket, and William of Sens," *Speculum* 68 (1993): 969–91; and James Barnaby, *Religious Conflict at Canterbury Cathedral in the Late Twelfth Century: The Dispute between the Monks and the Archbishops, 1184–1200* (Woodbridge, 2024), p. 49 (though see also ibid., pp. 116–19). Duggan rightly dismissed this notion, noting that the monks' delay in thinking of Becket as a martyr "lasted short of 12 hours" after his death: see Duggan, *Thomas Becket*, p. 214. Prior Odo and the living Becket had a strained relationship, but I see no evidence that he was opposed to Becket's cult. For letters about miracles addressed to Prior Odo, see IV.11, IV.85, and William no. 12 below.

[42] See the Prologue, II.1, and II.6.

[43] See below, III.18, III.21, and III.64. In III.18, he gives a specific date for a vision (namely May 2, 1171) that he places in "the first days of miracles."

[44] See *Gervase* vol. 1, p. 230, and William of Canterbury, *Miracula*, I.9, p. 148. Ralph Diceto also dated the beginning of Becket's miracles to Easter 1171: see Ralph de Diceto,

the *Miracles*, Benedict's account of his own visions of the archbishop. He began seeing Becket in his sleep the very night of the martyrdom. Eventually, he found the courage to speak, asking a question that would seem impertinent if it were not so despairing. If he were truly a martyr, Benedict asked, why wasn't he performing any miracles? The archbishop lifted up a lantern in response, and Benedict saw that a dense cloud was obscuring its light. He interpreted this as a "cloud of persecution" (I.1).

That there were serious consequences for anyone speaking of Becket as a saint in the aftermath of the murder is confirmed by numerous sources besides the *Miracles*. William FitzStephen wrote that the de Brocs were keeping watch by day and by night in Canterbury so that they "might carry off anyone speaking good of the archbishop and drag him before their court. And so the faithful did not dare at first to speak of the great works of God."[45] John of Salisbury, too, noted that "wicked men" had a "hate for [Becket that] was beyond sating" and they "forbade, on the government's authority, that anyone dare publish the miracles which were being performed."[46] There were people who claimed to have experienced miracles in this early period, but, as Benedict notes frequently, they were often too fearful to come to Canterbury to give thanks for them. Most of the earliest miracles that Benedict describes in his collection were ones that the monks first heard about weeks or months after the fact.[47]

Some of the most historically valuable chapters of Benedict's *Miracles* are those in which he describes the response of the Christ Church monks to this perilous situation. Not everything he writes should be taken at face value, but it is nevertheless clear that decisions the monks made during these "first days" had long-term implications for the nascent cult. When the monks had to bury Becket on the day after the murder, a marble sepulchre, sunk into the floor of the easternmost chapel of the crypt, was empty and available. The monks placed the body inside a wooden coffin, then the coffin into the sepulchre, and barred the doors to the crypt. Except for a few individuals the monks secretly admitted, no-one could visit the burial site in January, February, or March 1171. In early April, though, they took the brave decision to unbolt the doors and allow free public access to the crypt. Benedict supplies a precise date – the Friday following Easter (that is, April

---

Ymagines Historiarum, Historical Works, ed. W. Stubbs, RS 86 (London, 1876), vol. 1, pp. 346-7: "Circa Pascha Dominus Jesus Christus... gloriosissimi martyris sui... crebris coepit irradiare miraculis."

[45] William FitzStephen, *Vita Sancti Thomae Cantuariensis Archiepiscopi et Martyris*, MTB, vol. 3 (London, 1887), pp. 1-154, at p. 151.

[46] LJS no. 305, pp. 724-39, at p. 735. See also The Lansdowne Anonymous, MTB, vol. 4, p. 160.

[47] See below, Book I.

2, 1171) – for this major milestone (II.6). Interestingly, he presents this decision as largely the result of public pressure: he states that "the people" told the brothers they were "sinning," and they needed to open up the crypt, "lest it be said that we envied the martyr's glory and begrudged the infirm their health" (II.6).

The monks had given the nascent cult its natural physical focal point, and with this came a spurt of people claiming miracles at the tomb. The monks' nightmare seemed to be coming to an end: "our spirit was first greatly revived, and, as if we were awoken from a bad dream, so we were consoled" (II.6). Politically speaking, though, this was a dangerous decision. In a set of remarkable chapters in Book II, Benedict describes how the monks heard that there was "a multitude" of armed men planning "to seize the martyr" on the following night (II.26). The monks decided to remove the wooden coffin that held Becket's body from its marble sarcophagus and to hide it behind the altar of St. Mary. The attack the monks feared never came, but when they returned the coffin to the sarcophagus, they reinforced the site to make it more secure: "Around the marble sarcophagus, a wall of great hewn stones was set up and bound together most solidly with cement, iron and lead. The wall had two windows in each side through which people could insert their heads in order to kiss the sarcophagus. A large slab of marble was placed on top. There was a hollow space between the top of the sarcophagus and the slab which was hardly a foot high" (II.29).

Benedict did not think it important to provide dates for the feared attack or the reinforcing of Becket's burial site, and it is now impossible to pinpoint exactly when these events occurred. What can be said, though, is that the cemented-together stone structure with windows in its side would be the focus of pilgrims' devotions for the next fifty years, long after the political threat to the cult had ended.[48] In a remarkable chapter, Benedict described their enemies' new line of attack: they were saying that miracles at the tomb were being "feigned by diabolical art." The monks were casting incantations such that people felt sick, and when they came to the tomb, they would release them: "In this way, with the diabolical influence lifted, they would seem to be cured when they had not actually been ill" (II.43). According to Benedict, this problem was solved by another cultic growth spurt, this time well outside of Canterbury: "suddenly, the number of prodigies and signs was multiplied… so many witnesses to the truth came to us from all corners of England that our enemies could not resist or contradict them" (II.43).

An early decision made by the Christ Church monks about Becket's blood was a major factor – probably, in fact, the most crucial factor – that drove up the number

---

[48] On this tomb and the shrine to which Becket would be translated in 1220, see William Urry, "Some Notes on the Two Resting Places of St Thomas Becket at Canterbury," in Raymonde Foreville (ed.), *Thomas Becket: Actes du colloque international de Sédières 19–24 août 1973* (Paris, 1975), 195–209.

of people claiming Becket miracles in "all corners of England." They started to give out the blood they had collected from the martyrdom site, diluted with water, to people seeking miracles. Benedict provides an exact and very early date for when the monks began to do this, namely the eighth day after Becket's death, Tuesday, January 5, 1171. The story concerns a speechless priest of London named William. After William spent a night in vigil at Becket's tomb, the monks put a drop of blood on his tongue, plus "a drink of water made holy by a similar drop… which was without doubt begun by the divine will and is done frequently to the present day." Benedict proclaims that William "was the first of all to taste the blood of the martyr" (I.12).

We must be cautious with Benedict's spin on this story. While William may well have been the first person to whom the Canterbury monks gave a drink of Becket's blood, it is unlikely that he was *the* first, as Benedict would have it, to try drinking the blood in pursuit of a miracle. A great deal of blood left the cathedral the night of the martyrdom. Tests of its potency as a medicine probably began all but immediately. There are six other surviving accounts of William of London's miracle, and only one of them, written by the monk Gervase, attributed the miracle to a drink of Becket's blood provided by the Christ Church monks (other accounts stressed the priest's vigil at the tomb).[49] Benedict, though, was determined to see William's miracle as the beginning of the use of the blood, and to place the origins of the mixing of Becket's blood and water in the hands of the Christ Church monks. He knew that his readers might think that the monks had been too audacious. Should they have encouraged this practice, so similar to the drinking of the blood of Christ in the form of wine in the Eucharistic ritual? He assured them that "this was not begun without great fear; but, seeing that it gave profit to the ill, fear receded, and little by little security came" (I.12: see also I.23).

The truth behind the beginnings of drinking a mixture of Becket's blood and water was likely a good deal more complicated than Benedict makes it. What is clear, though, is that the monks decided very early on to distribute such a mixture to people seeking miracles. The consequence was that anyone who could make the trip to Canterbury could tap into a free supply of a very powerful and portable relic. Once the water relic began to filter back into the homes of pilgrims far

---

[49] See *Gervase* vol. 1, p. 229. For the other accounts, see Biographical Notes, William priest of London. For further discussion of the water relic, see Alyce A. Jordan, "The 'Water of Thomas Becket': Water as Medium, Metaphor, and Relic," in Cynthia Kosso and Anne Scott (eds.), *The Nature and Function of Water, Baths, Bathing, and Hygiene from Antiquity through the Renaissance* (Leiden, 2009), pp. 479–500; Pierre-André Sigal, "Naissance et premier développement d'un vinage exceptionnel: L'eau de saint Thomas," *Cahiers de civilisation médiévale* 44 (2001): 35–44; and Rachel Koopmans, "Water Mixed with the Blood of Thomas: Contact Relic Manufacture Pictured in Canterbury Cathedral's Stained Glass," *Journal of Medieval History* 42:5 (2016): 535–55.

outside of Canterbury, many miracles were claimed within those homes, resulting in more pilgrims heading to Canterbury to give thanks, more bringing the water relic home, and so on. Had the monks chosen instead to jealously guard their supply of Becket's blood and to continue to restrict access to Becket's tomb, the story of the cult could have been very different indeed. As it was, the "first days" began to give way to days with more reports of miracles, and with that, the monks took another decisive step: one of their number, Benedict, began to write down miracle stories.

THE PIONEER: BENEDICT BEGINS THE *MIRACLES* AND THE MONKS' FIRST PETITION FOR BECKET'S CANONIZATION

The best evidence for when Benedict began the *Miracles* is found in two successive stories in Book I. The first concerns a servant who had a vision and was cured of a toothache (I.14). Benedict explains that the miracle happened "around the time of Lent" (i.e., February 10–March 27, 1171), but, since the servant was too frightened to come to Canterbury at first, the miracle "was revealed to us around the sacred day of Pentecost" (May 16, 1171). Benedict begins the next story by writing, "In those days" (that is, around Pentecost) "when the church of Canterbury already shone forth with many miracles, and I was directing my attention to the ill people suffering throughout the entire church, according to the task assigned to me, I came upon a clerk… leaving the memorial of the martyr" (I.15). Benedict uses similar language when he discusses his work in the Prologue: "by the will and precept of the brothers, I am compelled to commend [the miracles] to the memory of letters. Although my wisdom does not suffice nor my eloquence assist me, I take up the burden freely and with devotion."

"The task assigned to me" and the "burden" "compelled" upon him by his brothers must have been one and the same: miracle collecting, which Benedict began around Pentecost, or put another way, in the late spring of 1171. In contrast to the tears and silence of the winter months, the monks were now witnessing electrifying scenes. In his accounts of a miracle on the Invention of the Cross (May 3, see II.33) and another on the day after Pentecost (May 17, see III.2), Benedict describes how throngs of people were present in the cathedral. When candles relit in the crypt without any human intervention on May 17, the crowd was thrilled: "It would be most difficult to relate how great was the exultation of all, how many showers of tears they shed, and how many thanks were rendered to God" (III.2).

As more scenes like this occurred and the numbers of stories brought to the monks rose, it must have become clear that miracles would forgotten if they were not written down. Someone needed to "commend them to the memory of letters." To convince Becket's enemies and detractors, this record had to be unimpeachable. Benedict assured his readers that stories of miracles "are doubted by us, lest they be doubted by others: we showed ourselves hard and as if unbelieving in the examination of the truth, so that the adversaries of the truth might be ground down into believing, or proved wrong by a strict examination of the truth and so confounded" (I.9, see also II.32, III.77, and IV.63).

The monks' resolution to record Becket's miracles was a bold move on the post-martyrdom chessboard. Miracle collecting was an unambiguous signal that they considered the dead archbishop to be a saint. Why was Benedict, among so many brothers, chosen for this "examination of the truth"? Was he eager – or reluctant – to take on this role? He does not tell us, but however he came to his task, he was clearly determined to do it well and to confound "the adversaries of the truth." He and his brothers were not alone in thinking this was a critical undertaking. Abbot Peter Celle, a great friend of the Becket camp, implored Prior Odo in a letter "with all supplication and earnest request" that "all those of you who will transmit to posterity the memory of the miracles of your and our martyr" would not write anything "about him or his miracles except what has been examined, purified, and sieved seven times."[50]

A lot was riding on the *Miracles* for Becket's budding cult, for the Christ Church monks, and for Benedict himself. As far as we know, none of the authors of the Becket Lives started working so early. The only well-known hagiographic account of Becket that has been dated earlier is a long letter composed by John of Salisbury that was sent to the bishop of Poitiers. This letter, which John later expanded into a short and widely circulated *Life* is, generally dated "early 1171." However, there are very good reasons to think that John's letter, which alludes to copious and widespread miracles "in both English provinces," cannot have been written before Benedict began miracle collecting around Pentecost or the late spring of 1171.[51] When we think of Benedict taking up his pen, we need to think of

---

[50] *The Letters of Peter of Celle*, ed. and trans. Julian Haseldine, OMT (Oxford, 2001), p. 522 (Haseldine's translation). Benedict transcribed part of this letter (see IV.87). Haseldine mistakenly dated this letter to Benedict's priorate rather than Odo's.

[51] For the letter (sent to John of Canterbury, the bishop of Poitiers), see *LJS* no. 305, pp. 724–49. For a dating of this letter to October 1171–April 1172, see Karen Bollermann and Cary J. Nederman, "John of Salisbury and Thomas Becket," in Chrisophe Grellard and Frédérique Lachaud (eds.), *A Companion to John of Salisbury* (Leiden, 2015), pp. 63–104, at pp. 81–5. For disagreement with this date, see Michael Staunton, "John of Salisbury and the Church of Canterbury," in Christophe Grellard and Frédérique Lachaud (eds.), *Jean de Salisbury, nouvelles lectures, nouveaux enjeux* (Florence, 2018), pp. 185–207. Staunton concedes that "a date after Easter [is] more plausible" (p. 203), and Anne Duggan has stated that it dates "certainly after Easter 1171": see Anne Duggan, "Becket is Dead! Long Live St Thomas," in Paul Webster and Marie-Pierre Gelin (eds.), *The Cult of Thomas Becket in the Plantagenet World, c.1170–c.1220* (Woodbridge, 2016), pp. 25–51, at p. 27. In my view, summer 1171 is the earliest possible date for the letter, and it

him as the pioneer he was, the first to embark on a major writing project devoted to portraying the dead archbishop as the great new martyr and saint of the age.[52]

Not long after Benedict started collecting, the monks made another move to boost Becket's cult. They sent one of their brothers to petition Pope Alexander III to canonize Becket. In 1171, papal canonization had almost none of the characteristics that we are familiar with today. The vast majority of people celebrated as saints in the late twelfth century had been acclaimed by local populations and confirmed by local ecclesiastical authorities. There was as yet no "canonization process," no need of a "canonization dossier," and none of the bureaucratic machinery that so characterized papal canonization procedures in the late medieval period.[53] The monks' canonization request needs to be understood as an attempt to gain political help and pressure from one of the very few places where the dead Becket's supporters hoped they could find it.

We know of this early petition from two sources: first, a statement in an anonymous author's *Life of Thomas* that a first petition had failed (this author is thought to have been a Christ Church monk),[54] and a second, particularly revealing source: a letter written by Pope Alexander himself. Dated to the late summer or early autumn of 1171, the letter was directed to the papal legates Albert and Theodwin.[55] The pope informs his legates that the Christ Church monks "have sent to us a certain one of their brothers" as well as "letters" requesting that Becket be "inscribed in the catalogue" of saints.[56] Given the travel time to Rome, this brother must have left Canterbury carrying the letters sometime in the summer of 1171. Alexander writes to instruct his legates to "seek to know the truth of this more fully from bishops and other secular persons concerning those miracles which are said to happen in the church. Write to us about the miracles and make known to us the certainty of the thing with all diligence... such that we are able to

---

could easily have been written later than this. John's letter deserves notice as the earliest known description of Becket's murder, but Benedict started collecting miracles before it was written.

[52] For a summary of the generally accepted dating for the Becket *Lives*, see Staunton, *Thomas Becket*, pp. 3–7. No modern edition of any of the Becket *Lives* has yet been published, and much remains to be worked out concerning their dating and interrelationships.

[53] See Christian Krötzl and Sari Katajala-Peltomaa (eds.), *Miracles in Medieval Canonization Processes: Structures, Functions, and Methodologies* (Turnhout, 2018).

[54] Anonymous II, *Vita S. Thomae*, MTB, vol. 4, pp. 80–144, at p. 143. On Anonymous II, see Staunton, *Thomas Becket*, pp. 39–43.

[55] For the letter, see *Decretales Ineditae Saeculi XII*, ed. by Stanley Chodorow and Charles Duggan, Monumenta Iuris Canonici Series B: Corpus Collectionum (Vatican City, 1982), vol. 4, no. 36, pp. 36–7. Anne Duggan dates the letter to the late summer or early autumn of 1171: see her discussion in Duggan, *Thomas Becket*, pp. 217–18.

[56] *Decretales Ineditae Saeculi XII*, vol. 4, no. 36, pp. 36–7 (my translation).

give assent to the petition of the aforesaid brothers securely and confidently, if it ought to be approved."[57]

This passage strongly suggests that the letters the Christ Church monk brought to the pope must have contained some kind of account of miracles within Canterbury Cathedral, an account that the monk would no doubt have supplemented with his own oral testimony. While Benedict was the obvious person to compose such an account, it would be a mistake to try to tie a section or sections of the *Miracles* we now have before us to the 1171 petition. Not much of the *Miracles* would have existed at this stage, and what did exist was not necessarily identical to the text we now have before us. Benedict would not write the Prologue until 1172–3, and most if not all of Book I, too, appears to be a later composition.[58] The letters that the Christ Church monk traveling to Rome carried with him were likely just that: letters written by the prior and community of Christ Church that included accounts of a number of miracles within Canterbury Cathedral. The most likely candidates for these miracles are some of those that now appear in Book II, but it is impossible to say which or how many might have been recounted.

Alexander's reaction to the petition was not what the monks had hoped. He wanted more testimony and wondered aloud "if [their petition] should be approved." In a precarious political situation due to an ongoing papal schism, Alexander dealt with Henry II very gingerly in the immediate aftermath of Becket's death.[59] In late March 1171, he stipulated only that Henry had to meet with papal legates to determine whatever penance he might need to perform, and should, in the meantime, refrain from entering churches. When the Christ Church monk arrived in Rome with the canonization petition, Henry had not met with the legates, and in fact would not do so until May 1172.[60]

The monks themselves likely realized that their 1171 request was a long shot. Alexander declined to canonize Becket, buying time by asking his legates to look into the miracle question themselves. Interestingly, he told Albert and Theodwin

---

[57] Ibid.
[58] The dating of the Prologue and Book I is addressed in more detail below, pp. 50 and 52.
[59] On Alexander's cautious dealings with the Becket dispute and its aftermath, see Anne J. Duggan, "*Alexander ille meus*: The Papacy of Alexander III," in Peter D. Clarke and Anne J. Duggan (eds.), *Pope Alexander III (1159–1181): The Art of Survival* (Farnham, 2012), 13–49, at pp. 25–37. For Alexander and Becket's canonization, see Donald S. Prudlo, *Certain Sainthood: Canonization and the Origins of Papal Infallibility in the Medieval Church* (Ithaca, 2015), pp. 33–41.
[60] The best account of Henry II's meeting with the legates and reconciliation at Avranches is Anne Duggan, "Diplomacy, Status, and Conscience: Henry II's Penance for Becket's Murder," in Peter Herde, Karl Borchardt, and Enno Bünz (eds.), *Forschungen zur Reichs-, Papst- und Landesgeschichte: Peter Herde zum 65. Geburtstag von Freunden, Schülern und Kollegen dargebracht* (Stuttgart, 1998), vol. 1, 265–90.

to question "bishops and other secular persons" – pointedly *not* the monks – about the truth of the accounts of Becket's miracles. At Canterbury, meanwhile, Benedict was occupied with his "task" and "burden" of miracle collecting.

Part Two

LISTENING, ASSESSING, LETTERS, AND NOTE-TAKING

The composition of medieval miracle collections has sometimes been envisioned as a rather mechanical activity, as if a writer merely sat at a tomb or shrine and wrote down all the stories he heard. Even a brief perusal of Benedict's *Miracles* makes it clear that its construction was far more complex and considered than this.[61] It is the product of two and a half years of intensive effort that involved listening, assessing, questioning, note-taking, investigating, hosting, and sorting through notes and letters, activities that likely ate up considerably more of Benedict's time than the actual writing.

In an important passage found early on in the collection, Benedict informed his readers that "we will tell the story only of these miracles: those which we saw with our own eyes, or we heard from the actual ill people already healed and their witnesses, or those things we learned from the testimony of religious men, who had seen them with their own eyes" (I.7). When one looks at the *Miracles* as a whole, it becomes clear that he really did view the stories he heard in these three categories, and that he assessed stories differently depending on which category they were in.

The first category, "those which we saw with our own eyes," meant, in essence, miracles happening within the cathedral – the kind of miracles that had first "consoled" and "revived" the monks after Becket's death (II.6). The "we" of this statement should be underlined: gathering miracles was often a group project. Benedict frequently refers to "we who were there" to hear or see something, "we" meaning the brothers and their servants, and "there" meaning Becket's tomb in the crypt.[62] Benedict must have spent many hours in the crypt, but he was not present every minute of every day, and probably not often on duty alone. He wrote of a monk named Roger who was also "assigned to the care of the sacred body," described how Robert, the monastery's sacrist, cured a man with Becket's belt, and refers to other unnamed monks and servants at work in the crypt chapel.[63] In one chapter,

---

[61] For a recent helpful survey of the composition of miracle collections, see Louise Elizabeth Wilson, "Writing Miracle Collections," in Sari Katajala-Peltomaa, Jenni Kuuliala, and Iona McCleery (eds.), *A Companion to Medieval Miracle Collections* (Leiden, 2021), 15–35.

[62] See, for example, II.32, II.40, and III.9.

[63] See IV.59, II.38, III.1, III.19, and III.20 and Biographical Notes, Roger, monk of Christ Church and Robert, sacrist of Christ Church.

Benedict described himself as traveling by night with a servant (IV.58), a story that underlines the fact that he was not always at the cathedral, much less in the crypt. There must be stories in the *Miracles* that he heard about from his brothers and/or their servants rather than being there himself.

The "seeing with our own eyes" rhetoric, meanwhile, should not be taken too literally. There certainly were occasions when the monks felt they had personally eyewitnessed a miracle, such as when a monk and a servant were in the process of getting a girl's candle relit at Becket's tomb when it flamed up of its own accord (III.1), or the time Benedict saw a lame man kneel to pray at Becket's tomb, get up, fall down, and then get up and stand without using a crutch (III.8). What the monks more commonly saw, though, were people who were visibly ill who, some time later, appeared to be improved. Some miracles would not have been visible no matter how carefully they watched. One man regained his sense of smell when he entered the church (II.15), while a woman was freed from something like tinnitus when she prayed at the tomb (III.16). Complicating matters further was the fact that people experienced miracles in other places in the cathedral, not just at the tomb.[64]

Whether or not the monks and/or their servants caught a glimpse of something, stories still needed to be told. The crucial importance of what we might term an exit interview is underlined by Benedict's frustration that not everyone who felt themselves healed in the cathedral came forward to tell the monks about it. He frets about these lost stories more than once.[65] For those who did present themselves, not all interviews were satisfactory. Benedict wrote that one boy claiming he had been enabled to see did not satisfy him because "he produced no witness or person to attest to his blindness" and "I did not see him blind when he came" (IV.56). In other cases, Benedict felt that people left the cathedral before the monks could be certain about their recoveries.[66] Still, cathedral miracles allowed Benedict and his fellows to question people very close in time to their experiences, as well bystanders who may have seen things they had not. Cathedral miracles make up a significant portion of the *Miracles*, about 30% of the whole, with many of them appearing at the beginnings of Books II and III.[67] Benedict was

---

[64] For miracles at the "doors of the church," see II.1, II.38, III.3, and III.33; for miracles at the martyrdom site, see II.33 and II.40; for a miracle at the "marble pavement," see III.7; and for miracles simply "in the church," see II.53 and IV.83.

[65] See II.34, III.39, and III.46.

[66] See IV.23, IV.33, and IV.35.

[67] The percentages of stories I cite for cathedral miracles, outside miracles, and religious men's miracles are from my count of the number of chapters devoted to each category. Another person's count might be slightly different from my own. Not all chapters concern a specific individual's story, and for those that do, it is not always clear to which category a chapter belongs. For a more in-depth discussion of Benedict's treatment of stories in these three categories, see Koopmans, *Wonderful to Relate*, pp. 159–80 and 282 n. 8.

so comfortable vouching for these stories that he even devoted two chapters to non-miracles, cases in which ill boys did not find healing at the tomb (II.16–17).

Benedict's second category of stories, those "we heard from the actual ill people already healed and their witnesses," encompassed an extremely broad range of stories: in effect, any miracle experienced by a lay person that happened outside of the cathedral. About 45% of the chapters in the *Miracles* fall into this category. Outside miracles could be far more spectacular than anything the monks had seen inside the cathedral, including resurrection miracles and the amazing story of the blinded and castrated Eilward of Westoning.[68] However, they were not easy to authenticate. Nearly all the people telling these stories were strangers. Aside from inspecting objects that these visitors brought with them, examining their bodies for signs of illness and healing, and noting what kinds of gifts they gave, the monks and their servants could not claim any degree of eyewitness for their miracles.

In this situation, Benedict assured his readers, they sought out "witnesses." He rarely named such witnesses in the *Miracles* (doing so would have taken time and bulked out the text considerably), but he did attach comments to certain miracles to reassure his readers that he and his brothers did not blindly accept everything they heard. One of the most interesting of these is a coda he added to the story of Beatrice, a pauper who claimed to have been healed of blindness partly on her way to Canterbury and partly after a vigil at the tomb. Beatrice wore poor clothing and her only witness was a girl, and Benedict openly doubted her story: "now I demanded more harshly for witnesses, now I presented to her an unmerciful appearance as if I were contradicting her. She answered back with hard and bitter words" (III.31). Beatrice convinced Benedict in the end, but there must have been other low-status, poor individuals who did not.

Benedict was also careful to state that they gathered stories from "the actual ill people." What he meant was that they did not accept secondhand stories. The person who experienced a miracle had to be the one who told them about it. In practice, Benedict recorded miracles involving infants and very young children who could not have told their stories themselves, and he may have silently bent this rule on other occasions. Still, the content of the *Miracles* strongly suggests that the monks did indeed wave off stories that people could have told them about their relatives, friends, neighbors, and acquaintances. Dismissing hearsay strengthened the credibility of the *Miracles*, and it also freed the monks from a great deal of labor. The time they spent listening to people would have ballooned alarmingly if they had opened the gate to such stories.

There were certain people, though, from whom Benedict would gladly hear secondhand stories. His third category of stories was "those things we learned from

---

[68] See IV.2, IV.62–6, and IV.94.

the testimony of religious men, who had seen them with their own eyes." While a person like Beatrice had a hard time being believed when she described her own cure, Benedict felt that men dedicated to the religious life – men like himself – could be counted on to tell true stories not only about themselves, but also about others. Benedict knew that nearly all of his readers would be religious men (that is, monks, clerks, canons, priors, abbots, and bishops), so he was effectively saying that he trusted them to know and tell the truth. In practice, Benedict extended this same trust to high-ranking laymen and women, such as Earl Simon, who told about the cure of his baker (IV.29), and Countess Rohese de Vere, who told a story about a canon of Bedford (IV.51). Religious women do not seem to have come into Benedict's calculations. His collection contains only two miracles concerning nuns. One story was told at Canterbury by the nun's high-ranking mother, while the other may well have been conveyed by letter.[69] Priests were also in a more marginal group. They often came from quite humble source origins, and while Benedict did include priests' secondhand stories, he also often added statements testifying to their veracity.

About 25% of the *Miracles* is made up of stories from religious men, the secular elite, and priests, and a remarkable two-thirds of these stories are secondhand – that is, stories about people other than the speaker. Benedict was writing at a time when most high-ranking members of English society, both secular and religious, had to be convinced of Becket's sanctity. In this context, one can imagine the excitement at Christ Church when someone of standing, such as an abbot, venerable knight, or countess, appeared at the monastery with stories of miracles to tell. These early adopters of Becket's cult were key witnesses, and Benedict was keen to hear and record their stories. Such valued guests must have been warmly received, hosted in comfortable quarters, and listened to with deference and delight. An unarticulated but clearly crucial subcategory of stories that Benedict also wanted to hear were those that showed Becket's enemies the errors of their ways, such as the story of a certain Simeon, described three times in a short chapter as an "enemy of a martyr," who was punished for mocking the efficacy of the water, or the miracle of a leprous boy who had connections to Queen Eleanor of Aquitaine, Godfrey, Bishop of St. Asaph, and Jocelin, Bishop of Salisbury.[70] Demonstrating that people of distinction testified to or were forced to confront the truth of Becket's miracles was a central goal of his project.

The written sources Benedict utilized in the *Miracles* are a subset of the "religious men" category. Benedict copied nine letters, salutation and all, into his collection.[71]

---

[69] See III.58 and IV.10.
[70] See III.25 and IV.74. See also I.14, III.17, and III.45.
[71] See II.52, IV.2, IV.4, IV.11, IV.65, IV.84–5, IV.87, and Addition 7. See also IV.86, which we know is the text of a letter from a monk of Reading Abbey because William copied the letter directly into his collection, including its salutation: see Parallel Miracles no. 12.

Religious men wrote eight of these. The ninth was written by the burgesses of Bedford (IV.2), but, as Benedict carefully explained, it was solicited by the highborn Hugh de Puiset, Bishop of Durham, so it came with his impressive imprimatur. Benedict's inclusion of these letters was clearly promotional, advertising that men like Albinus, the Abbot of Darley, Bishop William Turbe of Norwich, and Geoffrey, the Dean of Gloucester, had all testified to Becket's miracles in writing.[72] Some of the letters were carried to Canterbury by the very people who had experienced the miracle.[73] Benedict mentions receiving letters from priests, but – underlining their more marginal authority – he does not copy their letters directly into his collection.[74] He also stated that William son of Ranulf, the Lord of Whitchurch, notified the monks of miracles via letter (see III.40: either the letter or Benedict's introduction to it had some remarkably harsh inventive about the 'uncouth' and 'savage' Welsh population). Benedict may well have plagiarized from the Whitchurch letter, and he very likely lifted text from other letters in ways that cannot now be traced.[75]

Gathering material for the *Miracles*, then, meant countless hours of listening and questioning, leavened with an exciting flash of seeing something remarkable or a welcome visit from an honored guest. On a number of occasions Benedict mentions sending out messengers to check up on rumors of miracles or to discover how someone fared after they left the cathedral.[76] In the case of certain miracles that happened in Kent near Canterbury, he appears to have gone out himself to investigate.[77] All of these miracles, though, were ones that Benedict had first heard about at Canterbury. He did not go to London or Rouen or further afield to find out what people were saying in the way a modern investigative reporter might. He stayed put: the stories came to him. The only set of stories that Benedict might have heard about outside of Canterbury is the long block of stories concerning a cross set up in the martyr's honor at Newington, Kent, found at the close of Book III (III.64–78). Even here, though,

---

[72] See IV.11, IV.65, and Addition 7.
[73] See IV.4, IV.65, IV.84, Addition 7.
[74] See IV.64 and IV.66.
[75] There are very close verbal correspondences between Benedict's and William's account of the miracles of Cecilia of Plumstock (see IV.65 and Appendix no. 8). It seems they were both cribbing from a letter written by a local priest. For more analysis of the letters found in Benedict's and William's collections, see Rachel Koopmans, "Testimonial Letters in the Late-Twelfth Century Collections of Thomas Becket's Miracles," in David C. Mengel and Lisa Wolverton (eds.), *Christianity and Culture in the Middle Ages: Essays to Honor John Van Engen* (Notre Dame, 2014), 168–201.
[76] See IV.4, IV.11, IV.21, and IV.87.
[77] See II.2, IV.34, IV.63, and Addition 8.

it is more likely that Benedict was drawing on a letter or written account rather than collecting stories there himself.

Benedict was discriminating. The people with (by far) the best chance of having their stories recorded were religious men and the secular elite, followed by people who experienced miracles under the eye of the monks in the cathedral, with those who came to give thanks about miracles that happened elsewhere in last place, especially if such pilgrims ranked low in social hierarchies or otherwise struck Benedict as unreliable or uninteresting. He likely had other ways of ranking, sorting, and discarding stories that are now more difficult to discern. The clerk William FitzStephen heard the collection being read aloud, and he complained that "the writer fails to commend to memory" the miracles that the martyr was performing in France, Ireland, and elsewhere.[78] This is in fact a fair criticism of Benedict's *Miracles*, which does indeed concentrate very heavily on stories from English tellers.[79] In the earliest year or so of the cult, English pilgrims no doubt predominated, but later on, it could be that Benedict simply felt more comfortable with stories told by people residing in England.

For all its length, then, the *Miracles* is a subjective and highly limited account of Becket's early miracles. Still, for the most part, we can trust that the people named in the collection really did exist. Benedict wanted the people in his text to be traceable, and he takes care to tell the reader their names, family relationships, places of origin, and, in the case of children, their ages. To manage this across the entire collection, listening must have been accompanied by note-taking.

Benedict never explicitly stated that he used notes. William did, and he was clearly picking up on a process that was underway when Benedict was creating the *Miracles*. In the prologue to his *Life* of Becket, William explained that when he was asked by the brothers to collect Becket's miracles (in June 1172), there were many that were "concealed in uncorrected and defective notes [*in schedulis occultabat incorrecta et imperfecta*]." He then had a vision of Becket telling him to "choose what you will," which he interpreted to mean that he could pick and choose among the stories, concerning himself only with the ones he thought deserved to be heard.[80] Late in his collection, just before taking a break from collecting, William spoke of

---

[78] FitzStephen, *Vita*, p. 151.
[79] Benedict devotes two blocks of stories in Book IV to miracles in France (IV.17–23 and IV.60–1), and there are some individual stories concern French tellers: see, for instance, IV.21, the story of Mary of Rouen. He includes one story of a German (Matilda of Cologne, IV.37), and one of a Scot (John of Roxburgh, Addition 9). William would include far more non-English miracles, including discussion of Ireland: see Marcus Bull, "Criticism of Henry II's Expedition to Ireland in William of Canterbury's Miracles of St Thomas Becket," *Journal of Medieval History* 33 (2007): 107–29.
[80] William of Canterbury, *Vita*, pp. 2–3.

notes again, stating that though there were stories about resurrections "noted down in our tablets [*in tabulis nostris praenotentur*]," the times were difficult, and so "they must await another pen than mine."[81]

Notes, tablets – these were evidently notations about miracles written on scrap pieces of parchment, a roll or rolls, and/or wax tablets. In one chapter, William had a couple conclude their story by saying, "We ask that we be recorded in the register [*matricula*] and dismissed quickly, lest our return home be slowed, since we have traveled from the territory of York."[82] This all suggests a process of notation immediately on hearing someone's miracle story, with the writing of the miracle collection a separate activity, an activity made especially challenging if the miracle collector had to deal with inadequate notes or sort through great masses of them. A contemporary example of note-taking as a preliminary step to writing a miracle collection is found with the collection compiled from 1172–3 at the shrine of the Virgin at Rocamadour in south-central France. At one point, the collection's anonymous writer stated that a number of miracles could not be described in full because "the notary was unwell on the days when these things became known, and so he did not write down [the miracles] in the correct manner and with proper headings."[83] At the beginning of Book IV, Benedict contrasted the writing speed of a scribe with that of a notary, stating that the miracles were so numerous that "if I were given hands that could write not just speedily like a scribe, but record most rapidly like a notary, my talent would nevertheless be overcome, my tongue would fail, and my fingers become senseless" (IV.1). Though this passage does not prove that Benedict enlisted the help of a notary, the Christ Church monks certainly had the wherewithal to hire notaries or enlist literate servants to help them. Note-taking could have changed over time. Benedict might have relied on his memory at first, started note-taking himself, and then sought aid as the number of stories needing to be noted down increased.

However note-taking was being managed, by June 1172 there were clearly many notes that Benedict had not utilized, so much so that William felt oppressed by their number and their quality. In terms of the contents of the notes, the name of the male head of household seems always to have been noted. Women could go unnamed even if they were the key players in the story. A place of origin or a family name was also noted, however obscure it might be. The basic circumstances of people's illnesses and their cures must also have been noted down, including how long someone had suffered: eight months, for instance, or three years, or whatever the

---

[81] William of Canterbury, *Miracula*, VI.90, p. 484.
[82] William of Canterbury, *Miracula*, V.30, p. 396.
[83] *The Miracles of Our Lady of Rocamadour: Analysis and Translation*, trans. Marcus Bull (Woodbridge, 1999), p. 137.

individual said. Some of the extremely short chapters in Benedict's collection may reflect the content of such notes. One chapter, for instance, reads in total: "What I relate happened in the house of the knight Hugh de Bodebi. A seven-year-old boy, Alexander, could not hear in one of his ears. When the water was poured in his ear, he recovered perfect hearing" (IV.82). Benedict so often provides the age of children that it must have been standard to ask how old a child was. For speakers beyond childhood, he might say that the person was adolescent or elderly, but age was otherwise unimportant.

That the notes were inadequate, or that Benedict relied on his memory for certain details or entire stories, is clear from his occasional admissions that he had forgotten certain details, such as the name of a village, the extent of an illness, the range of infirmities, the name of a peasant, or the circumstances of a cure.[84] One case in which Benedict's notes seem to have failed him is the pair of chapters concerning miracles experienced by Constance, a nun of Stixwould (III.58), and the nun's ill sister-in-law, Matilda (III.59). Benedict stated that the patriarch of the family was the deceased Robert son of Gilbert in the diocese of Lincoln, a man who appears in a number of contemporary documents (see Biographical Notes). These documents show that Robert had a daughter-in-law named Matilda – the Matilda of Benedict's story. So far so good, but the documents record the name of Robert's widow as Matilda, whereas Benedict called her Constance, and the name of the ill Matilda's husband as William, whereas Benedict called him Robert. One way to explain this is that Benedict's notes only provided the names of the deceased patriarch of the family, Robert, and the two people who experienced miracles, Constance and Matilda. When he came to write down this story, perhaps he surmised that Robert's son would most likely be named Robert and Constance's mother would most likely be named Constance.

This mix-up is visible only because we have enough documentation about Robert son of Gilbert to be able to fill in the names of the family ourselves. There is another case of the same problem later on in the collection. Benedict gives a father and his son the same name (Ingelram), though we know from other documentary records that the father was in fact named Stephen (IV.52).[85] There must have been other problems moving from notes to the *Miracles* that are now not possible to trace. Some notes must have been so garbled, or the stories themselves uninteresting to the collectors, that neither monk decided to put them into their collections.

When people told their stories at Canterbury, questions were asked, notes were taken, and any letters were received. Actually composing the *Miracles* was a more

---

[84] See I.15, II.37, II.67, III.28, and IV.53.
[85] William gives the father his correct name in his version of the story: see Parallel Miracles no. 6.

deliberative process, when Benedict sat down to sort through notes, letters, and his memories of conversations. The material he had to choose from would have been constantly shifting as he selected and wrote up certain stories and gathered notes on more and still more. Composing would have required concentration, and Benedict very likely wrote the *Miracles* in the monastery's scriptorium rather than the hubbub of the crypt chapel. Whereas he seems to have plenty of help with the gathering process, the composition was on him, and it is here where his vision and skills as a writer really came into play.

MIRACLE MATCHING: A DEFINING FEATURE OF THE *MIRACLES*

A good way to envision Benedict's composition process is to compare the miracles to beads of a great variety of colours, shapes, and sizes, and the text to a very long thread. When Benedict settled down to a writing session, it was time to decide which beads to string together and the order in which he would put them. His chief preoccupation was to select beads – miracles – that matched together well. The energy he put into pairing and linking stories together is remarkable. There are unconnected stories, but they are far outnumbered by deliberately and carefully matched pairs, sets, and runs of miracles. Apart from a reading of the whole text, a fine-grained listing of these connections, provided below, is the best way to see how Benedict constructed the *Miracles*. I have noted unconnected chapters and transitional chapters (that is, chapters without a specific miracle story) with italics.

Book I

I.1–6	Six chapters recounting visions
I.7	*Transitional chapter from visions to miracles*
I.8–12	Becket's first five miracles
I.13–15	Three early miracles, the first dating to shortly before and after the martyrdom, and the second and third occurring in Lent 1171
I.16–18	Three early miracles relating to Becket's blood
I.19–21	Three miracles told by William of Bishopsbourne about Becket's blood and clothing
I.22–4	Three stories of Canterbury citizens using the blood-and-water relic acquired from the monks

Book II

II.1–3	Two miracles on Easter Sunday, plus miracles experienced by relatives of the subject of II.2

II.4–5	Miracles of two Canterbury residents
II.6	*Transitional chapter regarding the opening of the crypt*
II.7–8	Two lame women of Canterbury cured in the cathedral
II.9–10	Two people expelling noxious material after drinking the water relic
II.11–12	*Two unconnected miracles*
II.13–15	Two people experiencing miracles from the same village
II.15	*Unconnected miracle*
II.16–17	Two boys denied healing
II.18–22	Miracle of the water relic and a disappearing worm, then four miracles of wooden pyxes unable to hold the water relic
II.23–4	Two miracles happening in the cathedral
II.25	*Unconnected miracle*
II.26–8	*Transitional chapter regarding the removal of Becket's coffin and its concealment behind the altar of St. Mary,* plus a miracle of a man with bent back feet at this same altar of St. Mary, paired with a miracle of a boy with contracted and bent back feet
II.29–32	*Transitional chapter recounting the reinstallation of Becket's coffin and the making of a secure marble box with openings along its side,* plus three miracles regarding these openings
II.33–4	Miracle on the day of the Invention of the Cross and others occurring very soon after this miracle
II.35	*Unconnected miracle*
II.36–7	Two miracles resulting from washing with the water relic
II.38–9	Two miracles connected to use of Becket's clothing
II.40–2	Two miracles of boys who had been unable to walk for years, plus a story of a woman carried to Canterbury on a litter
II.43–7	*Transitional chapter regarding accusations that the monks were using incantations, accusations proved wrong by many miracles experienced outside the cathedral,* followed by four stories of people cured outside of the cathedral
II.48–9	Two miracles of men suffering from fistula
II.50	*Unconnected miracle*
II.51–4	Two stories told by Prior Robert of Cricklade; miracle of man suffering very similar ailment to Prior Robert; miracle of this man's son
II.55–6	Two stories about religious men who cured themselves and others using the same method
II.57–8	Two cures from the use of Becket's clothing
II.59	*Unconnected miracle*
II.60–1	Two recoveries of sons near death
II.62–4	Three miracles concerning severe headaches

32   THE PASSION AND MIRACLES OF ST. THOMAS BECKET

II.65–7   Two stories of knights who died good deaths, plus a miracle of the son of second knight
II.68–9   Two miracles at sea
II.70–1   Two men healed of serious problems with their arms
II.72   *Unconnected miracle*
II.73–6   Two cures of people from the marshes, the second from blindness, plus two cures of long-term blindness
II.77   *Unconnected miracle*

Book III

III.1–4   Four miracles of relighting candles in the cathedral around the date of Pentecost
III.5–7   Three miracles of seriously disabled people carried into the cathedral
III.8–9   Two cures of neighbors at the tomb witnessed by Benedict
III.10–11   The father of a crippled daughter confesses his sins, followed by a *transitional chapter in which Benedict muses on the "medicine of confession"*
III.12–14   Three cures of blindness in the cathedral
III.15–16   Two miracles in the cathedral
III.17   *Unconnected miracle*
III.18–25   Early vision regarding the wide distribution of the water relic; three miracles about odd occurrences with wooden pyxes holding the water relic; *transitional chapter with account of changeover from wooden pyxes to metal ampullas*; three miracles concerning metal ampullas
III.26–7   Woman with flux, man with dysentery, both cured with the water relic in the cathedral
III.28   *Unconnected miracle*
III.29   *Transitional chapter regarding cathedral miracles not being reported to the monks*
III.30–1   Two cures of people before they came to the cathedral
III.32–5   Four cures in the cathedral
III.36–7   Cures of a girl and her mother
III.38–9   Two cures of abnormal menstrual flow
III.40–3   Miracles at Whitchurch (in the Welsh Marches); miracle of Welsh pilgrims told by Abbot Richard of Sulby; miracle experienced by Abbot Richard
III.44–6   Three cures of blindness
III.47–8   Three cures of gravely ill women
III.50–1   Cure of infant daughter of Edric, priest of Ramsholt; miracle of a lost cheese told by Edric
III.52   *Unconnected miracle*
III.53–6   Two miracles involving coins, plus two miracles relating to Ralph, a fowler, one

of them involving a coin, the other a hawk

III.57 *Unconnected miracle*

III.58–9 Cure of Constance, daughter of Robert son of Gilbert, and cure of her sister-in-law, Matilda

III.60–2 Three stories told by John of Kinstan, Abbot of Jervaux

III.63–4 Two stories told by Master Henry of Houghton

III.65–78 Thirteen chapters devoted to miracles at a cross erected in Becket's honor at Newington, Kent; a fourteenth chapter concerning similar happenings at a similar place

Book IV

IV.1 *Transitional chapter about the great number of miracles*

IV.2 *Unconnected miracle* (the blinded and castrated Eilward of Westoning)

IV.3–4 Two miracles of lepers

IV.5 *Unconnected miracle*

IV.6–7 Two miracles of averted fires

IV.8–9 Two miracles told by people traveling to Canterbury together

IV.10 *Unconnected miracle*

IV.11–15 Two chapters about the water turning into blood, the second told by Ranulf, priest of Froyle, plus three more stories told by Ranulf

IV.16 *Unconnected miracle*

IV.17–23 Seven miracles happening in northern France, three of them concerning the water relic supplied by Tetion son of Hertran

IV.24–6 Three miracles concerning the clerk Philip of Alnwick, his son, and a woman in their household

IV.27–8 Two miracles of lepers

IV.29 *Unconnected miracle*

IV.30–1 Two cures of blindness

IV.32–5 Four stories of blindness as miraculous punishment

IV.36–7 *Two unconnected miracles*

IV.38–40 Three stories involving coins

IV.41–6 Six sea stories

IV.47–51 Five miracles resulting from the use of the water relic

IV.52 *Unconnected miracle*

IV.53–5 Three miracles of swollen/dropsical women

IV.56–7 Two recoveries of insane people, one doubtful cure of a blind boy

IV.58–9 Two miracles resulting from the invocation of the name of the martyr by Christ Church monks

IV.60–1 Two stories of people from France suffering from fistulas on their jaws

IV.62–6   Five resurrection stories of children dead or thought dead, three of them from drowning
IV.67–71   *Five unconnected miracles*
IV.72–6   Five cures of leprosy
IV.77–80   Four stories regarding people helped or acquitted in a judicial duel, trials by water, and a lawsuit
IV.81   *Unconnected miracle*
IV.82–3   Two cures of deafness
IV.84–7   Four letters about miracles (in IV.86, Benedict omits the letter's salutation)
IV.88–9   *Two unconnected miracles*
IV.90–1   Two miracles told by a dean
IV.92–3   Two miracles about neighbors, both of them cured by drinking the water relic
IV.94   *Unconnected miracle* (The resurrection of the son of Roger de Clare)

Additions

Addition 1–2   Two recoveries of boys near death (similar to IV.94)
Additions 3–5   Three blindness cures, the first two in the same village
Addition 6   *Unconnected miracle*
Additions 7–9   Three stories concerning individuals buried, fallen down a well, and submerged

Benedict matched up stories from the very beginning to the very end of the *Miracles*. Though one can find some long runs of similar miracles, such as seven vision stories, six stories about perils at sea, and a particularly notable set of five child resurrection miracles, most of his matches are in sets of two or three. He found an extraordinary number of ways to do this matching. He often linked up miracles by type of illness (blindness, leprosy, fistula, dropsy, mental illness, etc.), by type of disability (lameness, deafness, problems with arms, bent back feet, etc.), and/or by severity, such as a complete inability to walk, near-death illness, and long-term blindness. He matched up miracles by type of accident or rescue, such as drownings, fires, and judicial trials, or by the strange behaviour of material objects such as coins, candles, wooden pyxes, and metal ampullas. The use of specific relics often links together stories, most often the drinking of the water relic, but also the application of items of Becket's clothing. He also employed the place of a miracle as a binding device, matching together miracles about the openings in Becket's tomb, miracles at the martyrdom site, miracles happening at Newington, miracles in France, and miracles happening more generally inside or outside of the cathedral. He connected other miracles by their timing, devoting sets of chapters to miracles that happened in Lent, at Easter, at Pentecost, and others that he says happened in quick succession.

The type of person experiencing a miracle also served as a binding device, such as dropsical women or drowned boys. Reflecting his desire to record stories from religious men and high-status tellers, another very common way he linked together chapters was by teller, such as the stories told by John of Kinstan and Master Henry of Houghton towards the end of Book III. There are many inventive pairings, such as the two stories about monks invoking the name of the martyr, two about religious men who cured themselves and then cured others using the same method, two about boys denied healing, two about knights who died good deaths after drinking the water relic, and two about dangerous abnormalities in menstrual flow, one woman having none and coughing up blood, while the other had too much.

In addition to coupling and placing similar miracles together, Benedict often provided introductions or conclusions to chapters that were designed to link stories together, including otherwise unmatched miracles. For example, in Book II, he wrote about a lame woman with a painful knee who was brought to Becket's tomb and was not entirely healed (II.7). He began the next chapter by writing "We know that he who strengthened her disabled knee could also have fully restored the bases and soles of her feet so that she could step correctly again, because we know without doubt that he granted this to Wlviva of Canterbury" (II.8). After telling the story of the lame Wlviva, who prayed before Becket's tomb, he turned next to the story of Edmund, who "had brought himself there as well." This Edmund lacked sight in one eye and had felt something painful in his chest for a long time. After drinking the water relic, he regained the sight in the eye and the thing inside of him ruptured and came up through his mouth (II.9). This story led Benedict to tell another about someone with something stuck inside of them, the first sentence of the chapter reading, "There was no less praise or glory in what we know to have happened to a woman named Muriel." After being gravely ill, Muriel received a drink of the water relic, and was close to death when she began to vomit up cherry, plum, and acorn pits (II.10). Benedict transitioned to the next story, about a woman with a painful arm, with this reflection, "To these things the Lord added another miracle, concerning a lesser illness – though why do I say lesser? No-one thinks that the illness he or she suffers is small" (II.11). He began the following by writing "A blacksmith of the Isle of Thanet, Robert, also found the grace of healing" (II.12). And on and on it goes, with Benedict carefully tying stories together in one way or another.

Benedict had at least two reasons for putting so much effort into linking and matching miracles. The first is that it gives the *Miracles* a great deal of forward momentum, pulling the reader on from the next story to the next. The way Benedict constructed the *Miracles* replicates the way people exchange stories in conversation, with one story provoking thoughts of a similar one, prompting the memory of another and then another. We know from two sources that, even as Benedict was in the process of composing the *Miracles*, it was read aloud to his brother monks and their elite guests in the chapterhouse, the monks' daily gathering place.[86] Such readings, very likely performed by Benedict himself, were no doubt intended as a means to keep all the brothers informed about the saint's ongoing marvels, but they also must have encouraged Benedict to please and engage his listeners. By matching up miracles and recreating some of the natural connectiveness of conversation, he made his text easier and more pleasurable to listen to, and later, easier and more pleasurable to read. He was careful not to put too many miracles of the same type together, fearing, as he said in one chapter, that "distaste would be produced by the constant repetition of the same miracle" (IV.4). He aimed to "ward off distaste, as it were, by a variety of dishes" (IV.64).

The second reason Benedict matched together miracles was to give his text more credence. He believed that a repeat miracle made the first more convincing, a point he makes many times. After describing how a woman found that the blood of Becket that she had wiped out of a vessel had returned the next day, Benedict added on a similar miracle, so that "those who do not give much weight to the first sign might marvel at the second" (I.17). A miracle of a relighting candle happened a second time "so that a subsequent miracle would confirm the earlier one" (III.3). In the case of a man who found coins in his purse that he had given away, Benedict argued that he was "more faithfully and firmly to be believed," because another man "asserts that something similar happened to him" (IV.40).[87] The logic here – that a story of one miracle should be believed if someone claimed that a similar miracle had occurred – may not seem very sound today. For Benedict and his readers, repetition made it clear that the first miracle was no aberration and could be trusted.

Benedict played miracle Mah-jongg in order to make his text more engaging, interesting, and convincing. Readers interested in a specific story are advised to check if Benedict linked it with others, and if so, how the stories might build on or contrast with each other. "Thematic" is a term that is frequently used to describe the composition of a miracle collection, but it does not sit well with the *Miracles*. "Connective" is better, highlighting Benedict's efforts to shape, organize, and fuse together a large mass of unwieldly and disparate material. To return to the analogy of beads and thread, his intent was to string together a long and beautiful necklace

---

[86] See FitzStephen, *Vita*, p. 151, and William of Canterbury, *Miracula*, p. 138.
[87] For similar statements, see also IV.62 and IV.85.

that would be enjoyed and admired by his audience as it pulled them from one story to the next. Besides matching together miracles by type, there was another kind of linking that enthused Benedict. He was determined to rivet Becket's miracles to the Bible and the Bible to Becket's miracles.

BIBLICAL PARALLELISM:
ANOTHER DEFINING FEATURE OF THE *MIRACLES*

The Bible that Benedict knew was a Latin translation of a large collection of books, starting first with the Hebrew Scriptures, the "Old Testament" in Christian terms, and then the Greek "New Testament," starting with the four Gospels concerning Jesus's life and death. Hunting for correspondences between the stories of the Old and New Testaments, and from them to contemporary events, was a major cultural phenomenon of Benedict's late twelfth-century world. Scholars use a number of labels for this exercise, including typology, historical allegory, or exegesis. I will term it biblical parallelism. Present in a remarkable number of literary, historical, liturgical, and artistic works, biblical parallelism was bedrock practice among the literati in the late twelfth century.[88] It permeated the Becket dispute. For example, Becket and his supporters liked to compare King Henry II to King Herod, the Jewish king of the Christmas story.[89] Medieval Christians viewed Herod as an archetype of an evil ruler because of his (supposed) attempts to kill the infant Jesus. Meanwhile, one of Becket's opponents, Archbishop of York Roger de Pont L'Évêque, likened Becket to Pharaoh, the leader of the Egyptians who tried to prevent Moses from leading the Israelites into the Promised Land.[90]

Benedict infused the *Passion* with comparisons between Becket and Christ,[91] and in the *Miracles*, he was forever seeking resonances and harmonies between a

---

[88] For studies, see Beryl Smalley, *The Study of the Bible in the Middle Ages* (Notre Dame, 1964), Tibor Fabiny, *Figura and Fulfillment: Typology in the Bible, Art and Literature* (Eugene, OR, 2016), Hugh T. Keenan (ed.), *Typology and English Medieval Literature* (New York, 1992), and Christopher G. Hughes, "Art and Exegesis," in Conrad Rudolph (ed.), *A Companion to Medieval Art: Romanesque and Gothic in Northern Europe* (Oxford, 2006), pp. 173–92. Canterbury Cathedral has the remains of a remarkable typological series of stained glass windows dating to the late 1170s and 1180s: see Caviness, *Windows*, pp. 77–156 and Madeline Caviness, *The Early Stained Glass of Canterbury Cathedral* (Princeton, 1977), pp. 115–38 and 168–75.

[89] See *CTB*, vol. 2, no. 216, p. 939 and *MTB*, vol. 7, no. 735, pp. 429–33, at p. 432.

[90] See *MTB*, vol. 7, no. 777, pp. 525–9, at p. 527. See Staunton, *Thomas Becket and His Biographers*, for many instances of biblical parallelism in medieval writers' descriptions of the dispute, and for a full-length study focused on letter-writing, see Julie Barrau, *Bible, lettres et politique: L'Écriture au service des hommes à l'époque de Thomas Becket* (Paris, 2013).

[91] See above, pp. 11–12.

miracle story and biblical events, figures, and passages. For example, after describing how a lame woman was healed at Becket's tomb, he wrote that "the people saw her *walking about and praising the Lord*, and *they were full of wonder and elation because of what had happened to her [Acts 3:9–10]*" (II.7). The italicized phrases, drawn from the Book of Acts in the New Testament, describe the reaction of a crowd of onlookers to the healing of a lame man by the Apostle Peter. Another good example is found a few chapters later, where Benedict introduced a story by stating "*It was the feast day* when the Invention of the Cross is celebrated every year [Jn 5:1], and lying here and there in the church of Canterbury *was a great multitude of the sick, the blind, the lame, the withered, those awaiting* and asking for health [Jn 5:3], and *the power of* the martyr *was there to heal them [Lk 5:17]*." Here Benedict drew from the description of healing cures on a Jewish feast day at a place called the pool of Bethesda in the Gospel of John, adding on a phrase from the Gospel of Luke about Christ's healing of a paralyzed man. Benedict was especially fond of citing phrases from the Psalms, poetic songs found in the Hebrew Scriptures. To take one of many examples, when he described how an elderly, paralyzed knight decided to seek help at Becket's tomb, he lifted favourite passages from two different Psalms: "Finally, realizing that *there is no salvation in men [Ps 107:13]*, and that *it would be good for him to cling to God and put his hope in the Lord God [Ps 72:28]*, he asked to be put on his horse and brought to Canterbury" (II.23).

For the most part, Benedict would not have had to look up such passages in order to cite them. Benedictine monks sang the Psalms multiple times a day every day of their lives. Novices would soon have them all memorized. Other books of the Bible were not memorized wholesale in the same way, but passages and stories from them would have been deeply embedded in the minds of religious men and women as a result of their education, private reading, and most especially from participating in tens of thousands of church services over the course of their lifetimes. Each service had its own defined liturgy, a set of spoken prayers, chants, lessons, rites, and readings that were largely made up of passages and phrases drawn from the Bible. These liturgies were in Latin, and so their full meaning was only accessible to those who knew the language well. For those who did and spent hours every day hearing and participating in such liturgies, constant aural repetition stocked their minds with biblical images, stories, phrases, and events.[92]

[92] For further analysis of this phenomenon, see Frans van Liere, "The Bible in Worship and Preaching," in Frans van Liere (ed.), *An Introduction to the Medieval Bible* (Cambridge, 2014), pp. 208–36. On the medieval liturgy, see Richard W. Pfaff, *The Liturgy in Medieval England: A History* (Cambridge, 2009); M. Cecilia Gaposchkin, *Invisible Weapons: Liturgy and the Making of Crusade Ideology* (Ithaca, 2017), esp. pp. 4–7 for an excellent explanation of medieval liturgy; and Heather Blurton, *Inventing William of Norwich:*

Most of the biblical echoes found throughout the *Miracles* probably simply occurred to Benedict as he was writing. He must have put more work into the sections of the *Miracles* thick with biblical echoes (such as the Prologue, where there are numerous citations from the book of Lamentations), but most of what he needed was in his head. Nearly all of Benedict's medieval readers, in turn, were so well versed in liturgical and biblical texts that such phrases would have sounded chords deep within them. It would have worked rather in the same way that someone who today brings up a famous line from a pop song does not have to explain where it came from or what it means. When religious men read, "lying here and there in the church of Canterbury was a great multitude of the sick, the blind, the lame, the withered, those awaiting and asking for health," Benedict did not have to say, "readers, looking around the cathedral, it was just like the pool of Bethesda in New Testament times." They would have known what he meant without the need of any of the italics and citations I have provided below.

The point of biblical parallelism in the *Miracles* was to lift stories of Becket's miracles into an elevated religious register, heightening their significance with phrases and allusions instantly recognizable to Benedict's reading audience. Many medieval writers and hagiographers engaged in this kind of echoing, but did not always employ it so cleverly or to such an extent. Benedict, who would prove himself to be a talented liturgical composer, did it particularly well, adding great depth and richness to his text. What especially enthused Benedict were the times he could draw similarities between Becket's miracles and Christ's miracles. For instance, in the Prologue he writes "By [Becket's] merits, *the blind see, the lame walk, the lepers are cleansed, the deaf hear, the dead are risen up*, the mute speak, *the poor are evangelized* [Mt 11:5], the paralytic healed, the dropsical cease to swell, the mad return to their senses, the epileptic are cured, the feverish recover, and, to conclude in brief, all manner of infirmity is cured." Medieval readers would have understood that Benedict was echoing a well-known listing of Christ's miracles found in the Gospel of Matthew, and that by adding more miracle types, he was declaring, in effect, that Becket's miracles did not just replicate but expanded upon Christ's. While Christ attended to those who were blind, lame, leprous, deaf, and dead, Becket did this and *also* cured the mute, the paralyzed, the dropsical, the mad, the epileptic, the feverish, and "all manner of infirmity."

Another example of such linking of Becket to Christ is found in Benedict's description of Becket's first miracle. The story concerns a blind woman named

---

Thomas of Monmouth, Antisemitism, and Literary Culture, 1150–1200 (Philadelphia, 2022), esp. pp. 24–34. For a study of iconography and liturgy at Canterbury Cathedral, see Marie-Pierre Gelin, *"Lumen ad revelationem genium": Iconographie et liturgie à Christ Church, Canterbury, 1175–1220* (Turnhout, 2006).

Emma, in Sussex, who recovered her sight three days after Becket's death. Christ's resurrection was three days after his death, and Benedict found this parallel "quite beautiful" (I.8). He may also have been thinking of the story of Mary Magdalene, the first person to see the resurrected Christ on that third day (Jn 20:11–18), as a parallel to the blind woman Emma, the first to recover her sight and experience a miracle after Becket's death. He came up with a particularly striking adaptation of verses to describe Emma's story, writing, "*This was the beginning of the signs of Jesus* in Sussex of England, and *the glory of* his martyr *was manifested to his disciples* [Jn 2:11], *to us, who had eaten and drunk with him* [Acts 10:41], before he had been killed in the womb of the virgin and mother church." The full verse from the Gospel of John reads, "This was the beginning of the signs of Jesus in Cana in Galilee, and manifested his glory, and his disciples believed in him," while the passage in Acts describes how Christ's resurrection was shown "to us [i.e., Christ's disciples], who had eaten and drunk with him, after he arose again from the dead." By echoing and adding his own phrases into these verses, Benedict was declaring that Becket's death and miracles were like Christ's and that Benedict and his fellow monks were like Jesus's disciples.

A modern Christian might find such connections to be audacious, even blasphemous, but to Benedict, they were beautiful. Hearing harmonies, rhymes, resonances, and echoes between the Bible and Becket's miracles made them more meaningful and emotionally rewarding, creating a dense web of interconnections that Benedict expected to his readers to find pleasurable on an aesthetic level and persuasive on an intellectual one. Readers interested in a specific story or section of the *Miracles* containing such citations are advised to look up the passages and register the subtexts. This is important not only in order to grasp the full import of Benedict's account, but also because this echoing can lead a reader astray. For instance, Benedict concludes his story of how a woman named Wekerilda was cured of a number of ailments by writing "Up to ten people recovered from various infirmities that day, but we were not able to call back those who had slipped away and we drove out those without witnesses" (II.34). This looks like a straightforward factual statement, but Benedict was likely thinking of a story in the Gospel of Luke about ten lepers cured by Christ of whom only one came back to give thanks (Lk 17:12–17). It is especially critical to understand how frequently Benedict sought out and employed biblical parallelism when considering when and why he provided specific dates for some miracles.

DATED MIRACLES: MORE BIBLICAL PARALLELISM

No aspect of the *Miracles* has pleased scholars more than Benedict's decision to provide dates for certain miracles and events within Becket's early cult. Raymonde

Foreville praised the early books of the *Miracles* as providing "chronological details of the utmost interest," while Benedicta Ward described Benedict's work as "a chronological account of [Becket's] early miracles."[93] Didier Lett spoke of Benedict adopting a "strict chronological plan" for the first three books of the *Miracles*, while Nicholas Vincent terms the text a "simple chronological survey."[94] The *Miracles* is without question the best source we have for investigating the development of Becket's early cult. However, it is easy to overestimate Benedict's capacity to string together miracle stories in chronological order, his desire to do so, and his impartiality on the occasions he did attempt it. He was simply not concerned about grouping or lining up miracles in chronological order in the ways we might expect or wish.

Benedict's reasons for including dating references in some chapters are easiest to discern with a full listing, provided below. Some of his time references refer to the date a miracle occurred, while others concern the beginning, duration, or stages of an illness. It is the former type – dated miracles – that have most interested scholars and will be the focus of my discussion below, but to be comprehensive I have listed both types. I have also included the handful of occasions in which Benedict stated that a story or stories should have appeared earlier or would appear later in the text. He usually referred to a date by means of the Christian liturgical calendar (for example, "the day of the Lord's Supper" or "the Sunday before the first Ascension of the Lord"), though on occasion he used the Roman calendar ("the fourth nones of April"). Anno Domini ("year of our Lord") dating appears only once, at the end of the *Passion*, where Benedict provided a very precise accounting of the day, month, year, and hour of Becket's death. Otherwise, Benedict rarely specifies a year. For stories found in the early parts of the *Miracles*, it is obvious that the year is 1171, but later on, especially in Book IV, the year can only be determined where we now have a means of cross-referencing with other texts. The most important stories in Book IV for which cross-referencing can provide dates are those of Eilward of Westoning, who must have arrived at Canterbury in late 1171 or early 1172; Jordan Fitz-Eisulf, who came on pilgrimage to Canterbury with his family shortly after Easter 1172; and James, the young son

---

[93] Raymonde Foreville, "Les *Miracula S. Thomae Cantuariensis*," in *Actes du 97e Congrès National des Sociétés Savants, Nantes 1972* (Paris, 1979), pp. 443–63, at p. 444; Benedicta Ward, *Miracles and the Medieval Mind: Theory, Record, and Event* (Philadelphia, 1987), p. 90.

[94] Lett, "Deux hagiographes," p. 207 and Vincent, "William of Canterbury," p. 363. See also Ronald Finucane, *Miracles and Pilgrims: Popular Beliefs in Medieval England* (London, 1977), p. 125, Lenz, "Construire un recueil," p. 27 and Kay Slocum, *The Cult of Thomas Becket: History and Historiography through Eight Centuries* (London, 2019), p. 25.

of Roger de Clare, Earl of Hertford, who was brought to Canterbury by his mother twice, once on Candlemas (February 2) 1173, and again in the later parts of Lent or around Easter of that same year, that is, late March/early April 1173.[95]

For ease of reference, I have included renderings of Benedict's dates in a day/month/year format. Where the year can only be determined by cross-referencing, I have indicated this by brackets and italics. Most stories have no dating references.

Passion

Extract XI In the year of our Lord one thousand one hundred and seventy, in the fifty-third year of his life, on the fourth day before the kalends of January, on the third day of the week, about the eleventh hour, so that the fifth day of the Lord's Nativity might… be the day of [Becket's] birth from misery to glory (Tuesday December 29, 1170)

Book I

I.1   Benedict's own visions, starting the night of the martyrdom (December 29, 1170)

I.2   A vision "the night before the sorrowful day when the sorrowful news of the death of the martyr" arrived in Argentan, Normandy (early January 1171)

I.3   A vision "a few nights after the setting of our sun" (early January 1171)

I.4   A vision "in the week of the octave of the martyr's passing" (December 29–January 5, 1171)

I.6   A vision four or five weeks before Easter week (mid to late February 1171)

I.8   Becket's first miracle on "the third day" after the martyrdom (December 31, 1171)

I.9   Becket's second miracle on "the fifth day" after the martyrdom (January 2, 1171)

I.10 Becket's third miracle on "the third nones of January, a Sunday and the sixth day from the martyr's triumph" (January 3, 1171)

I.11 Becket's fourth miracle on "the next day" (January 4, 1171)

I.12 Becket's fifth miracle "after eight days" (January 5, 1171)

I.13 A miracle happening in part before Becket's murder, in part after the news of his death was known

I.14 "This miracle was done around the time of Lent, and was revealed to us around the sacred day of Pentecost" (Lent ran from February 17 –March 27, 1171; Pentecost was on May 15, 1171)

I.15 A miracle happening "around the middle of the days of the period of Lent" (late February/early March 1171), which was revealed to the monks "in those days" (referring to the time around Pentecost)

---

[95] For these stories, see IV.2, IV.64, and IV.94 below. I provide a detailed account of the dating of these miracles in Koopmans, "Benedict of Peterborough's Compositions," pp. 252–8.

INTRODUCTION 43

I.23   A miracle happening on "the day of the Lord's Supper" (Maundy Thursday, March 25, 1171)

I.24   Chronological framing at close of Book I, "The Lord worked these and many other miracles before the days of Easter" (before March 28, 1171)

Book II

II.1–2   Miracles on Easter Sunday (March 28, 1171)

II.3   Miracle four or five weeks after Easter (early May 1171)

II.5   Miracle in "the same period of Easter"

II.6   Opening of the crypt on "the fourth nones of April, on the Friday of Easter week" (April 2, 1171)

II.22   "There are more of these delightful miracles, but I wish to place first in the text's narration those things that preceded them in time"

II.24   Illness "from the time of the Lord's nativity up to the day of Easter" (December 25, 1170 up to March 28, 1171)

II.33   Miracle on the day of the Invention of the Cross (May 3, 1171)

II.52   References to the state of an illness in Lent (February 17–March 27, 1171), a remission from the day of the Lord's Supper to the Wednesday after Easter (March 25–March 31, 1171), and a worsening after this time

II.63   Reference to the severity of an illness in "the sacred time of Lent" (February 17–March 27, 1171)

II.66   A pious death on the day of the Ascension of the Lord (May 6, 1171)

Book III

III.1   Miracle on a day shortly before Pentecost (mid-May 1171: Pentecost was on May 16 in 1171)

III.2–3   Miracles on the second day of Pentecost (May 17, 1171)

III.4   Miracle on the third day of Pentecost (May 18, 1171)

III.18   Vision "on the Sunday before the first Ascension of the Lord after the passion of the martyr" (May 2, 1171): Benedict comments that this was "a marvel that I ought to have told earlier, but which I had forgotten"

III.40   Miracles that occurred on "the [Sunday] that precedes the nativity of the blessed John the Baptist"; "the feast-day of the precursor of the Lord"; and "the feast of the apostles Peter and Paul" (June 20, June 24, June 28, 1171, dates very likely copied from a letter sent to Canterbury)

III.73   Reference to a curse and an illness starting on St. Cecilia's Day (November 22), in the period when Becket "seemed to have obtained peace in the church through a concordance of king and priesthood" (a reference to the peace of Fréteval of July 22, 1170, dating the curse and beginning of the illness to November 22, 1170)

Book IV

IV.2 Eilward's theft occurring on "a feast day after the passion of the blessed martyr" [*from cross-referencing, the feast day must have been in 1171, and Eilward must have arrived at Canterbury in late 1171 or early 1172*]

IV.3 Leper at Canterbury "from Pentecost almost to Advent" [*from context, this is most likely Pentecost 1171–beginning of Advent 1171, May 15–late November 1171*]

IV.5 A long-term eye injury healed "in the year in which the glorious high-priest Thomas had completed his life, in the summer after he had exchanged life temporal for life eternal through his death" (summer 1171)

IV.64 Pestilence "from August to Easter" [*from cross-referencing, must be August 1171 to April 16, 1172*], with one son revived from death and a pilgrimage promised for "mid-Lent" [*late March 1172*]. Sickness of another son on "the Holy Saturday that precedes Easter" [*April 15, 1172*], death on "the Friday of Easter week" [*April 21, 1172*], pilgrimage from Yorkshire [*arrival in Canterbury sometime in May 1172*]

IV.65 An illness runs from "the time of harvest to the month of March" [*from context, this is most likely fall 1171 to March 1172*]

IV.69 Punishment starts on the feast of the Chair of St. Peter (February 22), pilgrimage around "the time of Easter" [*from context, this is most likely February 22 and Easter 1172*]

IV.72 "This was the time when the martyr shone forth in his first miracles... This [miracle about a leper] could have been written with the first signs of the martyr"

IV.94 Birth of James, son of Roger de Clare, "around Michaelmas" [*from cross-referencing, this must be September 29, 1171*], hernia forty days after his birth, suffered for "a year and some months" until brought to Canterbury by his mother, Matilda de St. Hilary, on Candlemas [*February 2, 1173*]. "After some weeks, in the middle of the following Lent" [*March 1173*], James falls ill, dies, is restored by relics. Thanksgiving pilgrimage to Canterbury [*arrival late March/early April 1173*]

Additions 1–9

No specific dates

When one excludes the stories with time references about the duration of an illness and looks just at the miracles Benedict pegged to a specific date, it is remarkable how concentrated such stories are in the early parts of the *Miracles*. The first and shortest book of the *Miracles* is full of them. Benedict provided dates for nearly two-thirds of Book I's miracles, fifteen out of twenty-four chapters, and stated that all of Book I's miracles had happened before Easter 1171 (I.24). He clearly put considerable effort into seeking out pre-Easter vision and miracle stories. In fact, he spoke about doing this, stating that many miracles "were done throughout England by the favor of the martyr before Easter – though not openly, but as if in secret. Some of these *we heard as if in the ear* shortly after the martyrdom, others with the passing of time, and we received them in order to *preach upon the housetops* someday [*Mt 10:27*]" (I.6). Also striking is the fact that he worked to line up vision stories and then miracle stories in Book I into something approaching chronological order, even aiming to describe Becket's first five miracles from December 31, 1170, to January 5, 1171 (I.8–12). In sum, Benedict worked hard at historical reconstruction in Book I, and a good part of it can fairly be described as chronological. Whether we should accept his reconstruction as hard historical fact, though, is another matter, to be discussed further below.

At the start of Book II, Benedict carried on in the same vein, tying all but one of the first seven chapters to Easter or the time period around Easter (March 28, 1171). After this, though, the number of dated miracles falls off dramatically. Book II is twice as long as Book I, but after the Easter stories, Benedict pegged just two further miracles to specific dates, namely to the Invention of the Cross (May 3, 1171) and Ascension Day (May 6, 1171). At the beginning of Book III, Benedict reverted back to what he had done in Book I and the beginning of Book II, fixing the occurrence of four miracles to a specific date, namely, the time around Pentecost (May 16, 1171). But that is it – nearly all the other dating references found the rest of the *Miracles* concern the duration of an illness. There is just one miracle in the remainder of Book III that Benedict tied to a date, namely a vision that he stated occurred on May 2, 1171 and that he said he wished he had told earlier (III.18). Another chapter connecting miracles to specific dates in Book III (III.40) looks very much like it was derived from a letter. Book IV, the longest of the collection, has no blocks of stories tied to a date and only one chapter (IV.5) in which the year something occurred can be identified without seeking cross-references or making assumptions from context.

Thus, after Book I and the initial chapters of Book II, Benedict's chief organizational principle was not chronological, but the connective, matching and linking aesthetic described above (and indeed, even in Book I, he matched up miracles in non-chronological ways).[96] Though we today might find it incompatible to construct one section of a text within a defined chronological time frame and then not construct the rest of the text in the same way, or to organize a few chapters by tying them to a specific date and then silently shift over to nonchronological ways of tying stories together, for Benedict, this was fine. When one looks closely at the dated miracles, it becomes clear that while Benedict seems to have been genuinely curious about the miracles that happened before Easter, the big point of the dated miracles in the *Miracles* was biblical parallelism, not chronology. Benedict was working to put Becket's miracles within Christian chronological frameworks in both big and small ways. The overall chronological

---

[96] See p. 30 above.

framework he gave the *Miracles* replicates the three main seasons of the Christian liturgical calendar: the pre-Easter period, the time around Easter, and the time around Pentecost. Importantly, Benedict did not just date miracles to these times. He also made the mood of the miracles replicate the mood of the liturgical seasons. The monks are plunged in anguish and unhappiness in the "first days of miracles." His readers were to understand the time after Becket's death not just as running (in part) over the period of Lent, but as *a kind* of Lent, a time of grief and darkness (Book I). Then comes Easter, which Benedict portrayed as a period of joyous rebirth and the outpouring of miracles, like to the glory of Christ's resurrection (beginning of Book II). At the beginning of Book III, he tied miracles to Pentecost. All of his readers would have known the biblical story of tongues of fire appearing above the heads of Christ's apostles on Pentecost, and that this event marked the coming of the Holy Spirit and the launch and spread of Christianity. For Benedict, the relighting of candles in the cathedral replicated the tongues of fire miracle, and from there, Becket's miracles go from one splendor to the next, spreading the same way that Christianity spread after Pentecost.

With dated stories in the first part of the *Miracles*, Benedict produced a chronology of Becket's posthumous cult that duplicated the grand liturgical narrative played out in Christian churches every year, from desolation in Lent to the joy of Easter and the spread of the gospel at Pentecost. In my reading, I do not doubt that it truly was a difficult time at Canterbury before Easter, nor that the events Benedict said happened in the cathedral around Easter and Pentecost did indeed happen in some shape or form. But would a modern historian whisked back to 1171 have highlighted the same events or framed the story in the same way? Was Easter/Pentecost 1171 the major pivot point in the development of Becket's cult? In my view, Easter/Pentecost 1171 is far too early to view Becket's cult as firmly established. When one considers political and religious developments during the period Benedict was writing, it seems highly likely that the cult's tipping point, that is, the point when it took on an unstoppable momentum of its own, occurred well after the spring of 1171.

Benedict himself said little about post-murder political and religious developments. He did mention an early vision through which news arrived about Pope Alexander III's censures of the murderers (I.14), and spoke frequently about the "enemies" of Becket, who are very much live threats in the text. He pounced on stories of miracles happening to or witnessed by kinsmen of the de Brocs and Gilbert Foliot, as well as miracles happening on territories owned by Becket's enemies, which he clearly felt were meant to show them the truth.[97] Yet he did not provide dates for these miracles, nor provide any account of how the major players acted in

---

[97] See III.17, III.45, III.65, and IV.2.

the wake of the murder. Though he had to have known about King Henry's decision to go on campaign in Ireland in the fall of 1171 and his reconciliation with the papal legates at Avranches in May 1172, nothing about this appears in the *Miracles*.[98] Benedict also must have known about the monks' early failed canonization petition, and he surely rejoiced when news arrived in Canterbury in the spring of 1173 that Becket was canonized, but again, there is no account of this in the *Miracles*. It is especially interesting that Benedict never mentioned the reconsecration of Canterbury Cathedral on December 21, 1171, despite repeatedly complaining early in the text about the monks' inability to conduct services in the desecrated cathedral. Even the cultic developments he did mention, such as the reinforcement of Becket's tomb (II.29) or the switch-over from wooden pyxes to metal ampullas (III.22), he did not this it was important to date.

Pegging stories to the pre-Easter period, to Easter, and to Pentecost was more important to Benedict than any of this. Indeed, if he had provided dates and discussion of political and religious developments, it would have muddied the grand narrative he wanted to construct. Benedict's efforts to put Becket's miracles on Christ's chronological track created pitfalls for the unwary reader. One of the main ones is the dating of stories in Book II. Since this book starts with Easter miracles and Book III starts with Pentecost miracles, one might think that all of Book II's miracles date to the fifty-day period between Easter and Pentecost 1171. When one reads through the book, however, it is clear that this simply cannot be the case. Book II is full of pairs and sets of miracles, with nothing of the careful chronologizing that one sees in Book I. Benedict surely did not worry whether the miracles he described of two young men suffering torments from fistula (II.48–9), or the three men suffering from severe headaches (II.62–4), all fell within that fifty-day period. When one looks closely at the two non-Easter miracles that Benedict aligned to a specific day, namely to the Invention of the Cross (May 3, II.33) and Ascension Day (May 6, II.66), it is clear that he again had biblical parallelism in mind. He saw the Invention of the Cross miracle as a parallel to the story of the pool of Bethesda, and the entrance of a dying man into heaven with Christ's Ascension into heaven. Benedict placed no less than thirty-two stories between these two chapters: he certainly did not expect his readers to think that they all occurred on May 4 and 5. Many of the stories in Book II likely date to mid to late 1171.

The most chronologically oriented section of the entire *Miracles* is Benedict's account of Becket's first five miracles in the week after his death (I.8–12). Benedict stated that these miracles happened in Sussex, Gloucester, Berkshire, Canterbury,

---

[98] William's collection would have much more direct discussion of Henry II, some of it negative, some of it very positive: see Koopmans, *Wonderful to Relate*, pp. 156–7, and Bull, "Criticism of Henry II's Expedition to Ireland."

and inside Canterbury Cathedral. Only the last of these stories was definitely known to him at the time. Like so much else in Book I, this set of chapters represents a painstaking reconstruction of a sequence of events well after the fact. When one looks these stories with a critical eye, it is clear that he did not make this effort for the benefit of later historians. In both the "first" and the "fifth" miracle, Benedict made fervent arguments for viewing Becket as a second Christ, and the sequence as a whole makes an argument for the liturgical celebration of Becket as a saint.

The first miracle, already discussed above, concerns the blind and ill Emma, wife of a knight in Sussex, who heard the news of the murder, appealed to Becket, and recovered her sight "most beautifully" on the third day after Becket's death, which Benedict explicitly states is a parallel to Christ's resurrection on the third day after his death (I.8).[99] I believe it is safe to assume that Emma did exist, that she was blind, and that she did indeed experience some kind of recovery of her sight shortly after Becket's murder. What is extremely doubtful, though, is Benedict's labeling of Emma's miracle as Becket's *first*. Given the nature of a cult, it was (and is) next to impossible for anyone to identify the first person to attribute a miracle to a given saint. Most medieval miracle collectors steered clear of identifying "first" miracles, much less the first five. William FitzStephen was the only contemporary besides Benedict who tried to pinpoint Becket's first miracle. He placed it in Canterbury on the very night of the martyrdom, stating that a woman was healed by means of drinking water containing some of the blood that her husband had gathered in the cathedral.[100] While we cannot trust that this was Becket's first miracle either (there could have been other people who did something similar before this particular woman did, or other scenarios in which a first person invoked Becket's aid), it is inherently far more probable that a woman at Canterbury with access to Becket's blood on the night of the murder experienced a "first" miracle rather than someone in Sussex a couple days later.

The chances are very good that Benedict knew of stories like the one William FitzStephen related, but decided to bypass them. He chose to tell a "third day" miracle instead. What this suggests is that we cannot rely on Benedict to tell the whole truth as he knew it, especially if other motives, especially a terrific opportunity to trumpet biblical parallelism, came into play. Turning to the miracles that Benedict labeled Becket's second, third, fourth, and fifth, I think it highly likely that the people of these stories – a girl in Gloucester named Huelina, a knight of Berkshire named William Belet, a blind woman in Canterbury named Brithiva, and William the priest of London (I.9-12) – all existed and all had experiences that were at least somewhat similar to those Benedict describes. Indeed, two of these individuals (the knight William Belet and William, the priest of London) appear

---

[99] See above, pp. 39-40.
[100] FitzStephen, *Vita*, pp. 149-50.

in other contemporary documents, underlining Benedict's basic credibility as a recorder. But were these stories the only ones Benedict had heard regarding this very early period? How probable is it that miracles were experienced at the pace of one per day? Why would he bother to line up stories like this, informing the reader about miracles supposedly happening on the fifth, sixth, seventh, and eighth days after Becket's death?

He had at least two reasons. First, the liturgical celebration of a saint occurred in an octave, counting the day of the saint's death as the first day with the octave falling eight days later. Dating miracles within Becket's very first octave was a flashing beacon that he thought that the dead Becket was a saint deserving of liturgical celebration. He dated early visions to this octave as well (see I.1–4). The second reason was to build a crescendo to the "fifth" miracle, about William, a priest of London, which he places on the day of the octave (January 5, which was also the last day of the Christmas liturgical season). As discussed above, Benedict saw tremendous significance in William of London's miracle, which he states was the first instance of anyone drinking Becket's blood in pursuit of a cure, like to the drinking of Christ's blood in the Eucharist (I.12).[101]

The point of counting out and describing the first five miracles, then, was almost the exact opposite of what one might think today. Benedict's goal was not to provide disinterested historical information. Where he was the most chronological, he was also the most interested in swaying and influencing his readers, giving them more reasons to think of Becket as Christ-like and a great saint worthy of veneration. Historical reconstruction with something as inherently nebulous as people's stories about miracles was no easy task, and Benedict was unusual among miracle collectors to put so much effort into it. But one must be careful not to over-read the results. Outside of the short Book I and the beginnings of Book II and III, Benedict was not engaged in historical reconstruction, and even there, his idea was to link Becket's posthumous history to Christ's history and the rhythm of the Christian liturgical calendar. Benedict's work is often more complex than it may first appear. This is certainly the case when one considers how and when he wrapped up and finished the *Miracles*.

THE ADD-ONS (THE *PASSION*, THE PROLOGUE, AND BOOK I), THE MONKS' SECOND CANONIZATION PETITION, AND THE LITURGICAL OFFICE

The texts now found at the beginning of the *Miracles* were not written first. Like many authors before and since, Benedict added on material when he was bringing the *Miracles* to completion. This includes the *Passion*. Its lost prologue may

---

[101] See above, pp. 17–18.

well have contained dating indicators, but there is a pointer within the surviving text that can provide an approximate date for its composition. In Extract VIII, Benedict described how the dead Becket had a line of blood running across his face, and commented that the saint "appeared to many people in visions bearing this mark. These people knew nothing about it, and yet described it as if they had seen it with their own corporeal eyes." Benedict could not have written this before such visions occurred. He described two of them partway through the *Miracles'* last and longest book. In the first story, he wrote that a woman saw Becket "having the crosswise trail of blood across his face that we have also mentioned in his *Passion*" (IV.37). In the second, a boy saw "the track of blood running sideways across his nose from his forehead to his left jaw which we also saw on him when he lay in his church killed by the swords of the impious" (IV.52). Nowhere else in the *Miracles* does Benedict mention the line of blood. These tight cross-references strongly suggest that Benedict had written the *Passion* not long before he reached this part of the *Miracles*, most likely sometime in 1172. This puts the *Passion* on par with other early accounts of the martyrdom found in John of Salisbury's *Life* and the first recension of Edward Grim's *Life*, both usually dated c.1171–2.[102]

The Prologue, too, was clearly composed by Benedict after a considerable portion of the *Miracles* was complete. In it, Benedict referred to the miracle of Eilward of Westoning: "new eyes and new genitals were created for a certain one who constantly invoked the martyr, his eyes and genitals having been mutilated." Eilward's story is found at the beginning of Book IV (IV.2), and would have been known to the monks in late 1171 or early 1172. The Prologue also contains a notable reference to the vacancy of the archbishopric of Canterbury: "Whoever succeeds our martyr in the seat of Canterbury should not fear to fight again for its dignities which the martyr defended to the death." Negotiations for the election of a new archbishop, in which the monks of Christ Church were deeply involved, started in the fall of 1172. Benedict had to have written the Prologue before these matters were resolved with the election of Richard of Dover, a former Christ Church monk, in June 1173.

Late 1172 or early 1173 is the most likely time frame for the composition of the Prologue. It was right around this time that the monks prepared and sent a second canonization petition to Alexander III. We know of this petition from William of Canterbury's miracle collection. He described how the Christ Church monks sent the cleric William of Monkton to the curia "in order to petition the lord pope in

---

[102] The long-held dating of Benedict's *Passion* has been to 1173–4 (see Staunton, *Thomas Becket*, pp. 3–4 and Barlow, *Thomas Becket*, pp. 4–5), but this was based on a misunderstanding of the timing of Benedict's composition of Book IV of the *Miracles*. For a detailed examination of the dating evidence, see Koopmans, "Benedict of Peterborough's Compositions."

the name of the brothers of Canterbury" to canonize Becket. However, William added, the clerk set off not knowing that Becket "had already been enrolled in the catalogue of martyrs."[103]

Pope Alexander canonized Becket on February 21, 1173. His letter to the papal legates Albert and Theodwin announcing the canonization is dated March 10, and his letters to the Christ Church monks and the people of England March 12.[104] William of Monkton, then, must have left for the papal curia sometime in the early part of 1173. We do not know what the monks' second petition looked like, nor whether William of Monkton brought along portions of the *Miracles* for the pope's inspection. When one looks at the Prologue, though, it is striking how much Benedict dwelled on the papal schism between Alexander and Octaviano Monticelli, the Italian cardinal who took the title Pope Victor IV. Benedict argued forcefully that since Becket supported Pope Alexander, and Becket was performing miracles, that proved Alexander to be the rightful pope and the schismatics to be wrong. Towards the end of the Prologue, Benedict came close to addressing the pope directly: "let the holy fatherhood of the highest see rejoice to have had such a son [i.e., Becket] at the ends of the earth and the end of the ages."

There is so much in the Prologue that Pope Alexander would have liked to hear that it is possible Benedict had drafted or was drawing upon a letter that was part of the second canonization bid. The effort that Benedict put into the Prologue is evident from its extraordinary exuberance of biblical references. Prologues were places for medieval authors to show off their literary prowess, and Benedict took full advantage of the opportunity, perhaps with a specific important reader in mind. To be clear, I do not think that it is safe to assume that what we have with the Prologue is identical to the petition carried by William of Monkton, but rather that it has the ring of something composed at that time and for that particular audience. Whatever William of Monkton brought with him, the pope was once again uninterested in accounts of Becket's miracles compiled by Christ Church monks. Not only did he canonize Becket without having seen the monks' second petition, but he stressed in his canonization letters that it was the papal legates' account of Becket's miracles – Albert and Theodwin's – that had made up his mind to canonize Becket.[105]

The news of the Becket's canonization would have taken approximately six weeks to travel from the papal curia to Canterbury. The monks likely heard the good news sometime in April or early May 1173. Soon, Benedict was chosen (or nominated himself) to write Becket's liturgical Office. This new task included

---

[103] See William of Canterbury, *Miracula*, IV.9–10, pp. 321–3, at p. 321: "de celebranda solennitate martyris nomine fratrum Cantuariensium dominum papam petiturus; quem jam ipsis ignorantibus catalogo martyrum ascripserat."

[104] The texts of the canonization letters are found in *MTB*, vol. 7, nos. 784–6, pp. 545–8.

[105] See *MTB*, vol. 7, nos. 784–6, pp. 545–8.

writing both the music and the texts (readings, antiphons, etc.) that would be used to celebrate Becket's feast day. Benedict had taken on a heavy new burden, but one that was particularly suited to his talents. It may well have seemed providential that right around this time, in early April 1173, Matilda de St. Hilary, wife of the earl Roger de Clare, arrived in Canterbury celebrating what she believed to be Becket's resurrection of her young son James. This miracle, concerning such a high-ranking family, was an ideal story with which to bring the *Miracles* to an (initial) close (IV.94).

Mid-1173 is a safe estimation for when Benedict wrapped up the *Miracles* and the first manuscript copies began to be made and circulated. Finishing the text meant writing through the story of young James, completing the Prologue, if he hadn't already done so, and stitching the *Passion* and the Prologue onto the body of the text. Part of this stitching may well have included composing and/or reworking parts or even all of Book I. There are striking echoes of the vision stories Benedict recounts at the beginning of Book I (I.1–7) in the Office, so much so it seems likely there was some overlap in the composition or reworking of these vision stories and Benedict's composition of the liturgy. In one remarkable case, Benedict utilized – to the letter – the responsory and verse heard in an early vision as a responsory and verse in the Office (see I.5).[106] It might be, too, that this finishing-up stage was when Benedict decided to enumerate and describe Becket's first first miracles in the form we now have them (I.8–12). That a considerable amount of time had elapsed from the early days of the cult to Benedict's composition (and/or reworking) of Book I is shown in a story about a religious woman named Wlviva. Since the time of her miracle, Wlviva had made not one but two career changes: "At this time, this woman was the custodian of an almshouse ministering to the poor and pilgrims. Afterwards, she took upon herself the chains of a harsher service, given over to the service of lepers, until at length she transferred herself to the repose of an anchorage" (I.17). It could well be that Wlviva became an anchorite in 1172 or early 1173.

Once the *Miracles* began to circulate in mid-1173, the Office was Benedict's primary task. It had to be completed by the time of Becket's first feast day as a canonized saint, December 29, 1173, and he wanted it to be impressive.[107] Sherry Reames has noted that Benedict put much more effort into writing this Office

---

[106] See Reames, "Liturgical Offices," pp. 570–1 and Slocum, *Liturgies*, p. 188; for more overlaps between the *Miracles* and the Office, see the notes provided with the stories below and Koopmans, "Benedict of Peterborough's Compositions," pp. 262–7.

[107] For this dating of the Office, see Anne Duggan, "A Becket Office at Stavelot: London, British Library, Additional Ms 16964," in Anne J. Duggan, Joan Greatrex, and Brenda Bolton (eds.), *Omnia Disce: Medieval Studies in Memory of Leonard Boyle, O.P.* (Aldershot, 2005), pp. 161–82, at pp. 163–7.

than many contemporary composers: "Benedict's chant texts are newly written poems in demanding kinds of accentual verse, using very regular meters and difficult rhyme schemes" that are "full of surprises as well – paradoxes, wordplay, [and] unexpectedly rich combinations of images and allusions."[108] Andrew Hughes termed it "a particularly interesting and superior office, both textually and musically, characterized by regularly rhymed and accentual verse set to music with features rather distinctive in themselves."[109] Today, the Office survives in hundreds of medieval manuscripts that were made and used throughout Latin Christendom.[110] Part of the reason it is so good is that Benedict worked out many of its ideas and themes in the *Passion and Miracles*.[111]

By mid to late 1173, Benedict very likely knew that Archbishop Richard of Dover (elected but not yet consecrated) intended to appoint him as his chancellor, and he may have already begun to serve in that post. Meanwhile, William carried on with his independent collection of miracles. He would work until c.1175, when he halted for a time. He made a final, very lengthy addition to his text c.1176–7.[112] For the most part, Benedict was content to leave miracle collecting to William. He made just two short additions to his *Miracles*, one addition consisting of two stories and a second of seven.[113] These stories can be dated to the second half of 1173 from their overlaps with William's collection. All four of the last stories (numbered below as Additions 6–9) are also found in William's *Miracles*. Benedict told these stories at length and clearly thought they were particularly important. In one story, Benedict states that he himself went and measured the well that a young woman had thrown herself down in a fit of despair (Addition 8). Another is about a workman who was buried by a landslide, but survived after calling on the martyr. This struck Benedict as a "new" kind of miracle, and he

---

[108] Reames, "Liturgical Offices," p. 561.
[109] Andrew Hughes, "The Story of O: A Variant in the Becket Office," in Maureen Epp and Brian E. Power (eds.), *The Sounds and Sights of Performance in Early Music: Essays in Honour of Timothy J. McGee* (Farnham, 2009), pp. 27–59, at p. 28.
[110] See ibid., p. 30, as well as Andrew Hughes, ed. by Kate Helson, *The Becket Offices: Paradigms for Liturgical Research* (Lions Bay, 2014).
[111] See Koopmans, "Benedict of Peterborough's Compositions," pp. 262–7; for discussion of the wide influence of the Office, see Duggan, "Becket is Dead!" pp. 28–36 and Estelle Joubert, "New Music in the Office of Thomas Becket from the Diocese of Trier," *Plainsong and Medieval Music* 18:1 (2009): 33–60, at pp. 33–4. See also Katherine Emery, "Architecture, Space, and Memory: Liturgical Representation of Thomas Becket, 1170–1220," in Tom Nickson (ed.), *The Cult of Thomas Becket: Art, Relics, and Liturgy in Britain and Europe*, special issue of the *Journal of the British Archaeological Association* 173:1 (2020): 61–77, at pp. 61–7.
[112] For this dating of William's collection, see Koopmans, *Wonderful to Relate*, pp. 153–5.
[113] See above, pp. xi–xii and 2.

could not resist a bit of glib biblical parallelism in his introduction to the story: "We longed for something new, for by something new we are kindled to new love of the new martyr of the English. *The Lord has done a new thing on the earth* [Jer 31:22] – or rather, under the earth" (Addition 7).

It looks as if Benedict could not bear to leave these stories to William, despite the fact that his collection was already in circulation. He appended them to his *Miracles* and put his own spin on them. But with that, he had finished. He never gave the *Miracles* a conclusion. He may have thought that he would come back to it again, but his time was consumed by administration and collecting miracles became William's sole job.

For the reader's convenience, I have summarized my suggested date ranges of components of the *Passion and Miracles* below.

The *Passion*: Composed 1172

The Prologue and (possibly) parts, perhaps all, of Book I: Composed between early 1172 and mid-1173, most likely early 1173

Book I (?), Books II and III: Composed between late spring 1171 and early 1172, with earlier sections likely revised when the Prologue was added on

Book IV: Composed between early 1172 and mid-1173

Additions: Composed in two sessions sometime between mid-1173 and late 1173

The Office for Becket's feast day: Composed mid-1173 to late 1173, completed by December 29, 1173, the first celebration of Becket's feast day

The speed with which Benedict produced these works is impressive. After 1173, Benedict would be elected to other posts and eventually have to leave Canterbury, but Becket's cult and his connections to Christ Church would remain central to him the rest of his life.

CONCLUSION: BENEDICT'S CAREER AND BECKET'S CULT AFTER THE *PASSION AND MIRACLES*

Benedict was Archbishop Richard of Dover's chancellor when a critical milestone in Becket's cult was reached, in some ways more important than Alexander III's canonization. In July 1174, King Henry II came to Canterbury on a penitential pilgrimage to Becket's tomb. The king's acknowledgement that Becket was a saint, and the confirmation that his old friend looked on him in favor (due to his forces' victory in battle at this very same time), lifted the last checks on the growth of

Becket's cult in Henry's realms.[114] Just two months later, there was a disaster. On September 5, 1174, a fire began in the roof over the choir of Canterbury cathedral. The choir, dedicated just a little over four decades before (in 1130), was renowned for its beauty. The fire did not touch the crypt where Becket's tomb was housed, nor did it reach the nave, but the destruction of the roof and upper portions of the choir was bad enough. Gervase described how the Christ Church monks had to retreat from the choir to the nave, "wailing and howling" their offices, while the townspeople tore their hair and hurled curses at God and the saints of the church.[115]

One wonders how Benedict felt on December 29, 1174, the second time his Becket Office was performed in the cathedral, when he and his fellow monks had to sing in the nave rather than in their beloved, now fire-damaged choir. He would soon take on the primary responsibility for its rebuilding. In 1175, Prior Odo left Canterbury to become the abbot of Battle Abbey, and in July of that year, the monks elected Benedict as their new prior. Benedict's writing of the *Miracles* and the Office, and the enthusiastic reception of these compositions outside of Canterbury, must have been major factors in his selection.

Two particularly interesting stories from Benedict's tenure as prior show how important Becket's miracles and relics continued to be for him. One concerns an encounter between Prior Benedict and King Henry II. In versions of the story found in Edward Grim's *Life* and the Chronicle of Battle Abbey, the king became angry at Benedict for some unnamed offense.[116] In another version, found in William of Canterbury's *Miracles*, the king had not fulfilled his promises to protect the liberties of Christ Church and Prior Benedict was trying to get him to do so.[117] In the Battle Abbey account, Odo, the former prior of Christ Church, steps in, soothes the king's anger, and reconciles him to Prior Benedict (the story is found in a section singing Odo's praises). But in Edward Grim's and

---

[114] A good description and analysis of Henry II's 1174 pilgrimage is found in Duggan, "Becket is Dead!" pp. 36–40.

[115] Gervase, vol. 1, p. 5. For a translation of Gervase's account of the 1174 fire and rebuilding of the cathedral, see Robert Willis, *The Architectural History of Canterbury Cathedral* (London, 1845), pp. 32–62. A good overview of much scholarly discussion is Peter Draper, "Recent Interpretations of the Late-12th-Century Rebuilding of the East End of Canterbury Cathedral and Its Historical Context," in Alixe Bovey (ed.), *Medieval Art, Architecture and Archaeology at Canterbury Cathedral*, British Archaeological Association Conference Transactions 35 (London, 2013), pp. 106–15. See also Carol Davidson Cragoe, "Reading and Rereading Gervase of Canterbury," *Journal of British Archaeology* 154 (2001): 40–53.

[116] Grim, *Vita*, pp. 448–50; *The Chronicle of Battle Abbey*, trans. and ed. Eleanor Searle, OMT (Oxford, 1980), pp. 308–9.

[117] William of Canterbury, *Miracula*, IV.97, pp. 493–4.

William's accounts, the king had a vision in which he was walking across a bridge and fell through a hole. Hanging onto the bridge, he invoked a number of saints until finally calling on Becket, at which point Prior Benedict appeared and saved him from his predicament. The next day, the king was reconciled to Benedict and granted him what he wished.[118] Both Grim's and William's accounts appear to have been written in very close proximity to the events, and there seems little reason to doubt that the outlines of the story are true. This is the only known instance in which Henry II had a vision of Becket, and it must have seemed fitting that the man who had described so many visions in the *Miracles* would reap such benefits from this one.

The second story is about Roger, the monk of Christ Church whom Benedict describes in the *Miracles* as being "similarly assigned to the care of the sacred body" (IV.59). In 1176, Roger was elected as the abbot of St. Augustine's, the large and ancient Benedictine monastery also located in Canterbury. According to a later chronicler, Roger was elected abbot because the monks hoped that through him, St. Augustine's would acquire relics of Thomas Becket. The chronicler was unimpressed with this motive, but notes that Roger did indeed bring to the monastery "a great part of the blood which [Becket] shed, a certain small portion of his head cut away, along with a considerable part of the brain of the said martyr."[119] He then writes that in order to get these relics, "an agreement was published between us and the prior of the same place, an agreement which was very disadvantageous and inconvenient to us." That this prior was Benedict is clear from what comes next: the text of a charter issued by Prior Benedict that concerns the exchange of some Christ Church lands for some of St. Augustine's.[120]

The story regarding this agreement may be a later invention, but Benedict's ability to do hard-nosed bargaining in pursuit of the rights and privileges of his community was surely part of the reason he found himself elected Abbot of Peterborough in July 1177, after just two years as prior of Christ Church. The chronicler Robert of Swaffham recorded that Benedict secured particularly impressive Becket relics for

---

[118] See the interesting discussion of this vision in Gesine Oppitz-Trotman, "The Emperor's Robe: Thomas Becket and Angevin Political Culture," *ANS* 37 (2014): 205–19, at pp. 218–19. For the charter confirming the liberties of Christ Church, see *The Letters and Charters of Henry II, King of England 1154–1189*, ed. Nicholas Vincent, OMT, 7 vols. (Oxford, 2022), vol. 1, no. 464, pp. 461–4.

[119] *William Thorne's Chronicle of Saint Augustine's Abbey Canterbury*, trans. A. H. Davis (Oxford, 1934), p. 100.

[120] Ibid., pp. 100–1. For the notification by Roger of the agreement and for confirmations of exchange of lands between St. Augustine's and Christ Church by Archbishop Richard of Dover and Henry II, see William Urry, *Canterbury under the Angevin Kings* (London, 1967), nos. 26–8, pp. 405–9; for Henry's charter, see also *LCHII*, vol. 1, no. 466, pp. 468–9.

Peterborough, certainly better than those given to Roger: "He acquired numerous relics of St. Thomas, namely his shirt, his surplice, and a great quantity of his blood in two crystal vessels, and two altars made from the stones on which the holy martyr lay in death."[121] Benedict also worked to stock Peterborough Abbey's library, very likely using manuscripts from Canterbury as exemplars. Swaffham listed a remarkable fifty-five items that he acquired for the library. With his enthusiasm for biblical parallelism, it is no surprise that these gifts included a complete set of glossed manuscripts of the books of the Old and New Testaments as well as legal and scholastic works.[122] He also gave them a *Life* of St. Thomas and copy of his *Miracles*,[123] and – along with other building projects – he completed a hospital and chapel dedicated to St. Thomas, which were located at the monastery's gate.[124]

Though he was praised for his accomplishments in Peterborough, Benedict probably regretted having to leave Canterbury as much as Odo had before him. Swaffham described how Abbot Benedict, at a time when he was "in great distress" and weighed down by the difficulties of freeing Peterborough from its debts, "set out for Canterbury, taking just one monk as a companion, and stayed there for some time."[125] We know that Benedict was in Canterbury in 1183, 1184, and 1187, and no doubt he travelled there other times as well.[126] As someone who was once in charge of the cathedral's rebuilding after the 1174 fire, he was likely keen to see how the work was progressing. By the mid-1180s, much of the construction of the new eastern arm of Canterbury cathedral was complete. This new construction included not only a magnificent new upper chapel, which was to serve as a home for Becket's relics, but also an expansion of the crypt chapel in which Becket's tomb was situated. The fresh, light, and roomy space in the crypt would have looked very different from the chapel in which Benedict, his fellow monks, and their servants had spent so much time and listened to so many stories.

The first stained glass windows of the upper chapel were being installed by the mid-1180s. It is a safe guess that Benedict looked forward to seeing these, as the

---

[121] Swaffham, p. 71.

[122] Swaffham, pp. 65–9 and *The Library of Peterborough Abbey*, eds. Karsten Friis-Jensen and James M. W. Willoughby, Corpus of British Medieval Library Catalogues 8 (London, 2001), pp. 15–22.

[123] *The Library of Peterborough Abbey*, nos. 47–8.

[124] On Benedict's building work at Peterborough, see Peter Fergusson, "Architecture during the Rule of Abbot Benedict," in Ron Baxter, Jackie Hall, and Claudia Marx (eds.), *Peterborough and the Soke: Art, Architecture, and Archaeology*, British Archaeological Association Conference Transactions XLI (London, 2019), pp. 179–99, and Lisa Reilly, *An Architectural History of Peterborough Cathedral* (Oxford, 1997), pp. 92–3.

[125] Swaffham, p. 65.

[126] See Edmund King, "Benedict of Peterborough and the Cult of Thomas Becket," *Northamptonshire Past and Present* 9 (1996): 213–20, at pp. 216–17.

glaziers' source text was his own *Passion and Miracles*.[127] The glazing and other preparations for Becket's translation were interrupted by a major dispute between the Christ Church monks and their new Archbishop, Baldwin of Forde, starting in 1184.[128] Benedict was called in to help resolve the dispute in 1187, but he would not see its conclusion before his death in 1193. The dispute dragged on into the thirteenth century, and it was not until c.1213 that glazing could recommence in the ambulatory of the upper chapel designated for Becket's shrine. They filled its windows with stories drawn almost entirely from Benedict's *Miracles*.[129] The translation of Becket's relics to his glorious new shrine did not occur until 1220. With the translation, and with the deaths of Benedict and the generation that witnessed the beginning of Becket's cult, the story of Canterbury's martyr entered a new phase.[130]

Benedict's *Passion and Miracles* provides an unparalleled and enthralling account of how one of the great European pilgrimages began. It invites us to weep with the Christ Church monks after Becket's death and to rejoice with them as evidence mounted that the murdered archbishop lived again as a saint, a saint more powerful

---

[127] On the glazing of the first windows in the ambulatory surrounding Becket's shrine (Canterbury Cathedral windows nVII, nVI, and nV), see Madeline Caviness, *The Windows of Christ Church Cathedral, Canterbury*, Corpus Vitrearum Medii Aevi: Great Britain, Volume II (London, 1981), pp. 175–9; Rachel Koopmans, "Pilgrimage Scenes in Newly Identified Medieval Glass at Canterbury Cathedral," *Burlington Magazine* 161 (issue no. 1398, September 2019): 708–15, and Koopmans, "Gifts of Becket's Clothing." For surviving panels connected to this early glazing campaign, see notes to I.6, I.12, I.13, III.22, IV.72, and Extract VIII in the *Passion*.

[128] For a narrative and analysis of this dispute, which carried on long after Baldwin's death, see Barnaby, *Religious Conflict at Canterbury Cathedral*.

[129] For this glass, see Caviness, *Windows*, pp. 180–214. Canterbury Cathedral's windows are numbered according to their position within the church: "n" for north aisle, "s" for south aisle, and a Roman numeral counting back from the east end of the church. For stories pictured in this later glazing campaign (encompassing the windows numbered nIV, nIII, nII, sII, sVI, and sVI), see below, I.22, I.24, II.13, II.23, II.24, III.60, III.62, III.69, III.77, IV.2, IV.3, IV.21, IV.30, IV.62, IV.64, IV.66, IV.76, IV.77, IV.88, IV.94, and Additions 7 and 9. The "miracle windows," as they are termed, are undergoing a major reexamination. In my notes below, I have included updated assessments of which stories are portrayed in the glass.

[130] For the cult's development in this new period, see Louise Wilkinson, "'Is Still Not the Blood of the Blessed Martyr Thomas Fully Avenged?': Thomas Becket's Cult at Canterbury under Henry III and Edward I," *History* 105 (2020): 673–90, and Anne Duggan, "The Cult of St. Thomas Becket in the Thirteenth Century," in Meryl Jancey (ed.), *St. Thomas Cantilupe: Essays in His Honour* (Hereford, 1982), pp. 21–44. For a well-illustrated overview of the cult through the Tudor period, see Lloyd de Beer and Naomi Speakman, *Thomas Becket: Murder and the Making of a Saint* (London, 2021), and for a survey that reaches to the present day, see Slocum, *The Cult of Thomas Becket*.

than anyone in Canterbury – or Britain – had ever seen before. The *Passion and Miracles* is by far the most important historical source we have for the first years after Becket's death, but for all its charms, it must be read with care. Benedict was not an investigative reporter. He had clear goals in mind, chief among them drawing parallels between Becket and Christ, presenting the reader with pleasing pairings and sets of similar miracles, and broadcasting Becket's extraordinary qualities as a saint. He gloried in miracles that proved "enemies" wrong, and he had a complex of prejudices all too typical of religious men of his time and place: against the Jews, against the Welsh, and very much for men like himself. In a widespread cult, his perspective was limited to what he heard at Canterbury, and even there, he felt under no obligation to report everything that he knew. He selected stories for his own reasons, and might well have discarded stories that today we would most want to hear.

Nevertheless, when one opens almost any page of the *Miracles*, it is hard not to be carried away with his descriptions of the people who came to Canterbury rejoicing in or seeking a miracle from the new martyr. Adolescent serving-maids and shepherds, the wives of knights and their children, priors, canons, priests, and clerks, Londoners, town-dwellers and people from the rural regions, minor barons and countesses, bakers and shoemakers, the very young and the very old – so much of the glittering spectacle of medieval society is found in these pages. Robert of Swaffham wrote that Benedict was well named (*bene dictus*), because he was given the blessing (*benedictio*) of many graces.[131] The martyr's first miracle collector was an administrator, builder, prior, abbot, and friend of kings. However, it is his splendid work from the time when he was still a mere monk, when much remained in doubt about the future of a dead archbishop, that he was and is still most remembered.

[131] Swaffham, p. 64.

The Passion of St. Thomas Becket

The surviving extracts from Benedict's Passion *begin with a vivid description of the confrontation between Thomas Becket and four of Henry II's knights in the archbishop's palace on the day of his death, Tuesday, December 29, 1170. The chief point of contention was the coronation of the Young King Henry in June 1170 and the ensuing excommunications and suspensions of the archbishop of York and the English bishops who had officiated at the ceremony. After a heated argument, their tempers raised, the knights left to arm themselves.*

Benedict was an eyewitness to the chilling events he describes. He draws numerous parallels between Becket's last hours and death with the story of Christ's passion in the Gospels. Though we are missing Benedict's account of the first blow that struck the archbishop, it is likely that we have a very significant proportion of the original text. The headings included below may have been Benedict's, but they were most likely written by the compiler of the Quadrilogus II, *the text in which the extracts from Benedict's* Passion *were preserved.*

Extract I

How the knights came to the archbishop and greeted him.

On the fifth day of the Nativity of the Lord, the archbishop was seated in his chamber around the eleventh hour.[1] Many clerks and monks were seated on this side and that discussing business and issues with him, when the four aforenamed knights,[2] who, with their father *Satan, had gone forth from the*

---

[1] In today's reckoning, this is sometime after 3pm on December 29 (the "fifth day" after Christmas, counting Christmas as day one). Before the advent of the mechanical clock in the fourteenth century, medieval Europeans split up the time between daybreak and sunset into twelve "hours," which meant that their daytime hours were quite long in the summer and quite short in the winter. In Canterbury in midwinter, the sun sets a little before 4pm.

[2] That is, Reginald Fitz-Urse, Hugh de Morville, William de Tracy, and Richard de Brito. Here Benedict uses the term *satellites* to refer to the four knights. He employs the same

presence of the Lord [Jb 2:7], came into the archbishop's chamber. As is the custom, they were greeted by several of those sitting near the entrance. They returned the greeting, but in subdued tones, as they advanced to the archbishop. They sat on the ground before his feet and did not greet him either in their name nor in the king's name. They were like those from whom salvation was far off, but death and perdition near. For some time, they pressed their lips in silence, holding back the venom of snakes, hidden behind their lips, so that it could later burst forth with more force. The Lord's anointed,[3] wholly blameless, was silent as well.

After some time had passed in this silence, not without the amazement of those sitting there, Reginald fitz Urse, bear-like in temper rather than descent,[4] addressed himself to the saint:[5] "We have been sent to you by our lord the king across the sea,[6] and we bring you royal injunctions. We want to know whether you prefer that they be discussed secretly or in public." The man of God, who did not hope for the world's fortunes nor fear its misfortunes, responded in a simple and humble tone, saying, "I leave this to your choice and pleasure." "Then let them be spoken of in secret," said Reginald, "and let those who are present be absent for a time." The saint, who did not see security in their number nor fear solitude, told his people to leave. When they had left and only the four knights remained in the chamber with the archbishop, the doorkeeper ran up and left the door open, so that those who were now seated outside could look back at their lord, the Lord's anointed, and could see him as well as those enemies of God. When the aforesaid Reginald had presented some of the royal mandates, the very prudent man

---

word frequently in the *Passion* and in the *Miracles* as well (see below, I.10, I.19, and II.35), but it is not easy to render in English. It means that knights were closely connected to the king (we get our English word "satellite" from this word: see *DMLBS*, entry for *satelles*), but possible translations, such as "attendants" or "ancillaries," are awkward and potentially misleading. I will render the word simply as "knight" or "knights."

[3] The term that Benedict uses here to describe Becket, *christo Domini* (the Lord's anointed), is found in the Hebrew Scriptures to denote the Messiah and the Christian New Testament to describe Christ. Benedict speaks of Becket as the Lord's anointed later in the *Passion* and in the miracle stories as well (see below, II.41 and III.64).

[4] The name "fitz Urse" means "son of a bear." See Biographical Notes, Reginald fitz Urse.

[5] The sole surviving panel from two medieval windows in Canterbury Cathedral picturing Becket's life may represent this scene of Reginald and the knights speaking to the archbishop: see Caviness, *Windows*, Appendix 1 no. 5, and Madeline Caviness, "A Panel of Thirteenth Century Stained Glass from Canterbury in America," *Antiquaries Journal* 45 (1965): 192–9.

[6] That is, King Henry II, who was in his domains in Normandy in December 1170.

of God considered them in a clear light. When he saw that they did not offer peace nor any good, with a presentiment of the future he called to mind the gospel, *Jesus did not trust himself unto them, for he knew all men* [Jn 2:24]. He summoned the doorkeeper and ordered that his clerics and monks who were there should come in, with all the laity excluded. When they had come in, the saint said to the knights, "Sirs, you can say what you like in the presence of these men." Reginald replied, "Since you have chosen that these matters come out in public rather than be kept secret, we will, in accordance with your will, reveal them to those who are here."

Presentation of the mandates of the king, and the response of the archbishop

"We bring an order from the lord king, who is currently across the sea, that you go to his son the new king, on this side of the sea, and that you do for him what you ought to do for your lord and king."[7] The saint said, "And what is it that I ought to do for him?" Reginald said, "This is something you should know, not us." He replied, "If I knew this, I would certainly not deny that I knew it. In truth, I think I have done for him whatever I should have done." Reginald contradicted him, "By no means: there is much still to be done, and much to be corrected."

The archbishop asserted that he did not know what he ought to correct with regard to the king's majesty, unless they would declare this by their good will, of which there certainly was none. Reginald said, "Since you say that you know nothing of this, we will reveal what you should do. Our lord the king charges you to go to his son the king, who is on this side of the sea, as soon as possible, in order to make an oath of fealty to him and to correct the sin that you have committed against the king's majesty." The man of the Lord responded, saying, "Why must I confirm my fealty to him with an oath on relics? In what way have I offended the king's majesty?" The knight skipped over the second question, since he was not able to answer it, and addressed the first one in this way: "Fealty, confirmed by an oath, is demanded of you for the barony which you hold of our lord the king, and an oath of security must be made by the clerics you have brought into his territory, if they wish to remain here."

---

[7] The "new king" is Henry II's eldest son, Henry, referred to as Henry the Younger or "the young king" after his coronation in June 1170. He was in England, "this side of the sea," in December 1170: see Matthew Strickland, *Henry the Young King, 1155–1183* (New Haven, 2016), pp. 100–7. Henry II's desire to crown his eldest son in the hope of ensuring a peaceful succession became a major source of contention with Becket. When the coronation went ahead without him, Becket, who was exiled in France, saw it as deeply offensive and a threat to the rights of the archbishop of Canterbury.

The archbishop replied, "Regarding the barony, I am prepared to do whatever justice or reason dictates for my lord the king. But let him be in no doubt whatsoever that he will be unable to extort an oath from me or from any of my clerics. Many oaths beyond measure have been coerced, and the perjured and excommunicated are already without number. But thanks be to God, I have already absolved most of them from the crime of perjury and the chains of anathema that had bound them. When it pleases the Lord, I will deliver the rest from these perils." "We know," said Reginald, "that you will do none of the things that we have declared to you. In addition, our lord the king commands you to absolve his bishops, excommunicated or suspended by you without his licence, both of the sentence of damnation and of silence, and to obey the law regarding these offences as well as others with which he will want to charge you."[8] The archbishop replied, "I did not suspend or anathematize the bishops. It was the lord pope, to whom it is well known that the Lord has granted this power. If you want to reopen the case about these matters, it should be done between you and him. It is not my concern to discuss this matter with you." Reginald said, "Although you did not do this yourself, yet it was done through you and by your instigation." The saint said, "If the lord pope, seeing the great injury inflicted on my church and me, has taken retribution, I confess that it does not displease me."

The son of unrighteousness had until now been exerting all his powers in the hope that by speaking cunningly, he might ensnare the most prudent lamb of God[9] in speech, or that he might turn him away from a state of rectitude and against the honor of God and the church, of which he was an invincible defender. When he saw that *a net had been spread in vain before the eyes of*

---

[8] Reginald refers here to the pope's excommunications and/or suspensions of figures such as Roger de Pont l'Évêque (archbishop of York), Hugh de Puiset (bishop of Durham), Gilbert Foliot (bishop of London), and Jocelin Bohun (bishop of Salisbury) (on these individuals, see Biographical Notes). Becket asked the pope for these excommunications and suspensions in retaliation for their participation in the coronation of the Young King Henry, performed in Westminster on June 14, 1170 in Becket's absence. Becket issued the pope's pronouncements shortly before he returned from France to England in late 1170. When Roger of York, Gilbert Foliot, and Jocelin of Salisbury heard of their sentences, they went to Normandy to complain to King Henry II in person. Henry was furious, and this was the point when he uttered the fateful words that impelled the four knights to travel to Canterbury. For accounts of the coronation, excommunications and suspensions, and the knights traveling to Canterbury, see Barlow, *Thomas Becket*, pp. 207–37 and Duggan, *Thomas Becket*, pp. 181–209.

[9] In the New Testament, the term "the lamb of God" is frequently used to describe Christ. In the miracle stories, Benedict often refers to Becket's blood as "the blood of the lamb": see below, Prologue, p. 78, n.8.

the one with wings [Prv 1:17] he attacked him with offensive accusations: "You show by clear signs that this pleases you. You have disgraced and shown contempt for the king's majesty by excluding his bishops from their bishoprics and preventing them from entering the holy mother church, all because they dared to crown our lord the new king, whose inheritance is proven by law, for he is the son of the king and queen and bears the sign of command on his shoulder. When you oppose his elevation and presume to do such a thing, it is easily believed and very likely that you intend to steal away his crown, invade the kingdom, and to be named and become the king of the land. But by God's will, you will not be able to achieve the title of royal dignity."

The saint, not unaware of the saying in which it is said, *an angry man stirs up strife, but a wise man appeases those that are stirred up* [Prv 15:18], applied the medicine of a mild response to the bitter soul of the knight, saying, "By no means, Reginald, by no means do I aspire to the name or dignity of a king, nor do I desire to tear away his crown from him. I would freely place three or four such crowns on him, if I had the power to do so. Nor do I believe that there is anyone in the world besides his father, my lord the king, who loves him more dearly than I do, or who wishes more good to him.[10] If the Lord assents and my life continues, I will prove this to him by deeds. As for the bishops, whom you say were suspended or excommunicated by me or through me, know for certain that whatever was done, was done with the king's consent and council. In the feast of the blessed Mary Magdalene, peace was restored between us, and he received me in my earlier grace.[11] Concerning the injuries and violence done to me and those belonging to me, and especially concerning the bishops, who disdained their mother, the church of Canterbury, and did not fear to usurp my office, I deposited my quarrel with the king. By his grace, he granted that I could seek from the lord pope any punishment compatible with justice and equity. He did not just consent to this, but also deigned to promise me aid."

Reginald, as empty of courtesy as he was full of anger, exclaimed, "Ah! What are you saying? It would be an unparalleled and unheard-of act of treason, if the lord king granted you licence to excommunicate or suspend his bishops who, by his order, participated in his son's coronation. This never came into his mind. You know that you are the author of great evil, you who accuse our

---

[10] In his youth, Henry the Younger had been entrusted to Becket's care and spent time in his household: see Strickland, *Henry the Young King*, pp. 34–40.
[11] A reference to the peace of Fréteval on July 22, 1170, when Henry made a number of concessions regarding the coronation and Becket's other complaints: see Barlow, *Thomas Becket*, pp. 209–13 and Duggan, *Thomas Becket*, pp. 179–200.

lord the king of such treason." "Reginald, Reginald," said the archbishop, "I do not accuse the king of treachery. Nevertheless, it is certainly not a secret that concord is restored between us and we have an agreement. Archbishops, bishops, many exalted men, very religious men, and fifty or more knights were there and heard these things. And you too, lord Reginald, you were present."[12] The enemy of truth responded, "Truly I was not there, and I did not see or hear this." The saint, most temperate in word and in tone, affirmed humbly and simply, "No, God knows. I am certain that I saw you there." But he again, perjuring himself that he had not been there, and injuring himself by his denial, said, "It is unprecedented and astonishing that you place a stamp of such treason on our lord the king. He will not be able to bear this from you any longer, nor will we, his faithful men, bear this any longer." Then the other knights also exclaimed and burst out in the same threats, swearing many times by the wounds of God that they had borne too much from him. *The hearts of the foolish were troubled* [Ps 75:6] and they *spoke their iniquity on high* [Ps 72:8], piling insult on insult, threat on threat.

But the man of the Lord, who had come not only to be struck by threats and insults, but also willingly to expose his head to the sword for the defence of church's liberty, responded mildly, according to what the ethicist says, *while its fury is at full speed, give way to its furious speeding.*[13] He said, "From the time I arrived in this land, at peace with God and the king, and with the king's safe conduct, I have endured many threats, many insults, and many injuries. For example, my men were taken captive and their possessions violently taken from them; the tails of my horses were cut off by Robert de Broc; and my wine was violently seized by Ranulf de Broc, the wine that the lord king had caused to be transported across his territories beyond the sea and brought to England.[14] I was wronged by many other injuries and insults, despite the fact our lord the king mandated and ordered to his son the king, both by letters and by the oral report of messengers, that there was to be a lasting peace with me and those belonging to me. And in addition to these things, you have come and made these threats to me. You should know that I bear such things very badly."

Reginald said to him, "If anyone presumed to do something that seemed to involve injury to you, why didn't you make it known, and you would have received whatever justice or reason might demand?" "Before whom," said the

---

[12] Another reference to Henry II's and Becket's agreement at Fréteval.
[13] Ovid, *Cures for Love*, line 119.
[14] On these incidents, see Biographical Notes, Ranulf de Broc and Robert de Broc.

archbishop, "would I make my complaint?" The knight replied, "To the king on this side of the sea."

"Friend," said the archbishop, "I have complained enough, I have laid out the injuries inflicted on me enough times, I have made enough vain attempts to achieve satisfaction. So many injuries have been piled on me every day. I have been distressed by so many and such grievous evils, and so many complaints of my impoverished men ring in my ears both day and night, that I would never find enough messengers necessary for their individual needs. Moreover, if I set forth my injuries, the benefit of justice and reason would be denied to me. As for the king on this side of the sea and his justices, they are dependent on the council of the king across the sea; they do nothing without consultation. For me, justice and equity are denied, and for my people, the opportunity of crossing the sea and approaching the king is prohibited. And so, I am treated very badly. In truth, I do not find rectitude or justice either here nor there from anyone, but I will exercise it as an archbishop can and should, never forsaking it for any mortal." In reply to this, one of them shouted, "Threats, threats: will you put the whole realm under interdict, and excommunicate us all?" Another said, "So help me God, he will not do this: he has put countless people under the chain of anathema."

And so they leapt to their feet, and with the bridle released from their anger and insults, they threw around their gloves, flung their arms about in rage, and as much by the gestures of their bodies as the vehemence of their cries, they presented clear indications of insanity. The archbishop also stood up. On account of the great noise and confusion of voices it was not easy to distinguish the poisonous words that each of them hurled at the Lord's anointed. Finally the sons of Belial[15] turned to the monks who happened to be there and attempted (though without success) to provoke them against their father and the father of the whole realm though these words: "On behalf of the lord king, we command that you not let this man depart, but keep him in custody, so that he may brought again to the king when he wills it." They repeated this same speech again and again, and the kind father responded for his sons: "What is this? Do you think I wish to escape and be a fugitive? I will not become a fugitive for the king nor for any living man. I did not come to flee, but instead await the frenzy of the attackers and the wickedness of the impious." "True," said the knights, "true, by the will of God, you will not escape." It was not pride that had supplied that word in contempt of the king to the most

---

[15] Belial is another name for Satan. Wicked people are termed "sons of Belial" in both the Hebrew Scriptures and the Christian New Testament.

holy man, but rather constancy, founded on Christ and made perfect as an example of virtue.

And so they went out with great tumult and many insults and threats, and the archbishop followed them to the chamber's door, crying out to Hugh de Morville,[16] who ought to have been above the rest as much by virtue of sound reason as on account of his noble descent, that he come back and speak to him. But they were so enraged that they could not control themselves, and he went away with the others in pride and indignation. The man of the Lord came back and sat down, and in the presence of his clerks he lamented over these commands of the king and the knights' slanderous words. One of his clerks, namely Master John of Salisbury,[17] a man of many letters, great eloquence and wise council, and, what is greater than these, a man rooted in the fear and the love of God, responded to the one lamenting in this way: "Lord, it is a very remarkable thing that you take no-one's counsel. And why was it necessary for a man of such excellence to get up, further inciting those evil men, and to follow them to the door? Would it not have been better to take council with those present here, and to give them a more mild response, these men who devise evil against you in whatever way they can, in hopes of provoking you to anger and at least ensnaring you in what you say?" But the saint, who longed for justice and the liberty of the church to the very point of death, as if it were a delightful repose, sighed and said, "I have already received every manner of council. I know well enough what I ought to do." And Master John said, "I hope, by God's will, that it turns out well."

How the knights armed themselves

And so the wicked knights went out, hurrying to their companions and accomplices in the court. Having very quickly armed themselves, they returned in armour, with swords and axes, bows and arrows, and also two-edged axes and other tools, either to break down locks and doors or to commit the outrage that they were planning. Several people ran to the archbishop shouting, "Lord, lord, they are arming themselves!" And he said, "What's the trouble? Let them arm themselves."

In that cursed company was that son of perdition, Robert de Broc, whom, as we said above, the holy man anathematized on the day of the Lord's Nativity and cut off from the communion of the faithful on account of the enormity of

---

[16] See Biographical Notes, Hugh de Morville.
[17] See Biographical Notes, John of Salisbury.

his crimes.[18] He knew all the entrances and exits in the palace because he held the custody of the whole archbishopric under his lord Ranulf de Broc[19] when the archbishop was exiled. The company had hastened to seize the door of the hall, but they could not get through due to the precaution of the servants. When they found that the door was shut and bars prevented their entry, they immediately turned aside, led by the aforesaid Robert, to a hidden staircase which led down from the outer chamber into the orchard, and having broken through a nearby window, they opened the door. When the servants running everywhere called out to the most brave champion of God that he should flee, he was not moved in spirit, nor did he move from that place. To him, nothing was more vile than to fear death for Christ. Both clerks and monks implored and very strongly urged him to flee. He remembered his previous promise, namely, that he would not flee those who kill the flesh for fear of death, and he remained seated, fearless. Like them, he did not know those who *believe for a while and in time of temptation fall away* [Lk 8:13]. But the few monks who were there broke the bolt on the door that led to the church through the cloister, and they urged their unwilling father to be led away, suggesting an honorable reason for him to depart, namely that it was the hour in which he ought to be performing the praise of vespers in the church.[20] Others, laying hands on him, lifted him up and used force on him. Then the saint ordered that his cross be carried before him, not forgetting to observe to the letter the precept of the Lord, *if any man will come after me, let him deny himself, and take up his cross, and follow me* [Mt 16:24]. He went out, but when he was forced by his companions to hurry, he stopped his step as if ashamed to flee. The monks still urged him on and compelled him to move along. Either because their behavior was more irreverent than usual, or in order to reassure and console them, he kept repeating these words, saying to them, "What is this, sirs? What do you fear?" When they came to the cloister door, they were not able to break it open, and they did not have the key, but the two cellarers of the church of Canterbury, Richard and William, who had heard the tumult and the crashing of arms and had hastened towards him by means of the cloister walk, pulled back the bolt and opened the door for the archbishop as he approached.[21]

---

[18] See Biographical Notes, Robert de Broc. The compiler of the Quadrilogus may have added the words "as we said above" to Benedict's narrative.
[19] See Biographical Notes, Ranulf de Broc.
[20] The last monastic service of the day, vespers was held at sunset.
[21] Other chroniclers suggested that this door opened miraculously.

Extract II

Concerning the archbishop's entry into the cathedral

Some of the monks left vespers, ran to their pastor, and brought him in, though he resisted. They hurried to close the doors of the church to keep out the enemy. However, turning back immediately, the holy father rebuked them, saying, "Allow my people to enter." He ran to the door and opened it, moving both them and others away from the doorway. With his most holy hands, he pulled into the church those who had been left outside to the bites of the wolves, saying, "Come in, come in quickly." And so he could say with the Lord, "*of them whom you have given me, I have not lost any one*" [Jn 18:9]. Finally the importunate demands of his own sons wrenched him away, and with the enemies already coming near, he left the doors open, not wishing to hinder their path nor his martyrdom, which he had known and predicted as his future blessing. While he was still across the sea, he had clearly foretold to two abbots, namely of Pontigny and Vauluisant, of whom we wrote above,[22] that he would undergo martyrdom and be killed in a church. To both, he had foretold that he would go to England not on the pope's order, but rather for the revelation of his martyrdom.

Extract III

When the man of God could have turned away from that hour of death if he had wished, the aforenamed knights came into the monastery, some calling out, "Where is that traitor?" and others, "Where is the archbishop?" The saint, in his spirit *knowing all things that should come upon him* [Jn 18:4] met them on the steps, some of which he had already ascended,[23] and with no fear on his face he said, "Here I am, no traitor, but an archbishop," so imitating the Lord when he went to meet the Jews seeking him, saying, *I am he* [Jn 18:5]. The first of them approached and said to the saint, "Flee, you are a dead man!" But the saint

---

[22] Pontigny and Vauluisant Abbeys were Cistercian monasteries located 120–60 kilometers southeast of Paris. Becket spent nearly two years of his exile in France at Pontigny Abbey (December 1164–November 1166) and would have known these abbots well. The phrase "of whom we wrote above" was likely added by the Quadrilogus II editor, who here included a lengthy passage from the *Life* of Herbert of Bosham describing the conversation between Becket and these two abbots at length: see Bosham, *Vita*, pp. 405–6, and Quadrilogus II, *MTB*, vol. 4, pp. 352–3.

[23] That is, the steps going up from the northwest transept into the choir.

said, "I certainly will not flee." The sacrilegious knight laid his hand on him and knocked off his cap with the tip of his sword. "Come this way," he said, "you are a prisoner." But the saint said, "I will not come. You will do to me here what you wish to do," and he shook off his hand from the hem of his cloak.

Extract IV

When he saw another armoured man approaching him with a drawn sword, he turned and said, "What is this, Reginald? I have given you many benefits, and you come to me armed in the church?" By these words, does not the imitator of Christ seem to resemble Christ when he said to the Jews, "*You are come out, as it were to a robber, with swords and clubs to apprehend me?*" [Mt 26:55]. The knight, filled with furious rage, said to him, "You will know soon. You are a dead man."

The Quadrilogus compiler utilized other authors to supply more details regarding the last words spoken by Becket and a description of the knights' first blow. Edward Grim and William of Canterbury said that Reginald Fitz-Urse struck Becket first, while William FitzStephen said it was William de Tracy.

Extract V

With his head bowed, he awaited the arrival of the second blow. When the second wound was inflicted on his head, he fell to the ground, his body lying straight as if he were prostrated in prayer. A third man cut off a large part of his skull, dreadfully enlarging the preceding wound. The fourth man, who was criticized by one of them for being slow to strike, hurled his sword with great force at the same wound, and the sword broke on the marble floor. He left both the tip and the hilt of the sword in the church. It seems to be true that this portends a great deal. What would the breaking of the enemies' sword seem to signal unless it were the true casting down of the hostile power and the victory of the triumphant church by means of the martyr's blood? It did not seem to be enough for that son of Satan to have committed such an outrage on the priest of God, for then – it is horrible to describe – he inserted his sword into the most holy head to pull out the brains of the dead man and to spread them, most cruelly, onto the pavement. He cried out to his partners in this crime: "He's dead: we should go right away." From this it may be supposed that they were afraid that some of the knights or servants of the holy martyr might come upon them and revenge the blood of their lord. As they went out of the monastery, they cried out the sign of a remarkable victory, as is customary on the field of battle: "The king's knights, the king's!" Others mockingly said, "He wished to be king, and wished to be more than the king. Let him be king now, let him be king now!" And in this they were similar to those who insulted the Lord hanging on the cross, *passing by and wagging their heads* [Mt 27:39] and among other things saying, *"For he said, 'I am the Son of God'"* [Mt 27:43].

Extract VI

Has any martyr earned a more glorious title? Each of the others took on an individual cause of martyrdom in an individual struggle for their own salvation, but he took up the cause of the universal church. He strove against princes and tyrants, against the mercenaries, rather than the shepherds, of the holy church. In order to vindicate the church, he permitted the knights to bear away their triumph over his body. People of another sect killed them, but Christians and his own sons killed him.[24]

Extract VII

Concerning the booty and clothing that the knights divided amongst themselves

The doers of evil, drunk on the effusion of innocent blood but no less thirsty for works of greed, ran back as quickly as they could, with their accomplices, to the palace of the archbishop. Some violently removed horses from the stables, others struck his servants, others went through all the furniture of the house and broke open packsaddles and chests. Whatever they found of gold or silver, clothing or various ornaments, they divided amongst themselves according to their individual desires. It pleased divine piety, which mightily and wisely disposes all things, that they were in this way made imitators of those who divided Christ's clothing amongst themselves, so that they might make the passion of the servant more similar to the passion of the Lord.[25] By the clear similarities between these events, all the faithful might recognize that the church should

---

[24] In other words, Becket was a superior martyr because he was killed by Christians who were under his jurisdiction as archbishop. Most of the martyr saints renowned in the medieval church had been killed by pagan Romans in times of persecution.

[25] All of the Gospel writers described how the soldiers who crucified Jesus cast lots for his clothing: see Matthew 27:35, Mark 15:24, Luke 23:34, and John 19:23–4.

be released from the world's servitude by the martyr's blood, just as the church was redeemed from the devil's power by Christ's death. Moreover, all the deeds and privileges that the malicious men found were given to that son of perdition, Ranulf de Broc, to be conveyed to the king in Normandy. This was so that he could, according to his will, tear into pieces, or never allow to be seen, those that seemed to be contrary to the customs of his realm, or those that protected the liberty of the universal church or the privileges of the church of Canterbury. And the knights certainly did these things.

Extract VIII

When the holy body was taken up from the ground, a small iron hammer and double-edged axe, left by the parricides, were found under him. He had taken possession of them as he fell, as if he were claiming power over them for himself. This demonstrated that in the future he would be a hammer of the wicked, and that no one would be able to evade his sentence of vengeance except by doing penance. Blood lay around his head in the likeness of a crown, perhaps as a sign of sanctity, but his face had no blood on it, except for a thin track that went from the right side of his forehead down to the left side of his face across his nose. Afterwards, he appeared to many people in visions bearing this mark. These people knew nothing about it, and yet described it as if they had seen it with their own corporeal eyes.[26] As he still lay on the pavement, some daubed their eyes with blood, others, bringing vessels, took a portion away as best they could, and others eagerly dipped in pieces of cloth cut from their clothing. Afterwards, no one considered themselves to be fortunate who did not carry off some portion, however small, of that precious treasure.[27] Since everyone was disordered and confused, each person could do as he liked. However, the part of the blood that they had left in the church was gathered most decently in a very clean vessel and kept back in the church to be preserved.[28] His cloak and outer garment, stained with blood as they were, were given to the poor on behalf of his soul with indiscreet piety. They would have been happy enough, if they had not immediately and unwisely proffered them for sale at a small price.[29]

[26] See below, IV.37 and IV.52.

[27] For miracles in Book I relating to this blood taken away from the cathedral, see below, I.12, I.17, and I.23.

[28] For Benedict's account of the first person to drink some of this blood (mixed with water) that had been gathered up by the monks, see below, I.12.

[29] For the purchase and use of this cloak, see I.19 and I.21; for a miracle relating to the

Extract IX

That sorrowful night was passed in suffering, groans and sighs, without a moment of happiness or forgetfulness of sorrow, and with expectations of greater evil the next day.

Extract X

How the body of the holy martyr was brought for burial

The next day, many armed men congregated outside of the city walls once again, and it was said everywhere that they had come intending to commit a greater atrocity, namely, to wrest the body of the holy martyr out of the bosom of the holy mother church by force and to drag it behind horses through the whole city, or to hang it from a gibbet, or to cut it into bits and throw it into a bog, or into a more vile place, which it is not decent to name,[30] in greater contempt of God and of the church. They said that a traitor's corpse should not be buried among the holy archbishops. The monks, alarmed for themselves as well as for the saint, fearing either that he would be treated foully, or that they would lose their precious treasure, made preparations to bury him with all speed. And so they could not wash his most sacred body, nor anoint it with balsam, as is the custom of the holy church of Canterbury. It is believed that this happened not so much because of human wickedness but by divine mercy. For the person the Lord ordained to be anointed in his own blood, what need is there for the scent of an ordinary perfume? When they took off his outer garments in order to dress him in an archbishop's vestments, they found that his body was enveloped in a hairshirt. This was painful not only on account of its harshness, but also because his undergarments, extending down to the knees, were made of haircloth, something we have never read nor heard as being copied by any other saint.[31] Above this, he was dressed as a monk, namely with the hood and coarse woolen shirt. They looked at each

---

outer garment, see II.58. This clothing was pictured in Canterbury Cathedral's stained glass: see Koopmans, "Gifts of Becket's Clothing Made by the Monks of Christ Church, Canterbury," in Tom Nickson (ed.), *The Cult of Thomas Becket: Art, Relics, and Liturgy in Britain and Europe*, special issue of the *Journal of the British Archaeological Association* 173:1 (2020): 39–60.

[30] By "a more vile place," Benedict likely means a cesspit or latrine.
[31] The discovery of the hairshirt was mentioned in many contemporary accounts of Becket's murder. For miracles relating to the hairshirt, see below, III.40, III.61, IV.19, and IV.94.

other, stunned by the sight of such hidden religion beyond what would have been believed, and with their reasons for mourning so multiplied, their tears began again.

How could it be thought that there was greed or treachery in such a man? How could this man, who secretly preferred a hairshirt above worldly comforts, have desired an earthly kingdom? How could he have been a traitor of the king's majesty? Was he not, rather, betrayed? He did not wish to yield to or to resist his betrayers, the sons of iniquity, though he could have done so. If he had wished, he could have prudently turned away from the enemy's deceit and rage or repelled them with a more powerful force. He had the power, the foreknowledge, and the forewarning. As for the power, even if the enemy had come multiplied by ten, he could have, if he had wished, driven them back one hundredfold. As for the foreknowledge, on the day of the Lord's Nativity, when he had administered the bread of the word of God to the people, he said, among other things, that he did not return from exile for any other reason than either to cast aside the yoke of servitude that had been placed on them, or to undergo the punishment of death among them and for them. He had also, as noted above, made mention of his passion to the abbots across the sea.

Moreover, just as he was informed of these things by divine kindness, he was also forewarned and forearmed by human zeal. It would be possible to speak of how numerous people acquired merit due to their good will in this matter, but two examples can be stated with certainty. A certain knight, well-known to him, informed Richard, the cellarer of Canterbury, on a pledge of faith, that the Lord's saint would not see the evening of the third day – though this was against his faith, since he had been bound to those murderers in the killing of his father. He preferred to put his faith, by which he was bound to them, in jeopardy, than to incur the guilt of such a terrible homicide in silence. When Richard told this to the most blessed servant of God, he smiled and replied, "They are threats." When he was told for certain by a citizen of Canterbury named Reginald that those who conspired his death had already landed in England, he began to weep bitterly, either to *blot out their iniquities* [Is 43:25] or because peace had not yet been obtained for the church, and he said, "They will find me prepared for death. Let them do what they wish. For I know, my sons, and I am certain, that I will die by arms. However, they will not kill me outside of my church." By these words, is it not proved that he not only knew about his passion, but also had foreknowledge about its manner and place? But since *his kingdom was not of this world, for if it were, his ministers would certainly have striven that he should not be delivered* to them [Jn 18:36], he chose by his own free will to drink the cup of the Lord cheerfully, rather than to stain the virtue of his former constancy by ineffectual flight, or to call to his defense those who would battle with arms. In this he imitated the one who could have asked his Father for twelve legions of angels for his defense,[32] but did not wish to do so. We believe that it would not be easy to find a passion of any other martyr that would seem to accord with such similarity to the Lord's passion.

Extract XI

The passion of that extraordinary champion of God, Thomas, archbishop of Canterbury, primate of all England and legate of the apostolic see, took place in the year of our Lord 1170, in the fifty-third year of his life, on the fourth day before the kalends of January, on the third day of the week, about the eleventh hour, so that the fifth day of the Lord's Nativity might, by the will of our same Lord Jesus Christ, be the day of his birth from misery to glory, our same Lord Jesus Christ, to whom, with the Father and Holy Spirit, is honor and glory, virtue, power and dominion, world without end. Amen.[33]

---

[32] See Matthew 26:53, where Christ states that he could request twelve legions of angels if he wished.
[33] The closing "our Lord Jesus Christ, to whom, with the Father and Holy Spirit… world without end. Amen" is a common conclusion for prayers or other devotional texts.

The Miracles of St. Thomas Becket

Prologue

After the most blessed martyr of Christ, Thomas, *rested from his labors* [Rv 14:13] and migrated from the transitory festival of the Nativity of the Lord to the joys of the inner and eternal festival,[1] *our dancing was turned into mourning* [Lam 5:15] and *our organ into the voice of those who weep* [Jb 30:31]. The *crown fell from our head* [Lam 5:16], the glory of the English, indeed even of the angels, the matchless flower of our pastors, the ornament and the splendor of the entire church. For us, our floods of tears were matched with many reasons for weeping, because we were made *orphans without a father* [Lam 5:3], and *the Lord had closed the mouths of the singers* [Est 13:17] since his holy church was polluted by the shameful act of parricide.[2] The mother *lamented and* the daughters *did not mourn* [Mt 11:17], and she *looked for someone who would share* her *sorrows, and there was none, and who would console* her, *and found none* [Ps 68:21]. The mother was mourning, and the daughters' singing increased the maternal suffering; she only experienced in herself *music in mourning, a tale out of time* [Sir 22:6].[3] We had to mourn the effusion of innocent blood, the contempt of the temple and of God, the continuing silence of our most noble church, the cruel audacity of those applauding this. The house of our holiness was desolate, *the lady of the nations sat in sorrow, all her friends scorned her, nor was there one who would console*

---

[1] By "the transitory festival of the Nativity of Our Lord," Benedict means the celebration of Christmas from December 25 to 31.

[2] Blood shed inside a church desecrates it, meaning that it cannot be used for services until it is reconsecrated in a formal ceremony. Monks would normally hold eight services (the "monastic offices") within their church per day, plus more for feast days and Sundays, but Becket's murder in the cathedral's northwest transept brought this all to a halt for almost a year. The cathedral was not reconsecrated until December 21, 1171.

[3] By the "mother mourning" and "daughters singing," Benedict meant that while no church services could be held in the desecrated "mother" cathedral, all the churches under Canterbury's jurisdiction, the "daughters," continued to conduct services.

her out of all those dear to her [Lam 1:1–2]. You would think that Canterbury, as much as Jerusalem, was lamented by the dirges of the prophets. *All our ways of Sion mourned, because there was no one who might come to the feast* [Lam 1:4]. *The Lord caused feasts and sabbaths to be forgotten* in her [Lam 2:6], and she who was accustomed to *bless the Lord in hymns and confessions* [2 Mc 10:38], *clothed in gold, a multi-coloured garment* [Ps 44:10] before the many churches of the earth, was now consumed day and night with tears and mourning and was filled with disgrace.

I speak in Christ before God – the sons of the church were not even able to restrain their tears at table, but eating they silently mourned, and mixed their drink with tears. Unless *the East had visited us from on high* [Lk 1:78] and from the kernel of our grain left to us a seed of blessing,[4] the house of the Lord would have been stained with eternal disgrace and would not have survived further to rise again. But blessed be the Lord who *did not suffer us to be tempted above that which we were able: but made also with temptation a way of escape, that we might be able to bear it* [I Cor 10:13]. Blessed be the Lord, who looked on the sad, and healed our sadness, who turned to us and gave pardon, who left blessing in his wake. Behold, *for this all generations will call us blessed, since he who is mighty did great things for us* [Lk 1:48–9]. For shortly after his martyrdom, *our young men saw visions and our old men dreamed dreams* [Acts 2:17], and from this, we breathed up to the time of hope of a greater consolation. Miracles ensued, and we knew that the Lord *had indeed lifted on high the horn of his Christ* [1 Sm 2:10] and that *in his hand he directed our salvation* [1 Mc 3:6] – and not only ours, but that of the entire English church. For when the flowers of virtues had been eradicated, and the seed of the one who had come forth from the bosom of the Father to sow his seed had been trampled down and eaten, dried, and choked,[5] the nettles of crimes filled the field of the church. Wolves raged in the Lord's sheepfold, and those who sat in the watchtowers did nothing, like mute dogs that were not able and did not even wish to bark. The sheep were dispersed and the hirelings fled, and there was no one to stand up against the foe,[6] no one to stand with the lord of Canterbury against the workers of iniquity. The apostate, I say, who had set himself up in the throne of pestilence, to the injury of the apostolic see, also polluted a very large portion of the world by

---

[4] See the parable of the grain of wheat, John 12:24–6.
[5] See the parable of the Sower, Luke 8:4–18; esp. verses 5–8 in which the seed is trampled, eaten, dried, and choked.
[6] This passage has close resonances with John 10:12–13, a passage in the parable of the Good Shepherd.

his worship of the idol Baal, which the schismatics set up and adored.[7] Of the rest of the evil deeds, who can comprehend them, when they were without number? By means of *the blood of the lamb* of Canterbury [Rv 7:14/Rv 12:11][8] the benevolence of the Almighty provided for everyone, and either corrected each person, or invited them to correction. For with the flashing of miracles, little by little the darkness of vices ceased, the seed of the word of God grew in the good earth, and the buds of reviving virtues sprouted in the field of the church. By the flashing of miracles, every day innumerable people *are turned from their evil ways* [Jer 26:3], and, *striking their breasts, they return* to the Lord [Lk 23:48]. By the flashing of miracles, every day wolves are made into sheep in the passages of the Lord's sheepfold, and persecutors become the defenders of the church. Finally, at this late hour, led at least by the example of their subjects, the priests of the Lord may be clothed in justice, having before them an example of patience in the long tribulation of their fellow priest, an example of constancy from his death,[9] and from the signs of miracles, hope of a glorious reward.

The schismatics, too, may look to *our lamp* which the Lord *placed on the lampstand* [Mt 5:15], and they may see whether they are set in the bosom of the church, or whether they are cut off from the communion of ecclesiastical unity. For Christ our Gideon carried in his hand, as long as it pleased him, a pitcher with this lamp inside of it, but when the clay of the flesh of the martyr was broken,[10] it was not only the light of his religion and sanctity that shone out, but also the light of miracles, and he showed *the people who walked in darkness* [Is 9:2] the way of truth. For this is the light that shone through the western church at the beginning of the schism by which it *divided light from darkness* [Gn 1:4], and, with Octavian repulsed, chose the catholic pope Alexander for its pastor.[11] If he had been a schismatic, our martyr would by no means have been able to pass by untouched by such a stain, nor would he

---

[7] This is a reference to the papal schism of 1159–78.

[8] The Christian idea of Christ's blood as "the blood of the lamb," evoked the lambs sacrificed in the ancient Jewish festival of Passover (see Exodus 12). By referring to "the blood of the lamb of Canterbury," Benedict is making a direct association between Becket and Christ.

[9] The text reads *ex morte constantiam* here. Robertson wondered whether *ex morte constantiae* was what was meant (see *MTB*, p. 23 n. 7), an emendation I have utilized here.

[10] See Judges 7: 16–22 for the story of Gideon's army carrying clay pitchers with lamps hidden inside of them. When the army attacked an enemy camp, they broke the pitchers and revealed the lamps' light.

[11] This is a reference to the contest between Pope Alexander III (1159–81) and Octaviano Monticelli, an Italian cardinal who took the title Pope Victor IV.

have been able to touch tar without being polluted by it. The frequency of miracles proves every day that he was unpolluted, for no-one can perform such miracles as he has unless God is with him. But if *the hand of God is with him* [Lk 1:66], who was the special son of Pope Alexander and *the staff of his old age* [Tb 5:23] in the western regions,[12] they err *who bow their knees before the idol* [Rom 11:4] in contempt of the Lord who *destroyed their Baal and slew the dragon* [Dn 14:27]. And so, *return, transgressors, to the heart* [Is 46:8] and *let there not be among you a new god* [Ps 80:10] and *do not adore any strange god* [Ex 34:14]. *You worship what you do not know, we worship what we know* [Jn 4:22], since *the Lord he is God* [Ps 99:3], he who found in Alexander *a man after his own heart* [1 Sm 13:14] and *chose him above all flesh* [Sir 45:4] *to feed Jacob his servant and Israel his inheritance* [Ps 77:71]. If he were not chosen by the Lord, how could the blessed martyr Thomas be both a supporter of his election and a saint? How could he both adhere to a schismatic father and please the Most High Father? How could he both die a schismatic and after his death shine forth with miracles?[13] It is certain that, unless he were from God, he would not be able to do any of it. Therefore, it is clear that the cause of his sanctity is his zeal for catholic unity and defense of ecclesiastical liberty. For he would not abandon unity, and he rooted out, as he could, both old and new abuses which seemed to detract from the dignities of the church of Canterbury, the English church, the Roman church, and indeed the universal church. Nevertheless, though he died for the defense of the universal church, yet he devoted himself especially to obtaining justice for Canterbury.

The older sons saw the labor of the father and the imperiled liberty of the mother, and they set aside their birthright for a worthless pottage of lentils,[14] and *turned to a crooked bow* [Ps 77:57]. But the most powerful champion of God, not wishing, like *the sons of Ephraim, to bend and shoot with the bow and turn back in the day of battle* [Ps 77:9], acted manfully, and his heart was strengthened, such that he was no less reluctant to embrace a death of unheard-of cruelty, than he had been before to take up an exile of unprecedented harshness.[15] Whoever succeeds our martyr in the seat of Canterbury should not fear to fight again for its dignities which the martyr defended to the death, nor

---

[12] For the pope's relationship with Becket, see Duggan, "*Alexander ille meus*," pp. 25–37.
[13] John of Salisbury made a similar argument in a letter he wrote to the archbishop William of Sens: see *LJS* no. 308, p. 751.
[14] In a biblical story (Genesis 25:25–34), Esau sold his birthright to Jacob, his younger brother, for a bowl of lentils.
[15] Becket was in exile in France from 1164 to 1170.

should he condemn the rights of the universal church, nor should he shrink from subjection to the lord pope Alexander and his successors.[16] For the great deeds of our martyr are seen both to commend Alexander and to protect the rights of the whole church, and to bear the witness of justice to the dignities of the martyr of Canterbury.

And so, let the holy fatherhood of the highest see rejoice to have had such a son at the ends of the earth and the end of the ages. Let the sons of the church of Canterbury rejoice to be given the consolation of such miracles. Let the whole orb of the earth, and all those who live on it, rejoice to be under the patronage of such a martyr. For who is there, of whatever status in the church, whatever sex or age, whatever grade or order, who has not found something useful in this our treasury? He has given the light of truth to the schismatics, confidence to fearful pastors, health to the ill, and pardon to petitioners and the penitent. By his merits, *the blind see, the lame walk, the lepers are cleansed, the deaf hear, the dead are risen up*, the mute speak, *the poor are evangelized* [Mt 11:5], the paralytic healed, the dropsical cease to swell, the mad return to their senses, the epileptic are cured, the feverish recover, and, to conclude in brief, all manner of infirmity is cured. By his merits, nearly all the miracles of the gospel are fulfilled multiple times. And what was more admirable to all, and unheard of in all ages, new eyes and new genitals were created for a certain one who constantly invoked the martyr, his eyes and genitals having been mutilated.[17] Nor have we read that any other saint of earlier times flashed out with so great and so many miracles so suddenly and in such a short time after his death. Therefore, by the will and precept of the brothers, I am compelled to commend them to the memory of letters. Although my wisdom does not suffice nor my eloquence assist me, I take up the burden freely and with devotion, trusting in him who said, "*Open your mouth and I will fill it*" [Ps 80:11]. I will come first to the visions and revelations of the Lord, by which his mourning servants were consoled and the sanctity and glory of his martyr were gradually made known to the world. And let no-one be enflamed against me, as if I were someone who put dreams at the base of the following work, for I do not lay the foundation of my narration on dreams. Rather, as a prelude, I begin with

---

[16] After Becket's death, the archbishopric remained vacant until Richard, a former Christ Church monk and the prior of Dover, was elected archbishop in June 1173. Richard received his pallium from Alexander III on April 9, 1174.

[17] A reference to the story of Eilward of Westoning: see below, IV.2.

certain great and wonderous visions. And since among the saints whose way of life is in heaven, I am still in the body, and regard my life as still being earthly, let me begin by speaking of something concerning myself, so that my narrative might rise from lesser to greater things.

The Chapters of Book I

1. A first and a second vision
2. A third vision
3. A fourth vision
4. A fifth vision
5. A sixth vision
6. A seventh vision
7. What happened after the visions, or which miracles are to be recorded
8. Concerning Emma, wife of Robert de Sancto Andrea in Sussex, who invoked the martyr on the third day after the martyrdom and recovered from the illness that had held her
9. Concerning Huelina, the daughter of Aaliza of London, who was healed at Gloucester five days after the martyrdom, with a sudden disappearance of a swelling of the head that she was accustomed to suffer every month
10. Concerning William Belet, whose swollen arm lost its swelling on the sixth day after his passion
11. Concerning Brithiva, a blind woman of Canterbury
12. Concerning William, a priest of London, from whom a paralysis of the tongue was removed
13. Concerning Stephen, a knight of Holland, freed from a demon's infestation
14. Concerning William Patrick, freed from a toothache
15. Concerning Robert, who had a hepatic complaint
16. Concerning Alditha of Worth, freed from the anguish of childbirth
17. Item concerning the multiplication of the holy blood
18. Item concerning the multiplication of the blood
19. Item concerning the same
20. Concerning the boxwood pyx that suddenly split when contacted by the blood, and how that blood vanished
21. Concerning the daughter of Ralph of Bourne, who was healed by the martyr's cloak
22. Concerning Etheldreda, freed from a quartan fever
23. Concerning the boy William of Canterbury, freed from a terrible swelling by drinking the blood of the saint and water
24. Concerning Goditha, of a certain Matthew of Canterbury, who, brought to the martyr's tomb by two women, left on her own feet

BOOK I

I.1. A FIRST AND A SECOND VISION

I saw in a vision on the night of his martyrdom [Dn 7:13], *our beloved, white and ruddy* [Sg 5:10], beautiful in face and pleasing of aspect. He was dressed in the vestments and ornaments of an archbishop and going to the altar of God, as if to celebrate the mysteries of the mass. When I had seen this again on the following night or on the third, I at last began to reflect, and chiding myself, I said to myself, "Has not my lord appeared to me again and again in a vision? Why do I shy away and say nothing to him? I will go to him and let him speak with me, or I will definitely speak and he will answer me." And so, going near to him, I asked for and received benediction, and then said, "Do not, I beg you, lord, be angry if I question you." And he said, "Speak." "Lord," I said, "are you not dead?" And he, having been asked in French, responded in Latin: "*I was dead, but I have risen*" [Rv 1:18/Lk 24:6]. Then I said, "If you have truly risen, and should, as we believe, be counted among the martyrs, why do you not show yourself to the world?" The saint said to this, "I carry a light, but on account of the interposing cloud it cannot appear." When I hesitated and did not understand the meaning of this, he added, "Do you wish to see?" "I do, lord," I said. And so he held up before him, with his right hand, a great lantern with a candle burning inside of it, and he told me to look around. I looked, and I saw that the empty air had been filled with a cloud of such density that the lamp seemed to be hidden from the eyes even of those standing nearby. I considered the words that he had said and understood the vision in this way. His *good works would shine out before men* [Mt 5:16],[1] but a cloud of persecution was intervening. The saint, having replaced the light, went to the altar, and those who were there began a festive and joyful introit for the mass, namely, as I remember, *Laetare, Jerusalem, et conventum facite, omnes qui diligitis eam*, etc. [Rejoice, Jerusalem, and come together all you who love her, etc.].[2] The pious father indicated to them that it should not be performed, and in a low voice, began an office of sorrow and prayers, without musical modulation, in this way, *Exsurge, quare obdormis Domine? exsurge, et ne repellas in finem; quare faciem tuam avertis, obliviseris tribulationem nostram? adhaesit*

---

[1] In this part of Matthew's Gospel, Jesus tells his followers to be like lamps on lampstands.
[2] This is the introit for Laetare Sunday (the fourth Sunday in Lent): Cantus ID g00776.

in terra venter noster: exsurge, Domine, adjuva nos et libera nos! [Arise, why do you sleep, O Lord? arise, do not cast us off to the end. Why do you turn your face away and forget our trouble? Our belly is on the ground: arise, O Lord, help us and deliver us].³ Therefore, from him saying, "I was dead but I am risen," I began to understand (when I had woken), that although he was dead from infirmity, yet he lived by means of the power of God.

In the same way, Bartholomew, the bishop of Exeter,⁴ was greatly mourning the martyr's death, when he saw, in his sleep, a man standing near him. The man said, "Why do you mourn?" and the bishop responded, "For our lord of Canterbury, because he is dead." The man said, "It is true that he is dead, but his hands and his arms live."⁵ And so our martyr lives, since, if I may give the bishop's interpretation of this vision, his hands live to do good works and his arms for his vindication. Concerning the vision in which I saw him praying with such devotion, I understood that he prays a great deal for the people and all the holy city of Christ, the true Jerusalem. We know that for those who love him, his prayers *shall be a great confidence before the most high God* [Tb 4:12]. His *voice is living and effectual, and more piercing than any two-edged sword* [Heb 4:12], just as was shown to a certain venerable man in his dreams.

I.2. A THIRD VISION

When the martyr's contest was completed, a certain man *gave sleep to his eyes and slumber to his eyelids* [Ps 131:4] when suddenly a voice resounded in his ears, as one ascending to the heavens, crying out horribly and saying, "Behold, *my blood cries out* more *to the Lord from the earth* [Gn 4:10] than the blood of Abel the just who was killed at the beginning of the world."⁶ This happened at Argentan the night before the sorrowful day when the sorrowful news of the death of the martyr was first heard there.⁷ The aforesaid man was terrified, and though he thought these things over carefully, he could not fathom what

---

3   This is the introit for Sexagesima Sunday (the second Sunday before the start of Lent): Cantus ID g00640.
4   See Biographical Notes, Bartholomew, bishop of Exeter (d.1184).
5   The hand and arm of God are often referenced together in the Bible: see, for instance, Deuteronomy 5:15, Psalms 43:4, Jeremiah 32:21, and Ezekiel 20:33.
6   Abel and Cain were sons of Adam and Eve. For the story of Cain killing Abel, see Genesis 4:1–16.
7   What Benedict does not mention here (but what he and many of his contemporaries would have known) is that King Henry II was at Argentan, a town in Normandy, when he heard the news of Becket's death.

they might portend. On the next day, several people came to sit with him and talk over various events among themselves. He presented his wrapped-up mystery to them that they might unravel it, but their interior eyes were prevented from understanding it, because up to that time, nothing had been heard in that region about the death of our Abel. As they talked and discussed these things together, it happened that someone arrived who asserted that the lord of Canterbury had been killed in his church by the sword. They were stunned, and turned to the one who had told them about his dream and said, "This must be the loud voice that you heard, since there is no doubt that this innocent blood cries out to God with great force." Therefore all of them testified that his dream was true and that this was its interpretation, and we know that their testimony is true. For from the time of the blood of Abel the just to the time of the blood of this just man, which was spilled in the temple of God, no similar noise has been heard in Bethlehem and in all its region, which has so suddenly filled all corners of the world.[8] *That his sound would go forth into all the earth* [Rom 10:18] and *all peoples tell of his glory* [Ps 85:9] was prefigured and manifestly predicted in a certain man's dream.

I.3. A FOURTH VISION

A few nights, rather than days, after the setting of our sun, a boy of an innocent age, too young to be suspected of lying, was shown a multitude of both sexes and all orders convening in the choir of the church of Canterbury. He saw the martyr lying without breath before the altar of Christ, all dressed in silk, and under his head there was a cushion also made entirely of silk. A reverent person in monastic habit supported his head with his hands. And suddenly, from both sides of the martyr, two branches grew up, as if from one trunk, and in a very little time they had grown so high that they seemed ready to break through the roof of the church. Everyone stood and gazed at the rods growing so quickly, wondering greatly, when the one in monastic habit said, "*Men, brothers, why do you stand here looking* [Acts 1:11] and wondering at the sight of the rods? This is a prefiguration of the fame and glory of the holy martyr. For in the same way that you see them going up to heaven, so too the glory of the saint will grow and multiply in the sight of the Lord.

---

[8] Benedict compared Becket to Abel in the Becket Office (Cantus ID 601463 and 601463a): *Novus Abel/ Succedit verteri/ Vox cruroris,/ Vox sparsi cerebri/ Caelum replet/ Clamore celebri* [A new Abel succeeds the old; the voice of blood, the voice of spattered brain, fills the heavens with a loud cry]. See Slocum, *Liturgies*, p. 190; and Reames, "Liturgical Offices," pp. 571–2.

They will grow to a great height and will shoot out branches to all the earth, and there will be no end to their length." That man said many similar things, and worthily extoled the worthy saint to God, but the boy was only able to remember a few of the things that were said because he was young and lacked capacity. Woken from sleep, he wished to accompany his father when he went to the church of Christ,[9] and, being persistent, he received permission to do so. When they both entered the choir, he did not find anything that he had seen, and he was amazed. When the father saw his son's troubled face, he was concerned for him. In response to his father's questions, the boy described what he had seen and what he had heard. The father understood, and he predicted to the innermost ears of some people that the great martyr had risen among us, and that he would truly be exalted and elevated and brought to the heavens. Already we have seen that *the Lord has magnified him in the sight of kings*,[10] and *the earth is full of his praise* [Hb 3:3].

How he was exalted and elevated, and *crowned with glory and honor* in heaven [Ps 8:6], can be considered by means of the following vision.

I.4.   A FIFTH VISION

In the week of the octave of the martyr's passing,[11] a brother who had died many days before appeared to a certain monk of Lewes.[12] Bearing in mind that the one he saw was dead, the monk asked him about many things, and also closely questioned him about the state of the lord of Canterbury who had recently been killed. The brother standing before him spoke a great deal in his praise and glory, but (so that it might be said shortly), he finished his account by saying that he had been presented by the blessed Virgin Mary and the holy apostles, as well as some of the martyrs, confessors and virgins, before the great golden throne[13] which has two doors which open and close. From the throne there rose *a most beautiful form beyond the sons of men* [Ps 44:3], in whose presence alone the souls of the faithful live and are made glad. He embraced the blessed Thomas and gave him the kiss of his benediction, and

---

[9] That is, Canterbury Cathedral, which was dedicated to Christ.
[10] This is an antiphon from the Common office for a martyr: Cantus ID 003671. Here Benedict might be making a veiled reference to the visit of the Young King Henry to Becket's tomb in the fall of 1172. For this visit, see Strickland, *Henry the Young King*, pp. 116–18.
[11] I.e., December 29, 1170 through January 5, 1171.
[12] Lewes Priory, located in Sussex, was the first Cluniac abbey founded in Britain. It was a large and important monastic establishment by the late twelfth century.
[13] See Revelation 4:1–11 for John's vision of the heavenly throne.

then he took the martyr from the saints and placed him most reverently with the apostles. The monk who heard this marveled, and wished to know the reason for this: why the martyr would be granted a more worthy seat than the rest of the martyrs, especially the first martyr Stephen and the saints Lawrence and Vincent.[14] The brother responded that he was of a more worthy position and order. The other martyrs entered individually into single combat and fought for the cause of their own selves, but the lord of Canterbury was killed for the cause of the whole church. While the other martyrs were killed by the Gentiles, he was slain by his own sons.[15]

I have said these things without injury to the holy martyrs, for it has been my intent to describe simply the sum of the vision rather than to dare to claim anything about matters so unknown.[16] And yet, twelve years earlier, something happened in the uttermost ends of England which appears to offer the testimony of firm and true weight to the present vision. A certain young man, of the name of Orm, was led out of the body for several days.[17] When he was returned to his body, he described what he saw in that world, marvelous things that aroused amazement in those who heard them. Among the things that he recounted, he said, "I was led to the highest order of the saints, and I said to my guide, 'Lord, who are they?' And he said, 'They are the apostles of Christ.' And I looked, and I saw an empty seat among the apostles and martyrs. I asked why there was a vacant place and who would fill

[14] For the stoning of Stephen, considered to be the first Christian martyr, see Acts 7:54–60. St. Lawrence (d.258) and St. Vincent (d.304) were martyred during periods of Roman persecution of Christians. They were both very popular saints in the medieval west.

[15] In other words, while Stephen, Lawrence, and Vincent were killed by pagan Romans ("Gentiles"), Becket was killed by Christians, his "sons" because he was their archbishop. Benedict comments on the fact that Becket was killed by Christians in the *Passion* as well: see above, Extract VI.

[16] To view Becket as better than all other martyrs, belonging instead in the company of the apostles (that is, Christ's original disciples), is quite extraordinary. For an excellent discussion of the types and hierarchies of saints, see Robert Bartlett, *Why Can the Dead Do Such Great Things: Saints and Worshippers from the Martyrs to the Reformation* (Princeton, 2013), pp. 137–238, with discussion of apostles and martyrs at pp. 167–85.

[17] An account of the vision of Orm, a thirteen-year-old boy from Yorkshire, was written down in 1126 by a neighboring priest. For an edition and discussion of the text from the sole surviving manuscript, see Hugh Farmer, "The Vision of Orm," *AB* 75 (1957): 72–82. This one known account of Orm's vision does not contain a reference to an empty seat, so Benedict seems to have been familiar with a different version. For a discussion of Orm's vision within the context of similar texts, see Carl Watkins, "Sin, Penance and Purgatory in the Anglo-Norman Realm: The Evidence of Visions and Ghost Stories," *Past and Present* 175 (2002): 3–33.

it. And the angel said to me, 'That is a seat for a priest of the English.'" As his informant stopped speaking, he returned to his body.[18] Many people had faith in his words, and took his unexpected death as additional confirmation. They believed that the priest he spoke of was a hermit of a most celebrated name, whose equal in religion and in merit of sanctity was not known.[19] But now, due to the agreement of the visions, the prerogative of a martyr, and the name and dignity of a priest, we deduce that the seat in heaven was prepared for our martyr, rather than for that hermit, especially as the latter was the priest of one region only, while the former was the high priest of all England. And yet I do not assert my own opinion in these things, nor do I exalt, with great daring, our martyr above all other martyrs. Even so, as far as I can judge from his words and actions, no-one could ever have had either a more glorious cause of martyrdom, a soul more powerful in suffering adversity, nor a greater desire to die for Christ and the Church. And so *his soul pleased God; therefore, the Lord hastened to bring him out of the midst of iniquities* [Ws 4:14], so that the angels of God in heaven would have joy in his triumph, and that joy would be returned to the church, for so long mired in the filth of sorrowful affliction, by the flashing of miracles. A certain sleeping brother of the church of Canterbury was given future notice of the same thing in a most beautiful way.

I.5. A SIXTH VISION

He thought that in the choir of the aforesaid church a diverse crowd had gathered, as if for a feast day, and solemn matins had begun. After the fourth lection was read, however, there was no-one to sing the responsory.[20] As they were standing as if stupefied, and there was a great silence in the choir,

---

[18] The Latin of Robertson's edition reads: "as his informant stopped speaking, he left the body," but it seems rather that he *returned* to his body, as I have rendered it here. Phyllis Roberts has catalogued a fourteenth-century sermon that includes a story very similar to this. It concerns a "dead youth… [who] was miraculously restored to life after telling of how he had seen in heaven a beautiful seat standing empty among the apostles being held for Thomas Becket": see Roberts, *Thomas Becket in the Medieval Latin Preaching Tradition: An Inventory of Sermons about St Thomas Becket, c.1170–c.1400*, Instrumenta Patristica 25 (The Hague, 1992), no. 151, p. 208.

[19] Given the Yorkshire origins of Orm's vision, the hermit Godric of Finchale (d.1170), is the most likely candidate for the "hermit of a most celebrated name." On Godric, see *Reginald of Durham: The Life and Miracles of Saint Godric, Hermit of Finchale*, ed. and trans. by Margaret Coombe, OMT (Oxford, 2022), and Tom Licence, *Hermits and Recluses in English Society, 950–1200* (Oxford, 2011), pp. 100–5, 166–71, and 186–90.

[20] Such a silence would sound very strange, because a responsory always follows the reading of a lection.

a young man of great beauty rose, and sang this refrain with a most sweet modulation of voice in the sight of all:

> *Ex summa rerum laetitia*
> *summus fit planctus in ecclesia*
> *de tanti patroni absentia;*
> *sed quum redeunt miracula,*
> *redit populo laetitia*
> [Out of the heights of happiness, the greatest lament is made in the church because of the absence of such a patron; but when miracles return, happiness returns to the people].

Having finished the responsory, the young man added on the verse:

> *Concurrit turba languidorum*
> *et consequitur graciam beneficiorum*
> [The crowd of the ill comes forward, and they receive the grace of benefits].[21]

When the brother woke, he told what he had heard to the rest of the brothers cast in sorrow. He warmed some with the hope of future happiness, but he renewed and increased the grief of the father's death in others.

I.6. A SEVENTH VISION

One monk was undone by grief to a greater extent than the rest. He said to several of us that death would put an end to his pain and his life at the same time. His pious father could not bear his sorrow for long. *As a mother consoles her children, so also he consoled* him [Is 66:13] and turned his sadness into joy. He visited him while he slept, and beginning the fiftieth Psalm, urged him to pray with him.[22] Having alternated verses, they were already nearing the

---

[21] Benedict utilized this responsory and verse, with this exact wording, in the Becket Office: Cantus ID 600814 and 600814a. In the Sarum liturgy, they follow the fourth lection for Matins, replicating where it was sung in the vision: see Reames, "Liturgical Offices," pp. 570-1. In the monastic Office, they follow the sixth lection: see Slocum, *Liturgies*, p. 188.

[22] Psalm 50 (numbered 51 in Hebrew and Protestant Bibles) was recited at the conclusion of each of the monastic offices. On the central importance of this Psalm in medieval thought and devotion, see Bruce K. Waltke and James M. Houston with Erika Moore, "Psalm 51: 'The Psalm of All Psalms' in Penitential Devotion," in idem, *The Psalms as Christian Worship: An Historical Commentary* (Grand Rapids, MI, 2010), pp. 446-83.

end, when the saint little by little moved away, as if he intended to leave. The monk wailed when he noticed this. Kindled with greater desire for the fatherly presence, he tried to hold him back with tears. The father returned, as if compassionate for a crying son, and said, "Why, son, are you troubled? Do not be sad or sorrowful, but rather refrain from suffering, for before the seventh week ends, you will hear something that will make you rejoice greatly. Cease from your mourning, and *be of good courage, for you will soon* receive consolation" [Tb 5:13]. The promise of the saint was a true one, as became clear in Easter week, which was the fourth or fifth from that day.[23] For in that week, miracles clearly began to multiply, the doors of the church were unlocked, and the sick who had gathered were admitted to the tomb of the martyr. The Lord granted so much grace of healing to the ill that every single day we were able to say, with joy, the words of the gospel, "*We have seen wonderful things today*" [Lk 5:26].

Many signs, however, were done throughout England by the favor of the martyr before Easter – though not openly, but as if in secret. Some of these *we heard as if in the ear* shortly after the martyrdom, others with the passing of time, and we received them in order to *preach upon the housetops* someday [Mt 10:27]. We *did not wish to sound the trumpet before* us immediately [Mt 6:2], nor to *enlarge fringes* [Mt 23:5], but we were mute and did not speak of the good things,[24] until the Lord stilled the tempest's wind.[25] We awaited the father's promise concerning what would happen to the city of Canterbury that a certain English pilgrim, returning from Jerusalem, had heard ten years before the martyr's passion from the mouth of a monk. It seemed that this monk was like a prophet: as the spirit mounted in him, he would foretell many things that the hearers very often saw to come to pass. And so, on a day when the monk saw the pilgrim standing near him, he said, "Friend, where are you from?" "From England," he said. And the monk replied, "O England, England! How lovely is your future!" Turning again to the pilgrim, he said, "Have you ever been to Canterbury?" When he said that he had never seen the city, the monk said, "O Canterbury! how lovely, how delightful is

---

[23] This dates the grieving monk's vision to mid to late February 1171.
[24] Writing quite soon after Becket's death, a monk of Reading, Robert Partes, complained in a poem that Canterbury was not proclaiming Becket to be a martyr: see W. H. Cornog, "The Poems of Robert Partes," *Speculum* 12 (1937): 215–50, p. 249.
[25] A reference to the story of Christ calming the storm: see Matthew 8:23–7, Mark 4:35–41, and Luke 8:22–5.

your future![26] For there will come a day when the people will flood to you in the same way they now visit the blessed Giles, or the blessed James, or Rome, or Jerusalem."[27] Returning from Jerusalem, this pilgrim told this to not a few people nearly ten years before the martyrdom of our most pious father Thomas. Moreover, when he heard that the city of Canterbury was illuminated by many miracles, he said to his lady, Bertha of Gloucester, a very venerable woman,[28] "Do you remember, lady, those things I heard from that monk when I was returning from Jerusalem, and that I told them to you when I came back?" And she said, "I well remember that." Then the pilgrim said, "Surely, I believe that the things which were then told to me about Canterbury have been fulfilled in these days." This was related to us by the pilgrim and the lady with most truthful attestation.

With whatever spirit these things were predicted, we discerned a great source of truth, for we conjectured that these things were fulfilled by the frequency of miracles and the arrival of many people. And indeed, the thronging of the people seemed to be more wonderful than the miracles, unless this too is a miracle. For what is more miraculous or more marvelous, than that the world today adores a man whom yesterday they hated; that today they run toward him, from whom yesterday they fled; that they implore his patronage in the presence of God today, when yesterday, either from fear of earthly powers or from the wickedness of their own minds, they would not associate with him. Many of the wise see this to be the greatest miracle among great miracles.[29]

---

[26] Benedict echoed this idea of the good fortune of specific places associated with Becket in an antiphon in the Becket Office (Cantus ID 201809): *Felix locus/ felix ecclesia/ in qua Thome/ viget memoria./ Felix terra/ que dedit presulem/ felix illa/ qua fovit exulem./ Felix pater/ succurre miseris,/ ut felices/ iungamur superis* [Blessed is the place, blessed is the church in which the memory of Thomas flourishes; blessed the land that bestowed the archbishop, and blessed the land that welcomed the exile. Blessed father, help us wretched ones so that we, blessed, may be united with those above]. See Slocum, *Liturgies*, p. 208 and Reames, "Liturgical Offices," pp. 573–4.

[27] Rome, Jerusalem, and Compostela (the resting place of St. James) were the three principal pilgrimage sites for medieval Christians. The relics of St. Giles (d.c.710) were held at the Abbey of Saint-Gilles in the Languedoc region of southern France. The abbey became a major pilgrimage church, serving as a waypoint for pilgrims going to Compostela in particular, but also to Rome and Jerusalem.

[28] See Biographical Notes, Bertha of Hereford.

[29] A panel in Canterbury Cathedral window nV shows a throng of pilgrims traveling to Canterbury: see Koopmans, "Pilgrimage Scenes," 708–15.

I.7. WHAT HAPPENED AFTER THE VISIONS, OR WHICH MIRACLES ARE TO BE RECORDED

Since God lessened the cloud of persecution which, as has been said above, had been obscuring the light of the martyr, the discourse now passes from visions to the mention of miracles. Putting them aside, it is agreeable to add on these, lest we seem to dally over the trifles of dreams for a lack of signs. We will tell the story only of these miracles: those which we saw with our own eyes, or we heard from the actual ill people already healed and their witnesses, or those things we learned from the testimony of religious men, who had seen them with their own eyes. It is foolish to wish to conceal the grace and glory that the Lord gives and be like the impious, *who sit in darkness and the shades of death* [Lk 1:79] and do not wish to speak of the joy of light. For behold, the most blessed martyr of Christ, Thomas, lights up the world again, and more abundantly than he used to. He has again been made into a refuge for the world, who, for as long as he was in the world, was *a light of the world* [Jn 9:5] and *a tower of its strength in the face of* the enemy [Ps 60:4]. The setting of such a sun could not be hidden from the world's darkness, nor did the fall of such a tower fail to make a great sound. *The alabaster was broken* in the church of Canterbury, and the whole *house was* suddenly *filled with the scent of the perfume* [Jn 12:3].[30] The glorious triumph of the most constant champion was not unknown in the halls of princes, nor passed over the hovels of the poor, for everyone, far and wide, knew of his death very soon.

I.8. CONCERNING EMMA, WIFE OF ROBERT DE SANCTO ANDREA IN SUSSEX, WHO INVOKED THE MARTYR ON THE THIRD DAY AFTER THE MARTYRDOM AND RECOVERED FROM THE ILLNESS THAT HAD HELD HER

On the third day, the news of the accursed deed came to the house of a knight of Sussex, by the name of Robert de Sancto Andrea,[31] whose wife Emma lay oppressed by a grievous illness and deprived of light. By the vehemence of the

---

[30] For the story of the woman who came to Christ with an alabaster of perfume, see Matthew 26:6-13, Mark 14:3-9, Luke 7:36-50, and John 12:1-8. Benedict reused this imagery in the Becket Office (Cantus ID 202016): *Granum cadit, copiam/ germinat frumenti,/ Alabastrum frangitur/ fragrat vis unguenti* [The seed falls and puts forth an abundance of grain; the alabaster is broken, and the potency of the perfume is fragrant]: see Slocum, *Liturgies*, p. 204 and Reames, "Liturgical Offices," pp. 576-7.

[31] See Biographical Notes, Robert de Sancto Andrea, with thanks to John Jenkins for this identification.

illness, she had been made blind. The woman heard, *her belly was troubled* [Ps 30:10], and her heart trembled. Sighing from deep within her chest, she said, "Truly, Christ has made for himself a precious martyr." She did not just call him a martyr: she also invoked him, adding these words, "Holy Thomas, precious martyr of Christ, I vow myself to you. If you restore the sight taken from me and bring me back to health, I will visit your resting place to offer my prayers to you, together with gifts." This wonderful flower of faith was followed by more wonderful fruit of faith, for suddenly, it was as if the martyr turned to her and responded with the voice of the Lord, "*O woman, your faith is great, let it be to you as you wish*" [Mt 15:28], for within half an hour of making the vow, she received her sight, and within six days, she rose from her bed. Having received what she wished, she delayed fulfilling her vow for a long time, either from negligence or from forgetfulness. For her correction, she was again struck with the scourge of a graver illness. She renewed her vow. She became well at once, and she hurried to Canterbury with her husband and household to give thanks to the martyr for the doubling of grace in her. *This was the beginning of the signs of Jesus* in Sussex of England, and *the glory of* his martyr *was manifested to his disciples* [Jn 2:11], *to us, who had eaten and drunk with him* [Acts 10:41] before he had been killed in the womb of the virgin and mother church.[32] His miracles began, quite beautifully, on the third day.[33] In the same way that the saint had fixed himself to the cross of Christ in circumstances marvelously similar to Christ's, because he suffered similar kinds of treachery and ignominy, so too he merited the honor of a swift manifestation.[34]

I.9. CONCERNING HUELINA, THE DAUGHTER OF AALIZA OF LONDON, WHO WAS HEALED AT GLOUCESTER FIVE DAYS AFTER THE MARTYRDOM, WITH A SUDDEN DISAPPEARANCE OF A SWELLING OF THE HEAD THAT SHE WAS ACCUSTOMED TO SUFFER EVERY MONTH

The glory of a second sign made the fifth day from the martyrdom noteworthy.[35] A great length of distance was traveled in a short space of time, for on this day the lamentable news arrived in Gloucester. Huelina, the daughter of

---

[32] By this, Benedict means Becket's death inside Canterbury Cathedral, the mother church of England.
[33] That is, December 31, 1170.
[34] In other words, Becket died a Christ-like death, and in the same way that Christ rose three days after his death, Becket's first miracle came three days after his death.
[35] January 2, 1171.

Aaliza of London, was beginning her sixteenth year. From her fifth year, her head had swollen up every month and had almost immobilized the rest of her body. In the winter months, the pain and swelling went away after two or three days, but in the summer, it would often remain for a whole week. Lying with her head supine, the girl would not be able to turn or move onto her side. She had no rest while she was awake and very little or no ability to sleep. Although she was still of a tender age, she was given many medicines and draughts and bore many caustics, but they did not correct or expel the disease. The mother of the ill girl heard of the passion of the venerable father, and she believed and trusted in the martyr, thinking that the land had received rather than lost a patron. The mother made a promise to the martyr for her daughter, and obligated her by a vow to a devout pilgrimage if the martyr would unbind her from the tie of such an infirmity. She had hardly finished speaking when the girl, who then happened to be suffering in the usual way, turned herself onto her side and slept. When she woke, the disease was plucked out from its roots, such that she felt no remnants of it remaining in her. Afterwards, we heard and looked upon them both with our eyes, and we judged that this miracle, corroborated by irrefutable testimony, was worthy of faith. Otherwise, the miracle of the following day would accuse us of incredulity, since it seemed to support the preceding sign with unshakeable testimony. Yet because of others, and mainly because of the belittling of those speaking evil, it was not useless that we doubted each one. They are doubted by us, lest they be doubted by others: we showed ourselves hard and as if unbelieving in the examination of the truth, so that the adversaries of the truth might be ground down into believing, or proved wrong by a strict examination of the truth and so confounded.

I.10. CONCERNING WILLIAM BELET, WHOSE SWOLLEN ARM LOST ITS SWELLING ON THE SIXTH DAY AFTER HIS PASSION

The Lord Jesus again revealed his martyr on the sixth day in a town of Berkshire, which the English call Enborne; *he revealed in this way* [Jn 21:1]. In that place there was a venerable knight, William Belet,[36] well known and of good repute. For three months, he was tortured by pain in his left arm and had endured the heavy burden of being confined to bed. His arm was so swollen that it grew to the size of his thigh, while his hand expanded so much

---

[36] See Biographical Notes, William Belet.

that it looked like a fist rather than a hand. His fingers were so thick that they no longer seemed to have the shape of fingers. Then came the third nones of January, a Sunday and the sixth day from the martyr's triumph,[37] when the mother of the household, returning from church, began to cry most bitterly. Thinking that she wept out of compassion for him, he urged her to hold back her tears, chiding her with soothing words and saying that the scourge of the Lord would be to his good: he would improve when the divine piety willed it. But the woman replied, "It is not what you think, most dear lord. I am not only distressed on your account. I weep for our father and the father of our whole land, the lord of Canterbury, who was killed in his own church by the swords of the most wicked knights." And so, having begun, she told him everything that she had heard about it. Then he said, "Truly, he is a precious martyr of God," and turning to prayer, he said, "Precious martyr Thomas, since it is true that you underwent your passion for the love of God and the defense of the liberty of the church, and since I believe that you are a martyr of Christ, so may you deign to release me from the misery of this illness that I am suffering. If you grant me the grace of this release, you will have me as a pilgrim to your holy tomb." Oh how firm was the faith of the ill man, how full of merit, how quickly rewarded! With the end of the prayer came the beginning of the end of pain. On the following night, eased by a sweet and sufficient sleep beyond that which was usual, he woke to find himself restored. The pain was expelled, the swelling gone, and his left arm again had the appearance of his right. *This was the third time that Jesus revealed himself* in his martyr [Jn 21:14], after he was in him again crucified.

I.11. CONCERNING BRITHIVA, A BLIND WOMAN OF CANTERBURY

On the next day,[38] at Canterbury, the light of the fourth miracle shone forth. A poor woman named Brithiva had become blind. As it was her darkness, so it was also her light. She was touched by the spirit of majesty, for despite being simple, illiterate, and blind in body, yet she saw that someone who was killed in such a way could be nothing other than a martyr. And so, grounded

---

[37] January 3, 1171.
[38] The Latin reads *altera autem die*, which is generally translated as "a few days ago" or "the second day." What Benedict appears to be saying here is that Brithiva's miracle happened the "second day," by which he means the day following William Belet's miracle. This would place Brithiva's miracle on the seventh day after Becket's martyrdom. To avoid confusion, the translation for *altera autem die* adopted here is "the next day."

and rooted in faith, she went to lodgings in the vicinity. She asked the mother of the household if she had procured something of the martyr and whether she would lend it to her, so that she might touch it to her eyes lacking light. She produced a reddened cloth that was still moist with the martyr's liquid blood.[39] The blind woman wiped her eyes and wiped away the fog of blindness. She had come being led; she left without any guide.

I.12. CONCERNING WILLIAM, A PRIEST OF LONDON, FROM WHOM A PARALYSIS OF THE TONGUE WAS REMOVED

And after eight days,[40] the joy of the fifth miracle came to us. When William, a priest of London,[41] a man of innocent simplicity and simple innocence, had sat down to dine on the fourth day before the death of the blessed Thomas, namely on the feast day of the protomartyr Stephen,[42] a sudden paralysis took away his tongue's function. Two experienced doctors were called and he engaged them both. The ill man received an antidote from each of them individually, antidotes recommended by them as most excellent, but they had no effect and gave the ill one no improvement. When the most holy priest of God offered himself as a sacrifice to God to Christ, in Christ's church and for Christ's church, and *by his own blood entered in the holy of holies* [Heb 9:12], a man of most illustrious and reverend aspect appeared to another clerk of London in his sleep, saying, "Rise, go and tell William the priest that he is to hasten to Canterbury to the new martyr of Christ. If a drop of the holy blood is placed on his tongue, his speech will be restored." And again, when he was departing, he said, "Do you hear what was said to you? Beware lest you neglect the command." He went and spoke to the priest as he had been ordered to do. *The man believed the word which* the messenger *said to him* [Jn 4:50], and he immediately set out and went to Canterbury. Having asked for permission, he kept vigil overnight in prayer at the tomb of the martyr.[43] A drop of blood was given to him, as he asked. Moreover, a drink of water made holy by a

---

[39] In the *Passion*, Benedict described how people dipped pieces of cloth of Becket's blood: see above, Extract VIII.

[40] I.e., eight days after Becket's martyrdom (counting the martyrdom day as the first day): Tuesday January 5, 1171.

[41] See Biographical Notes, William, priest of London. William's miracle is pictured in two panels of Canterbury Cathedral window nV: see Caviness, *Windows*, p. 179 (where the first of the two panels is incorrectly identified as the miracle of William Patrick with Toothache).

[42] Stephen's feast is held on December 26.

[43] The doors of the crypt were kept locked until the Friday of Easter week (see below, II.6). Anyone seeking access to Becket's tomb would have needed the monks' permission.

similar drop was given to him, which was without doubt begun by divine will and is done frequently to the present day. For he who said, *"every one shall be perfect, if he be as his master"* [Lk 6:40], and made the blessed Thomas a most perfect imitator of himself in his life and passion, also wished to give Thomas a perfect and admirable resemblance to himself after his death. In the same way that the blood of Christ with water benefits the growth of souls,[44] so also, when the blood of his servant is drunk with water, it benefits the health of bodies. We do not believe that there has been anyone else to whom God has granted this special privilege of resemblance: it is observed that only *the blood of the lamb* of Bethlehem and *the blood of the lamb* of Canterbury is drunk in the whole world.[45] Yet this was not begun without great fear; but, seeing that it gave profit to the ill, fear receded, and little by little security came.

And so, this priest was the first of all to taste the blood of the martyr, and he received the grace of speaking, although at first less than perfectly. When he was at Canterbury, less was restored to him, but when he turned back, his speech was granted more fully. And so he returned exulting and greatly praising the Lord in his martyr, yet secretly, on account of the fear of the Judaizing persecutors – Judaizers, since in the same way the Jews endeavored to extinguish the name of the slain Christ, so also those people endeavored to extinguish the glory of the murdered martyr and to erase his memory from the earth.[46] And so, *no one yet spoke openly* about him, nor confessed his marvels in public, but *there was much murmur about these things among the people* [Jn 7:12-13]. At this time, God's and the martyr's enemies conspired that wherever they found men of such conviction, they were either immediately punished or led in chains to their prisons. *An edict went forth* from them [Lk 2:1], as if under the name of a public power, lest anyone speak further of him. But they tried in vain to hide the rays of the sun. They were able to give pain to his glory, but not to destroy it, *for his magnificence was elevated above the heavens, and his glory above all the earth* [Ps 107:6]. So also we, since we ought *to serve God rather than men* [Acts 5:29], cannot but speak *about the things which we have seen and heard* [Acts 4:20].

---

[44] Benedict is referring here to the practice of mixing wine with water in the Eucharistic ritual, in which the wine/water mixture was considered to be the blood of Christ.

[45] On "the blood of the lamb," see above, Prologue, p. 78, n.8, and for the weight Benedict places on William's miracle as supposedly the first time anyone drank Becket's blood, see the Introduction, pp. 16-18 and 49.

[46] For other markedly anti-Semitic statements made by Benedict, see below, II.20 and II.76.

I.13. CONCERNING STEPHEN, A KNIGHT OF HOLLAND, FREED FROM A DEMON'S INFESTATION

We saw a knight of Holland by the name of Stephen,[47] who was notable both by name and by his great devotion to the blessed Thomas. For no less than thirty years, he had been afflicted by a demon every single night as he slept, such that he was so pressed down and suffocated that unless he woke up quickly, he would die. Oppressed in this way, he used to cry out in his sleep and call to his servants by name, ordering them to run to his aid. Woken from sleep, or sometimes even keeping watch around him on his orders, they shook the shouting man roughly, and sometimes raised him up so that he sat or stood erect. He had told them many times that he should be made to stand on his feet, and he asked them to wake him by pulling hard on his hair. In such distress he passed around thirty years, to the point that he would have preferred to renounce all of his possessions than continue to be vexed by this terrible phantom. He spoke to many doctors, increased his gifts to them and offered them still greater ones, but it brought him no benefit at all. For they said it was *ephialtes* (what we would term, in Latin, over-lying)[48] but he always insisted that it was a demon. Our lord of Canterbury still lived *in the flesh beyond the flesh*,[49] and, having been called back from exile, he was in his patriarchal see awaiting the reward of his struggle. At one time before that same lord's passion, the knight was sleeping and suffering his usual affliction, when it seemed to him that he begged the Lord by the merits of each of the saints whose names he was able to remember that the demon would be cast off and he would receive the benefit of rest. This had done nothing for him, when by chance, or rather by divine will and instigation,

---

[47] See Biographical Notes, Stephen of Holland (Lincolnshire), knight. I am grateful to John Jenkins for this identification. A panel in Canterbury Cathedral Trinity Chapel window nV pictures this miracle: see Caviness, *Windows*, pp. 178–9 and Rachel Koopmans, "Demons and Discoveries in a Miracle Window of Canterbury Cathedral," *Vidimus* 123, January 2019 issue (online journal), https://vidimus.org/issues/issue-123/feature.

[48] *Ephialtes* is a transliteration of Greek term meaning a nightmare of crushing or throttling: see *DMLBS*, entry for *ephialtes*. In one manuscript, there is additional explanation: "which the common people call an incubus, the literate an oppressor" [*quod vulgus incubonem, Latini oppressorem, appellant*]: see Robertson's note, *MTB*, vol. 2, p. 44 n. 6. For discussion of this story and its vocabulary for an incubus, see William F. MacLehose, "Fear, Fantasy and Sleep in Medieval Medicine," in Elena Carrera (ed.), *Emotions and Health, 1200–1700* (Leiden, 2013), 67–94, at pp. 67–8. See also Stephen Gordon, "Medical Condition, Demon or Undead Corpse? Sleep Paralysis and the Nightmare in Medieval Europe," *Journal of the Social History of Medicine* 28:3 (2015): 425–44.

[49] In other words, he was living a heavenly life while still on earth. See Romans 8:3–9 and compare with a widely cited quotation attributed to Jerome: *Profecto in carne praeter carnem vivere non terrena vita est, sed caelestis* [Truly, to live in the flesh beyond the flesh is to live not the earthly but the heavenly life].

he added, "Lord, free me for the love of the archbishop of Canterbury who was exiled for you and the freedom of your church!" When nothing resulted from this request, he thought that many of the archbishops of Canterbury had been banished for the same cause, and he added, "Lord, for the love of the archbishop Thomas!" But when no peace came to him from this, he thought that many of the lords of Canterbury had the same name. So that there would not be any uncertainty and to avoid any ambiguity, he said, "The Thomas who was last exiled for you!" Immediately, that which had harassed him disappeared and he was freed.

On another night, suffering from the same trouble, he rejoiced to find himself freed at once with an invocation of the same name. But after the passion of the saint, when, having heard [the news] of his death which had immediately filled the whole world, he had a mass celebrated for him, and he wholly escaped the punishment which had been inflicted on him since his boyhood. On another occasion, the same demon appeared to him in the form of a bird.[50] It seemed that it was unable to approach him in his bed, and so circled him from afar. The knight spoke to and taunted it, saying, "I trust in the merits of the blessed martyr Thomas and do not fear you: his grace will protect and recover me from your control." From this hour, no phantom troubled the knight in this way. After a period of time in which he made certain of his liberation, he went to the memorial of the saint on foot. The humble dress he wore indicated the humility of his heart, and the way he told the story suggested the wonderful happiness of his mind. In our presence, he praised the martyr with wonderful affection, the martyr who, while living, had delivered him from this terrible distress once and then twice. After his death, he delivered him once more, and then there was no need to do it again.

I.14. CONCERNING WILLIAM PATRICK, FREED FROM A TOOTHACHE

There was no less cause or abundance of joy for William Patrick, the servant of William of Warbleton, who was miraculously released not from the illusion of a phantom, but from a real and terrible toothache. He had a very large swelling on his jaw, and was in such unbearable pain that those not knowing

---

[50] The manuscripts differ in the form the demon took at this point. Some read "bird," others "ship," and others "dwarf": see Robertson, p. 45 n. 1. Robertson follows the manuscripts reading "dwarf," but a bird would seem to be more likely to "circle from afar." The late twelfth-century stained glass picturing this miracle in Canterbury Cathedral shows a demon flying down from above, supporting the reading of bird.

the reason for his cries and gestures might think that he was mad rather than in pain.[51] Except for the fact that the Lord had quickly stayed his hand and lifted him up, he would have been placed in chains as a madman. By divine mercy, he escaped the hardness of chains by the pleasant embrace of the sweetest dream. When he was asleep, he saw a young man of most elegant appearance standing near him, and when he asked him who he was, he said he was a clerk of the lord of Canterbury. The dreamer warned and advised him not to tell this to anyone, for it was not safe for anyone in England to make an avowal of this sort on account of the martyr's enemies. But he said, "I am not afraid of them. I should not quake with fear – they should. Look, I carry letters from the lord pope. Those who transgressed by the death of the martyr are to be punished: the rest, where-ever they might be in England, are free from punishment to the same degree that they are free from guilt."[52] And when the ill one said the name of the person whom the blessed Thomas used to call "the son of perdition" in his writings,[53] the other said, "He is heading straight into the pit of hell. But you, young man, what is wrong with you?" He spoke of what he suffered, and he heard him reply in this way: "Open your mouth, and I will bring comfort to you by means of the lord of Canterbury's cloak in which he was dressed in the hour of his passion."[54] Taking up the edge of the cloak, he waved a little air into his mouth. He placed that same cloak on the swelling on his face. When the dreamer woke, he found himself freed from all pain. What was to him even more marvelous, which those listening to him heard with great admiration, he could accurately describe what the cloak of the saint was like, though he had never seen it. *These things his disciples did not know at first* [Jn 12:16] but after miracles were multiplied, and *many bodies of the saints, which seemed to have slept* in an idleness of torpor or fear, *rose* on account of devotion and flocked in crowds to the martyr, the young man, too, *came into the holy city* of Canterbury with his lord, and he *appeared to many* [Mt 27:52–3]. He removed a swelling of doubt from our hearts about this event, the fame of which had preceded his

---

[51] Benedict frequently states that people in extreme pain look as if they were insane. For these references, and for analysis of Benedict's stories about cures of the insane, see Claire Trenery, *Madness, Medicine and Miracle in Twelfth-Century England* (New York, 2019), pp. 79–109, esp. 86–8.

[52] This appears to be a reference to Alexander III's proclamation of March 25, 1171 that Becket's murderers and all who helped them were excommunicated. See Vincent, "Murderers," pp. 252–3 and *MTB*, vol. 7, no. 751, pp. 475–8.

[53] See Biographical Notes, Ranulf de Broc.

[54] For more on this cloak, see Extract VIII of the *Passion* and I.19 and I.21 below.

arrival. This miracle was done around the time of Lent and was revealed to us around the sacred day of Pentecost.[55]

I.15. CONCERNING ROBERT, WHO HAD A HEPATIC COMPLAINT

In those days, when the church of Canterbury already shone forth with many miracles, and I was directing my attention to the ill people suffering throughout the entire church according to the task assigned to me, I came upon a clerk nearing the age of an adult, who, having completed his prayer, was leaving the memorial of the martyr. He said that he was Robert, the son of a knight called William of the province of Surrey: the humble name of the village has not remained in my memory. The young man asserted that he had been suffering from fever for some weeks. Having been advised to flee to the merits of the blessed Thomas, he ignored the admonition. At length, he had himself carried to London so that he might be cured by the doctors there. He had been in a dangerous position from fevers for a long time, and he learned, by the judgement of the doctors, that he had a hepatic complaint.[56] Pain occupied the right side of his body from his shoulder to his groin, his face was parched with pallor, the fevers ate up his body, a dry cough exhausted his panting chest, and the hardness of his liver, which the doctors term sclerosis,[57] was such that if one were to lay a hand on it, it felt like a stone, and fingers could not press in under the ribs. By these indications, he was understood to have a hepatic complaint, a condition that cannot be cured by the work of any doctor, no matter how industrious. And so, with the fevers only moderated, and despaired of by all, he was sent back to his own home, and for several weeks he was confined to the tedium of bed. However, he changed within himself and was converted to the holy Thomas: he began to ask that he be favored by his merits. O, what a worthy spectacle, delightful to relate! In the same hour that he poured out his prayer, he began to feel better. Brought back to vigor, that same day he left his bed, and he did not need to lie down again due to any weakness. This strength and health was granted to him around the middle of the days of the period of Lent,[58] and in his heart he wished to go

---

[55] Lent fell between February 10 and March 28 in 1171; Pentecost Sunday was May 16.
[56] Benedict uses the word *hepaticus*, a transliteration of a Greek word meaning liver, to describe Robert's condition: see the DMLBS entry for *hepaticus*.
[57] Sclerosis is a Greek term meaning hardening: see the DMLBS entry for *sclerosis*. This word is spelled *sclirosim, scliorsin, sclyrosyn,* and *scyrosim* in different manuscripts: see Robertson, *MTB*, vol. 2, p. 48 n. 1 and Duggan, "Santa Cruz," p. 47.
[58] That is, about the beginning of March 1171.

to Canterbury with all haste. But seeing that the wind of persecution was still strong, he feared to go there, and put off the accomplishment of his desire until a less dangerous time. For the Lord had not yet commanded the wind and the sea that they might be calm.[59] The ship was still tossed in the midst of the waves, and the persecutors of the martyr attempted to erase his name from the earth, though the Lord added glory to his saint against them.

I.16. CONCERNING ALDITHA OF WORTH, FREED FROM THE ANGUISH OF CHILDBIRTH

A pregnant woman, Alditha of Worth, came to the time of birth, but did not have the power of birthing. She was in labor for three full days and nights, but did not give birth. From the distress of so much pain, she was approaching death. Her priest was called, a man who was also her kinsman. She received the viaticum and commended herself most strongly to his prayers, worrying that though he had loved her chastely when she was alive, he might forget her when when she was dead. Having compassion on the sufferer's pain, the priest said, "Look, I have a stole blessed by the martyr of God, Thomas the archbishop of Canterbury.[60] Trust that you can be freed by his merits, and without any doubt, you will be freed." She applied herself to faith. With faith, she invoked the name of the martyr, and the stole was wrapped around her. The priest had hardly gone a mile from the home when, brought back by her husband, he knew the woman *had brought forth,* and already *she remembered no more the anguish, for a person was born into the world* [Jn 16:21].

I.17. ITEM CONCERNING THE MULTIPLICATION OF THE HOLY BLOOD

A certain religious woman, Wlviva, acquired a portion of the precious blood that had been shed in the church of Christ in Canterbury for Christ. It was as much as could have been held in the shell of a hazelnut. At this time, this woman was the custodian of an almshouse ministering to the poor and pilgrims. Afterwards, she took upon herself the chains of a harsher service, given over to the service of lepers, until at length she transferred herself to the repose of an anchorage. Having acquired, as we said, a portion of the precious blood,

---

[59] For the story of Christ calming the wind and the sea, see Matthew 8:23–7, Mark 4:36–41, and Luke 8:22–5.

[60] When priests were ordained, archbishops would bless their stoles, long strips of cloth that hung around priests' necks and were worn whenever priests conducted a service.

she returned to her almshouse, rejoicing for the precious relic, but anxious on account of its small amount. She worried that the wooden vessel would drink up all the liquid of the blood, or that it would diffuse through the bottom of the vessel and congeal, such that she would not be able to remove the blood when she wished to. Having thought these things over, she wiped out the blood from the wood most carefully with a cloth. She thought that if the cloth were stained with the relic, it would serve more bountifully for those desiring a part of it, and that the vessel itself might be necessary for another purpose. And so she wrapped up the vessel in a cloth and placed it back in a chest. The next day, she unlocked the chest and opened the little vessel in order to see the relic. She found liquid blood in it, about the same amount, as far as she could judge, that she had, the day before, wiped out from its base. Stupefied and marveling at the new thing, she secretly told one of her familiars what had happened to her, as happy at the duplication of the blood as she was certain she had carefully wiped it all out. When this came to my notice, I called the woman to me, and demanded that she show me both the blood and the cloth stained by the blood. In order to be certain, I began to adjure her, by the name of the Lord, that she was certain that she had wiped out the blood such that nothing remained in the little vessel. She proved herself to be most certain by such assertions that to fail to put faith in her words would seem to be a sign of incredulity. Yet, lest the scrupulous be brought to doubt by these things, it has pleased divine piety that those who do not give much weight to the first sign might marvel at the second.

I.18. ITEM CONCERNING THE MULTIPLICATION OF THE BLOOD

When the lord of Canterbury had been exiled, the Lord, *who sits to purge and cleanse the sons of Levi* [Mal 3:3], who *makes good* the elect *like gold in a furnace* [Ws 3:6],[61] who *looks away in opportunities and in tribulation* [Ps 9:22], imposed upon our heads men who mocked the name of the exiled martyr, detested his works and hated his person.[62] *Kindled like fire in thorns* [Ps 117:12], they questioned the friends of the martyr and most cruelly persecuted all those who favored him. Many were mute and would not speak to the good, such that no one dared even to mutter against them. But even if they had spoken, they would have inflicted harm on our party and done nothing to

---

[61] This phrase is part of an antiphon from the Common office for several martyrs: Cantus ID 005100.
[62] See Biographical Notes, Ranulf de Broc and Robert de Broc.

promote the business of the lord of Canterbury. While their malice prevailed, Ralph, a monk of the church of Canterbury, was driven by this tempest to the church of Colchester.[63] Having a special love for his lord of Canterbury, Ralph was zealous in his resistance to his enemies, even though his zeal profited neither himself, nor us, nor our father.[64] When the lord was reconciled to us, he was recalled with honor, and when he saw that the martyrdom was accomplished, with blood shed for the liberation of the church, he acquired a small amount of the blood of the church's liberation. He sent it to the church of Colchester, giving it to them out of a debt of honor and sense of mutual affection. In his glass ampulla, there was such a small amount of blood that it could hardly make a circle on the bottom. He had stopped up the fragile vessel with care. Fearing that it would be broken, he had closed and encased it in very dense wax. It was presented to the abbot of Colchester[65] by means of master Raymond, a man of good repute. With the ampulla sealed up in this way, it was kept in careful custody until the abbot was free to turn his attention to viewing and displaying the relic. The vessel was brought forth the next day and the wax was removed. The ampulla was found most full, the blood having increased. Likewise, the wax that had stopped up the vessel was stained with the superfluity of blood. This was seen, but it was not yet marveled at, as they believed that Ralph had filled it up entirely. They were wholly ignorant that a miracle had occurred and ascribed to his benevolence and generosity what was the work of divine majesty. When he later heard from the sacrist of that church that they had received the ampulla full of blood, he did not dare to reject these tantalizing rumors as false, nor to believe them as being true, until the opportunity arose that he could go to Colchester in order to examine and be certain of the cause. When they were reunited, he showed them how much he had sent, and they showed him how much they had received. By the testimony of their eyes, both parties were made certain and amazed. They also told him that they had given the water that had been used to wash the wax of the ampulla to a neighbouring church. The priest had put a pyx with the water upon the altar, but then, taking it off the altar, he brought it to his home. When he got up the next day, the pyx had split open and not a single drop could be found. And so, to those to whom the will of God wished it, blood that

---

[63] That is, St. John's Abbey, a Benedictine monastery in Colchester. There were least two Christ Church monks named Ralph in the late twelfth century: see BR, p. 260. One Ralph became the abbot of Shrewsbury in 1175; another is recorded as a subsacrist in a charter dated 1175-7: see Urry, CUAK, no. XXIII, pp. 402-3.

[64] In one manuscript, the phrase about the uselessness of Ralph's zeal for Becket was omitted by the scribe: see Robertson, MTB, vol. 2, p. 51 n. 3.

[65] See Biographical Notes, Walter de Walensis.

was given increased, and *to whom it was not given, even that which he seemed to have was taken away from him* [Mt 25:29].

I.19. ITEM CONCERNING THE SAME

Another miracle of the augmentation of the blood, no less glorious than the two described above, was told to us by a priest of Bourne, William,[66] a man of honest conduct and commendable religious bearing. He was very well known to those of Canterbury both on account of his close proximity as well as his goodness. When he heard that the athlete of Christ had offered sacrifice of himself to God, he began to consider how patiently he had endured his injuries and seven long years of exile, how calmly he had borne the deportation of his relatives, his friends, and even their infant children at the breast,[67] and how resolutely, for Christ, he had offered his head to the blows of the knights. Thinking over all the circumstances of his passion, he foresaw with clarity that everything pointed to the martyr's glory and earned him the title of a glorious martyr. From this contemplation of the past, he considered what would happen in the future, and in his heart he became convinced that it was impossible that he would not be glorified by manifest miracles soon. He conjectured that the relics of such a martyr would, in a short time, be precious in the future, and so he devoted himself entirely to acquiring them, fearing that if he awaited the time of miracles, the very abundance of miracles would deny him the opportunity of acquiring them. *The Lord gave this desire to his heart, and he was not cheated* of his desire [Ps 20:3]. When he found the cloak of the holy martyr for sale, the cloak in which he was martyred, such that it was blood-stained, and which had been given away for his soul,[68] he purchased it, and he also acquired an ampulla full of liquid blood. When another priest, an acquaintance of his, heard about this, he asked that he be found worthy to be given a portion of the blood. When he was preparing to give this portion to him, he transferred the liquid blood into a clean vessel in order to see its quantity. He put the gritty mixture he found at the base of the ampulla into the basin of the

---

[66] See Biographical Notes, William, priest of Bourne.
[67] The exile of Becket's relatives and friends was described with horror by contemporaries. John of Salisbury wrote, "what is unheard of anywhere in history, [the king] sentenced to exile all the archbishop's kinsmen and all who were connected to him by friendship or any pretext at all, without distinction of rank or order, of status or fortune, of age or sex, for both women lying in childbirth and infants wailing in their cradles were driven into exile": Ronald E. Pepin, trans., *Anselm and Becket: Two Canterbury Saints' Lives by John of Salisbury* (Toronto, 2009), p. 87.
[68] See above, *Passion*, Extract X.

altar. Then, having set aside a large portion of the blood for the petitioner, he poured the remainder back into the ampulla. He who had multiplied the oil for the widow under the direction of the prophet[69] so augmented the blood that he found that the ampulla was as full as it was before.

I.20. CONCERNING THE BOXWOOD PYX THAT SUDDENLY SPLIT WHEN CONTACTED BY THE BLOOD, AND HOW THAT BLOOD VANISHED

The same venerable man granted a small portion of the blood to a certain preacher, one of those who travel the earth and walk about,[70] in a boxwood pyx. When contacted by the holy relic, the pyx instantly split. To prevent the blood from pouring out onto the ground, the pyx was reinforced with wax. The preacher returned to his inn and put down his pyx, but the next morning, when he opened it, he found no blood or trace of blood in it, though the wax had not allowed it to pour out, nor could the hard solidity of the boxwood absorb it. Many were in doubt as to the reason why such a grace was taken away from the preacher, although several conjectured that it was likely and probable that he was guilty of greedy intention.

I.21. CONCERNING THE DAUGHTER OF RALPH OF BOURNE, WHO WAS HEALED BY THE MARTYR'S CLOAK

The same man of God came upon the sickened daughter of Ralph of Bourne, an honorable man. She was so ill that she had lost the use of all her senses. She lay as if she were insensible, and her parents despaired of her: she brought nothing to them except a cause for mourning. But he brought our martyr's cloak and wrapped the girl in it. With those caring for her at watch around her and expecting the mercy of God, she began little by little to feel the power of the cloak and to recover her senses. What is the use of words? The next day the priest came in order to visit the ill girl, and he found her secure in her health and at play with other children.

---

[69] See 2 Kings 4:1–7 for the story of Elisha and the widow's oil.
[70] That is, a wandering preacher. Such preachers were becoming a common feature of medieval society by the late twelfth century. They were frequently viewed with suspicion by the ecclesiastical hierarchy: see Giles Constable, *The Reformation of the Twelfth Century* (Cambridge, 1998), pp. 62–5.

I.22. CONCERNING ETHELDREDA, FREED FROM A QUARTAN FEVER

For nearly a year, a quartan fever[71] had oppressed a certain Etheldreda, who lived in Canterbury but had been born elsewhere. Her bluish color and wax-like appearance indicated that she was near death. Coming, therefore, to the monk attending at the martyr's tomb, she asked that she might drink the blood of the martyr. The monk mixed it [with water], as it was done for the rest, lest the taste or the color of blood induce horror in the drinker. Having drained what was in the cup, the woman's usual color returned and her former vigor was restored. Afterwards, she was neither touched nor saddened by fevers, nor troubled by any vexation.

I.23. CONCERNING THE BOY WILLIAM OF CANTERBURY, FREED FROM A TERRIBLE SWELLING BY DRINKING THE BLOOD OF THE SAINT AND WATER

On the day of the Lord's Supper,[72] William, a son of a citizen of Canterbury, was snatched from the jaws of death by the same experiment. Although many had already experienced the efficacy of this medication, yet it was not given without fear to those seeking it – and no wonder, for it is very unusual for humans to drink human blood. But it was made known to us in the following way that the ill might faithfully drink the purest blood of the vine of Canterbury,[73] and also that a great boldness might be granted to us to mix the same with water.

This adolescent of whom we speak was struck with a grave illness. After he had most gravely suffered from it for about fifteen days, in his sleep the precious martyr of Christ and the glory of the martyrs showed himself to him, as if he stood at the altar of Christ in the choir of the church of Canterbury and celebrated the solemnities of the mass with many reverend and glorious persons ministering to him. Catching sight of the ill boy, he seemed to speak to a monk holding a vessel full of his blood among those who were standing

---

[71] A quartan fever is one that recurs every fourth day, that is, every seventy-two hours. Etheldreda's miracle is portrayed in two panels in Canterbury Cathedral window nIV: see Caviness, *Windows*, pp. 184–5.
[72] That is, Maundy Thursday, which fell on March 25 in 1171.
[73] "Blood of the vine" is a reference to the Eucharistic ritual in which wine becomes Christ's blood (see John 15:5 for Christ's declaration that he is a vine). With "blood of the vine of Canterbury," Benedict draws yet another parallel between Becket and Christ.

about him, saying, "A grave illness oppresses that boy. Bring a little drink of my blood to him, so that he might drink and become well." It seemed to the boy that he drank, and that the drink of holy blood *delighted* him *as in all riches* [Ps 118:14], for it seemed to him like the sweetness of honey in his mouth. Illness soon woke the sleeper, and from the sweetness of the vision, he returned to pain. When he was awake, he described the joy of the vision to his parents, asserting that he had hope of recovering his health if he merited to receive a drop of the precious blood in a drink. The father thought to satisfy his son's desire, but he spent that day and the next in fruitless work. Finally, on the third day, the day on which the Lord's Supper is annually celebrated, the adolescent swelled so much about his stomach and vitals that he wholly lost the ability to speak. It was remarkable that he had swollen to such an extent; it was even more remarkable that his middle had not burst. And so the anxious father ran about here and there, until, by the clemency of divine mercy, he obtained the health-giving water that he had sought. Hastening home, he offered the little drink to the ill boy. The pain immediately eased, the swelling decreased, and such vigor, along with health, was restored to the boy that on the fifth day[74] he was able to present himself to the martyr to give thanks.

I.24. CONCERNING GODITHA, OF A CERTAIN MATTHEW OF CANTERBURY, WHO, BROUGHT TO THE MARTYR'S TOMB BY TWO WOMEN, LEFT ON HER OWN FEET

Goditha, of a certain Matthew of Canterbury, also presented herself, though she was supported on the feet of others rather than her own: two women held up the third.[75] A terrible swelling was seen from her knees on down. The medicine of the blood and water was applied and the swollen members were brought back to their original size. The woman was brought secretly, and she left secretly as well. Improving continuously each day, she was soon brought back to full strength.

The Lord worked these and many other miracles before the days of Easter and so showed the beginning of the glorification of his champion. However, these are small things, and in comparison to those that followed, almost deserving of scorn.

---

[74] Counting from Maundy Thursday, this would be March 29, 1171, the Monday after Easter.

[75] Goditha's miracle is portrayed in two panels in Canterbury Cathedral window nIV: see Caviness, *Windows*, p. 182 (where the panels are incorrectly identified as the story of Petronella of Polesworth), and Koopmans, "Water Mixed with the Blood of Thomas," pp. 545–50.

The Chapters of Book II

1. Concerning the mute Samson
2. Concerning Geldewin, the son of Godefrid the baker, whose recovery seemed hopeless
3. Concerning two other sons of the same man, who were beset by fevers
4. Concerning the blind Manwin
5. Concerning the lame Emelina
6. When and for what reason the doors of the crypt, in which the body of the martyr reposed, were opened
7. Concerning Edilda of Canterbury, who had not been able to walk on the sole of her foot for more than a year
8. Concerning Wlviva, who walked with the support of a staff
9. Concerning Edmund, who could see nothing with one of his eyes
10. Concerning Muriel, who vomited cherry pits, plum pits, and acorns
11. Concerning Ethelburga, who lost the use of her arm from an acute gout
12. Concerning the blind Robert, blacksmith of the Isle of Thanet
13. Concerning the insane Henry of Fordwich
14. Concerning a deaf woman
15. Concerning Eilward of Tenham, who was not able to smell anything
16. Concerning a crippled boy to whom the saint denied healing
17. Concerning another boy, blind, who was similarly denied
18. Concerning Agnes, from whose putrefying face a worm came out
19. Concerning the pyxes of Ralph of Sheppey which split open when contacted by the blood and water
20. Concerning the pyx of Godeliva, which, full of the water, split open when she entered the house of a certain Jew
21. Concerning the pyx of another woman, from which the water vanished
22. Concerning the pyxes of Peter and Haimo, from which the water was subtracted in a similar way
23. Concerning the paralyzed William of Dene
24. Concerning Saxeva of Dover, who suffered from stomach spasms and pain of the arm
25. Concerning Richard of [Northampton], suffering from lientery

26. Concerning the private translation of the martyr and a vision of the martyr seen the same night
27. Concerning the miraculously crippled Richard of Bearsted, who was cured miraculously on the day after that translation
28. Concerning the crippled Ralph *de Tangis*
29. Concerning the replacement of the martyr in the prior location, and of the edifice of the tomb
30. Concerning a certain Matilda of Canterbury, who was not able to put her head into the window of the tomb
31. Concerning a certain insane Elward who thrust his whole body through one of the windows and exited through the other, which afterwards, when he was healed, he was not able to do
32. Concerning William of London, who, having inserted and pulled out his head, immediately recovered the sight of an eye
33. Concerning Ansfrid of Dover, deprived of nearly all his senses
34. Concerning Wekerilda, crippled and blind in one eye
35. Concerning the blind Elvida of Beckenham
36. Concerning Emma, who had a terrible ulcer on her [shin] and foot
37. Concerning the blind Matilda of Ipswich
38. Concerning Brian de Insula, whose chin was stuck to his chest
39. Concerning Frodo, who had disabled feet
40. Concerning the son of Eilmer *de Cleche*, who had never had the ability to walk, stand upright, or get to his feet
41. Concerning the son of a certain William of Lincoln, who was unable to walk on his feet because of a swelling on his kidneys
42. Concerning the ill Eremburga of London, a hopeless case
43. How the persecutors of the martyr maligned the monks of the church of Canterbury in order to cloud the glory of the miracles
44. Concerning Thomas of Etton, who was struck with quinsy when he maligned the martyr [*see Parallel Miracles no. 1*]
45. Concerning Juliana, the wife of Robert Puintel, who was distended by an enormous swelling
46. Concerning a certain [Ralph] of Lincoln, who was not able to stem a nosebleed
47. Concerning the son of Matilda, who lay as if insensible until a vow was made for him to the martyr, when he immediately turned to his mother's breasts

48. Concerning Gilbert, a shoemaker of London, who was cured of fistula
49. Concerning Hugh of Bourne, also freed from an agonizing fistula
50. Concerning a pyx in which the martyr's water disappeared, proving the carrier to be a thief
51. Concerning Robert, canon of the church of St. Frideswide of Oxford, who was weakened by severe diarrhea
52. Concerning Master Robert, the prior of the same church, whose leg, afflicted by a grave and chronic disease, the martyr cured
53. Concerning William, a knight of Earley, freed from a similar affliction
54. Concerning the son of the same knight, seized by madness
55. Concerning Master Peter de Melida, released from high fevers, and certain others who were cured
56. Concerning Roger, a clerk of London, who, when he was feverish, slept in a place where the saint had lain and woke well. Collecting the dust of that same place, he administered it as a drink to many others for their health
57. Concerning Guncelin, a monk of Norwich, who was healed of a swollen and painful arm by means of the martyr's stole
58. Concerning Ansfreda of Canterbury, whose quinsy of the neck the mantle of the martyr repressed
59. Concerning Solomon, nearly one hundred years old, whose blindness the martyr illuminated
60. Concerning Henry, son of William of Kelvedon, who tasted the martyr's water and vomited a worm half a cubit long
61. Concerning Nicholas, son of Hugh de Beauchamp, whom the martyr healed of dropsy
62. Concerning Richard, knight *de Rokeleia*, healed of a dangerous headache
63. Concerning Adam *de Hadlega*, gravely ill from the extremes of the same disease
64. Concerning John of the Chapel, who, after he tasted the saint's water, sneezed and ejected a cherry stone that he had borne for nearly four years
65. Concerning [Robert] of Springfield, who obtained the health of his soul after drinking the health-giving water, as he had requested
66. Concerning Roger, son of Herbert of Bisley, to whom something similar happened
67. Concerning the son of this Roger, the clerk Thomas, who was cured of three infirmities

68. Concerning the pilgrims in peril on the sea who escaped to dry land by invoking the martyr, though other ships in their company sank
69. Concerning others who suffered on the sea with the breeze of winds withdrawn
70. Concerning the knight William of Chester, whose arm was [folded up]
71. Concerning Ralph of Essex, oppressed by a similar trouble
72. Concerning Ada of London, who was not able to turn herself onto her side nor move from her bed
73. Concerning Thomas, son of Adam, who had the stone
74. Concerning Lefseda, whose right eye was blind
75. Concerning Godiva of Chelmsford, blind for five years
76. Concerning Geoffrey of Chalgrave, blind from birth
77. Concerning the daughter of [Gilbert] of the Isle of Thanet who had contracted feet

BOOK II

II.1 CONCERNING THE MUTE SAMSON

The day of the Resurrection of the Lord had come,[1] *the day which the Lord had made*, the day in which the whole church *rejoices and is made glad* [Ps 117:24]. In that day, only the church of Canterbury wailed and wept. It heard of its daughters filled with joyful sweetness, and it was filled with bitterness.[2] However, lest we be overwhelmed by overflowing grief, he who had closed our mouth opened the mouth of a mute man in the church in our presence. When he entered the church, a spirit suddenly disordered him, and he was struck down and fell to the earth. He rolled about, foaming at the mouth, injuring himself by casting about repeatedly and rending himself, until he became quiet again. In a distinct but hardly intelligible voice, he asked for a drink to be brought to him. The people were then absent because divine services had been suspended, yet almost in a moment the rumor of the new miracle attracted a multitude that was hard to number. Each of them asked who he was, where he was born, and what had happened to him. He was not able to satisfy their wishes easily because they hardly understood his stammering: he was often compelled to repeat what he had said. He said that he had been born in the region of Oxford and had lost his speech five years before while sleeping in a meadow. He had gone to sleep in good health, and woke a mute.[3] Recently, he had had a vision in which two men of venerable appearance told him that he should hurry to Canterbury to the new martyr of Christ, saying that if he asked in faith without hesitation, he would recover his speech there: in no other place in the world would he regain his health more quickly. To those wishing to know his name, he said his name was Samson.

Many of the hearers had faith in his words, but others doubted. Although he had no witnesses to his assertions, we nevertheless obtained considerable

---

[1] Easter Sunday, March 28, 1171.
[2] Canterbury Cathedral stood silent on Easter Sunday 1171 because Becket's death had desecrated the cathedral, whereas "its daughters" – other churches in England – held Easter services, and so were filled with "joyful sweetness." Benedict complains about this enforced silence in the Prologue as well.
[3] On waking ill after sleeping outside, see also II.28, III.63, and IV.76.

support of their truth. He spent many days with us, and every day, little by little, he became more proficient in forming words and expressing himself, though he never was able to speak perfectly. We sent to the city of Rochester, where he had stayed for some time, and did not find anything that would undermine his claims. Afterwards, I spoke with his innkeeper, with whom he had stayed many days. He said that he had often seen him inebriated, and yet he was never able to draw a single word out of the drunk lad. The old proverb is true that it is only possible to gain the truth from children and drunkards.[4] And so, we were able to exclaim, as did the other churches, though in a different way and from a different cause, *"This is the day that the Lord has made, let us rejoice and be glad in it"* [Ps 117:24].

II.2. CONCERNING GELDEWIN, THE SON OF GODEFRID THE BAKER, WHOSE RECOVERY SEEMED HOPELESS

On the same day of the Lord's Resurrection, the martyr called back to life the dying son of a servant of the church of Canterbury. Geldewin, the son of Godefrid the baker,[5] had been enfeebled for more than four months by a grave illness. He was thought to be at the point of death, for he had gone three days and nights without food or drink, and lay as if he were insensible, without voice or feeling. His father, returning from church after receiving the Eucharist, had acquired a scrap of cloth stained with the blood of the martyr. He sat down by the little boy, washed and wrung out the cloth in water, and was about to bring that water to the ill one and in fact was on the point of pouring it into the dying boy's mouth. Marvelous to relate, as his father sat next to him, it was as if (as in truth it was) that the boy was recalled by the power of the presence of the relic. Beyond all hope, he opened one of his eyes, and said to his father, who was not a little amazed, "Am I to drink this, father?" He drank the drink given to him, and in a short time he tasted food. Within five or six days, his strength was restored and he was seen at play with his playfellows.

---

[4] Benedict is echoing a well-known proverb, "the drunkard, the fool, and the child speak truth": see *The Oxford Dictionary of Proverbs*, ed. by Jennifer Speake, 6th ed. (Oxford, 2015), p. 51.

[5] See Biographical Notes, Godefrid, baker of Christ Church, Canterbury.

II.3. CONCERNING TWO OTHER SONS OF THE SAME MAN, WHO WERE BESET BY FEVERS

This same man had two more sons who were both weakened by the force of fevers, one of them in longer intervals, the other in shorter. When the father saw that the power of the relic brought perfect health to the first son, he divided the cloth and hung it round the neck of each of the others. These sons too were immediately freed from the bane of fevers. After four or five weeks, when the father no longer feared the return of the disease, he unfastened the relic hanging from one son's neck. Hardly had he taken it away and was turning to go, when the boy was seized by revived fevers and his whole body shook. Marvelling at the new event, the father took up the medicine and hung it around the neck of the feverish boy again. Immediately, and not without the amazement of those seeing this, he stopped trembling and was released.

II.4. CONCERNING THE BLIND MANWIN

As the miracles gradually became frequent and the martyr's fame grew, the rest of the ill people of Canterbury, little by little, fled to the aid of the martyr. Among them was the lame Manwin, who, though he was a pauper, was nevertheless very well known in the city. He had been blind for nearly two years. Sometimes his son and sometimes his wife led him about in order to beg. Taking measures such that he would not need to depend on someone else's sight, he asked for and received a drop of the sacred blood from a certain person. When he returned home, he had just applied it to his eyes when his infant son, who was not yet entirely able to walk, fell to the ground and began to cry and wail. Anxious for the little boy because there was no-one to pick him up, he forgot himself, wiped the blood from his eyes, and rose to pick him up from the ground. He saw the boy before he was able to lift him up. The city of Canterbury knew him to be blind and afterwards judged him to have recovered his sight.

II.5. CONCERNING THE LAME EMELINA

A certain lame woman of Canterbury, Emelina, was lifted up in the same period of Easter. Four years before, she had fallen and injured her knee. Possibly because of a lack of medicine, the nerves had contracted, and she remained crippled, not without shame. She regained the use of her feet by means of a staff, but without its support she was unable to take a single step.

Roused by the fame of miracles, she came to the church of Christ in order to petition the martyr, and shortly became disordered and fell in the same place the mute man mentioned above had fallen.[6] Throughout the day, until evening, she rolled about in continuous torment. As the light of day was overtaken by the darkness of night, she withdrew, exhausted, but healed. In fact, she was so exhausted that we ordered her to support herself with the staff, but she refused. She felt herself to be leaving altered from how she had come, and did not wish to take up again what the saint had taken away.

II.6. WHEN AND FOR WHAT REASON THE DOORS OF THE CRYPT, IN WHICH THE BODY OF THE MARTYR REPOSED, WERE OPENED

The doors of the crypt were still held closed by bars and bolts. The people were not generally admitted to the tomb of the martyr. If anyone was brought in, this was done secretly. Because of this, a substantial portion of the people were upset. Many of them confronted many of us in the convent, declaring that we were sinning because the people did not have access to their father. They said that our reputation was being tarnished because we seemed to be hiding away the talent loaned to us.[7] The doors of the crypt should be opened, lest it be said that we envied the martyr's glory and begrudged the infirm their health. When we saw their faith, we determined that though the church was prevented from holding divine services, their petition should be granted. On the fourth nones of April, on the Friday of Easter week,[8] the doors of the crypt were opened, and the ill were admitted to the sarcophagus of the saint. A glorious spectacle was then to be seen every day. There you could see *the font of David open for the washing of the sinner and the menstruating woman* [Zec 13:1], the pool moved by the angel, and not one healed but many.[9] You could see both the upper and the lower irrigated ground being given to Axa,[10] that is, given to those weeping for the weakness of their body and to those weeping for wounds of their souls. You could see the jar of oil not run out and mercy abounding in the saint.[11] You could see the vessels brought to the prophet and

---

[6] See above, II.1.
[7] See Matthew 25:14–30 and Luke 19:12–28 for the parable of the talents, in which a servant buries the talent (an amount of money) that his master had given him.
[8] April 2, 1171, the Friday following Easter Sunday.
[9] Reference to the healings at the pool of Bethesda, John 5:2–17.
[10] Reference to the story of Caleb granting his daughter Axa both dry and irrigated land, Joshua 15:14–19.
[11] Reference to the story of Elijah and the widow's jar of oil, 1 Kings 17:13–16.

the oil poured into them multiplied,[12] for the ill were carried and conveyed there, and they went back full of the martyr's mercy. Then our spirit was first greatly revived and we were consoled as if we were awoken from a bad dream. And yet, pain still triumphed over joy because we were not able, as we wished, *to bless the Lord in his works, and glorify him with the voice of our lips* [Sir 39:19–20]. Yet we *gave back the measure of our service*,[13] as far as we were able, by singing and saying Psalms in our hearts *to the Lord who alone does wondrous things* [Ps 71:18]. For great and very wonderful things were being worked every day around the tomb of the martyr.[14]

II.7. CONCERNING EDILDA OF CANTERBURY, WHO HAD NOT BEEN ABLE TO WALK ON THE SOLE OF HER FOOT FOR MORE THAN A YEAR

A woman of Canterbury, Edilda,[15] was cast down there, having been carried by the help of three women. She had come to the middle of the second year in which she was not able to stand on her foot. For all of that time, she was confined to her bed and lived in the vicinity of death. The power of the disease was especially strong in her left knee. Its nerves contracted, such that she was deprived of the ability to walk with her foot. The knee could not bear a touch, even if the woman herself touched it very lightly. She was brought to the martyr by three women, as was already stated, and was leaning on a staff. With the pain receding, she returned home. In testimony of the reception of her health, in our presence she let her raised fist fall with great force upon the knee which since the second year, had been too painful to touch. The people saw her *walking about and praising the Lord*, and *they were full of wonder and elation because of what had happened to her* [Acts 3:9–10]. Why she still

---

[12] Reference to the story of Elisha and the vessels filled with oil, 2 Kings 4:1–7.

[13] *RB 1980: The Rule of St Benedict in Latin and English with Notes*, ed. Timothy Fry, OSB (Collegeville, 1981), 49.5.

[14] A remarkable late twelfth-century panel in Canterbury Cathedral window nV shows pilgrims crowding around Becket's tomb in the crypt. It may well have been meant to illustrate the results of the opening of the crypt after Easter: see Rachel Koopmans, "Pilgrims at Becket's Tomb and Shrine: Stained Glass Portrayals at Canterbury Cathedral and St. Mary's Church, Nettlestead, Kent," in Alyce A. Jordan and Kay Brainerd Slocum (eds.), *Images of Thomas Becket in the Middle Ages and Beyond: The Uses and Reception of a Celebrity Saint* (Woodbridge, 2025).

[15] In the survey of cathedral holdings in Canterbury compiled 1163–7, four Edildas/Eadildas are mentioned: see Urry, *CUAK*, Rental B, pp. 234 and 243 (Edilda the daughter of Eadmeie), p. 242 (Edilda the wife of Elred Wran), p. 232 (Edilda the wife of Galfridus), and p. 241 (Edilda the widow of Osbert).

remained lame and not all of her health was restored, we refrain from discussing, thinking it best to remain silent concerning the secret judgments of God rather than to dare to divine them.

II.8. CONCERNING WLVIVA, WHO WALKED WITH THE SUPPORT OF A STAFF

We know that he who strengthened her disabled knee could also have fully restored the bases and soles of her feet so that she could step correctly again, because we know without doubt that he granted this to Wlviva of Canterbury.[16] *Satan had bound her* for three years [Lk 13:16]. She was bent over, not able to move herself without the use of a staff. Shortly after she prostrated herself in prayer near the saint, she stood up straight without the staff. The pain was gone from her loins and she did not wish to carry the staff that once carried her.

II.9. CONCERNING EDMUND, WHO COULD SEE NOTHING WITH ONE OF HIS EYES

Edmund, a youth born in Canterbury and well known there, had brought himself there as well, although he was led by the guidance of only one eye. He appeared to have a left eye, but it did not have the power of sight. In addition, something that seemed to be coagulated and very heavy had grown inside of his chest. Sometimes it felt as if it were impelled up higher, and sometimes it fell lower. He suffered terrible stabbing pain and exceeding torments from this for two years and was driven to the point of death, as his colorless and wasted appearance suggested. A drop of the most sacred blood was dropped into his eye, and he drank blood and water mixed together. The potency of this drink was amazing. After having gone some distance from the tomb, he fell flat on his face, turned upon his side, and twisted about, shouting. He often tried to get up, but was too unstable to stand. He fell down, striking his face on the pavement. He seemed to have come to harm: you would have thought him to be insane as the divine power healed him. At last, he fell into a slumber and slept supine. The saint of God stood before the sleeping man, gripped his shoulder and shook him, saying, "Rise, go." And he suddenly awoke, and that mobile thing that had tormented his insides shifted. He felt it

---

[16] In the survey of cathedral holdings in Canterbury compiled 1163–7, two Wlvivas are mentioned: see Urry, *CUAK*, Rental B, p. 237 (Wlviva the sister of Maria), and p. 241 (Wlviva the widow of Ingenulf).

move up to the lower part of his throat, and, nearly suffocating, he threw his hand to his throat, wishing to touch it to find out what it was. Then, suddenly, as if a sack inside of him had ruptured, by some divine power it was expelled through his mouth. It seemed to him to have the bitter taste of gall. Quickly getting up, he threw off his cloak and went to the tomb of the martyr to give thanks, having received perfect health in his eye as well as in the rest of his body. For the love of the martyr, he soon thereafter took up the cross to go to Jerusalem, *and all the people who saw this gave praise to God* [Lk 18:43].

II.10. CONCERNING MURIEL, WHO VOMITED CHERRY PITS, PLUM PITS, AND ACORNS

There was no less praise or glory in what we know to have happened to a woman named Muriel. Enfeebled by a grave illness for two or more years, she thought that the only remedy to her pain would be death. However, when her husband saw the glorious things that were happening by means of the glorious martyr of God, he gave his ill wife a drink of the health-giving water. She drank, and up to the third day she gradually grew more troubled than usual with weakness. On the third day, she was so debilitated that she was taken off her bed, lest she die lying on a bed of feathers, contrary to the Christian religion. A priest was summoned with great haste in order to give her last rites. But she was suddenly gripped by nausea and vomited up the material of the disease, and all that day she continued to vomit in hourly intervals. It was found that she vomited up many whole pits of cherries, plums, and acorns, and that some of them had germinated in the coolness of her stomach. Some of these were shown to us, and it was a marvel that the woman had carried the pits of the fruits in her stomach for such a long time, and also that pits could germinate in a stomach. There is no doubt that she would have died if she had not been assisted by the drink of the holy liquid. And so the woman was relieved and snatched from the jaws of death. She who was so enfeebled that, as we have said, she was not able to step beyond the threshold of her house for two years, was brought back by divine power to such strength that on the next day she walked to the martyr. *And all the people rejoiced together at all the things that were gloriously done by him* [Lk 13:17].

II.11. CONCERNING ETHELBURGA, WHO LOST THE USE OF HER ARM FROM AN ACUTE GOUT

To these things the Lord added another miracle, concerning a lesser illness – though why do I say lesser? No-one thinks that the illness he or she suffers is small. We knew a certain matron Ethelburga, full of alms-giving and good works, who suffered an acute gout in her left shoulder and arm for many days. She arranged to have the length of her useless arm measured in order to make a candle to its length to the honor of the martyr. There you could see the martyr respond to the woman with the rendering of grace that the Lord promises to those who turn to him, *Before you invoke me I say to you, "Behold, here I am"* [Is 58:9],[17] for hardly had she measured the wick to the length of her arm when all the pain lessened, as she felt and confessed. The candle made, she gave it to the martyr and returned to full health.

II.12. CONCERNING THE BLIND ROBERT, BLACKSMITH OF THE ISLE OF THANET

A blacksmith of the Isle of Thanet, Robert, also found the grace of healing, but his healing was preceded by a vision no less wonderful than the health granted to him. He had lost the light of his eyes for at least two years. The poverty of his household made him more anxious about losing his sight. When our venerable father had returned from his exile, and the time drew near for him to be called to heaven from his exile on earth, this man received advice in a dream: "Go, Robert, to Canterbury, to the church of Christ, and a monk will place milk in your eyes. You will receive your sight." He thought this was a delusion at first and so did not believe the promise nor follow the command. But later, when he heard that the saint of God was shining forth with so many miracles, he remembered what he had heard. He considered that the innocent blood of a most sweet lamb was like the sweetness of milk, and began to hope for his healing. He arrived in the place he had been ordered to go to, guided by his family members, for we saw both his wife and his daughter come with him. His eyes were smeared with the desired blood of the martyr and he prostrated himself in prayer. As he was lying there, he felt his head to be in an uproar, as if beset by the sound of a great clap of thunder. Having received his sight, he got up and publicly preached the grace of God to the people.

II.13. CONCERNING THE INSANE HENRY OF FORDWICH

What is easier – to give health to the mind or to the body? The one who illuminated the eyes of this man's body also restored the mind of Henry, a youth from

---

[17] Benedict drew this from the Prologue of Rule of St. Benedict, which in turn draws on Isaiah 58:9.

Fordwich.[18] He had been insane for several days and had inflicted on his friends an unexpected wound of pain. His hands were tied behind his back and he was dragged to the saint. Though he resisted and cried out, he was presented to the saint. All that day he remained insane, and then, as the light of the sun receded, he began gradually to recover the light of rationality. He spent the night in the church and left the next day in most perfect health.

II.14. CONCERNING A DEAF WOMAN

We received a woman from the vicinity of the same village who not only found it impossible to hear anything, but was also vexed with an intolerable headache. The common medicine of the sick, the water mixed with blood, was dropped into her insensible ears; she also drank it and gave herself to prayer. As she prayed, her pain became even more acute. She thought it was as if many twigs were being snapped into small pieces in her head. She asked those standing near her if they could hear what resounded in her head. While she was being oppressed in this way, she cried to the Lord, and he heard her. As she cried out, it seemed as if an interior abscess had broken, for a great deal of bloody matter began to flow out of her ears. Blood followed on the bloody matter, and after the blood, the grace of the missing hearing followed on as well.

II.15. CONCERNING EILWARD OF TENHAM, WHO WAS NOT ABLE TO SMELL ANYTHING

Eilward, a man of Tenham, had lost the pleasures of smell for several years, being unable to smell anything. He entered the place where that good odor of Christ rested everywhere, that sweet sacrifice, that aromatic tree, the fragrance of which was already being wafted through the whole world. Before he had reached that fragrant flower of England, a most sweet odor met him and filled his nostrils, and he rejoiced to have received his sense of smell back again.

II.16. CONCERNING A CRIPPLED BOY TO WHOM THE SAINT DENIED HEALING

We do not think it is right to say nothing of the one who was patently denied among so many asking for and receiving their health. A crippled boy who was begging the martyr for the grace of walking had placed his head on the

---

[18] Henry of Fordwich's miracle is portrayed in two panels of Canterbury Cathedral window nIV: see Caviness, *Windows*, p. 184.

sarcophagus and happened to fall asleep. The holy father appeared to him, demanding, "Why are you lying on me? You will certainly not receive your health. Go. I will do nothing for you." As he heard these words, he woke, and told us and his mother what he had heard with great and heartfelt anguish. He was certain that this judgment would not change, and had himself placed in a different spot. We still urged him to press on with his prayers, and he did, but as time went on there was no improvement to his health.

II.17. CONCERNING ANOTHER BOY, BLIND, WHO WAS SIMILARLY DENIED

The reason why he refused to cure this boy though he responded to the rest, he knows who mandated a similar judgment for another boy who was blind and also resting upon the tomb. He did not hide the reason for this judgment. A certain figure appeared to the sleeping boy and said, "why are you lying here? The archbishop orders that no healing will be granted to you. Health is taken from you on account of a sin committed before you were born." And yet, we do not believe that *the son carried the iniquity of his* parents,[19] but rather that that the Lord wished to chastise the parents through their son, such that the bodily loss of their son would bring the punishment of grief to the parents. After a few days, this boy departed from this light. I confess that we greatly mourned over both boys, and the denial of health to each of them saddened us, but the martyr made us rejoice in other cases.

II.18. CONCERNING AGNES, FROM WHOSE PUTREFYING FACE A WORM CAME OUT

Of these, the first that should be discussed is what the water of Saint Thomas – for so the people of the surrounding region call it, the "water of Saint Thomas" or "the water of Canterbury" – did for a certain Agnes of Canterbury.[20] A pain that could not be checked had invaded the woman's face, which was disfigured by a horrible swelling. Contorted on one side, her mouth displayed a form of corruption from its normal state. A huge amount of phlegm flowed from her mouth unceasingly and copiously. This flow brought no remedy to the swelling or the pain and it caused her no little amount of shame. At length, the inner part of her face was infected as well, making it necessary for the

---

[19] See Ezekiel 18:20, where it is stated that the son will not carry the iniquity of the father.
[20] An Agnes, daughter of Simon the clerk, is found in the survey of cathedral holdings in Canterbury compiled 1163–7: see Urry, *CUAK*, Rental B, p. 226.

woman to subsist on milk rather than solid food. Since she was not able to eat, she refreshed herself with little sips, until finally she was in so much pain that she abstained from this as well for three full days. You would not have been able to bear the smell of her putrid face. Five weeks passed in these torments, until the woman thirsted and took up the water of the saint. O marvelous water, which not only quenched the thirst of the drinker, but also extinguished the pain! O marvelous water, which not only extinguished the pain, but also reduced the swelling! I will tell of a wonder. In order to catch up the phlegm, the woman used to place a basin under her mouth. When she lay down flat with her mouth open, it would catch up the phlegm running from her mouth. But when she lay down again after taking a drink of the water, a worm came out of her mouth. It had a fair-sized head that was red like a live, burning coal, and its tail was like a very sharp needle. It was one and a half inches in length, crawled about on four feet, and moved with such liveliness that many said that it was from the evil side. It was thought that the worm had sunk into the phlegm, but when the bowl was placed up in an elevated window, it was not found.[21] And so all the pain ceased in the sufferer, and in a short time, with the swelling deflating, her face was returned to its original state.

II.19. CONCERNING THE PYXES OF RALPH OF SHEPPEY WHICH SPLIT OPEN WHEN CONTACTED BY THE BLOOD AND WATER

Among the other miracles, there happened a certain delightful miracle that is also worthy of memory. The power of the water of Canterbury was known far and wide, and already all the region flocked to the water. Among those who came, Ralph of Sheppey brought a wooden pyx with which to receive the water, but he did not bring it back filled. He was about to leave, fearing no misfortune and moving this way and that, when the pyx split along its side. Astonished, the man paled with fear, and as the contents of the pyx were flowing out, he took pains to fill the cleft with wax. However, when he turned the pyx to its other side, he found that it had not remained whole on that side either. In order to stop all the water that was left from flowing out, he again applied wax to it. You would have seen there a remarkable thing: water rose upwards from the base through the mouth of the pyx and violently boiled over. You would think it was a cooking pot with a fire kindled under it, unable to retain the water against the force of the hostile element. However,

---

21   In other words, the worm could not be seen in the bowl even with the light from the window.

the man thought that this came about from some natural cause, namely that the power and force of trapped air could make this happen, and so he lifted off the cover and placed it back on. When the cover was replaced, the vessel split from its base all the way to its top, and a crack appeared nearly the width of the thickness of a human finger.

This event seemed wonderful to us for three reasons. First, the pyx was made from very thick wood; second, it was old and very hard material; and third, water usually reunites cracks in wood, but here, on the contrary, it divided the whole. The man was stupefied and afraid, and wondering beyond what could be believed possible, he immediately and quickly transferred the modicum of water that remained into another pyx. But this pyx too, in another marvel, could not hold the power of the relic. The water, as if it wished to run through the pyx, opened up a path for itself in the middle across the side of the pyx. There was a marvelous combat between man and element, for, when he brought the remedy of wax to this crack, at which point the water was tilted to the other side of the pyx, the evil that he was trying to avoid occurred. The pyx was split apart from top to bottom, and so ended up exactly the same as the first. Everyone who was there was amazed, but for him, his fear and shame increased.

We were present and carefully investigated the cause of this event. Nothing appeared certain, yet we suspected either that the man who carried the water or the one to whom he carried it was unworthy. Still, so that he would not have to go both ashamed and lacking that which he desired, we kept the two pyxes and gave him a third to see what would happen with that. Joyful, he left carrying the water, but as he was going, it boiled and he lost it. Though he tried to take the lid off to see the boiling water, he was not able to remove it, nor even to budge it. One of his companions asserted that he who was not worthy either to carry the relic or to see it must be unworthy. The truth of what he said was plainly shown by what happened next, for although the lid could not be lifted while the water was present, in the end he removed it gently and without any difficulty, but found the vessel completely empty. If the man was astonished, if he mourned, if he feared for himself, he knows, who had been shown to him so that he might fear for himself. He told us later that he was so full of grief and so gripped by fear that he confessed everything that he could remember doing wrong not just to one priest, but to thirteen. Following his heart's contrition, he filled the empty vessel with the water of the font, which also makes the ill well who drink it in faith.

Did not the martyr seem to sport with the man here, such that he at last, recognizing himself, might sport with the enemy who was sporting with him?[22] Should this be called a sport or a censure of the martyr? If we wish to call it a sport, it is an honest sport, if a censure, it is of praiseworthy piety. He did not wish to blame in anger a person coming to the relic unworthily, and he did not wish to rebuke in wrath. He sustained the ill patiently; he reprimanded with mercy; he healed the converted with wonderful grace of sweetness.

II.20. CONCERNING THE PYX OF GODELIVA, WHICH, FULL OF THE WATER, SPLIT OPEN WHEN SHE ENTERED THE HOUSE OF A CERTAIN JEW

We know a certain Godeliva of Canterbury to have been rebuked by means of a similar mode of piety.[23] She had carried away the water in a wooden vessel. As she returned home, she was passing the lodgings of a certain Jew, and entered at the request of a Jewish woman.[24] An expert in certain charms and incantations, she had been accustomed to say charms over the disabled foot of the Jewish woman. Hardly had she set foot in the impious house when her pyx split in three places, and by the loss of the water she recognized her interior fault of mind. Realizing that she had been rebuked for her error, she did not visit the Jewish woman any more. We should marvel even more at the cracks in the pyx because, though the foot of the pyx was large and solid, and was separated from the hollow part by the interposition of a kind of delicate neck, yet not just the hollow part, but also the solid foot of the pyx had been split.

---

[22] What Benedict apparently means here is that the martyr made the pyxes and the water act strangely so that Ralph would realize that the devil ("the enemy") had been sporting with him, and that he needed to "sport back" by confessing his sins and stopping his unworthy activities.

[23] Two women named Godeliva are found in the late twelfth-century surveys of the holdings of Christ Church: the widow of Adam son of Gode (Urry, *CUAK*, Rental B, p. 235), and the wife of Solomon the Mercer in Canterbury (see Urry, *CUAK*, p. 177 and Rental F, no. 660, p. 374).

[24] Canterbury was home to a synagogue and a sizeable Jewish community in the late twelfth century. See Michael Adler's discussion in *The Jews of Medieval England* (London, 1939), pp. 47–124, and for the location of some of the homes of Canterbury Jews in this period, see Urry, *CUAK*, pp. 119–20. For discussion of this miracle story, see Ephraim Shoham-Steiner, "Jews and Healing at Medieval Saints' Shrines: Participation, Polemics, and Shared Cultures," *Harvard Theological Review* 103:1 (2010): 111–29, at p. 116, and Matthew Mesley, "*De Judaea, muta et surda*: Jewish Conversion in Gerald of Wales's *Life of Saint Remigius*," in Sarah Rees Jones and Sethina Watson (eds.), *Christians and Jews in Angevin England: The York Massacre of 1190, Narratives and Contexts* (York, 2013), pp. 238–49, at p. 248.

II.21. CONCERNING THE PYX OF ANOTHER WOMAN, FROM WHICH THE WATER VANISHED

Another woman also mourned that the water was taken away from her, though it happened in a different way. The first woman's portion of water visibly poured out from a split pyx; this woman's portion was invisibly taken away. She had returned carrying the water to her lodging, which was about two or three furlongs away from the tomb of the saint.[25] She opened the pyx after she had put it down, and she found it not only empty but dry as well.

II.22. CONCERNING THE PYXES OF PETER AND HAIMO, FROM WHICH THE WATER WAS SUBTRACTED IN A SIMILAR WAY

In a similar manner, two men from Essex, Peter and Haimo, were cheated of what they desired. After they crossed the river Thames, they found that their vessels were empty, though they had taken them away from Canterbury full. One of them said to the other, "Truly, all my water is gone." The other man, fearing that something similar had happened to him, picked up and opened his vessel. He said, "Assuredly, not a drop of mine remains." Haimo addressed the cart-driver, who had transported them both coming and going, and said, "Check and see whether any of your relic is left, and give a gift of this great blessing to us." But the cart-driver said, "I will not look at it until I go into my home." His humble cottage was by the river, and once he arrived there and found his pyx full, he transferred half of his water to Haimo's pyx and gave it to a boy to carry to him. The power of the divine will is wonderful. The boy was still standing in his house and speaking with the man, and as they were talking he opened his pyx and saw that it was empty of water. They were both stupefied: the boy went away without water. We heard about these events from the cart-driver. There are more of these delightful miracles, but I wish to place first in the text's narration those things that preceded them in time.[26]

II.23. CONCERNING THE PARALYZED WILLIAM OF DENE

The knight William of Dene in the region of Canterbury had reached old age when he was struck with paralysis, and so he suffered from two complaints,

---

[25] That is, about half a kilometer away from Canterbury Cathedral.

[26] For more stories of pyxes, ampullas, and the water acting oddly, see below, II.50, III.19–25, III.51, III.52–4, and IV.38–40. For analysis of these stories, see Koopmans, "The Smallest Matters."

paralysis and old age.[27] The illness did not affect his whole body, but his feet and legs were impaired. He was carried about by the aid of two or three men wherever his bodily needs called him. For half a year, he weakened and withered as he trusted in doctors, in the sons of men, in whom there is no salvation. Finally, realizing that *there is no salvation in men* [Ps 107:13], and that *it would be good for him to cling to God and put his hope in the Lord God* [Ps 72:28], he asked to be put on his horse and brought to Canterbury. Since his powers were not sufficient to guide himself nor his horse, he was held by other hands so that he would not fall. When he was off his horse, two young men took him up. Supported by them and also by a staff, he was brought to the tomb of the holy martyr. There he most devotedly invoked God and God's martyr, and he felt his legs and feet coming back from insensibility, his nerves warming up, and the grace of mobility being renewed in all his body. Thinking, as was in fact the case, that by divine means he had been given the ability to stand, he cast aside his cloak and leapt up, as many stood by and watched. And so he both sensed and experienced that his health had been granted by the manifest power of God. Rejoicing, he seated himself in that place and took off his shoes. With bare feet, in great devotion and thanksgiving, he prostrated himself before the saint. He gave his staff to the saint as a sign of the reception of his health, and he left on his own feet without the help of any other support. To the joy of those looking on, he mounted his horse, and reported the reason for his great happiness to those of his house.

II.24. CONCERNING SAXEVA OF DOVER, WHO SUFFERED FROM STOMACH SPASMS AND PAIN OF THE ARM

What are we to say of Saxeva of Dover?[28] Was there less happiness for her, whose suffering had been greater? From the time of the Lord's nativity up to the day of Easter, she had learned what the opposite of health was from continuous stomach spasms and pain in her arm. And yet, she had as much pain of the heart as of the body, for she was not able to work, and she was ashamed

---

[27] William of Dene's miracle is portrayed in two panels of Canterbury Cathedral window nIV: see Caviness, *Windows*, pp. 182–3 (where the panels are incorrectly identified as portraying Prior Robert of Cricklade's miracle). Though William cannot be identified in contemporary documents, a "Thomas of the Dene," the seneschal of the curia of Christ Church, and a "Godefrid of the Dene" are known from late twelfth-century charters and rentals from Canterbury: see Urry, *CUAK*, pp. 306, 412–13, 428–9, 432–3, and 436–7.

[28] Saxeva of Dover's miracle is portrayed in two panels of Canterbury Cathedral window nIV: see Caviness, *Windows*, pp. 183–4 (where the panels are incorrectly identified as picturing the miracle of Juliana Puintel).

to beg: her soul wearied of her life. She fled to the martyr, prayed, and slept. As she was sleeping, the martyr showed his presence to her and said "Rise, offer your candle." She woke and felt herself healed. She obeyed the command and showed herself healed and quickened, so much so that she said, extravagantly, that she felt she could fly.

II.25. CONCERNING RICHARD OF [NORTHAMPTON],[29] SUFFERING FROM LIENTERY

May the reader pardon me if I speak at a little more length about a man with dysentery, or rather of lientery, who was marvelously healed among us. For a better knowledge of this miracle, it is necessary to begin the story a little further back. When the cause and the mode of the illness are known, the conclusion is also better understood. A scholar of Northampton, Richard, son of Walter,[30] had been exhausted by a stomach flux, which the doctors call diarrhea, for the period of a month. One night, when he had fallen asleep, a man of great height and terrible appearance terrified him with this question: "You, tell me what you would prefer – to suffer continual illness for nine years, or after nine days to satisfy nature by the debt of death." When he rejected both, the man turned to him again and said, "Choose quickly from the alternatives, for you cannot evade both fates." Seeing that he could neither avoid misfortune nor refrain from answering the question, he decided that it would be better to suffer illness for the whole of the fixed time with the hope of recovery than to end the sweetness of life, which cannot be brought back, by the bitterness of premature death. At that, the man struck him with his upraised fist on the top of his thigh with such force that when he woke, he had no power at all in his thigh.[31] For a whole year he could not walk. At times he would recover from the stomach flux, and then with the disease reviving, he would be brought to the point of death. In the second year, although he could walk again, at intervals he was exhausted by the loosening caused by the same disease. Afterwards, when he was in the region of Worcester, by this time a confirmed sufferer of dysentery, a doctor promised to give him aid and took him into his care. And while he pursued diverse medicines for dysentery, that

---

[29] The chapter heading incorrectly reads Richard "of Norwich."
[30] Northampton was home to a prospering school in this period: see H. G. Richardson, "The Schools of Northampton in the Twelfth Century," *English Historical Review* 56 (1941): 595–605.
[31] This has close similarities to a biblical story in which Jacob wrestles through the night with a mysterious man until the man touches the socket of his hip, disabling him and making him limp: see Genesis 32:22–32.

cruel tormentor appeared again, and accosted the woman giving him lodging, saying, "Why does the doctor waste time trying to cure that ill man? His work is useless, for the foreordained conclusion has not yet come when the sick man will escape the scourge of that illness." The woman did not know of the conclusion of which he spoke, but the young man told her about his earlier dream. And so the industry and efforts of the doctor were overcome, and he suffered from dysentery for five years, tortured by a constant death without death. Then the dysentery turned into lientery. He consumed food and drink, but would excrete it undigested. The looseness of his excretions both in the form of urine and of feces was such that he completely lost control of himself. He could not satisfy either necessity without a violent flux of the other. He was also tormented by a great swelling of his stomach, and he presented a miserable sight to those seeing him. In such misery he carried on his miserable life for nearly two years. When, therefore, *it pleased Him who had separated him from his mother's womb* [Gal 1:15] that *he might remove his blows from him* [Ps 38:11] and *the works of God might be manifested in him* [Jn 9:3], a young boy, a brother born of the same womb as the ill man, saw a splendid man appear to him in a dream and say, "Advise your brother that he should not delay going to the martyr of Canterbury. Through his merits, he will be given perfect health again."

It was now the ninth year of his illness, the year the Lord was pacified, the year of his benevolence, the year in which his athlete the most blessed Thomas was *crowned with honor and glory* in heaven [Ps 8:6], and he gave the glory of miracles to his church on earth. And so, the man suffering lientery was put into a cart (for he was not able to walk nor ride a horse), and the closer he came to Canterbury, the more he felt the illness recede. Leaving the cart, he walked to the martyr. I do not remember seeing anyone living who had such a destroyed and discoloured face. His skin hardly adhered to his bones, and as for his face – I would not say that it had a pallor, but rather that it was fouled by a blackish putrefaction. He looked like someone raised up after having been dead three or four days. Let the description end: it would seem to be beyond belief. He tasted the water of the saint, and he prayed prostrated on the ground. Suddenly, as if in great torment, he began to wail and shout, to twist and turn. Falling into a lassitude, he slept, and he woke healed. Both to make certain of his health and for devotion, he stayed for several days at Canterbury. He told us that on the following night he only had to get up once to answer the call of nature, whereas on the previous night his illness had compelled him to get up sixteen times. On the next day, the taste of water unexpectedly provoked a nausea. This happened so that the seeds of the illness would not remain in him. After a great deal of vomiting, the health that followed was complete. Since he seemed to be possessed from his bodily actions, we asked him whether his mind was also being held captive or if he was able to know what he did or to feel what he suffered. He answered that it was as if he were in an ecstasy. At first, it felt as if his inflated stomach was being shrunk, and then very much constricted, and the church seemed narrow to him. He remembered nothing more. We asked others about this as well, those who through similar actions gained a similar benefit, and they gave the same answer. And so he left full of joy, his devotion to the saint increased to the same degree that his misery had been long extended.

II.26. CONCERNING THE PRIVATE TRANSLATION OF THE MARTYR AND A VISION OF THE MARTYR SEEN THE SAME NIGHT

In all this, the fury of the evil ones *was not turned away, but* their *hand was stretched out still* [Is 9:12]. It was reported in the church of Canterbury that some of those who had been present at the death of the martyr had gathered together a group of powerful allies, and that they were ready to seize the martyr on the following night with a multitude of armed and well-equipped men. We heard that they were not congregated in a single group, but were dispersed in several places and had made mutual agreements according to what seemed suitable to them. For security's sake, we assembled a contrary force. We also removed the body of the saint from the marble tomb, placed it in a wooden coffin, and hid it behind the altar of the blessed Mary. In that way, if the strength of the evil ones prevailed, they would not find the martyr in the sepulchre and would leave cheated and confused. All that night, there were nearly as many people on vigil as there were monks in the church. The Lord also stood vigil for us, *he who does not slumber nor sleep* [Ps 120:4], and *he dispersed them by means of his power* [Ps 58:12], just as one of our brothers saw in a vision. This brother was ill and entirely ignorant of what was happening in regards to the saint. Above the pinnacle of the temple, he saw an angel radiant beyond reckoning, and many monks were walking around it upon floor-boards spread there for them. When he turned to look at another part, he saw something like a fiery rope placed upon the front of the church. The head of it had split into two and was threatening to encircle the entire church. When he cast his eyes again on the angel, it looked as if a thunderbolt were hanging in the air next to it. As he stood looking at this, trembling and stupefied, a man stood next to him and said, "Why do you look? Don't you know what this means? The resplendent angel is the archbishop. The monks, whom you see circling him, are the sons of this church who are on watch around him this night. The fiery rope, its ends lying upon different areas, is the jealousy of the evil-doers coming from diverse places and conspiring to do ill to us. The thunderbolt, which you see near the angel, is divine terror, preventing them from doing the evil they have planned." With this, the monk woke, and as he rested in his bed he prayed to the Lord to defend the church. *And suddenly there came a sound from heaven* [Acts 2:2] and the air rumbled with a tremendous thunderclap and flashed with fire. There was thunder and flashing and lightening, the waters poured from heaven, and a storm of a fury not seen for many days broke out. We blessed the God of the heavens who sent forth thunder and lightening and scattered them, and we also rejoiced to be freed from fear of the enemies by means of this vision.

II.27. CONCERNING THE MIRACULOUSLY CRIPPLED RICHARD OF BEARSTED, WHO WAS CURED MIRACULOUSLY ON THE DAY AFTER THAT TRANSLATION

On the next day, the Lord cured Richard, son of Eilnold of Bearsted, who is thought to have spent thirty-four years paying the penalty for a single sin. After the death of the first King Henry, when the peace of the English was disturbed and the kingdom was divided against itself and made desolate,[32] this Richard attached himself to a knight and worked day and night robbing and plundering the poor. For *the Lord had shut up his people under the sword* [Ps 77:62] and *the powerful fed upon the vineyard of the Lord, and the faces of the poor were laid waste* [Is 3:14–15]. Among the transgressions of his youth, this man laid waste to a field of a poor woman who had cut it in the time of harvest. The woman saw him and cursed him in the name of the Lord. After a short time had passed, his feet and shins were struck such that he was not able to run to commit such an act again. His shins were bent into a bow. His feet bent inwards and the soles of his feet faced one another. He used the joints of his feet and the nodes of his shins (which we commonly call ankles) as if they were the soles of his feet. And so, in this way he was punished for thirty-four years for what he had done in an hour.[33]

---

[32] This is a reference to the period of anarchy and civil war in England after the death of Henry I in 1135 until the accession of Henry II in 1154. See Hugh M. Thomas, "Miracle Stories and the Violence of King Stephen's Reign," *Haskins Society Journal* 13 (2004 for 1999): 111–24, and for a notable study of military men's stories in William's collection, see Bull, "Criticism of Henry II's Expedition to Ireland."

[33] Assuming that Richard came to Canterbury in 1171, his crippling illness began around 1137.

When *the time for his mercy came* [Ps 101:14], and he came to Canterbury and stood before the sepulchre of the holy father, his entire body was struck, the visible motion of his body attesting to the presence of an invisible power. Even if a very strong man had taken him by the shoulders and shaken him with all his strength, he could not have been struck in this way. Pulled backwards as if by a violent dragging force, he went before the altar of the blessed Virgin Mother, where the body of the saint had been hidden the night before, and there he was prostrated. There he fell and rose, rose and fell many times. At last, he sprang onto the altar so speedily and with so much agility that it would seem terribly difficult even for someone with perfect health and dexterity to do likewise. And then again, as if he were thrown into agony, he cast himself headlong down from the altar. We were amazed that he had not broken his neck. And so, having been greatly vexed, he rose from the floor and stood erect on the soles of his feet, which were again able to carry him from that time. When he was asked how or by what impulse he was able to leap with such agility onto the altar, he said that he could do nothing except what he had been forced to do by the power of the Mother of God and the martyr of the Lord.

II.28. CONCERNING THE CRIPPLED RALPH *DE TANGIS*

Great is the martyr *and great is his power,* and already his miracles *cannot be numbered* [Ps 146:5]. A year before, a boy *de Tangis*,[34] Ralph, slept in a meadow, and after he woke and rose to go, he could not extend his feet.[35] The nerves of his knees were contracted, such that one of his heels was attached to his buttocks, and the other was not far from it. The big toe of his left foot was bent under the sole of his foot while the remaining four toes were bent back and adhered to the bony framework of the foot. Many pustules were on the back of the other knee. Until the time of miracles, he moved about by crawling. In pain and misery, he came to the martyr, crawling and dragging himself along the ground. As he came, he received the clemency of the martyr. His nerves were stretched out, a torture that made the boy cry out. In the midst of his cries, the pustules burst and bloody matter came out. His heels were straightened away from his buttocks, his large toe left the sole of his foot, and the remaining toes were released from the bony framework. He got up and left, but from the great pain of the extension of his nerves, he remained lame until the third week.

---

[34] The place is unidentified.
[35] For other stories in which sleeping outdoors results in illness, see II.1, III.63, and IV.76.

II.29. CONCERNING THE REPLACEMENT OF THE MARTYR IN THE PRIOR LOCATION, AND OF THE EDIFICE OF THE TOMB

And so, seeing how God had multiplied his mercy for us, we knew that the abundance of signs and prodigies would act as kindling to the hatred and jealousy of the evil-doers. So they might not again attempt what they had earlier been unable to do, we placed the martyr in the former location, *and made the sepulchre secure, sealing the stone and setting guards* [Mt 27:66]. Around the marble sarcophagus, a wall of great hewn stones was set up and bound together most solidly with cement, iron and lead. The wall had two windows in each side through which people could insert their heads in order to kiss the sarcophagus. A large slab of marble was placed on top. There was a hollow space between the top of the sarcophagus and the slab which was hardly a foot high. Certain marvelous things happened regarding these windows which are worthy of being told.[36]

II.30. CONCERNING A CERTAIN MATILDA OF CANTERBURY, WHO WAS NOT ABLE TO PUT HER HEAD INTO THE WINDOW OF THE TOMB

We knew a woman by the name of Matilda, the wife of Ertin, a man of Flanders who was a citizen of Canterbury.[37] When she tried to put her head through a window to kiss the sarcophagus, she was not able to do so, even though her body was slim and narrow. As she was returning home and conversing with a matron, her lady, she asked, "My lady, were you able to kiss the tomb of the martyr?" She replied, "I kissed it not once but many times." And she said, "How were you, a large and fat woman, able to reach the sarcophagus, when I, though I am small and thin, was not able to get through the window? I put in enough effort: I tried for a long time with no success." Her lady said, "Examine your conscience, and ask carefully whether you may have spoken ill of the saint when he was in the flesh or living with God." Sighing and gravely rebuking herself for her guilt, she returned to the place of the sepulchre and gave herself over to prayers and great wailings. She showed that she had obtained the forgiveness she sought by a clear sign. Approaching the window with due reverence, she was able to insert her shoulder-blades as

---

[36] A stained glass panel in Canterbury Cathedral window nV shows a man with his head inside one of these windows: see Koopmans, "Pilgrims at Becket's Tomb."

[37] For other residents in Canterbury in this period who were neither English nor Norman, see Urry, *CUAK*, p. 171.

well as her head without any difficulty, and she rejoiced that she was able to acquire the desired kisses almost from the top of the sarcophagus. When she went home and told her fellows over a meal what had happened, she heard from her husband that something similar had happened to him.

II.31. CONCERNING A CERTAIN INSANE ELWARD WHO THRUST HIS WHOLE BODY THROUGH ONE OF THE WINDOWS AND EXITED THROUGH THE OTHER, WHICH AFTERWARDS, WHEN HE WAS HEALED, HE WAS NOT ABLE TO DO

In a great and stupendous miracle, the saint who had contracted the opening in the case of these two people expanded it for someone else. A certain man from Selling of adult age and large stature, Elward by name, had gone insane. Wherever he turned, he thought the enemy of the human race confronted him. He ordered him to be gone in the name of the Lord and spat as if spitting into his face. He was led to the saint and placed next to the sepulchre, and there he saw that diabolical phantom that seemed to be striking him. Not knowing where to turn, he fled to the martyr, and in a wonderful way he thrust his whole body through the narrow aperture that was hardly able to admit a human head. Without any difficulty, he wound himself inside this very narrow space in such a way that his head was at the martyr's feet and his feet at the martyr's head. Once he was stretched out upon the body of the saint in this way, he became quiet for a little while. We became concerned about how he would get out, and thought that the structure would definitely have to be broken apart for him to exit. Beyond all expectation, he came out of the other opening. Later, when he was in his right mind, we ordered him to go inside again. No matter how hard he tried, he could not get his shoulders into the aperture, not even with his clothes off. We made an adolescent with a thin and boyish body also try to do it, and we saw that his attempts were useless.

II.32. CONCERNING WILLIAM OF LONDON, WHO, HAVING INSERTED AND PULLED OUT HIS HEAD, IMMEDIATELY RECOVERED THE SIGHT OF AN EYE

Afflicted by blindness, William of London washed his eyes with the holy water of Canterbury. He could see in one eye, but the fog of blindness remained in the other. Again and again he made use of the same medicine, but he was not able to produce any further improvement. Realizing that his vision was not going to improve, he wondered, and thought it likely, as he heard his friends impartially thought as well, that the saint had given him sight in one eye and had put off the gift of the other for a time. This was in order that the recuperation of the one might inspire hope for the recuperation of the other, and that he might hasten to Canterbury and the memorial of the saint, both to give thanks for the healed eye and to offer prayers for the one without sight. Coming to the sepulchre, he made an offering, put his head inside the window, and very quickly pulled it out again, with his hand against his healed eye pressing the eyelid closed. He looked around with the eye that had been blind, and he shouted, "What is this? I can see!" Those of us who were there marvelled, and closely examined the occurrence and the truth of this event. We found everything satisfactory to our wishes, except that in his pupils, which were not fully purified, a portion of a cloudy white spot still remained. In a short time, it had entirely disappeared.

II.33. CONCERNING ANSFRID OF DOVER, DEPRIVED OF NEARLY ALL HIS SENSES

It was the feast day when the Invention of the Cross is celebrated every year [Jn 5:1],[38] and lying here and there in the church of Canterbury *was a great multitude of the sick, the blind, the lame, the withered, those awaiting* and asking for health [Jn 5:3], and *the power of* the martyr *was there to heal them* [Lk 5:17]. There was among the others a boy about ten years old, Ansfrid, the son of Edwin of Dover. Nature had denied him the gift of clear speech since his birth. This affliction seems to have come from this: he could not hear anything at all in one ear, and in the other, he could hear only a very little or nothing at all. Moreover, one of his eyes was half closed, and the other was completely hidden under its sealed eyelid, such that he barely had the use of half an eye. The nerves of his right hand were so contracted that his fingers were clenched tightly inwards and their tips were driven into their base, with his nails digging into the flesh. Three pustules had grown on one of his thighs. These had vanished, but they had left him lame.

And so on the day of the Invention of the Cross, this unfortunate and miserable boy, deprived of nearly all his senses, had been placed by his parents on the spot where the precious blood of the precious martyr had been split. While they knelt in prayer, he burst out in tears and cries. As he indicated his

[38] The Invention of the Cross, celebrating St. Helena's discovery of the relic of the cross, is celebrated on May 3.

many torments by means of gestures as well as his wailings, many of those standing there shed tears as well. After weeping and lamenting, he fell asleep, and there before him was the venerable friend of God, dressed in his pontifical garments. He said to him, "What are you doing here? What do you want?" And he said, "Lord, I seek my health." Then the saint grasped the boy with two fingers by the locks on the top of his head (for his head had been shaved and the hair had grown back a little), and he shook him like a kind father playing with his son, saying, "Rise, go home." When he woke after this sweet and joyful vision, he brought no little cause of joy to the people standing round about. For God, *who closes and no one opens, and opens and no one closes [Rv 3:7]*, kindly unlocked the mouth and ears of this boy, granting him perfect hearing. Having unbound his fettered tongue, he made him able to learn to speak clearly. Though he was laboriously imitating others, yet he was able to copy the words that people spoke. His eyes were also opened, and he received sight without any imperfection. His fingers, which before had been bent to the palm of his hand, he now could extend freely and quickly. He got up and, without the lameness he had before, he ran to the tomb of the saint along with his parents, as much as the multitude of people rushing to and crowding around him would allow. You could see the sons of piety rush to the pious spectacle, *lifting* their *hearts and* their *hands to the Lord [Lam 3:41]* and erupting in praise of God and the martyr. Their tears overflowed due to joy rather than the pain or loss which often furnishes the cause.[39]

II.34. CONCERNING WEKERILDA, CRIPPLED AND BLIND IN ONE EYE

Hardly had we been sated with the sight of this delightful vision when we were drawn to another no less glorious spectacle. Wekerilda, a little woman of Horton, had lain in the church for three days and nights, fasting continuously and giving notice of her terrible punishment by her cries and groans. Her left eye had been wholly darkened for about six years. For no shorter length of time, her left hand had been bowed all the way up to her arm, such that the palm of her hand nearly seemed to be joined to her arm. Her right leg had been bent almost up to her thigh for something like eleven years, and her foot was so curved that her toes and heel faced each other, her large toe seeming to join the inside of her foot below her ankle. We saw this woman improved to such an extent that she saw equally clearly with both eyes, she held both

---

[39] Robertson suggested that the phrase "furnishes a cause" [*ministrat opes*] echoes a passage in the *Epistolae ad Ponto* by Ovid: *Has fortuna tibi nostra ministrat opes.*

hands out equally, she extended both knees the same way, and the toes of her injured foot returned to their ordinary place, with the toes of both feet similarly straight. Yet in one matter the grace of healing was not fully granted to her. One foot was still a little curved, making her lame, and so she walked with a staff. Thus in one woman four miracles were done, to the great happiness of the confluence of people. Up to ten people recovered from various infirmities that day, but we were not able to call back those who had slipped away and we drove out those without witnesses.[40]

II.35. CONCERNING THE BLIND ELVIDA OF BECKENHAM

A woman from Beckenham near London, whose name was Elvida, had not been able to open either eye for around five years, for her eyelids were stuck together as if they were glued. Led by her son, she fled to the manifest light of the English, with the intention of receiving light herself. When she approached the place where that light was thought to have been extinguished by the hands of the savage knights, she felt, as we learned later from her own telling, that her head was in uproar, as if her brain had been violently shaken. It was as if it had been put into a lit furnace and completely set on fire. She threw back the veil from her head and ripped the clothing from her breast, and suddenly fell prone on the ground, staying there for about an hour, until she opened her eyes and got up, bursting forth with these words: "Precious lord, saint Thomas, I give thanks to you for now I see!" The people ran to the glorious and pious spectacle, as full of joy as this was worthy of wonder. Each of them tested whether she could really see, asking her what they held in their hands, how they moved their hands and their fingers, and many similar things in order to find out the certain truth of the event. She answered every question from each questioner correctly, and she inspired not only rejoicing among the bystanders, but tears of delight.

II.36. CONCERNING EMMA, WHO HAD A TERRIBLE ULCER ON HER [SHIN][41] AND FOOT

The foot of Emma of Thanington, in the vicinity of Canterbury, was flayed and eaten away by the worst kind of ulcer. Anyone who saw it, even someone with an iron heart, would have been softened to compassion. For four years

---

[40] This echoes Luke 17:12–17, a story about Christ healing ten lepers, only one of whom came back to give thanks.
[41] The caption writer added "shin": Benedict only mentions an ulcer on Emma's foot.

she suffered such sharp pains and terrible burning that she was being undone. Her groans and colorless face told the truth of this as much as her words. When she washed the ulcer with the saintly water, the burning stopped, the pains ended, and all manner of discomfort ceased. The raw flesh of her eaten-away foot seemed to be partly covered with hardened bloody matter, but in a short time, new skin covered it over and she was entirely healed.

II.37. CONCERNING THE BLIND MATILDA OF IPSWICH

So too, Matilda, the wife of Geoffrey Paris of Ipswich, who had been blind and led by another's eyes for roughly sixteen years, experienced the power of the saintly water of Canterbury in our presence. When she washed her eyes, she also, as I would put it, washed away the blindness from her eyes.

II.38. CONCERNING BRIAN DE INSULA, WHOSE CHIN WAS STUCK TO HIS CHEST

Brian de Insula[42] was also brought there, lying on a bed. In his region, he held the power of a provost, and he aimed to be feared rather than loved. His chin was all but stuck to his chest and his neck was rigid and inflexible. He was not able to lift his head nor to turn it at all. He was brought on a litter, for he was unable to ride or walk. Intense pain and fear of death had made him humble and devout. He was set down at the door of the church, and it was as if the martyr met him there and said to him, "*Rise, take up your bed and walk*" [*Jn* 5:8], for he left the bed and walked to the tomb of the martyr. The sacrist of the church of Canterbury, Robert,[43] encircled his neck with the blood-stained belt of the martyr and sent him away improved. His chin lifted and he departed on foot, leaving the litter with the martyr, but he did not regain full health for many days.

II.39. CONCERNING FRODO, WHO HAD DISABLED FEET

We also saw Frodo, from the region of the holy martyr Edmund,[44] who had so much intolerable pain in the joints between his feet and his shins that he was not able to dig or do any other work of that kind for around twelve years.

---

[42] See Biographical Notes, Brian de Insula, provost.
[43] See Biographical Notes, Robert, sacrist and monk of Christ Church.
[44] That is, the region of Bury St Edmunds in Suffolk, the burial site of St. Edmund (d.869), the king of East Anglia killed by the Vikings.

If the pain ever lessened and he was able to apply himself to work, in a short time he would have to return to his bed, and then he would be unable even to walk. He said that in his sleep he was told that he would find a remedy for this great trouble if he were to put the shoes of saint Thomas on his feet. When these were not able to be acquired, he placed them in his slipper and full health followed.

II.40. CONCERNING THE SON OF EILMER *DE CLECHE*, WHO HAD NEVER HAD THE ABILITY TO WALK, STAND UPRIGHT, OR GET TO HIS FEET

Eilmer *de Beche*[45] and his wife Edilda, the wretched parents of a wretched child, merited to feel the delights of parental joy at Canterbury. Divine piety had brought them offspring, but the gift of offspring was marred by the imperfections of nature. Their son, Henry, was about nine years old. When his mother gave birth to him, she gained rather than deposited a burden. He never had the ability to walk, stand upright, or get to his feet. For nine years, the only way he could move from place to place was by being carried. The parents, along with the boy, fell prostrate where the martyr had been killed. After a little while, he rose with the gift of walking granted to him. An untrained and unpracticed traveller, he walked here and there with the help of a staff or by holding someone's hand. And so the soles and base of his feet were made solid, and what nature had not given him, he recovered by means of exercise.

II.41. CONCERNING THE SON OF A CERTAIN WILLIAM OF LINCOLN, WHO WAS UNABLE TO WALK ON HIS FEET BECAUSE OF A SWELLING ON HIS KIDNEYS

A woman no less unfortunate, the wife of William of Lincoln, became equally happy. An enormous swelling had grown up on the kidneys of her son William two or three years after his birth. From the swelling came pain, from the pain infirmity, and from the infirmity he was so crippled that up to the end of his fifth or the beginning of his sixth year, he could not walk. The swelling made it impossible for him to stand on his feet. Sitting was intolerable, and even when he was lying down at rest, his suffering continued. There was no human remedy because there was no cause of the illness and punishment, and also

---

[45] The place is unidentified. In addition to *Cleche* and *Beche*, it is spelled *Deche* in some manuscripts: see Robertson, *MTB*, vol. 2, p. 88 n. 7, and Duggan, "Santa Cruz," p. 51.

no interruption. Whatever respite there was, it did not alternate with rest: the name and the benefit of rest was removed. And so, the mother took up the little boy, and, groaning, she carried him in her arms to Canterbury, the one whom she had before laboriously carried in her womb. When they were still two days distant from the city, health started to appear in the boy. We saw him afterwards regain the ability to walk near the sepulchre of our father, and hardly anything remained of the swelling.

II.42. CONCERNING THE ILL EREMBURGA OF LONDON, A HOPELESS CASE

We know of a matron of London, Eremburga, who was so ill that both she and all her family and friends thought her case was hopeless. Bequeathing everything that seemed to be hers, she requested that she be buried with the canons at the church of the blessed Virgin and Mother.[46] The priest of the parish to which she seemed to belong contested this and said he required either burial or five shillings for benefit of burial.[47] The woman's husband, not wanting her petition to be denied, nor to satisfy the priest's wishes, thought of a clever way to bring the lawsuit to naught. He put the woman on a ship and accompanied her as her custodian. He did this more out of fear than hope: he expected that a corpse rather than a woman would be taken to Canterbury. But she was insensible to it all, and was taken away feeling neither fear nor hope. Disembarked from the ship, she was put onto a litter, and so went to the church of Canterbury. She was carried, not led there, and she arrived being helped by many, not just one. For a short time she lay near the martyr, and she received back her mind and power of speech. Her strength returned and she sat up. She stormed the martyr with prayers, asking that she either quickly die in that place or quickly recover and be able to walk home. Those of us who were there marvelled at the presumptuous beginning of the prayer, but we marvelled no less that a prize of faith so quickly followed in response to her worthy devotion. After a short delay, she jumped up, as *if the Spirit of the Lord had come upon* her,[48] and she speedily and with a firm step walked many

---

[46] St. Mary Overie, a house of Augustinian canons at Southwark (now Southwark Cathedral), is probably the house referred to here.

[47] The priest of a parish would usually receive a burial fee for a parishioner. Eremburga's wish to be buried at a house of canons would deny him this fee.

[48] This is a common phrase in the Bible: see Judges 6:34, 1 Samuel 16:13, Isaiah 61:1, Ezekiel 11:5, and Luke 4:18.

times around the mausoleum of the saint until she made her way to her inn. She walked there herself as she had wished.

On the following day, she and her husband quarrelled over an issue of money. When he demanded a sum he had seen her to have, she stated that she had not had it and polluted her faith. She did not fear to call the blessed martyr Thomas as witness to her lie, and as she swore and perjured herself, she immediately became ill again and out of her mind. When she returned to a quiet state, she openly confessed her offence. She was led again to the martyr, and she again implored for pardon and health. She laboured with such severe punishment at the sepulchre of the saint that it is thought that she atoned for her perjury. By divine regard, she again departed on her feet, healed in body, though her mind was still disordered. In time, she fully recovered.

II.43. HOW THE PERSECUTORS OF THE MARTYR MALIGNED THE MONKS OF THE CHURCH OF CANTERBURY IN ORDER TO CLOUD THE GLORY OF THE MIRACLES

In all this, the fury of the evil ones *was not turned away, but* their *hand was stretched out still* [Is 9:12]. They sharpened their tongues *like a sword* [Ps 63:4] and unwisely endeavored to contradict or cleverly to distort each of God's mighty deeds. They imitated *those that said that the Lord ejected devils by means of Beelzebub, the prince of devils* [Lk 11:15], and told everyone that the monks of Canterbury were engaged in magical incantations. They said that miracles were being feigned by diabolical art and so were not really happening. People arriving would be suddenly seized by their incantations, and then, at the monks' will, would be released from insanity. In this way, with the diabolical influence lifted, they would seem to be cured when they had not actually been ill. However, their testimony did not accord with the truth nor with each other. The martyr *performed great deeds in God*, and so that *he might bring to nothing those that afflicted us* [Ps 59:14], he struck this blow to their accusation: it was necessary for them either to stop maligning our innocence or to accuse all England of this crime. For suddenly, the number of prodigies and signs was multiplied throughout England, and with the multiplication of witnesses to the truth, our innocence and reputation was vindicated. It brought grief to those wishing us evil; our glory brought them embarrassment. So many witnesses to the truth came to us from all corners of England that our enemies could not resist or contradict them.

II.44. CONCERNING THOMAS OF ETTON, WHO WAS STRUCK WITH QUINSY WHEN HE MALIGNED THE MARTYR

When the Lord's anointed was still being maligned by some of them, a knight of the region of York, Thomas of Etton,[49] heard this, and he too did not blush to denigrate his sanctity and glory, even though he once served the saint when he was the provost of Beverley.[50] No sooner had he scattered poisonous words of slander upon his lord, the Lord's anointed, than, as it is written, *the Lord scourges every son whom he receives* [Heb 12:6]. He was struck and nearly suffocated by a dangerous sickness, by quinsy, as it was thought.[51] When he considered how suddenly he had been taken ill, he realized that he had been slanderous and at fault, and he turned to the Lord with all his heart. He did not delay to moderate the flagellation of the martyr with the flagellation of a spirit of penitence and contrition. The remarkable justice of the Lord was followed by the Lord's remarkable pity. As soon as he had repented of his offence and the martyr granted him the gift of inward tears, the pain vanished and everything returned to normal. When an opportune time came, he hastened to the memorial of the martyr. He testified that after this happened, he also had been freed from acute fevers by means of invocation of the martyr. [*See Parallel Miracles no. 1 for William's account of this miracle.*]

II.45. CONCERNING JULIANA, THE WIFE OF ROBERT PUINTEL, WHO WAS DISTENDED BY AN ENORMOUS SWELLING

Juliana, a woman as lovely in appearance as she was honest in her habits, was the wife of Robert Puintel of Essex,[52] a knight known to me. At one time, several days after she had given birth, she was careless about her diet and ate a noxious fish. She suddenly became ill and began to swell up. Both her husband and her family expected time to bring her a cure or alleviation, but the illness of the sick woman and their sadness both grew. Around the middle of the following night, her swelling had increased to such an extent that none of them hoped for a remedy any longer. As people despaired of her exterior

---

[49] See Biographical Notes, Thomas of Etton, knight of the region of York.
[50] Becket received the provostship of Beverley c.1154 and retained it until 1163.
[51] Quinsy is a medieval term for severe throat pain and inflammation.
[52] A William Puintel, possibly a son or another relation of this Robert, appears in the Essex section of the 1198 *Rotuli curiae regis*: see *Rotuli Curiae Regis, Vol. 1: Rolls and Records of the Court Held Before the King's Justiciars or Justices*, ed. Francis Palgrave (London, 1835), p. 203.

health, she turned to provide for her interior salvation. She summoned a priest with the greatest haste, but before she was graced by his presence, she lost the power of speech. Now no-one had any hope of happiness whatsoever.[53] There were no bounds to the sorrow of each of them. The nurse of the ill woman was there, and she alone called to mind the blessed Thomas, arguing that recourse should be made to his merits. A vow should be made for her, and a candle the length and breadth of her body should be made quickly in the saint's honor. The knight acquiesced to the advice of the nurse. When she had been measured by a stretched-out cord, she suddenly turned to her side and slept for a short time, about the time in which one can walk a furlong at an easy pace.[54] When she woke, she got up immediately, showing that she was slender and wholly sound and so bringing their lost happiness back to everyone. When she came with her husband to Canterbury, she joyfully told this miracle to us, and in order to give reverence to the holy martyr, she spent a night in vigil in the church of Canterbury praying and giving thanks.

II.46. CONCERNING A CERTAIN [RALPH][55] OF LINCOLN, WHO WAS NOT ABLE TO STEM A NOSEBLEED

A young man of good habits, Ralph son of Ralph of the province of Lincoln, wasted away with weakness as blood poured out of his nose and continued to flow incessantly for two days. It put him in a desperate state. The efficacy of incantations, the power of herbs, the potency of stones – all were in vain. He received the sacrament of last rites and prepared to depart from his body. The martyr was brought to mind by his parents and desperate friends. Taking on both the faith and the pain of the woman of the gospel crying out for her demon-possessed daughter,[56] with devotion and supplication they implored the martyr, asking that by the blood that he had shed with rejoicing for the liberty of the church, he would stop the young man's dangerous flow of blood, so keeping him from dying, obtaining an interval of life for him, and granting him the grace of health. The martyr is *near to all those who invoke him in truth* [Ps 144:18]. As they all rose from prayer, they saw that the nosebleed was checked and he had recovered from the illness. Though he did not have his full vigor, he recovered this later with nourishment. With his strength

---

[53] Unable to speak, Juliana would be unable to confess her sins.
[54] That being just a few minutes (a furlong was equivalent to about an eighth of a mile).
[55] The text of the caption reads "Robert" rather than "Ralph."
[56] See Matthew 15:22–8 for the story of the woman with a demon-possessed daughter.

restored, he presented himself to the martyr with an oblation. His parents accompanied him and gave testimony to this miracle.

II.47. CONCERNING THE SON OF MATILDA, WHO LAY AS IF INSENSIBLE UNTIL A VOW WAS MADE FOR HIM TO THE MARTYR, WHEN HE IMMEDIATELY TURNED TO HIS MOTHER'S BREASTS

Matilda and Roger of London tarried together at a wine-seller's shop, and the son born of their fornication fell ill after a few days. All the signs of approaching death were clearly evident in his face and he lay completely cold. Both parents wept, but the mother, who loved the child more dearly, wept more. She considered this thoroughly, and concluded that after her fault of neglecting chastity, she deserved to suffer swift punishment for her fornication. Mindful of the martyr, she renounced her former life. The situation reversed marvellously. No sooner had the infant and the infant's cradle been measured for a candle in the honor of the saint, than the boy, made whole and happy, suckled at the breasts offered by his mother.

II.48. CONCERNING GILBERT, A SHOEMAKER OF LONDON, WHO WAS CURED OF FISTULA

A young man of London practicing the art of shoemaking, by the name of Gilbert, was struck with the disease of fistula.[57] He became more and more imperiled every day. The infection perforated his stomach and abdomen in five places, and one of the holes was so wide that it appeared broader than the width of three fingers. With his stomach being eaten away like this, his intestines could be seen. Despaired of by those close to him, and lacking human help, he fled to divine aid. He went, with much difficulty, to Canterbury. After he made his prayer, his wounds were daubed with the blood of the martyr. Having asked for a portion of the blood, he brought back some with him, though a small amount, to London. Each day, he anointed each of the wounds, and in a short time they healed over and he received his health. He flew back again to the saint. In order to repay the debt of thanks for the reward of his health, he ran the distance from London to Canterbury, some fifty miles, in one day. He showed his naked body to us, perfectly cured, and he did not fear to challenge others to a run.

---

[57] In medieval terms, a fistula was a narrow, open sore that oozed pus or bodily fluids.

II.49. CONCERNING HUGH OF BOURNE, ALSO FREED FROM AN AGONIZING FISTULA

Hugh of Bourne, the son of William, was also plagued by a fistula. After three years' continuous suffering, he was close to death. The flesh under his armpit was eaten away to his ribs; an egg would fit in the hollow. This large opening divided itself into nine channels: one went up sideways into his chest, another went in the opposite direction to his back, the third went all the way up to his neck, the fourth went down and across to his kidneys, and I do not remember where the rest curved around him. The young man consulted a skilled doctor, from whom he heard that he was wholly incurable, leaving him desperate. He fled to the saint, asked for the water and received it. That same week, all the openings dried up. Feeling himself well and robust, he soon began to press on with a peasant's works and labors. As he worked, the disease revived, and he again resorted to the earlier medicine and again was cured. He washed himself and left, and he saw that no fistula now flowed with bloody matter. Before eight days had passed, the flesh healed over and he was completely cured.

II.50. CONCERNING A PYX IN WHICH THE MARTYR'S WATER DISAPPEARED, PROVING THE CARRIER TO BE A THIEF

A certain Richard was having a banquet in Essex with his friends and acquaintances. As they were feasting, the shepherd of the house entered the house, carrying a pyx in his hand. Richard said to him, "What are you carrying, shepherd?" "I bear the water of the martyr of Canterbury," he said. And Richard said to him, "If you have served me well in the work entrusted to you and there is no wickedness in your hands, you will have brought water; but if the saint has not left a drop for you in the vessel, he will have proved you to truly be a thief." They both agreed to these terms. Richard took the pyx from him and opened it in the midst of the company. He found it not just empty, I declare, but dry, as if water had never been put in it. "Son," he said, "give glory to God: confess what you have done." He was stained as a thief and evildoer on all scores, for he did not have anything to bring to his defence. The wood was solid and not a type to absorb moisture, nor had he traveled a long way, since he had brought the water from a neighbouring house, not from Canterbury. And so, terrified, he immediately confessed that he had been less than faithful to his lord in the cheese and butter accounts. But pardon was granted to him for the love of the saint, and with his transgression transformed into jest and laughter and the glory of the martyr, the pyx was hung in the church in exhibition and remembrance of such a delightful miracle.

II.51. CONCERNING ROBERT, CANON OF THE CHURCH OF ST. FRIDESWIDE OF OXFORD, WHO WAS WEAKENED BY SEVERE DIARRHEA

Robert, a canon and the chamberlain of the church of St. Frideswide of Oxford, was weakened by severe diarrhea. Once the flux had eased, he became so constipated that the new problem was worse than the earlier one. Seeking to resolve this beyond the mode of nature, his earlier illness turned into excessive vomiting. And so, returning to his bed, he was brought to such a state that all the signs of approaching death had appeared. No one thought a remedy was possible for him. One of the brothers came to the ill canon, and ardently tried to get him to call to mind the memory of the martyr Thomas. The ill man tried to say the name of the martyr, and though he managed to say the first syllable, he was too ill to say the second. The canon who had been helping him recalled that that water of holy memory was being held in the monastery. He ran and quickly brought it to him, but found on his return that the ill man's eyes were closed and he could not speak. However, he opened his mouth and poured in several drops as he invoked the martyr with supplications. Without any delay at all, the ill man exclaimed freely and clearly, "O lord, saint Thomas, have mercy on me!" He said this, and immediately sat up, and recovered so much of his strength that day that on the next day he returned to the convent. He was not afraid to take up the rigours of the order with the others in the customary way, because he had been loosened and no longer suffered from constipation. When the prior of the church, Master Robert of Cricklade,[58] saw this, he called two of the canons who had never had any faith in the things that were being said about the martyr. He said, "Do you believe, or do you still waver?" And they confessed that no scruples of ambiguity remained in them, bringing no little joy to the questioner. And so divine pity, by driving off a bodily ailment from one, cured the wound of disbelief in two others. We heard these things from the mouth of the venerable prior, who also fled to the martyr, suffering greatly from an ailment himself. Later, he wrote to us describing how he became ill and how he escaped it by means of the martyr, which follows below, the salutation removed.[59]

---

[58] See Biographical Notes, Robert of Cricklade, prior of St. Frideswide.
[59] A version of this salutation is preserved in a copy of the letter found in a fourteenth-century Icelandic account of Becket's life and miracles. The text (in the nineteenth-century translation) reads: "Prior Robert, the least slave among the servants of God, to brother

II.52. CONCERNING MASTER ROBERT, THE PRIOR OF THE SAME CHURCH, WHOSE LEG, AFFLICTED BY A GRAVE AND CHRONIC DISEASE, THE MARTYR CURED

"It has been twelve years or more since I have been in Sicily. I wished to go from the city of Catania to Syracuse walking along the Adriatic sea, and so my journey took me.[60] The south wind and the fluctuation of the sea, which was to my left, inflicted a swelling with a very pernicious redness to my foot and leg. In the lodging in which I stayed in Syracuse, I improved with the application of hot poultices and plasters. I became better when I returned to Rome and was cleansed by medicines there, and on my entire journey home to England I had no trouble with it at all. However, a short time after I had returned to England, the swelling returned, though not as severely as before, and I drove it away by various treatments. It is now the third or fourth year, as I make it, since that disease struck me so severely that I was not able to rid myself of it by draughts or bloodletting, when many leeches were applied, nor through plasters, poultices, ointments, or any other medication. It was a severe swelling, so much so that the swelling on the foot was thought to be thicker than the foot itself. My leg was like this all the way up to the knee. Abscesses appeared both on the inside and outside, and not just in one place but many, such that I could hardly touch them for the pain. When bloody matter came out from one of the abscesses and there seemed to be some hope of healing, before it dried up another would emerge that was just as bad or worse. With these afflictions succeeding one another, I found no rest. Where my shin had seemed smooth, itching sores appeared which, growing together, stripped off the skin. The pain was no small thing. Blisters also appeared, filled almost to the thickness of a thumb. They emitted a great deal of pus when they broke open, but this brought about only torment rather than a cure. Later, two of the abscesses upon the foot broke open. Whenever I put on or took off a shoe, the pain was excruciating.

What more? I knew that it was a chronic illness, which could not be cured by human hands, for as the physicians say, chronic diseases bring death.[61]

Benedict sendeth the greeting that he may live with God. What thou didst ask of me in the strength of thy love, I have now done to the best of my power, though failing to do it as well as I should have wished, inasmuch as my clerkship sufficed not to write the miracle in such a fair fashion as duty demandeth and exacteth of me, for the honour of God and the blessed Thomas" (*Thómas Saga* vol. 2, pp. 93–5).

[60] It appears that the primary purpose of Prior Robert's trip to Italy and Sicily was to collect papal privileges from Adrian IV for the priory of St. Frideswide: see A. J. Duggan, "Cricklade, Robert of," *ODNB* and Biographical Notes, Robert of Cricklade, prior of St. Frideswide.

[61] Prior Robert appears to be making a general statement here rather than quoting from a specific medical text.

The people of my city are my witness. When I spoke with them on feast days, urging them, according to my custom, to take on the way of righteousness, I sat while I spoke with them, including when clerics from various places in England were present, with the excuse that I could not stand because of the pain. In the Lent now past, I languished with sorrow because I could not be present at divine services as I was accustomed to be and especially because the mystery of the Lord's passion was coming near. I worried that I would not be able to celebrate it as I ought, and I prayed to the Lord in my heart that he would turn his face from my sins and hear me, so that at least on these days, by his gift, I might be able to do what pertained to my ministry. And though I am unworthy, he to whom salvation belongs granted that my pain so lessened from the Lord's Supper to the Wednesday after Easter that I was able to perform everything to my desire, to my amazement and to that of the brothers who knew of my illness. After this was accomplished, the pain returned.

It came into my mind that I should go to visit the sepulchre of the most blessed martyr and archbishop Thomas because I had heard of the signs of his martyrdom. By the time I came to Canterbury, the length and great labor of the journey had made the illness worse and the swelling great. Lying at his sepulchre, I prayed to the Lord that he would free me from my infirmity by the merits of his martyr. I prayed to the martyr that he would pray for me to the Lord. Not knowing if I had been heard, I returned to my inn anxious and groaning, not knowing if I would be able get back to my own home on account of the pain. At last it came into my mind to use the saint's water that had been given to me as an ointment for my foot. Putting my foot in a basin, I made the sign of the cross with the water over my foot and my shin in the name of the Holy Trinity and in memory of the most blessed martyr, and I anointed both of them with the water. I threw what remained into the fire, lest it be trampled underfoot. I started on my journey the next day, returning to my own country, feeling a lessening of the pain and a reduction of the swelling. When I had reached my lodging in Rochester, I took off my shoe, hoping to see the reduction I had sensed, but I could not yet see what I had felt. Having faith in the recovery of health, I again anointed it in the same way. As I went to London the next day, I felt the pain lessen and the swelling reduce even more. When I took my shoe off in London, I was able to see the difference easily. In the third stopping place, the reduction was even greater, and I felt little pain.

When I arrived at Oxford, despite having made such a journey in which I would ordinarily have grown worse as each day passed, I found myself wholly healed, such that no vestige of the abscesses, sores, or blisters remained, with the exception that the skin was still somewhat reddened. All the inflammation was gone and all the pain had vanished, such that I was not the only one who marvelled, I who did not discern how I had been cured by the hand of the mercy of God and the merits of the most blessed martyr. Everyone who had seen my disease before was amazed and glorified God and his most blessed martyr. I showed my foot and leg to many religious persons and to others wishing to see the miracle. I say to you in truth before God that all these things are as I have written. I have omitted many things so that the reader would not be bored with an account that was too lengthy. I add here that I am able to walk and stand on this foot and leg just as well, indeed I think even better, than on the foot that was not afflicted by this infirmity."

These things, as they are put down here, we had asked the prior to write about himself. He wrote back with haste, aiming to explain the event rather than to concern himself with the phrasing of the words.

II.53. CONCERNING WILLIAM, A KNIGHT OF EARLEY, FREED FROM A SIMILAR AFFLICTION

A knight of Earley, named William,[62] endured a very similar disease for around three years. Blisters the size of nuts appeared on his legs and feet. They were a horrible colour and burned like fire. They broke open and more and more burst out, and he miserably wasted away. In the places where they broke open, the flesh was stripped off. It would sting and burn and then become covered over with hardened bloody matter like a poultice. When the *time had come* when the Lord *would have mercy* on him [Ps 101:14] a young man appeared to him as he was lying on his bed, saying to him, "William, why do you not go to Canterbury? Vow yourself to the martyr Thomas and go there. Beware if you do not do this, whether it pleases your wife or not." And he said, "I will go, since it pleases God." As he said these words, sleep departed from his eyes, he immediately sat up, and the stupefied man stupefied his wife who was on watch. She asked what had happened, and he concealed it from her. He was again seized by sleep, and behold, he saw the martyr standing very near. The martyr's eyes were fixed on him, and he had a friendly aspect that promised that he would easily grant the grace he was asked for. It seemed to the man that he went up to the saint and humbly beseeched him for sound

---

[62] See Biographical Notes, William of Earley.

health. Waking, he got up and told his wife what he had seen and what he wished. She assented, and he started off.

On the first day he was hardly able to travel for a mile, and this was on horseback, not on his feet. He grew better day by day and came to Canterbury. He slept in the church, where his pain grew greater than usual, but his hope of healing also grew. He gave as an oblation two wax legs weighing twenty-four pounds that were made to resemble the full size of his legs. On the next day, when we took him for a walk, he confessed that he was entirely free of pain. And so, when he went back home, he ordered that his shoes be taken off his feet. When he revealed his unshod feet, they were so free from the impediment of the disease that there was no mark, relic or sign of infirmity to be seen. Even his skin was free from any red mixed in with the white, for with the ulcers healed, his skin came back together. All redness and blackness was expelled, and his skin was left uniformly clear.

II.54. CONCERNING THE SON OF THE SAME KNIGHT, SEIZED BY MADNESS

On a later occasion, we spoke with the wife of the knight at Canterbury,[63] asking her why she too had come. She said, "I have come to give thanks and render oblations to the saint for my young son, not yet seven years old. He went out of his mind one day, shouting, 'Look where they come! Look where they come!' He would go silent when sudden fits came on him, and when they had passed he would burst out again with the same words, 'Look where they come! Look where they come!' My husband was stupefied, I was stunned, and all the family was amazed. We all rushed to implore the martyr and ask for his help. My husband ran to bring the little piece of his vestments which your liberality had granted him, and he hung it around the neck of the afflicted boy. Immediately he rested his head on his father's knee and slept a short time. When he woke, he was sound. When we were going to bed, we removed from the boy's neck that which had freed him from the chains of madness. Hardly had we fallen asleep when the boy was afflicted again with madness and exclaimed, 'Look where they come! Look where they come!' Rising from bed, we ran to him, repeated the medicine, and made promises to the martyr for the boy. Soon he was wholly restored to his senses. This is the reason I have come to this place: that I might give to the martyr what I promised him."

---

[63] See Biographical Notes, Aziria of Earley.

II.55. CONCERNING MASTER PETER DE MELIDA, RELEASED FROM HIGH FEVERS, AND CERTAIN OTHERS WHO WERE CURED

A clerk of celebrated name of the church of Lincoln, Master Peter de Melida,[64] was held fast by severe fevers, worse than any he could remember having before. At the hour the fever was to return, he drank the water and evaded the fever. And *so he went and preached to the* people *that it was* Thomas *who had made him well* [Jn 5:15]. On account of this, many people with ailments came to his house so that they could drink of the blessed water, and they were cured there of their illnesses. The water drove out fevers from many, repressed swellings of the viscera, relieved cutting pains of the vitals, curbed dropsy entirely in a certain person, and conquered paralysis in another before it could take hold and bring doom as it had already begun to do. A three-year-old boy was refusing the breast of his mother and held his tongue out of his mouth constantly because he was so overheated. When a drop touched his tongue, he instantly cooled down and turned to his mother's breasts.[65]

II.56. CONCERNING ROGER, A CLERK OF LONDON, WHO, WHEN HE WAS FEVERISH, SLEPT IN A PLACE WHERE THE SAINT HAD LAIN AND WOKE WELL. COLLECTING THE DUST OF THAT SAME PLACE, HE ADMINISTERED IT AS A DRINK TO MANY OTHERS FOR THEIR HEALTH

A clerk of London, Roger, also burned with acute fevers. Since he did not have any of the water and was too sick to be able to go to Canterbury, he lay down to sleep in a certain place where he had heard the martyr had slept. The repose of sleep was followed on at once by the repose of the desired health. He collected some of the dust of that place and brought it about with him, and he administered the happiness of health to many people who took up the dust mixed with water. Among so many sufferers from fever, we wanted to make special mention of this case, so that it may be known how much power there is in his blood when the dust of his bed can do such things.

---

[64] See Biographical Notes, Peter de Melida.
[65] This chapter may well be derived from a letter sent by Peter de Melida to Christ Church.

II.57. CONCERNING GUNCELIN, A MONK OF NORWICH, WHO WAS HEALED OF A SWOLLEN AND PAINFUL ARM BY MEANS OF THE MARTYR'S STOLE

The convent of the church of Norwich knows how much the arm of the monk Guncelin had swollen and how painful it was. His arm was wrapped in the stole of the martyr, and in a very little time all the burden of the infirmity was unwrapped from him.

II.58. CONCERNING ANSFREDA OF CANTERBURY, WHOSE QUINSY OF THE NECK THE MANTLE OF THE MARTYR REPRESSED

We are also not unaware of how Ansfreda, daughter of Hubert of Canterbury,[66] suffered from quinsy. She was dressed in the blood-stained outer garment of the martyr, which in a moment dissolved the great swelling on her neck.[67]

II.59. CONCERNING SOLOMON, NEARLY ONE HUNDRED YEARS OLD, WHOSE BLINDNESS THE MARTYR ILLUMINATED

Solomon, a citizen of London, was known to be nearly one hundred years old. His eyes darkened, and he was not able to see. In that year when the light of the English illuminated heaven and was illuminated throughout the earth, he had been deprived of the light of his eyes for around six years. He determined to amend his life and opened his blind eyes by means of the martyr's relics. *In the evening* he cried to the martyr, and *in the morning he heard* his *voice* [Ps 54:18]. In the morning, when he was led to church, he opened his eyes and said to his guide, "Shameful woman, why are you walking along beside me dressed in such a way? Go, put on your clothes, and do not walk by me half covered in skimpy linens." Stunned, she said, "Does this mean, lord, that you see me?" "I see, and see well," he said, "by the grace of God and our new martyr." His *neighbours and kin heard that the Lord had magnified his mercy with* him, *and they congratulated* him [Lk 1:58]. Many Londoners came there to see Solomon, and left with greater devotion for the martyr, because they saw *that he had done this sign* [Jn 12:18].

---

[66] A cordwainer named Hubert is found in a Canterbury rental dated c.1206: see Urry, *CUAK*, Rental F, pp. 370 and 374.

[67] For the gift of this outer garment to the poor after Becket's murder, see *Passion*, Extract VIII above.

II.60. CONCERNING HENRY, SON OF WILLIAM OF KELVEDON, WHO TASTED THE MARTYR'S WATER AND VOMITED A WORM HALF A CUBIT LONG

A miracle of great wonderment and most worthy of everyone's praise occurred in Kelvedon in Essex. Henry, the only son of William, knight and lord of the manor, was more than ten years old. He had lost his appetite in his second year, and with his shrunken and pale appearance, he reached his tenth year seeming more dead than alive. He was choked with fits nearly every single day, and it seemed as though his intestines were being cut with sharp razors. The son designated as the heir was preceding his parents in death. Their anguish was immense. And *the Lord saw their affliction and heard their cry* [Acts 7:34]. It happened one day that as the boy was suffering more greatly than usual from the infirmity, someone came in who carried the antidote of the water of Canterbury. The boy tasted it, but it seemed to bring no improvement – in fact, he became much worse. When he was brought to a desperate point and his life hung in the balance, he suddenly vomited out a worm half a cubit long,[68] along with pus and putrefaction. All who saw what came out of his mouth marvelled. With loud voices, they praised the martyr and the potency of the draught. The boy soon slept, sweated, and woke cured. The worm was hung in the church.

II.61.[69] CONCERNING NICHOLAS, SON OF HUGH DE BEAUCHAMP, WHOM THE MARTYR HEALED OF DROPSY

Hugh de Beauchamp had a son with dropsy named Nicholas.[70] The dropsy made his stomach distend, genitals swell, hands puff up, and feet inflate. This brought despair to the doctors, grief to his parents, and horror to all those seeing him. No doctor could be found who would dare to take on the cure of the boy, fearing that they would appear to be driven by greed to deceive his noble parents by receiving payment from them for their work and yet killing the boy by their attentions. All of them abandoned him as incurable. Prayers were directed, therefore, to the doctor of Canterbury. A thread was brought to measure the length of the boy. As it was being stretched out between the measurers' hands, it broke. The severed section was placed alongside the boy's body, and it was found to be not greater nor lesser, but exactly equal to the

---

[68] I.e., around nine inches long.
[69] Robertson numbered this as chapter 62 of Book II.
[70] See Biographical Notes, Hugh de Beauchamp, baron of Eaton Soton, Bedfordshire.

boy's length. Everyone marveled at the thread, but they were more gladdened by the boy's health. Without any earthly medicine whatsoever, he deflated. In a short time, he offered himself healed to his doctor.

II.62.[71] CONCERNING RICHARD, KNIGHT *DE ROKELEIA*, HEALED OF A DANGEROUS HEADACHE

A severe headache led the venerable knight, Richard *de Rokeleia*,[72] to tire of living. For nearly four years he wasted away inwardly. For two years, he was so often apprehensive of death that he ran to the bath of confession not once, but seven times every single week, believing that *every day that shone for him was his last*.[73] By the advice of friends, he was instructed and persuaded to bind himself by a vow of pilgrimage to the martyr.[74] After he made the vow, he gave sleep to his eyes and rested for a time. When he woke, he found the pain was gone. And so he went to his liberator without delay. According to what is said, *vow and pay to the Lord your God* [Ps 75:12], he paid his vow and gave gifts to God and the martyr *in the sight of all the people, in the courts of the house of the Lord, in the middle of Jerusalem* of Canterbury [Ps 115:18–19]. The same malady did not touch him later; he was protected by the patronage of the martyr.

II.63. CONCERNING ADAM *DE HADLEGA*, GRAVELY ILL FROM THE EXTREMES OF THE SAME DISEASE

Adam *de Hethlega*[75] was gravely ill for a long time from the extremes of the same disease, so much so that in the sacred time of Lent he was not able to

---

[71] Robertson numbered this as chapter 61 of Book II.
[72] This Richard is most likely from Rokesley/Ruxley, which is part of Greater London today but was in Kent in the medieval period: see Edward Hasted, *A History and Topographical Survey of the County of Kent* (Canterbury, 1797), pp. 1–2, 142–4. It is also possible that he was a member of the Rokele family. There were two Richard de la Rokeles active in the mid and late twelfth century: see Robert Adams, "The Rokeles: An Index for a 'Langland' Family History," in Andrew Cole and Andrew Galloway (eds.), *The Cambridge Companion to Piers Plowman* (Cambridge, 2014), 85–96, at p. 89.
[73] Echoing Horace, Epistle 1, iv.13: "believe that each day which shines on you is your last" [*omnem crede diem tibi diluxisse supremum*].
[74] Here I follow Robertson's emendation of *martyri* for *martyris*: see Robertson, *MTB*, vol. 2, p. 106 n. 4.
[75] The place is unidentified. It is spelled *Helega* and *Hedlega* in various manuscripts: see Robertson, *MTB*, vol. 2, p. 107 n. 1 and Duggan, "Santa Cruz," p. 52. This might refer to Hadleigh, Suffolk.

fast past the third hour of the day. The most excellent martyr of God did not find him unworthy to be shown his presence in a dream. When he was deep in sleep, he saw him standing nearby, saying, as it seemed to him, "Adam, do you sleep?" He denied it and said, "No, lord, I am awake. Who are you?" He said, "I am Thomas the archbishop of Canterbury, who has come to bring you a remedy for your peril. Do you care to be cured?" "Lord," he replied, "I desire nothing as much as a cure." And it seemed as if the saint drove his thumb into the top of his head and turned it in the brain, not without great pain to the sufferer. When he pulled it out, he showed it to him smeared with white corruption and most foul putrefaction. He said, "Look, you are fully cured!" And he added, "Come! Come!" – repeating himself. From that hour the man was made completely well, but, not knowing what he was called to do, he was heedless of the words of the saint who had called him and went about his own business. After a few days spent in such negligence, the saint appeared to him in a dream again, saying "Why are you still delaying here? Don't dawdle. Come as quickly as you are able to come." The man then got up and consulted an elderly priest, seeking his sensible advice on the thrice-repeated command. When he heard that he was being called to render thanks at Canterbury, he obeyed, and appearing at Canterbury, he opened all these things to us.

II.64. CONCERNING JOHN OF THE CHAPEL, WHO, AFTER HE TASTED THE SAINT'S WATER, SNEEZED AND EJECTED A CHERRY STONE THAT HE HAD BORNE FOR NEARLY FOUR YEARS

A young men of excellent qualities, John of the Chapel, who was a clerk of Roger, archdeacon of Shrewsbury,[76] came and eloquently told the story of his miracle to us. He had suffered a blocked-up nostril for four years. He consulted doctors, and they said it was a polyp – that is, a bit of dead flesh which sometimes grows in a nostril – and he found no cure. When the fourth year was nearing its end, all the cause and material of this infirmity moved up between his eyebrows. He feared he would go insane on account of an intense headache. In the end he was confined to bed. His hands, feet, and all his body lay useless, and he could not turn himself from side to side, open or close his hands, or stretch out or pull back his feet. Just as if he were weakened by a sudden paralysis, he lay five or six days without taking any food or drink. Only his power of speech remained. A drink of the water of Canterbury was

---

[76] See Biographical Notes, Roger, archdeacon of Shrewsbury.

brought from that neighborhood to the one in peril. After he had confessed his sins and promised to change his way of life, he vowed to go to Canterbury and in the course of time to erect an altar in honor of the martyr. He then drank the water. Wonderful to relate, and hardly credible even to the faithful, as soon as he had swallowed the water, it felt to him as if it descended like a cold wave through all the limbs and joints of his body, and then rose up again slowly through his whole body. As if it were pursuing the disease, it especially froze his brain, and his head was full of so much more uproar than usual that he was terrified, thinking that the life-giving medicine might send him into sudden death. In the middle of this torment, he sneezed, and it felt as if something dropped into his mouth from his brain. He put his fingers in his mouth and pulled out a cherry stone. He immediately received back all the power of his limbs. He asked for his shoes, put them on and got up without delay, walking here and there through the yard of the house. Made well, though very weakened by continuous fasting, he came to us. He showed us the stone, but he unyieldingly took it away with him.

II.65. CONCERNING [ROBERT][77] OF SPRINGFIELD, WHO OBTAINED THE HEALTH OF HIS SOUL AFTER DRINKING THE HEALTH-GIVING WATER, AS HE HAD REQUESTED

Concerning the health-giving liquid of Canterbury, it is memorable and worthy to remember that just as it brought corporeal health to many ill people, so too, by the martyr's gift, it brought the health of souls to many. Robert, son of Jocelin of Springfield in Essex, a knight of praiseworthy life, full of virtuous deeds and works of mercy, became gravely ill. He summoned one of his acquaintances from London, Anselm, a priest of the church of St. Swithun,[78] for he had heard that he had gone to Canterbury and brought back the water of the most holy martyr. And when he had tasted the relic, the priest urged him to ask with firm faith for the health of his body from the saint. He replied, "Far be it from me to categorically ask for a remedy of a bodily infirmity. May the Lord grant me health of the soul, or what he knows is right for me, through the merits of his saint and the virtue of his relic." He passed the rest of that day and half of the following night with much relief and great contentment of heart, resting with both his lips and eyes closed. Waking after

---

[77] The caption writer mistakenly gave his name as Jocelin.
[78] This is probably St. Swithun, London Stone in Cannon Street, which was established by the late twelfth century: see John Schofield, "Saxon and Medieval Parish Churches in the City of London: A Review," *Transactions of the London and Middlesex Archaeological Society* 45 (1994): 23–146, at p. 131.

a little while, he urgently asked for the viaticum and the rest of the necessities for the dying. The priest and the rest of those who were there wondered at this, and said that it was not necessary, especially since he seemed to be more cheerful than usual. To those earnestly seeking out the reason for his request, he said, "I just saw the blessed martyr Thomas. He seemed to be gloriously dressed and in a beautiful orchard, and he asked me who I was, where I was from, and whether the illness that I had was serious. I answered each question truthfully. 'Do not fear,' he said, 'and do not be sad, for you will come very soon to my society.' And so I cannot stay here with you long, so do not delay in administering to me those things that are appropriate for the dying." When he took the viaticum, he said, "Into your hands I commend my spirit. You have redeemed me, Lord God of truth." And so, more as if he were going to sleep than dying, he sent forth his spirit into the hands of the Lord and the martyr. If there is anyone who does not wish or dare to call this a miracle, and does not disdain to hear our judgement on this, let him know that when we consider the prayer of the knight, the appearance and promise of the saint, and the knight's manner of dying, it seems to us to be a much more glorious miracle than if he had received his health and recovered, for doctors may have been able to accomplish that.

II.66. CONCERNING ROGER, SON OF HERBERT OF BISLEY, TO WHOM SOMETHING SIMILAR HAPPENED

Roger, the son of Herbert of Bisley, a knight of the region of Gloucester, lived a most esteemed life, for he lived like a knight of God rather than a knight of the world. He suffered from a constriction inside his chest, like the pressure of phthisis,[79] such that he could hardly breathe enough air to live. He consulted industrious doctors and gave them generous fees, but when he knew that *the hand of the Lord was heavy upon him* [I Sm 5:6], since *there is support in the midst of plague* [Ps 72:4] for those who *make flesh their arm* [Jer 17:5], he turned his whole heart to the Lord. Because he feared that the words of prayers would not be accepted on his own merits, he asked that the merits of the most holy martyr commend him to God. On the advice of friends, he dispatched and directed a messenger to Canterbury for the water of his relics. He received him back, with the water, on the vigil of the Ascension of the Lord.[80]

---

[79] Here Benedict uses the Greek medical term for consumption or tuberculosis.
[80] The feast of the Ascension, the day when Christ went up to heaven (see Acts 1:6–11), is forty days after Easter. In 1171, the vigil of Ascension Day was on May 5, the feast itself on May 6.

Those who were there wished that he would taste the relic, but since he was a man of great devotion as well as discretion, he said that he thought it would be something like a sin of irreverence to pour such sacrosanct liquid into innards still distended with food. Thus, at his command, it was brought into a nearby church and placed in the custody of a priest, so that when it had been guarded reverently for the night, the knight might more reverently receive the water the next day. On the next day, when he had devotedly strengthened himself with the Lord's sacrament, and when he saw the most holy water brought, as he had asked, in a consecrated cup of the altar, he said to the priest, "Now present to me, lord, the water of the blessed martyr, yet on this condition: that I will, by the intercession of the glorious friend of God, either recover physically in three days, or win the eternal health of my soul this very day." He drank what was in the cup, and then, as if he had premonition of the divine will, he was brought at once, by his own order, from the solitude of an inner chamber to an outer hall. The hour had nearly come when that solemn feast, celebrated throughout the world, was to be celebrated. When he heard the voices of the clerics in the procession modulated in song, he prayed that he might be placed upon ashes and sackcloth, according to the customs of the Christian religion. Everyone resisted and did not do as he asked, as it did not yet seem necessary, but he held sway by means of the keenness and authority of his orders. And so, he was placed on ashes and sackcloth, and he poured out his prayer in this way: "O Lord Jesus Christ, glorious king, who on this day ascended bodily to heaven amongst an ineffable heavenly procession, by the merits of the glorious martyr and your friend Thomas, the archbishop of Canterbury, and the virtue of the holy water, which I received in his name, take me today in your procession, Lord Jesus, and let me merit to come into the society of your martyr." Hardly had he finished saying this when, immediately, without any interval of time, he breathed forth his spirit as if falling into a most sweet sleep. Many clerics, more knights, and a very large number of ordinary people had gathered there, to whom God had granted that they should be present at such a spectacle. They could not wonder enough that by an invocation of the martyr, he should so suddenly be heard, both as to his desire and as to his salvation.

We know of these things from the account of his son, Thomas, a venerable clerk, who came to Canterbury to fulfill his vows to God and the martyr. He declared that he himself had been snatched from the jaws of death by an invocation of the martyr.

II.67. CONCERNING THE SON OF THIS ROGER, THE CLERK THOMAS, WHO WAS CURED OF THREE INFIRMITIES

In this clerk, various infirmities ran together, of which only one, constipation, remains in my memory. After he was deprived of his strength for nearly five weeks, he tasted the aforementioned water. Immediately his bowels were loosened and the chains of all his illnesses were dissolved, and he escaped, healthy and whole.

II.68. CONCERNING THE PILGRIMS IN PERIL ON THE SEA WHO ESCAPED TO DRY LAND BY INVOKING THE MARTYR, THOUGH OTHER SHIPS IN THEIR COMPANY SANK

Pilgrims took ship to go to Saint James of Compostela. After a favorable voyage, they were nearing the port when they were driven back by an opposing wind and a great storm, and for days they were blown here and there. For many days they were driven before various winds, until, with the storm growing in fury, they had no hope of safety or means of defending their lives. Setting the merits of the martyr against the wrath of God, they invoked the saint, asking for his aid, *lest the tempest of water drown them and deep water swallow them up* [Ps 68:16]. If they were rescued, they promised to go to Canterbury and honor the saint with gifts and oblations. The martyr prayed to the Lord for them, as we believe, and he was heard on account of his esteem. Other ships foundering in the same dangerous storm disappeared, but this one, which had been bound by these vows, was driven to the port of Sandwich, where that same saint and martyr of God had taken ship when driven into exile, and where he disembarked at the end of his exile.[81] Other ships *went into the height of the sea, and the tempest swallowed* them [Ps 69:3]. But they left the ship and hastened to Canterbury. They discharged their vows, and, as we believe, told us about these things faithfully. Many of them left crosses with their liberator, Thomas, that they had, by English custom, intended to offer to Saint James.

---

[81] Landlocked today, Sandwich was an important port in the medieval period. Thomas Becket embarked for France from Sandwich on November 2, 1164 and landed there on his return from exile on December 1, 1170.

II.69. CONCERNING OTHERS WHO SUFFERED ON THE SEA WITH THE BREEZE OF WINDS WITHDRAWN

Others suffered on a calm sea. With the breeze of winds withdrawn, the ship stood fixed on the calm waters. The air was immobile, the ship's sail unmoving. And they cried to the Lord, *who produces winds from his treasury* [Ps 134:7], and they put forward the merits of the glorious martyr in commendation of their prayers. They made a collection and promised wax to the martyr. Suddenly, plentiful wind rushed into the sail, and they safely made their way to the port of their desire. All of them began to marvel at the martyr and to say that *the winds and the sea obey him* [Mt 8:27].

II.70. CONCERNING THE KNIGHT WILLIAM OF CHESTER, WHOSE ARM WAS [FOLDED UP][82]

The right arm of William, a knight of Chester, was folded up such that he could not extend it nor remove it from his chest. He invoked the martyr and promised to make the journey to him without delay. Right then, the pain fled and he was brought back to perfect health. He extended the arm freely and easily.

II.71. CONCERNING RALPH OF ESSEX, OPPRESSED BY A SIMILAR TROUBLE

The arm of another man, Ralph of Essex, swelled up, and he was in such a desperate state that no-one held out hope for his life. His arm was thicker than his thigh, and he was not able to bend or move it at all. Confined to his bed for about five weeks, it appeared that the only remedy for the malady would be death. Anxious and not knowing what he ought to do, he at last took a penny, made the sign of the cross on his arm from every angle, and offered the same penny to a poor man in the name of the martyr. In addition, he ordered a wax arm to be made to the length of his arm, to be offered to the martyr after he received his health. The pain vanished instantly, and little by little the swelling subsided.

---

[82] The caption writer mistakenly writes that William's arm was "greatly swollen."

II.72. CONCERNING ADA OF LONDON, WHO WAS NOT ABLE TO TURN HERSELF ONTO HER SIDE NOR MOVE FROM HER BED

Ada, a young woman of London, wasted away from a long illness. Towards the end, she had so little strength that she was unable to lift herself or to turn onto her other side in her bed unless she had someone's help or pulled herself up by a rope hanging above her. After a second remonstrance in a dream, she was transported by boat to a landing ground near Canterbury. She was put onto a horse and held on it by another person's hands, and in this way she was conveyed to Canterbury. When she came to the western suburb of the city, she heard that there was a priest there of good reputation and upright life, and she was put down from her horse in order to bewail her sins in his ears. Wonderful to relate, though she had not been able, as mentioned above, to sit on the horse without someone else's help, when she had been taken down from it, she stood on her feet, and, as the men who had come with her stood by astonished, she went with the priest to the church.[83] She deposited her little burden of sins with the elderly priest, and was filled with hope for greater health by her sudden strength. She hastened to the tomb of Thomas, the friend of God. On that same day, she recovered her former health and left rejoicing.

II.73. CONCERNING THOMAS, SON OF ADAM, WHO HAD THE STONE

A boy of the marshes,[84] Thomas, son of Adam, was being undone by the distress of the stone.[85] He cried and groaned so miserably every time he had to urinate that the hearts of those hearing him were moved to compassion. When he, along with his parents and other ill people, had begged for the martyr's aid, he closed his eyes in a light sleep. When he woke, he needed to urinate and went out of the monastery. Along with the urine, he painlessly passed the stone broken up into very fine sand. He did not have to bear any more trouble from that source.

---

[83] This may well refer to the church of St. Dunstan, located outside the city walls near Canterbury's West Gate. Another possibility is the chapel of St. Nicholas Hospital in Harbledown, located two kilometers west of Canterbury Cathedral.
[84] This likely means Romney Marsh in the south of Kent.
[85] That is, a kidney stone.

II.74. CONCERNING LEFSEDA, WHOSE RIGHT EYE WAS BLIND

The woman Lefseda, who came from the same region, lamented that her right eye was blind. When she had tasted the holy water, she returned to the place of the martyrdom, and she received sight in her right eye that was not much worse than that of the left, even though it had earlier endured a great deal.

II.75. CONCERNING GODIVA OF CHELMSFORD, BLIND FOR FIVE YEARS

Godiva, a woman of Chelmsford, had also been condemned to blindness for five years. Falling down before the sepulchre of the martyr, she saw a ray of the sun. She could discern shapes and colors, but she did not receive perfect sight.

II.76. CONCERNING GEOFFREY OF CHALGRAVE, BLIND FROM BIRTH

At the sepulchre of the glorious martyr Thomas, we saw and testify to the repetition of the miracle in the gospels of the man born blind, the man who replied to the Jews who wondered and maligned, *"from the beginning of the world no-one has heard that anyone has opened the eyes of one born blind"* [Jn 9:32]. A fourteen-year-old boy blind from birth, Geoffrey, son of Liviva of Chalgrave, came to Canterbury by means of the guidance and aid of his mother. His eyes were touched by the precious blood of the martyr. On the following night, his eyes swelled up incredibly. They emitted so much bloody matter that if the true amount were described, it would seem to exceed the bounds of truth. We saw this to happen to innumerable others, both for the torment of unworthy healthy people and for the health of worthy sick people. After the third day, the swelling was reduced, and though his eyes still appeared reddened with congealed blood, he opened them, and proved by clear indications that he was able to see whatever he looked at. Although he was able to perceive different colors of things, he could not put names to any of them with the exception of white. I do not know why he could only name this color, unless it may be that light and brightness, like love and joy and similar things, seem to be akin to human nature and naturally beloved of the soul. Perhaps he was ignorant of the rest of the colors, those that are less natural and less pleasing, and could only easily conceive the conception of pleasing whiteness. The blood left his eyes little by little. Having grown better, to the great joy of his mother as well as others known to him, he went back to his home.

II.77. CONCERNING THE DAUGHTER OF [GILBERT][86] OF THE ISLE OF THANET WHO HAD CONTRACTED FEET

Gilbert, of the Isle of Thanet, brought his small daughter to the martyr and offered her to be straightened out. All of the toes of her right foot were contracted and joined to the sole of her foot. She carried herself on a staff rather than her feet and used the top part of her foot as a sole. She was cast before the sepulchre. Her nerves were stretched out and her toes lifted up. She leapt up with her toes perfectly aligned, and placed her sole, which had never touched the ground, on the ground, though still not confidently.

---

[86] The chapter heading reads "Wibert."

The Chapters of Book III

1. Concerning a candle on the martyr's tomb lit by divine means
2. Item concerning a similar miracle
3. Item concerning the same
4. Item concerning the same
5. Concerning Gunnilda *de Elfiestun*, whose feet had such tender soles that she could not even bear to stand on a pillow
6. Concerning Albreda of Malling, who was wholly unable to move about
7. Concerning Ailmer, a young man of Canterbury, who was so paralyzed that he could not feel the heat of a fire or the cut of a knife
8. Concerning Eilwin of Berkhamsted, who was varicose
9. Concerning Walter, his neighbour, who suffered from two ailments
10. Concerning the daughter of Wedeman of Folkestone, whose fingers on both hands were bent to their base
11. Concerning the fact that hardly anyone presumes to approach the saint's tomb without first driving out all their sins through the door of confession
12. Concerning the blind Liveva *de Lefstanestun*
13. Concerning Robert of London, who recovered sight in one eye but brought back the other blind
14. Concerning Henry, son of Elias, to whom the same thing happened
15. Concerning Avisa of Goshall, who was lame on both sides from birth
16. Concerning the deaf Godiva of Stratford
17. Concerning a certain [William] de Broc who was gravely ill
18. Concerning the extraordinary vision of a boy of Salisbury that he saw with his bodily eyes
19. Concerning the broken pyx of Liveva of Darenth
20. Concerning the water that boiled in a certain person's pyx
21. Concerning another pyx that sprang out of a monk's hand and was split
22. Why and how ampullas were invented to carry the water of the holy martyr
23. Concerning a certain man who denied a poor man requesting the water, and later found his ampulla empty when he was about to give some water to a rich man
24. Concerning another who found his ampulla empty when he wished to share the water with one requesting it, but when he showed the ampulla later, he found it full

25. Concerning a third man who carried away two filled ampullas and found that neither had liquid
26. Concerning Gunnilda *de Hameldene*, swollen and cured by means of a stomach flux
27. Concerning a certain Richard, who had dysentery
28. Concerning William of Higham Ferrers, who was not able to walk on account of contracted sinews
29. Concerning those who went back cured who are unknown to us
30. Concerning [Godfrey] of Lillingston, who had a diseased spot in the pupil of an eye
31. Concerning a certain blind Beatrice, who was cured before she came to the martyr
32. Concerning a boy of St. Valery, Thomas, who carried his foot suspended above the ground
33. Concerning William, the son of Payne *de Pech*, whose arm had been made useless by paralysis
34. Concerning the blinded Alvida *de Aedgardintona*
35. Concerning the crippled Godwin of Braithwell
36. Concerning Iselda, the daughter of certain knight Henry, who was deaf for [six] years
37. Concerning the epileptic wife of the same knight
38. Concerning Gunnilda of Luton, whose menses entirely ceased
39. Concerning a certain Emelina, whose menses continually flowed
40. Concerning those who were cured at Whitchurch
41. Concerning Griffin the Welshman, who, having seen a beautiful vision, was beautifully cured
42. Concerning two others from Wales who were cured
43. Concerning the overturned vessel in which the saint's water was retained and did not flow out of its uncorked mouth
44. Concerning the man who received the eye-salve of the holy blood of Canterbury in his eyes and was cured at the city of Rochester
45. Concerning a certain man born blind, who received sight in the middle of the street
46. Concerning another who received sight at Canterbury
47. Concerning [Wivelina] of Littlebourne whose head had swollen up

48. Concerning Matilda of Thornbury, who had been ill for a long time
49. Concerning Aeliza, wife of Alan of Ratling, who was suddenly cured through vomiting
50. Concerning the daughter of Edric of Ramsholt
51. [Concerning] a certain cheese that was lost and miraculously found through an invocation of the martyr
52. Concerning a certain man freed from quinsy
53. Concerning the gold that the saint gave to a certain man
54. Concerning the silver that the saint wittily took away from another
55. Concerning a certain Flemish man's daughter whose leg was broken
56. Concerning a hawk that the same Flemish man had not been able to capture except by means of an invocation of the martyr's name
57. Concerning a certain man who had a dislocated arm for five weeks
58. Concerning a certain nun who was mute and recovered when the glove of the martyr was placed on her chest
59. Concerning a certain Matilda who was greatly swollen
60. Concerning Hugh, the cellarer of the church of Jervaulx, who was gravely ill
61. Concerning the monk Radulf healed at Byland
62. Concerning the feverish Richard, a knight of Stanley, who also had contracted fingers
63. Concerning a certain boy on whose eye a pustule grew so large that the boy was not able to close the eyelid
64. Concerning a certain priest whose hand and arm were useless from paralysis, and how crosses were erected in three places where the martyr had dismounted from his horse, and of the miracles that happened there
65. Concerning [Odilda] of Southwell, who received her sight at one of the crosses
66. Concerning another woman who similarly received her sight there
67. Concerning a three-year-old boy who was brought forth blind from his mother's womb
68. Concerning Eliza of Dunton with a disease of the heart
69. Concerning Goditha of Hayes, suffering from dropsy
70. Concerning the blind Aldida from the county of Staffordshire
71. Concerning the similarly blind Hedewic from the region of Gloucester
72. Concerning Leuric of the region of Barking in [Suffolk], whose hand was struck by paralysis

73. Concerning Luciana, the daughter of Walter Torel, who was struck by paralysis and lost the use of her tongue on account of her father's curse
74. Concerning a certain man with a hernia
75. Concerning the blind Robert *de Baalum*
76. Concerning a little boy named Henry, whose right foot was fixed over his left foot in the shape of a cross
77. Concerning the two lame daughters of Godbold of Boxley
78. Concerning candles relit in another place where the martyr dismounted from his horse

BOOK III

III.1. CONCERNING A CANDLE ON THE MARTYR'S TOMB LIT BY DIVINE MEANS

The great festival day on which Mount Zion glowed with heavenly fire and the Holy Spirit descended on the disciples of Christ in tongues of fire was already near at hand.[1] Oh happy day, not only because of the feast's celebration, but also because a miracle that preceded the feast was similar to it, making us happier still. The kindness of the Lord Jesus would not allow a delay of the glory of such a miracle until the day of the feast. Anticipating that day of glory with this day of glory,[2] he sent heavenly fire upon the tomb of the saint. By the similarity of the miracle, he pointed out that Thomas was the co-disciple and co-heir of those apostles[3] and gave to the still grieving church the grace of a new consolation.

For two entire days, the daughter of Aylward, a citizen of Canterbury, had fallen on the ground, unwittingly struck herself, and filled the church with her cries. By means of an invocation of the saint, the illness that she had was at last taken away, but she remained concerned about an offering which she did not have. A certain matron who chanced to be passing by and carrying a small amount of wax in her hand took pity on her. She took some thread for a needle from her garment, doubled it over on itself and pressed a good deal of wax around it. Then she gave it to the girl so that she could offer it to the martyr. The candle was lit, and, by the order of the superintending monk, it was placed in the middle of the sepulchre in order to burn there – though the happiness of the ensuing miracle altered his design. A short time later, a light wind blew in the window opposite. Among all the candles placed around there, it only extinguished the girl's candle: its wax was thicker and its wick

---

[1] Benedict is referring to the Christian feast of Pentecost, when, after Christ's resurrection, his disciples received the Holy Spirit in the form of tongues of fire appearing above their heads: see Acts 2:1–4. The traditional understanding was that this happened on Mount Zion in Jerusalem.
[2] Which day that was Benedict leaves unclear. It must have been sometime shortly before Pentecost, which is celebrated on the Sunday falling fifty days (effectively seven weeks) after Easter. In 1171, Pentecost Sunday fell on May 16.
[3] For another story linking Becket and the apostles, see I.4 above.

more slender. Since the abundance of wax and thinness of the wick were not in due proportion to one another, the candle was barely able to burn and was easily extinguished. The monk saw the smoking wick, called a servant and said, "Do you see that the girl's candle has been extinguished? Relight it." He hastened to do so, and as he was putting down what he had in his hands, the candle was seen to relight without any human assistance. Not just one man, I say, was present at this glorious vision, but the people, who had seen that candle so far extinguished that it was sending up a lot of smoke. It appeared to be divinely relit such that its flame produced a long tail. Although the wick was thin and the wax dense, as was said above, it was so quickly consumed by fire that it was nearly all devoured. It was extinguished as quickly as possible so that at least some of it would be left, in order that the wax too would not be lost along with the flame.

Now let those traitors and parricides who killed the saint, accusing him of being a traitor, say where they have ever read or heard that any traitor or criminal has ever been been glorified by such a miracle. Fire from the Lord descended on Nadab and Abiud, the sons of Aaron, but it destroyed rather than dazzled them.[4] The fire of the Lord was kindled against the murmurers in the desert, but it was a devouring rather than life-giving fire.[5] Heavenly fire fell down on two hundred and fifty supporters of Korah, but it killed them all.[6] At the time of Elijah, fire from heaven surrounded the two battalions of fifty, but it destroyed rather than illuminating them.[7] Light from heaven shone about Saul, but it did not illuminate him: it blinded him.[8] But when fire descended from the Lord upon our Thomas, it fell not on a criminal for punishment, but rather upon the innocent for his glory. And so let the evil ones cease persecuting the glorious friend of God even when he is dead, and reckon up the brightness of his innocence and the fervour of his charity from his miraculous deeds. For what does light descending on light mean, unless

---

[4] See Leviticus 10:1–2. Nadab and Abiu were destroyed by the Lord's fire after they made offerings of "strange fire" against the Lord's commands.

[5] See Numbers 11:1–3. During the exodus, the people of Israel complained about fatigue. The Lord became angry and sent down fire that killed a number of them.

[6] See Numbers 16:35. In the course of the exodus, a man named Korah challenged the authority of Moses. Two hundred and fifty of his followers were destroyed by fire sent by the Lord.

[7] See 2 Kings 1:10–12. When the king Ahaziah sent a commander in charge of fifty men to the prophet Elijah, Elijah called down heavenly fire on them, and he did so again when Ahaziah sent a second delegation of fifty men.

[8] See Acts 9:3, the famous story of Saul (the future apostle Paul) being blinded on the road to Damascus.

that the martyr was the *son of light, a lamp of the whole church, a dwelling of the Holy Spirit,* in whom *the fire that the Lord came to cast upon the earth* had burned?[9] It seems to mean for our Thomas what it meant long ago for the wondrous Martin, for a heavenly light appeared upon Martin as well, though he was then standing at the altar, not lying in his tomb.[10] The Lord gave glory of this kind to Martin only once, to Elijah twice,[11] but he privileged our Thomas with four occurrences of this miracle.

III.2. ITEM CONCERNING A SIMILAR MIRACLE

The martyr favoured the second day of Pentecost for us in a similar way.[12] He deigned to bestow on us and allow us to conserve that heavenly light which we mourned to have lost earlier. A teenage girl, Goditha, whose father was Baldwin of Wye, was seriously ill, and on that day the saint gave her the gift of his customary mercy. The girl had two lit candles. One was resting on the pavement and the other was affixed to the wall. Unsteady on her feet and weak in body, she was unable to stand, and collapsing to the ground, she extinguished the candle on the pavement. When she got up to relight it, her hand shook, and she knocked off the candle fixed to the wall. She took up the candles deprived of light in both her hands and turned to the multitude that had assembled, saying, "Oh woe is me! Look, both of my candles have gone out!" Becoming more upset as she saw no light in that entire crowd of people, she saw her sister far off in the church and said, "Sister, don't you see? Light my candles." Her sister refused, saying that she was afraid to touch her or to come near to her. Sighing and moaning, the girl said, "Oh most sweet Lady, virgin Mary, oh holy lord Thomas, martyr of Jesus Christ, what am I to do? Look, my candles have gone out." Oh, the kindness of the martyr! Oh, his compassion, as sweet as honey! Truly, *his eyes are on the* afflicted, *and his*

---

[9] In this passage, Benedict draws on very familiar Christian imagery: for "son of light" see Matthew 5:14, Luke 16:8, John 12:36, Ephesians 5:8, 1 Thessalonians 5:5, etc.; for "lamp of the church" see Matthew 5:15, Mark 4:21, Luke 8:16–18 and 11:33–6, etc.; for "dwelling of the Holy Spirit," see John 14:17; Romans 8:11; 1 Corinthians 3:16, etc. At the end of the sentence is a reference to Luke 12:49, in which Christ says, "I am come to cast fire on the earth."

[10] For this miracle of St. Martin of Tours (d.397), see *Sulpicius Severus: The Complete Works,* trans. Richard Goodrich (New York, 2015), II.2, p. 213. See also IV.58 below, where Benedict references another miracle of St. Martin.

[11] Here Benedict refers again to 2 Kings 1:10–12.

[12] By the "second day of Pentecost," Benedict means the day following Pentecost Sunday. In 1171, this was May 17.

ears are held to their prayers [Ps 33:16]. As the girl looked here and there, and between her plaintive groans turned her eyes back to the candles, they were both aflame with new fire. She looked at the great crowd which had come to the feast day and had seen the glory of this miracle, and she said, "Did you see, my lords? Look, the blessed martyr Thomas has relit my candles." It would be most difficult to relate how great was the exultation of all, how many showers of tears they shed, and how many thanks were rendered to God. With bent knees and hands held high, they gave glory to God. After many expressions of thanksgiving, they dispersed in order to communicate their joy to the whole city of Canterbury. From the fire of the candles, all the lights of the church were lit. The candles were preserved in part: what was left was divided and handed out to petitioners. Through it all, the Lord was blessed, whose *fire is in the Zion* of Canterbury, *and furnace in the Jerusalem* of heaven [Is 31:9].

III.3. ITEM CONCERNING THE SAME

At once, the gift of grace which he had given he doubled in the same moment, so that a subsequent miracle would confirm the earlier one. The people were rushing in throngs to the new fire and bringing back the heavenly sign with them to their own homes. A woman was hastening with the rest with her lit candle intending to light the hearth of her home. A gust of wind at the door of the church extinguished the candle she carried. "Saint Thomas, martyr, help!" she said, "I have lost the light I was carrying." Hardly had she called upon the saint when suddenly, by divine will, she received a flame. The priest Frederick, a most reliable witness to this event, was there, as well as several clerks and a great crowd of the laity. But as to the rest of the candles upon which the divine fire came, though we have countless witnesses, we have not recorded in writing due to the crudeness of their names.

III.4. ITEM CONCERNING THE SAME

The third day of Pentecost was marked by the same sign in our presence. A certain Alan was praying at the sepulchre of the martyr, assisting his little son, whom he had brought contracted. The boy was holding a candle in his right hand. So that it would not slip from his weakened hand, the father was helping him by placing his own hand under his son's. By chance, the candle went out. The man was standing without light before the lamp of England, and it was as if in that moment light came forth from our light: a new fire lit the extinguished candle. And so in the festival of the Paraclete of the Holy

Spirit, the Paraclete[13] caused those upon whom He looked favorably to rejoice four times by means of fire, the miracles in beautiful harmony with the feast.[14]

III.5. CONCERNING GUNNILDA *DE ELFIESTUN*, WHOSE FEET HAD SUCH TENDER SOLES THAT SHE COULD NOT EVEN BEAR TO STAND ON A PILLOW

In those days, there was no lack of the grace of healing for the sick as well. For about two and a half years, a grave illness ate away at the wretched limbs of Gunnilda, from the village which the English call *Elfiestun*.[15] In the end, all the substance of the disease settled in her feet, and she was unable to walk at all or to stand for a moment, not even on a pillow. The soles of her feet were so tender and painful that they were oppressed by the lightest touch. Confined to her bed, for six months she had lived a hateful life, as if she were passing through a continual death. She was carried by two servants to the place where the martyr exchanged temporal death for life eternal. Resting there awhile, she had pressed on with her prayers when suddenly, her strength restored, she rose to her feet. Her servants hastened to hold her up, but she said, "Go and leave me to myself. I will try to go the sepulchre of my lord on foot." She came, though with a slow and faltering gait, and she produced witnesses to her illness to those of us sitting there. Having made her prayer, she went to her inn, which was located a considerable distance away, with a firmer step. She regained her health and left.

III.6. CONCERNING ALBREDA OF MALLING, WHO WAS WHOLLY UNABLE TO MOVE ABOUT

Albreda, the wife of Eustace of Malling, had a miscarriage due to an injury to her side. Taking to her bed, she wasted away with sickness for about a year.

---

[13] "Paraclete," a Greek word meaning counselor or comforter, is found a number of times in the Gospel of John (see John 14:15, 14:26, 15:26, and 16:7). The Greek term was retained in the Latin Vulgate translation. Medieval Christians interpreted the Paraclete to be synonymous with the Holy Spirit, the third member of the Trinity.

[14] Benedict included an antiphon celebrating these relighting miracles in the liturgical Office for Thomas Becket (Cantus Database ID 200111): *Ad Thomae memoriam/ quarter lux descendit/ et in Sancti gloriam/ cereos accendit* [At the tomb of Thomas, light descends four times, and lights candles to the glory of the saint]. See Slocum, *Liturgies*, p. 206, and Reames, "Liturgical Offices," p. 577.

[15] The place is unidentified. Robertson suggested that this might refer to Elvaston in Derbyshire. It could also be Alfriston in East Sussex (I am grateful to John Jenkins for this suggestion).

After this, although she was delighted that her ability to rise from her bed returned, she was unable to walk about both from weakness of heart and from distress of body. She was brought to the place made holy by the blood of the martyr and gave herself to prayer. She rose healed and able to walk correctly and steadily. We both saw and spoke to her, and she declared to us that she was not distressed by any impairment due to illness or weakness.

III.7. CONCERNING AILMER, A YOUNG MAN OF CANTERBURY, WHO WAS SO PARALYZED THAT HE COULD NOT FEEL THE HEAT OF A FIRE OR THE CUT OF A KNIFE

A young man of Canterbury, Ailmer, was completely paralyzed from his navel on down and was carried about in a basket every day. For nearly two years, he had lived only half alive. If you were to thrust a red-hot knife through the deadened parts of his body, you would have seen him carrying on with his face unchanged, demonstrating by an absence of signs that he felt nothing at all. His feet were once placed in the fire, and he did not pull them out or show any terror of the flames. For some days, as was said, he was brought in a basket to the saint. He was placed on the marble pavement of the church and gradually received the motion and use of his limbs. The martyr *set his feet upon a rock and directed his steps* [Ps 39:3]. Because he was weak from the long illness, he took up crutches as aids at first. In a short time, he became so strong that he left them with the one who had made him strong. And so *the Lord put a new canticle in the mouth* of the people, *a song to our God. Many saw this and feared and hoped in the Lord* [Ps 39:4].

III.8. CONCERNING EILWIN OF BERKHAMSTED, WHO WAS VARICOSE

Eilwin of Berkhamsted was afflicted with pain in the kidneys and the thighs. Eventually he became unable to do any work and was made physically incapable. For more than sixteen years, he moved about relying wholly on two crutches. We thought he was varicose on account of the curvature of his back, for he was bent over and was not able to look up.[16] He had wrapped leather and rags on the tops of his crutches to prevent them from abrading or injuring his armpits, and also put iron on their tips to keep them from being worn

---

[16] It is difficult to understand why Benedict speaks of Eilwin as being "varicose," as varicose veins usually impact the legs and not the spine. Perhaps he meant *gibbosus* [hunchbacked] or some version of *scoliosis*.

away from constant use. After about sixteen years, as noted above, without any improvement in his condition, he saw very many people return in good health from the memorial of the martyr, who is most deserving of praise and commemoration. He knew these people had gone there ill and infirm. He set out on the journey in the company of others and headed to Canterbury, though he could not travel as far each day. He finally arrived at the place and, kneeling as best he could before the sarcophagus of the martyr, he undertook with offering and prayer to appease God and the martyr in order to escape the infirmity inflicted on him for his sins. Right after he made his oblation, he rose up from the ground, and then, with his whole body trembling, he again fell prostrate on the ground. He immediately got up again and stood upright on his feet without using a crutch. I was there, and when I saw this, I led him and another ill man from his neighborhood (of whom I will speak more subsequently), apart from the crowd, though he was still leaning on one crutch as he walked. He lay for a time in prayer, and then called over a boy, giving him the crutches to carry to the martyr. And so, with his hands held up to heaven, he followed the boy who went before him carrying the crutches. When the people saw this, they fell to the earth on bended knees and dissolved in tears for joy. He left his crutches with the saint in thanksgiving and departed rejoicing, healed and whole.

III.9. CONCERNING WALTER, HIS NEIGHBOUR, WHO SUFFERED FROM TWO AILMENTS

He had a companion for his journey from his neighborhood, Walter, who had come being led by his wife on account of the darkness of his eyes. His genitals had swollen to an immense size, and against his will he had lived a life that for ten years had become a sort of living death. Incurable by men, he sought a cure from the martyr. With such offering as he was able to make, he was honoring God in his martyr, God, who does not attend to the mere size of a gift, but rather to how much is given out of the giver's means. Just as he was the companion of his neighbor in the labor of the journey, so too he became his companion in the joy of health restored. He confessed himself to have as much restoration of sight as he had absence of pain, and his genitals were no longer swollen as well. To tell it briefly, these two needy men came to the tomb together. Both fell to the ground together, both rose together, together they were cured by divine mercy, and together they departed with great joy. All of us who were there and witnessed this event were left by them rejoicing, or, rather, weeping with joy. I saw both of them later. They were not clad in rags as before, but were well-dressed men of robust strength.

III.10. CONCERNING THE DAUGHTER OF WEDEMAN OF FOLKESTONE, WHOSE FINGERS ON BOTH HANDS WERE BENT TO THEIR BASE

The fingers on both hands of the seven-year-old daughter of Wedeman of Folkestone were bent to their base. She was fed by the hands of others: her sinews had been contracted since her birth and she had never been able to feed herself. Her father put her on a horse and brought her to the martyr. He placed her in the middle of the church and assiduously commended her to God and the martyr. The following day, all her fingers were stretched out with the exception of the middle finger of her right hand, which heavenly power left somewhat curved. Through confession of his sins and suitable penance, the father had taken precaution lest his sins or those of the girl hinder her healing, or lest he fail to escape the sorrow he had suffered on her account for so long a time.

III.11. CONCERNING THE FACT THAT HARDLY ANYONE PRESUMES TO APPROACH THE SAINT'S TOMB WITHOUT FIRST DRIVING OUT ALL THEIR SINS THROUGH THE DOOR OF CONFESSION

In this way, through the merits of his blessed and glorious martyr, the mercy of the Almighty makes even more provision for the health of souls than for the health of bodies. Now hardly anyone presumes to approach the saint's sepulchre to ask for anything, or even to enter the doors of the church of Canterbury, unless such person is first rebaptized in the fountain of confession and of shed tears, promising a more correct form of life in the future. We dare say without any doubt in *the word of truth*[17] that many enmeshed in sin for many years had sickened spiritually without the medicine of confession. On account of their reverence for the martyr, they renounced their old lives and the darkness of their sins before they dared to approach his most holy body, fleeing for refuge to the light of innocence by the way of confession. It does not seem to be off subject to have touched on this briefly. Since the soul is humanity's greater part, so likewise its cure constitutes the more glorious miracle.

---

[17] "The word of truth" is a phrase found in the New Testament: see 2 Corinthians 6:7, Colossians 1:5, and James 1:5 and 1:18.

III.12. CONCERNING THE BLIND LIVEVA *DE LEFSTAN-ESTUN*

Among those who *had eyes but saw not* [Ps 113:13] was Liveva, the wife of Godric *de Lefstanestun*.[18] We saw that once her blindness was wiped away, she could see so clearly that she was able to thread the narrow eye of a needle in our presence, a feat that many onlookers asked her to repeat again and again for the sake of curiousity or delight. In addition, her hands, which were once dreadfully swollen, she brought home slender and thin, the swelling reduced.

III.13. CONCERNING ROBERT OF LONDON, WHO RECOVERED SIGHT IN ONE EYE BUT BROUGHT BACK THE OTHER BLIND

A certain Robert of London, who had not been able to see the soil nor the sun for four years, received light at our light. It came out well for him in the right eye and badly in the left, for the right eye was given light, but the left he took home in the same condition as when he came.

III.14. CONCERNING HENRY, SON OF ELIAS, TO WHOM THE SAME THING HAPPENED

Much the same thing happened to a boy of the marshes,[19] Henry the son of Elias. He came with both eyes blind. When he returned home, one eye had sight.

III.15. CONCERNING AVISA OF GOSHALL, WHO WAS LAME ON BOTH SIDES FROM BIRTH

Avisa of Goshall,[20] the daughter of Ordgar the skinner, was rolling around, shouting and wailing, with the others in the church. Her mother had brought her into this light lame on both sides. The pain she had been suffering from the lengthening of her sinews ceased, and in a panting voice she declared that she had been straightened. We sought witnesses of her illness and found two trustworthy ones. Moreover, since what sight proves is more credible than

---

[18] The place is unidentified. Robertson suggested it was Leytonstone, but it could also be a similarly named manor near Rayleigh, Essex: see Percy H. Reaney, "Lestenston or Harberts in Rayleigh," *Transactions of the Essex Archaeological Society* 20:1 (1930): 95–6.
[19] Benedict likely means Romney Marsh in Kent.
[20] This probably refers to Goshall near Ash, Kent.

that which is received by hearing, she was ordered to walk here and there in the churchyard, and she left us in no doubt at all. The girl was already of marriageable age, about sixteen years old.

III.16. CONCERNING THE DEAF GODIVA OF STRATFORD

The woman Godiva, coming from Stratford, *had become like one who hears not* [Ps 37:15]. She heard a roaring in her head like the sound of loud thunder, which kept out the sound of voices and all other sounds from her ears. She did not know how to describe the pain in her head precisely. A drop of the water that expels every kind of illness was placed in her deaf ears. As she prayed for a short while at the tomb, an adequate and complete cure of her former pain was given to her by God. With her ears restored to their use and quiet restored to her head, she went home cured, carrying back a worthy reward of deserving devotion and faith.

III.17. CONCERNING A CERTAIN [WILLIAM][21] DE BROC WHO WAS GRAVELY ILL

If the saint should *love those who love him*, how could this be said to be great? Even *the publicans and heathens do this* [Mt 5:46–7]. Charity's embrace is narrow if it admits only the friend and excludes the enemy. The honey-sweet benevolence of our most kind father Thomas not only patiently bore with his enemies and brought them to repentance, but also most kindly converted and admitted them to grace. Robert de Broc, the usher of the king's chamber,[22] had a brother of the same surname, William, whose members had been wasted by severe fevers for four years. In addition, he was tortured by sharp pains of the stomach and vitals: it seemed as if he were being cut into small pieces by sharp razors. With the disease rooted in him, he was frequently, though not continuously, confined to the tedium of bed, at one point for three weeks, at another for four or five weeks, and then he lay there for the space of an entire year. Both his chest and his stomach swelled up in an unusual manner and he felt no benefit from any medication. Then, when the glory of miracles by which the Lord exalted his saint was made known to him, he was contrite at heart, because he had denigrated the saint both when he lived in the flesh and when he was glorified after the deposition of his flesh. He hastened to Canterbury

---

[21] The caption writer mistakenly named Robert as the subject of the miracle.
[22] See Biographical Notes, Robert de Broc.

to make amends so that he might gain his health. He drank the health-giving liquid, and had hardly returned to his inn when he vomited out the material of the disease, a green and multi-colored poison. On the next day, he used the same medicine again, and merited to experience the same efficacious grace. After he received the water on the third day, his nausea ceased, and he did not vomit. Having been given his former health back, he promised not to deny any of these things to any of the evildoers.

III.18. CONCERNING THE EXTRAORDINARY VISION OF A BOY OF SALISBURY THAT HE SAW WITH HIS BODILY EYES

A marvel that I ought to have told earlier, but which I had forgotten, I will tell as it has now come back to mind. At dawn on a Sunday, Richard, the son of a certain Roger of Salisbury, rose and left Salisbury on his way to Marlborough, bringing to his uncles and friends the news of his mother's death. Having left the city, he came across an old woman who asked him for alms. The boy had purchased two loaves, one smaller than the other; of these, he divided the larger one and offered it to the poor woman. When he was on the great plain, having gone about five miles along his way, he encountered three men of tall stature who were dressed in white woolen clothing as if they were hermits. The one in the middle was a little taller than the others. He had a small amount of grey hair and held in his hands a bronze vessel full of blood. When the boy saw them, he was terrified and his hair stood on end, especially when he saw the blood. He thought that they had killed someone, for the plain was very large, and the place was far from any human dwelling. Yet they seemed like very venerable and religious persons, especially the one who carried the blood. He alone spoke to the boy, and he proceeded to ask him where he came from and where he was going. "Do you carry bread?" he added. "I am carrying it, lord," he said. Then he said, "Offer part of it to us." The boy, looking on the speaker's face that deserved reverence, showed reverence to him as he was able, and gave him the loaf of bread that was whole. Then he said to him, "I do not want the whole one, but the divided loaf, the other half of which you gave to the old woman this morning." To the boy wondering at this, he then said something of greater admiration: "Do you remember what was shown to you this night in your dreams?" The astounded boy said, "I remember well." In his dreams, he had seen a young man with an angelic face who had guided him and had showed him, as if he were standing on a high wall, the torments of hell and the delightful house of Paradise. The boy said that he remembered these things and marvelled that he knew all of it. Emboldened, he questioned the one who had questioned him: "What is it, lord, that you carry?" He said, "The blood of the blessed Thomas, archbishop of Canterbury," and added, "Do not go on, son, but turn back immediately, and say to the dean and canons of Salisbury that they are to make a procession around the city. If they do not do this, let them know that a great storm will come to the town." And when the boy was leaving, he said, "go quickly, and beware lest you look back before you have gone a furlong from us." The boy looked back, therefore, only after he had gone a furlong, and he found that he alone was on the plain. No matter how far or where he looked about him, he was able to see no-one, in a place where for five or six miles not even a little fellow could have hidden himself. And he returned, marvelling over this more than anything else. He told the canons what he had seen and heard, and they believed him.

These things happened in the first days of miracles, namely on the Sunday before the first Ascension of the Lord after the passion of the martyr,[23] before the blood and water of the martyr had been carried to distant regions. He who wishes to ascribe these things to a miracle, let him do so. Having pondered these things as I am able, it seems to me that the blood that the three men carried could be meant to signify that the blood of the lamb of Canterbury[24] would be carried through the entire earth, as is the case in the present day. Indeed, in a short time his miracles were greatly multiplied, the fame of the martyr spoken of far and wide, and the water with his blood carried off to all the regions of England.

III.19. CONCERNING THE BROKEN PYX OF LIVEVA OF DARENTH

All eagerly drank in joy from the waters of our health-giving fountain and carried the water home with them in vessels of wood or clay. In the multitude, a young woman of Darenth, Liveva, put forward her pyx and asked that it be filled with the life-giving drink. But when the brother who was preparing it for the ill ones at that hour raised his eyes and saw the great crowd coming to him, he apportioned a smaller amount than usual to each one. He was fearing and guarding against a scarcity of the water, which was already insufficient. The young woman, having received a portion of the water in her vessel, insisted that she receive more. When he refused and attended to the others, she stole what he had denied her. She secretly took up a cup that she had seen

---

[23] I.e., Sunday May 2, 1171 (in 1171, Ascension Day fell on May 6).
[24] In the New Testament, Christ is frequently compared to a sacrificial lamb: for references to "the blood of the lamb," see Revelation 7:14 and 12:11 and 1 Peter 1:19. See also p. 78, n.8 above.

placed near her and poured the liquid it held into her vessel. As soon as the pious theft of the water touched the pyx, the pyx split in the midst of the crowd of people, and she lost both what she had been given and what she had stolen. Reproached by the monk, she mourned greatly. Having left the vessel to be hung up with the others similarly broken, she left most sad and weeping, and not a little perplexed on account of this.

III.20. CONCERNING THE WATER THAT BOILED IN A CERTAIN PERSON'S PYX

Something of considerably greater, or at least of equal shame happened to my schoolfellow, who was commended both for his knowledge of letters and the grace of his manners. For *nothing is altogether blessed*.[25] There is no man who lives who does not sin. Even *the just fail seven times in a day* [Prv 24:16]: *all have sinned and fallen short of the glory of God* [Rom 3:23]. So let him not be aggrieved with me, as I do not write this to disturb him, but rather for the glory of the martyr, especially as *he who says he has not sinned is a liar, and there is no truth in him* [1 Jn 1:8]. This young man, having received water in his pyx before the altar next to the tomb, was holding it in his hand when the water boiled up through the mouth of the vessel. He was not able to retain or stop it. The monk who had filled it with water said, "Put the pyx back down on the altar: it does not seem to want to be held by you." He put it down and immediately the water subsided. Wiping and drying off the exterior of the vessel and the interior of the lid, he received the relic in his hand and moved away, but he found he could not go freely through the mausoleum of the martyr. He had hardly gone two or three steps when the water again came out of the vessel. It was like a boiling pot that cannot subside. The monk said, "What is this? Where are you coming from? I think you were in a place of ill repute. Take your hands off the vessel." He put it back on the altar again, and when it stood there, the overflowing water and *the waves were stilled* [Ps 106:29]. Having carefully turned and dried the vessel, the cleric picked it up for a third time, and with slow steps he reached the middle of the tomb. The waters leapt up and flowed out in abundance, with much more force than the first or the second time. The monk called to him and said to bring back the vessel. He disregarded this and went to the man from whom he had received it. He gave it back to him, and hardly had it come into the hand of the other man when all the force of the waters stilled and the water stayed within the vessel. We all marvelled, and we did not find a cause for the

---

[25] Horace, *Odes*, book II, poem 16, lines 27–8.

unnatural event. Yet there certainly must be a cause, for nothing happens on earth without a cause. There was a clear enough cause when a no less delightful miracle happened in the hand of the aforesaid monk. This monk, who had earlier laughed at the clerk, was later himself made an object of laughter for all.

III.21. CONCERNING ANOTHER PYX THAT SPRANG OUT OF A MONK'S HAND AND WAS SPLIT

There were already many vessels split open by means of contact with the water that had been hung on the wall as a sign. In the first days of miracles, they split to a greater degree, then less so as time passed. The aforesaid brother was holding in his hand a vessel with a little crack that a woman had left with him. He was silently thinking to himself: "Why is it that the martyr shows the glory of his strength to a lesser extent and exercises the power of his forces to a lesser degree than usual? At first, the pyxes cracked open with such great fissures that everyone was amazed. Some of them even broke into pieces. But now, the clefts are hardly the width of a needle or straw. Why should this one be hung up with the rest? If the saint had split this one to the same degree as the others, it would be worthy, I confess, to be numbered with the others, but it will stay with me: I will not hang it up. Is it not very beautiful, and could it not be useful for me for another purpose? I will not hang it up for such a tiny fissure." While he was silently reflecting on these things, the lower part of the pyx, which, by turning it upside down, he had made into its top, was suddenly torn out of his hand by a divine impulse, such that he only held on to the lid. It tumbled a long way upon the straw and made such a sound that the brother marvelled and trembled along with the others who were there. He quickly threw the lid onto the ground as well and said, "Go from me, devil, you are from the evil side!" At length, later on, when he picked the pyx up from the ground, he found it marvellously cracked from the top down. We asked the brother what he had done, that he had become like one of the people? Fearing that he would be suspected of having done something worse, he revealed his greed, if this ought to be censured by the word greed, to everyone. And so, this miracle was as much a joke and source of laughter to many as of admiration.

III.22. WHY AND HOW AMPULLAS WERE INVENTED TO CARRY THE WATER OF THE HOLY MARTYR

I would bore my readers if I put each case of a broken vessel into a separate chapter. In order to move on to different stories, many must be condensed and discussed briefly. Some vessels were cracked, some were split into parts, and the water of others boiled, either upwards through the mouth or through the medium of the solid wood. In others, the water suddenly disappeared. In order to test whether the breaking of their vessels should be credited as a miracle, many people kept them full of water overnight, but when these pyxes were filled with the holy water, the people lost both the water and the pyxes. In the lids of many of the broken pyxes, we found women's mirrors. Even a pyx made of boxwood did not remain intact when contacted by the water. Many people did not trust vessels made of wood and relied instead on ceramic vessels, but they found themselves leaving equally confounded, because when the pots were filled with the liquid, some immediately shattered. In others, the liquid suddenly disappeared. There was, therefore, great fear and anxiety in all who came to the water. They worried that the water would be subtracted in some way or that they would be the subject of mockery or derision to those looking on. At last, so that the special and greatest cause of the breakings be brought to people's notice, and the will of God and the martyr be known to all, it came into the heart of a young man that he should make ampullas out of lead and out of tin by the work of casting, and the miracle of breaking ceased. We know that this was the divine will, such that the ampullas of the physician of Canterbury might be carried throughout all the earth, and that the whole world might know his sign in his pilgrims and in those he cured. For the first vessels were carried hidden under their clothing, but the ampullas were openly hung around the neck.[26]

III.23. CONCERNING A CERTAIN MAN WHO DENIED A POOR MAN REQUESTING THE WATER, AND LATER FOUND HIS AMPULLA EMPTY WHEN HE WAS ABOUT TO GIVE SOME WATER TO A RICH MAN

Even in some people's ampullas, the water disappeared. A man in Bedfordshire refused a pauper who asked him for a portion of the water. The next day, a rich man asked for the water. He wished to give him some, but he found that his ampulla, despite being sealed up, was empty. Although I learned about

---

[26] A panel in Canterbury Cathedral window nV shows pilgrims with ampullas around their necks queuing to receive the water relic: see Koopmans, "Pilgrimage Scenes," 708-15. On these ampullas, see Jennifer Lee, "Searching for Signs: Pilgrims' Identity and Experience Made Visible in the *Miracula Sancti Thomae Cantuariensis*," in Sarah Blick and Rita W. Tekippe (eds.), *Art and Architecture of Late Medieval Pilgrimage in Northern Europe and the British Isles* (Leiden, 2004), 473-91.

this from a venerable knight to whom this man had confessed it, yet because this man did not return to us nor send back his ampulla, I prefer to pass over it than to assert it by writing.

III.24. CONCERNING ANOTHER WHO FOUND HIS AMPULLA EMPTY WHEN HE WISHED TO SHARE THE WATER WITH ONE REQUESTING IT, BUT WHEN HE SHOWED THE AMPULLA LATER, HE FOUND IT FULL

Another person who was carrying an ampulla filled with the same relic came upon a pauper who asked for a portion. When he opened the little vessel that he thought was full, he too found it empty. When he was going to show the empty vessel to another asking for the water, he found it full to the top.

III.25. CONCERNING A THIRD MAN WHO CARRIED AWAY TWO FILLED AMPULLAS AND FOUND THAT NEITHER HAD LIQUID

A third who had carried away two filled ampullas lodged with a man named Simeon who was an enemy of the martyr. When Simeon saw them hanging on the post of the house, he said, "What do you have in those ampullas?" "The water of the blessed martyr Thomas," he replied. The enemy of the martyr supplied some mocking statements, and said, "Give me one of those so that I can pour it into my lake. The fish will fatten and multiply, the water of the lake will be sanctified, and no-one in our neighborhood will have to take the trouble to travel to Canterbury to draw it up." After he said this, he took up the ampullas, and he found one to be empty and the other, too, without any liquid. The enemy of the martyr confessed this to the sacrist of the church of Canterbury,[27] compelled by the dean Simon, his uncle.

III.26. CONCERNING GUNNILDA *DE HAMELDENE*, SWOLLEN AND CURED BY MEANS OF A STOMACH FLUX

The stomach of Gunnilda *de Hameldene*,[28] married to William, the son of Leuric, swelled up tremendously after her first delivery, so much so that it seemed that she was again great with child and inflicted with the distress of childbirth. It was not a case in which the swelling and pain evaporated after

---

[27] See Biographical Notes, Robert, sacrist and monk of Christ Church, Canterbury.
[28] The place is unidentified. Robertson suggested Hambledon.

a short time. Instead, this condition, rooted and fixed within her for many years, grew old along with her. It was restrained many times with draughts and different kinds of medications, but never driven off. When the doctor who had labored for her cure put aside the burden of the human condition, the swelling grew distinctly and with so little restraint that when she was sitting, her uterus nearly protruded to her knees. A messenger was sent to Canterbury to bring back the water of unusual power to her. The woman tasted it and immediately felt some relief, such that she took up the journey and labor of a pilgrimage to the saint. Once she was stationed in Canterbury and first tasted the relic there, the swelling of her stomach subsided through frequent vomiting and an unexpected flux. This improvement made her very happy, yet the runs shamed her even more, so much so that she regretted, with feminine bashfulness, that she had come to Canterbury. Just as nothing is too impudent for dishonest women, so too nothing is without shame to the modest. She wished to be in the church, but she could not remain there for an hour, for she was frequently compelled to run out by her stomach flux. The remedy of the flux did not cease until her stomach returned to its natural limits and usual slenderness. And so, made thin and slender, she returned home. She most devoutly *blessed the Lord God of Israel, who has raised up a horn of salvation to us in the house of David his servant* [Lk 1:68-9].

III.27. CONCERNING A CERTAIN RICHARD, WHO HAD DYSENTERY

The same power that brought healing by loosening the stomach of the aforesaid woman restrained the flux of a certain man no less favorably. For nine months, a certain Richard with the surname Wise, a man of the household of the Countess Rohese,[29] had been exhausted by a diarrhea or dysentery and brought to a desperate condition. Any night on which he only had to rise seven or eight times seemed – by his own judgment – to be merciful. As he journeyed to that place made most celebrated by the memorial of our martyr, that vexation forced him to draw apart to answer nature's call fifteen times between London and Rochester. Yet on the following day, when he traveled twenty-five miles along the route, he only had to withdraw seven times for the same purpose. When he could see the church of Canterbury some two miles away, he dismounted from his horse and walked the rest of the way. Entering the church of God, he was troubled above all by the fear that he

---

[29] See Biographical Notes, Rohese de Vere, and IV.51 below.

would be frequently called away from prayer by his usual trouble. However, the martyr approved of his pious desire, and having tasted the relic, it did not go as he had expected. For all of that day, all of the following night, and much of the following day, he remained in the church, and he did not feel anything adverse at all. And so, healed, he returned to his own people giving thanks to the Lord for grace and glory.

III.28. CONCERNING WILLIAM OF HIGHAM FERRERS, WHO WAS NOT ABLE TO WALK ON ACCOUNT OF CONTRACTED SINEWS

A villein from a village called Higham Ferrers near Northampton was named, as I remember, William. He constantly carried about that which carried him for at least three years, for his sinews were so constricted and contracted that the power of walking had been taken from him. He was taken to Canterbury on a horse, and as he stretched out his prayers in the course of his vigil, the sinews of his knees were stretched out. Gradually, without much distress, he extended them their full length and a most sweet sleep stole upon him. When he woke, he ran to the tomb of the saint at a rapid pace. He offered his crutch on which he had supported himself so long, and so the obligated one eagerly paid his thanks to the martyr.

III.29. CONCERNING THOSE WHO WENT BACK CURED WHO ARE UNKNOWN TO US

We believe that the miracles that have been written down are few and insignificant in comparison to those that have not reached our notice. We do not know how many of the simple and ignorant received the benefit of health and departed secretly without our knowledge: only God knows their number. At that time, the office of reeve in the city of Canterbury was held by John son of Vivian.[30] When he saw a driver passing by on his cart, he said, "Friend, take care: if you have sold your goods, pay the tolls required by law." The driver said, "I paid a toll that the blessed and admirable martyr Thomas has received. In this cart, I brought in people weighed down by various illnesses, of whom only two remain for me to carry back. The rest lead the way, scorning the cart, and I follow them alone. I brought in a burdened cart and leave with it nearly empty." And so, unknown to us, these and many others are very often cured.

---

[30] See Biographical Notes, John son of Vivian, borough reeve.

186 THE PASSION AND MIRACLES OF ST. THOMAS BECKET

III.30. CONCERNING [GODFREY][31] OF LILLINGSTON, WHO HAD A DISEASED SPOT IN THE PUPIL OF AN EYE

A certain knight, surrounded by a multitude of witnesses, showed himself among the rest of those cured by the martyr. Godfrey, son of Adam of Lillingston,[32] came to Canterbury with the intention of discharging a vow. He said that the vision of one of his eyes had been disabled by a diseased spot in the pupil to the point that he had eventually lost its use. But the spot had shrunk immediately after his vow, and in a short time, against all expectation, it had vanished. And so, he did not come to be cured. Instead, he was cured so that he might come.

III.31. CONCERNING A CERTAIN BLIND BEATRICE, WHO WAS CURED BEFORE SHE CAME TO THE MARTYR

It is a wonder, a most pious thing worthy of record among many pious things, that our most pious father's grace anticipates the vow of some people, so compelling them to the obligation of a vow. For others, it provides health immediately after a vow. It encounters some when they are on their journey and still far from the city of Canterbury. It takes up some when they enter the city, and it awaits others at the point when they stand in the church or at his sepulchre. It takes hold of some when they leave. Still others are kept waiting for a long time, and it restores them to health when they have returned home.

A certain pauper of Woodstock, Beatrice, took on the labor of a pilgrimage, and she had not completed half of the journey before she was set free along the way. One of her eyes had been entirely blind for seven years; the other had been similarly plagued for four years. As she made her way, holding the same hope with which everyone else in the four regions of the world was now accustomed to come to Canterbury, the splendor of the sun gradually began to shine on her. At first she wondered, and fluctuated between truth and falsity, hope and fear, joy and sadness. She summoned the girl by her own name who was leading her and asked whether the sun's ray had appeared on the earth. And so that which we read, *draw near to God, and he will draw near to you* [Jas 4:8], seemed to happen to her, though in a different way and sense. The closer she came to the church of Canterbury and the memorial of the martyr, the more her vision improved and the blindness receded. In one of her eyes, she felt only the beginnings of health as she came. During the

---

[31] The caption mistakenly provides the name Adam rather than Godfrey.
[32] See Biographical Notes, Godfrey, son of Adam of Lillingston.

night she spent in vigil in the church, she rejoiced to have received its use back entirely. There was also a most fetid ulcer on her lip. It itched constantly and flowed with putrid matter each and every night, alternating from bloody matter to blood. When she washed it with the holy water, it dried up then and there and was no longer polluted with a flow of corruption or blood.

I confess my incredulity, if indeed it is to be called incredulity as I did not doubt for myself but for others, so that the bar of incredulity might be thrown away from everyone's heart. Doubting in myself over those things that she said had happened to her, who was despicable by clothing and appearance, and who had no witness to commend her except the girl, now I demanded more harshly for witnesses, now I presented to her an unmerciful appearance as if I were contradicting her. She answered back with hard and bitter words, as if they came from the action of an angry soul. She called me hard and bad and incredulous, and ill-advisedly and unworthily appointed to the service of such a martyr, as I seemed to envy his glory, and to impugn his miracles with too much care for the investigation of truth.

III.32. CONCERNING A BOY OF ST. VALERY, THOMAS, WHO CARRIED HIS FOOT SUSPENDED ABOVE THE GROUND

Thomas of St. Valery,[33] who had already reached the age of adolescence, had borne a painful injury for more than half a year. He was carried by one foot; he carried the other suspended above the ground. When he was before the sepulchre of the saint, he tasted the water and washed his foot. He rejoiced that he then received the gift of perfect health without feeling any torment or distress or any preceding suffering whatsoever. As a memorial of the grace given to him, he gave a wax foot in the shape of his own foot.

III.33. CONCERNING WILLIAM, THE SON OF PAYNE DE PECH, WHOSE ARM HAD BEEN MADE USELESS BY PARALYSIS

The arm of another, William, the son of Payne *de Pech*,[34] who had reached the age of boyhood, had hung useless at his side from paralysis for nearly three

---

[33] St. Valery [*Sancto Walerico*] refers to St. Valery, Normandy. There was a family living in England in the late twelfth century that termed itself *de Sancto Walerico*, as Thomas is described here, so he could well have lived in England rather than Normandy.

[34] The place is unidentified. It is spelled *Peth* and *Beth* in some manuscripts: see Duggan, "Santa Cruz," p. 52.

years. He had hardly come into the church, with his mother as his companion, when he fell on the earth shouting and crying. When he at last got up again, he reported that the favor that he had come to ask for had been granted.

III.34. CONCERNING THE BLINDED ALVIDA *DE AEDGARDINTONA*

The loss of sight saddened Alvida, the daughter of Edith *de Eggerdintuna*.[35] She turned to the saint, and by means of a devout vow, she accomplished the recovery of one eye, though its sight was not perfect. She was led to Canterbury by the guidance of her mother's eyes. When she poured out prayer at the tomb of the martyr, she obtained full and perfect restitution of both eyes, though not without much torment.

III.35. CONCERNING THE CRIPPLED GODWIN OF BRAITHWELL

Godwin of Braithwell, a manor in the diocese of York, was bedridden due to pain from swelling of his legs, shins, and feet. Nearly a year went by before he regained a small measure of his strength and left his bed. With the help of two crutches, the fault of one foot was amended, and he went to the martyr. For some days he sought the gift of sound health through urgent prayers, but, having no success, he thought of returning home. He had hardly gone a mile, which was the whole of his first day's journey, when in the silence of the dead of the night the saint appeared to him in his sleep and spoke with him, saying: "Godwin, where are you going?" He replied, "I endured the pains of a long journey and came to the holy martyr Thomas with the hope of procuring good health. Now I am miserable, because I am returning not only without improvement, but also in considerably worse condition from the effort." Then the saint said, "Return to Canterbury, return, and plead with the saint more earnestly." When he woke, he ignored this great admonition and returned to the labour of the journey he had begun. By chance, he came across two knights from his region. When they asked how much success he had found, he told them everything that had happened to him in order. They vehemently insisted that he should return to the town when they heard about the vision. They wished to see a sign with their own eyes, and from the

---

[35] The place is unidentified. It is spelled *Aeggerdintona* and *Eggearduitona* in various manuscripts: see Robertson, *MTB,* vol. 2, p. 141 n. 3 and Duggan, "Santa Cruz," p. 52. Robertson suggested Egerton in Kent.

pauper's vision they had conceived a hope of doing so. And so he returned with them, and he had hardly bent his head to the martyr's feet when all of his pain was expelled and the swelling reduced. Healed, he sprang up. It would be difficult to say whether the knights' wonder was deeper or whether their joy was more abundant. Of this one thing we can be certain, that each and all of us felt joyful admiration and admiring joy. The man walked and jumped up before everyone and greatly praised the Lord in his martyr. He threw down his wooden feet and returned to his own region on his own feet, one of which he had previously not been able to bend or to move.

III.36. CONCERNING ISELDA, THE DAUGHTER OF CERTAIN KNIGHT HENRY, WHO WAS DEAF FOR [SIX][36] YEARS

We also saw a knight of Peterborough, named Henry de Longavilla,[37] present to the holy martyr Thomas his daughter Iselda, who heard no more with her ears than she did with her elbows. She had been wholly deaf for at least six years, as we learned from the testimony of Henry, his son-in-law Richard, and those who came with them. After she had persisted in her prayers to the ninth hour,[38] she returned to her inn, and as she was eating she exclaimed, "I hear the whistling of a pipe, though it is far away'. Her father said, 'It is not far off, but nearby – but whether it is far or near, does this mean, daughter, that you think you can hear?" "I can hear," she said, "thanks to God and the martyr." Everyone congratulated her, and the feasting was intermingled with tears of joy. The following day, the woman returned to the memorial of the saint. As a sign of devotion and humility, and as testimony to the reception of her health, she did not delay to offer the hair cut from her head to the martyr.

III.37. CONCERNING THE EPILEPTIC WIFE OF THE SAME KNIGHT

This same Henry returned to his own fields, rejoicing over his daughter, but concerned for his wife espoused to him. She had been vexed with epilepsy nearly every single day, and she was not able to perceive immediately *whether the Lord had heard* her *petition* [Ps 6:10]. And the woman went, and she became well. Her face was no longer changed by the epilepsy into different

---

[36] The caption writer wrote "eight" years, misreading Benedict's text.
[37] See Biographical Notes, Henry de Longavilla.
[38] That is, until mid-afternoon.

expressions except for one single occasion, when the Lord took the disease from her and gave her perfect health.

III.38. CONCERNING GUNNILDA OF LUTON, WHOSE MENSES ENTIRELY CEASED

The menses of a woman of Luton by the name of Gunnilda had entirely ceased. Her menstrual blood had been turned into vomit, and for eight months she was not able to stop herself from coughing up blood. Pressed by the distress of such an affliction, she came to the martyr. When she *entered the gates of the Lord in confession* [Ps 99:4], she smelled an inexpressibly sweet scent, as if it were wafted out of the church. She was so refreshed by this great sweetness that she wondered whether she had already changed from how she had come. She progressed step by step, and a second and then a third time she smelled the same fragrance. Having profited from this remedy, she returned with the joy of recovered health. She was struck again by the same illness, again sought out the martyr, and from the martyr she returned healed.

III.39. CONCERNING A CERTAIN EMELINA, WHOSE MENSES CONTINUALLY FLOWED

With the same ease, the martyr drove away the inverse infirmity of the woman just mentioned. The miracles concerning the two opposing evils do not differ greatly because the infirmities themselves are not very different in their quantity of danger. Both too much flux and none at all summon the payment of death from women. Too much empties to the point of death, while none at all engorges to the point of death. While the aforesaid woman was in danger due to the cessation of her menses, a flux seized Emelina and brought an overflow of the woman's discharge. It was too great and continuous. She invoked the martyr, renounced the pleasures of her old life, and for the rest, she promised that she would be more anxious of her virtue in the future. She vowed to go to the sepulchre of the saint if she were able to escape this shameful malady. Very soon, about two or three hours later, the flow of her blood stopped. She rose from her bed and hastened to Canterbury, intending to give thanks and fulfil her vow. She told us what had happened to her, not without shame, and in what manner she was quickly healed. She also disclosed to us that the horse on which she rode had been struck on the eye, causing a swelling so great that all those seeing it thought that the eye would be permanently blinded. However, when she made a wax eye in the shape of the injured eye of the horse and marked it in the name of the martyr, on the next day, the horse was found wholly healed, beyond everyone's expectation.

III.40. CONCERNING THOSE WHO WERE CURED AT WHITCHURCH

William son of Ranulf,[39] a nobleman of not inconsiderable power in the province of Cheshire at Whitchurch, came to Canterbury in part in order to pray and in part for the purpose of acquiring relics. As he was situated on the border of the Welsh, he was sometimes attacking them and sometimes being attacked by them. He believed that the presence of such relics would bring him the benefit of greater safety. The aforesaid race of people are as uncouth in mind as they are in body. They thirst, with savage hearts, for the blood of those living near them.[40] However, they have great reverence for relics of the saints and especially for those that they know without doubt have performed some miracle. He was given several portions of the hairshirt of saint Thomas and of his vestments stained with his blood. We asked him to report back to us in writing whether the Lord thought it worthy to grace these relics with miracles. This was done. The aforesaid William notified us after a very few days that Whitchurch had received the relics with great honor and a solemn procession. On the following Sunday, the one that precedes the nativity of the blessed John the Baptist, five men were freed from various illnesses.[41] Three more were liberated on the feast-day of the precursor of the Lord, and fourteen more on the feast of the apostles Peter and Paul.[42] Among them, a

---

[39] See Biographical Notes, William, son of Ranulf (d. after 1203).

[40] For another notable case of the vilification of the Welsh in the context of Anglo-Norman colonization and the Becket cult, see David Winter, "Becket and the Wolves: Imagining the Lupine Welsh in a Thirteenth-Century Latin Preaching Exemplum from Llanthony Secunda Priory," in Tristan Sharp with Isabelle Cochelin, Greti Dinkova-Bruun, Abigail Firey, and Giulio Silano (eds.), *From Learning to Love: Schools, Law, and Pastoral Care in the Middle Ages, Essays in Honour of Joseph W. Goering* (Toronto, 2017), pp. 590–612. See also Kathryn Hurlock, *Medieval Welsh Pilgrimage c.1100–1500* (New York, 2018) and Keith Williams-Jones, "Thomas Becket and Wales," *Welsh History Review* 5 (1971): 350–65.

[41] The nativity of John the Baptist (the "precursor of the Lord"), is celebrated on June 24. In 1171, the Sunday preceding this feast fell on June 20.

[42] The feast of the apostles Peter and Paul is celebrated on June 29. Benedict's description suggests that William son of Ranulf requested the relics in the early summer of 1171 and wrote a letter (or had a priest or local religious man write a letter for him) concerning miracles at Whitchurch sometime in July 1171. Perhaps the letter was carried to Canterbury by Griffin, whose miracle is related at length in the following chapter.

paralytic woman who had been brought there left her bed and returned perfectly healed to her own region.[43]

III.41. CONCERNING GRIFFIN THE WELSHMAN, WHO, HAVING SEEN A BEAUTIFUL VISION, WAS BEAUTIFULLY CURED

A Welshman named Griffin was brought to that monastery.[44] After he spent three days in vigils and prayers, he left improved on the fourth day. His right leg had swollen up immensely and the sole of his foot had lost its skin and seemed to be eaten away. It appeared to be seized by the foulness of a cancer. He returned home from the monastery, and when he rested his tired limbs in sleep, he saw a bird as large as a swan, very beautiful and whiter than snow, which was perched in the branches of a nearby tree. He took up a bow, bent it, and shot an arrow at the bird, though without using his full strength. The bird flew up and perched further off. When he saw this, he attacked it with a second arrow. Then the bird seemed to speak to him, as if in a human voice, saying, "Why are you shooting arrows at me, Griffin? Stop, no more." Then it seemed that the bird brought him a most beautiful lance, and it spoke again, saying, "Take this lance, Griffin, and care for it well." Amazed, he took it up eagerly and with great joy. When he woke, he thought over the dream silently within himself, wondering what this vision meant. He began to think that the bird signified a powerful man, perhaps his lord or some other person, and that the gift of the lance meant that he would receive the power or strength to take back lost possessions of his inheritance from the hands of his enemies. This made him very happy and hopeful. When he again fell into a light sleep, he saw a person standing by who was splendidly clothed and of venerable appearance. He said, "You saw a vision, Griffin, and how are you interpreting it? You do not know how to conjecture wisely. This is its interpretation: the snow-white bird signifies the new martyr of the English, Thomas the archbishop of Canterbury. The short flight of the arrow, the first one you shot when you held your strength in check, you should understand as the short journey you made to Whitchurch to the relics of the martyr. The second shot of the arrow, of greater length, means the toil of the greater journey to the

---

[43] For the relics held at Whitchurch, see also William of Canterbury, *Miracula*, II.82, pp. 244–5.

[44] The Latin name for Whitchurch was *Album monasterium*, so by "monastery" [*monasterium*], Benedict likely means a church or chapel at Whitchurch rather than a monastery as such.

martyr's sepulchre that you must undertake in order to receive your health. As for the lance kindly given to you, know that it means that the saint will give you the perfect strength that you desire." This was the end of speaking for the one, of sleeping for the other. He got up, and he started the journey on foot having asked for and received the blessing of his father. Since he spurned the ease of a vehicle, he did not think that he would be able to go as much as a mile a day, yet he journeyed five miles on the first day, twenty on the second, and then forty or even more on every following day. He did all this without weariness. When he came to Canterbury, we saw him so improved that hardly any vestige of the disease remained under the new skin.

III.42. CONCERNING TWO OTHERS FROM WALES WHO WERE CURED

Others of the Welsh came to beg for the help of the martyr. We learned that one of them, who had already passed through some years of his youth, had been mute from birth. When he was returning from Canterbury and had passed through the city of Rochester, *the chain on his tongue was loosened* [*Mk 7:35*] and he began to speak in English as well as Welsh, though he spoke the Welsh language more easily because he had learned it by hearing it from his earliest years. A man esteemed of religion, Richard, canon and abbot of the church of Sulby in Welford,[45] met the Welsh along the way as they were departing. They were dancing about in such exultation that language would hardly suffice for someone wanting to explain it fully. A woman among the Welsh had also received her sight, increasing their happiness still further. Though they wished to return to the martyr, they did not have enough money to do so, and so they sent us word about what had so delightfully occurred to them along the way by means of the aforesaid abbot.

III.43. CONCERNING THE OVERTURNED VESSEL IN WHICH THE SAINT'S WATER WAS RETAINED AND DID NOT FLOW OUT OF ITS UNCORKED MOUTH

On an occasion when this same abbot was going on a journey, he was carrying the health-giving water of the martyr with him. He had carefully closed the mouth of the little vessel with wax and held it inside his shirt with reverence. The vessel was upright on the middle of his chest, but as he was going along

---

[45] See Biographical Notes, Richard, abbot of Sulby.

he discovered that it had fallen onto its side. Thinking little of it, he continued his journey, negligently confident that the wax was doing its work, or, rather, confidently neglecting the relic. Very often he tried to right the vessel as it was lying on its side, but, driven by negligence, he left off his intent. Rebuking himself as lazy, he put his hand to his chest, and was sadly shocked to find the vessel without its cork. He thought it would be entirely empty, but when he pulled it out, it was full to the brim. The man of the Lord was not able to contain himself, immediately showing to those traveling there the glory of God and the power of the relic. It was a great marvel to them that not a drop of the liquid placed inside of the vessel had come out of its mouth's wide opening. We confess that to us, it appears indisputable that He who caused the vessels of those less worthy to break open by the power of the relic, or for the relic to be suddenly extracted from the vessels, was also able to stop up the open mouth of the man of God's vessel invisibly and prevent any of the relic from being lost.[46]

III.44. CONCERNING THE ONE WHO RECEIVED THE EYE-SALVE OF THE HOLY BLOOD OF CANTERBURY IN HIS EYES AND WAS CURED AT THE CITY OF ROCHESTER

A man of Gloucester in the darkness of blindness, a condition settled in him for many years, desired to escape it. The blood of the martyr was placed in his eyes by us. He received it with hope for his health, but it was the cause of swelling and anxiety for him. He had expected a good result from the holy medicine, yet he went away with unexpected pain. He came full of hope that he would see, but his hope vanished when this did not happen. On his return journey, he went into the church of Rochester, emitting sharp cries of pain and terrible groans. Fearing that his life was coming to a sudden end, he anticipated the moment of death by summoning a priest to make confession. He was then taken up by the monks of that church and placed before the memorial of the blessed confessor Ithamar. There, praying in the midst of the secrets of the divine sacrifice,[47] he unexpectedly received the divine grace of sight. Though we believe this to have happened through the power of our relic, yet the aforementioned servants of God ascribe it to the blessed Ithamar. We do not contradict them, but we know of a similar miracle that unquestionably

---

[46] For stories about these other vessels, see above II.19–22, II.50, and III.19–22.
[47] In other words, during the liturgy of the Eucharist. St. Ithamar was appointed as the first bishop of Rochester in the seventh century.

happened in the middle of the public street that no-one can presume to steal away or extort from the glory of our martyr.

III.45. CONCERNING A CERTAIN MAN BORN BLIND, WHO RECEIVED SIGHT IN THE MIDDLE OF THE STREET

Several pilgrims of the martyr once came upon Gilbert Foliot, related by blood to Gilbert, the bishop of London.[48] This Gilbert was then the steward of all the external matters in the bishopric and on a journey.[49] A man blind from his mother's womb was being led among them with his eyes covered up. Having finished the years of youth, he already seemed to be entering the age of maturity. Asked where he was coming from, the blind man answered that he was returning from the martyr of Canterbury. Asked what he had done there and with what profit he might be returning, he said, "I have nothing to report, lord, except what is detrimental to me. I was brought forth blind from my mother's innards, and thus far I have remained blind. I was led blind to Canterbury, but my eyes were unharmed and painless; I return blind with the distress of incalculable pain. That relic, in which I had hoped to find a remedy, made my eyes swell up with incredible pain, and to this day fouled my face with a constant flow of bloody matter." The aforementioned Gilbert went to the blind man, and, impelled by curiosity, lifted the veil that had been put before his eyes to protect them from wind and dust. Suddenly the blind man began to cry out, as if overwhelmed by pain, repeating in a great loud voice, "Holy Lady Mary, Holy Lady Mary!" Frightened by these cries, the steward was concerned that he had injured him in some way by his touch. He asked him whether his cries meant that he was hurt. But he said, "Not at all, lord, I am not hurt at all: rather, I can see. Lord God!" he said, "the human form is so beautiful. This is the first day in which the beauty of the human face has appeared to me."

And so, the seeing man greatly exulted, the companions of his journey rejoiced, and the enemy of the martyr, namely Gilbert, clung to doubt, but a great amazement seized them all. The man distinguished the shapes and colors of things, though he had not been taught which names to put to them. Tested by many questions, he brought satisfaction to the doubting steward, and by the suitability and truth of all his answers, the man born blind proved that innate sight had been given to him. Truthful and religious men heard these things from the mouth of the same steward and poured them into our ears

---

[48] See Biographical Notes, Gilbert Foliot, bishop of London.
[49] See Biographical Notes, Gilbert Foliot, steward of Gilbert Foliot.

196 THE PASSION AND MIRACLES OF ST. THOMAS BECKET

to be committed to writing. For just as these things are worthy to relate for his glory, so also, by the testimony of the said Gilbert, they very often compel faith, because no-one ought to doubt the glory of the martyr when even his enemy is compelled to declare it.

III.46. CONCERNING ANOTHER WHO RECEIVED SIGHT AT CANTERBURY

The prior of Folkestone came across a man near Winchester.[50] He asked him who he was, where he had been, and where he was going. He said that he was born and brought up in Cornwall and had been blind for seven years. By another person's eyes he had been led to Canterbury, he had received his sight at Canterbury, and now he was returning home from Canterbury. The redness and disfigurement of his eyes seemed to contradict his tale that he had received his sight, and so the prior, with many questions, aimed to get at the truth of the matter. In addition to answering his questions satisfactorily, he also described the trees, groves, and everything about them in that area. He said that his neighbours and acquaintances had preceded him home and had left him at Canterbury. He had remained for two weeks, at last received his sight through the urgency of his prayers, and now was returning. We know of many others cured by the merits and intercession of the blessed martyr, for whom, although with different numbers, it seems to be as it said in the gospel: *Were not ten made clean? And where are the nine? There is no one found to return and give glory to God* [Lk 17:17–18].

III.47. CONCERNING [WIVELINA][51] OF LITTLEBOURNE WHOSE HEAD HAD SWOLLEN UP

The entire head of Wivelina, a poor little women of Littlebourne, was horribly swollen and hardly retained the appearance of being human. Having received the heavenly sacraments, she was lying as if she were dead when her only daughter came to her. She bent a coin over the head of the dying woman to be offered for her to the blessed martyr. The mother was healed by the faith of the daughter, for, as the horror of the night receded, so too did the horror of the swelling. And so she fulfilled with devotion the vow of the daughter made for her, and showed herself cured in our presence among the others cured by our father.

---

[50] The alien Benedictine priory of Folkestone, which originated as a community of nuns, had been made a dependent of the Benedictine abbey of Lonlay in France in the late eleventh century. The name of its prior in the 1170s is unknown.
[51] The caption mistakenly reads "Liviva."

III.48. CONCERNING MATILDA OF THORNBURY, WHO HAD BEEN ILL FOR A LONG TIME

The sickness of Matilda, wife of Silewin of Thornbury, had progressed into its thirteenth year and worn her out with pain and misery. For all this time she had either been confined to her bed, or could get up and walk, but not without the support of a crutch and only for two or three steps. She longed to go to Canterbury, but when she told her neighbours of her desire to go on pilgrimage, she seemed to be deranged. They knew that she was not able to walk a furlong with a crutch nor cross the threshold of her home without its support. The hardship of a dangerous and unbearable journey could not dissuade her. She trusted in the martyr and was not confounded; she went in faith and did not fear. On the first day, she went sixteen miles with no pain. On each day that followed, her strength increased. She took on the labor of the journey with no labor, and when she entered the city of Canterbury, she felt no debility in her body. Rather, she had obtained the joy of perfect health from the martyr before she came to his tomb to fulfill her vow.

III.49. CONCERNING AELIZA, WIFE OF ALAN OF RATLING, WHO WAS SUDDENLY CURED THROUGH VOMITING

This woman, therefore, was saved from a great bodily detriment by means of her own faith, but Aeliza, wife of Alan of [Ratling],[52] was saved from a more perilous danger by means of another person's faith. She was thought to be at the brink of death on account of sudden and almost unbelievable torments. Her friends were called and came together, including those who were related to her by blood and those made like family by the strength of their friendship. They were able only to sigh with desperation, having no hope for a remedy for her. All of them predicted a death for her which she could neither evade nor delay. At last it happened that the water of holy memory came into the mind of one of them, the water that had brought unexpected help to so many desperate people, even to those who were already dying. It was fetched and brought into the house, accompanied by a manifest power. It was poured into the mouth of the ill woman, and it flowed back in return by a sudden ensuing nausea. By vomiting she returned to health, and, speeding to the tomb of the martyr, she obligated herself to an annual payment for her life.

---

[52] The caption reads *uxore Alani de Retlinges* (wife of Alan of Ratling) whereas Benedict's text describes him as *Alani uxore de Redingis* (wife of Alan of Reading). Though usually the caption writer is in error, here "Ratling" seems to be the best reading. See Urry, *CUAK*, p. 56 and Biographical Notes, Alan of Ratling.

III.50. CONCERNING THE DAUGHTER OF EDRIC OF RAMSHOLT[53]

A large bulging pustule suddenly broke open in the middle of the left side of the face of the infant daughter of Edric, priest of Ramsholt. It emitted bloody matter that hardened on her face. Other pustules then grew up around it and her entire face was covered with them. The parents applied medicines and charms, and while they awaited her improvement, the pestilence constantly grew, such that they began to lose hope for her life. Finally, they measured around her head, made a candle in honor of the martyr, and awaited the mercy of the Lord. That was around the tenth hour. As the evening was drawing on and the day had already come to a close, a large portion of the hardened bloody matter fell off. Underneath it, her skin appeared white and healthy. On the third day, they found her cured, such that her face was not darkened by even a tiny mark.

III.51. [CONCERNING] A CERTAIN CHEESE THAT WAS LOST AND MIRACULOUSLY FOUND THROUGH AN INVOCATION OF THE MARTYR[54]

In the same village, there happened a miracle of a more minor affair, but much more amusing in the telling. A certain person had presented a cheese to the wife of a man named William. She entrusted its care to her small daughter, Beatrice. Having put away the cheese, she turned her attention to the amusements and games one plays at that age and immediately and entirely forgot about it. Several days went by before the cheese came back to the girl's mind, but she could not remember where she had put it. With the cheese lost, she feared that she would receive a beating in punishment, and she told her secret to one of her brothers, also a young child, whom she loved above the rest and by whom she was especially loved. She asked him whether he could remember where the cheese had been put. He answered that he didn't know. It was now nearing the Friday of the following week. They feared that the cheese would be asked for, and again and again they searched everywhere, turning their home upside down. They sought the cheese but could not find it. Though they

---

[53] The full caption reads "Concerning the daughter of Edric of Ramsholt and a certain cheese that was lost and miraculously found through an invocation of the martyr." Robertson's edition has two separate chapters for the miracle of the daughter and the story of the miracle of the cheese, and so I have split this caption into two.

[54] The caption writer did not provide a separate title for this chapter; this is the second part of the caption he supplied for III.50.

deliberated together frequently and for long periods, no ideas came to them. Then something that seemed good to her came into the girl's mind, namely that they should go to the aforesaid man, although he lived far away, and ask him for a cheese like the first one. But the boy said, "We definitely should not do that. God willing, it would be much better if we did this. I have heard – already it is well known everywhere – that the holy martyr of God, Thomas, shines forth with countless miracles. If we decide to flee with devotion to his aid, we will certainly not be saddened by the rejection of our request. So, let's pray for his mercy, so that he will make us dream about where the cheese is." This childish plan pleased them both, and having said the Lord's Prayer, they hastened to their beds.

And so the saint stood before the sleeping girl, his appearance and clothing most beautiful, and said to her, "Why are you sad?" She told him the cause of her sorrow, namely, the missing cheese and the fear of punishment. The saint indicated a very old vessel that was once used for the making of butter and said, "Don't you remember that you put the cheese into that old vessel? Get up, you will find it there." Waking from the dream, she ran to the place he indicated. Taking up the cheese, she ran even faster to her brother, saying, "Hugh, I found the cheese." The boy said to her, "To be sure, I know where you put it." When she asked where, he stated the place correctly and emphatically. Marvelling over his answer, the girl said, "How did you know?" The boy said, "A man of pleasing appearance who was dressed like a priest stood before me and asked me the reason of my sorrow. When he had learned about it from me, he showed the cheese to me, saying, 'Get up, you will find it in that old vessel.'" The girl said, "To be sure, the same man also appeared to me in my sleep and used the same words." And so they went to their mother and explained how everything had happened, and she did the same with the village priest Edric. The priest met with the boy and the girl separately, and he heard the same story without the smallest difference from them both. When he came to Canterbury, nearly everyone to whom he told these things burst out in laughter.

III.52. CONCERNING A CERTAIN MAN FREED FROM QUINSY

An abscess that seemed to be a type of quinsy grew in the throat of John of Bennington, a village in the diocese of Lincoln. The swelling filled his whole face, and the mounting pain took away his ability to hear in his left ear. For about fifteen days, he found all food abhorrent: only the refreshment of water brought any relief to his fasting innards. The water of the blessed martyr was brought from nearby and he was doused in both his ear and his mouth. Suddenly, the pain completely vanished. With the sudden easing of pain, he thought, until he felt it, that the swelling had left too. When he woke after being refreshed by a sweet and unaccustomed sleep, the interior of the abscess ruptured and a great deal of bloody matter flowed down his throat. It was thought that this was leading him to his end, and accordingly, friends and acquaintances came to the dying man. As is the custom in that region for those about to die, he was laid out on the ground on ashes and a burning candle was placed in his hand. But after a little while, he got up, something beyond the hope of those sitting there. After coughing up a great deal of corruption, he told them that he heard a voice while he slept that said, "Behold, you will be given back your health through St. Thomas the archbishop of Canterbury." At once, he got up healed, and in a short time, with his vigor re-established, he did not delay to go to give thanks to the martyr.

III.53. CONCERNING THE GOLD THAT THE SAINT GAVE TO A CERTAIN MAN

There was a young man named Curbaran from the port of Dover who sought the necessities of life for himself through the shoemaker's craft. With a wonderful and pure simplicity, he used to say the Lord's Prayer every day for the soul of the holy martyr, not understanding that he who prays for a martyr does injury to the martyr. He did this without any interruption until the saint thought it worthy to show himself to him in his dreams, saying, "Curbaran, are you sleeping or awake?" He declared himself to be awake, and the saint pointed out a mill to him and spoke again, "Do you know that mill?" And the young man said, "I do, lord – who are you?" "I am Thomas, archbishop of Canterbury. Go to that mill, and take up that which you will find there under the elder tree, for it is right that I repay you something for your devoted service." At dawn he got up, and according to the precept of the Lord, *first seek the kingdom of God and his justice* [Mt 6:33], he hastened to the church to pray. When he returned, the vision came to his mind and he turned to the mill. When he was under the elder tree, he immediately found a very thick and rusty coin. At first he thought it was made of brass or copper, but when he showed it to a man who was a good deal more shrewd than him, he discovered it to be gold when he bit into it with his teeth.[55] When he carefully cleaned the

---

[55] Biting (or cutting into) a coin was a way to determine whether a coin was made of precious metal or whether it was merely base metal that had been plated to appear gold or silver.

rust off the coin, he found it to have the image and inscription of Diocletian Augustus. It was clear that its worth was more than forty pieces of silver, for it was pure gold of the highest quality and weighed as much as five silver coins.[56]

III.54. CONCERNING THE SILVER THAT THE SAINT WITTILY TOOK AWAY FROM ANOTHER

The martyr who gave gold to this man with pious kindness, rather wittily extorted silver from another. One of our servants would ask us daily for a penny for himself, not because any need compelled him, but rather due to shameless greed. He unexpectedly came down with fever and was exhausted to the point of death. He slept and saw the martyr saying to him, "Get up quickly and offer a penny upon my tomb, and the fever will not seize you again." He got up and did what he had been ordered without delay: willingly or unwillingly, he put a penny on the tomb. We were amazed to receive money from the man who had daily stated that he wished to take away rather than offer anything to us, and we wished to know about this man's new devotion and the reason for it. We asked, and, marvelling, we heard. In this way the martyr suppressed both the heat of the fever and the heat of greed in him.

III.55. CONCERNING A CERTAIN FLEMISH MAN'S DAUGHTER WHOSE LEG WAS BROKEN

The daughter of Ralph, a fowler of Flanders,[57] had fallen, and her broken leg would not heal. "What are we to do," the parents asked themselves, "since the broken bone will not mend, and the little girl is perishing?" They made a plan: they wrapped a farthing of oblation onto the broken leg, invoked the martyr's aid, and promised a farthing to the martyr every year. Before the eighth day, the girl was perfectly cured by means of the silver poultice. She ran about everywhere with a firm and steady step. She was brought to Canterbury by her parents, and she gave the medicine that had made her well to her physician for his reward. And so, the one and the same farthing served both as medicine and oblation.

---

[56] During Diocletian's reign as Roman emperor (284–305), a heavy gold aureus with the inscription "Diocletian Augustus" was minted. This coin circulated in Britain.

[57] Ralph and his family may well have lived in England rather than Flanders. A number of people from Flanders lived in Canterbury at the time Benedict was writing: see Urry, *CUAK*, p. 171 and above, II.30.

III.56. CONCERNING A HAWK THAT THE SAME FLEMISH MAN HAD NOT BEEN ABLE TO CAPTURE EXCEPT BY MEANS OF AN INVOCATION OF THE MARTYR'S NAME

The father of the same child had attempted to capture a hawk for eight days without success. He made a vow to the martyr and said, "Blessed Thomas, glorious martyr, I offer you a penny if you will give me a hawk." At that moment, one came to the fowler as if it had been broken to his hand. We saw the hawk, and we received the penny of oblation.[58]

III.57. CONCERNING A CERTAIN MAN WHO HAD A DISLOCATED ARM FOR FIVE WEEKS

Edric, a man from the region of Worcester, endured a dislocated upper arm for five weeks. The head of the bone was separated from the shoulder. Every time he moved it, it struck against his ribs. Although the arm was pulled every day, it was not possible to move it back into place. At last, after five weeks, he made a vow to the saint on the advice of a doctor. Then the arm bone sprang back into place when pulled by the doctor, even though he had hardly touched it. The doctor was amazed, because before the vow was made, he had often pulled on the arm without success.

III.58. CONCERNING A CERTAIN NUN WHO WAS MUTE AND RECOVERED WHEN THE GLOVE OF THE MARTYR WAS PLACED ON HER CHEST

A noble matron of the diocese of Lincoln by name of Constance,[59] the widow of the illustrious man Robert son of Gilbert,[60] told us about her daughter, Constance, a nun of Stixwould.[61] She was struck by a grave illness, and at the end she had no use of her limbs. For about fifteen days she was entirely mute. It happened by chance – or rather by divine arrangement, which leaves nothing to the rule of fortune – that a certain person traveling through and

---

[58] On this miracle, see Gesine Oppitz-Trotman, "Birds, Beasts and Becket: Falconry and Hawking in the Lives and Miracles of St Thomas Becket," in Peter Clarke and Tony Claydon (eds.), *God's Bounty? The Churches and the Natural World* (Woodbridge, 2010), pp. 78–88.

[59] From other documentation, we know that her name was actually Matilda: see Biographical Notes, Robert, son of Gilbert (d.1166).

[60] See Biographical Notes, Robert, son of Gilbert (d.1166).

[61] Stixwould Priory, founded in 1135, was located about fifteen kilometers east of Lincoln.

lodging there boasted that he had a glove that was once the blessed martyr Thomas's. When he made this known to the nuns, they obtained the glove and placed it upon the bosom of the sick virgin. Hardly had it touched the naked chest of the handmaiden of God when she opened her eyes. Her speech returned, the condition of her entire body was restored, she sat up, and she felt no further annoyance from that illness. She would have visited the sepulchre of the martyr herself, but the rigor of her order would not allow anyone to leave after she had once entered and taken up the holy habit.[62] Her mother devotedly took up her place. She came to Canterbury with her son Robert and daughter-in-law Matilda, who had also been cured by the martyr.[63]

III.59. CONCERNING A CERTAIN MATILDA WHO WAS GREATLY SWOLLEN

After she was freed from the tribulation of childbirth, the uterus of this Matilda[64] swelled up again: it was so much greater than the previous swelling that it appeared to be double the size. Physicians tried to help her, but their work failed. Praying many prayers, she asked that true doctor of all doctors, whom all nature obeys, would *turn his face away from her sins* [Ps 50:11] and look to the merits of his holy martyr, that with his mediation he might help her in her peril. She heard that an anchorite serving God in her vicinity had a portion of the holy water. She first employed the remedy of confession, and then had herself brought there. By having herself carried to the saint, she declared that she was not worthy to receive the relic if it were brought to her. And so she drank from the hands of the religious man, and immediately, without any voiding or bouts of nausea, she deflated to such an extent that when she returned home, she could put on her tightest clothing without any difficulty – the clothing she was not able to wear unless she was slim and well. In a marvellous way, she was made slim in less time than it would have taken her to gallop a mile on a horse.

---

[62] Stixwould was a Cistercian priory.
[63] Here again, Benedict seems to have made a mistake with the names of this family. The first son of Robert son of Gilbert and his wife Matilda was named William, not Robert. William was married to a Matilda and is very likely the son referred to here. See Biographical Notes, Robert, son of Gilbert.
[64] This is most likely the daughter of Robert of Ropsley named Matilda who married Robert son of Gilbert's son William. See Biographical Notes, Robert son of Gilbert.

III.60. CONCERNING HUGH, THE CELLARER OF THE CHURCH OF JERVAULX, WHO WAS GRAVELY ILL

A doctor devoted himself to the cure of the gravely ill Hugh, cellarer of the church of Jervaulx.[65] Warned again and again not to disregard the merits of the blessed Thomas or to put his hope in mortal man rather than in one skilled in medicine, he did not acquiesce, but trusted instead in the power of herbs. However, after much time, much expense in medications, and much zeal and labor, the doctor left Hugh in a desperate state, showing all the signs of approaching death. In that same monastery, several men suffering fevers had already become well by tasting the health-giving water. Hugh was getting worse by the hour when John, the abbot of that place,[66] seeing both the benefit to the other ill men and his deterioration, came to him and tried to impress upon his mind the memory of the martyr. Finally he acquiesced, and with an invocation of the martyr, he tasted the water. With a sudden and violent outpouring of blood from his nose, he became well. The aforesaid abbot came to us and left certification concerning these things.

III.61. CONCERNING THE MONK RADULF HEALED AT BYLAND

The same abbot also described how he went to the place which is called Byland by the inhabitants, which in Latin means "beautiful glade,"[67] and found there Radulf, a monk who was already breathing his last. He had taken the viaticum and had been anointed with oil, as is the custom of those in the church. Having already lost the ability to speak, he appeared to be insensible to everything: those who were present awaited only the hour of his death. By chance this abbot had brought with him the little piece of the hairshirt of saint Thomas that had been furnished to him. He placed it in water and made the sign of the life-giving cross over it. They opened the mouth of the dying man and poured in the water. Shortly thereafter, the man who was ill not only received the ability to speak, but he also rejoiced that his appetite had been restored. To everyone's astonishment, he asked that food be brought to him. And so, his vigor returned, he was given back his former health.

---

[65] Jervaulx was a Cistercian abbey in Yorkshire. This miracle is portrayed in three panels of Canterbury Cathedral window nIII: see Caviness, *Windows*, pp. 191–2.
[66] See Biographical Notes, John of Kinstan.
[67] Before becoming abbot of Jervaulx, John of Kinstan had been a monk of the Byland community. It was located about forty-five kilometers from Jervaulx.

III.62. CONCERNING THE FEVERISH RICHARD, A KNIGHT OF STANLEY, WHO ALSO HAD CONTRACTED FINGERS

We have commended to memory a third miracle by the certified testimony of the same abbot. A knight of the region of York, Richard of Stanley, was being housed at the abbey of Jervaulx.[68] He was feverish and in excruciating pain from a trouble of the kidneys. He had, moreover, lost the natural flexibility of the fingers of his hands. They were bent, although not curved all the way to the palm of his hand. He had heard that many people there, both laymen and monks, had been restored to health by a taste of the water, and so he too tasted the water. On the next night, when he lay fast asleep in the first part of the night and the hour of his fever's onset had come, he thought that he saw in his dreams the true presence of saint Thomas. With the gentlest touch of his hand, he smoothed his head as well as the rest of the members of his body. This vision did not fail to be fruitful for him. He went to sleep surrounded by many troubles, and when he woke, he was cured of them all. When he dined with the abbot the next day, he told him about the manner and the result of the vision, and by displaying his spread-out fingers, he compelled faith to be had in him.

III.63. CONCERNING A CERTAIN BOY ON WHOSE EYE A PUSTULE GREW SO LARGE THAT THE BOY WAS NOT ABLE TO CLOSE THE EYELID

A knight and Henry of Houghton,[69] a clerk of the holy martyr, were once both traveling in the territory of the blessed Alban.[70] As they approached each other, they exchanged greetings, and the knight was asked which region he lived in or where he had come from. He answered that his native land was the county of Berkshire and that he was returning there from Canterbury. Asked what he had seen in Canterbury worthy of telling, he said, "I saw the manifest glory of God in others and I sensed grace in myself. After a long illness, I was conveyed to Canterbury, partly in the bed of a soft litter, and partly in the more comfortable transport of a ship. And look, as you see, I return rejoicing and entirely recovered. I boldly dare to declare that I do not remember ever

---

[68] Richard of Stanley's miracle is pictured at the top of Canterbury Cathedral window nIV: see Caviness, *Windows*, pp. 181–2.
[69] See Biographical Notes, Henry of Houghton, master and clerk of Thomas Becket.
[70] Killed sometime in the third or the beginning of the fourth century, Alban was renowned as Britain's first Christian martyr. The monastery of St. Albans, located about thirty-five kilometers northwest of London, was one of England's great Benedictine establishments.

being more well or agile. My servant boy, whom you see here, was no less successful. In fact, although I am grateful beyond words for my own healing, yet I am struck with a greater amazement concerning the remarkable grace divinely granted to him. Some years earlier, as he slept under a bramble-bush as shepherds customarily do, a large blister covered the entire pupil of one of his eyes.[71] In the days that followed, it grew and became hard as stone. From a distance, it looked to be much larger than the size of a very large acorn. Two years went by, and after that, due to how much it protruded from his eye, he could not close his eyelid. After he had received no profit at Canterbury, he came back with me, in pain and groaning, as far as the city of Rochester. He was satisfying his body's need for sleep when the saint showed himself in a vision. It seemed as if the boy's eye received the touch of the most holy hands, and at length he marked it with the sign of the cross, as it pleased him, and he slipped away from his sight. The boy woke up with an itching eye, and suddenly, with the little sack of the swelling having broken, he felt putrefaction flowing. Waking those of us who were there with his persistent cries, we ran to him with lit candles. We thought that we were running to some sorrowful scene, but divine grace met us with joy. From that hour, it has not stopped constantly leaking bloody matter and blood mixed together, which we and the boy hope will bring a remedy."

When Henry had heard these things from the knight, he dismounted from his horse and uncovered the boy's eye, which had been covered to protect it from the wind. He found the eyelids already able to close themselves together. When he separated the eyelids, he used a thorn to lift out the little sack, which was deflated and emptied of putrefaction, and he found the pupil of the eye to be pure, healed, and entirely without corruption. The boy cried out that he could see perfectly, and the boy's lord and Henry also both exclaimed and rushed to perform thanksgiving. Although our eyes did not see these things, yet, since they are certified by the mouth and eyes of this Henry, we have no doubts about incorporating them as if our eyes had seen them.

---

[71] On waking ill after sleeping outside, see also II.1, II.28, and IV.76.

III.64. CONCERNING A CERTAIN PRIEST WHOSE HAND AND ARM WERE USELESS FROM PARALYSIS, AND HOW CROSSES WERE ERECTED IN THREE PLACES WHERE THE MARTYR HAD DISMOUNTED FROM HIS HORSE, AND OF THE MIRACLES THAT HAPPENED THERE

There was a time when a group of the great men of the kingdom of England had come together and were discussing among themselves the diverse marvels of the martyr. That same clerk testified that he heard one of the men, who had once been an enemy of the holy martyr, to have responded in this way: "The things being described are wonderful and utterly exceed the bounds of faith. My mind would retreat and draw back from belief in them all, except for the fact that eyewitness faith has made me certain about one of them. For I know and am certain that a priest, who dwells at one of my fortifications, had a right hand and arm made useless for a long time from an unusual malady of paralysis, to the point that he could not move his hand nor put it to his mouth. This suffering kept him from the office of the altar for some years. But now that he has come back from Canterbury, not only does he perform a priest's duties freely and without encumbrance, but he also competed with my squires and sergeants to determine who could throw the heaviest stone. In this game, he was seen to carry off the victory from them all." Having said these things, the magnate turned to Henry and asked, "Henry, how can we regard the wonderful occurrence of these things to be just and reasonable? How can it be that the man who, when he was chancellor, was the most severe of any of us on the church of God, now surpasses every single saint of whom the church reads or sings in both the multitude and the magnitude of his miracles?" Although he would have been able to object to the question by pointing out the arduous and most saintly life of the holy martyr, he assumed a more humble principle for speaking[72] and explained it in this way: "Which seems to you to be a greater crime: to renounce Christ, or to exercise severity on the church of Christ, which is what you accuse both yourself and the saint of doing? If Peter could be absolved of such a great crime by such a short lament;[73] if the thief, sanctified by the confession of his crime and a momentary penance,

---

[72] With reference to a question [*quaestio*] and principle [*principium*], it looks as if Benedict (or possibly Master Henry himself, who might have written this for Benedict) intended to evoke the method and language utilized in late twelfth-century schools.

[73] A reference to the story of Peter renouncing Christ three times before he heard a rooster crow in the morning (Matthew 14:66-72, Mark 26:69-75, Luke 22:60-1, and John 18:16-27).

could be taken up to paradise before the remaining saints,[74] then what ought to be conferred on the Lord's anointed and the defender of the church? He suffered the injury of nearly seven years of exile, the violent dispossession of his goods, the deportation of his parents and the imprisonment of his friends, a hairshirt, and, at the end, that which is greater than all of these things, such a cruel cause, time and place of death. Surely divine mercy did not expend itself entirely on Peter and the thief and leave nothing remaining for the future? That mercy is wholly what it was: it suffers no decrease." After the clerk discussed these things and more in this way, the magnate became so satisfied that he gave him the reward of his blessing, crying out, "Truly, you have removed a tumor from my heart that I would not have wished to have remained rooted there for twenty pounds."[75]

In respect to this, I wished to add the following briefly, so that it might be known to the readers by what compassion the most kind martyr *has heaped coals of fire on the heads of his enemies* [Rom 12:20]. Not ceasing to pursue him, even when he was dead, with old hatreds,[76] they were brought to charity by the sweetness and certitude of miracles, lest by adding sin to sin they be brought to death. In order to insert his love into the mind of his renowned enemy, the saint worked wonderful grace of healing in one of his villages, which is called Newington in English, or "New-Village" in Latin.[77] In the first days of miracles, a cross was erected in the middle of this village, although by whose direction it is not known. The place where the cross stands is holy ground, full of grace and renowned for the glory of miracles. When the saint had been called back from exile and was going to London, he dismounted

---

[74] A reference to the story of the thief crucified alongside Jesus who asked to enter the kingdom of heaven (Matthew 27:38, Mark 15:27, and Luke 23:32–43).

[75] Twenty pounds – equivalent to 4,880 silver pennies – was a tremendous amount of money. Though Benedict does not name this magnate, the "renowned enemy" in the next part of the chapter can be identified as Richard de Lucy (see Biographical Notes), so perhaps Henry of Houghton's conversation was with him.

[76] The text edited by Robertson reads: "ceasing to pursue him, even when he was dead, with old hatreds," but the sense requires a negative. I have emended the text to read: "*not* ceasing to pursue him, even when he was dead, with old hatreds."

[77] Newington is located about thirty kilometers west of Canterbury on the road to London. In the early 1170s, it was held by Richard de Lucy (see Biographical Notes). In the first recension of his Life of Becket, Edward Grim discusses the healing miracles that occurred in the place where Becket had confirmed children (Grim, *Vita*, pp. 427–8). Newington appears three times in William's collection: see William of Canterbury, *Miracula*, pp. 168, 188, and 310. On Newington in the late twelfth century, see Diana Webb, "The Saint of Newington: Who Was Robert le Bouser?" *Archaeologia Cantiana* 119 (1999): 173–87, at pp. 176–7.

from his horse at Newington, and he stood on that spot while he placed his hand on children, confirmed them with the chrism, and invoked the presence of the fullness of grace. For it was not his custom, as it is for many, in fact nearly all bishops, to perform the ceremony of confirmation while sitting on his horse. Instead, on account of his reverence for the sacrament, he would dismount and stand as he placed his hand on the children. Moreover, in two other places where he dismounted for the same reason, he devoutly satisfied the needs of the people coming there. On account of the frequency of miracles and admonition of the martyr in dreams, a wooden cross was erected in each place. There is so much glory of signs in these places, so much grace of healing, such a great concourse of the people, and such great feeling of devotion from those coming there, that the church can sing of its servant as it does of the Lord: *those who slandered you will come and worship the prints of your feet* [Is 60:14], for even the enemies of the martyr ran there in groups, vying with one another, and they worshipped in the place where his feet had stood.

III.65. CONCERNING [ODILDA][78] OF SOUTHWELL, WHO RECEIVED HER SIGHT AT ONE OF THE CROSSES

We know of an old woman of Southwell, Odilda, who was coming to Canterbury to ask for the honey-sweet grace of the martyr when she obtained it at that place, namely, at Newington. She had been deprived of the sight of her eyes for four years. Three years before, moreover, her eyelids cohered together, such that her eyes were stuck shut as well as blind. When she threw herself down along with her other co-sufferers next to the above-mentioned cross, her head was filled with pain. In the midst of the torment, she thankfully received the opening of her eyes and the delight of friendly light.

III.66. CONCERNING ANOTHER WOMAN WHO SIMILARLY RECEIVED HER SIGHT THERE

A woman of Woolwich also sat in the jail of blindness for ten years. When she obtained at that place what she had been going to Canterbury to request, she was greatly gladdened. A sharer in longed-for sight, she roused the throng of people standing there to give thanks and praise to God.

---

[78] The caption writer mistakenly supplies the name Edith.

III.67. CONCERNING A THREE-YEAR-OLD BOY WHO WAS BROUGHT FORTH BLIND FROM HIS MOTHER'S WOMB

A three-year-old boy, who was brought forth blind from his mother's womb,[79] was brought to that place and rested there. After vespers were finished and the light of day was seen to be concluded by the darkness of night, with many standing around him he miraculously received, with opened eyes, the sight that nature had denied him. His sad start to life was to be brought to a more joyful ending.

III.68. CONCERNING ELIZA OF DUNTON WITH A DISEASE OF THE HEART

Eliza of Dunton, the daughter of Roger, suffered greatly and with much anxiety from that illness which the physicians call *cardia*.[80] Her breath was so constricted that nearly every moment it seemed that she would expire instead of respire. She brought her drooping limbs to rest under that aforementioned cross. She was restored, and after resting, she left healed.

III.69. CONCERNING GODITHA OF HAYES, SUFFERING FROM DROPSY

The swelling of dropsy had possessed the whole of the little body of Goditha of Hayes.[81] All of the beauty of the human form had been removed from all of her limbs. There was no health in her from the sole of her foot to the top of her head. When she arrived at the aforesaid place, a drink of the water of Canterbury was the sole means by which she was drained of fluid. It was as if by tasting the most efficacious draught, a laxative for the stomach had been procured for her. Then she went to Canterbury, the universal and solemn refuge of the wretched. The same laxative persisted through five days, until her limbs were made slender and thin and she left slight and wholly slimmed down.

---

[79] The phrase "who was brought forth blind from his mother's womb" scans as a hexameter and Robertson treats it as a quotation.

[80] Robertson emended Benedict's *cardia* to *cardia[cus]*. I have retained the Latin term here: in the DMLBS, *cardia* is defined as cardiac fever.

[81] Goditha of Hayes' miracle is portrayed in three panels of Canterbury Cathedral Trinity Chapel nIII: see Caviness, *Windows*, p. 188. The second panel is very heavily restored and today contains an insertion of a scene from another window.

III.70. CONCERNING THE BLIND ALDIDA FROM THE COUNTY OF STAFFORDSHIRE

For no less than three years, a woman named Aldida from the county of Staffordshire was a stranger to light. After she poured out her prayers to the Lord in that place and invoked the name of the martyr, the desired health of her body followed.

III.71. CONCERNING THE SIMILARLY BLIND HEDEWIC FROM THE REGION OF GLOUCESTER

It was similar for a certain tanner, Hedewic, from the region of Gloucester, who had likewise been condemned to the blindness of his eyes for three years. Divine grace, through invocation of the martyr, poured out the grace of light. Yet at first he bore many torments, and by his pain he moved others to the state of tender compassion. We did not keep in mind the name of the village from which he said he came, but let it suffice to have it noted here, for the sake of testimony, that his lady and the companion of his journey was Bertha, the widow of Elias Giffard,[82] from whose fief he holds his land.

III.72. CONCERNING LEURIC OF THE REGION OF BARKING IN [SUFFOLK][83] WHOSE HAND WAS STRUCK BY PARALYSIS

Also in that same location, Leuric of Barking in Suffolk, of the region of the blessed virgin Etheldreda,[84] rejoiced to have his paralyzed hand restored to him, though not without great signs of preceding torment. He spent two days crying and wailing without cease, but on the third day, the benefit of hoped-for healing came at the same time as quiet returned. He *stretched out his hand* [Ps 54:12] and showed it to be entirely healed.

---

[82] See Biographical Notes, Bertha, widow of Elias Giffard.
[83] The caption writer mistakenly states that he was from Norfolk.
[84] The relics of St. Etheldreda, an Anglo-Saxon queen who died in 679, were kept by the Benedictine monks of Ely. By the late twelfth century, Etheldreda was a popular saint and Ely a large and powerful community with many possessions in Suffolk.

III.73. CONCERNING LUCIANA, THE DAUGHTER OF WALTER TOREL, WHO WAS STRUCK BY PARALYSIS AND LOST THE USE OF HER TONGUE ON ACCOUNT OF HER FATHER'S CURSE

Around that time when the blessed athlete of God, Thomas, seemed to have obtained peace in the church through a concordance of king and priesthood,[85] it happened that Walter Torel, a man of Warwickshire of the village named Austrey in English, cursed his daughter Luciana, at that time in her fourteenth year. She had been spinning on the feast day of the blessed virgin and martyr Cecilia which is kept as a great and solemn celebration in that region.[86] Her father had returned from church and found her spinning. Led by his zeal for the festival, he punished her with a curse. As soon as her father's curse fell on her, she withered away and was deprived of the use of the right side of her body and her tongue. When her father saw that he had been heard in his evil-doing, he wept and cried. By his evil-doing, he had inflicted a retribution of pain: she, punished herself, heaped up the punishment of pain. He put the half-dead girl on his shoulders and brought her to the resting places of many saints. At last, in a certain church of the blessed virgin Edith, her tongue alone was freed from the curse.[87] With his pain lessened somewhat, though not his labor, as he was burdened again with the sad and miserable burden, he turned his feet and his soul to the memorial of the martyr of Canterbury. When he came across the cross mentioned above, he cast the girl down in the place where his feet had stood. He prayed for a long time. The native vigour and heat of the nerves of both her hands and her feet returned and the whole of the mortified part of her body lived again. Her father rejoiced with the unexpected joy and went on to Canterbury. He was delighted to leave with a companion whom he had brought as a burden. And so, before he came to the martyr, he was heard by the martyr.

III.74. CONCERNING A CERTAIN MAN WITH A HERNIA

Another person, in contrast, was returning from Canterbury and came to that place. He had had a hernia for not much less than seven years. After making his prayer, he sensed the effect of the prayer. Into nearly the middle of the

---

[85] That is, the period after Henry II and Becket agreed to the peace of Fréteval on July 22, 1170.
[86] St. Cecilia's day is celebrated on November 22.
[87] The relics of St. Edith (d.984), an Anglo-Saxon princess, were held at Wilton Abbey in Wiltshire, located about 200 kilometers south of Austrey.

night, he was rolling about here and there and from one side to another. His innards, coming together and returning to their proper place, were divinely repaired, and he marvelled at the power of the martyr that he had in this way experienced in himself.

III.75. CONCERNING THE BLIND ROBERT *DE BAALUM*

Robert *de Baalim*,[88] whose eyes had not had the ability of vision for nearly ten years, was coming from Essex, led by his wife, to beg the favor of the martyr. He had gone through the city of Rochester when he was trodden on by the foot of the horse ridden by a blind man behind him, and he lamented that his heel was injured. Having learned that the one who was following him was blind, and that they both were drawn to the saint for the same reason, he cried out loudly, either on account of his injury, or for his own and the other's blindness, because of which neither could take precautions either for himself or the other. He bent his knees both bodily and mentally to the Lord. He appealed to the Lord that the lost happiness of sight would be summoned back to him thorough the merits of the martyr. When he had fallen prone to the ground upon asking this for a third time, he saw and took up a stone lying before his eyes. He began to kiss it for joy. Scorning the guidance of his wife, he ran and quickly flew before his companions, such that none of the company were able to accompany him. As he ran ahead in this way, and fell to his knees to worship God at nearly every furlong, those who followed him did not believe him to be sane in his mind nor unhurt in body. They thought that insanity impelled him to run, a stumbling-block had brought about his fall, and the fall an injury. He, however, ran headlong and without ceasing for nearly six miles to Newington where the first cross in the honor of the martyr had been erected. He worshipped in the place where his feet had stood. Afterwards, with indescribable joy, he proceeded to Canterbury.

III.76. CONCERNING A LITTLE BOY NAMED HENRY, WHOSE RIGHT FOOT WAS FIXED OVER HIS LEFT FOOT IN THE SHAPE OF A CROSS

Aliza of Northampton, wife of the tanner Roger, also brought her little three-year-old boy Henry to that place. From the hour of his birth, his right foot had

---

[88] The place is unidentified, though "Baalim" or "Baalum" may refer to a family name rather than a place. A family with the surname "de Baalun" was active in England in the late twelfth and early thirteenth centuries.

been immovably fixed over his left foot in the shape of a cross. The bones in his shins were either non-existent or too slender. In order to be made certain of this, his mother very often grasped them most firmly, but she could never feel the solidity of bones in the softness of flesh. What benefit is there in lengthy description? It is the mother and tinder of disgust. She put the boy in this miserable condition down in that holy place, and took him up erect and his feet separated from each other.

III.77. CONCERNING THE TWO LAME DAUGHTERS OF GODBOLD OF BOXLEY

Two girls, the daughters of Godbold of Boxley, were brought to that place.[89] From their cradles, they had carried themselves about by crutches rather than their own feet. Both importuned the martyr for their health, and the older was seized by sleep. The saint visited and spoke with her in her dreams, and she was promised and granted health. When she woke, the sinews of her knee had wonderfully straightened out and there was great rejoicing among the clerics and the people. As the bells of the church were rung as a sign,[90] she was brought into the church. When the younger one saw this, she yielded to a flood of tears, for she was saddened by her misery to the same degree that the older sister had been made joyful by her success. She blamed the saint because she remained lying there while her sister departed. You could see there the weeping of Esau on account of the gift of his father's blessing, crying out: *Do you only have one blessing, father? I beg that you bless me too.* And when she *wept with a loud cry,* the pious father *was moved* [Gn 27:38–9].[91] He visited her in her sleep on the following day and restored her health in the same manner as he had the first. With the repetition of the miracle, praise to God and joy to the people were doubled. There were innumerable other people to be seen there who had been freed from the suffering of many kinds of illnesses. But since some of them did not produce witnesses, or were not sifted down by us to the purity of truth, we let not a few that had easily entered

---

[89] This miracle is pictured in three panels in Canterbury Cathedral window nIII: see Caviness, *Windows*, p. 189.

[90] Bells were commonly rung as signs of miracles: see also below, IV.2.

[91] These citations come from the biblical story in Genesis about two brothers. Esau, the older brother, is lamenting the fact he has not had a blessing from his father, unlike his younger brother, Jacob, who has. In the case of the sisters from Boxley, the older sister receives her health first while the younger one laments, but Benedict does not seem to mind this slight mismatch.

our ears go out just as easily. We did not wish to mix chaff with the grain or insert doubtful things among the certain.

III.78. CONCERNING CANDLES RELIT IN ANOTHER PLACE WHERE THE MARTYR DISMOUNTED FROM HIS HORSE

We do not think it should be buried in silence that in another place where the venerable father similarly stood, before a cross was erected there, it has been said that a great light shown out. There are four witnesses asserting to this event: Henry *de Topindenne*,[92] a truthful man of commendable way of life, Samuel the cleric, and two others, whom common report also praises for their faithfulness and truthfulness. As they were making a journey not far from the place, all of them – together and at the same time – saw thirteen lit candles there. At the time there was still some daylight, and wishing to see it from a closer distance, they all dismounted from their horses and approached the place on foot. When they were about half a stone's throw away from the candles, they suddenly disappeared from their eyes. Struck with wonder, they went back. Having gone back, they looked, and they again saw the lit candles and counted them. Mounting their horses, they discussed among themselves what it could mean that with the sun setting, such a light shone out in that place against the shadows of night. The aforementioned Henry remembered that the blessed athlete of God had traveled through that place. Turning aside to a cottage that he had spotted, he learned from a little woman that the saint had stood there when he had administered confirmation to children. Afterwards, that place was marked out and its sanctity made more evident by the grace of many instances of healing and the great frequency of miracles, and so a sign of cross was also erected there by the faithful. In addition, a third place in which his feet had stood was made similarly venerable by no less glory of prodigies, of which it is not necessary to speak specifically now. By such silence, I do not condemn them, but rather defer them, for with such a great multitude of miracles, I hesitate to know what I should bring forward first, and what later, for *abundance makes me poor*.[93]

---

[92] The place is unidentified. It is spelled *Tropindenne* and *Trobindenne* in various manuscripts: see Robertson, *MTB*, vol. 2, p. 171 n. 2. Robertson suggested Tappington, Kent.
[93] Ovid, *Metamorphoses*, book III, line 466.

The Chapters of Book IV

1. How it is not easy for the writer to write of all the martyr's great deeds
2. Concerning Eilward, to whom the martyr Thomas restored gouged-out eyes and cut-off genitals [*see Parallel Miracles no. 2*]
3. Concerning Ralph of Longueville, perfectly cured of leprosy and struck by the contagion of leprosy again
4. Concerning Humphrey of Chesterton, released from a similar ailment
5. Concerning Odo of Falaise, who, having been struck in the eye, lacked sight for seven years
6. Concerning the house of Gilbert, baker of the bishop of Rochester, which was freed from fire in the midst of flames
7. Concerning the houses of William of Yarmouth similarly freed
8. Concerning William of Parndon, son of Eudes, who was dying or dead
9. Concerning Baldwin, from the same place, who had weakened from an acute illness
10. Concerning a nun who remained half dry in the midst of a heavy rain
11. Concerning the saint's water turning into blood
12. Item concerning the same
13. Concerning Seileva of Froyle, from whose breast a swelling of extraordinary size protruded
14. Concerning Everard of Winchester, weakened by a sudden paralysis
15. Concerning his brother [Ranulph] the priest
16. Concerning the wife of [Anfrid] of Ferring, in whose uterus a fetus had putrefied
17. Concerning Alelm who, having cut his thumb, invoked the martyr, and after the meal did not find a scar of the wound
18. Concerning Weremund, son of Wielard of Béthune, whose bowels spilled out of his anus
19. Concerning Hermer, son of Tetion, who had movements and tremours in all his limbs
20. Concerning [Vidoch] *de Anoch*, whose water boiled out of its vessel on account of his anger, but when he became pacified, the water was pacified too
21. Concerning Mary, who wept at one moment and laughed the next
22. Concerning Durand, the son of Osbern of Eu, into whose ear a stone had fallen

23. Concerning Ernald, Ernulf, and Amalric, three ill men from the border region of Thérouanne and Ponthieu
24. Concerning Philip of Alnwick, whose genitals had swollen up
25. Concerning his son John, whose entire body was possessed by pustules
26. Concerning a certain epileptic woman in the aforesaid Philip's household
27. Concerning the leprous Walter
28. Concerning the leprous Eilgar
29. Concerning Ernold, the dropsical baker of the earl Simon
30. Concerning Juliana, the daughter of Gerard of Rochester, who was not able to open her eyelids
31. Concerning the girl named Laeticia, who lost an eye from the piercing of a straw when she was in her cradle
32. Concerning the knight Geoffrey, surnamed Malaeartes, who was blinded by the water of the saint
33. Concerning Aliza, the wife of the fisherman Martin of Leicester, who was blinded by the martyr
34. Concerning a peasant of Abingdon, who was curbed by the martyr with a similar blow
35. Concerning the son of William *de Benewella*, to whom a similar misfortune occurred
36. Concerning [Segiva] who had borne an ear of rye in her esophagus for nearly three years
37. Concerning Matilda of Cologne, a demoniac
38. Concerning a penny the saint restored to a certain matron named Sibilla
39. Concerning Richard, the cleric of the sheriff of Devon, to whom the martyr administered halfpennies according to his intent
40. Concerning Ralph, the subprior of the church of St. Augustine, apostle of the English, whose pennies the martyr multiplied
41. Concerning Henry, a youth of London, who transferred his goods to another ship when he was sailing from Norway as a result of the martyr's admonition, and who was saved from the peril of death
42. Concerning the ship that followed the sailors who had abandoned it without any navigator [*see Parallel Miracles no. 3*]
43. Concerning another ship that the saint visibly freed [*see Parallel Miracles no. 4*]

44. Concerning [Ailred], a young man from Exeter, who was benevolently freed by the virtue of the martyr when he was entwined in an anchor's rope and carried headlong

45. Concerning a man of Dover, who recovered three lost anchors through the saint [see *Parallel Miracles no. 5*]

46. Concerning other men freed from a storm on the sea by the martyr

47. Concerning a certain ill man who asked for the saint's water, drank water deceptively brought to him from a well, and was healed

48. Concerning Warin, surnamed Grosso, whose swollen arm the saint beautifully healed in a dream

49. Concerning a certain canon of Croxton, whose expelled eye was put back into its place by the water, without the touch of any hand

50. Concerning another, a certain swollen man in the same abbey

51. Concerning a certain canon of Bedford, on whose neck burning blisters emerged, which suddenly vanished by means of the martyr's water

52. Concerning Ingelram son of [Stephen] of Goulton, whose arm the saint struck with an affliction and afterwards cured in a dream [see *Parallel Miracles no. 6*]

53. Concerning the swollen Mabel *de Aglandre*, who was judged incurable by doctors

54. Concerning the dropsical Eliza of Middleton of Oxfordshire

55. Concerning a dropsical woman of Merston

56. Concerning a blind boy and an insane [girl] from Wales

57. Concerning the insane Walter of Grimsby

58. Concerning dogs silenced with the name of the martyr

59. Concerning Eda of Scotland, who could not walk, and who rose and walked by means of a monk commanding her in the name of the saint

60. Concerning [Hugo] *de Tukin*, exhausted by a fistula

61. Concerning [Melania] of Fontenay, who had a similar fistula

62. Concerning a boy of Rochester who fell in the water

63. Concerning a boy of Sarre who was submerged in a bath

64. Concerning the dead son of Jordan son of Eisulf [see *Parallel Miracles no. 7*]

65. Concerning the daughter of Jordan of Plumstock, who was thought to be dead [see *Parallel Miracles no. 8*]

66. Concerning the drowned son of Hugh *de Benedega* [see *Parallel Miracles no. 9*]

67. Concerning the wife of Peter de Arches, who had a flux of blood

68. Concerning Gerard of Flanders, who had kidney stones
69. Concerning the smith Geoffrey, who worked at an inappropriate time and whose fingers adhered to his palm
70. Concerning the dropsical William of St. David's
71. Concerning Juliana of Godmersham, whose arm was mortified
72. Concerning Elias, monk of the church of Reading, who was struck, it was thought, with leprosy [see *Parallel Miracles no. 10*]
73. Concerning the leprous Gerard
74. Concerning the leprous Gilbert of St. Valery
75. Concerning the leprous Peter of Abingdon [see *Parallel Miracles no. 11*]
76. Concerning the leprous Richard
77. Concerning two men, of whom one miraculously triumphed in a duel over the other
78. Concerning others who were accused concerning the game of the lord king that they had taken
79. Concerning others accused of the same thing
80. Concerning Agnes, whose stepson took her dower and returned it to her in a sudden change of mind
81. Concerning Peter *de Denintona*, who was suddenly cured of an enormous swelling
82. Concerning Alexander, partially deaf
83. Concerning Robert, also partially deaf
84. Concerning Osbern of Lisieux, who had a hernia
85. Concerning a certain John who was blinded and afterwards could miraculously see again by means of the water of the martyr
86. Concerning a monk of the church of Reading, who was freed from a devil that had closed up his throat and nose by means of the martyr's water [see *Parallel Miracles no. 12*]
87. Concerning a monk of Mont-Dieu, Geoffrey, suffering from dropsy, who deflated when he stroked an account of the martyr's miracles over his body and was healed
88. Concerning a boy of Winchester on whom a wall fell [see *Parallel Miracles no. 13*]
89. Concerning the ale that did not purify itself as ale usually does, and suddenly received the necessary condition with the application of a string that had held an ampulla holding the saint's water

90. Concerning Elias *de Sibburnia*, whose viscera were so constricted they seemed to be attached to his back
91. Concerning a certain Hadewisa, who had an interior rupture
92. Concerning Robert *de Beveruno* with the stone
93. Concerning his neighbor Hingan, who suffered sudden fits
94. Concerning the son of the earl of Clare, resurrected from the dead [*see Parallel Miracles no. 14*]

BOOK IV

IV.1. HOW IT IS NOT EASY FOR THE WRITER TO WRITE OF ALL THE MARTYR'S GREAT DEEDS

If the Lord increased the grace of my humble gifts by multiples, *if I spoke in the tongues of men and of angels* [1 Cor 13:1], if I were given hands that could write not just speedily like a scribe, but record most rapidly like a notary, my talent would still be overcome, my tongue would fail, and my fingers become senseless. If I attempted to touch on each of the mighty deeds of the martyr briefly, much less to explain them fully and clearly, the warning of the ethicist would sting me, and not without purpose, for I should have mused on this warning at the beginning:

You who write, select a subject equal to your powers,
And consider carefully what your shoulders can and cannot bear.[1]

But now, since I sought out something greater than my powers, against the counsel of the other wise man, it is as if I were *a searcher of majesty overwhelmed by too much glory* [Prv 25:27]. For the great deeds and merits of our martyr are indeed very glorious and inscrutable, and though they entice me by their sweetness, they are an onerous weight on my feeble perception. However, *seeing that I have begun, I will speak of my lord though I am but dust and ashes* [Gn 18:27].

IV.2. CONCERNING EILWARD, TO WHOM THE MARTYR THOMAS RESTORED GOUGED-OUT EYES AND CUT-OFF GENITALS

From what already has been said it is clear that the memory of saint Thomas deserves to be eternal in the bosom of the Mother and Virgin Church. However, so that the Lord might declare him to be higher in merit and glory, he thought it right to favour him with a miracle more marvelous and unusual,

---

[1] Horace, *Ars Poetica*, lines 38–40.

for it is more unusual for new members to be substituted for those that had been cut out than for weakened ones to return to strength.

In the royal town of Westoning in the region of Bedfordshire,[2] there was a common man by the name of Eilward.[3] One of his neighbors, Fulk, owed him two pennies for ploughing half a measure of land. He paid one penny, but he put off payment of the other until the following year, saying he did not have it. On a feast day after the passion of the blessed martyr, when by chance they were both going to the tavern (for it is the English custom to indulge in eating and drinking on a feast day, such that their enemies see their sabbaths and mock them), he asked for the debt, but Fulk said that he owed nothing. Eilward asked that he at least pay half of what he owed as he was going to get ale, and he could keep the rest for a similar occasion. When the debtor refused this, the creditor threatened that he would get what was due to him. After they both got drunk at the tavern, Eilward left first and went to Fulk's house, where he tore down the bar of the door and stormed into the house, a burglar as much from rashness as drunkenness. He turned over everything in the house looking for things he could carry away, and he hit upon a large whetstone and on gloves which country dwellers use to guard their hands against the pricks of thorns. The pauper thief carried off both these things, together hardly worth the value of a penny. Boys playing in the yard of the house cried aloud and ran together to the tavern, calling to their father in order that he might get back the plundered goods. Pursuing the man, Fulk

---

[2] Westoning is located twenty kilometers south of Bedford.
[3] Benedict described Eilward's miracle in an antiphon in the Becket Office (Cantus Database ID 601515): *Novis fulget/ Thomas miraculis:/ membris donat/ castratos masculis/ Ornat visu/ privatos oculis* [Thomas gleams with new miracles: he gives masculine members to the castrated, he grants sight to those deprived of eyes]. See Slocum, *Liturgies*, p. 200 and Reames, "Liturgical Offices," p. 575. Eilward's miracle is pictured in six panels in Canterbury Cathedral window nIII: see Caviness, *Windows*, pp. 187, 189–91 (the second panel of Eilward's narrative is listed as "Becket's Appearance at a Shrine"). Robert of Cricklade discussed Eilward in his *Life and Miracles of Thomas Becket*. This text is now lost, but it was used by the author of an early fourteenth-century Icelandic saga on Becket: for passages concerning Eilward, see *Thómas Saga*, pp. 103–7. On some of the legal aspects of Eilward's miracle, see John Hudson, *The Formation of English Common Law: Law and Society in England from the Norman Conquest to Magna Carta*, 2nd edition (New York, 2018), pp. 148–9. On the punishment suffered by Eilward, see Klaus van Eickels, "Gendered Violence: Castration and Blinding as Punishment for Treason in Normandy and Anglo-Norman England," *Gender & History* 16:3 (2004): 588–602. Benedict frequently uses the historical present in Eilward's story in order to give his account more verve, but to avoid confusion I have decided to provide past tense verbs throughout.

snatched away the whetstone and hurled it on the head of the thief, such that he broke the whetstone with Eilward's head and Eilward's head with the whetstone. He also drew the sharp knife that he bore and pierced Eilward's arm with it. He prevailed against him, took the miserable man to the house that he had ransacked, and tied him up as a thief, a robber, and a burglar. He summoned the beadle of the village, Fulk, who asked what Eilward had done and said, "As a cause for an arrest, this is too small and insufficient. However, if you can increase the theft and produce him weighed down with other goods he supposedly stole, you will be able to accuse him of a punishable crime." He agreed, and tied a drill, a double-edged axe, a net, and not a small amount of clothing around Eilward's neck along with the whetstone and gloves. On the next day, he presented him to the king's officials.

Having been brought to Bedford, Eilward was held in public custody for a month. He sent for a certain venerable priest, Paganus, and, as one exposed to extreme danger, he prepared himself for death – or, that is, for life. He unfolded all the secrets of his conscience, pouring into the secure ears of the priest everything that he found opposed to his salvation. He also committed his hope for the liberation of his body to divine mercy, saying, "My dearest lord, if I can evade this moment of grave danger, I will go on foot to the land which the Son of God, our Lord Jesus, sanctified by his life on earth and by his death. And so, I also ask that I might be branded with the sign of the cross by a hot iron on my right shoulder, so that even if my clothes are removed, the sign might not be taken away from me."[4] The priest did as he was asked, advising him to flee devoutly to the intercession of the saints, especially to the intercession of the glorious martyr Thomas whom the Lord had exalted with such glory of miracles. Moreover, the length and breadth of his body was measured with a thread, so that the man, when freed, could offer a candle to the holy martyr. He also gave him a scourge made of rods, saying, "Take these rods, and, with an invocation of the martyr, torment yourself five times a day before you eat anything. Do not stop bending your knee to the martyr day and night and making invocations to him, except when, overcome by the need to sleep, you are forced to remedy nature's deficiencies." Having diligently advised him in this way, he left, stating that the judges had determined that no priest would be permitted to see him again. However, he often sent a man to him who would – secretly, through the window – rouse him from negligence

---

[4] Those pledging to go to Jerusalem, as Eilward is doing here, would ordinarily sew a cross onto their clothing.

or encourage him to even greater effort. Moreover, [Auger],[5] the prior of the canons of Bedford,[6] from whom we also have witness to this admirable miracle, often sent food to meet the captive's needs and visited the jailed man. So that he might breathe freely for an hour at least, he would have him taken from the jail to walk under the open sky.

Four weeks had passed, and the beginning of the fifth had come, when the miserable man was taken from jail to the council to be judged. The accuser charged him of the crime of theft. He assiduously denied the crime he was accused of, casting away all the things that had been hung around his neck except for the whetstone and the gloves, which he acknowledged he had taken as surety for the debt. He wholly denied theft or any other crime. Judgement was delayed and he was again sent back to jail. After the fifth week, he was again brought to the council and accused by his adversary of the theft of only the whetstone and the gloves. The accuser feared to undergo the trial by ordeal demanded by the defendant. Though he was condemned by his silence concerning all the things he had accused him of taking before, he had the favour of the sheriff and the justices, and so he was able to excuse himself from the necessity of a duel, while having the other tried by the ordeal of water. It was, however, a Saturday, and the trial by ordeal was put off until the Tuesday of the following week. He was again held in jail, and his jailer's cruelty did not allow him to keep vigil in the church, which the piety of the Christian religion allows for persons purging themselves from sin. Nevertheless, he devoutly celebrated in jail the vigils that he was not allowed to celebrate in church.

As he was being led to the water, the priest Paganus met him on the way. He advised him to bear all things with equanimity for the forgiveness of his sins, not to have hatred or anger in his soul, to forgive his enemies from his heart for everything they had done, and not to despair of God's mercy. He said, "May the will of God and the martyr Thomas be done in me!" Plunged

---

[5] Robertson's edition lists the prior's name as Gaufridus (Geoffrey). Anne Duggan has collated three manuscripts in which the prior's name is recorded as "Angerius": see Duggan, "Santa Cruz," p. 53. The prior of the Augustinian priory of Bedford who was appointed April/May 1170 was named Auger (see *HRH*, p. 177), so I have emended "Geoffrey" to "Auger."

[6] A canon of Bedford named Philip de Broi was the cause of a sharp dispute between Henry II and Becket on the question of the treatment of criminous clerks: see Barlow, *Thomas Becket*, pp. 93 and 104. The regularization of Bedford's canons and the foundation of Bedford's Augustinian priory occurred c.1166, possibly as a direct result of this notorious incident. Though Benedict does not mention Philip de Broi's case in his discussion of Eilward's miracle, he and many of his readers would have known of it.

into the water, he was found guilty, and was seized by the aforesaid beadle, Fulk, who said, "Here, you criminal, you will come to me here." He replied, "Thanks be to God and the holy martyr Thomas!" He was taken to the place of punishment, deprived of his eyes, and his genitals were mutilated. They tore out the entire left eye right away, but they were hardly able to extract the right eye, lacerating it and cutting it into pieces. They buried the members that had been cut off under the turf, and, according to what is read of the one who was set upon by robbers, *they stripped him, and, having wounded him* (as has been described), *they went away, leaving him half dead* [Lk 10:30]. Not a small crowd of people had come to the spectacle, some compelled there in the name of public power, some by the tug of curiosity. His accuser Fulk, the king's official of the same name (by whose instigation and council, it is believed, he was brought to such misery), and two other officials mutilated him. When they asked him for pardon, however, he granted it freely for the love of God and Saint Thomas the martyr. He cried aloud with wonderful faith that though he was deprived of light, he would go to the memorial of the martyr. He did not despair of the kindness and virtue of the martyr, knowing that it would be more glorious for the martyr to restore lost eyes than to save those that had not been removed. The only person with him was his twelve-year-old daughter, who had also begged for food for him when he was in jail.[7] Everything he had had been confiscated, *all his friends despised him, and of all those who were dear to him, there was no-one to console him* [Lam 1:2]. His wounds bled so much that those who were there sent for a priest, fearing for his death, and he confessed to him. After a little while, however, the flow of blood lessened, and he was led by the young girl back to the village of Bedford. He threw himself down beside the wall of a house and stayed there until nightfall. During that day, no-one extended any human kindness to him. When night came, a man by the name of Eilbrict had mercy on him, especially because of the poor weather and heavy rain that was greatly troubling him as he lay out in the open. *He received him with joy* into his house [Lk 19:6].

He spent ten days in darkness, dedicating himself to the labor of prayers and vigils. In the first vigil of the night of the tenth day, after mourning, groaning and sighing, he fell asleep. The one he had invoked appeared to him, dressed in dazzling, snow-white clothes. Marking the sign of the cross on his forehead and eye-sockets with his pastoral staff, he was seen to depart in silence. He woke up and, heedless of the vision, lay down again and slept. A second time

---

[7] Robert of Cricklade noted that Eilward's daughter was traveling with him after he left Canterbury: see *Thómas Saga*, p. 103 and Biographical Notes, Robert of Cricklade.

before dawn the one who was dressed in white and had *whitened his garments in the blood of the Lamb* [Rev 7:14] returned and said to him, "Good man, are you sleeping?" He said that he was awake, and he said, "Do not, do not sleep, but instead keep vigil and persist in your prayers. Do not despair, but rather put your trust in God and the blessed Virgin Mary and Saint Thomas, who comes to visit you. If you keep vigil tomorrow night with a burning wax candle in the church of the blessed Mary nearby,[8] before the altar of the same Virgin, and do not hesitate, but apply yourself in faith to prayer, you will rejoice in the restoration of your eyes." Waking, the man silently thought over what this vision might portend, and whether, with its meaning uncovered, the promise of the saint might come about. As he was thinking over this in secret, a female servant said to him, as if she were a messenger of a good omen, "Eilward, last night I saw in a dream that you would receive sight in both of your eyes." And he said, "This may happen, when it pleases God and his blessed martyr Thomas." When evening began to fall and the day was nearly done, the lids of his left eye became itchy. In order to scratch them, he removed the wax poultice that had been put on his empty eye sockets to draw out the corruption or to keep the eyelids closed. Opening his eyelids, by the wonderful power of God it seemed to him that the opposite wall of the house was lit up as if with the brightness of a lamp. It was in fact a red ray of the sun, which was almost at the point of setting. Unsure of the truth, and incredulous about this himself, he called the lord of the house and pointed out what he thought was there. And he said, "Insane, Eilward, you are insane. Be quiet. You don't know what you are talking about." He replied, "I am definitely not insane, lord. It really seems to me that I see this with my left eye." His host still wavered, wishing to have certainty about this, and waved his hand before his eyes, saying, "Do you see what I am doing?" He responded, "I think you have moved your hand back and forth in front of my eyes." Then he told him, in order, what he had seen from the beginning of the first vision, what he had been ordered to do, and what was promised to him.

This word went out among the neighbors [Jn 21:23], and the novelty of the new things attracted not a small multitude of people. The dean Osbern, the lord, or rather the servant of the aforesaid church, ran to that place, and having heard the man's vision, he brought him into the church. He placed him before the altar of the blessed Virgin, building him up and comforting him in the faith. When a light was put in his hand, he said he could clearly see the altar cloth, and then the image of the blessed Virgin Mary, and last other objects

---

[8] This is very likely the parish church of St. Mary's in Bedford.

of smaller size. The amazement of the people grew in proportion to the grace of sight given to the man, and they tried to discover how he had the power of sight, whether from new eyes or from his empty eye-sockets without pupils. They discerned two small pupils lurking deep inside his head, scarcely as large as the pupils of a small bird. These pupils continued to grow, and their slow augmentation increased the indescribable and incredible astonishment of all those seeing them. And so the clamour of the people was lifted to heaven, the praises owed to God were rendered, the bells of the church were rung, and many came who had earlier retired to sleep. With their illuminated man, they stayed awake and awaited the sun. In the morning, a crowd of the entire village massed together as one, and in the bright light they looked at him carefully. They noticed that one eye was grey in colour, while the other was entirely black, though when he was born both eyes were grey. Among the rest of them, the priest of the church of St. John, who had received his confession when he had been mutilated, also ran there, and seeing the wonderful power of God, he said, "Why must we wait for the precept of papal authority? I will not wait any longer. I will begin a divine service of the glorious friend of God, Thomas, as of a most precious martyr, and I will say it to the end. Who can doubt him to be a martyr, when he does such things?"[9] Running to the church, he did what he said he would, with the bells ringing.

And so the man was no longer deprived of light, I declare, but rather he was ornamented by it. In the same way that he had been ignominiously dragged through the middle of the village to punishment, he was now brought back along the same path, with the glory and favor of the people, to the church of St. Paul, where he spent the night of the Lord's day sleepless. He then left and took up the journey to Thomas, *the author of his salvation* [Heb 2:10]. Wherever he went, a great multitude of the people followed him, for his fame preceded him and roused everyone to meet him. Whatever gifts were given to him, he distributed to the poor for the love of the martyr. When he had gone about four miles, he put his hand down to scratch an itch on the scrotum of his testicles, and he discovered that his members had also been restored to him. They were very small, but they grew bigger, and he did not deny those who wished to feel them. When he came to London, Hugh, the bishop of Durham,[10] received him with congratulations, and did not wish to

---

[9] Usually, a mass for a martyr would only be said for someone who had been officially recognized as such by the Church. Eilward's miracle dates to late 1171 or early 1172, a year or more before Pope Alexander III's canonization of Thomas Becket in February 1173.
[10] See Biographical Notes, Hugh de Puiset, bishop of Durham.

dismiss him before he sent a messenger to Bedford so that the truth would be certified by a diligent investigation. When we received him, moreover, although the testimony of many had preceded him, we were not satisfied with the substance stated above until we had heard them confirmed by the letters and testimony of the citizens of Bedford. They sent writing to us which stated the following:

"Greetings from the burgesses of Bedford to the convent of Canterbury and all the faithful in Christ.

Let it be known to the convent of Canterbury, and all catholic people, that God has worked a marvelous and remarkable miracle in Bedford through the merits of the most holy martyr Thomas. It happened that a certain rustic of Westoning by the name of Eilward was captured, for a theft worth only a single penny, and led before the sheriff of Bedford and the knights of the county. By them, he was publicly condemned, and outside the village of Bedford, with clerics, laity, and women present, he lost his eyes and testicles. The chaplain of St. John of Bedford, to whom the aforesaid rustic confessed after his mutilation, testifies to this. His host, by name of Eilbrict, with whom he was afterwards given hospitality, also testifies that he was wholly lacking eyes and testicles when he was first given hospitality by him, and afterwards, often invoking the merits of saint Thomas the martyr, through a glorious and wonderful vision of the same martyr, he was restored to health."

So reads the testimony of the burgesses of Bedford concerning this miracle. What will the enemies of the martyr say about this? Every objection of the malefactors is countered in this, as I might say, miracle of all miracles, nor does the adverse party have any means of avoiding a shameful reproach. The fact that he was truly deprived of his aforementioned members is established by the power his enemies were granted to harm him and their eagerness to do so. The ones who mutilated the man were the ones who hated him the most. But even if they had spared him, not only they themselves, but all those who were there as witnesses to make sure that the sentence of the judgment was not frustrated, as well as the many people who had condemned him, would have imperiled themselves if, injuring the king's majesty, the condemned man had escaped unharmed. Thus the wonderful wisdom of God, *who catches the wise in their craftiness* [Jb 5:13], so miraculously ordained that it was necessary for them either to overcome all their fear to testify to the miracle, or to expose themselves to inevitable peril if they denied the sign. The testimony of the truth is also supported by the multitude of witnesses who were there, as well as the firmest grounds of truth, the contrast of the new eyes, and also the smallness at first both of them and of the other members. In place of the eyes of grey colour that nature had given him, he received one that was grey and the other black. Who has ever heard the like? Who has seen something similar? Great was the faith of the man, great the merit of his faith, great also the reward of the merit. [*See Parallel Miracles no. 2 for William's account of this miracle.*]

IV.3. CONCERNING RALPH OF LONGUEVILLE, PERFECTLY CURED OF LEPROSY AND STRUCK BY THE CONTAGION OF LEPROSY AGAIN

A young man of no less faith or merit of Longueville named Ralph,[11] who had been struck by the contagion of leprosy, entered into an agreement with his fellow-lepers of a leper hospital, having determined what he ought to give to them for his living. At this point, due to his hoarse voice, fetid breath, ulcerous limbs, and pustules rising up again and again on his swollen and sallow face, he was not able to live with the healthy. But when the glory of miracles had spread about, he trusted in the merits of the martyr to the same degree that he was ashamed of his own and went to the holy church of Canterbury. He prostrated himself before the tomb of the saint, and, completely dissolved in tears, he was heard in his prayers to obligate himself to astounding vows, with astounding devotion conceived from his astounding pain. He promised to go to Jerusalem for the love of the martyr. Of all the bread by which he was fed, he would make three alms. He would fast on Lenten fare twice in the week: namely, on Tuesday, the day the martyr was killed, and on Friday, the day Christ was crucified.[12] As a sign of his devoted servitude, he would also redeem his own head from the saint by an annual offering of four pennies. He remained at Canterbury for nine days. Each day, he drank and washed with

---

[11] Ralph's miracle is portrayed in three panels in Canterbury Cathedral window nIII. For *Longa villa*, which I have decided to translate as Longueville, Robertson suggested Langton (presumably meaning Langdon?) in Kent. It seems more likely that Ralph either hailed from Longueville in Normandy or was a member of the Huntingdonshire family called *de Longavilla* (for miracles concerning the knight Henry de Longavilla, see III.36-7 above). Ralph's ability to make provision for himself at a leper hospital, give alms, and vow a trip to Jerusalem indicates that he came from a family with some means.

[12] This appears to be the earliest reference to special devotion to Becket on a Tuesday. For other references, see Duggan, "The Cult of St. Thomas Becket in the Thirteenth Century," p. 40 n. 105.

the holy water, and he left improved. But we hoped a better end would result from this good beginning, and as he was going we strongly urged him to consider returning when he was fully cleansed. He promised to do so. And it happened that as he went, he was cleansed. Then he brought back joy concerning himself to his friends. We had dismissed him corrupted with leprosy, and in the space of a month, we welcomed back a young man of most elegant form. Therefore from Pentecost almost to Advent he stayed with us, being most whole, healthy, handsome, and without a mark. At length he left us, as if he intended to travel to Jerusalem, and returning home – I do not know by what hidden judgment of God – he was seen to be leprous to such a degree, that no one ever existed more fouled by the contagion of leprosy. The reason for his deterioration He knows, who said to him whom He had cured, *Behold, now you are healed: now sin no more, lest something worse happen to you* [Jn 5:14].

IV.4. CONCERNING HUMPHREY OF CHESTERTON, RELEASED FROM A SIMILAR AILMENT

The repetition of the first miracle doubled the joy kindled in us. For, as we had been informed by the kindness of the venerable master Edmund, the archdeacon of Coventry,[13] a leper of his archdeaconate returned from the memorial of the memorable martyr without any blemish. Although we had faith in his words, since this archdeacon had only heard of this thing and *what we hear rouses the mind less vividly than what the eyes reliably report,*[14] we did not wish to commit it to writing unless the leper came back to us with certifying letters from his dean. The execution of our wishes followed, and *as we had heard, so have we seen* [Ps 47:9]. Since the letter corresponded with the archdeacon's narration, we dismissed the man in peace. We have thought it fitting to include the dean's letter, retained for testimony, for it is in this tenor:

"To the convent of the church of Canterbury, from Saffrid, dean of Chesterton,[15] greetings and prayers in the Lord.

Since the innards of our minds delight in the multitude of the blessed Thomas' miracles, we have determined to lay bare for you those that have happened

---

[13] See Biographical Notes, Edmund, master and archdeacon of Coventry.
[14] Horace, *Ars Poetica*, lines 180–1.
[15] A charter dated 1160x1176 that was witnessed by Edmund (see Biographical Notes, Edmund, master and archdeacon of Coventry) includes a witness named "Sasfredo." This might be the writer of this letter: see *EEA: Coventry and Lichfield, 1160–1182*, ed. by M. J. Franklin (Oxford, 1998), p. 74.

among us, so that they might produce an increase in joy along with the others collected by you. Here, therefore, is what has happened, what the Lord has done and shown to us. In our diocese, we know that a certain man, Humphrey by name, was truly ill for three years. Nearly all the strength was drained from his limbs and he had shaggy and prominent ulcers. He was said to be struck by leprosy by those who lived with him and that he should be segregated from human fellowship so that his company could be avoided. Shamed as well as pained by his body's illness, the man went to the holy places of many saints in the hopes of gaining bodily health. After many days, it came into his mind to seek the places[16] of the blessed king and martyr Edmund[17] for the sake of a cure, where the miracles of the glorious martyr Thomas were already being publicized round about. He heard that through his merits it was certain that *lepers were cleansed, the lame could walk, sight was restored to the blind* [Mt 11:5/Lk 7:22], and the feverish were brought back to their former color of face. Though he was weak, when he heard these things he hastened (as he could) to travel to the holy Thomas. And so, having turned his prayers to him, hardly had he tasted the health-giving water when he felt the descent of the long-standing illness from his head to his chest, from his chest to his stomach, from his stomach to his legs, and from his legs into nothingness. Returning home, he neglected to give back in return the thanks he owed to God and the saint for his health. Hiding the miracle in his heart which the Lord made visible in his face, he returned to us, and at length he told me what had happened. Hearing the nearly incredible truth of this, I send him back to you, so that he might supply the saint what he did not do."

This is the tenor of the letter his pen set down, which we had begged the archdeacon to obtain for us. What will we say to this? Among the servants of God, can we find anyone who fully equals the martyr of Canterbury? To whom will we compare him? If you place him next to his contemporaries, you will find no one like him. If you have recourse to the ancients, although there is a similarity, yet you will not find a similar abundance. Moses put leprosy to flight, but only in Miriam.[18] *There were many lepers in the days of Elisha,*

---

[16] Robertson's edition supplies the word *merita* ("merits") at this spot (see Robertson, p. 184 n. 3). Anne Duggan has collated three manuscripts in which the word *loca* ("places") is found (Duggan, "Santa Cruz," p. 53), a reading I have adopted here.

[17] St. Edmund (d.869) was the famed saint and miracle-worker whose relics were held at Bury St Edmunds in East Anglia. For a full-length study of his cult, see Rebecca Pinner, *The Cult of St Edmund in Medieval East Anglia* (Woodbridge, 2015).

[18] See Numbers 12, in which Moses asked the Lord for the healing of his leprous sister Miriam.

but no-one was cleansed except Naaman of Syria [Lk 4:27].[19] We believe that neither in the course of the Old Testament, nor in the time of grace,[20] can any servant of God easily be found through whose merits so many lepers were purified or improved. This will be demonstrated by all that follows, but since distaste would be produced by the constant repetition of the same miracle, we will put off the rest of the lepers and interpose a few things.

IV.5. CONCERNING ODO OF FALAISE, WHO, HAVING BEEN STRUCK IN THE EYE, LACKED SIGHT FOR SEVEN YEARS

One of the king's officials, Odo of Falaise,[21] a knight of good repute and, saving the king's honor, a friend of the martyr during his lifetime, took too little care to protect himself with his shield in the lists and was severely struck in his right eye by the lance of his sporting opponent. It followed that for nearly seven years, he carried out the office entrusted to him with only the use of his left eye. He was a reckoner of the king's accounts. In the year in which the glorious high-priest Thomas had completed his life, in the summer after he had exchanged life temporal for life eternal through his death, there came a day in the course of the mysteries of the mass when the knight prayed more devoutly than usual. Remembering the cruel murder of the martyr, whom he had dearly loved, he began to weep bitterly. The tears poured forth, and he was not able to contain himself. When he moved his hand to wipe away the tears, his eye, restored to perfect use, saw his outstretched hand before it felt it. Uncertain, he closed his left eye, and verified that the right eye could truly see. We saw him coming to the memorial of the martyr with votive offerings and gifts, yet so humbly and so cast down that one might wrongly think him to be a beggar by his bearing and dress.

IV.6. CONCERNING THE HOUSE OF GILBERT, BAKER OF THE BISHOP OF ROCHESTER, WHICH WAS FREED FROM FIRE IN THE MIDST OF FLAMES

A pilgrim returning from the memorial of the martyr entered the town of Rochester in order to spend the night there. Though his entrance was denied

---

[19] For the story of Elisha's healing of Naaman, the leader of the Syrian army, see 2 Kings 5:1–14.
[20] By "the time of grace," Benedict means since the time of Christ.
[21] Charles Homer Haskins speculated that this Odo could be identified with the *Odo hostiarius* (Odo the doorkeeper) who appears in the Pipe Rolls in this period: see Haskins, *Norman Institutions* (Cambridge, 1918), p. 163.

everywhere, the maidservant of the household of Gilbert, the baker of the bishop of Rochester, received him for the love of the martyr. This Gilbert was absent. Several of the young men of the bishop's household, for whom the same house was accustomed to serve as a dining room, had arrived at nightfall, as was their usual habit. The pilgrim had brought with him a tin ampulla full of the holy water of Canterbury. *In the middle of the night, when everything was silent* [Ws 18:14], the city was beset by fire. The fire raged everywhere, and with a dry summer heat aided, as usual, by the force of the wind, the entire city was threatened with destruction. Everyone was terrified and confused, and everyone despaired of themselves; no-one had the strength to attend even to their own affairs. The young men and the pilgrim leapt up and climbed on top of the house to try to repel the advancing conflagration, but the fire, growing in strength, was already consuming the neighboring house. Repelled by the heat, they quickly descended. Only the pilgrim, whose faith blazed more hotly than the physical fire, remained undaunted on the roof of the house. He asked for a pole or something long, and a forked stake was held up to him. Taking it, he attached the reliquary that had been hanging from his neck to the top of the stake and he set it closer against the fire. It is believed that the reliquary's cooling defense had sustained him against the heat of such near and large flames.

The extraordinary faith of the man was followed by an even more extraordinary display of power. The fire, which had been blazing about in different directions and was licking the ridge of the house upon which he stood, suddenly seemed to stand still in the sky, as if it were terrified of an opposing element, or rather, more truly, of the power of the martyr in the element. Many who were there have testified that they saw the whole globe of flame turned aside when the pilgrim thrust the ampulla towards it. Among them was a wealthy inhabitant of the city. Having seen this marvelous sight, he tried to entice the pilgrim away with the offer of twelve shillings, such that his house, which he expected to meet a similar end to the rest, might be protected by the presence of the reliquary. But the pilgrim said, "Even if you brought together all the wealth of the city, I would not now leave this place. This house gave me hospitality for the love of the blessed martyr Thomas. By his merits, it will be freed from the present danger." And so the whole city was fodder for the flames and destroyed by the combustion. In the midst of the fire, only that house remained unharmed.[22]

---

[22] There are documentary references to a major fire in Rochester on April 11 or 12, 1179: see Martin Brett, "The Church at Rochester, 604–1185," in Nigel Yates with the assistance of Paul A. Welsby (eds.), *Faith and Fabric: A History of Rochester Cathedral, 604–1994*

IV.7. CONCERNING THE HOUSES OF WILLIAM OF YARMOUTH SIMILARLY FREED

The kindness of the martyr also preserved the houses of William of Yarmouth from fire. When the village was aflame and the peril to his houses seemed unavoidable and imminent, he said, "Saint Thomas, glorious martyr, come to my aid and repel the fire. If you will be the liberator of my houses, I will be your servant and pilgrim very soon." The fire was at once restrained. He obtained what he had requested, and he fulfilled with his action what his mouth had vowed.

IV.8. CONCERNING WILLIAM OF PARNDON, SON OF EUDES, WHO WAS DYING OR DEAD

Infirmity had brought down William, the son of Eudes of Parndon, to such an extent that he lay without any sign of life and seemed to have departed human affairs. The parents of the boy, thinking that he had without doubt died, got up weeping and lamenting, the mother going out to call together neighbors, the father going into the garden to weep alone. Distressed for their son – dying or dead, I do not know which I ought to say – they called upon the martyr of Canterbury as they anxiously ran about. From their loud cries of lament, the name of the martyr rang through the whole area. Once he had entered the garden, the groaning father looked in the direction of the city of Canterbury and knelt to pay his respects to the body of the martyr, though it was far away.[23] After a little while, both of them re-entered the house, and they found the boy revived, whom they believed to have left truly dead. After eight days, restored to his former vigor, he was presented to his liberator and shown to us.

IV.9. CONCERNING BALDWIN, FROM THE SAME PLACE, WHO HAD WEAKENED FROM AN ACUTE ILLNESS

We also saw another with them, Baldwin, who testified that he had been confined to his bed for five weeks. In all that time, he had taken nothing except for

---

(Woodbridge, 1996), p. 27. However, Benedict finished writing the *Miracles* long before 1179. Fires were a common peril in medieval towns and cities, and this chapter must refer to an earlier, otherwise unrecorded fire in Rochester. Given the reference to the "dry summer heat," it most likely occurred in the summer of 1171 or 1172.

[23] Canterbury is located about 100 kilometers southeast of Parndon, a village in Essex that was absorbed by the village of Harlow in the mid-twentieth century.

water, with the exception of Sundays, when, as is the custom, he was carried to the church and received blessed bread as if for communion. When he tasted the health-giving water of the martyr, he immediately assumed not only good condition, but even greater vigor.

IV.10. CONCERNING A NUN WHO REMAINED HALF DRY IN THE MIDST OF A HEAVY RAIN

A nun of a certain church some twenty-seven miles from Canterbury[24] was sitting outside and making, with great devotion, a little gift – a belt to be offered to the martyr. Suddenly, water began to pour down from the sky. Her fellow nuns took refuge under shelter, but she, pressing on with the work she had begun, would not move from the place. "Come in," said the other sisters, "Lecarda, come in quickly." But she said, "I will not go in, nor will I move from here: am I not the worker of St. Thomas the martyr? If he wishes, he will keep his work and his worker unharmed by the rain." The rain became heavier and there was a powerful rainstorm all around her, but the martyr's worker, sitting in the middle of the downpour, remained half dry and half wet. From the top of her head, her back part was soaked by rain, but not a drop touched the belt nor the front part of her body except for her feet. She called to two of the sisters and showed herself to them, so that they might be witnesses and knowers of such a miracle. The belt was sent to us, and it was hung up next to the body of the martyr as a memorial of the miracle.

IV.11. CONCERNING THE SAINT'S WATER TURNING INTO BLOOD

We also heard about a remarkable miracle shown in the village of Stafford, namely of the water turning into blood. I could describe how this happened, but I prefer the letter and testimony of the faithful religious man Albinus, abbot of Darley,[25] to my narration. I sent a messenger to him in order to find out the truth of this event, and he sent letters to the prior of the church of Canterbury to this effect:

---

[24] This church is most likely the priory of Minster in Sheppey, which is located about forty kilometers from Canterbury. Another possibility is the Benedictine nunnery of Higham or Littlechurch, about fifty kilometers from Canterbury, which was founded c.1148.
[25] See Biographical Notes, Albinus, abbot of Darley.

"To Odo, most dear friend in Christ and prior of the church of Christ of Canterbury,[26] from Albinus, abbot of Darley. Eternal greetings in Christ.

Just as he who tells a falsehood from his heart should be charged with the offense of falsity, so too he who fails to testify to truth in his time is guilty of falsity, for this, as the scripture tells us, is to deny Christ.[27] *Having been requested for the truth, we therefore bring forward testimony to the truth; we know that our testimony is true* [Jn 21:24]. Thus, let it be known to you that a certain burgess of Stafford, Reinard, was afflicted by a severe illness. He asked for the water of the blessed martyr Thomas from a knight named William de Warenne,[28] who had acquired the water from you. When a messenger brought the vessel in which the blessed water had been contained to Reinard, it was found to be empty, and the hands of the messenger appeared bloody. The wife of Reinard and Nicholas his son saw and testified to this miracle. Having seen this, Reinard gave thanks to God, and disclosed in the spirit the things that had happened to a priest named William. Reinard asked that the vessel be filled with holy water, and the water poured into it was turned into blood. I and Henry and William and Osbern, priests, and Nicholas and Odo, deacons, and the aforesaid woman Aileva and her son Nicholas,[29] saw and testify to this. The same Henry saw the water of the blessed martyr that he had acquired from you turn into blood, and I also saw this. He presented this water with its ampulla to the prior of Lenton."[30]

So runs the testimony of the abbot about this miracle. Moreover, the clerk administering the archdeaconate of the county of Stafford, who had come from those parts to reverence the martyr, was questioned by us. He confessed that he had sent for the priest who had blessed the water poured into the pyx and had placed the blood made from it in his church, with two clerks accompanying it. The clerk demanded an oath from the priest on the right hand of the Most High concerning this transformation, and he, with his hand on the holy book, maintained his testimony to such a miracle.

---

[26] See Biographical Notes, Odo, prior of Christ Church, Canterbury.

[27] This is a reference to the denial of Christ by Peter, told in Mark 14:66–72, Matthew 26:69–75, Luke 22:5–62, and John 18:15–27.

[28] William son of Ranulf, lord of Whitchurch (see III.40 and Biographical Notes) was sometimes termed William de Warenne, and Whitchurch is only about fifty kilometers from Stafford. However, the Warenne family was large and William a common name, so this knight could be someone else entirely.

[29] See Biographical Notes, Nicholas son of Aileva.

[30] See Biographical Notes, Robert de Broi, prior of Lenton.

IV.12. ITEM CONCERNING THE SAME

But since what has been written might seem to be in the realm of the impossible – as if the One who made wine from water and changed wine into his own blood were not able to change water into blood[31] – we will bring forth the truth of how this same sign was confirmed by a fourth repetition,[32] so that no uncertainty might remain in the hearts of doubters. A certain knight, Elias, the reeve of the manor of Froyle (as it is termed in English),[33] returned from Canterbury and hung the filled ampulla that he had brought back in the church, not daring to keep in his own home the common medicine of the sick. However, the squire of the knight, being less circumspect and cautious than his lord, kept the ampulla he had brought back from Canterbury, which was filled with the same relic, in his house. Those who needed medicine in the parish hastened to the church, and they experienced in themselves the virtue of the Canterbury medicine. However, the priest, Ranulph, a man who is by our judgment very devoted to God and the holy martyr, did not administer the health-giving liquid to anyone without instructing them to fast for two or three days first. Hearing this, many of the parishioners turned back, saying, "This is a harsh message: why should we fast for him when he never abstained for us?"

A certain woman who was appointed the custodian of the house of the aforesaid knight heard that the priest had denied the water to many people. To one of the women who had been refused, she said, "Why would you fast? Come to me, and I will give you plenty of the same liquid." Going back to the house, she secretly stole the ampulla of the squire. As she was about to give the water to the woman who had followed her there, she saw the lord of the house coming in, and she was afraid. She poured the water into a beaker that was at hand. So that her theft would not be noticed, she filled the ampulla with other water and put it back in its place, bidding the woman to come back the next day. In the morning, when she was coming to take away the promised gift, the

---

[31] Benedict is referring to Christ turning water into wine at the Marriage at Cana (John 2:1–11) and the miracle of the Eucharist, the turning of water into Christ's blood.

[32] Benedict counted three transformation miracles in the chapter above. He celebrated these four miracles in an antiphon in the Becket Office (Cantus Database ID 200355): *Aqua Thomae quinquies/ varians colorem/ in lac semel transiit/quater in crurorem* [The water of Thomas, varying its colour five times, transformed once into milk, four times into blood] (see Slocum, *Liturgies*, p. 205 and Reames, "Liturgical Offices," p. 577). Benedict does not tell a miracle of the water changing into milk in his collection, but there is such a miracle in William's collection: see William of Canterbury, *Miracula*, IV.45, pp. 354–7.

[33] See Biographical Notes, Elias of Froyle.

other woman went to the chest to fulfil her promise, took out the beaker, and found thick and congealed blood. She paled from fear, and she broke out in great cries as women do. The servants of the home ran there, asking for and hearing about the reason for the uproar. The lord of the house, the knight, also came, and from the voice of the one confessing, he considered that there was some reason for such a change. And so the priest Ranulph, mentioned above, was sent for, and he came. Like the others, he was completely horrified seeing this thing. The blood, as was said above, was thick and coagulated, such that it was able to be divided into pieces. It had blackish streaks in the midst of it like the blood of a person with a smashed skull. Whatever was touched by it was tinged as if by a purple dye. Taking the beaker with its blood, the priest placed it in the church and preserved it there for many days. Fearing lest the substance of the blood might be diminished by drying out, or even to be wholly reduced to nothing, he added water, by which it was dissolved. Finally, it dried out completely. However, the bottom of the beaker remained completely stained by the dried blood. The priest brought the beaker and bestowed it on us.

Dear brothers, what do we think the Lord wished to impress upon our hearts by this event? Let others say what they perceive. To me, it seems that three things are suggested. First, the degree of similarity between Christ and the martyr. Just as one turns the wine into blood, so the other turns water into blood, yet both here and there the Lord has worked. Second, how great of a relic is acquired by those who carry away the water sanctified by the blood of the martyr. Many of those who carry it away would complain very much to leave without it. Third, with how much reverence and devotion the water ought to be drunk, when a woman who wishes to give it away irreverently finds that no-one is able to drink it. I could expound further on each point, but as I believe enough has been said for the wise, I proceed to other things, for the way before me is great.

IV.13. CONCERNING SEILEVA OF FROYLE, FROM WHOSE BREAST A SWELLING OF EXTRAORDINARY SIZE PROTRUDED

We heard three miracles from the mouth of the same venerable priest that are pleasing and worthy to be repeated. An abscess of extraordinary size protruded from the breast of Seileva, one of his parishioners. To use the words of the priest, it seemed equivalent to the thickness of the end of a large beam. She came and showed herself to the priest, and, instructed by him, took up the three-day fast. With the time completed, she washed the swelling with the sacred liquid, and the next day she found it reduced to the smallness of a nut or acorn. She washed again, and the next day revealed to the priest that it had wholly disappeared. He rejoiced greatly. Because it is said that the humors of the entire body flow to the breasts, he had been in a state of great fear and agitation that the swelling might rupture and the woman would be drained until she exhaled her spirit and died.

IV.14. CONCERNING EVERARD OF WINCHESTER, WEAKENED BY A SUDDEN PARALYSIS

The second miracle he told us was about his brother Everard, chaplain of the church of the blessed Virgin Mary at Winchester, a man very well known in the entire city.[34] One night when he was resting in the chamber of the prior at the church of Southwick,[35] he was rising from his bed to answer the call of nature when a paralysis suddenly struck him. As he was trying to walk forward, he fell down steep steps. Awakened by the noise of his fall, the prior woke other sleepers. They swiftly ran towards him, carrying lit candles, and found him to be entirely without the use of his senses. The ill man was carried to the infirmary, and there he remained for seven days, neither seeing, nor eating, nor drinking. He lay there like a dying man. In Winchester, it was heard that he had died, and his prebend was given to another cleric, his books were handed away, and his estate disposed of. Many of his friends and relatives gathered around him. In this group was his brother, from whom we heard about this, namely the above-mentioned priest, Ranulph.[36] Although the prior wished to make the paralyzed man, already dying, into a canon, Ranulph dissuaded him saying, "What good can it be to a man without sense or reason to take on the religious habit? The habit which he assumes unknowingly would bring him no merit, but it could be a cause of ill to him. Such a change of habit would be a confirmation of the gift of his prebend and the distribution of his goods." After a short while, Ranulph said, "Is there anyone in this village who might have even a small amount of the water of saint Thomas the martyr?" The water was found and brought, and it was poured three times into the mouth of the ill

---

[34] A man named Everard, possibly this same Everard, appears as a witness to a charter issued by Henry of Blois, the bishop of Winchester, between 1154x1171: see *EEA VIII: Winchester, 1070–1204*, ed. by M. J. Franklin (Oxford, 1993), no. 130, p. 93.

[35] Southwick, an Augustinian monastery near Brighton, was founded c.1145x53. It is about thirty kilometers from Winchester to Southwick. The prior in the early 1170s may have been named Philip, who is known to have been prior there 1174x88: see *HRH*, p. 184.

[36] Froyle, where Ranulph was priest, is about forty-five kilometers away from Southwick.

man, who was barely breathing. He suddenly spoke, saying "If it pleases God, I will go to Canterbury" – and again he lay mute as he had lain before.

Leaving that place, his brother Ranulph went to Winchester in order to recall the items of his brother that had been dispersed or to deal with them in a better way. When he had sat down at table, a servant of the same brother whom he had left paralyzed came in and said to him, "Your brother and my master is here." Thinking that he had been brought as a corpse, he answered, "Shouldn't he have been buried there with the canons?" But the messenger said, "By no means – see, he comes." "How does he come?" said the priest. "Is he brought on a bier?" "Not on a bier," he said, "like an ill or dead man, but as a vigorous and living man he comes on horseback." All those who heard him were stupefied, and wondered if the things that were said could be true. They wondered especially in regard to the brother, when they heard that he was coming whom the brother had left all but dead. The rumor spread through the city, and not a small crowd of men went out of the city to meet him, wishing to see revived the one they had heard was dead. Impatient at any delay, they went well out of the city, to the distance of about two miles, to intercept the arriving man. Seeing him, they were made glad with great joy. And they conducted him into the city and congratulated him, either because they greatly esteemed him, or rather because to them, *he was dead and is come back to life again, was lost and is found* [Lk 15:24]. *On account of this a great crowd came out to meet him, since they had heard that this sign was worked in him* [Jn 12:18]. His prebend was restored to him and all the rest of those things which belonged to him by right. The cleric to whom the prebend had been transferred died a few days later. These things, as they are written in unpolished style, the aforesaid Ranulph, the brother of the ill man, asserted to us, which *he both saw with his eyes and heard with his ears* [Mt 13:15]. The ill man, now well, said that he could not remember either his illness nor those things that had happened around him, excepting that, when he returned to himself, he asked that his horses be brought to him, and, mounting, he hastened the twelve miles to Winchester, where he was stupefied by the stupefied crowd coming to meet him.

IV.15. CONCERNING HIS BROTHER [RANULPH][37] THE PRIEST

The aforesaid Ranulph visited the martyr, drawn there not only by these miracles but also by another need. For three weeks he had been weakened by an

---

[37] The caption writer has "Ralph" rather than "Ranulph" here.

acute illness. He had eaten nothing in that time and the doctors despaired of him. Disposing of all that he had, he awaited nothing less than the coming of death. On a certain Saturday, he called to mind the new martyr of the English and made a vow to him, saying, "Raise me up from this bed, glorious martyr, and I will come to you." He ate that very day, got up, and, getting on a horse, he went as far as the barn, which had been built for him two miles off. He then returned to his house, for on account of his infirmity, he was hardly able to stand. On the next day, however, returning from the church and feeling himself to be better, he ordered his horses to be saddled so that he might go on the journey he had vowed. Those who knew his debility attempted to dissuade him, but he would not give in. Undertaking the journey, that same day he traveled some forty miles. Rather than being worn out by this exertion, it was as if he received strength from it. He came to the martyr in excellent health.

IV.16. CONCERNING THE WIFE OF [ANFRID][38] OF FERRING, IN WHOSE UTERUS A FETUS HAD PUTREFIED

I will tell of a very wondrous sign in a few words. A man of the knightly order, Anfrid of Ferring in Sussex,[39] spent his days well *with his espoused wife, who was with child. The time of delivery had come* for the woman [Lk 2:5–6], but she was not able to give birth. She had conceived a son, but she would not be his future mother: she would be his sepulchre. For fifteen days the fetus had not moved in the mother's womb. A corpse lay in a corpse, a dead body in the dying one; the child was gone before it was seen, buried before it was born. The living woman seemed to have putrefied from the dead body. She was rendered senseless and her case seemed hopeless. "What are we doing?" said the father of the house, "what are we doing? We sit despairing, and we do not remember the martyr of Canterbury." Taking up a string, he measured the dying woman with an invocation of the martyr's name, promising a gift of an oblation to the martyr which she was not able to vow for herself. After the vow was made, no-one would have been able to take a thousand paces before she gave birth. The dead fetus was so wasted away that it seemed to have the appearance of meat boiled in a pot. And so the woman, whom they thought had rotted inside, escaped, and she visited the martyr in the company of her

---

[38] He is named "Hamfrid" by the caption writer and in one manuscript: see Robertson, *MTB*, vol. 2, p. 196 n. 1. Robertson's edition gives his name as *Ansfridus*, but Duggan has collated three manuscripts that provide *Anfridus* (see Duggan, "Santa Cruz," p. 53), which I will follow here.

[39] See Biographical Notes, Anfrid of Ferring.

husband. We heard their own voices relating these things, and we had faith in their witnesses and their many tears.

IV.17. CONCERNING ALELM WHO, HAVING CUT HIS THUMB, INVOKED THE MARTYR, AND AFTER THE MEAL DID NOT FIND A SCAR OF THE WOUND

A certain man at St. Omer by the name of Lambert *prepared a great feast and invited many guests* [Lk 14:16]. Among the revelers and feasters was a distinguished young man named Alelm. When he took up a little loaf in order to slice it, his knife slipped, and he cut his left thumb all the way to the middle of the nail. He immediately exclaimed, "Help, God and saint Thomas!" Blood flowed out forcefully. The young man, embarrassed, hid his misfortune as best he could by wrapping his thumb with the border of his cloak. His fellow diners asked whether he was hurt, to which he said, "By no means, by the will of God and saint Thomas." After they had eaten, water was brought to wash away the blood and a cloth to bind up the thumb. The blood was washed; the hurt was gone; the wound was sought but not found. Everyone was astounded. They saw the water completely colored by the blood and the blood-stained cloak, but they could not discern where the blood had come from. The doctor on whom he had called had not only healed the wound, but did not even leave a scar of the wound on the thumb. The young man told all the listeners of the dream he had had the night before, which he had already told some of them that morning before the accident. "I thought," he said, "that I was sitting and eating at table with the blessed martyr Thomas, and the saint gave me some of his hairshirt and relics." They said, "truly, the martyr was at table with you today, by whose invocation you were so quickly healed."

IV.18. CONCERNING WEREMUND, SON OF WIELARD OF BÉTHUNE, WHOSE BOWELS SPILLED OUT OF HIS ANUS

Weremund, son of Wielard of Béthune, a boy nearly three years old, sickened in his mother's lap, and under the torment of a prolapsed rectum was suddenly heading to death. Women experienced in countering this peril were called in, but despite applying all their care, they were not able to succeed. In the end, his bowels spilled out of his anus and his parents' cries were raised up. Alerted by the terrible cries, the neighbors hastened to see him. A priest also came, and he bound the despairing parents to still greater despair, saying, "If there were no other man in this world, the boy would not be able to escape this death." An unknown man came to the same spectacle, and he said to the despairing father, "If you had the water of the martyr of Canterbury, you would certainly get your healthy son back. It freed me from insanity, and it would be able to return this boy's bowels to their place." They made inquiries about the martyr's water, and someone said it could be found in a neighbouring village about a mile away. When the father heard this, he hastened to the place. Returning with water he had received from Tetion, the son of Hertran, he poured it into the mouth of the boy on the brink of death, promising an oblation of the boy to the martyr if he received him back well. The crowd and the priest were still there and they awaited the end of the matter. Hardly had the water descended into the interior of the child, then little by little his bowels were mended and gathered up in his stomach. In the sight of all those there, the boy rose up sound, as if he had not suffered any injury.

IV.19. CONCERNING HERMER, SON OF TETION, WHO HAD MOVEMENTS AND TREMOURS IN ALL HIS LIMBS

When Hermer, the son of the aforenamed Tetion, was about seven years old, he was seized by an illness and recovered after the space of a year. He seemed to be well again, but then was suddenly struck with a grave affliction. His steps were always unsteady and his hands and arms were constantly in motion. With the look of someone insane, his head constantly turned about in a circle, such that it seemed his mind was seized. He was condemned to such a silence that it almost seemed as if he were mute and speechless. The father consulted many doctors, but all except one pronounced him to be incurable. Because that one doctor required a fee so high that the father of the boy, constrained by poverty, was not able to pay it, he took refuge in the merits of the saint. He heard that relics of the martyr of Canterbury were to be had at the port of Wissant at the church of the blessed Nicholas.[40] He visited that place, and asked that the portion of the hairshirt, which was held there, be dipped in water. After the boy had drunk and was taken away from the church, the motion of all his body stilled, and his ability to speak returned along with restored health. When asked how he was, with his freed voice he answered that he was healed and well. He was brought back into the church and thanks were made to God.[41]

---

[40] Wissant was one of the major embarkation points from France to England. Becket departed from Wissant in late 1170 on his return to Canterbury.
[41] On this and other stories concerning children who appeared insane, see Claire Trenery, "Insane Innocents: Mad Children in Benedict of Peterborough's *Miracula Sancti Thomae Cantuariensis*," *Family & Community History* 18:2 (2015): 139–55.

IV.20. CONCERNING [VIDOCH][42] *DE ANOCH*, WHOSE WATER BOILED OUT OF ITS VESSEL ON ACCOUNT OF HIS ANGER, BUT WHEN HE BECAME PACIFIED, THE WATER WAS PACIFIED TOO

Vidoch *de Anoch*[43] received water in a little vessel from the same Tetion. When he left, he saw that two men were coming towards him, neither of whom he liked, and he resolved that he would walk by without speaking to or greeting them. Suddenly the water began to flow out of the vessel, like a pot boiling over, as if it wished to visibly say to him: "there will be no friendship between me and you, you who do not love your neighbor." The bearer realized that he had made a bad decision, and with a changed mind he said, "I will certainly greet them." He marvelled that at the moment that his heart was pacified, the water was pacified as well.

IV.21. CONCERNING MARY, WHO WEPT AT ONE MOMENT AND LAUGHED THE NEXT

We marvelled no less at the afflictions of a certain Mary of the diocese of Rouen, which she had suffered for nearly a year.[44] At one moment she would cry and in the next break into laughter. She would clap her hands, and after clapping, she would suddenly fall and lie in an ecstasy for an hour or a half hour. She was advised that every day that she heard the Mass, she should place her head underneath the Gospel while it was being read. She very often felt a good effect from this remedy. After hearing the Mass, she often remained quiet, but she was not freed. The same affliction used to return ten or more times a day. Unwillingly laughing and crying, the girl was fatigued to the point of death. When, at last, she invoked the martyr and made a vow of pilgrimage, she was rewarded with fifteen days of peace. She put off fulfilling her vow, and was returned to the earlier scourging, so much so that the latest attacks seemed worse to her than the earlier ones. She considered the cause of her deterioration, and she set off on the promised journey and was not attacked again. We later sent a messenger to her, who might make us more certain of her liberation. Although he did not find her at home, he learned of her freedom from her neighbors and reported this to us.

---

[42] The caption writer has "Judoc."
[43] The place is unidentified but was very likely located in northern France.
[44] Mary's miracle is told in three panels of Canterbury Cathedral window nII: see Caviness, *Windows*, pp. 196-7, where they are labeled "Cure of Matilda of Cologne."

IV.22. CONCERNING DURAND, THE SON OF OSBERN OF EU, INTO WHOSE EAR A STONE HAD FALLEN

Durand, the son of Osbern of Eu, was playing with stones. Having by chance been called by his mother, he tossed up the stones, and then one fell into his ear and caused him pain. He put his finger into his ear to try to get the stone out, but after greater and greater probing he gave up, tormented. His parents came and tried the same thing, but their attempts were useless. Then they put in a curved needle in order to draw out the stone, but this drove it in more deeply. As the stone vanished from their eyes, so the hope of getting it out vanished from their hearts. The boy began to be in great anguish. His cries and wailing and rolling about of his body made him seem as if he were insane. He was kept safe by the binding of his hands, and the next day he was brought to church. The father invoked the martyr for his son, and turning to the boy he said, "Son, vow that you will go to Canterbury and visit the tomb of the martyr." "I promise, my father," he said. Wonderful to relate, at the same moment that the word came from his mouth, the bloody stone came from his ear. He who wishes to see it, let him come to the martyr, and he will find the fulfillment of his desire.

IV.23. CONCERNING ERNALD, ERNULF, AND AMALRIC, THREE ILL MEN FROM THE BORDER REGION OF THÉROUANNE AND PONTHIEU

From the border region of Thérouanne and Ponthieu we received three sick men: Ernald, his brother Ernulf, and their neighbor Amalric. Ernald had been fatigued for four months by a fistula. With a swelling abounding in his throat and on his face, he was deprived the sight of one of his eyes. For a similar length of time, Ernulf had been weakened by diarrhea by day and by night. Amalric's sinews were so stiffened and contracted that he carried himself about supported by two crutches. When Amalric reached the threshold of the church, his feet and shins became like lead and his progress was halted as if he were pressed down by a weight. Yet when, with much effort, his companions had dragged him to the tomb of the martyr and he prayed there, the pain ceased, the weight lifted, and the whole of his lost health was restored. On the next day, he offered his crutches, and, leaping about in our presence, he gave us a clear indication of his health. The other man came saying that the flux that he had suffered from had fluxed into nothing. The third, too, received improvement: the very large swelling on his diseased jaw shrunk down so that it had nearly reached the slender size of the healthy jaw. However, he left with his companions and left us in doubt of the completion of the healing begun in him.

IV.24. CONCERNING PHILIP OF ALNWICK, WHOSE GENITALS HAD SWOLLEN UP

A clerk of Alnwick named Philip suffered with the detriment of two infirmities: a dangerous debility of the feet and a dreadful inflammation of the genitals. The second illness had brought him to despair of his life and the doubled pain fixed him to his bed. When the doctors despaired of him, he fell asleep. He thought he was lying in a church near the shrines of two saints. The blessed and glorious martyr Thomas rose from one of the shrines and spoke to him, saying: "Philip, you saw me, and you loved me very much when I lived in the world. And this will benefit you, in this life and in the future." With his hand, he stroked the recumbent man from his head to his groin. He grasped the greatly inflamed and swollen scrotum with two of his fingers and let go after piercing it with his nails. He said to someone standing by, "Take the shoes off his feet." When this was done, the cleric woke from sleep, and at the same moment the pain left his feet and the terrible swelling left his genitals. And he realized that this was not a dream of the sort that men are often deluded by, especially as he found that the skin of that area was indeed burst by the nails of the martyr. He found himself lying in a great deal of water, with his scrotum drained and shrunk back to its proper size. He rose healed, and from a great distance he came to Canterbury.

IV.25. CONCERNING HIS SON JOHN, WHOSE ENTIRE BODY WAS POSSESSED BY PUSTULES

His son, John, had a headache, and his whole body, front and back, was covered with pustules. He washed each one with the water of the martyr, and he was rewarded with a visitation of the martyr in his sleep, who promised him health with this stipulation: "If you vow to go to Canterbury, you will soon be cured." Waking, he found all the ulcers burst. Made whole in a short time, he took on the owed journey of pilgrimage.

IV.26. CONCERNING A CERTAIN EPILEPTIC WOMAN IN THE AFORESAID PHILIP'S HOUSEHOLD

An epileptic woman from the household of the aforesaid Philip came to Canterbury. She drank the water of the martyr, went back and afterwards did not fall from the falling sickness.

IV.27. CONCERNING THE LEPROUS WALTER

A leprous knight of Lisors named Walter lived for more than a year in a leper hospital. Having received a license from his fellow lepers, he went to Lisors to his wife, and, taking up funds for the journey, he hastened to Canterbury. After having stayed there for a time, he returned, and as he returned he sensed returning health in himself. Having turned back to his own lands, all that had legally belonged to him was restored, and so he had fellowship with men and lived with them. When I heard this, I sent one who would inquire diligently into the truth of the matter. He found him gravely ill, but having no mark of leprosy.[45]

IV.28. CONCERNING THE LEPROUS EILGAR

The body of Eilgar of Calne, similarly tainted by leprosy, was wasting away. Pustules stood out on his entire body. His hands and feet were contracted and covered with ulcers, and for the most part had no feeling. His nostrils were blocked up and his breath stank. Even his wife shunned his company and sent him away. He fled to the martyr, and before his tomb, having poured out tears and prayers, he slept. And it seemed as if he saw someone passing by him and saying, "Man, get up, go home, and be healed" [Mt 9:6/Mk 2:11/Lk 5:24]. And so, when he got up, he obeyed the commands. On his return home, from his renewed vigor in walking he felt a great beginning of health in himself. He passed everyone who was walking in front of him, though when he came to Canterbury, he had not been able to keep up with the slowest. And so with his flesh made whole and blooming again he was greatly improved, but by my judgment he was not completely cleansed. The cured ulcers began to come forth again, such that those who had not seen him before might think him to be a leper, but those who knew him marvelled at the change.

---

[45] Perhaps the same messenger who checked on the epileptic Mary of Rouen (see IV.21) also went to Lisors to see how Walter was faring. Lisors is a little over thirty kilometers from Rouen.

IV.29. CONCERNING ERNOLD, THE DROPSICAL BAKER OF THE EARL SIMON

I know what I tell from the relation of an illustrious man, namely, Earl Simon.[46] Dropsy had enormously distended his baker, Ernald. When he had been ill for nearly two years, always growing worse, he was finally confined to his bed and declined for half a year longer. His lord was grieved because he was going to lose him. Doctors were called in, but not one was found who would venture to take charge of his treatment, for there were clear signs in him that his liver had rotted. He placed all his hope for his healing in the doctor of Canterbury. Solely by the invocation of his name, he was restored to the point of walking. He hastened to Canterbury, slept by night in the church, and with a sudden loosening he dishonored the place dedicated to God. But in the morning, when he felt very ashamed of himself, he found the pavement clean and quite unpolluted, with nothing indecent present. And so his lord received him back lean and healthy, and he gave great thanks to God and the martyr.

IV.30. CONCERNING JULIANA, THE DAUGHTER OF GERARD OF ROCHESTER, WHO WAS NOT ABLE TO OPEN HER EYELIDS

Gerard of Rochester led his daughter, Juliana, whose eyelids were fastened together and inseparably united.[47] This was put to the test, and it was proved that there was nothing in this of fiction or fraud. For four months she had not been able to distinguish day from night. With her eyelids anointed by the marvelous blood, father and daughter turned back, the daughter in the night of blindness, the father in the night of sorrow. On returning home, they rebuked the martyr because he had not heard them. With her eyes suddenly opening, the martyr restored the grace of seeing to the girl and the cause of delight to the father.

---

[46] See Biographical Notes, Simon de Senlis III, earl of Northampton.
[47] Juliana's miracle is pictured in three panels of Canterbury Cathedral window nII: see Caviness, *Windows*, pp. 193–4.

IV.31. CONCERNING THE GIRL NAMED LAETICIA, WHO LOST AN EYE FROM THE PIERCING OF A STRAW WHEN SHE WAS IN HER CRADLE

A girl named Laetitia was also a cause of joy to us.[48] She was born of a noble father but humble mother. I omit the names of the district and estate on account of their crudeness. When she lay in her cradle, the pupil of her eye was injured by the piercing of a straw, and up until her fourteenth year she suffered the loss of its vision. One of her aunts, who had raised her, was going to pray at Canterbury, and, whether the aunt wished it or not, the girl followed her. She lay with her head upon the martyr's head and fell asleep. When she woke, she pressed together the eyelids of her healthy eye with her hand, and looked around with the eye that was then healed: "Aunt," she said, "I definitely see with the eye with which I did not see." And she said to her in secret, "Hush, daughter, hush, and put your head on the saint's sepulchre again." She put her head back, and after a little while rose completely cured.

IV.32. CONCERNING THE KNIGHT GEOFFREY, SURNAMED MALAEARTES, WHO WAS BLINDED BY THE WATER OF THE SAINT

The saint who, in this manner, brought light to the innocent, struck with blindness a knight of Gloucestershire who came to him in an unworthy way. He was called Geoffrey, surnamed Malaeartes, of the manor called Charlton.[49] Healthy, he came to the martyr among the sick. He asked that the blood and water mixture be put in his eyes. We denied him, seeing that he had little need, but he insisted, and having conquered with his persistence, he left. About seven miles distant from the city, he was struck with blindness, and was afflicted with such pain that it seemed he was able to say, "*O all you that pass by the way, attend, and see if there be any sorrow like to my sorrow*" [Lam 1:12]. Turning into himself, he gazed into the interior of his heart, and overturning the whole house of his conscience, he found the drachma that he had lost.[50] And so he lifted up his soul, bowed down under the feet of the passersby, to

---

[48] A literal translation preserves Benedict's wordplay: "A girl named Joy [*Laetitia*] was also a cause of joy to us."

[49] This seems to refer either to the manor of Charlton Kings, part of the hundred of Cheltenham, or to the manor of Charlton Abbots, owned by the Benedictine abbey of Winchcombe.

[50] Referring to the parable of the woman who lost a drachma (a coin) and turned over her whole house until she found it (Luke 15:8–9).

the Lord. He ejected the filth of his sins through the doorway of confession and took the sacrament of the Lord's body and blood. Thus, with his interior illumined, he was led back to Canterbury. In blindness, he carried out three days of penance there, and he recovered the light he had lost. He testified to us that because of this blindness he was purged of many sins that he had always held secretly shut up in his heart, and that he would never have brought them forth except by the lash of blindness.

IV.33. CONCERNING ALIZA, THE WIFE OF THE FISHERMAN MARTIN OF LEICESTER, WHO WAS BLINDED BY THE MARTYR

Things like this also happened to several others, of whom one was the woman Aliza, wife of the fisherman Martin of Leicester. Returning from Canterbury, she was riding in a wagon with two women when she heard one of them complaining that she saw nothing, and that she had received an eye-salve of the saint's blood in her clouded eyes to her harm. Breaking into laughter, Aliza said, "Others whom the martyr receives sick he sends away well, but you came well, and leave blind. With signs like this, be sure to visit the tombs of the saints again." And as she laughed heartily, it felt to her as if burning hot coals from an oven were dropped into her own eyes. Her eyes were greatly troubled from the heat, and before she had rubbed them four times, the light of her eyes had wholly left her; it already was not with her. And so she continued to be blind for around ten weeks. When she had paid sufficient penalty for her mocking behavior, she returned to Canterbury, having been admonished to do so in a dream, and she obtained her sight, though not fully. We do not know whether or not she afterwards regained the full extent of her earlier vision in the cleansed eyes.

IV.34. CONCERNING A PEASANT OF ABINGDON, WHO WAS CURBED BY THE MARTYR WITH A SIMILAR BLOW

We declare that we are certain of a miraculous and long-term blindness that came upon a peasant of Abingdon. Since many have turned from the reality of this miracle and have darkened truth's brightness by a cloud of facetious lies, let the hearers know that by diligent investigation I have come upon the truth, such that they might be able to discern light from the darkness. The aforesaid peasant sought the martyr with his healthy wife and his sick brother, but his severity would not allow them to remain at Canterbury as long as they wished. Having loaded them into a cart against their will, he brought them back to the city of Rochester. He rejected the same lodging that he had stayed at when he came, having seen that several of the blind and disabled pilgrims of the saint had been received there. He said, "Far be from me to spend the night with the blind of St. Thomas. They are nothing to do with me." He ordered his family to leave, despite their resistance, and he brought them to another house. Little by little, the Lord drew the darkness of blindness over the peasant's eyes. By the next day, the one who had, the day before, shunned the blind going to the martyr as if they were a contagion, was wholly blind. He often went to the martyr afterwards, but once he was blinded, he reported that he, without light, was never once illumined from our light. Even to this day, he lives and does not see.

IV.35. CONCERNING THE SON OF WILLIAM *DE BENEWELLA*, TO WHOM A SIMILAR MISFORTUNE OCCURRED

This also happened to a boy, the son of William *de Benewella*,[51] as a result of his father's curse. He, having brought his blind father to Canterbury, did not wish to yield to his wish that they stay there for a time. He departed, and his father cursed him in this manner: "May the glorious martyr avenge my injury on you, you who abandon me, deprived of light, in a distant and unknown region. Since I cannot exist without you, and it is not your desire to stay with me, I will return with you to my house from which I departed. If you would stay here for a short time, you would perhaps see me sighted, but now, against my hope, I will leave as I came." And so the son led the father away, and in the entrance to the city he lost the light of one of his eyes. Lamenting, he went on for another seven miles, until, wholly darkened by the darkness of blindness, he sat down in the middle of the king's road with his father, whom he was leading. Having been given recompense by passersby, they were both led to Canterbury. However, afterwards they left without our knowledge, leaving us uncertain about their health.

IV.36. CONCERNING [SEGIVA][52] WHO HAD BORNE AN EAR OF RYE IN HER ESOPHAGUS FOR NEARLY THREE YEARS

For nearly three years, Segiva, the daughter of a certain Richard of Essex, had borne about half an ear of rye in the mouth of her stomach. When she was

---

[51] The place is unidentified. Robertson suggested Banwell.
[52] The caption writer gives her the name of Sara.

playing with others on the threshing floor, she sucked a flying ear through her panting mouth into her throat. When the sickened girl was already judged to be dying, a certain dropsical woman arrived who was going to the martyr. She spent the night there. When she returned from Canterbury, entirely healed, she brought with her the water of the martyr, and she gave the drink to the imperiled girl. Suddenly the ear sprang up to the lower part of the throat, and there it sat some fifteen days. And so by divine will, and, as we believe, the virtue of the relic, the ear was expelled. It was covered in dense and coagulated blood as if it were a lump of bloody flesh.

IV.37. CONCERNING MATILDA OF COLOGNE, A DEMONIAC

We saw a little woman filled with a demon, named Matilda, who was brought from the region of Cologne. We shuddered at her amazing raging in our presence. She tore to shreds the linen garment that alone covered her body, and with no mean strength she struck a blow on a certain person who wanted to move her away. She would have suffocated a young boy who came near her if he had not been quickly pulled away by the bystanders. And so, bound, she raged near the martyr for four or five hours, until the martyr regarded her with the favor of health. The evil spirit was expelled and left behind the indecent traces of its going. Returning to herself little by little, she was fully restored to wholeness by the next day. Speaking in her dialect, which we could hardly understand, she told us that she had seen the martyr in a dream. He was dressed in his pontifical vestments and had the crosswise trail of blood across his face that we have also mentioned in his *Passion*.[53] He inquired about the manner of her illness, and she revealed her suffering in body and mind to the questioner. Then the saint promised her health, charging her with a journey of pilgrimage to the dwelling of the apostles, or to the church of blessed James, promising her that in this way she would be released.[54] We asked her how she had become insane, and she said that her brother had killed a young man who had loved her wrongfully. She was so seized by madness that she struck her little one, only baptized the day before, with her fist, and removed him from this world. And so she went away from the martyr healed and joyful, grieved only for the magnitude of her crime and its pardon.

---

[53] See above, *Passion*, Extract VIII, and also below, IV.52.
[54] In other words, Matilda was to make a pilgrimage to Jerusalem or to Compostela.

IV.38. CONCERNING A PENNY THE SAINT RESTORED TO A CERTAIN MATRON NAMED SIBILLA

For the sake of refreshment, it is pleasing to insert among the serious items even a few of the martyr's sports, since to him even his sports are serious. The esteemed matron Sibilla was drawn into court before the judges concerning her dower, which her stepson wished to take away from her. A girl who had been cured of insanity by the martyr came and asked in the name of St. Thomas that she be given some money for food or clothing. The matron showed reverence for the name and granted a penny to the petitioner, at which point she knew and was quite certain that she had only a halfpenny left. We found her ready and eager to swear on relics that nothing remained in her purse except the halfpenny, so much so that we do not doubt that her simple word is to be believed. Later, when she was seated and waiting for the judges to arrive at a judgment on her case, she happened to put her hand in her purse, and she found a penny similar to the former one but of larger size.[55] She marvelled greatly, and turning to a knight among those sitting there she said, "The penny I gave away for the martyr has been returned to me." Other knights turned ears to these murmurings, and not a few lovers of novelty surrounded her. Realizing that it was not possible to hide what had happened, the woman openly confessed what she had before discovered in secret. She showed the penny to the many people standing there, and it was not seen without admiration, but no-one could separate it from the woman, for the silver was made *more precious to her than gold*, and this penny more *than the finest of gold* [Is 13:12].

IV.39. CONCERNING RICHARD, THE CLERIC OF THE SHERIFF OF DEVON, TO WHOM THE MARTYR ADMINISTERED HALFPENNIES ACCORDING TO HIS INTENT

I make note of a miracle not very dissimilar to the previous one. When Richard, the cleric of the sheriff of Devon, was going to visit the memorial of the blessed Thomas, he made a vow in his heart that when he was on pilgrimage, he would not deny anyone seeking alms who asked in the martyr's name. So, he ordered one of his servants to obtain small change for him. He gave away all the farthings the servant had supplied and his soul was moved

---

[55] Unlikely our industrially produced coins made of base metals, medieval pennies were cut out of sheets of hammered silver. Being hand-made, they could vary in size. A larger penny had more silver content and so was more desirable than a smaller one.

to realize that his provision was inadequate. He would either have to give each pauper a whole penny or he would have to break his heart's vow.[56] When a pauper came upon him and sought a payment in the saint's name, he put his hand in his purse and pulled out a halfpenny. He met with a second beggar, and he found another halfpenny. A third came and received the same. A fourth poor man arrived, and the giver did not lack a fourth halfpenny. He presented a fifth halfpenny to a fifth postulant. Not being asked after that, he came to Canterbury: the way was traveled, the money expended. The esteemed man asserted to us with an oath that he was most certain that he had not brought a halfpenny with him.

IV.40. CONCERNING RALPH, THE SUBPRIOR OF THE CHURCH OF ST. AUGUSTINE, APOSTLE OF THE ENGLISH, WHOSE PENNIES THE MARTYR MULTIPLIED

He is more faithfully and firmly to be believed, because Ralph, the subprior of the church of St. Augustine, apostle of the English, or the church of the apostles Peter and Paul, outside the walls of the city of Canterbury, dedicated in honor of the apostles, but known by the name of the blessed Augustine[57] – this Ralph asserts that something similar happened to him. Ralph was going to the city of Rochester on church business. He received five shillings[58] for his expenses from the steward of the house, Haimo, son of Roger. Pennies were spent on horseshoes, on saddlecloths, and on his servants' other business. He also gave out three halfpennies to paupers asking for alms for the love of the martyr. When he returned home after the business was concluded, he counted the pennies, and he found not only five shillings, but also three halfpennies above that sum. He called one of his servants to him and said, "Didn't we spend those coins?" And he said, "We spent them in this and in that business, and you also gave three halfpennies to paupers for the name of the blessed Thomas." "Then how," he said, "did I bring back not only as much

---

[56] In the medieval period, a farthing was made by cutting a penny into quarters (a "farthing" means a fourth of a penny). A halfpenny was literally half a penny, made by cutting a penny down the middle. It would take a sharp chisel, a hammer, a hard surface, and some force to cut a penny into such pieces – not something easily done while on a journey.

[57] The large and important Benedictine monastery of St. Augustine's, founded in 598, was located very near Canterbury Cathedral and the monastery of Christ Church.

[58] There were no shilling coins in the medieval period. A shilling was a unit of account: it was another way to say twelve pennies. Reading that Ralph "received five shillings," medieval readers would have understood that Ralph was given sixty pennies.

as I took away, but also three halfpennies over that sum?" And they marvelled, knowing that to their knowledge, no-one had returned the money they had spent nor had increased any reimbursement. We, like them, do not doubt this to be a miracle, considering the exact similarity between the amount given out in alms and the amount of superabundance.

IV.41. CONCERNING HENRY, A YOUTH OF LONDON, WHO TRANSFERRED HIS GOODS TO ANOTHER SHIP WHEN HE WAS SAILING FROM NORWAY AS A RESULT OF THE MARTYR'S ADMONITION, AND WHO WAS SAVED FROM THE PERIL OF DEATH

Ships sailing from London went to the shores of Norway and were moored there. The ships were loaded with their various goods, and when they were preparing for their departure, the most pious martyr Thomas appeared to Henry, a young man of London, who was then resting on a bunk in one of the ships because he was suffering grievously from fevers. "Are you sleeping, young man?" he asked. He said, "I was sleeping, lord, but you woke me: who are you?" "I am Thomas, the archbishop of Canterbury. You must, in every possible way, guard against returning in the same ship in which you came. Board another, and you will escape imminent peril. That ship will break up on its return voyage and no-one will rescue his belongings from it, but you, if you comply with me, will also be freed from fevers." The young man woke and then again fell asleep. Again the saint came in his dreams, and again ordered and impressed upon him what he had before. The young man related the warning he had received to one of his companions that he valued more than the rest. When both of them had transferred their goods to another ship, namely that of Rainier of London, they were brought to London by a favorable wind, and the feverish young man got rid of his fever in the middle of the voyage. But the ship that he had left ran blindly against rocks and was broken up. Those who had been in the ship left it and all its goods to the rocks and the waves, and leapt into a boat that they might at least save their souls. We heard these things from the young man, who came to offer to the martyr a gift of oblation with prayers of thanks.

IV.42. CONCERNING THE SHIP THAT FOLLOWED THE SAILORS WHO HAD ABANDONED IT WITHOUT ANY NAVIGATOR

From another man's oblation, we learned of an unusual miracle of great piety. A man named Ailwin came from Bristol to the martyr, gave gold, and withdrew. When the monk who was sitting at the tomb noted that the oblation did not at all accord with the clothing of the man (for he was dressed very poorly), he called him back and asked why a pauper had presented gold to the saint. He said, "I made a vow to the martyr and have fulfilled it. When I was sailing from Ireland not long ago, my ship came upon quicksand and stuck fast in it. The harder we worked to get it out of danger, the more the sand pulled it in. When it was nearly submerged to the highest deck, in desperation we disembarked onto a little boat, hoping that our lives at least might be saved, for there was no hope for the preservation of the ship nor of our things. Then I said, 'Thomas, martyr of God, if you have merit with God, if you can do it, if you ever performed another miracle, restore my ship to me. If you do this, I will visit your tomb and make an oblation of gold to you.' And so, we left the ship and sailed off in the little vessel in order to escape to land. We went about eight furlongs from the ship, but as long and as hard as we rowed, the ship always seemed to be the same distance from us. We encouraged each other to the work in turns, but the farther we sailed, the closer we came to the ship. Stopping the useless labour, we waited a short time, and look! We came upon the ship that was coming without any navigator, that ship we had left with a spread-out sail and nearly sunk. We recovered it coming to us like an oblation from God, boarded it, and landed favorably without any damage. I have visited the martyr for this reason, and given gold." When he had said these things, we believed him, though he lacked witnesses. We obtained evidence for truth from his simplicity and the poor correspondence of his oblation to his clothing. [*See Parallel Miracles no. 3 for William's account of this miracle.*]

IV.43. CONCERNING ANOTHER SHIP THAT THE SAINT VISIBLY FREED

In our judgment, he is no less to be believed than three others who testified to a sign of no less magnitude. They said that they were in a ship that came into the same kind of peril at night. When, in fear of death, they had all cried out to the saint, and, kneeling down in the ship, had said the Lord's Prayer, a man appeared to them in shining white garments walking upon the moving waves of the sea.[59] He took hold of the prow of the ship and thrust it back far into the sea, such that the sound of its wake could be heard far and wide. He then vanished from their sight. The three men stood as witnesses to this. They were prepared to certify to us with their hands on relics that they were in that ship and that, in the darkness, they saw that person with their eyes. [*See Parallel Miracles no. 4 for William's account of this miracle.*]

IV.44. CONCERNING [AILRED],[60] A YOUNG MAN FROM EXETER, WHO WAS BENEVOLENTLY FREED BY THE VIRTUE OF THE MARTYR WHEN HE WAS ENTWINED IN AN ANCHOR'S ROPE AND CARRIED HEADLONG

Tossed about in an extremely violent storm, other men were driven by a whirlwind into a most dangerous area of the sea that sailors call the Gatteraz.[61] In the ship was a young man from Exeter, Ailred, and a certain cleric in whose mouth the name of the martyr constantly resounded. The cleric said that there was nothing to be feared, because with his eyes he himself had seen the martyr in the ship. Greatly encouraged, the sailors threw out the ship's anchor, but the ship was being driven by the heaving of the sea and the violence of the wind and the anchor's rope ran out with force. As it ran, by chance it ensnared the leg and thigh of the above-mentioned young man and dragged him headlong. He said, "St. Thomas, martyr of God, since it does not please you to save my body, save my soul." Three young men standing nearby seized the running line and the ring of the anchor was broken. The anchor was carried off into the deep, while the rope, with the young man, was held back. Where the rope had wrapped around his leg and thigh, the flesh had been abraded away all the way to the bone. This provides much to marvel at for those accustomed to peril at sea. For those who are expert in these matters, it is no small wonder that the ring of the anchor was broken and that a rope going out with such speed could be held back by only three men. In a storm it is usual for the anchor, not the ring, to be broken. Moreover, unless precautions are taken that it be sent forth in a certain way, a thousand men cannot hold back the rope from being carried off into the deep.

---

[59] See the story of Jesus walking on water to rescue a floundering ship: Matthew 14:22–36, Mark 6:45–56, and John 6:16–24.

[60] The caption reads "Alfred" rather than Ailred.

[61] The Gatteraz is a rocky region offshore Gatteville in Normandy (near Barfleur) that has a strong current. It is sometimes spelled Catteraz (Benedict's Latin is *Cataras*). The White Ship carrying the son and heir of King Henry I foundered in this area in 1120.

IV.45. CONCERNING A MAN OF DOVER, WHO RECOVERED THREE LOST ANCHORS THROUGH THE SAINT

Eilwecher of Dover was sailing to Brittany when a storm came upon him. He cast out three anchors and lost them all to broken ropes. Having invoked the martyr, he nevertheless escaped to land. When the sea was calm again, he returned with his companions to seek for the anchors, since the area in which he had lost them was not far from land. They hunted for them for three days and could not find them. One of them said, "We should promise to give a wax anchor to the martyr of Canterbury if he restores our iron ones to us." All of them agreed. They put the implement with which they searched the bottom of the sea back into the water, and pulled out all the anchors. And so, returning to England, they came to the martyr, bringing with them the gift that they had promised. [*See Parallel Miracles no. 5 for William's account of this miracle.*]

IV.46. CONCERNING OTHER MEN FREED FROM A STORM ON THE SEA BY THE MARTYR

A storm caught Ivo of Lynn and many other ships seeking the far-off region of Norway. A priest was sleeping in this Ivo's ship, and the saint appeared to him and said, "Priest, do you sleep? Get up, and tell your companions that they should each say the Lord's prayer for the soul of my father twenty times, and then none of you will perish."[62] It was done as he ordered, and, without any damage, they were favorably driven back to the port from which they had set out. All the rest of the ships were dispersed. Some were smashed and broken up, and not a few sunk. I received this story from Robert, a clerk of Lincoln, who escaped from that same danger in the same ship. There are many more tales of such sort, but one and the same food cannot be constantly taken without disgust.

---

[62] This is an interesting early reference to Thomas Becket's father, Gilbert Becket, who was of Norman origin and gained wealth by renting properties in London. A later legend held that Gilbert Becket went on Crusade and that his wife, Matilda, was the daughter of a Muslim ruler who followed him back to London: see John Jenkins, "St Thomas Becket and Medieval London," *History* 105 (2020): 652–72, at pp. 668–72.

IV.47. CONCERNING A CERTAIN ILL MAN WHO ASKED FOR THE SAINT'S WATER, DRANK WATER DECEPTIVELY BROUGHT TO HIM FROM A WELL, AND WAS HEALED

A young man suffering with an acute illness was at the point of death. The anxious man asked for the martyr's water from the friends in attendance. None of them had any. One of them ran to a well, filled a vessel, and brought it to him, saying, "Here is the water of the saint that you requested." The ill man believed and drank, and, wholesomely deceived, he immediately regained his health. Shortly thereafter, the illness having left, he left his couch, and felt nothing adverse except for a weakness. The young man himself not only told us of these things, but also brought the one who drew the water from the well and others as witnesses.

IV.48. CONCERNING WARIN, SURNAMED GROSSO, WHOSE SWOLLEN ARM THE SAINT BEAUTIFULLY HEALED IN A DREAM

After bloodletting, the entire arm of a knight of Norfolk, Warin, surnamed Grosso, swelled up and hardened like a stone from the hand to the shoulder. The swelling seemed to extend into his chest and the region of his heart. You would hardly be able to tell how much smaller his arm was than his torso. Comparing their size, you would say there was little or no difference. Many plasters and salves were applied, but instead of receding, the swelling thrust out. The knight was despaired of, and careful watch was kept over him as if he were in extremis. The latest of medicines, the Canterbury remedy, was applied, and the arm of the dying man was washed several times with the wonderful water of the wonderful martyr. When the knight lay as if he were dying, it seemed to him that the martyr stood before him and said, "Get up, Warin, and prostrate yourself before me." It seemed to him that he did as he was commanded. Then the saint said, "Do again what you have done." He obeyed and heard a third time from the martyr, "You will do the same thing a third time." Having done this, it seemed that the martyr turned to some people standing there and spoke these words: "Wipe away his sweat in the place of the blessed water." With these words, the dying man suddenly roused himself and sat up, to the wonder of those who were caring for him. The pain having gone, he held out his arm, which before he had not been able to bend in any part, with the same agility as the other. Within six or seven days the swelling disappeared. Asked by the knight how I understood the words of the saint, I left a more subtle understanding of these things to the subtle and explained it simply to him in this way: "Wipe away his sweat, that is, take away the labor of his infirmity. Wipe away in the place of the blessed water, that is, I say, in the arm, where my blessed and holy water was placed."

IV.49. CONCERNING A CERTAIN CANON OF CROXTON, WHOSE EXPELLED EYE WAS PUT BACK INTO ITS PLACE BY THE WATER, WITHOUT THE TOUCH OF ANY HAND

There was a canon in the valley of St. John of Croxton in the region of Leicestershire[63] by the name of Robert, a man full of days and reaching the age of decrepitude. Above his eye, he had a great swelling that appeared to be about to dislodge the eye – in fact, to expel it altogether.

One day, when he was sitting outside the choir with his eye greatly protruding, one of the brothers who happened to be passing by noticed that his face was bloody and his eye had come out and hung upon his face. He was brought to William, the abbot of the church, from whom I also received that which I tell,[64] who was greatly alarmed and did not know what was to be done, for with the eye thrown out, the pupil seemed to be expelled from the white of the eye in an astonishing way. At last, he told the brothers who were there to lead him into the choir to the altar and wash the eye with the water of the blessed martyr, which was kept there, with this idea: that through the merits of the saint, the pupil might return to its place and the eye might be restored to its former state. He was led to the choir, washed with the sanctified liquid, and led back to the cloister. A person would scarcely have had time to go a furlong at a steady pace, when a certain person came to look at him who had not seen him with the eye pushed out. He pulled aside his cowl and found the pupil restored to the eye and the eye restored to its place. He turned to the abbot and said, "Why are you sad, lord? There is nothing wrong with this man except what was wrong before; there is nothing in addition to his former infirmity." And for each and all this was a joyful wonder and a wonderful joy.

---

[63] This is Croxton Abbey, also known as Croxton Kerrial, a Praemonstratensian community founded c.1160.
[64] See Biographical Notes, William, abbot of Croxton Kerrial. Benedict may well have drawn this account (and that in the next chapter) from a letter written by the abbot.

IV.50. CONCERNING ANOTHER, A CERTAIN SWOLLEN MAN IN THE SAME ABBEY

In the same abbey, there was another greatly swollen up. To say it briefly, having tasted the martyr's water, his stomach was brought back to its former slenderness.

IV.51. CONCERNING A CERTAIN CANON OF BEDFORD, ON WHOSE NECK BURNING BLISTERS EMERGED, WHICH SUDDENLY VANISHED BY MEANS OF THE MARTYR'S WATER

When the canons of the church of the blessed Paul of Bedford[65] were sitting and speaking together in the cloister at the appointed hour, one of them, Stephen by name, felt something like a burning coal on his neck. He said to the canon who was sitting next to him, "Look and see what is burning my neck so badly." He looked at him and said, "There is a blackish blister that looks very misshapen." After a very short time, Stephen said again, "Look and see what it might be, for I am being terribly tormented and burned." He looked and began to cry aloud to the blessed Virgin and Mother of the Lord, declaring that four blisters had now arisen that were exactly the same as the first. The bell having been rung, everyone hastened to the service, but pain was tormenting him, so he first went to the altar and wet his neck with the holy water of the holy martyr. He then returned to his own seat or station in the choir. All distress departed, and he found by touch that all the blisters had disappeared. The countess Rohese told these things to me as she had heard them from the same Stephen.[66]

IV.52. CONCERNING INGELRAM SON OF [STEPHEN][67] OF GOULTON, WHOSE ARM THE SAINT STRUCK WITH AN AFFLICTION AND AFTERWARDS CURED IN A DREAM

When great crowds were rushing to our martyr and were hastening from the cities to him, the same desire came in the mind of the wife of [Stephen] of

---

[65] This is the Augustinian church of Bedford whose prior, Auger, was involved in Eilward of Westoning's miracle: see above, IV.2.

[66] See Biographical Notes, Rohese de Vere.

[67] The caption reads "Ingelram son of Ingelram of Goulton," providing the correct name of the boy (which, notably, Benedict never mentions – it seems the caption writer had knowledge of this miracle from another source), but reflecting Benedict's incorrect

Goulton,[68] a knight of Yorkshire. She made this known to her lord and added, "Let us also bring our son with us." The boy was standing and listening to his parents, and he responded to his mother's words in this way: "I am healthy and well. What would I achieve with the martyr?" His father rebuked the boy's foolish response and lifted his hand to strike him, but he did not hit or touch the fleeing boy. The boy left and occupied himself with scholarly matters, thinking the offence of his mouth to be nothing. That night, his arm was mortified and made completely insensible. He was not able to feel the application of either fire or iron. Though his arm was often pricked and scored by a needle, he felt nothing. The boy was sent by his parents to many places and many doctors were consulted concerning his case, but no help was found. His parents said, "Look, look: you have something to do with the martyr of Canterbury. Promise quickly what you dared to deny before." And he promised. The following night, he saw the saint in his sleep. He had the track of blood running sideways across his nose from his forehead to his left jaw which we also saw on him when he lay in his church killed by the swords of the impious.[69] He said to the boy, "See to it, boy, that you give yourself to the religious life this year. Get up, be healed." He spoke and so it was. Sleep lifted from his eyes, and he showed that the death of the arm, as one might say, was lifted from the arm as well. He stretched out his arm and, healed, he began the labor of the journey that he had thought to undertake while ill. We heard afterwards from the priest of that same village that the boy took on the religious habit at Fountains.[70] After the boy had returned home, the saint again appeared to him in his sleep, and again warned him that he was to give himself to a monastic order. The boy was answering him, and at brief intervals asking, "Where, lord? When, lord?" and much else along these lines. The parents heard the boy speaking with intervals of silence, but they could not hear the voice of the person he was speaking to. Nor was the person

---

understanding of the father's name. William accurately gave his name as Stephen. See Biographical Notes, Stephen de Meinil.

[68] Benedict's incorrectly text reads "the wife of Ingelram of Goulton." In fact, her husband's name was Stephen and her son's name was Ingelram. See Biographical Notes, Stephen de Meinil. From a charter issued by Stephen, we know that his wife's name was Joan.

[69] For Benedict's discussion of this line of blood on Becket's face, see above, *Passion*, Extract VIII, and the story of Matilda of Cologne, IV.37.

[70] Fountains Abbey was a Cistercian abbey in Yorkshire. For the grants that Ingelram's father made to Fountains and his intent to become a monk there himself, see Biographical Notes, Stephen de Meinil. The position of this sentence is odd: it would have made more sense to say where the boy became a monk at the close of the chapter. This may indicate that Benedict was working from a written source or sources and/or that he decided to expand the story at some point.

seen, yet a wonderful brightness lit up the whole house and chased away the shadows of night, such that they clearly saw the boy and the rest of the things in the house. They said to each other, "Let's stay back: he sees something that we cannot see." With the brightness fading, the boy awoke and told his parents what he had seen and heard, and a few days later, he devoted himself to the monastic life in the cloister that saint had assigned to him. [See Parallel Miracles no. 6 for William's account of this miracle.]

IV.53. CONCERNING THE SWOLLEN MABEL *DE AGLANDRE*, WHO WAS JUDGED INCURABLE BY DOCTORS

At the castle of William de Vernon that is commonly called Néhou,[71] a swelling rose up in the uterus of Mabel, daughter of Stephan *de Aglandre*,[72] that had the hardness of a stone. For nearly three years, though doctors strove against it, it took root there. Many practiced in the art of medicine worked toward her cure, but all despaired and abandoned her as a hopeless case. She was brought to her bed tormented by such intense pain, with terrific and strange thrashing of her limbs, that it seemed to be pushing her over into insanity. For fifteen days she went without food, and yet two men could hardly hold her down in bed. Now she was too hot and then exceedingly cold; now the swelling grew, then it diminished; now she was fixed down and immobile, then she was loosened and in motion and hurled about here and there – these things followed on one after another. And so, while the girl was dying without death, one of those known to her, having come back from Canterbury, brought the water of the martyr. He urged her to lift up her mind to the blessed one that he might lift her up. She should raise prayers to him, that he might raise her from her bed. But she said, "He is not able to help me. He would certainly have helped if he could, for I have cried to him many times, and he did not hear me." "Still press on," he said, "make a vow to the martyr that you will go to his tomb casting off linen garments, disdaining a cart, and with bare feet." And so she vowed and, as I remember, tasted the water of the martyr. In that very moment the tumor inside of her burst, and the corruption of her body flowed out through the uncorrupted virgin's virginal passage, not little by little but in one gush: it was like thick black water, most foul. In that same

---

[71] See Biographical Notes, William de Vernon. The castle is referred to as *Nean, Neaho,* and *Neau* in various manuscripts of Benedict's collection: see Robertson, *MTB*, vol. 2, p. 221 and Duggan, "Santa Cruz," p. 54. Though Robertson read this as a reference to Neen in Shropshire, it must refer to William's castle at Néhou in Normandy.

[72] The place is unidentified.

hour the girl got up, trim and healed but weak. She soon wanted to fulfil her promise, but those close to her did not allow her to walk about much. They feared that by such exertion she, in her weakened state, might be brought back into grave peril. Clean coverings were put on her bed and she was forced to rest a few days. One of the doctors heard that Mabel had recovered, and he said, "Those who say this are lying. It is impossible that someone threatened with such an illness could escape death." He came to see her. Hearing of her mode of healing, the happy man was astounded, and astounded, he believed.

IV.54. CONCERNING THE DROPSICAL ELIZA OF MIDDLETON OF OXFORDSHIRE

Dropsy took hold of the pregnant Eliza of Middleton. From day to day, it increased the swelling of her uterus dreadfully. She fell into her bed and lay in a desperate state. Every time she turned onto her side, she heard a sound in her womb like the sound *of many waters [Rv 19:6]*. She took it to be waters by its husky-sounding murmur. No matter what herbs, tonics, or medicines were given to her, she received no strength, efficacy, or utility from them. The woman abandoned earthly medicines and invoked heavenly doctors. She vowed herself to the blessed martyr Edmund, to the admirable confessor Leonard, to the glorious virgin Margaret, and to others.[73] But just as the herbs did her no good, so none of the saints she invoked wished to aid her. She became agitated about her unborn child, preferring that it should be brought out into light than that her own life should be lengthened in such pain. She asked that her uterus be opened and the infant be extracted, so that although it was not born, yet it might be reborn by the health-giving font, and *whether it lived or died it would be unto the Lord [Rom 14:8]*.[74] However, no-one could be found who would perform this impious piety. She labored for five days as if she were giving birth, yet she could not move the fetus in her womb at all. Seven midwives were there, whose council was that the help of the Canterbury martyr be sought. She vowed that she would visit the martyr if she first felt a visit from him. These words were still in her mouth when the wonderful mercy of God descended upon her. For suddenly there was a

---

[73] St. Edmund (d.869) was one of England's most prominent saints. Medieval hospitals were often dedicated to St. Leonard of Noblac, an early Frankish saint. The virgin martyr St. Margaret of Antioch was widely revered in medieval England.

[74] Eliza's idea was for her child to be extracted and immediately baptized, despite the fact that this would likely result in Eliza's own death. If her child were stillborn or died in the womb, it could not be baptized, with grave consequences for its soul.

great sound, heard through the whole house, that came from the womb of the prone woman. Whatever was inside her was ruptured, and a great amount of water sprang forth from the birth canal. The midwives' hands were not able to bear its touch because of its heat. The woman thought she had given birth, and said, "There's still one in my womb: unless I'm deceived, I have twins." But her mother said, "Daughter, you still have the burden that you think is gone: you still have it in your womb." A second and a third time, as before, a great deal of water came forth, such that it seemed to be able to fill two or three barrels. And so what had hindered the infant's exit was ejected, and the woman gave birth to a boy. Regaining her health, she did not forget what she had promised to the holy martyr.

IV.55. CONCERNING A DROPSICAL WOMAN OF MERSTON

I can also add a story about another case of dropsy concerning a woman of Merston, but lest the readers become weary when they ought to have pleasure, it will suffice to say just this: having inflated frightfully, by drinking the water of Canterbury and invoking the martyr, the swelling deflated and she regained her original size and beauty.

IV.56. CONCERNING A BLIND BOY AND AN INSANE [GIRL][75] FROM WALES

A woman from the borders of Wales, those who call themselves Britons, was leading a little boy blind from birth and an insane girl. The girl was restored in mind on the road. The boy was improved at Canterbury to the point that I do not dare to say whether he was blind or not, for when a light was held before his eyes, he could follow it here and there, but he still could not see the path he walked on. I say this about it, because I do not want to appear *to magnify fringes* [Mt 23:5] by speaking much about little things. Several people have done this both with regard to this boy and to another young man, William of Horsepool near Sherwood, who was wholly unknown to us. He said that he came blind, but he produced no witness or person to attest to his blindness. I confess I saw him seeing when he left, but I did not see him blind when he came. Although he lingered with us for many days so that his vision might improve, it seemed to me that he always remained in the same state.

---

[75] The caption writer has "woman."

IV.57. CONCERNING THE INSANE WALTER OF GRIMSBY

A clerk of Hatcliffe near Grimsby named Walter was of unsound mind for five weeks. The devotion of his friends and relatives procured his health for him from the martyr. Having vowed that they would take him to the saint, he soon recovered his reason, and he gave himself to the promised journey.

IV.58. CONCERNING DOGS SILENCED WITH THE NAME OF THE MARTYR

Among the other miracles of the blessed and glorious friend of God Thomas, we can tell of what we read of Martin, namely this: in addition to the miracles Martin performed himself, many were also done in his name.[76] I will first describe what happened to me. Driven by urgent necessity, I was traveling by night accompanied by only one servant. Three dogs came upon us, barking most fearfully, and they followed on relentlessly, making us tremble and pale with fear. I call the Lord as my witness that I was terribly afraid that they might injure me or pull the boy off his horse and tear him in pieces, for it is natural for dogs to be more savage and ready to bite at night than in the day. By chance I remembered that in the Life of the blessed Martin, I had read of someone who had silenced the mouths of barking dogs in Martin's name.[77] And so, I turned to the dogs and said, "In the name of blessed Thomas, be silent." I speak in Christ before God: all of them suddenly became mute. After this statement, not one of them barked even once. You would think that their mouths had been stopped up or their tongues cut out; they fled as if they had received blows by those words. To my wonder, the same thing happened to me a second time on the same night. By God as my witness, I do not tell these things on my own account, nor do I seek my own glory, but that of the martyr. Moreover, something of equal or greater wonder also happened to Roger the monk, who was similarly assigned to the care of the sacred body.[78]

---

[76] St. Martin of Tours (d.397), a soldier, hermit, and bishop, was one of the most popular saints of the medieval period. He was renowned for cutting his cloak in two and giving one half to a beggar.

[77] The story is found in Sulpicius Severus' *Dialogues*: see *Sulpicius Severus: The Complete Works*, III.3, p. 233.

[78] See Biographical Notes, Roger, monk of Christ Church, Canterbury.

IV.59. CONCERNING EDA OF SCOTLAND, WHO COULD NOT WALK, AND WHO ROSE AND WALKED BY MEANS OF A MONK COMMANDING HER IN THE NAME OF THE SAINT

Eda, a venerable woman of Scotland with illustrious relations, had a most grave infirmity that settled in her knee and deprived her of the ability to walk. For ten years she had not been able to take a step and reclined in a cloak or some sort of covering: that which supported her in mind also bore her in body. She was brought to Canterbury on a bed and placed near the martyr's tomb. On the third day, it happened that as she rested near the sepulchre, she asked for a drink of the health-giving water. The monk refused unless she got up and came to him. She said, "For ten years, lord, I have not taken a step. How can I now to come to you?" To this, the monk said, "In the name of the martyr, I command that you get up and come to me."[79] Marvelous to see and delightful to hear, she immediately got up and not only came to the monk, but also circled the tomb three times and walked a long way from the tomb, though she was only able to walk on tiptoe. On the following day she was able to plant her whole foot on the ground. Though she did not dare to relinquish her bed at the beginning of her healing, she scorned it on her return and went home mounted on a horse. She progressed little by little from day to day, and a great gain of health followed.

IV.60. CONCERNING [HUGO][80] *DE TUKIN*, EXHAUSTED BY A FISTULA

Hugo *de Tukin*,[81] a knight from a manor in France, which by its own name is termed Provins, presented himself healed to our martyr. He had been wounded in the jaw with a lance and a fistula had taken root in the same spot. It pervaded his jaw and extended all the way to his eyebrows and his forehead. Doctors with great expertise labored toward his cure. Cutting the flesh of his jaw, they scraped the bones and applied medications. Having done all this, they gave up and departed, declaring him incurable. By chance it happened that a cleric came into that region carrying the water of the martyr. The knight drank and washed the putrid jaw. In about eight days, the fistula was dried up,

---

[79] This passage echoes Christ's command to a paralyzed man lying on a bed to get up (see Matthew 9:6 and Mark 2:11) and his similar command to an ill man lying on a bed (see John 5:8).
[80] The caption writer has Henry rather than Hugo.
[81] The place is unidentified.

the flesh had amalgamated, and the skin had come together. Healed in a short time, he visited the martyr.

IV.61. CONCERNING [MELANIA][82] OF FONTENAY, WHO HAD A SIMILAR FISTULA

For six years, a fistula disfigured the jaw of Melania, the wife of William of Fontenay. She went about eight furlongs to a place where she had heard the water of the saint was held, washed her jaw, and returned home. Before she had reached her home, the fistula disappeared, the wound was invisible, and the woman found herself completely healthy.

IV.62. CONCERNING A BOY OF ROCHESTER WHO FELL IN THE WATER

Little Robert, son of Liviva of Rochester, was playing with boys when, by chance, he fell into the river Medway and was pulled under.[83] The playing boys scattered, shouting that little Robert was submerged in the river. A large crowd amassed and searched for the boy, but he was not found. The mother of the lost boy also ran there, crying and saying, "Thomas, glorious martyr of God, return my son to me!" She kept saying only this. The boy had fallen in the water at nones, and he was pulled out with an iron hook as the bells were ringing for vespers.[84] He had fallen in the water when the tide had filled the river up to its banks. When he was pulled out, the tide had almost receded completely. The pallid boy was suspended by his feet, his rectum was stopped up, and a wedge was put in his mouth to allow the salty water with which he was swollen to flow out. He had no voice or feeling, and not a drop of water emerged. He was spun in a tub to bring on nausea, and was worked on up until the beginning of the coming night without any effect. The boy lay without the breath of life such that many said he was dead. Then the mother, invoking the martyr, measured the boy with a thread, and promised

---

[82] The caption writer has Metania rather than Melania.
[83] This miracle is portrayed in Canterbury Cathedral window nII: see Caviness, *Windows*, pp. 195–6. Originally a six-panel story, only the first three panels have survived. For the imagery of the first panel, the glaziers amalgamated little Robert's story with that of another drowned boy, Philip Scot: see below, IV.66.
[84] The monastic services of nones (at the "ninth hour") is held in the middle of the afternoon, while vespers is at sunset. The exact amount of time between the services varied according to the time of year.

the martyr a thread of silver of that length for the life of her son. Straightaway, he vomited out what had been suffocating him and was suddenly restored to health. The next day he went out to play with the boys as usual. Although we are able to say that he was submerged from nones, when he fell in the river, all the way to vespers, and that he lived without breath, yet we will desist on account of the jeers of the mockers. We do not wish to test the great deeds of the martyr by argument, since those things that are clear do not need proof. He who weighs this miracle lightly, let him note how that saint magnified it by a similar miracle.

IV.63. CONCERNING A BOY OF SARRE WHO WAS SUBMERGED IN A BATH

Two small children were sitting in a bath, one about three years old, the other about six months old. The mother, hoping that the older would take care of the younger, went to the threshing floor to do some winnowing. The older one got out in order to play, but the younger was submerged in the bath. The mother had winnowed the chief part of the barley when she ordered that a dish should be brought to her. A girl running to do so became the bearer of sad news: namely, that the baby boy was under water. The mother paled as she heard this, and, taking the baby out of the bath, she brought him outside of the house and cast him in the street. The women of the neighborhood hastened to the crying and lamenting mother. Nearly all of the men had gone off to fish or to reap. They suspended the child by its feet and vainly attempted to bring him back to life. One of her neighbors, who had returned from Jerusalem, said to her, "Why put in this pointless effort? Bury the baby: it has been a long time since its spirit was expelled." Then one of the widows said, "Do we not have five widows here? Let us invoke the blessed martyr Thomas nine times on our knees, and repeat the Lord's Prayer nine times in his name, and he may listen." And so it was done, but the boy did not get up. One of them said to the mother, "Run, get a thread, measure the child, and promise a candle of the length to the martyr." When this was done, blood and water immediately came out of the dead one's mouth, and soon afterwards the boy screwed up his eyes and began to howl. The name of the young boy was Gilbert, the mother Wulviva, the father Ralph, son of Brithwin of Sarre. I went to the village of Sarre that I might carefully sift out the truth, and know from the testimony of those who were there that the martyr truly raised him from the dead and returned him to his mother.[85] He was submerged in the bath from the third all the way to the sixth hour. After being pulled out at the sixth hour, he lay without the breath of life until the tenth or eleventh hour, until finally, as was said above, he was resuscitated and lived again. It may be that someone among the detractors dares to deny this, the assertion that a six-month-old infant could live without breath for half a day, for he who is incredulous both speaks and acts faithlessly. Let him hear what follows, so that, converted, he may repent, or, confounded, he may be shamed.

IV.64. CONCERNING THE DEAD SON OF JORDAN SON OF EISULF

The hand of the Lord came down heavily on a knight of great name, Jordan son of Eisulf,[86] striking his house with pestilence from the time of August to Easter. Very many were ill in his house, and no-one could help them. The nurse of his son William, who had the second name Brito,[87] was struck by the disease, died and was buried. The third day after the nurse's death, the Lord also struck the ten-year-old boy with the same illness. He was taken from them on the seventh day at about the third hour.[88] A priest came, and he commended the boy's soul into the hand of the Creator and performed the usual ecclesiastical rites for the dead. All that day and the following night a vigil was kept over the boy as over a corpse. I will not speak of the parents' terrible grief because even a simple man will be able to imagine it.

On that same day, about twenty pilgrims returning from the memorial of the martyr arrived there. For the love of the martyr, the father extended hospitality to all of them, and until the following day, when they wished to leave, he provided them with rest and refreshment. A priest came to take the lifeless body to the church and convey it to burial. But the father said, "My son will certainly not be carried away. My heart predicts that the martyr Thomas does not want me to lose him, for I was his man while he lived and his close friend."[89] Having received the water of the martyr from the pilgrims, he said

---

[85] The village of Sarre is less than fourteen kilometers away from Canterbury.
[86] See Biographical Notes, Jordan son of Eisulf. The miracle relating to Jordan's sons is told in nine panels in Canterbury Cathedral window nII: see Caviness, *Windows*, pp. 197–9.
[87] On William Brito, see Biographical Notes, Jordan son of Eisulf.
[88] In other words, mid-morning on the seventh day after the nurse died.
[89] There is no mention of Jordan son of Eisulf in surviving correspondence or the lives of Becket, but the archbishop had a large range of connections, and it is possible that Jordan had some kind of relationship with the living Becket.

to the priest, "Pour it into his mouth, and perhaps the martyr will return my son to me." The priest admired the faith behind this request, though he thought the father might be out of his mind. He poured in the water, and the boy did not get up. The burial of the lifeless corpse was delayed to the tenth or eleventh hour as the father awaited what the Lord would do. The priest, suspecting that this was the will of someone out of his head, said to him, "Lord, why should the burial of the dead be delayed? It is already nearing the end of the second day after the boy died." But he said against this: "My son will certainly not be buried, for my heart testifies truly in this: he will be returned to me by the martyr Thomas. Bring the water of my lord." After it was brought, he went to the body and uncovered it. He lifted his head, separated his clenched teeth with a knife, and poured in the water. As soon as the water went in, a slight rosiness appeared in the middle of the left side of his face. This greatly gladdened the father, and he poured in the water again, this time holding the boy erect in such a way that the water could travel down his throat. The boy opened one of his eyes, and seeing his parents wet with tears, he spoke, saying, "Why do you cry, father? Why do you weep, mother? Don't be sad, for the blessed martyr Thomas has returned me to you." Having said these things, he went silent, and said nothing more up to vespers. His father said, "Quick: bring four silver coins." He bent two of them for himself and his wife and two for the revived boy. He placed the coins in the boy's right and left hands, promising that he would offer the boy to the martyr at mid-Lent, and those sitting there observed him. As twilight came on, the boy sat up, took food and drink, spoke, and, returned to his parents, he became well.

The end of the period fixed for carrying out the vow was reached, but its execution was put off to another time because of some interfering hindrance. And so the martyr of the Lord, Thomas, appeared in the sleep of a certain leper who lived some three miles distant from the knight's home and was wholly ignorant of these matters. He said, "Gimp, do you sleep?" (for we heard that this was the name of that leper). He replied, "I was sleeping, but you have woken me. Who are you?" And the martyr said, "I am Thomas the archbishop of Canterbury. Do you know Jordan the son of Eisulf?" "Very well, lord, for he is a very good man who has given many gifts to me." Then the saint said, "Go and tell him from me that the time he determined has passed and he has not performed his promised vow. He should hurry to Canterbury and render his vow for his son, whom the Lord restored to life by my intervention. If he does not set out on this journey quickly, I will bring down evil upon him and his wife. To the same degree that he received joy from me through the resurrection of his son, so he will acquire sorrow from the loss of another." The leper replied, "Nearly twenty years have gone by, lord, in which I have not seen the light of the sky, and I am bedridden with bad feet. How can I go to the knight's house?" When he woke, the leper did not weigh what he heard as important and did not do what the martyr had told him to do. And so the martyr appeared to him again, and said, "Why haven't you done the things I told you?" "Lord, I cannot," he said, "I am bound by blindness and disability." And the saint said to him, "Call your priest, and put my words in his mouth so that he can tell the knight all the things that I have commanded." The leper summoned the priest and said to him, "The martyr of Canterbury has commended these things to you." But the priest said, "It was a dream. Am I to tell tales and trifles from dreams to such a man? He is powerful and a great man, and would take a story like this, and its teller, as mockery. You will not get me to bring a message like this to him." A third time the saint stood before the leper, and said, "Why hasn't what I ordered been done?" "Lord," he said, "I told your orders to the priest, and he scorned to hear them. What more can I do?" The saint responded, "In the morning, send your daughter to fetch the knight and his wife, and they will certainly come to you. But when they come, I warn you: do not hide from them a single word I have said to you." In the morning they were called, they came, and were amazed at what they heard. They therefore fixed a date which they would not go pass, namely the last week of Lent. However, with the arrival of the count of Warenne, the knight's lord,[90] they delayed the pilgrimage, turned themselves aside, and did not keep their pact.

When the last day of the agreed-on time came, namely the Holy Saturday that precedes Easter, the Lord struck another son of the knight with a severe sickness. This boy was dearer to them and a little older than the one who had been brought back to life. The next day, the parents themselves were taken ill, confined to bed, and despaired of. The disease gathered strength in the boy, and he slept in death on the seventh day, the Friday of Easter week.[91] The son's death increased the illness of the parents, especially in the case of the father, who had dearly loved the boy because his features so closely resembled his father's.[92] Seeing that the things that the saint had proclaimed through the

---

[90] See Biographical Notes, Hamelin de Warenne.

[91] Given the placement of this miracle at the beginning of William's collection (which he started in June 1172), this miracle all but certainly occurred in 1172. In 1172, the date of Easter was April 16, and the Friday of Easter week, the date of the elder son's death, was April 21.

[92] That is, the features of Eisulf, the man so important in establishing the dominance of the family in the West Riding. See Biographical Notes, Jordan son of Eisulf.

leper were fulfilled, he said to his wife, "Look, my lady, at the sorrow our delay has brought to us. Oh, such sorrow! We certainly delayed too long. We made a false promise to the martyr, for the second time, and look at the result: we lost our son. The punishments he promised have also descended on us, and we must expect a similar end. I prayed to the martyr for the other son, and he returned him to us, but how will we pray for this one or for ourselves? I do not dare to ask the offended martyr for anything more before I perform my vow. So, let us hurry, lest something worse happen to us."

Wonderful to relate, in that same moment the illness of both of them was lessened. Hearing that they were preparing themselves for a journey, some of their friends came and advised that they should not give themselves to such a labor when they were weak and ill, especially not the mother of the family, whose sickness was more dangerous. They feared that the journey's exertion might ripen the sickness into death. But the knight said, "If we live or we die, both of us will go to the martyr. I will go alive, or I will be brought there as a corpse. My wife, too, will be brought to the martyr alive or be carried there dead. If he doesn't want us living, he will have us lifeless." In the knight's household, some twenty men were also ill, of whom some had been bedridden for seventeen weeks, some for twenty weeks, some for twenty-six or twenty-seven weeks, and some twenty-nine or thirty weeks. Before setting out, he gave each one a drink of the water of the martyr that he had, and the taste administered health and brought vigor to them all. Everyone got up from his bed and no-one was left lying down. None of them failed to escort the departing lord a long distance outside the gate or at least all the way to it. His wife, who had fallen in a faint seven or more times on the first day on account of the toil of the journey, dismounted from her horse when she saw the pinnacle of the temple of Canterbury. She hastened on bare feet to the martyr's tomb, some three miles away, and was not troubled by the exertion. And so, the parents came together barefoot along with their boy. In the midst of floods of tears, they rendered to the martyr the vows that their lips had made.

Consider this one miracle and you will perceive four performed in one. A boy two days dead came back to life; warnings and threats of the saint were repeated three times; the vengeance that the saint had predicted came to pass; everyone who had sickened in the household of the knight suddenly became well. We secretly wrote about these things to his priest, and he brought forward testimony to the truth, writing back that the boy was definitely dead and resurrected from the dead by the water of the martyr. What testimony do we still ask for? Is this not enough for the commendation of the martyr?

Oh martyr of great merit! Oh great merits of the martyr! *Oh the depth of the riches of the wisdom and of the knowledge of God! How incomprehensible are his judgments, and how unsearchable his ways!* [Rom 11:33]. Who would have ever imagined this surpassing excellence of merits? This worthiness of the martyr? This singular similarity between Christ and the martyr? For in the same way that Christ's blood saves the soul from eternal death and confers on it life eternal, so the martyr's blood gave earthly life to a lifeless body. Since there is no miracle more glorious than bringing the dead to life, what has been written should suffice. To go on from a miracle such as this to one of less wonder would be like setting poor coarse food before diners after a delicious feast. However, since – as the blessed Gregory says – *among daily luxuries even common foods have a more agreeable taste, such that when poor food is consumed, one may, by adverse reaction, the more eagerly return to more delicate feasts,*[93] it is pleasing to place the lesser next to the greater, and to ward off distaste, as it were, by a variety of dishes. However, I will first add two miracles to this preceding one, miracles concerning two who were thought to have died that are no less wonderful nor much inferior in magnitude. [*See Parallel Miracles no. 7 for William's account of this miracle.*]

IV.65. CONCERNING THE DAUGHTER OF JORDAN OF PLUMSTOCK, WHO WAS THOUGHT TO BE DEAD

And so, in the diocese of Norwich, the fifteen-year-old girl Cecilia, daughter of a certain Jordan of Plumstock, was struck by cancer. While the modesty of a virgin made her wish to bear the pain rather than reveal her shame, the disease crept up bit by bit until it consumed her thighs and buttocks, to the point that the junctions of the bones were laid bare and the joining of the sinews were exposed. At last, when her bloodless face showed her to be unwell, her parents asked what she suffered, and elicited reports of great pain. The size of the ulcers was equal to the length of a foot. They emitted such a terrible stench that her mother desired her death, her family members avoided her presence, and the neighbors shrank from entering the house in which she lay. The ulcers of the devouring cancer were wrapped in bandages that needed to be changed every hour because of the great amount of pus the ulcers exuded. She was not able to sit or lie down, but instead supported herself on her knees and elbows and fell forward on her face. Suffering in

---

[93] Here Benedict adapted a passage from the preface to the Homilies on Ezekiel: see *Patrologia Latina*, vol. LXXVI, cols. 785A, and *Homilies on the Book of the Prophet Ezekiel by Saint Gregory the Great*, trans. Theodosia Tomkinson (Etna, CA, 2008), p. 23.

this way from the time of harvest to the month of March, she was brought to the end of life. For three or four days she took no food or water, but lay on a couch, leaning against a wall with her knees drawn together and her eyes open and unblinking. She seemed to take on the look of something neither living nor dead. Those seeing her thought she had been rapt out of her body, remembering a certain woman of the region, named Agnes, who, a few days before, had been rapt in her spirit as she slept, and for five days had been led about by the blessed Catherine and shown the rewards and punishments of the dead.[94] And so, thinking that she too had been drawn from her body, they kept watch over her with hope of her return.

And so it happened that while the girl lay unmoving, a woman of the area who loved her dearly came to her at the beginning of night. Believing that she was truly dead, she exclaimed, "You have done an evil deed, you who allowed this girl to die in her bed: why didn't you lay her out on a hairshirt, as is the Christian custom for the dying? You have acted thoughtlessly." And so she was carried into an outer building and exposed on the ground. Her limbs were rigid, her body cold, her eyes staring, the sinews of her knees contracted, and altogether she was as hard and stiff as if she were dead. Her legs could not be stretched or straightened out. And so a linen cloth was put over the corpse, and candles were lit as for a funeral. But the father, who had thrown himself down elsewhere, tormented by both pain and suffering, was woken from sleep and ran in, crying, "Surely my daughter is not dead?" "It is true," said the mother, "she is dead." Then he said, "O blessed Thomas, martyr of God, now repay my service, I who once attentively rendered service to you. Repay my service! Necessity now presses. I once zealously served you before you were given worldly honors. Repay my service! Remember, blessed martyr, how you were once ill in Kent in the house of Turstan the cleric and how I served you there.[95] You were not able to drink wine, cider, ale, or anything that could make one drunk, and I hunted throughout that whole region for whey for you to drink. Repay my service! You then had just one horse, and I looked after it. Martyr, repay my service, remembering all the work that I bore for you. Repay my service! You do not want me to have served you for nothing." He passed nearly half the night crying out in this way. He so often repeated "Repay my service" that his throat was stopped up by hoarseness. The devotion of the

---

[94] The virgin martyr St. Catherine of Alexandria was a very popular saint in medieval Europe. The story of Agnes' vision bears comparison with Benedict's account of the vision of Orm (see above, I.4).

[95] See Biographical Notes, Turstan of Croydon.

martyr approved of the prayers of the supplicant, and, lest he seem to be ungrateful for all his service, he restored the girl to her former health. For suddenly, as she lay beneath the cloth covering her, she put up her hand and pulled it off herself. When she tried to speak, though, she was not able to say anything intelligible on account of her extreme weakness. The following day, she was revived by food and drink. Within three days, even her cancerous thighs had dried up, and in three weeks, without any kind of earthly medicine, she was better.

With these events marvelously completed, the aforesaid man, the father of the girl, went to William, the bishop of Norwich,[96] telling him about the matter and asking for a letter of testimonial. But the bishop did not immediately have faith. He called the priest and those present who had seen the affair, and learned of the whole thing in order, so that by the certification of their testimony, he might be able to stand as a witness for the events. He also called in two married women of good repute who examined the vestiges of the cancer, and he proved her to be most healthy. Therefore he sent letters to us signed by his seal.[97] Although the letter brings forward testimony that she was dead and laid on the ground, yet it touches on some things too briefly which are treated more sufficiently, as we believe, by us above. The manner of the letter is as follows:

"William, by the grace of God bishop of Norwich, to his venerable brothers in the Lord, the prior and the holy convent of Canterbury: eternal salvation in Christ.

We desire with all desire to inform your holiness of the wonders of God that are happening in our diocese to people afflicted with various illnesses who direct all their devotion to St. Thomas and offer pure invocations of their hearts to him. When God does not wish to hide the things which glorify his saint, how can one presume to conceal them among men? We have heard from the testimony of William, a priest of our region, and many of our men, that the bearer of this letter, Cecilia, the daughter of one of our men, was held by the sickness of cancer for a long time. The disease spread implacably about her thighs, and at last she was so oppressed by the worsening illness that she

---

[96] See Biographical Notes, William Turbe, bishop of Norwich.
[97] Bishop William had prior experience investigating the miracles of William of Norwich: see Thomas of Monmouth, *The Life and Passion of William of Norwich*, ed. and trans. Miri Rubin (London, 2014), VI.10, p. 158.

was thought to be lifeless and was placed on the floor in the manner of a corpse. Her father's soul was turned to bitterness, but still trusting in divine mercy and the merits of the most blessed martyr, he burst out in a voice filled with suffering. With a most devoted mind, he invoked the saint of the Lord and begged for the restitution of health to his daughter by the will of divine grace. And so she was restored to her earlier health by the merits of the most blessed martyr, and to the glory of such a miracle we send her to you with our written testimony. Farewell." [*See Parallel Miracles no. 8 for William's account of this miracle.*]

IV.66. CONCERNING THE DROWNED SON OF HUGH DE BENEDEGA

On a manor in the region of Warwickshire called *Benedega*,[98] Hugh surnamed Scot was held to be of good repute and reputation among his neighbors. His son, Philip, was about eight years old. As boys do, he was throwing stones to crush toads that were coming out of a deep iron mine filled with water when, by chance, he fell in and was himself overwhelmed by water.[99] When his father came home and discovered that he was not there, he sought for him everywhere. He found him submerged in the water, and he pulled him out as the sun was setting. The boy was greatly distended with water and was lifeless, as he still believes. The corpse was brought into the house, and the common people gathered as one and sympathized with the anxious sorrow of the parents. Useless attempts were made to see if human help could bring him aid. The boy's very large tunic, wide enough for two boys, could not be pulled off of him because of the size of his distended stomach. It was cut from top to bottom. They hung the boy from his feet and struck his soles, but with the water failing to flow out, hope fell away from them. With the boy laid out on a table and a fire kindled in the hearth on either side, they watched over him until morning.

When the sun rose, by the advice of the mother they sent to the next village, and water of the blessed martyr Thomas was brought back. When the mother inserted a spindle into the boy's closed mouth to separate his clenched teeth, by accident she also inserted one of her fingers. When she pulled the spindle out, her finger

---

[98] The place is unidentified. In William's account of the miracle, Hugh Scot and his son live in Cheshire rather than Warwickshire.
[99] Canterbury's glaziers utilized the imagery of toads coming out of water and boys throwing stones at them Canterbury Cathedral window nII: see Caviness, *Windows*, p. 195.

was caught and nearly pierced through when his teeth came together. When she cried out, the father put a little knife between his teeth, but before he was able to free the mother's trapped finger, he had broken two of the front teeth, those that are called incisors. Some of those present wanted to call a priest so that the last rites could be performed and the boy buried. But the father protested, saying, "So help me God: unless the blessed Thomas restores him to me alive, he will have him dead at Canterbury. I will either bring him there alive or carry him there dead: he will not be buried here." When the water was poured in for both the first and the second time, it came out again, not finding an open passage. But when it was put in a third time, by divine will it descended down into his insides, and suddenly his muscles were seen to twitch. The boy unclenched his closed fist, drew it up little by little, and opened one of his eyes. His father, joyful to an inexpressible degree, said, "Son, do you wish to live?" He replied, "I do wish it, my father." Those who were standing about were still lamenting over the horrible swelling of his stomach, but it subsided little by little. In the sight of all, it recovered its natural size and slenderness, and yet not a drop of water had flowed out from his body, neither from the upper nor the lower parts. We know without doubt that this boy had died not only by the declaration of his father and many others, but also from the testimony of letters from his priest. [*See Parallel Miracles no. 9 for William's account of this miracle.*]

IV.67. CONCERNING THE WIFE OF PETER DE ARCHES, WHO HAD A FLUX OF BLOOD

The wife of a knight, namely Peter de Arches,[100] suffered from hemorrhoids for a long time. When she was lying down she could not get up by herself. Her husband put her on a litter and brought her to Canterbury. When she was brought into the churchyard, the sought-after grace of the martyr immediately appeared, for the woman at once got up from the bed. The martyr restored her in an upright and healthy state to the knight, and kept the litter for himself. Having abandoned her bed, she reverenced the saint, showing him to be worthy of her reverence by her speedily granted wellbeing.

---

[100] See Biographical Notes, Peter de Arches.

IV.68. CONCERNING GERARD OF FLANDERS, WHO HAD KIDNEY STONES

Gerard of Samford, a knight of Flanders,[101] knows from experience how much distress is suffered by a person with kidney stones. One night when he got up needing to urinate, a stone blocked the way and he was tormented almost to death. He thought that he would not live a single hour. Because of the intensity of his distress, he was not able to stay still in one place. He invoked the Lord, he invoked the blessed Virgin and Mother of the Lord, he also invoked many saints: finally, he invoked the martyr Thomas. Marvellous and nearly incredible to relate, except that *no word is impossible with the Lord* [Lk 1:37], at the same time the name of the martyr exited his mouth, he felt the stone exit from his penis. He rested, and the next morning got up and searched for the stone. He was able to find one half of it but not the other. It was like half of an almond nut, and in the hands of those handling it, it broke into grains like sand.

IV.69. CONCERNING THE SMITH GEOFFREY, WHO WORKED AT AN INAPPROPRIATE TIME AND WHOSE FINGERS ADHERED TO HIS PALM

It happened that Geoffrey, a smith of Linby, was making a knife's blade on St. Peter's Chair-Day, contrary to the reverence owed to the feast.[102] When he had ground it to perfection with the strop, the apostle, to whom was given *the power of binding and losing*,[103] so bound him that his little finger was suddenly inflexible and stuck to his right palm. On the next day when he got up from bed, he found that the next smallest finger, that is the leech or the ring finger, was also stuck to his palm. This punishment for untimely work continued to the time of Easter, and in the meantime, he was unable to do the work of a smith. He went to the martyr, came to the tomb, and his little finger was released. On the following day, he again touched the tomb, and gained the release of the other finger, though the area where the fingers had cohered to his palm remained peeled of flesh. And so what Peter bound, the martyr loosened, and he followed the same order in loosening as the apostle had in binding. First came the restitution of the first finger to be taken away. He regained his fingers on successive days, for he had lost them not on one day but on two.

---

[101] A knight Gerard from Flanders appears twice in William's collection: see William of Canterbury, *Miracula*, III.21, p. 280 and VI.72, pp. 470–1.
[102] This feast, honoring Peter the apostle as the first pope, is celebrated on February 22.
[103] See Matthew 16:19, where Christ gives Peter the apostle the power of binding and loosing.

IV.70. CONCERNING THE DROPSICAL WILLIAM OF ST. DAVID'S

A stomach flux weakened a youth of St. David's, William surnamed Crispin, for fifteen days. The flux next turned to constipation, the constipation into a swelling, and the swelling into dropsy. No-one could easily describe the full extent of his gross thickness and no-one could satisfy his thirst. He was given only very modest and sparing amounts to drink, but at length, it seemed hopeless. The signs of death were clearly becoming visible on his face. A priest was called, and he received the viaticum. Having fed on the body of the Lamb of Bethlehem, he asked that he might drink the blood and water of the lamb of Canterbury.[104] An ampulla was brought, and he himself poured water into the ampulla because it did not seem sufficient in itself to quench his multiplied thirst. He drank down everything in a first cup and in a second. He had drunk half of a third when the water rebounded in vomit, drawing out all of the disease and the seeds of the disease with it. What came out was so gummy that it seemed to excel the stickiest glue for gumminess. That same day the youth was made most slender and was freed from all distress, and in three days, restored to full vigor, he started on his journey to the martyr.

IV.71. CONCERNING JULIANA OF GODMERSHAM, WHOSE ARM WAS MORTIFIED

There is a manor of the church of Canterbury which in English is called Godmersham,[105] where the left arm of a certain Juliana, daughter of Edilda, was withered. Her fingers were inseparably stuck together, the thumb lay conjoined to the palm, and the arm always hung at her side wholly insensible. Brought to the sepulchre of the martyr, she suddenly sank down as if afflicted by a defect of the heart, and her fingers separated from each other seemingly in the space of a single moment. Her thumb was released from the palm and the whole arm was brought back to life.

---

[104] As part of the last rites, priests would put the viaticum (another name for the bread of the Eucharist, considered to be the body of Christ) into the mouths of the dying. Here Benedict is comparing the Eucharist and Christ ("the Lamb of Bethlehem") to the blood-and-water relic of Becket ("the lamb of Canterbury").

[105] Godmersham is located about fourteen kilometers away from Canterbury.

IV.72. CONCERNING ELIAS, MONK OF THE CHURCH OF READING, WHO WAS STRUCK, IT WAS THOUGHT, WITH LEPROSY

The person who wishes to know of the disease and means of cure of the monk Elias should convene with the holy convent of the church of Reading.[106] Many who were most skilled in the art of medicine said that he was struck with a terrible leprosy. The signs were runny and teary eyes, ulcerated limbs, and scales over his entire body: when he rose in the morning, you would see his bed covered in them. I leave his description to those servants of God, for something that is unmistakable needs no proof. Greatly distressed, and not knowing how he might go to the blessed Thomas, for he feared that if he asked the abbot would deny him permission,[107] the brother instead asked for leave for a feigned journey to the hot baths of the city of Bath. He started off to the west, and then retraced his steps and went east, to the city of the new-born martyr. This was the time when the martyr shone forth in his first miracles, when the storm winds still blew, before *iniquity would obstruct its mouth* [Ps 106:42], before *one would* openly *speak of the power of the Lord* [Ps 105:2] before *many would come and ascend to* the martyr *of the Lord and to the house of the God of Jacob* [Is 2:3/Mi 4:2]. This could have been written with the first signs of the martyr, except that either through forgetfulness or through investigation and making certain of the truth it was delayed until now. Along the route, the brother came across a knight who cared for him and for whom he had much affection. He asked where he was going, heard the answer, and advised against it: "Do not," he said, "do not, my lord, go to Canterbury, lest the magnates hear of it and you bring down evil on your convent. Look, I carry the water of the holy martyr Thomas. Drink this, if you will. The kindness of the martyr will be able to hear you here." The monk dismounted, and, prone on the ground, he reverenced the water, drank, and, as I remember, washed his face, which had earlier been washed by many tears. Then he turned aside to the blessed martyr Edmund,[108] and from one of his friends he obtained a cloth stained with the blood of the martyr Thomas. He soaked it in water, washed his corrupted body and washed away the leprosy. After some days he returned home, and they received

---

[106] Canterbury's medieval glaziers pictured the leprous monk Elias being examined by doctors, a panel now in Canterbury Cathedral window sVII: see Caviness, *Windows*, pp. 212–13. For discussion of Elias' miracle, see Rachel Koopmans, "Thomas Becket and the Royal Abbey of Reading," *The English Historical Review* 131:1 (February 2016): 1–30, esp. 11–15 and 28–9.

[107] See Biographical Notes, William the Templar, abbot of Reading and archbishop of Bordeaux.

[108] St. Edmund (d.869), the famed saint and miracle-worker whose relics were held at Bury St Edmunds in East Anglia.

him into it as if there were nothing wrong with him. From the marvelous change to his leprous body, the abbot suspected he had gone to Canterbury, not to Bath. Speaking with a calm demeanour to the one fearing to confess, he asked how he was cured. He heard of his mode of cure and, full of wonder, he believed. [*See Parallel Miracles no. 10 for William's account of this miracle.*]

IV.73. CONCERNING THE LEPROUS GERARD

A youth of Flanders, Gerard of Lille, had to be sequestered from the common dwellings of men for fear that the contagion of leprosy, which raged in him, might contaminate others. His fellows had borne with him for a long time because he was not meanly born and was greatly esteemed, until finally, with the pollution obvious, he received the sad sentence of his expulsion. Told that he would be living with the lepers and compelled, anxious for himself, to hasten his exit from the village, one night in a dream he saw himself at Canterbury lying prostrate at the tomb of our martyr. The sarcophagus was cracked, and through a cleft the saint blew into his mouth. This vision seems especially marvellous because when he later came to Canterbury, he found the condition of the tomb and marble and the entire structure to be just as he had seen it in his dream. Rejoicing greatly, and having found in hope, though not yet in reality, *the pearl of great price* of health, *he went and sold all that he had*, so that, going to Canterbury with faith and devotion, he might acquire it [Mt 13:46]. Having set out on his journey, in another dream he thought he was praying spread out in the shape of a cross in a great church unknown to him, and it seemed as if the martyr walked past him and struck him lightly between his shoulder blades with a staff, saying, "Rise, you are healed." And so, rising, he crossed the sea, prostrated himself before the martyr, and spent nine sleepless nights in the church of Canterbury. He was anointed with the anointment of blood and water and he drank the same medication every day. The skin of his feet and legs, where the leprosy was the worst, was spilt everywhere, as if he were cut by a razor. This gave the flowing disease innumerable paths through which to run out. The bloody matter passed into his shoes and he left with the anguish of the disease diminished. When he had boarded a ship and was out to sea, there was a sudden cessation of the pricking and burning pain and he felt himself cleansed. And behold, as if the saint said to him, "Now you are healed, *return and give glory to God*" [Lk 17:18], the ship was driven back to the port of Sandwich by a terrible storm. Since this port was in the vicinity of Canterbury, he returned and presented himself cleansed to us. Staying many days with us, he increased the devotion of many to the martyr.[109]

---

[109] For other lepers who stayed at the tomb for some time after their cures, see IV.3 and IV.76.

IV.74. CONCERNING THE LEPROUS GILBERT OF ST. VALERY

Leprosy had shown itself to a slightly lesser extent in the body of a nearly ten-year-old boy of St. Valery named Gilbert. The evil disease had sullied his hands and arms, feet and legs, and his entire body. Though his face was not marked out by horrible pustules, it was distended and swollen and marked by red and white patches. He was the cause of great pain and shame to his parents, though they still made supplication to the Lord with faith, that he might be made the cause of praise and glory to his martyr. And *God saw that this was good, and it was so* [Gn 1:9–10]. He was led to the martyr, and in three days he was so improved that the bloody matter that had flowed out and hardened all over his body had vanished, feeling had returned to his hands and feet, his skin appeared whole, and by sure signs he seemed to be disposed to perfect health. However, a short time after he had returned home, by what judgement of God I do not know, he became much worse than he was before.

IV.75. CONCERNING THE LEPROUS PETER[110] OF ABINGDON

Eleanor, queen of England,[111] found a cast-out infant, and gave it to Godfrey, bishop of St. Asaph,[112] to bring up. The boy was taught letters. After a few years, he was covered by a foul leprosy. Segregated from the fellowship of students, by the episcopal sentence of that same bishop he was barred from entering the jurisdiction of Abingdon. After four years had gone by, the protuberances on his face had grown greater and greater, and his entire body more and more consumed. The boy left secretly, fled to the martyr, was cleansed by a stomach flux, and returned sound. Those who knew him were stunned when he returned because his face was so altered, the leprosy was annihilated, the swellings had disappeared, and his skin bloomed again. Up until that time, the bishop had remained incredulous about the things which were said of the martyr. But when he saw the cleansed boy, the boy he had seen leprous, had cast out of the jurisdiction, and had abhorred, he was compelled to believe the blessed Thomas to be of great merits, venerable excellence, and wonderful power. The bishop of Salisbury's soul, too, by this

---

[110] Notably, neither Benedict nor William named the leper in their accounts. The caption writer appears to have known his name from another source, suggesting that this was a much-discussed miracle.
[111] See Biographical Notes, Eleanor of Aquitaine (d.1204).
[112] See Biographical Notes, Godfrey, bishop of St. Asaph's and titular abbot of Abingdon.

same sight, was converted to the love of the martyr.[113] [*See Parallel Miracles no. 11 for William's account of this miracle.*]

IV.76. CONCERNING THE LEPROUS RICHARD

It is pleasant to tell those who wish to hear of the glorious cure of a leper born and bred in the territory of Chester, in the village which is called Edgeworth by the English.[114] He appeared to have come to the first years of his adolescence when he was cleansed. His name was Richard Sunieve,[115] the son of a poor woman, but the servant of a rich knight, Richard son of Henry. The boy was tending his lord's horses and, as is the habit of shepherds, lay down in the shade of a thorn bush and slept. When he got up to go home, he appeared to have a swollen and speckled countenance.[116] Little by little over the course of eight years, *the Lord stretched forth his hand* and touched him.[117] Leprosy spread through his whole body, and his flesh was pained by dreadful ulcers. When at last he presented a dreadful and horrible sight to everyone, he was expelled not only from the household of the knight, but also from the village. He was followed only by his mother, to prevent his death. There was no health in him from the sole of his foot to the top of his head, and no spot on his entire body that was not ulcerated, not even the space of an arrow's point. There was so much heat in his decaying body that a cloudy smoke rose from him, as if from a sooty place, and so much putrefaction was expelled that changing his linens every hour did not suffice. The smell was so bad that even his mother shunned his presence, and for his meals, she either held out the food placed on a long pole, or laid out what he was to eat and then absented herself. The boy heard of the martyr's fame, and it greatly grieved him that he was not able to go to the martyr. His tears wet the bed on which he lay, until, through the invocation of the saint, he rose from his bed and made his way to Canterbury. He improved day by day as he traveled. He was admitted to the tomb, and when he was prostrate and kissing the tomb, a large pustule rather like a small apple, which protruded from his lip underneath his nose, vanished in the midst of the kisses. Thinking it had fallen off,

---

[113] See Biographical Notes, Jocelin de Bohun, bishop of Salisbury.
[114] By "territory of Chester," here Benedict means territory of the *earls of* Chester in Gloucestershire, where they held the manor of Bisley and a half-hide of the neighboring manor of Edgeworth. I am very grateful to John Jenkins for this information.
[115] Richard's story is told in six excellently preserved panels in Canterbury Cathedral window nII: see Caviness, *Windows*, pp. 194–5.
[116] On waking ill after sleeping outside, see also II.1, II.28, and III.63.
[117] Numerous passages in the Bible speak of the Lord "stretching out his hand" to punish (or, less usually, to heal): see, for example, Isaiah 5:25.

he searched for it with his hand, but he was not able to find it. When he tasted the health-giving liquid, he was in disorder and confused as if he were drunk. With tottering steps, he was hardly able to leave. It was as if he were thrown into an ecstasy. Rising, however, he sensed a new agility in his body, and his skin, which was still stretched out although the leprosy had gone, straightaway seemed thinner and more wrinkled. Delay in returning seemed tedious to him, and he hastened his return so that he could present himself healed to his own people, bringing joy to them before he did for us. His lord, who had been unsure about the martyr's miracles up to this time, saw this to be a clear and evident miracle, and *he himself believed, and his whole house* [Jn 4:53]. However, when he heard that the boy had secretly left us, he visited the martyr with his wife, family, brothers, kinsmen and friends, leading the healed and sound boy back to us. Having been asked many times, he released him to remain for a time with us.[118]

IV.77. CONCERNING TWO MEN, OF WHOM ONE MIRACULOUSLY TRIUMPHED IN A DUEL OVER THE OTHER

Two men were brought together for a duel of judgment.[119] One of them had by far the larger build and greater strength. He seized the weaker one and lifted him high in order to hurl him to the ground. So lifted up, the smaller man lifted up his mind to heaven, and prayed a brief prayer, saying, "St. Thomas, martyr, help!" He was in great and sudden peril and his time for prayer was short. Those who were there are witnesses. As if the name of the saint weighed down against him, the stronger one suddenly fell under the man he held and was overcome.

IV.78. CONCERNING OTHERS WHO WERE ACCUSED CONCERNING THE GAME OF THE LORD KING THAT THEY HAD TAKEN

Two men were accused and brought to trial by water concerning the woods and game of the lord king of England that they had taken. One applied himself to invoke the martyr and escaped, while the other was judged to be a thief and was hanged.

---

[118] See Parallel Miracles no. 15 for William's reference to a Richard cured of leprosy who stayed at the tomb for a long time, all but certainly this same Richard.

[119] That is, a trial by battle. This miracle was once represented in Canterbury Cathedral's stained glass. Two intact inscriptions that are clearly connected to this story survive in Canterbury Cathedral window nVII: see Caviness, *Windows*, p. 176.

IV.79. CONCERNING OTHERS ACCUSED OF THE SAME THING

I pass over in silence the names and number of the other men who were justly accused of the same thing, but who escaped from the imminent peril of death by invocation of the martyr. In a vision, he stood by one of them, ordering that they would go free. When sleep lifted from his eyes, his dream gladdened his companions. They were tried by water, and each of them escaped. Walking in bare feet and dressed in woolen garments, all of them came together to the martyr to give thanks.

IV.80. CONCERNING AGNES, WHOSE STEPSON TOOK HER DOWER AND RETURNED IT TO HER IN A SUDDEN CHANGE OF MIND

Agnes of the province of Cornwall, the widow of a certain William, also came walking barefoot and dressed only in woolen garments. She had been deprived of her dower by her stepson. The lawsuit was contested and the matter debated for a long time, and the case, at first hanging in doubt, was about to reach its end, with possession awarded to the stepson. Despairing within herself, she made a vow to the martyr Thomas that she would go to him barefoot and without linen if he would assist her in her forsaken state. Unexpectedly, the hatred of her stepson was converted into filial love. He restored to his stepmother everything he had before denied her when she had asked for it, without legal action, price, or prayer. Weeping for joy, she immediately fulfilled her vow.

IV.81. CONCERNING PETER *DE DENINTONA*, WHO WAS SUDDENLY CURED OF AN ENORMOUS SWELLING

The swollen head of Peter *de Denintona* in the province of Surrey[120] was like the head of a bull. He could hardly breathe. His friends and acquaintances came together and entirely despaired of him. The water of the martyr was brought and poured into the mouth of the desperate man. The house in which he lay was more separate, such that it was remote from the areas in which people usually congregated. Everyone left, with only one staying with him. Hardly had those who had left sat down at the table to eat, when the ill man got up, put on his

---

[120] Perhaps there was a misreading here of Surrey for Suffolk, and Peter was from Dennington in Suffolk.

shoes, and ran into the house with a cleansed body and restored head. He asked for water, washed his hands, and sat at the table with the rest. They marvelled that the one whom they had left barely alive had come to eat with them.

IV.82. CONCERNING ALEXANDER, PARTIALLY DEAF

What I relate happened in the house of the knight Hugh de Bodebi.[121] A seven-year-old boy, Alexander, could not hear in one of his ears. When the water was poured in his ear, he recovered perfect hearing.

IV.83. CONCERNING ROBERT, ALSO PARTIALLY DEAF

A similar thing happened in the church of Christ of Canterbury to Robert, son of Asketil, of the aforesaid region. He heard nothing in his left ear, as I had tested. After he slept in the church, his left ear had more acute hearing than his right.

IV.84. CONCERNING OSBERN OF LISIEUX, WHO HAD A HERNIA

We received a young man of Lisieux, Osbern, carrying letters for us of this kind:

"To the beloved brothers and friends in Christ, the prior and sacrist and the rest of the brothers of the holy mother church of Canterbury, greetings from Silvester, the treasurer of the church of Lisieux.[122]

We speak of what we know; we attest to what we have seen. This boy, the bearer of these letters, lived with us for a long time in the service of one of our canons, Roger the son of Ain. Many months have elapsed since he fell into a helpless bodily state, because he had a hernia, or what is commonly known as a rupture. The anguish of this infirmity pressed on him to such an extent that he wished for death rather than remain for long in such a life of tribulation. At last the Lord gave him the inspiration to fly to the help of your saint, the new martyr. He made a vow that within a certain amount of time he would make a journey to your church, in which the martyrdom took place, and visit the burial place of the holy martyr, from whom he hoped for healing. O how

---

[121] See Biographical Notes, Hugh de Bodebi.
[122] See Biographical Notes, Silvester, treasurer of Lisieux.

admirable is the name of Christ in his holy martyr! Within eight days after making the vow, he had received perfect health. Seek the truth of these things from him. *He is of age, let him speak* [Jn 9:21]. Farewell."

IV.85. CONCERNING A CERTAIN JOHN WHO WAS BLINDED AND AFTERWARDS COULD MIRACULOUSLY SEE AGAIN BY MEANS OF THE WATER OF THE MARTYR

We also heard of a marvel that happened in the village of Corbie: a man had recovered his gouged-out eyes by means of the blessed and glorious martyr. We sent a messenger there, and we heard that his eyes were not gouged out but rather savagely wounded by a sharp knife. His torturer, when he was working to take them out, was enraged and brought out a knife with a very sharp point. He cruelly stabbed into the eyes again and again, such that everyone thought that it was worse to have them wounded in this way than to be gouged out. They reproved him for this great wickedness, to kill a man rather than blind him. Our messenger knew the truth of this from men of the village who had seen this with their eyes. When he did not find the abbot of Corbie at home,[123] to whom we had written regarding the investigation of this miracle, he carried back a letter of testimony to us from the prior and convent which reads as follows:

"To the venerable lord Odo, by the grace of God prior of the church of Canterbury,[124] A.,[125] called the prior of the church of Corbie, and the convent: greetings and respect.

We are writing back to you regarding those things you thought worthy to inquire of us by means of your letter. A certain young man named John, born at the fortified town which is called Valenciennes, was discovered and proved to be thieving in our village. According to secular law, he was to be executed by hanging. When he was being dragged off to the punishment of this terrible death, it pleased our burgesses that he might only be deprived of his eyes, and so be dismissed. And so he was made blind and greatly wounded in his eyes. He was led to the house of the sick and received by the hospital's keeper, Ralph. Out of compassion, he bathed the eyes of the blinded man with warm water for that day and the following night, and he warmed them in order to

---

[123] Corbie Abbey was a famed and influential Benedictine monastery in northern France.
[124] See Biographical Notes, Odo, prior of Christ Church, Canterbury.
[125] The prior only provided his first initial rather than his full name.

ease the pain. On the third day, when he asked him with concern whether any access to sight was open to him at all after his blinding, he answered that no light remained in one eye, but in the other a little brightness came in, though so little that he certainly would not be able to find his way along a road without a guide. A certain poor young cleric had come there in the meantime, who confessed that he carried with him in a glass vessel the water of our most blessed patron, the martyr Thomas, Archbishop of Canterbury, glorified by God in our time, the water that very many know has performed numerous miracles. And so they received a small amount of the water, and in honor of the martyr we have spoken of, they reverently lit candles and carefully washed the eyes of the blind man with it. He regained his sight there, to such an extent that even the scars of the wounds inflicted on him during his blinding were healed. On the next day, he went to his own region healed and rejoicing. Lest these things leave any hesitation in your heart, we testify to you that one of our brothers was freed from a flood from the nose by drinking this same water."

IV.86. CONCERNING A MONK OF THE CHURCH OF READING, WHO WAS FREED FROM A DEVIL THAT HAD CLOSED UP HIS THROAT AND NOSE BY MEANS OF THE MARTYR'S WATER

Geoffrey, a monk of the church of Reading,[126] was encumbered by a very grave illness, to the point that it was thought he was in the last extremity, for he was deprived of the use of all his senses and all the members of his body. What more? All the brothers gathered together so that they might anoint him with holy oil, as is the custom. He received the sacrament, lost his speech, and was despaired of entirely. The prior, not knowing at all what should be done, said, "O brothers, if any of you know where the water of the holy martyr Thomas might be, let it be brought here in Christ's faith." Shortly thereafter an ampulla with water was brought by one of the brothers. After it was poured through the lips of the sick man, the chain upon his tongue was suddenly loosened, all his senses recovered, and all the members of his body received their earlier health, such that he said, "It is well." Afterwards, he cried out loudly, "Thanks be to God, who by the merits of his martyr, St. Thomas, completely freed me from an evil spirit that had quite closed up my throat and nose." And so

---

[126] See Biographical Notes, Geoffrey of Wallingford, monk of Reading. For discussion of this miracle and the early cult of Becket at Reading, see Koopmans, "Thomas Becket and the Royal Abbey of Reading."

the monk escaped both the hand of the demon and the injury of death. [*See Parallel Miracles no. 12 for William's copy of a letter from Augustine, a monk of Reading, which served as Benedict's source for this account.*]

IV.87. CONCERNING A MONK OF MONT-DIEU, GEOFFREY, SUFFERING FROM DROPSY, WHO DEFLATED WHEN HE STROKED AN ACCOUNT OF THE MARTYR'S MIRACLES OVER HIS BODY AND WAS HEALED

Peter, the venerable abbot of St.-Rémi,[127] wrote regarding our inquiry about the truth of a certain miracle,[128] and among other things says, "What I relate of the true events regarding the monk of Mont-Dieu named Geoffrey, I heard partly from him, and more fully from our monk who, at that time, was engaged in writing there. By chance, an account of miracles of St. Thomas had come to us from England, and from us to the brothers of Mont-Dieu. The said brother, his whole body swollen and distended, like someone truly afflicted with dropsy, was not able to leave the cell. Having received the account, with faith and invocation of the name of the saint, he touched it to his feet, shins, and the whole of his body, and recovered to such a degree that in a short time he was able to return to the church and his office, though he was not completely cured."

IV.88. CONCERNING A BOY OF WINCHESTER ON WHOM A WALL FELL

I know an honorable man of the city of Winchester whose son, Geoffrey, who was about a year and a half old, had been delivered from an acute illness by means of the water of Canterbury.[129] After some days, however, when the boy's mother sat alone in the house, and the boy rested in a crib opposite her, a great stone wall of the house collapsed and buried him in a heap of quarry-stones. The mother cried, "Lord, St. Thomas, save my son, whom you

---

[127] See Biographical Notes, Peter of Celle, abbot of St.-Rémi and bishop of Chartres.
[128] The full text of the letter Peter of Celle sent to Christ Church (of which this chapter is just an extract, with some alterations) was preserved in Peter's letter collection: see *The Letters of Peter of Celle*, no. 142, 522–5. The translation above is my own. Haseldine dates Peter's letter to 1175/76 (thinking that it was sent when Benedict was the prior of Christ Church), but a better date range is 1172/3.
[129] This miracle is portrayed in Canterbury Cathedral window sVII: see Caviness, *Windows*, pp. 210–11.

earlier restored to me!" When she had said this, she fell into a trance due to her extreme anguish. When some servants of the house came and saw her lying there as if she were dead, they applied the remedy of cold water, as it is usual to do. When she came back to herself and sat up, they said, "What has happened, lady?" "Oh, such sorrow! My son is dead. Look, he lies broken under the heap of rocks and stones." But they invoked the name of God and the martyr, and, calling many men to their aid, they dismantled the mound of rubble. After much work, they broke through to the boy, and they found him not only unhurt but laughing. The boy's crib, which was made of thick and solid wood, was broken into eighteen pieces. But the tender skin of the infant was entirely unhurt, with the exception of a small bruise under his eye, though a stone larger than the child was lying on top of him. *Those who saw this were amazed* [Lk 2:48] and *astonishment seized them* [Lk 5:26]. [See Parallel Miracles no. 13 for William's account of this miracle.]

IV.89. CONCERNING THE ALE THAT DID NOT PURIFY ITSELF AS ALE USUALLY DOES, AND SUDDENLY RECEIVED THE NECESSARY CONDITION WITH THE APPLICATION OF A STRING THAT HAD HELD AN AMPULLA HOLDING THE SAINT'S WATER

Ralph *de Hathfeld*[130] and his wife wished to visit the martyr but did not have the ability to do so. The poverty of their household's means hindered the accomplishment of their pious desire. They formed a plan to make ale and sell it, hoping in this way to gain the funds for themselves from the profits. The ale was made, but it was not able to purify itself, as this drink usually does, and did not emit any fermentation. The woman who had mixed it saw it come to nothing. She took the string which had held an ampulla of the water of the martyr, and, invoking the martyr, she placed it in the ale. Immediately the fermentation that alewives call barm[131] burst forth to such a remarkable degree that it could hardly be kept from overflowing. And so, the undrinkable drink was made drinkable and worthy of sale. I did not hear about this from

---

[130] The place is unidentified. It is spelled *Hadfeld* and *Hathfel* in various manuscripts: see Robertson *MTB*, vol. 2, p. 253 n. 1 and Duggan, "Santa Cruz," p. 55.
[131] The Latin word Benedict uses here is *flos*, which usually translates as flower, but could be used to describe a kind of surface scum or deposit. The first step in the making of ale is to make a wort by crushing barley, soaking it in hot water, and draining off the liquid. For the wort to become ale, it needs to ferment. When it does, a thick, foamy top – the barm – will form.

the woman herself, but rather from Master Richard, monk of Ely,[132] who had heard these things from her in confession.

IV.90. CONCERNING ELIAS *DE SIBBURNIA*, WHOSE VISCERA WERE SO CONSTRICTED THEY SEEMED TO BE ATTACHED TO HIS BACK

The viscera of Elias, the nephew of Richard the dean *de Siburna*,[133] were so constricted and contracted that his stomach and back seemed to be stuck together. He was in such anguish, and had such difficulty in breathing, that he seemed to be about to die every hour. The water was sent for, he drank, and in that same moment he became better.

IV.91. CONCERNING A CERTAIN HADEWISA, WHO HAD AN INTERIOR RUPTURE

Hadewisa, the servant of this same dean, seemed to have an interior rupture, such that the viscera had broken out from the interior membrane and gathered against the exterior skin, making a very large swelling. Hardly had she tasted the water when the swelling subsided and the viscera settled back into their place.

IV.92. CONCERNING ROBERT *DE BEVERUNO* WITH THE STONE

Among those suffering from the stone, who was more miserable than Robert *de Beveruno*?[134] He opened his mouth to make a vow of pilgrimage, drank the water of the martyr, and emitted the stone, which had been broken into pieces by the power of the drink.

IV.93. CONCERNING HIS NEIGHBOR HINGAN, WHO SUFFERED SUDDEN FITS

His neighbor, Hingan, suffered sudden fits. They seized him while he was sleeping, and his great anguish made those who saw him feel pain. When the fit

---

[132] See Biographical Notes, Richard, master and monk of Ely.
[133] The place is unidentified. It may be Shipbourne in Kent.
[134] The place is unidentified.

ended, he did not remember his suffering. It was thought to be another kind of the falling sickness. And so he drank of the healing water, and, after the drink, he lived in peace.

IV.94. CONCERNING THE SON OF THE EARL OF CLARE, WHO WAS RESURRECTED FROM THE DEAD

God does not cast aside the powerful, for he himself is powerful [Jb 36:5]. The powerful and noble received their dead back by resurrection. One of these was described above,[135] and here another will be specified. He who makes all breath sent back the missing breath of life to James,[136] the son of the earl Roger de Clare,[137] then still a nursing infant. The merits of the innocent martyr went to the aid of the innocent one not just once, but twice. Born around the feast of St. Michael,[138] the infant boy was forty days old when he ruptured himself by too much crying. Intestines filled the scrotum of his testicles. With things so disordered, what ought to have been in the stomach was in the scrotum, which was distended and hung down nearly to his knees. His father offered forty or even more silver marks for his cure,[139] but no-one would accept this unless they were allowed to cut into the tiny infant. His parents, however, fearing for his young age, would by no means consent to the use of a knife. And so, the infant's hernia remained for a year and some months. In the course of the second year from his birth, on the day of the Purification of the blessed Virgin and Mother Mary,[140] he was brought to the martyr by his mother.[141] Washed with the water of the martyr, within three days he was released from his infirmity, with no trace of it remaining.

---

[135] See the story of Jordan son of Eisulf, IV.64 above.
[136] James' miracle is pictured in Canterbury Cathedral window sVII: see Caviness, *Windows*, pp. 211–14, and for the panels picturing Matilda pulling her son away from a doctor and in church being notified by an older son of James' death, Rachel Koopmans, "Visions, Reliquaries, and the Image of 'Becket's Shrine' in the Miracle Windows of Canterbury Cathedral," *Gesta* 54:1 (2015): 37–57, at pp. 45–51.
[137] See Biographical Notes, Roger de Clare, earl of Hertford.
[138] Michaelmas, September 29. The year of his birth was 1171, and the recoveries and pilgrimages occurred in early 1173: for this dating, see Koopmans, "Benedict of Peterborough's Compositions," pp. 255–6.
[139] A mark was a unit of account equivalent to thirteen shillings and four pence, or two-thirds of a pound. Forty marks was the same as 6,400 pennies, an enormous sum reflective of both Roger de Clare's wealth and his concern for his son.
[140] The Purification of the Virgin, also known as Candlemas, was celebrated on February 2.
[141] See Biographical Notes, Matilda de St. Hilary.

After some weeks, in the middle of the following Lent, he was struck by another illness and breathed forth his spirit. The mother had gone to church to attend the divine office. The household had remained at home. Among them, no one could be found who would announce the boy's death to the mother's ears for fear of being called the cause of the calamity. At last a young boy, the brother of the dead boy, ran to the church.[142] Unable, like any boy, to keep a secret, he repeatedly cried out to his mother, "Lady, my brother is dead; lady, my brother is dead." Instantly going pale, she sprang up, and casting aside her cloak she ran back to the house. She found that the infant had been carried from the inner room to an outer chamber and was laid out on the floor. His mouth was open, but he was entirely without breath. His tongue and lips were pulled back and his eyes were sunken and turned up such that only the whites could be seen. He was entirely cold and rigid, and, to say it shortly, truly dead. She picked him up in her arms and said "St. Thomas, restore my son to me! On a previous day you saved him from hernia. Now he is dead. Holy martyr, restore him to life." She ran and extracted from the reliquary the relics of the saint which she had brought back from Canterbury. She poured the blood of the martyr in the mouth of the dead infant, and thrust the little piece of the hairshirt down his throat, constantly crying and saying, "Holy martyr Thomas, return my son to me. If you revive him, he will be brought back to your tomb. I myself will visit you barefoot. Hear me!" The knights who stood about, the countess of Warwick[143] and other women, all called upon her to be silent, but she knelt again and again on the ground with her bare knees and cried out even more: "Holy martyr, have mercy on me!" Then Lambert, her chaplain, an honorable man of good old age,[144] said "Why are you acting in this way, lady? You are being unwise and what you are doing is foolish: anyone who hears what you are doing and saying will think you are out of your mind. Is not the Creator allowed to do what he wishes with his creature? Cease. Put aside the infant, and let it be treated as a dead child. It is very foolish for you to make such an effort for something that is impossible." All of them spoke similarly, but she said, "I certainly will not stop, nor will I put the infant aside: I trust that he will be returned to me. Martyr, glorious martyr,[145] most pious, beloved martyr, have mercy on me, return my son to me." And when she had cried out in this manner for two hours, the martyr

---

[142] For James' brothers, see Biographical Notes, Matilda de St. Hilary.
[143] See Biographical Notes, Matilda de Percy (d.1204).
[144] On Lambert the chaplain, see Biographical Notes, Matilda de St. Hilary (d.1193).
[145] Here I have followed the manuscripts collated by Duggan, "Santa Cruz," p. 55, which do not have the repetition of *inquit* (she said) found in Robertson's edition.

had mercy on her and restored life to her infant. At first, a hint of redness appeared on his face, and a little while later, rolling his eyes, he burst out crying. And they blessed *the Lord who kills and revives, who leads to the depths and leads back* [1 Sm 2:6], and *there was great happiness in the* house [1 Mc 4:58], and in the end joy outstripped mourning, for *they obtained joy, and sorrow and mourning fled away* [Is 35:10]. The countess, the mother of the restored boy, took up an unusual labor, and made good her promised journey on bare feet to Canterbury with the boy. Following her were the countess of Warwick and many other women, the forenamed chaplain Lambert, and many knights, who all testified that they had seen the boy to be truly dead and that he was truly resurrected from the dead. [*See Parallel Miracles no. 14 for William's account of this miracle.*]

The Chapters of the Additions

1. Concerning Gilbert, son of William of Brun, freed from fever
2. Concerning Savaric de Vallibus
3. Concerning the daughter of William of Baldock
4. Concerning a woman living in the same village
5. Concerning the son of William the clerk
6. Concerning Hugh of Ebblingham, struck with leprosy [*see Parallel Miracles no. 15*]
7. Concerning a man completely buried in earth and yet not dead [*see Parallel Miracles no. 16*]
8. Concerning the daughter of Thomas of Ifield [*see Parallel Miracles no. 17*]
9. Concerning John, servant of Sweyn of Roxburgh, who was submerged in a river [*see Parallel Miracles no. 18*]

ADDITIONS

ADDITION 1[1] CONCERNING GILBERT, SON OF WILLIAM OF BRUN, FREED FROM FEVER

Death, by means of acute fevers, was claiming Gilbert, the son of William of Brun, from Caen. The boy hardly breathed and he was unable to speak. Friends had come to try to console and assuage the grief of the father, but he did not wish to find comfort. He retreated into his bedchamber, closed the door, and wept for his son, saying in his heart, "I will not watch the boy die." Then, thinking from a sudden tumult of voices that he was without doubt dying, he flew quickly and went to meet the martyr, as much to his memory as to the cause of happiness, saying: "O blessed friend of God Thomas, without any doubt my son will not die. I will give him to you, he will be yours, I entrust him to you, I give him over to your service. Have mercy on me, glorious martyr, and if it be your will, save this boy your servant. I will lead him to your holy sepulchre: have mercy on me, most pious martyr." Saying these words, he came to the boy and said, "Son, for the love of God and the martyr Thomas, speak to me if you are able." And immediately, as if he were woken from sleep, he lifted up his arms and embraced his father. The one who was all but dead sat up and began to speak. That same week, he was restored entirely healthy to his father.

ADDITION 2[2] CONCERNING SAVARIC DE VALLIBUS

Roger, the young son of Savaric de Vallibus,[3] an honored knight, was also being carried away by diarrhea. He had lived on water alone for twenty days. His parents made a vow for him that would shortly be paid to the martyr. I speak of marvels, but do not exceed the measure of truth. After making the vow they went to dine, and during the first course they received the first course of happiness. As they were eating, the boy, who had been left in his room hardly alive, got up, dressed himself, and came to where they were

---

[1] Numbered IV.95 in Robertson's edition.
[2] Numbered IV.96 in Robertson's edition.
[3] See Biographical Notes, Savaric de Vallibus.

dining, with boyish levity spinning and playing with a rattle[4] in their presence. The company of guests marvelled, and the parents rejoiced to receive such a guest.

ADDITION 3[5]   CONCERNING THE DAUGHTER OF WILLIAM OF BALDOCK

The daughter of William of Baldock had very swollen eyes for fourteen weeks. The injury of the swelling drove out the natural light of her eyes. The father washed the eyes of the infant with the martyr's water, and though the swelling of both eyes immediately went down, sight was restored only to one of them.

ADDITION 4[6]   CONCERNING A WOMAN LIVING IN THE SAME VILLAGE

A woman living in the same village was blind for eleven years. She departed and washed, and she came seeing.

ADDITION 5[7]   CONCERNING THE SON OF WILLIAM THE CLERK

A boy from the manor of the diocese of York called Kirkham was brought to us, the son of William the clerk. Witnesses were brought forth who attested that as a result of a great swelling, an eye was expelled from his head, and the pupil from the eye. The parents washed the eye with the eye-salve of Canterbury and offered a candle to the martyr to the measurements of the boy. The next day, the boy was found healed. The pupil was returned to the eye and the eye restored to its place.

---

[4] Benedict uses the unusual word *taratantara* to describe little Roger's toy: see the entry for this word in *DMLBS*.
[5] Numbered V.1 in Robertson's edition.
[6] Numbered V.2 in Robertson's edition.
[7] Numbered V.3 in Robertson's edition.

ADDITION 6[8]   CONCERNING HUGH OF EBBLINGHAM, STRUCK WITH LEPROSY

The omnipotent Father, who *strikes his son with the rod and saves their souls from death* [Prv 23:14], *who visits their iniquities with a rod and their sins with lashings, but does not scatter away his mercy from them* [Ps 88:33-4], struck Hugh of Ebblingham with a sudden leprosy in the time of harvest. His entire body was deformed by large protuberances. The man thought over his sin and *confessed his injustices against himself to the Lord* [Ps 31:5]. Having invoked the martyr, within eight days he felt himself improved and went to Canterbury. In a vision at night, he saw the face as of one crucified. With his hand, he touched the place of leprosy, and said, "*Behold, you are made whole*" [Jn 5:14]. He came to us, and *we saw him having no beauty or comeliness* [Is 53:2]. Although in many places only the vestiges of leprosy remained, in others the bulging protuberances had not yet been put to flight. And so, he washed with the marvellous water of the martyr, who was washed in his own blood and is entirely clean. The man was not yet clean when he came to the martyr. Through him he was made clean, for we dismissed him improved, and after some months, we received him entirely cleansed. Blessed in all things is the kind providence of God, who stole away the cleansed martyr from the world, that his cleanliness might cleanse the unclean of the sordidness of the world. There were very many for whom the martyr smoothed out skin roughened by leprous protuberances, but it is not necessary for each of them to be described individually and jointly. For even a sweet song, when it is repeated frequently, sometimes produces tedium. Lest, therefore, by wearing away we grind down to tedium, let us await something new. [See Parallel Miracles no. 15 for William's account of this miracle.]

ADDITION 7[9]   CONCERNING A MAN COMPLETELY BURIED IN EARTH AND YET NOT DEAD

We longed for something new, for by something new we are kindled to new love of the new martyr of the English. *The Lord has done a new thing on the earth* [Jer 31:22] – or, rather, under the earth. For a fall of earth surrounded a man, and though he was compressed from all sides, he was not destroyed. The man bore without injury what would have overcome many oxen. This

---

[8] Numbered V.4 in Robertson's edition.
[9] Numbered VI.1 in Robertson's edition.

happened in the village in the vicinity of Gloucester that the English call Churchdown, and the man's name was William.[10] That man was constructing an aqueduct and was in a pit extending lead pipe. It was about the tenth hour,[11] and it is said that the pit was twenty-four feet deep. The overhanging earth fell on the worker and filled up the pit such that it was level with the surrounding ground. Before he was buried as if he were dead, he said, "St Thomas, glorious martyr, if what is said about you is true, help me that I might be rescued alive. If you keep me alive, I will visit the place where you were living and dead." He was standing bent over, and praying in this position, his breath was already being blocked. Beyond hope, he coughed, then he vomited, and after the vomiting came freedom of breath. Buried, he cried constantly to the martyr all that night and the following day up to the third hour.[12] Everyone there shared the opinion that he must be dead. There was no doubt about his death, since he was covered by such a great weight of earth. Yet, by the martyr's virtue, this one small man carried the weight of one hundred cartloads or more.

The priest of the village was anxious for the soul of the dead man, not knowing that that soul was more anxious for its still living body. And so, the priest conducted the funeral rites for him, though they would not be the last ones, as he thought, but the first. In the morning, a young man of the same village, led by divine inspiration, came that way and heard a sound under the earth. Coming by chance across the herald of the village, he said, "The man buried yesterday is still alive." He said, "What you say is impossible: he died instantly." In response, the young man said, "If you doubt it, come and hear." He agreed and put his ears upon the earth, and the hesitating doubt was removed from his heart. The rumor sounded throughout the village. The people came with spades and mattocks and other digging tools. The earth was lifted, the man disinterred. He was brought out alive and uninjured, preaching the virtues of the martyr Thomas to all. Visiting the martyr, he certified this by letters in this mode, though the fame of the event had long preceded his arrival.

"Greetings from Geoffrey, dean of Gloucester, to his venerable lord and father, prior of the Holy Trinity of Canterbury, and all the convent.

Know that the bearer of these letters, William, was buried in a certain deep pit, twenty-four feet deep, his co-workers having fled, and he was buried there for

---

[10] This miracle is depicted in Canterbury Cathedral window sVII: see Caviness, *Windows*, pp. 213–14.
[11] That is, late afternoon.
[12] That is, mid-morning.

one night and up to the third hour of the next day. The funeral rites were conducted for him as if he were dead. He, however, feeling the approach of death, invoked God and prayed that he might be liberated from this great danger for the love of his most glorious martyr Thomas. Crying aloud, he made a vow that he would go to the place where saint Thomas had been killed. After he was heard by some people who were passing that place, they announced to the entire village that they had heard a human voice in the pit. The priest and more than a hundred men hastened there and drew him out. But also many other miracles are done among us every day through Thomas, the most glorious martyr of Christ, which I will relate to you when I come to you in a short time, God willing."

So the account ended, which concurred in every respect with the testimony of the people who had been present. For he, with many others, *came for a witness, to give testimony of the light* [Jn 1:7]. *If we receive the testimony of men, the testimony of God is greater. For this is the testimony of God, which is greater, because he has testified* in modern times *of his* martyr [1 Jn 5:9]. [See Parallel Miracles no. 16 for William's account of this miracle.]

ADDITION 8[13]   CONCERNING THE DAUGHTER OF THOMAS OF IFIELD

Led astray by the prompting of the servants of her father's house, Salerna, the daughter of Thomas of Ifield, stole a cheese of her mother and gave it to them. By chance, the mother discovered the cheese was missing. She accused the girl of the offence and threatened her when she denied it. When threats did not work, she also applied blows, declaring that if she did not confess, on the next day she would beat her until she exhaled her spirit. That day was the Sabbath, though not for her. More anxious for the future than remorseful for the past, she spent nearly the entire night sleepless, crying and wailing, and saying, "St. Thomas, take care of me. St. Thomas, help me. Help me, St. Thomas. Take care of me, St. Thomas." In the morning, when she knew that her mother had gone to church,[14] she left the house and went to a well of water in order to throw herself into it. In this way, if she could not escape death, she could at least change its means. When she came near the well, she saw near her something like a little woman going with her. It used its power to seek

---

[13] Numbered VI.2 in Robertson's edition.
[14] Probably the church of St. Margaret, Ifield, which may have been a timber church at the time.

her soul, forcing her to the edge and saying "Go, go. You will go in, you will go in." And so she sat on the edge of the well, then hung by her hands in the mouth of the well. By the instigation of he who is down below, she sent herself down headlong, crying with a loud voice, "May Almighty God and St. Thomas take care of me!" And she fell into the deep pit and was not dashed, since the Lord supported her with his hand. For he heard her and her voice, and *descended with* her *into the pit* [Ws 10:13] and *drew* her *out of many waters* [2 Sam 22:17] *lest* she *be swallowed by the deep* of the abyss, and *the mouth of the well* of hell closed over her [Ps 68:16].

And so she sank under three or four times. Each time she emerged, when she had breath she called out, "St. Thomas, help me!" By some divine force, the girl's entire body, all the way to her feet, was driven above the water, and God or the martyr, or rather both God and the martyr, placed her feet on a staff and put another staff in her shaking hands. She was standing on one staff set along the surface of the water, while she leaned on the other, which was propped against the wall of the well. She had no idea how she came to be standing on the staff nor who had put the second staff into her hands. We have established and made most certain that a young man had cleaned this same well a few days before, and he had not left a staff or stick in it, not even a twig. As the girl stood there, she heard a consoling voice often repeating itself in these comforting words: "Do not fear, daughter, you will go up safely. You will go up safely, daughter, do not fear." She testifies that she saw the person speaking to her standing near her, dressed in the whitest linen. And so, this is what was happening in the well.

A servant of the family, who was working in a nearby field, heard the voice of the girl as she fell. He had also seen her sitting on the edge of the well and, astonished, had reproached her. He ran and woke a sleeping young man in the house, calling him by name, repeatedly telling him that Salerna had fallen in the well. But he, as though waking in a dream, both heard the voice of the one speaking to him and yet was not able to cast off sleep. For he saw before him something in the shape of a hideous man. He was very tall, had a terrible visage, held a great cudgel in his hands, and repeated again and again, "If you get up, you are a dead man. If you move, I will kill you." At last, he was woken by the insistence of the one calling to him, and he ran with the boy to the well. He went down into it but became frightened by its depth and came out again. They both stood there distressed by the misfortune and not knowing what to do. Then one said to the other, "Be quick, get on a horse and hurry to the church, and make clear to our lady what dreadful misfortune has happened."

He got on a horse and went quickly, and, after some considerable delay, not only the lady, but also the entire parish that had, as usual, gone to church on that day, returned with him. The young man was sent down the deep pit of the well on a rope, and the girl was pulled out while he remained on the staff. She kept exclaiming and saying, "Measure me for St. Thomas, measure me for St. Thomas." She wanted the length of her body to be measured and a candle made that she could offer to the martyr for her delivery. When she had been pulled out, she was found to be uninjured, though she was afflicted with such cold that she was near death. She kept saying, "He was with me just now in the well, but now he is gone." "Who was with you?" they asked. And she said, "The blessed martyr Thomas dressed in white, and he said this and this to me in the well." All who stood there blessed the martyr of the Lord, *who does all as he will, in heaven, in earth, in the sea, and in all the deeps* [Ps 134:6].

And indeed, the great depth of the aforementioned deep pit makes this a great miracle. I measured its depth myself, and I found that from the level of the ground to the top of the water, the distance was around fifty feet, and the water went to the depth of more than sixty feet. I set this forth among the rest of the martyr's signs confidently, for it was certified by the testimony not only of the girl herself, but also of her parents and the faithful men of the vicinity, for *these have seen the works of the Lord, and his wonders in the deep* [Ps 106:24]. [*See Parallel Miracles no. 17 for William's account of this miracle.*]

ADDITION 9[15]   CONCERNING JOHN, SERVANT OF SWEYN OF ROXBURGH, WHO WAS SUBMERGED IN A RIVER

We also know of an extraordinary sign that happened in the river Tweed near the city of Roxburgh.[16] On no account should we be silent of what the Lord has done for the servant of Sweyn, the provost of the city: *John is his name* [Lk 1:63]. This man was washing or watering the horse of his lord in the aforenamed river in the evening. The horse was fearful, and, frightened by a hurdle that it happened to see before it,[17] it turned aside and leapt into the depths. The horse swam to dry land, while the young man, thrown off, remained in the river. When he fell into the river, the young man cried out, "St. Thomas,

---

[15] Numbered VI.3 in Robertson's edition.

[16] This miracle is depicted in Canterbury Cathedral window sVI: see Caviness, *Windows*, p. 206.

[17] A hurdle is a light and moveable fence. In his account of this miracle, William suggests that this hurdle was a weir for catching fish.

just as I was truly your pilgrim and went to you, I will go to you again, by your will. Help me so that I do not die!" The horse went back and was taken in without its rider. A sorrowful story of his drowning began to circulate. When the neighbours heard these rumours, they *went out immediately, and it was night* [Jn 13:30]. And they *passed by* here and there, *and behold, he was not: they sought him and his place was not found* [Ps 36:35]. He had already been pulled a long way off by the waves and was being held under the hollow of a large rock on the bottom of the river. So each of them went home, none of them having hope of finding the submerged man.

When he had lain on the bottom of the river until midnight, eight men appeared to him, looking as if they were crossing the river near him. He thought that he got up and followed them, but in truth he rose to the surface of the water and followed them by swimming. At length, as he reached the bank, he seized the branch of a willow tree. As he was pulling the tree toward him, the branch broke off, a large stone from the bank tumbled down on him, and he fell into the river again. After a little while, the same men went by as if crossing next to him, and he followed them. He thought that he was walking, but he was swimming upon the water,[18] until he felt himself to be in the water under a bridge. Suddenly, by the wonderful power of God, he found himself lying upon the bridge. He had no idea how he had been lifted from the water or how he had come upon the bridge, since the height of the bridge above the water was considerable, and no one could easily climb up onto the bridge from the water. He was swollen with the water he had been forced to drink, but it came out the same passage it had entered in. As he was vomiting in distress, he heard one of the aforementioned men, clothed in pontifical ornaments, say to him, 'It was to your benefit that you brought me to mind yesterday when you fell. See, you are freed from death. Be a good man, and do good while you are able'. When he lifted his eyes in order to see who spoke with him, he vanished from his eyes. Oppressed by cold, he was not able to get up, but by creeping along on his hands and feet he was able to reach a house near the bridge. He was almost not allowed in, since the people in the house at first thought that it was the spirit of the drowned man that groaned outside the door. His chilled limbs, frozen by the water, were nurtured by the aid of a fire and brought back to strength. When he received his former vigour, he, along with his lord Sweyn, went as he had vowed to Thomas, the Lord's anointed, and he gave thanks to him for grace. [*See Parallel Miracles no. 18 for William's account of this miracle.*]

[18] Christ was famed for walking on water (see Matthew 14:22–36, Mark 6:45–56, and John 6:16–21). Benedict did not want his readers to think that he believed that the servant John of Roxburgh replicated one of Christ's most famous miracles.

Biographical Notes

Alan of Ratling, occ. 1148x1180 [III.49]. The Ratlings took their name from a manor of Nonington, Kent, located about fifteen kilometers from Canterbury. Alan of Ratling held ground in Canterbury, was one of the men named in the 1169 excommunications issued by Becket for those who had taken possessions belonging to the church of Canterbury, and appears in the Pipe Roll for 1176–7: see *CTB*, vol. 2, letter no. 262, p. 1129; Urry, *CUAK*, pp. 55–6, 182; *PR 23 Henry II*, p. 206. None of the surviving documentation records the name of Alan of Ratling's wife, the subject of Benedict's miracle story.

Albinus, abbot of Darley, occ. 1151x1176 [IV.11]. Albinus was the first abbot of Darley (or Derby), an Augustinian house founded c.1146 just north of Darby (see *HRH*, p. 161). The abbot of Darley is mentioned in a letter sent to Thomas Becket before mid-1166 by Nicholas of Mount-Saint-Jacques, prior of the hospital of Mont-aux-Malades in Rouen (*CTB*, vol. 1, no. 94, pp. 386–7, on this hospital, see Elma Brenner, 'Thomas Becket and Leprosy in Normandy', in Paul Webster and Marie-Pierre Gelin (eds.), *The Cult of Thomas Becket in the Plantagenet World, c.1170–c.1220* (Woodbridge, 2016), pp. 81–94). Nicholas tells Becket that they know little of the gossip of the court, but that they will know more when the abbot of Darley arrives. This suggests that Albinus was long a friend of the Becket party. Canons from Darley staffed the Augustinian priory of St. Thomas the Martyr near Stafford founded c.1174. Albinus is named in its foundation charter: see F. Parker, ed., "'Chartulary' of the Priory of St. Thomas (A'Becket) Near Stafford," in *Collections for a History of Staffordshire*, The William Salt Archaeological Society (London, 1887), vol. 8, pp. 130–2. See also **Nicholas son of Aileva.**

Anfrid of Ferring, knight [IV.16]. "Anfridus de Fering" is listed in the carta of Hilary, bishop of Chichester, under the returns for Sussex: see *CB* no. XII (7), p. 16. "Anfridus (de) Feringes" is also a witness on a charter dated 1164 relating to the abbey of Fécamp in Normandy: see *Calendar of Documents preserved in France Illustrative of the History of Great Britain and Ireland, Vol. I, A.D. 918–1206*, ed. by J. Horace Round (London, 1899), p. 48. At the time of the Domesday survey, the manor of Ferring was held by a man named Ansfrid: see *DP*, p. 155. Unfortunately, we do not have any documentation that provides the name of Anfrid's wife.

Aziria of Earley [II.53–4]. Benedict does not name Aziria, the wife of **William de Earley**, but her name is known from a charter relating to Buckland Priory: see *A Cartulary of Buckland Priory in the County of Somerset*, ed. F. W. Weaver (Somerset Record Society vol. 25, 1909), no. 34; see also E. H. Bates Harbin, "Charter of Clemencia de Erleigh," in *Notes and Queries for Somerset and Dorset*, ed. by Frederic William Weaver and Charles Herbert Mayo (Sherborne, 1915), vol. 14, p. 70. The couple's eldest son and heir was named John: see "Parishes: Sonning with Earley, Woodley and Sandford," in *A History of the County of Berkshire: Volume 3*, ed. P. H. Ditchfield and William Page (London, 1923), pp. 210–25.

Bartholomew, bishop of Exeter (d.1184) [I.1]. A scholar and one of the leading lights of the English Church, Bartholomew, bishop of Exeter from 1161 to 1184, walked a fine line during the Becket dispute. He was suspended from office for his participation in the coronation of Young King Henry in 1170, but was reinstated soon after Becket's murder. The monks of Christ Church invited Bartholomew, along with the bishop of Chester, to perform the reconsecration ceremony for Canterbury Cathedral on December 21, 1171, a strong sign of their good favour (this may have been the occasion when Bartholomew told the Christ Church monks of his vision). **John of Salisbury** spent some time at Exeter after the murder. Bartholomew's importance in the aftermath of the dispute is also shown by the letter Henry II addressed to him regarding his reconciliation with the papal legates in Normandy on May 1172: see *LCHII*, vol. 6, Appendix 1 no. 3015, pp. 54–5. On Bartholomew, see Frank Barlow, 'Bartholomew', *ODNB*; A. Morey, *Bartholomew of Exeter, Bishop and Canonist* (Cambridge, 1937), esp. pp. 15–43 and Rebecca Springer, "Bartholomew of Exeter's Sermons and the Cultivation of Charity in Twelfth-Century Exeter", *Historical Research* 92 (May 2019): 267–87.

Bertha of Hereford [I.6]. The "Bertha of Gloucester" of Benedict's story may be Bertha of Hereford, the daughter of the powerful magnate Miles of Gloucester (d.1143), the first earl of Hereford. Bertha married William de Briouze/Braose (d.1192), who served as sheriff of Herefordshire from 1173–5. See Brock Holden, *Lords of the Central Marches: English Aristocracy and Frontier Society, 1087-1265* (Oxford, 2008), pp. 22–3 and 254. Another possibility is that this Bertha is the same woman Benedict names as **Bertha, the widow of Elias Giffard**, in III.71.

Bertha, widow of Elias Giffard [III.71]. Bertha, the daughter of Richard FitzPons, married Elias Giffard, the lord of Brinsfield in Gloucestershire, at an unknown date. Elias died in 1159 having become a monk of Gloucester. Bertha's death date is unknown, but her will, in which she granted property to the monks of Gloucester, is extant: see *Historia et cartularium monasterii Gloucestraie*, ed. William Henry Hart, RS 33 (London, 1863), vol. 1, p. 188. For a family tree that includes Bertha, see Scott L. Waugh, *The Lordship of England: Royal Wardships and Marriages in English Society and Politics, 1217–1327* (Princeton, 1988), p. 43.

Brian de Insula, provost [II.38]. Brian de Insula, of the Isle of Wight, was the son of Jordan de Insula and the father of Robert de Insula: see John L. Whitehead, "Genealogical and Other Notes Relating to the de Insula, otherwise de l'Isle, de Lisle, or Lisle Family," *Proceedings of the Hampshire Field Club & Archaeological Society* (6:1) 1907, 111–39, at pp. 117–21. The family owed their rise to their relationship to Richard de Redvers, a baron of Henry I (see also IV.53 and **William de Vernon** below). Brian de Insula witnessed four charters of Richard's son, Baldwin de Redvers (d.1155): see Robert Bearman, "Baldwin de Redvers: Some Aspects of a Baronial Career in the Reign of King Stephen," *ANS* 28 (1995): 19–46, at p. 26 and Robert Bearman, ed., *Charters of the Redvers Family and the Earldom of Devon, 1090–1217*, Devon and Cornwall Record Society 37 (Exeter, 1994), p. 38.

Edmund, master and archdeacon of Coventry (d.1179) [IV.4]. Edmund first appears as a witness to a charter dated 1146x47. He became archdeacon of Coventry c.1160, a post from which he retired c.1176, apparently in hopes of his nephew receiving the archdeaconry: see *EEA: Coventry and Lichfield, 1160–1182*, ed. by M. J. Franklin (Oxford, 1998), pp. 27–8. There is a charter witnessed by Edmund that includes a witness named "Sasfredo," quite possibly Saffrid, the dean of Chesterton, who wrote the letter Benedict copied into his collection: see ibid, p. 74. Edmund founded the hospital of St. John the Baptist in Coventry between 1160 and 1176: see Sethina Watson, "City as Charter: Charity and the Lordship of English Towns, 1170–1250," in Caroline Goodson, Anne Elisabeth Lester, and Carol Symes (eds.), *Cities, Texts and Social Networks, 400–1500: Experiences and Perceptions of Medieval Urban Space* (Ashgate, 2010), 235–62, p. 250 n. 52.

Eleanor of Aquitaine (d.1204) [IV.75 and William no. 11]. One of the most famous queens of the Middle Ages, Eleanor of Aquitaine married King of France Louis VII in 1137. After this marriage was annulled in 1152, she married Henry, soon to be King of England Henry II. Eleanor supported her son the Young King Henry in a major rebellion against Henry II in 1173, after which she was imprisoned until Henry died in 1189. During the reigns of her sons Richard I and John, Eleanor played a major role in the governance of the Angevin realms. For a convenient brief account of Eleanor's life, see Jane Martindale, "Eleanor [Eleanor of Aquitaine], *suo jure* duchess of Aquitaine," *ODNB*.

Elias of Froyle, knight and reeve [IV.12]. Elias is found under Hampshire in the Pipe Rolls for 1167–8: *PR 14 Henry II*, p. 175. For the Froille family and other documentary references to Elias, see *The Herald and Genealogist*, ed. by John Gough Nicholas, F.S.A. (London, 1870), vol. 5, p. 432.

Geoffrey of Wallingford, monk of Reading [IV.86 and William no. 12]. The letter copied in full by William notes that Geoffrey was from Wallingford and was a cantor. He is very likely the "G. cantor" noted in a late twelfth-century booklist from Reading: *English Benedictine Libraries: The Shorter Catalogues*, ed. Richard Sharpe, Corpus of British Medieval Library Catalogues 4 (London, 1996), B71 no. 14, p. 422.

Gilbert Foliot, bishop of London (d.1187) [III.45]. A Cluniac monk who became abbot of Gloucester (1139–48), bishop of Hereford (1148–63), and finally bishop of London (1163–87), Foliot was a learned man known for his sermons and biblical commentaries. A lengthy surviving collection of his letters and charters shows him to have been an active and conscientious diocesan administrator. Gilbert was Becket's most vocal and powerful opponent within the English church. Becket twice excommunicated him, the second time for his participation in the coronation of the Young King Henry in 1170. He was not reinstated as bishop of London until May 1172. See *LCGF* and C. N. L. Brooke, "Foliot, Gilbert (c.1110–87), Benedictine monk and bishop of London," *ODNB*.

Gilbert Foliot, steward of Gilbert Foliot, bishop of London [III.45]. Two kinsmen of Bishop Gilbert Foliot who were also named Gilbert Foliot are known from contemporary records. One was a canon of St. Paul's and later the archdeacon of Middlesex. The other, who seems more likely to be the steward referred to in Benedict's story, was the bishop's nephew and held land in Normandy. On Gilbert's family, see Dom Adrian Morey and C. N. L. Brooke, *Gilbert Foliot and His Letters* (Cambridge, 1965), pp. 32–49, esp. p. 41 n. 2 and p. 43.

Godefrid, baker of Christ Church, Canterbury [II.2–3]. Godefrid is recorded as holding two acres of land just outside of Canterbury's Worthgate (see Urry, *CUAK*, Rental A no. 19, p. 223). He took part in a major dispute between the archbishop and the Christ Church monks in the late 1180s, when Godefrid, along with a number of other servants, took the archbishop's side. Prior Honorius (1186–9) viewed Godefrid as the traitorous servants' ringleader and described him as a "man of Belial": see Urry, *CUAK*, pp. 162–3 and *EC*, no. 219, pp. 201–2.

Godfrey, bishop of St. Asaph and titular abbot of Abingdon [IV.75 and William no. 11]. Godfrey, a monk of Coventry, was appointed bishop of St. Asaph in 1160. In 1165, he fled from Wales due to the victories of Owen Gwynnedd. He settled at Abingdon, where he was the titular abbot between 1165 and 1175. In the late 1160s, Thomas Becket sent Godfrey a stern letter rebuking him for acting as a bishop outside of his see, and in 1170, he ordered him to resign or return to his see (*CTB*, vol. 1, no. 155, pp. 724–7 and vol. 2, no. 226, pp. 978–9). Godfrey participated in the coronation of the Young King Henry. In September 1170, the pope gave Becket permission to penalize Godfrey, along with David the archdeacon of St. Asaph, for their actions: see *CTB*, vol. 2, no. 307, at pp. 1294–5. Godfrey was forced to resign the bishopric at the Council of Westminster in 1175 and lost the abbacy of Abingdon in that same year. His death date is unknown. On Godfrey, see *Fasti Ecclesiae Anglicanae 1066–1300: IX The Welsh Cathedrals*, ed. by M. J. Pearson (London, 2003), p. 33.

Godfrey, son of Adam of Lillingston, knight [III.30]. Godfrey of "Lullingestan," very likely the same Godfrey discussed by Benedict, is found in the Oxfordshire section of the 1174–5 Pipe Roll (*PR 21 Henry II*, p. 13). Lillingstone Lovell was part of Oxfordshire in the medieval period.

Hamelin de Warenne, earl of Surrey (d.1202) [IV.64 and William no. 7]. The illegitimate son of Geoffrey of Anjou, Hamelin was the half-brother of King Henry II. When Hamelin married the heiress Isabelle de Warenne in 1164, he became one most powerful magnates in England. Hamelin denounced Becket at the Council of Northampton in 1164. After Becket's death, Hamelin would claim that his eye had been healed by the saint: his story is found in William of Canterbury, *Miracula*, VI.45, p. 452. Given the placement of this story towards the end of William's collection, Hamelin's miracle must have occurred after that of the family of Jordan son of Eisulf. In the late 1180s, the Christ Church monks would write to Hamelin requesting help in their dispute with archbishop Baldwin: see *EC*, pp. 85, 264–5, 268, and Barnaby, *Religious Conflict at Canterbury Cathedral*, p. 115. On Hamelin, see Thomas K. Keefe, "Warenne, Hamelin de, earl of Surrey," *ODNB*.

Henry of Houghton, master and clerk of Thomas Becket [III.63–4]. This is likely the Master Henry who was formerly of the royal chapel: see *CTB*, vol. 2, Appendix I, pp. 1374–5, and Barlow, *Thomas Becket*, pp. 131–2. In 1163, Becket sent Master Henry as his envoy to the papal curia, referring to him as "a loyal servant to both you and us": see *CTB*, vol. 1, nos. 12–16, pp. 30–41. Master Henry was said to be frustrated by Becket's stubbornness at Montmirail in 1169: see FitzStephen, *Vita*, pp. 96–7.

Henry de Longavilla, knight [III.36–7]. A knight named "Henricus de Longavill," is found in the 1166 carta of Nigel de Louvetot, a baron of Huntingdonshire (*CB* no. CXCVI (11) p. 207). For this Henry and the manor of Orton Longueville (located less than three miles from Peterborough), see "Parishes: Orton Longueville with Botolphbridge," in *A History of the County of Huntingdon: Volume 3*, ed. William Page, Granville Proby and S. Inskip Ladds (London, 1936), pp. 190–8. See also IV.3 for the miracle concerning the leprous Ralph of Longueville, possibly a member of the same family.

Hugh de Beauchamp, baron of Eaton Soton, Bedfordshire [II.61]. Hugh's parentage is obscure and not all of the details of his life are clear. He may have been a natural son of Simon de Beauchamp (d. c.1137). By the mid-1150s, he was in possession of the barony of Eaton Soton. Though there is no return for this barony in the *Cartae Baronum*, Hugh is found a number of its entries (see *CB* no. CXLV (20), p. 150; no. CXCV (2) p. 205; and no. CXCVII (1) p. 209) as well as in the Pipe Rolls: see the entries in *DD*, p. 311. A later Hugh de Beauchamp founded the Augustinian priory at Bushmead c.1195: for the foundation charter, which lists a Nicholas de Beauchamp (the son of the story?) as a witness, see *The Cartulary of Bushmead Priory*, ed. G. Herbert Fowler and Joyce Godber (Streatley, 1945), no. 17, pp. 28–30. On the Eaton branch of the Beauchamp family, see G. Herbert Fowler, "The Beauchamps, Barons of Eaton," in *Proceedings of the Bedfordshire Historical Record Society* 2 (1914): 61–91, esp. pp. 68–71. A Hugh de Beauchamp went on the Third Crusade and died at the Battle of Hattin in 1187, as is known both from Roger of Howden's *Gesta Regis* and a grant from Hugh's wife Phillipa to the Benedictine priory of St. Neot's: see BL Cotton MS. Faustina A iv, fol. 83, and "Parishes: Eaton Socon," in *A History of the County of Bedford: Volume 3*, ed. William Page (London, 1912), pp. 189–202.

Hugh de Bodebi, knight [IV.82]. In the Lincolnshire section of the *Cartae Baronum*, the carta of Maurice de Craon lists "Hugo de Boebi," very likely the same knight in Benedict's story. See *CB* no. CCVI (8), p. 220. Boebi/Bodebi may refer to Boothby Pagnell in Lincolnshire.

Hugh de Morville (d. c.1173/74) [*Passion*, William no. 6]. The most socially elevated of Thomas Becket's four murderers, Morville knew Becket when he was Henry II's chancellor. The murderers went to Morville's castle at Knaresborough after Becket's death. Later, c.1173, Morville went on pilgrimage to Jerusalem in penance for Becket's murder. He died on pilgrimage and never returned to England. On Morville, see Vincent, *Murderers*, esp. pp. 223–9 and 262–3, and R. M. Franklin, "Morville, Hugh de," *ODNB*.

Hugh de Puiset, bishop of Durham (d.1195) [IV.2]. The nephew of King Stephen, Hugh de Puiset became bishop of Durham shortly before Stephen's death and the accession of Henry II in 1154. He was a powerful secular magnate as well as bishop: see his return in *CB* no. CCXXXIV, pp. 250–2. Hugh kept the Becket dispute largely at arm's length, but in 1170 he was one of the bishops present at the coronation of the Young King Henry. He was suspended from office, a suspension lifted around Easter 1171. In late 1174 or early 1175, about three years after his encounter with the blinded and castrated Eilward of Westoning, Hugh sent a letter to the Christ Church monks describing the miracle of a blinded and castrated thief in Durham:

see William of Canterbury, *Miracula*, V.10, pp. 419–22. On Hugh, see G. W. S. Barrow, "Puiset, Hugh du, earl of Northumberland," *ODNB*, and for a full-length study, G. V. Scammell, *Hugh du Puiset: Bishop of Durham* (Cambridge, 1956).

Jocelin de Bohun, bishop of Salisbury (d.1184) [IV.75]. Bishop of Salisbury from 1142 to his death in 1184, Jocelin de Bohun initially sided with Becket. After Becket suspended him from office in 1166, Jocelin became closely allied with Becket's vociferous opponent, **Gilbert Foliot, bishop of London**. Jocelin, along with Gilbert and **Roger de Pont L'Évêque, Archbishop of York**, were excommunicated in late 1170 due to their participation in the coronation of the Young King Henry in June 1170. The news of these excommunications enraged Henry II, starting the train of events that led to Becket's death. Jocelin was reinstated in March 1172. See B. R. Kemp, "Bohun, Jocelin de," in *ODNB*.

John son of Vivian, borough reeve (d. by 1189) [III.29]. An important figure in Canterbury, John son of Vivian is known from entries in the Pipe Rolls, rentals, and a grant of wardship. His father, Vivian of Wigt, went to Jerusalem, possibly as part of the Second Crusade. John's son seems to have predeceased him, but he had three daughters who often appear in contemporary rentals and charters. On John, see Urry, *CUAK*, pp. 64 and 84–5.

John of Kinstan, abbot of Jervaulx (d. after 1190) [III.60-2]. John of Kinstan, a monk at Byland Abbey, was led to the foundation of Jervaulx (of which he would be the first abbot) by means of a vision of the Virgin Mary and Christ: see *The Foundation History of the Abbeys of Byland and Jervaulx*, ed. and trans. Janet Burton, Borthwick Texts and Studies 35 (York, 2006), pp. 25, 48–60. John was abbot of Jervaulx from 1149/50 to c.1185: see *HRH*, p. 135. Abbot John is pictured in three panels of Canterbury Cathedral window nIII: see Caviness, *Windows*, pp. 191–2.

John of Salisbury, scholar, bishop of Chartres (d.1180) [*Passion*]. One of the most learned men of his day, John of Salisbury wrote works concerning rhetoric, education, political science, and philosophy, and is also known for an extensive and important collection of letters. For an overview of his life and work, see David Luscombe, "Salisbury, John of," *ODNB*. John was a fervent supporter of Thomas Becket and spent much of the period of Becket's exile in France at the abbey of St. Rémi at Reims, headed by **Peter of Celle**. On his relationship with Becket, see Bollerman and Nederman, "John of Salisbury and Thomas Becket," and on his relationship with Canterbury, Michael Staunton, "John of Salisbury and the Church of Canterbury," in Christophe Grellard and Frédérique Lachaud (eds.), *Jean de Salisbury, nouvelles lectures, nouveaux enjeux* (Florence, 2018), pp. 185–207. John wrote a short and widely circulated *Life of Becket*: for an English translation, see Pepin, ed. and trans., *Anselm and Becket*, pp. 73–95. He was bishop of Chartres from 1176 to his death in 1180. For a Becket miracle at Chartres, see John's account in a letter he sent to Canterbury sometime between 1177 and 1179: *LJS* no. 325, pp. 804–5.

Jordan son of Eisulf, knight (d. c.1195) [IV.64 and William no. 7]. Jordan first appears in the documentary record c.1155; his last appearance is in 1194–5, after which he was succeeded by his son Richard. Jordan's father, Eisulf (also spelled Assulf, Assolf, Asolf, Essolf, Edulf, Esolf, and Aissulf in contemporary documents) was a major landowner in the West Riding of Yorkshire. While Jordan was not the eldest of Eisulf's sons, he was nevertheless a major actor in the region and started a family line later known as the Thornhills. Jordan was the constable of Wakefield for **Hamelin de Warenne**, earl of Surrey. He is named as such in a charter issued by Hamelin to the benefit of the priory of St. Mary Magdalen in Lincolnshire, a cell of St. Mary's Abbey, York: see *Monasticon*, vol. 3, p. 618b, num. V. A steward named William Brito witnessed a grant made by the earl of Albemarle to the priory of Pontefract c.1190–5. This could well be the boy of the miracle story: see C. T. Clay, "The Family of Thornhill," *Yorkshire Archaeological Journal* 29 (1929): 286–321, esp. 287–91. See also William Paley Baildon, *Baildon and the Baildons: A history of a Yorkshire manor and family* (privately printed London, 1912), vol. 2, pp. 26–33; and Hugh M. Thomas, *Vassals, Heiresses, Crusaders, and Thugs: The Gentry of Angevin Yorkshire, 1154–1216* (Philadelphia, 2003), pp. 106–11, 202–3. Jordan, his wife, and his sons are pictured in Canterbury Cathedral Trinity Chapel window nII: see Caviness, *Windows*, pp. 197–9.

Matilda de Percy, the countess of Warwick (d.1204) [IV.94]. The wife of the earl of Warwick (William de Beaumount (d.1184)), Matilda de Percy was closely related to the de Clare family. Her mother, Adelisa de Clare (d. by 1166, m. William II de Percy), was **Roger de Clare**'s sister, making Roger her uncle and his little son James her first cousin. Matilda de Percy was a generous benefactor of religious houses in Yorkshire and was buried at Fountains. See Susan M. Johns, "Percy, Matilda de, countess of Warwick," *ODNB*.

Matilda de St. Hilary, countess of Hertford and countess of Arundel (d.1193) [IV.94 and William no. 14]. The daughter and heir of James of St. Hilary, a baron of Norfolk, Matilda's first marriage was to **Roger de Clare** (d.1173). The honour Matilda brought to the marriage with Roger is listed separately in the *Cartae Baronum* returns: see *CB* no. CCXIII (68–85), p. 241. The couple had two daughters (Aveline and Mabel) and four sons. Richard de Clare (d.1217) was Roger's heir; the couple's other three known sons, John, another Richard, and James, all seem to have died unmarried. James is named as a witness in a charter issued by his mother granting a mill to St. Andrew's priory, Northampton, dated 1173–6: see F. M. Stenton, ed., *Facsimiles of Early Charters from Northamptonshire Collections* (London, 1930), pp. 130–1. Matilda's chaplain Lambert, named in Benedict's account of the miracle, is the first witness of this charter. A surviving impression of Matilda's seal shows Matilda being handed a hawk by an attendant: see Susan M. Johns, *Noblewomen, Aristocracy and Power in the Twelfth-Century Anglo-Norman Realm* (Manchester, 2003), 209–11. For an English translation of the grant made by Matilda de St. Hilary to the alien Benedictine priory of Stoke-on-Clare when she was married to Roger, see Jennifer C. Ward, *Women of the English Nobility and Gentry, 1066–1500* (Manchester, 1995), no. 73, pp. 93–4. Matilda's second marriage was to William IV de Aubigny, earl of Arundel and Sussex (d.1184), whom she married sometime before Michaelmas 1176. The couple had two sons, including William's heir, William (d. before 1221), and a daughter. Matilda's honour passed to William de Aubigny during his lifetime but became hers again after his death. It was escheated to the Crown after her death in 1193 and was acquired by her son Richard de Clare. Matilda, her son James, and one of James' older brothers are pictured in Canterbury Cathedral Trinity Chapel window sVII.

Nicholas son of Aileva [IV.11]. Nicholas son of Aileva (spelled Ailwena), is listed as a witness to the foundation charter to the Augustinian priory of St. Thomas the Martyr, which was located two miles east of Stafford. A "Henry, priest" and "William Speri Osberto, priest," also appear in the witness list, and may well be the same priests who were called as witnesses to the miracle described in the letter of **Albinus, abbot of Darley**. For the foundation charter, see Parker, "'Chartulary' of the Priory of St. Thomas (A'Becket)," pp. 130–2.

Odo, prior of Christ Church, Canterbury (d.1200) [IV.11, IV.65, IV.84, IV.85, William no. 12]. A learned and respected monk of Christ Church, Odo was elected prior in 1168 against Becket's wishes. Becket wanted him deposed, but Odo remained in his position and had the firm support of his monks. They would eventually propose him as a candidate to replace Becket as archbishop, a petition that failed. Odo was elected abbot of Battle in 1175. Though he did not want the position, he was eventually convinced to leave Canterbury for Battle. Benedict (author of the *Passion and Miracles*) was elected by the monks to take his place. See R. M. Thomson, "Odo of Canterbury, theologian and abbot of Battle (d.1200)," *ODNB*.

Peter of Celle, abbot of St. Rémi and bishop of Chartres (d.1183) [IV.87]. A Benedictine monk who became abbot of Montier-la-Celle near Troyes (c.1145–61), abbot of St. Rémi at Reims (1161–81) and bishop of Chartres (1181–3), Peter of Celle was a close friend of **John of Salisbury** and an ardent supporter of Thomas Becket.

He cultivated friendships with many of the leading figures of his day, including popes, bishops, and monks of differing orders. He was a prolific author, composing many sermons, treatises, and letters: see the introduction to *The Letters of Peter of Celle*.

Peter de Arches, knight [IV.67]. Probably the son of Peter de Arches (or de Arcis), Peter de Arches is stated to be "of Kettlewell" (in Yorkshire) and appears in a number of twelfth-century charters: see *EYC* vol. 11, p. 152 and nos. 133 and 136, and also *DD*, p. 288.

Peter de Melida, master and clerk of Lincoln (d. before 1181) [II.55]. A legal expert and donor of manuscripts to Lincoln Cathedral, Master Peter de Melida first appears in documents in the 1150s: see *Fasti Ecclesiae Anglicanae, 1066–1300: III. Lincoln*, compiled by Diana Greenway (London, 1977), pp. 133–4. He may have been from Meleti near Milan (see ibid, p. 133 n. 4). For surviving manuscripts donated by Peter de Melida, see R. M. Thomson, *Catalogue of the Manuscripts of Lincoln Cathedral Library* (Cambridge, 1989), pp. xv, 57, 138, 142, and 150.

Ranulf de Broc, king's official (d. c.1179) [*Passion*, I.14, I.18]. Henry II put Ranulf de Broc in charge of Canterbury's estates after Becket went into exile in 1164. He and his kinsman **Robert de Broc** were despised by the Becket party. Becket excommunicated Ranulf more than once and termed him "the most criminal son of perdition" in the last letter he wrote to the pope: see *CTB*, vol. 2, no. 326, at pp. 1346–7. Ranulf sent Becket's relatives into exile, plundered his estates, seized his wine, and hosted the four knights in Saltwood Castle the night before and the night after the murder. For the wine incident, see William of Canterbury, *Vita*, p. 117, and for an excellent study of the de Brocs, see H. F. Doherty, "The Murder of Gilbert the Forester," *Haskins Society Journal* 23 (2011): 155–204, at pp. 187–96.

Reginald fitz Urse (d.1173x75) [*Passion*]. Though Reginald fitz Urse was not the highest in rank of the four knights who murdered Thomas Becket, he served as their spokesman and leader. He had no sons and was certainly dead by 1175 when his daughter Maud petitioned for his barony of Bulwick in Northamptonshire. It seems likely that he died in the Holy Land on a pilgrimage to expiate the crime of the murder. See Vincent, "Murderers," and R. M. Franklin, "Fitzurse, Reginald (d. 1173x5)," *ODNB*.

Richard, abbot of Sulby [III.42–3]. Richard appears to have been the first abbot of Sulby in Welford, a Premonstratensian monastery in Northamptonshire: see *HRH*, p. 197. Early in William of Canterbury's miracle collection (*Miracula*, I.10, pp. 148–50), there is a letter written by this same Richard concerning a vision of one of the Sulby brothers, and later on, William describes two more miracles that Richard told to the monks (*Miracula*, III.34–5, pp. 291–2). Richard is listed as a witness to two charters edited by F. M. Stenton, *Documents Illustrative of the Social and Economic History of the Danelaw, from Various Collections* (London, 1920), no. 253, p. 189 and no. 277, pp. 209–10. In the second of these charters, dated by Stenton to late in Henry II's reign, **William, abbot of Croxton Kerrial**, is also listed as a witness.

Richard, master and monk of Ely [IV.89]. The Master Richard who spoke to Benedict is probably the same man who is commended by the author of the *Liber Eliensis* as "our brother Richard, a most studious man of letters and someone of the greatest eloquence": see *Liber Eliensis: A History of the Isle of Ely*, trans. Janet Fairweather (Woodbridge, 2005), III.44, p. 346. A Richard, perhaps this same Richard, was the subprior at Ely and became the prior c.1177: see *BR*, p. 434 and *HRH*, p. 46.

Richard de Lucy, royal justiciar (d.1179) [III.64]. One of the most powerful men in England, Richard de Lucy oversaw the kingdom when Henry was overseas and commanded the king's forces during the rebellion of 1173–4. Closely involved in the Becket dispute, de Lucy argued bitterly with Becket and was twice excommunicated by him. Richard de Lucy's possession of a knight's fee in Newington and Sheppey is recorded in the Pipe Rolls and in the *Cartae Baronum* (*CB* no. CLXXIII, pp. 183–4). For a story of Henry II's grant of 5/7s of the manor of Newington to Richard de Lucy, see *William Thorne's Chronicle*, p. 275. De Lucy gave away his holdings in Newington to the Augustinian abbey of Lesnes in Kent, which he founded in 1178 and dedicated to the Virgin and Thomas the Martyr. He was buried at Lesnes in 1179. See Emilie Amt, "Lucy, Richard de (d.1179)," *ODNB*.

Robert, sacrist of Christ Church, Canterbury [II.38, III.25 and IV.84]. As sacrist, Robert was the caretaker of the vestments and sacred vessels of Christ Church. He was clearly a leading figure in the monastery. John of Salisbury addressed two letters to him in early 1170 in which he urged him to support Thomas Becket (see *LJS* no. 299, p. 699, and no. 303, pp. 713–15), and Robert is also mentioned in Gervase's account of Becket's return from exile in 1170 (Gervase vol. 1, pp. 221–2). He was involved in the dispute between the Christ Church monks and Archbishop Baldwin in the late 1180s, at which point he appears to have been an elderly man. See the entry for Robert II in *BR*, pp. 265–6.

Robert de Broc, king's official (d.1194) [*Passion*, I.18, III.17]. Robert de Broc, a younger kinsman of **Ranulf de Broc**, was one of the despised *Brokeis* family who had control of the estates of the archbishopric when Becket was in exile. Like Ranulf, he was excommunicated more than once by Becket, including an excommunication on Christmas Day 1170, just four days before Becket's murder (see William of Canterbury, *Vita*, p. 120 and FitzStephen, *Vita*, p. 130). He was known for cutting off the tail of one of Becket's horses in December 1170, a grave insult: see Andrew M. Miller, "'Tails' of Masculinity: Knights, Clerics, and the Mutilation of Horses in Medieval England," *Speculum* 88:4 (2013): 958–95 and Hugh M. Thomas, "Shame, Masculinity, and the Death of Thomas Becket," *Speculum* 87:4 (October 2012): 1050–88. On the de Broc family, with special attention to Robert de Broc and a mention of the miracle recounted in III.17, see Doherty, "The Murder of Gilbert the Forester," pp. 187–96.

Robert de Broi, prior of Lenton [IV.11]. Lenton Priory, founded in the early twelfth century, was a Cluniac monastery in Nottingham. Robert de Broi became Lenton's prior c.1163 on the recommendation of **Gilbert Foliot**, bishop of London. By or before 1176, Robert had been replaced as prior by a certain Philip. See *HRH*, p. 119, and *LCGF* no. 147, pp. 192–3.

Robert de Sancto Andrea [I.8]. Likely a descendant of Morin de Sancta Andrea, who had holdings in Sussex (see J. H. Round, "The Early History of North and South Stoke," *Sussex Archaeological Collections* 59 (1918): 1–24, at p. 20), Robert de Sancto Andrea is listed as holding land in Catherington, near the Sussex border, in the 1170s: see *PR 23 Henry II*, p. 169.

Robert, son of Gilbert (d.1166) [III.58–9]. Robert son of Gilbert, sometimes further identified as "of Tathwell" or "of Legbourne," founded the priory of Legbourne, later identified as a Cistercian nunnery, c.1150. His co-founders were his wife Matilda and his brother Berengar. See Louise Wilkinson, *Women in Thirteenth-Century Lincolnshire* (Woodbridge, 2013), pp. 86–7. Robert and his wife Matilda had numerous children: see the genealogy in ibid., p. 72. Though none of these children is known to have been named Constance, it seems highly likely that this is the Stixwould nun's family. William, the couple's eldest son, was married to a Matilda, the daughter of Robert of Ropsley. This is very likely the daughter-in-law named Matilda in III.59 who had the badly swollen uterus.

Robert of Cricklade, prior of St. Frideswide (d.1174x79) [II.51–2]. A theologian and hagiographer, Robert of Cricklade was prior of the Augustinian house of St. Frideswide in Oxford c.1140–74. He wrote a *Life and Miracles of Thomas of Canterbury* which now survives only as extracts in a fourteenth-century Icelandic saga (see *Thómas Saga* and Margaret Orme, "A Reconstruction of Robert of Cricklade's Vita et Miracula S. Thomae Cantuariensis," *AB* 84 (1966): 379–98). It appears that Robert began his *Miracles* with the same letter that Benedict utilized for II.52. On Robert of Cricklade, see Andrew N. J. Dunning, "St Frideswide's Priory as a Centre of Learning in Early Oxford," *Mediaeval Studies* 80 (2018): 253–96, and A. J. Duggan, "Cricklade, Robert of," *ODNB*.

Roger, archdeacon of Shrewsbury (d. c.1182x83) [II.64]. The archdeacon of Shrewsbury oversaw the dioceses of Coventry and Lichfield. Archdeacon Roger appears as a witness to episcopal acta of the bishops Roger de Clinton (1129–48), Walter Durdent (1149–59), and Richard Peche (1161–82): see *Fasti Ecclesiae Anglicanae 1066–1300: XI, Coventry and Lichfield*, complied by Christopher Brooke, Jeffrey Denton and Diana E. Greenaway (London, 2011), p. 35.

Roger de Clare, earl of Hertford (d.1173) [IV.94 and William no. 14]. One of the great magnates of England, Roger de Clare succeeded his brother to become earl of Hertford and lord of Clare in 1153. When Becket attempted to regain Tonbridge Castle in 1163 and demanded that Roger pay homage to him for the possession, Roger refused. William FitzStephen reported that this demand angered Henry II, noting that Roger de Clare was related to almost all of the nobility of England and had a very beautiful sister whom the king had once desired (FitzStephen, *Vita*, p. 43). Roger was present at the Council of Clarendon in 1164. His participation in the dispute during Becket's exile is unknown, but he is recorded as being one of the leaders of Henry II's Inquest of Sheriffs in 1170 and as journeying with the king when Henry II departed for Ireland in 1171. Roger married **Matilda de St. Hilary**, with whom he had four sons and two daughters. His heir was Richard de Clare (d.1217). On Roger de Clare, see *CB* nos. CCXXIII–CCXXIV, pp. 239–42; Richard Mortimer, "de Clare, Roger, second earl of Hertford (*d*.1173)," *ODNB*; R Mortimer, "The Beginnings of the Honour of Clare," *ANS* 3 (1980): 119–41; J. C. Ward, "Royal Service and Reward: The Clare Family and the Crown," *ANS* 9 (1989): 261–78 and J. C. Ward, "Fashions in Monastic Endowment: The Foundations of the Clare Family, 1066–1314," *Journal of Ecclesiastical History* 32:4 (1981): 427–51.

Roger Pont de l'Évêque, archbishop of York (d.1181) [William no. 16]. None of the writers of the Becket *Lives* had anything good to say about Roger, portraying him as worldly and dissolute as well as Becket's enemy. In June 1170, Roger presided over the coronation of Henry the Younger. Becket was outraged and suspended Roger from office. He was not reinstated until December 13, 1171. See Frank Barlow, "Pont de l'Évêque, Roger de," *ODNB*.

Roger, monk of Christ Church, Canterbury [IV.58–9]. There appear to have been at least two monks named Roger at Christ Church in the late twelfth century: see *BR*, pp. 266 and 308. The most likely candidate for the Roger in Benedict's story is the monk who was made abbot of St. Augustine's in Canterbury in 1175 and died in 1213 (see *HRH*, p. 36). A charter dating to 1175–7 retains Roger's seal, on which he termed himself "Roger, chaplain of St. Thomas": see Urry, *CUAK*, charter no. XXVI, pp. 405–6. A late medieval chronicle states that Roger was the custodian of the altar at which Becket was martyred, and that he was chosen as abbot of St. Augustine's in the hope that he could acquire Becket relics for the house: see Davis, *William Thorne's Chronicle*, pp. 100–1.

Rohese de Vere [III.27 and IV.51]. Benedict's "Countess Rohese" seems to be the daughter of Aubrey de Vere and Adeliza de Clare who married Geoffrey de Mandeville, earl of Essex (d.1144), with whom Rohese had three sons. After Geoffrey's death, she married Payne de Beauchamp, a baron of Bedford (d. c.1155). Their son, Simon de Beauchamp (d.1206) followed his father as lord of Bedford. Rohese, along with her second husband, founded Chicksands, a Gilbertine priory in Bedfordshire. On his flight out of England in 1164, Thomas Becket briefly stopped at Chicksands. Rohese may well have been there, as she was known to have retired to the priory after Payne's death. In late 1170, Rohese's son by Geoffrey, William de Mandeville (d.1189), who was then the earl of Essex, was ordered by Henry II to apprehend Becket, but by the time he arrived at Canterbury the archbishop had been killed (see Barlow, *Thomas Becket*, pp. 236–7). On Rohese de Vere, see Kathryn Faulkner, "Beauchamp, de, family (*per. c.*1080–*c.*1265)," *ODNB*. In Faulkner's article, Rohese's death date is provided as 1166, but it seems that she lived longer than this.

Savaric de Vallibus, knight [Addition 2]. The de Vallibus or de Vaux family is well attested in the twelfth century. A Savaric de Vallibus appears in a charter dated to the early thirteenth century in the cartulary of Athelney abbey: see E. H. Bates, ed., *Two Cartularies of the Benedictine Abbeys of Muchelney and Athelney in the County of Somerset* (London, 1899), no. 31, p. 135.

Silvester, treasurer of Lisieux [IV.84]. The nephew of Arnulf, Bishop of Lisieux (1141–81), Silvester owed his position as treasurer of the cathedral's chapter to his uncle. Bishop Arnulf was opposed to Becket during the dispute. Silvester had very different opinions. He went into exile due to Becket, had a prebend at Waltham confiscated, and corresponded with the archbishop: see *CTB*, vol. 1, no. 122, pp. 582–5, and vol. 2, no. 262, pp. 1130–1 n. 15.

Simon de Senlis III, earl of Northampton (d.1184) [IV.29]. When Simon's father, Simon de Senlis II, died in 1153, Henry II gave the earldom of Northampton to the king of Scotland. Simon de Senlis III nevertheless continued to refer to himself as "Earl Simon," just as he appears in Benedict's miracle story. See *CB* no. CCV, pp. 217–20, and David Crouch, *The English Aristocracy 1070–1272: A Social Transformation* (New Haven, 2011), pp. 44 and 263 n. 32. Simon was formally recognized as the earl of Northampton from 1174.

Stephen de Meinil, knight (d. c.1190) [IV.52 and William no. 6]. The family name is also found as Mainel, Meynell, Menil, Menill, Meynhille, Meynil, and Maisnil.

Their family seat was Whorlton in the North Riding of Yorkshire (Goulton, mentioned in Benedict's story, is a hamlet within the parish of Whorlton). On the family, see "Parishes: Whorlton," in *A History of the County of York North Riding: Volume 2*, ed. William Page (London, 1923), pp. 309-19, and *EYC*, vol. 2, pp. 133-47, with genealogy on p. 134 and discussion of Stephen II on p. 137. Stephen is found in the Pipe Rolls as well: see *PR 22 Henry II*, p. 112; *PR 23 Henry II*, p. 78; and *PR 26 Henry II*, p. 67. He died c.1190 and his son Robert succeeded him. The name of Stephen's wife, Joan, is preserved in a charter issued by Stephen granting woods to Rievaulx Abbey: see *EYC*, vol. 2, no. 799, pp. 144-5. Stephen made a grant to Fountains for the making of fisheries: see *Cartularium abbathiæ de Rievalle*, ed. J. C. Atkinson, Surtees Society no. 83 (Durham, 1889), p. 175 n. 3, and John Burton, *Monasticon Eboracense* (York, 1758), p. 164. Joan Wardrop, *Fountains Abbey and Its Benefactors: 1132-1300* (Kalamazoo, 1987), p. 167, notes that in this grant Stephen "expressed the intention of entering Fountains as a monk," the same monastery his son Ingelram had joined. Stephen also made grants to Gisborough, an Augustinian priory: see *EYC*, vol. 2, no. 800, pp. 145-7.

Stephen of Holland (Lincolnshire), knight [I.13]. Stephen appears in the Pipe Rolls as a former tenant of Duke Conan IV of Brittany (d.1171), who had held the Honour of Richmond: see *PR 22 Henry II*, p. 122. Stephen's son Ralph was at Conan's court in Brittany 1160x1168: see *EYC* vol. 4, p. 62.

Thomas of Etton, knight of the region of York [II.44 and William no. 1]. Thomas of Etton was the son of Geoffrey Etton and the father of three sons, Thomas, Geoffrey and Odard: see John Bilson, "Gilling Castle," *Yorkshire Archaeological Journal* 19 (1906): 105-92, at pp. 107-9, and *EYC* vol. 9, pp. 191-4, nos. 105 and 106. Becket was appointed the provost of Beverley c.1154 and retained the post until 1163. Frank Barlow notes that as provost, Becket was likely "an absentee delegating his duties to an unidentified deputy" (Barlow, *Thomas Becket*, p. 38). The way William describes this miracle leaves little doubt that Thomas of Etton was that deputy (Etton is eight kilometers from Beverley). A grant he made 1154-c.1160 lists, as its second witness, a canon of Beverley named Simon (see *EYC* vol. 9, no. 105), indicating his connections to the chapter when Becket was provost. Thomas of Etton is also recorded as making grants to the Cistercian abbey of Meaux: see *Chronica monasterii de Melsa, a fundatione usque ad annum 1396*, ed. Edward A. Bond (London, 1866), vol. 1, pp. 316-19.

Turstan of Croydon, clerk [IV.65 and William no. 8]. William provides more information about Turstan than Benedict, stating that he was a native of Kent and that Archbishop Theobold (Becket's predecessor) had appointed him proctor of Croydon. Though there is little information about Croydon's connections to the archbishops of Canterbury in the twelfth century, in the thirteenth century the archbishops had a residence there and were using it as an administrative centre (see "Croydon: Introduction and Croydon Palace," in *A History of the County of Surrey: Volume 4*, ed. H. E. Malden (London, 1912), pp. 205–17). Turstan of Croydon is found in the returns for Kent in the Pipe Roll for 1174–5 (*PR 21 Henry II*, p. 217). In William FitzStephen's *Life*, Turstan is described as one of Becket's clerks who stayed behind when Becket was exiled. He was incarcerated for a night in a jail in London and paid 100 marks for his immunity (see FitzStephen, *Vita*, p. 78). John of Salisbury addressed a letter to a Turstin of Acolt (Acol, in Kent), in which he makes it clear that this Turstin had served Theobald and Becket and was a friend of the bishop of Poitiers (see *LJS* no. 264, pp. 535–7). This may the same man as Turstan of Croydon.

Walter de Walensis, abbot of Colchester (d.1184) [I.18]. The abbot of St. John's Abbey in Colchester from 1168 to 1184 (see *HRH*, p. 40), Walter appears in a number of charters of **Gilbert Foliot, bishop of London** (all of them dated well after Becket's murder): see *LCGF* no. 358, pp. 406–7; no. 401, pp. 441–2; and no. 464, pp. 491–2.

William, abbot of Croxton Kerrial [IV.49]. Croxton Kerrial was a Praemonstratensian abbey in Leicestershire founded c.1160. William was its second abbot: see *HRH*, p. 194. It was a daughter house of Newhouse in Lincolnshire, the first Praemonstratensian abbey in England. Abbot William must have known **Richard, the abbot of Sulby**, another Praemonstratensian house, as they are both witnesses to a charter regarding the possessions of Newhouse: see Stenton, ed., *Documents illustrative*, no. 277, p. 209.

William Belet, knight of Enborne, Berkshire (d. c.1175) [I.10]. William Belet is recorded as holding land in Enborne in the 1169–70 Pipe Roll: see *PR 16 Henry II*, p. 72 and also *PR 22 Henry II*, p. 132, where he is said to be dead. On William Belet and his family connections, see John Cloake, "Appendix: I: The Belet Family in the Twelfth and Thirteenth Centuries," in *Palaces and Parks of Richmond and Kew: Volume I, The Palaces of Shene and Richmond* (Chichester, 1995), 212–18, at p. 215.

William of Earley, knight (d. by 1185) [II.53–4]. This family took their name from Earley in Berkshire, but their principal residence was in Somerset, with their holdings centered on the manor of Somerton Erleigh. William of Earley succeeded his father, John of Earley, c.1165. He submitted a return for one enfeoffed knight in 1166 (*CB* no. LIV, pp. 55–6), and is found in the Pipe Rolls (*PR 13 Henry II*, p. 103; *PR 23 Henry II*, p. 49; *PR 25 Henry II*, p. 71, 87; *PR 31 Henry II*, p. 25 (at which point he had died)), as well as in a number of charters. William's uncle was Thomas of Earley (Thomas de Erlegh), a clerk of Henry II who was promoted to the archdeanery of Wells c.1169–70. The powerful Reginald FitzJocelin de Bohun, clerk to Henry II and later bishop of Bath 1174–91, spoke of Thomas de Erlegh as a relative, so William of Earley must have had some familial relationship with him as well (see *EEA X: Bath and Wells, 1061–1205*, ed. F. M. R. Ramsey (Oxford, 1995), xlvii–xlviii, pp. 68–73 and 134–6). William founded Buckland Priory in Somerset as a house of Augustinian canons in or after June 1170. He seems to have had some role in the refoundation of Buckland c.1180 as a house of Hospitaller nuns, sometimes known as Minchin Buckland, though the surviving documents regarding this refoundation date to c.1185, at which point he had died. See *EEA X: Bath and Wells, 1061–1205*, pp. 69–70 and *A Cartulary of Buckland Priory in the County of Somerset*, ed. F. W. Weaver (London, 1909), esp. pp. xviii–xix, nos. 1–3, 6, and 11). See also **Aziria of Earley**, William's wife and mother of his son John, their heir.

William de Vernon [IV.53]. The second son of Richard de Redvers (d.1155), William de Vernon married Lucy de Tancarville and inherited the family's possessions in Normandy near Vernon and Néhou. On William de Vernon, see Daniel Power, *The Norman Frontier in the Twelfth and Early Thirteenth Centuries* (Cambridge, 2004), p. 206; and on the castle at Néhou, see Thomas Stapleton, *Historical Memoirs of the House of Vernon* (privately printed in London about 1855), p. 67.

William, son of Ranulf (d. after 1203) [III.40]. On William son of Ranulf, the lord of Whitchurch and member of the Warenne family, see R. W. Eyton, *Antiquities of Shropshire* (London, 1860), vol. X, pp. 16–18, and *EYC* vol. 8, pp. 35–8. William appears in Pipe Roll entries starting in 1176. He made a number of grants to monasteries, including one to the Augustinian canons at Lilleshall, a little over thirty-five kilometers from Whitchurch, and another made before 1186 to Combermere Abbey, a Cistercian monastery eight kilometers from Whitchurch (for the Combermere Abbey grant, see *Monasticon* vol. 5, p. 326 no. 8). He was still alive in 1203.

William, priest of Bourne [I.19–21]. Described as *presbiter de Burnis* and *sacerdos de Burnis*, William is recorded as holding land near St. Margaret's Church in Canterbury: see Urry, *CUAK*, p. 184, Rental A 24, p. 223 and Rental B 223, p. 243. Bourne all but certainly refers to Bishopsbourne, Kent, located eight kilometers from Canterbury.

William, priest of London [I.12]. The story of William, the speechless priest of London, is described by six contemporary writers besides Benedict. See Gervase vol. 1, p. 230; FitzStephen, *Vita*, p. 150; "Quaedam miracula gloriosi martyris Thomae archiepiscopi Cantuariae," *AB* 20 (1901): 427–9, at p. 427; and notices in three anonymous passions edited by Robertson: *MTB*, vol. 4, p. 199; *MTB*, vol. 2, p. 289; and *MTB*, vol. 2, p. 288.

William the Templar, abbot of Reading and archbishop of Bordeaux [IV.72]. A friend and staunch supporter of **Gilbert Foliot, the bishop of London**, William the Templar was abbot of Reading from 1165 to 1173. He was promoted to the archbishopric of Bordeaux by King Henry II in 1173. He remained closely involved in the king's affairs. On William's career, see J. B. Hurry, "William the Templar, Abbot of Reading," *Berkshire, Buckinghamshire and Oxfordshire Archaeological Journal*, xxi–xxii (1916), pp. 108–10; and on his attitudes towards Becket, see Koopmans, "Thomas Becket and the Royal Abbey of Reading."

William Turbe, bishop of Norwich (d.1174) [IV.65 and William no. 8]. A Benedictine monk and prior of Norwich cathedral priory, Turbe became bishop of Norwich from 1146/7 to his death in January 1174. He was an elderly man in the early 1170s. John of Salisbury urged Turbe to support Becket in a letter written c.1168 (*LJS* no. 262, pp. 531–3), and Becket himself addressed one of his last letters to the bishop, noting that he hoped he would be able to see him again "before you depart and fly from this mortal sphere" (*CTB*, vol. 2, no. 328, pp. 1358–9). Turbe promoted the cult of William of Norwich, a boy whose death was (wrongly) blamed on the Jews of Norwich. Thomas of Monmouth's tale of the boy's death and subsequent miracles was dedicated to William Turbe: see *The Life and Passion of William of Norwich*, ed. and trans. Miri Rubin (London, 2014), pp. 3–7. On Turbe's career, see Christopher Harper-Bill, "Bishop William Turbe and the Diocese of Norwich, 1146–1174," *ANS* 7 (1985): 142–60, esp. pp. 153–4, and Christopher Harper-Bill, "William [*called* William Turbe]," *ODNB*.

Appendix:
William of Canterbury, The Parallel Miracles

William of Canterbury began his independent collection of Thomas Becket's miracles in June 1172. Until Benedict brought his collection to a final halt sometime in the second half of 1173, the two collectors were working at the same time and chose some of the same stories to recount in their separate collections. There are eighteen of these "parallel miracles," as they were termed by E. A. Abbot.[1] This is a tiny percentage of the hundreds of stories the two collectors described in their texts, but as stories that both collectors deemed important, they have outsized significance. It is highly unusual to have dual accounts of medieval miracles composed by writers living at the same time and in the same religious community. Most of the parallel miracles are found near the end of Benedict's collection and in the first three books of William's (William completed his collection, which is some 40% longer than Benedict's, c.1177). For ease of reference, I have listed the stories below in the order they are found in Benedict's collection, but it is important to note that the stories in William's collection do not mirror this ordering and are not all found together.[2] Benedict's collection – shorter, finished first, and generally more readable – circulated much more widely and was copied more often than William's.

The two monks' accounts are often strikingly different in tone, emphasis, and content. Where the two collectors differ on matters of fact (as frequently happens), it can be very difficult to decide whose account might have been more reflective of reality. Compared to Benedict, William was more preachy, more keen to point out the morals of miracles for his readers. He had a greater knowledge of medieval medicine than Benedict, enjoyed utilizing unusual words and rhetorical questions, and tended to provide more statistical information about sizes, numbers, distances, and so on. He could also be more overtly political. The murderer Hugh de Morville, Roger the Archbishop of York, King William of Scotland, and the bishop of Glasgow appear in stories which Benedict did not mention their names (see below, nos. 6, 16, and 18). However, William does not mention Hugh de Puiset, the bishop of Durham, in the story of Eilward of Westoning (no. 2), nor Jocelin, bishop of Salisbury, in the story of the leper of Abingdon (no 11).

[1] Abbott, *St Thomas of Canterbury*, vol. 2, pp. 76–273.
[2] For a figure illustrating the placement of these stories in the two collections, see Koopmans, *Wonderful to Relate*, p. 150.

The parallel miracles are especially valuable for revealing some of the ways in which Benedict and William utilized letters sent to the Christ Church monks. In a number of cases, they copied in the same letters as supporting evidence (see nos. 2, 8, 16). In the case of Cecilia of Plumstock's miracle (no. 8), the two accounts are frequently (though by no means entirely) the same word-for-word. Either William was copying off of Benedict's account, or, most likely, both were lifting passages from the same letter. The similarities one sees between the accounts of the miracles of Jordan son of Eisulf and of Hugh Scot (nos. 7 and 9) are also very likely the result of both collectors cribbing from the same letters. For the miracle of the leprous monk Elias of Reading (no. 10), Benedict appears to have composed his own story, while William simply copied in an account from a letter – a letter that probably came to Canterbury after Benedict had already written his account. In another case, William copied in a letter that Benedict silently plagiarized (no. 12). Where the wording of the two writers is the same, I have aimed to keep the wording of my translations the same as well.

1. THE MIRACLE OF THOMAS OF ETTON (BENEDICT II.44, SEE P. 142 ABOVE).

WILLIAM OF CANTERBURY I.13, P. 153, Concerning the knight who was struck with quinsy because he blasphemed the martyr Thomas

In the territory of York, the knight Thomas of Etton had administered the provostship of Beverley under the authority of the martyr while he, on his own account, also fulfilled the office of secretary.[3] When he had been told by the people about the miracles that the Lord made manifest in the martyr to the glory of those striving for the rights of the church, with the ease of a courtier he burst into blasphemy, *setting his mouth against heaven* [Ps 72:9]. He accused the martyr with the reproach of being lustful and a scoundrel, in this way thinking him to be now what he remembered to have seen many days ago, if he ever had been like that – or more likely, measuring another man's conscience by his own. And so, he was struck without delay by quinsy, and the passage of life-giving air became so constricted that every moment he thought he was going to be suffocated. Feeling the punishment of divine severity arriving within himself, he remembered what he had said, how he had not known respect, and not felt shame among the saints. And so he beat

---

[3] See Biographical Notes, Thomas of Etton.

his breast, confessed his fault with heavy sighs, and sought forgiveness. The martyr's mercy cannot – it cannot – reproach the repentant, nor spurn the truly contrite. For with the same speed it had struck the slanderer, it healed the repentant. Having spoken a curse, his breath was constricted. Having spoken in the holy spirit, the blockage in his throat was removed and freely flowing breath returned.

2. THE MIRACLE OF EILWARD OF WESTONING (BENEDICT IV.1, SEE ABOVE PP. 221–9).

WILLIAM OF CANTERBURY, II.2, PP. 155–6, Confirmation of the following miracle

"Therefore greetings from the burgesses of Bedford to the convent of Canterbury and all the faithful in Christ.

Let it be known[4] to the whole convent of Canterbury and all catholic people that God has worked a marvelous and remarkable miracle in Bedford through the merits of Saint Thomas the martyr. It happened that a certain rustic of Westoning by the name of Ailward was captured, for a theft worth only a single penny, and led before the sheriff of Bedford and the knights of the county. By them, he was publicly condemned, and outside the village of Bedford, with clerics, laity, and women present, he lost his eyes and testicles. John, the chaplain of St. John of Bedford, to whom the aforesaid rustic confessed, testifies to this. His host, by name of Ailbrict, with whom he was afterwards given hospitality, also testifies that he was wholly lacking eyes and testicles when he was first given hospitality by him, and afterwards, often invoking the merits of saint Thomas the martyr, through a glorious and wonderful vision of the same martyr, he was restored to health."

WILLIAM OF CANTERBURY II.3, PP. 156–8, Concerning him whose eyes were gouged out and genitals cut off

We think it is not aside from the point to elucidate the course of events to confirm posterity in the faith. So, a neighbor owed this Ailward a penny. When he asked for it back, and the other refused to pay it, he was seized by anger and broke into the house of the debtor, which he had fortified by a bar

---

[4] William's text reads *sicut: sciant* has been supplied from Benedict's copy of the letter.

hung on the outside when he had gone to the tavern. He ripped off the bar as a surety, and taking at the same time a whetstone placed against the roof of the cottage, as well as a drill and gloves, he left. The father was told by his children, who were at play shut inside the house, that a thief had broken into the house and had left with plundered property. He pursued and caught him, and ripping the whetstone from the hand of the one carrying it, he wounded his head. Taking out a knife, he pierced his arm. He brought him back as a thief caught in the act of thievery, together with the articles he had stolen, and bound him in the house that he had broken into. A crowd gathered, along with the bailiff Fulk. It was suggested by the bailiff that since a man would not be mutilated for the theft of things worth one penny, that the stolen goods be increased by other things as if they were stolen as well. This was done. Next to the bound man was placed a little bundle of skins, a cloak, a linen cloth and a gown, along with an iron tool that is commonly called a hatchet.[5] The next day, he was brought with that bundle also hanging on his neck to the cognizance of a certain Richard, the sheriff,[6] and the knights of the county. Yet lest sentencing in a doubtful matter be too hasty, he was held in public custody in Bedford with judgement suspended for a month. In the meantime, he confessed all his sins since childhood to the priest Paganus, who had been secretly called in. He was advised by him to humbly beg for the assistance of the blessed Mary and all the saints and especially the blessed Thomas, whom the Lord had thought fit to glorify with proofs of miracles and signs, to exclude all anger and incitement to hatred from his soul, to not despair of the mercy of God and, whatever he would suffer, to bear it with equanimity for the remission of his sins. He was to do this with all the more care because he could not be drowned in water nor burned by fire if he was forced to undergo either trial, because, as the common folk believe, he had as a little child been baptized on Whitsun eve.[7] He gave him a rod to receive discipline five times a day in order to summon the mercy of God for himself. He gladly listened to this advice, and having encircled his body with a thread, he devoted himself to the martyr, promising to improve his ways. Also, fearing that he would be deprived of his clothing, he branded the sign of the cross on his right shoulder with a hot iron. As it happened that there was a meeting of judges at Leighton

---

[5] William uses the highly unusual word *volgonium* for this iron tool: see the entry for *volgonium* in *DMLBS*.

[6] The sheriff of Bedfordshire and Buckinghamshire from 1170 to 1178 was actually named William son of Richard.

[7] Whitsun is another name for Pentecost Sunday, which is celebrated seven weeks after Easter. I have not found another reference to a folk belief about protection given to infants baptized on Whitsun eve.

Buzzard, he was brought there as an accused man. There he asked that he enter single combat with Fulk his accuser, or undergo the ordeal of fire, but due to the influence of the bailiff Fulk, who had received an ox for this purpose, he was condemned to the ordeal of water, which he was not able to escape by any means.[8] From there he was taken back to Bedford, where he was imprisoned for a month. With the judges convened, he was handed over to undergo the test of the ordeal of water, and he received the sorrowful sentence of his condemnation. He was led out to the place of punishment and was mutilated by having his eyes put out and his sexual organs cut off, which a multitude of people saw buried in the earth. In the midst of these punishments, he did not stop asking for divine help and invoking the blessed Thomas, forgiving the torturers everything they cruelly did to him. The punishment completed, he was brought to the town and given hospitality by a certain Ailbricht. After ten days had passed, one evening, before the first part of the night, he saw in his sleep the blessed Thomas, whom he had called on constantly, and who was dressed in white clothes. He marked the sign of the cross between his eyebrows with his pastoral staff and did the same again before dawn, saying, "Good man, are you asleep? Wake. Tomorrow you are to keep vigil at the altar of the blessed Mary with a lamp. Behold, Thomas comes to you, and you will receive your sight." After the sun had risen, a female servant said, "I saw in my sleep, Ailward, that you had regained your sight." He answered, "This is possible for the Lord, just as all things are possible." As the day waned, his left eye itched, and scratching with his fingernail, he removed the wax and the poultice that had been placed there to draw out the putrid matter. And catching sight of a ray of sunshine on the wall, he exclaimed, "God be worshipped! I see." To this, the stunned host said, "What is this? You are raving." He also waved his hand in front of his eyes, saying, "Do you see what I am doing?" He answered, "I see a hand moving." And so the dean of the village was called, a crowd gathered, and he was taken away and led into the oratory. Very small eyes were growing, the right wholly black, and the left grey, although since infancy they were both grey. His genitals, which he allowed anyone who wished to touch, could be estimated to be smaller than those of a cock. We saw and heard these things of which we speak and testify. For he of whom we speak was sent to Canterbury and spent many days with us, receiving sustenance from the assets of the martyr.

---

[8] Since Eilward supposedly could not drown due to his baptism on Whitsun eve, it was impossible for him to be successful in an ordeal of water. To be judged innocent in such an ordeal, the accused would have to sink under the water and not come up again. On the ordeal, see Robert Bartlett, *Trial by Fire and Water: The Medieval Judicial Ordeal* (Oxford, 1986).

3. THE MIRACLE OF A SHIP RETURNED BY THE MARTYR (BENEDICT IV.42, SEE ABOVE P. 256).

WILLIAM OF CANTERBURY III.45, PP. 301–2, Concerning a ship that the martyr propelled from the shallows

Certain sailors from Ireland came upon a sandbank that seamen call Colresand,[9] and the ship was stuck fast in the shallows, its sail slack. What was to be done? Its cargo weighed it down, for it was returning to its usual port loaded with hides and other items to be sold, and wealth was its injury. What was to be done?

Driven against the earth, where land, broken by the sea,
wrecks the ship, exposed to a double danger,
half the vessel is aground, while half floats on the waves.[10]

The unfortunate sailors, seeing the irrevocable threat to their ship (for as the tide went out the area of sand increased, and the ship was more and more run aground), leapt into the skiff, saving their souls and abandoning the ship and its goods, entrusting them to the care of the martyr Thomas. And when they had fled a long distance from the ship, the ship – as has never before been heard – followed the ones who were fleeing, and without human direction was brought up close. Yet their eyes were hindered for a time, and they did not realize that the coming ship was the one that they had left stuck in the shallows. They saw the sail hung up and those things that they had left, but they still did not perceive that it was theirs, for they had no expectation that what had been taken away was now being brought to them. And so they hailed the ship and asked who was in it, from where and to where it was heading, and there was no-one to reply. But the guardian to whom they had entrusted the ship opened their eyes, by whose power it was released from the Syrtes,[11] by whose direction it was borne after its own helmsman. And so, recognizing their ship, they boarded it, and made a safe voyage returning to the town of Bristol, which is where they had set out.

---

[9] This may mean "colorful sand." I have not been able to identify this location.
[10] Lucan, *Pharsalia* IX, ll. 335–9, slightly altered.
[11] The Syrtes are the sandbanks and shallows off the north African coast near Libya. The passage in Lucan's *Pharsalia* cited by William is about the dangers of the Syrtes.

4. THE MIRACLE OF THE MARTYR PUSHING A SHIP OFF A SANDBANK (BENEDICT IV.43, SEE ABOVE PP. 256–7).

WILLIAM OF CANTERBURY III.46, PP. 302–3, Concerning a ship in danger on a sandbank

Seized by the love of gain and the desire to catch herring, other sailors had ventured into the deep. Coaxed by calm weather, they were drawn on to their fate, and would have been dragged into death, if he who does not desire the death of sinners had not saved their vanishing life. As they were hooking the fish, the unwise sailors were hooked, and as they coveted their prey, led on by greed, they sank in the shallows and were immersed nearly to the deck. Sea and earth were so mixed that it was not possible to distinguish the nature of the elements, and, as the poet describes,

The land did not sink down deep, so as to admit the water of the ocean,
nor yet defend itself against the sea,
but the region lies untraveled, owing to the uncertain conditions that prevail there –
sea broken by shoals, and dry land severed by sea –
and the waves strike beach after beach before they collapse with a roar.[12]

And so the ship stood, only the stern protruding. With the rising sea, the prow was about to descend under the waves. The wretched mariners made diverse vows for their diverse souls, and at the end called to mind the new martyr, the man of God, who pitied the afflicted men and found it worthy to show himself in visible form. Walking upon the waters,[13] he seized the front of the prow and drove the ship back into the waves. After a successful voyage, the vessel brought its sailors into port.

---

[12] Lucan, *Pharsalia* IX, ll. 305–9.
[13] See Matthew 14:22–33, Mark 6:45–56, and John 6:16–24 for the story of Christ walking on water and saving his disciples' ship.

5. THE MIRACLE OF ANCHORS AND A MAN FROM DOVER (BENEDICT IV.45, SEE ABOVE P. 258).

WILLIAM OF CANTERBURY III.44, PP. 300-1, Concerning a lost anchor

Sailing on the sea, a certain Girard of Dover let down an anchor from his ship as a storm was rising. When he wished it to be pulled back up, two of the sailors, as is customary, stood in the prow to pull on the rope. They were not able to pull out the hook, and even though they all pooled their effort, everything they tried failed. As a last resort, they wrapped the top of the cable onto a beam that sailors call a windlass, so that with the help of the beam their attempt would be more effective. This is a beam placed across the stern and pierced through its side, which is used in larger ships for raising the sail. Spokes are inserted in the holes, and what is not possible with human power alone is possible by leaning on the spokes, for as the cable is wrapped around the revolving beam, help is readily given by the beam. And yet the tenacious anchor still did not feel the hands of the panting sailors. And so, destitute of all human support, they sought divine support, saying, "True martyr Thomas, with power over the sea and the land, return what our weakness cannot. Release the mooring cable, preserve the ship without damage. We know that you do not have need of our good works, but you wish reverence to be exhibited to you; you wish mortal devotion to be enhanced by vows and prayers. And thus we promise that your memorial will be visited and the form of the iron tackle will be made in wax. Return the instrument by which we are held back." With the vow made, they set to and recovered the anchor with little effort.

And yet, going on again, they threw out two anchors in different locations along with the one they had recovered, and they tossed about, held there by the deep. After a short time, they again stood in the prow to recall the anchor which they had recovered by divine gift. And behold, finding the cable to be broken, they began to call out, "Martyr Thomas, why have we lost what you returned to us? Return what you returned, and we will return what we promised." And so they lost all hope of recovery, but by the care of the martyr, what they had lost was recovered beyond all hope. For when they drew in the other anchors, they also received the one about which they had been concerned. For a fragment of the cable of the lost anchor had adhered to the cables of the others, tied up in a divine knot, such that the ship was preserved unharmed, and the martyr's power was shown in the waves.

6. THE MIRACLE OF INGELRAM, SON OF THE KNIGHT STEPHEN (BENEDICT IV.52, SEE ABOVE PP. 261–3).

WILLIAM OF CANTERBURY II.37, PP. 195–8, Concerning a cleric whose arm, struck by paralysis, became inert

A certain Stephen of the village of Whorlton[14] had made a feast for a certain rich man. While that rich man, named Robert, was dining with him, Hugh de Morville[15] sent to [Robert], saying these things: "I marvel at our mutual affection and our former fellowship, which has so easily cooled that you have not seen my face in a long time. Therefore I order that you show yourself and speak to me," and he established a place and set a time. Hearing this order, his face fell, and he neither ate nor drank, recalling in his soul the savage and appalling sin that [Hugh] had committed, and rejecting, as befits a Christian, the detestable fellowship, which, even by speaking, incurs the stain of ecclesiastical excommunication. Why, infamy of our age, do you seek out the fellowship of the white-clothed? Why, citizen of disgraceful Babylon, do you pollute the flock of the Lord? Do you not know that *the entire herd of pigs dies in the field, because of the disease and mange of a single pig*?[16] However, the mother of the family,[17] seeing the sadness of her guest, said to him, "Why is it a concern that that priest Thomas is dead? Who is moved by this? The churchman domineered beyond measure, rushing forth with such great arrogance that he even tried to trample on the necks of princes. He thought he could attack and subjugate the king? Feast, I urge you, and rejoice." In these words and others like them the morally unclean woman raved.

In time, her husband, going about his worldly business in the manner of the worldly, heard many things said about the illumination of the blind, the restoration of hearing to the deaf, the cleansing of lepers, and other wonders the Lord deemed worthy to work through the merits of the blessed martyr. And so, returning home, he recounted what he had heard and what the common people were saying, and he added that he himself wished to visit the tomb of the martyr. The mother and his elder son were seized by the same desire. The

---

[14] See Biographical Notes, Stephen de Meinil.
[15] See Biographical Notes, Hugh de Morville. After the murder, the four knights retreated to Morville's castle in Knaresborough and stayed there for about a year, during which time they faced little or no punishment. Knaresborough is about sixty kilometers from Whorlton. On Morville and Knaresborough, see Vincent, "Murderers," pp. 251–7.
[16] Juvenal, *Satires* 2, ll. 79–80.
[17] Her name was Joan: see Biographical Notes, Stephen de Meinil.

younger son said, "I have no need to go, since I am not mute nor lame, nor hindered by any other bodily trouble." And it happened that when he had given himself up to his schoolboy's studies, he was struck by paralysis and lost the function of one of his arms. After he was detained by this for some weeks, he was brought home, and, taken round the monasteries of the region, he consulted doctors. They pierced his arm with a needle and found it completely without feeling. The woman of whom we spoke who raged against the saint at last repented, realizing that her son was being punished for the fault of his mother. With fasting and beating, she chastised herself for her tongue's raving. And God saw the contrition of the penitent woman, for the blessed Thomas appeared to her suffering son and said, "Be healed. See to it that you change your state of life this year and put on the habit of a monk." With the splendor of the person and the great light of heaven, the house was enlightened such that every corner could be seen clearly. Wakened from sleep by these rays, the student leapt out of bed, and grabbing clothing with the hand that had been paralyzed, he called, "Father, father, I am healed!" Woken, the parents were amazed, as were certain of the king's servants who, at that time, had been received there as guests. Perhaps this mercy had been delivered on account of their presence, from he who wishes all men to be saved and to come to know the truth. Having learned how it happened, they went into the chapel that same hour and gave thanks, which they later performed more fully at the tomb of the martyr with him to whom the mercy had been extended.

When they had returned home from there, the young man, who had been flighty as youths are, became most steady and mature in his ways. And he asked through his priest, since he did not dare to do it for himself, for the reward of being allowed to put off his worldly clothing. But his father delayed, fearing lest he take on, though youthful frivolity, a hard and narrow path, and later draw back, weary of the burden and labour and repenting the penance. And it happened that as the boy was thinking over his conversion one night, the martyr Thomas appeared to him as before, attired as an archbishop and stained with blood. And his parents heard him in his sleep responding to the martyr: "Which monastic habit? Where? When? Lord, have mercy on me." They said to each other, "Let's be patient and not wake him: he's seeing a vision." And when the vision and sleep had departed, he exclaimed "Did you see the blessed Thomas? He was here and left just now. He said to me, 'I have twice spoken to you privately, Engelram. The third time I appear to you, the whole region will know'."[18]

---

[18] The story ends here, with no indication of whether there was a third time.

7. THE MIRACLE OF THE SONS OF JORDAN SON OF EISULF (BENEDICT IV.64, SEE ABOVE PP. 270–4).

WILLIAM OF CANTERBURY II.5, PP. 160–2, Concerning a dead ten-year-old boy

The knight Jordan, son of Eisulf,[19] from a village which he called Pontefract, along his wife and son about ten years old, whom, he asserted, had died and had been reawakened by the blessed martyr Thomas, came to Canterbury in order to give thanks for this grace. On the departure of the boy's nurse from human affairs, the boy likewise died. All the proper things were done to him as if he were dead except for burial, since his father did not permit him to be taken for burial. For he said, as if an angel were speaking through him, "The Spirit promises to me the restitution of my son. If I were to have even a small amount of the water of the glorious martyr Thomas to pour into his mouth, it seems to me that in this right faith and firm hope I would not be a mourning father." And so he received water from pilgrims to whom he had granted hospitality, and poured it into the dead boy's mouth, as much as rigor mortis would allow it to open, for he had lain lifeless from the third hour of the day up to about the eleventh hour of the following day. At first, nothing went down the closed passage into his insides, but little by little, the natural channels were relaxed and a redness infusing his cheek indicated the working of divine power. After a short time, he opened one of his eyes and said, 'Don't weep. The glorious martyr Thomas has returned me to you'.

And so, both parents vowed to go with the boy to the memorial of the martyr. The preparations for the journey extended to the time of *Laetare Jerusalem*.[20] Then, when everything was ready, something else impeded the journey. The earl of Warenne,[21] in whose name the aforesaid knight held land, came to that place and detained the ones about to depart on pilgrimage. It happened that the blessed Thomas appeared to a leper living in the domain of that knight, saying, "Brother, do you sleep?" "I slept," he said, "before you woke the sleeper. Who are you?" He answered, "Thomas, the archbishop of Canterbury. Tomorrow, go and tell the knight here that he should not delay his pilgrimage and vow

---

[19] See Biographical Notes, Jordan son of Eisulf.
[20] This is a shorthand way to describe the fourth Sunday in Lent, which falls sometime between March 1 and April 4 every year. *Laetare Jerusalem* means "Rejoice, Jerusalem": these are the first words spoken in the Mass for the fourth Sunday in Lent (Cantus ID g00776).
[21] See Biographical Notes, Hamelin de Warenne.

any further. Otherwise, he should know that he will lose something that he does not love any less than the boy I restored to him." He was afraid, however, to deliver such a message, and the following night the martyr came again. "See here," he said, "you did not comply with the command." He answered, "You know, lord, that due to my diseased feet I am not able to walk." He replied, "Call your priest, that he might carry out the command." When he did this, and the priest made an excuse on account of fear and the very short temper of a man of such rank, the martyr showed his presence for a third time, not thinking him to be unclean whom the Lord had sanctified in the washing of rebirth.[22] Charging the intermediary with contempt, he summoned him and said, "By means of your daughter, announce the message you have received to the knight and his wife." And this was done, yet they delayed further. When it was almost the time of Easter, the older son of the family, whom the father loved the more dearly since he so closely resembled his father's line in body and facial features, was struck by a disease and departed human affairs. Moreover, the knight with his wife were so gripped by the bodily disorder, and not just them but their whole household, that they despaired of life. And so, fearing the destruction of life, or a graver loss, they set out on the pilgrimage. They were accompanied by twenty-one of their servants, some of whom had recovered from long sickness by a drink of the healing water that very day. The mother of the family, who, within a short space of the trip, had fainted nine times, despaired on account of the length of the journey. But her husband, with firmness of soul, said, "Alive or dead, she will be brought to Canterbury." And their journey succeeded through the assisting merits of him whom they sought, according to the dictum, *to them that love God all things work together unto good, to those who, according to his purpose, are called to be saints* [Rom 8:28], such that the woman, when she was about to enter Canterbury, had walked three miles on foot.

8. THE MIRACLE OF CECILIA, DAUGHTER OF JORDAN OF PLUMSTOCK (BENEDICT IV.65, SEE ABOVE PP. 274–7).

WILLIAM OF CANTERBURY II.35, PP. 190–3, Concerning a girl cancerous and dead

I remember that I spoke of a certain Jordan whose son we saw recalled from death.[23] And let it now be declared that we saw the daughter of another of

---

[22] This seems to mean that the martyr did not consider Gimp to be unclean, though he was a leper, because he had been baptized.
[23] That is, the son of Jordan, son of Eisulf, whose miracle William had described thirty chapters earlier: see above, no. 7.

the same name, though of inferior condition, twice liberated from death by a marvel not inferior. In the diocese of Norwich, the girl Cecilia, who was about fifteen years of age, was struck by cancer. To say it briefly, while the modesty of a virgin made her wish to bear the pain rather than expose her shame, her thighs were consumed, to the point that the junctions of the bones were laid bare and the joining of the sinews were exposed. The size of the wounds was equal to the length of a foot. They emitted an unbearable exhalation of sulphurated gas, such that her mother desired her death and members of the household avoided her presence. Every day, corruption consumed even the bandages that were wrapped around the voracious disease. Tormented by this contagion from about the time of harvest to the first of March, she was brought to the end of life. So, from Tuesday to Friday, she was not refreshed by food nor drink, but lay on a couch, leaning against a wall with her knees drawn together and her eyes open and unblinking. She took on the look of something neither living nor dead. Those household servants seeing her thought she had been rapt out of her body, remembering a certain woman of the region, named Agnes, who, while she slept, had been led by the blessed Catherine through various places while she was in a spiritual rapture. She was shown the rewards and punishments of the dead, among whom she also saw a priest called Godwin, who had died a few days earlier, with his knees terribly wounded by repeated blows from a key. It was thought he suffered this punishment because when he was alive, he had carried off the key to the church of the blessed Mary while another priest was celebrating Mass inside of it.

And so it happened that while the aforesaid girl lay unmoving, a woman of the neighborhood arrived to pay her a visit, a woman who loved her dearly. When she saw her dead she exclaimed, "Why did you not lay out this girl, whom we have seen and left dead in bed, on a hairshirt, as is the Christian custom for the dying? You have acted thoughtlessly." And so she was carried into an outer building and, with her limbs rigid and eyes wide open, placed on the ground. A linen sheet was also placed under the corpse, and candles were lit as for a funeral. But the father, who had thrown himself down elsewhere, tormented both by pain and suffering, waking from sleep, ran in, crying, "If the Lord looks favourably on me, my daughter is not dead. O blessed Thomas, now repay my service, I who once attentively rendered service to you!" And he repeated the sorrowful cry, "Repay my service! Necessity now presses. Repay my service!" As for the reason he said this, we do not think it wrong to briefly append a succinct explanation.

The blessed Thomas, before he was exalted by the world's honors, before the smile of fortune expanded both his power and his reputation, received hospitality from a certain clerk named Turstan, a native of Kent, who, having been made a proctor in a place called Croydon under the archbishopric of Theobald,[24] took on the work vigorously and administered the affairs with industry. There, when Thomas was ill and could not drink neither wine nor cider nor anything else that could make one drunk, he drank whey, as his illness required, that this servant Jordan had sought out and inquired for throughout the vicinity. He also took care of the one horse that he held privately. For this reason, presuming on this liberal service, he repeated, "Repay my service." This he so often repeated that his throat was stopped up by hoarseness. The blessed one, moved by pity, did not wish to be held ungrateful. For he restored the woman to life, who right away drew her hand to herself and spoke, although she was not yet able to express herself in an intelligible voice, having been brought low by emaciation and death. The following day, she took food and drink. Within the space of three weeks, her cancerous thighs had dried up and were made whole.

With these events marvellously concluded, the aforesaid man, the father of the girl, went to his lord the bishop of Norwich,[25] telling him about the matter and asking for a letter of testimonial, so that, when he came to Canterbury, he would not be thought to speak without authority in describing an event beyond belief and credence. But the bishop did not immediately have faith, until he called the priest and those who had been present and seen this affair, as well as two married women of good repute to examine the vestiges of the cancer: he learned of all of the affair in order. It was divinely arranged that this diligent investigation would remove all doubt. Therefore, by a written document signed with his seal, he declared the deed to the brothers worshipping God in the church of Canterbury, which is as follows:

"William, by the grace of God bishop of Norwich, to his venerable brothers in the Lord, the prior and the holy convent of Canterbury: eternal salvation in Christ.

We desire with all desire to inform your holiness of the wonders of God that are happening in our diocese to people afflicted with various illnesses who direct all their devotion to God's most holy saint Thomas and offer pure

---

[24] See Biographical Notes, Turstan of Croydon. Theobald was the archbishop of Canterbury from 1139 to 1161. Thomas Becket was part of Theobald's household in the 1140s and 1150s before he became Henry II's chancellor in 1154.

[25] See Biographical Notes, William Turbe, bishop of Norwich.

invocations of their hearts to him. When God does not wish to hide the things which glorify his saint, how can one presume to conceal them among men? We have heard from the testimony of William, a priest of our region, and many of our men, that the bearer of this letter, Cecilia, the daughter of one of our men, was held by the sickness of cancer for a long time. The disease spread implacably about her thighs, and at last she was so oppressed by the worsening illness that she was thought to be lifeless and was placed on the floor in the manner of a corpse. Her father's soul was turned to bitterness, but still trusting in divine mercy and the merits of the most blessed martyr, he burst out in a voice filled with suffering. With a most devoted mind, he invoked the saint of the Lord and begged for the restitution of health to his daughter by the will of divine grace. And so she was restored to her earlier health by the merits of the most blessed martyr, and to the glory of such a miracle we send her to you with our written testimony. Farewell."

9. THE MIRACLE OF THE DROWNED PHILIP, SON OF HUGH SCOT (BENEDICT IV.66, SEE ABOVE PP. 277–8).

WILLIAM OF CANTERBURY II.40, PP. 200–2, Concerning a dead eight-year-old boy

Why do you marvel, reader? Marvel at the following, in which equally or more marvellously a person is recalled to life.[26] If you presume to oppose this, denying him to be dead whom we will raise to life, if neither the parents exhibiting the boy, nor suitable witnesses, though of the household, bring satisfaction, let the sequence of the event itself and the power or wonder of the martyr be persuasive.

In the region of Cheshire, the man Hugh, surnamed Scot, was of good name and reputation among his fellow countrymen. His son, Philip, about eight years old, was sitting by an iron mine and throwing stones, as boys do, to crush a toad coming out of the mud. Making his attempts without care, he was himself overwhelmed by water. When his father came home and discovered that he was not there, he sought for him everywhere, village to village. He found him submerged in the water, and pulled him out dead, greatly distended with water. Already the day had sunk to dusk. And so the father devoted himself to sighs and groans, the mother to tears and laments. They carried out the first

---

[26] William is referring to the story of a boy's resurrection that he had told in the previous chapter in his collection (II.39).

things that are thought to be efficacious in such matters. They cut off the tunic, which could not be taken off due to the distention of the body. Pounding the soles of the feet, they hung the corpse by the feet. But, hope falling away from them, the water failed to flow out. When these efforts failed to succeed, they spread him out on a table, lit a fire on either side, and passed through the length of the night without sleep. When the sun rose, by the advice of the mother, whose concern was more attentive, the water of Saint Thomas was brought back from the next village. When she was endeavoring, with her own hands, to pour it in the cold lips, and with the help of a spindle was separating his closed mouth and clenched teeth, along with the spindle she inserted her finger. When she pulled the spindle out, her finger was caught, and as his teeth came together, it was nearly pierced through. And when she was crying out, the father applied a knife and knocked out two of the front teeth, those that are called front incisors. Yet when the first health-giving drop was poured in, it did not find a way through and flowed out. But the third time, the faith and devotion of the parents succeeded such that it flowed in. His muscles were seen to twitch, and the boy began to draw in his hand and open one of his eyes. The father leapt up and asked whether he was able to live. He answered, "I wish to live." Wonderful is the Lord, and his mercy is not numbered, he who first restored that which was not there, and then consumed what was there in abundance. For when those who were there were lamenting the swelling of his stomach, the stomach began, before their eyes, to sink down little by little, recovering its natural size and slenderness, yet not a drop of the waves he drunk flowed out of his body from either the upper or the lower regions. When we speak of these things, we do not magnify by our fiction the truth of the great works of God, which need no such amplification. Rather, we tell what we have learned from the parent of the boy who gave thanks with the boy. If the blessed Thomas had not restored him to life, he had often said that he would have brought him dead from his region to the site of his resting place.

10. THE MIRACLE OF THE LEPER ELIAS OF READING (BENEDICT IV.72, SEE ABOVE PP. 281–2).

WILLIAM OF CANTERBURY VI.8, pp. 416–17, Concerning a leprous monk

[Note: this chapter was not composed by William. It is the second part of a lengthy letter written by Anselm, a monk of Reading, which was sent to Jeremy, a monk of Christ Church Canterbury. William copied this letter directly *into his collection. The rest of the letter is found in VI.7, pp. 415–16 and VI.9, pp. 417–19.]*

Elias, a monk of the church of Reading, suffered from leprosy or morphea. He was so ulcerous that he might be called another Lazarus,[27] for from the soles of his feet to the top of his head, no place, not even the smallest spot, was free from a multitude of protuberances and ulcers. Thinking that hot baths might bring him relief and his pain would be lessened by the sulfur's warmth, he went to Bath and sat in the baths for forty days. But since he had placed his hope in the warmth of sulfur rather than in the marvelous martyr whom the Lord *wounded for our iniquities, so that by his bruises we might be healed* [Is 53:5], he was not yet worthy to be cured. After he had spent everything that he had been able to collect on doctors, like the woman in the gospels who merited to touch the fringe of the Lord's clothing,[28] he turned to the martyr. Therefore, he traveled to London under the subterfuge of seeking medicine, anticipating an occasion to steal off to Canterbury, for our abbot deferred to the martyr less than was fitting, not allowing those of his house to go on pilgrimage.[29] In the meantime, he asked for the water from pilgrims returning from the memorial of the martyr. He drank, and was healed, so much so that he does not retain traces of the disease; rather, he displays an agreeable appearance, as is clear to those seeing him.

11. THE MIRACLE OF THE LEPER OF ABINGDON (BENEDICT IV.75, SEE ABOVE PP. 283–4).

WILLIAM OF CANTERBURY II.52, PP. 213–14, Concerning a leprous youth

Eleanor, the venerable queen of England,[30] found a little child cast out on the road and deprived of a mother's care, and ordered that he be brought up in the convent of Abingdon. There, after having filled many years learning letters, he was struck by elephantiac disease, and was removed from the school and from the convent by the order of the bishop Godfrey of St. Asaph,

---

[27] See Luke 16:19–31 and John 11:1-45 for stories of Lazarus.
[28] For the story of the woman spending all she had on doctors, see Mark 5:25–34 and Luke 8:43-8.
[29] See Biographical Notes, William the Templar, abbot of Reading and archbishop of Bordeaux.
[30] See Biographical Notes, Eleanor of Aquitaine.

who administered the affairs of the convent.[31] His tuberous face, flowing eyes, thin eyebrows, and wide ulcers on his arms and thighs, open down to the bone, provoked nausea. His hoarse voice hardly reached the ears of a person standing next to him, and his bandages had to be changed every day or every other day on account of the outflow of bloody matter. These things advised against his company or cohabitation. Yet the youth trusted in the mercy and the merits of the blessed Thomas, whom the grace of heaven had made illustrious in similar cases, and he set out for Canterbury. On the way, he felt the beginning of his cure in the excessive activity of his bowels. After staying two days at the tomb of St. Thomas, he returned cleansed, carrying back home vestiges of the disease. One day he took hold of the bishop's dress as he was walking past, and said that he had been cleansed by the merits of the blessed Thomas of Canterbury. The bishop, not knowing him due to his sudden transformation, asked him for his name and who he was. Stating his name, and by the same answer specifying who he was, he rendered the questioner stupefied. And so the bishop, thinking over the outcome of the matter and the length of the illness, which had increased in intensity through two years, consulted doctors. After he was unable to refute those asserting his health and their faithful eyes, he called back the rejected one to the courtyard of the convent and to people's company. He also took him with him when he came to the tomb of the martyr to pray and showed him to be seen.

12. THE MIRACLE OF GEOFFREY, A MONK OF READING (BENEDICT IV.86, SEE ABOVE PP. 289–90).

WILLIAM OF CANTERBURY II.50, PP. 210–11, Concerning a monk nearly dead

Let it be said without my labor what favour the church of Shrewsbury[32] and of Reading found in the martyr.

"To the venerable lord Odo, prior of Canterbury,[33] from brother Augustine, monk of Reading, greetings and much love in Christ.

We consider it right to reveal to your holiness a certain great and celebrated miracle in the house of Reading. For a certain brother of our congregation,

---

[31] See Biographical Notes, Godfrey, bishop of St. Asaph.
[32] William mentions Shrewsbury because the chapter following this one in his collection (II.51) is a copy of a letter about the miracle of the precentor of Shrewsbury.
[33] See Biographical Notes, Odo, prior of Christ Church, Canterbury and abbot of Battle.

named Geoffrey of Wallingford,[34] a vigorous man and worthy cantor, and one of the leaders of our house, was encumbered by a very grave illness, to the point that it was thought he was in the last extremity, for he was deprived of the use of all his senses and all the members of his body. What more? All the brothers gathered together so that they might anoint him with holy oil, as is the custom. When they had arrived at the point of the reception of holy communion, the prior called, 'Lord Geoffrey, open your mouth to receive your salvation.' He tried but could not, until he was just able to receive the tiniest particle between his teeth. Soon, when he had been replaced in his own bed, and remained in that same sickness such that we thought he would leave his body on that same day, after a short interval of time the prior came with a few brothers, investigating whether he could possibly receive any word of confession from the mouth of the ill one. They could expect nothing at all from him but death. The prior, not knowing at all what should be done, asked the brothers if any among them kept safe the water of the holy martyr Thomas. Shortly thereafter the health-giving water was brought, that which I had brought from the memorial of the martyr. Once it was poured through the lips of the sick man, the chain upon his tongue was suddenly loosened, all his senses recovered, and all the members of his body received their earlier health, such that he said, 'It is well.' Afterwards, he cried out loudly, 'Thanks be to God, who by the merits of his martyr, St. Thomas, completely freed me from an evil spirit that had quite closed up my throat and nose.' The witnesses to this miracle are the entire convent of Reading and nearly all the inhabitants of our town."

13. THE MIRACLE OF GEOFFREY OF WINCHESTER (BENEDICT IV.88, SEE ABOVE PP. 290–1).

WILLIAM OF CANTERBURY II.45, PP. 206–7, Concerning a boy on whom a wall fell

You have heard of a wounded boy.[35] Hear of a boy of younger age, who was freed from a greater danger.

The boy named Geoffrey, born in Winchester of the father Robert and mother Leticia, seethed with the heat of fevers about sixteen months after his birth. When he drank the water of St. Thomas, he gave joy to his parents by at once

---

[34] See Biographical Notes, Geoffrey of Walllingford, monk of Reading.
[35] In the previous chapter, William told a story about a boy kicked by a horse.

regaining coolness. However, without warning, happiness was darkened with sadness. For when his mother was sitting by herself in her house, a wall of the house was shaken and fell from top to bottom, under which the infant was at rest in his cradle. The wall was made of stone and thirteen feet tall, and the cradle was smashed into eighteen pieces, though it was made squarely, of solid boards, in the manner of a bedstead. Several of the fragments were driven down and buried in the ground. It was thought that the wall fell because of a storm the preceding day, but we believe that this was arranged by the Holy of Holies in order to glorify the holy one. When the mother saw that her little one was overwhelmed by ruin, she cried out, "St. Thomas, save the boy you returned to me!" and with the cry, because of her grief, she fell into a faint. Wonderful kindness of the saint! Wonderful power of the unconquered martyr, who hastened to hear the pious mother, and in accordance with his merits kept the boy, on whom the weight of four or three cartloads pressed down, unharmed in death itself. For when the son was seized by ruin here, and the mother by sorrow there, two men came and pulled the reclining woman to her feet. They asked for and heard the reason for her sorrow. Having called for help, they took down the heap of rubble. They found the cradle crushed into pieces, and they lifted out the boy not only uninjured, but also happy and laughing. Wonderful to relate, he did not have a sign of injury on his whole body except for a small bruise near one of his eyes that was hardly noticeable. As time went on, and they put off the thanks they owed for the boon of the martyr, the boy began to sicken and be claimed as repayment for these praiseworthy acts. And it happened one day that a certain woman came to the grandmother of the boy and said, "It is revealed to me about the boy that he ought to be sent to the memorial of the blessed Thomas. Know that this revelation proceeded from the Lord. For I do not say this either for the benefit of money nor for any other less than honest motive, but rather I am the messenger of divine admonition." Therefore, after a short time the boy was sent to Canterbury, and we learned what we have spoken.

14. THE MIRACLE OF JAMES, SON OF ROGER DE CLARE (BENEDICT IV.94, SEE ABOVE PP. 293–5).

WILLIAM OF CANTERBURY II.68, PP. 228–30, Concerning a dead boy, the son of an earl

There is no partiality of persons with God, but in every nation, he who fears God, that one is acceptable to Him [Acts 10:34–5]. *He does not cast aside the powerful, for he himself is powerful* [Jb 36:5], nor does he necessarily admit a poor man because of his poverty. He attends to the heart, not to the condition, to the possessor, not to possessions. For if someone has an abundance of merit in excellent works and makes a petition of the Lord, he will equally merit to be heard whether he be rich or poor. His poverty will not tell against him, nor his wealth. Therefore let everyone be keen to please God in mind and to strive to act for God in word, that God might act for him.

Matilda, the countess of Clare, had of her husband a son James.[36] A short time after his birth, he was struck by a hernia, and his intestines flowed down into the little sack of his testicles. When his father saw that he was dragged into pain at a young age and from the cradle into care, he assembled doctors, promising them a great number of coins if they could cure him. Determining that the cause of the rupture was excessive movement and wailing, they said they needed to do an incision. But the mother, having compassion for him on account of his tender age, would not permit him to be cut, instead placing all her hope in the Lord and blessed Thomas. Going to his resting-place on the day on which, as it is written, the blessed Mary Mother and Virgin presented her Son in the temple,[37] she herself also took care to present her son to the care of the martyr. There, she received the advice, which she had not presumed, to wash the infirm parts of the boy with the health-giving water. She washed, and she earned complete health for the one who was washed. No other form of cure was applied. Merely by faith, the intestines returned to their place.

After some time had passed, the same boy was seized by illness and taken from life. The grief of his guardians was great. When the rigor of his limbs most certainly declared the absence of life, they carried the body to an outer building, deferring the ceremonial and funeral rites for the mother's consideration. Since none of them dared be the messenger of the sad news and afflict the mother with sadness, a little brother of the dead boy ran and announced to his mother what he had seen. Throwing off her garment, she speedily returned from prayer and picked up the corpse in her hands. She pressed it to her breasts, enfolded it in her arms, did not fear to put her face next to its, and cried out, "St. Thomas, previously you returned my son to me. Why did you want to return him for his mother's grief? You cured the illness that tormented him terribly. Woe is me! What sin have I committed now, what command have I transgressed, that I am condemned to be bereaved? Holy martyr, the one you

---

[36] See Biographical Notes, Matilda de St. Hilary and Roger de Clare.
[37] The Purification of the Virgin, also known as Candlemas, is celebrated on February 2.

returned, return again now. I place myself under obligation: I will return to your tomb with devotion, clothed in woolen garments, barefoot and abject. Return, holy martyr, the one you returned before." Speaking in this manner, by turns she bowed her knees to the ground. The men and women who were there reproved her and urged her silence, especially the chaplain Lambert, who said, "What is this, lady? What are you doing? What are you saying? Such things do not suggest a healthy or wise mind. A dead body demands funeral rites, not entreaties like these. Return the body to ashes. Commend his spirit to his Creator, who, according to His desire, pours a soul into His creature or takes it away. Don't irritate God's mercy with foolish speech." She lamented nonetheless and said, "I will not leave off until the martyr has mercy on me and my son is restored from death." Furthermore, she poured the water of the martyr and thrust the portion of the hairshirt from the clothing of the same martyr between the closed lips of the deceased. As she groaned and wailed, she noticed a red spot appear on his face, and grasping the sign of divine mercy, she arose giving thanks for the announcement of returning life.

15. THE MIRACLE OF HUGH OF EBBLINGHAM (BENEDICT ADDITION 6, SEE ABOVE P. 299).

WILLIAM OF CANTERBURY IV.20, PP. 332-4, Concerning two lepers, one from this side of the sea, one from beyond the sea

"Never," said Galen, "in my life have I seen a man entirely cured of leprosy, unless he drank wine into which a snake had fallen and rotted. When this wine was drunk, I have seen it abrade off and strip the skin."[38] We, however, have seen two men perfectly cleansed and not retaining any sign of leprosy who had no other medicine than the blood and water of the martyr. One of them, by the name of Richard,[39] dwelled at the tomb of the martyr for a long time, *eating and drinking such things as we had* [Lk 10:7], and was a spectacle for the kings, earls, natives and foreigners who had come to pray. The other was a certain Hugh, of the village of Ebblingham, which stands about fifteen

---

[38] The works of Galen, the Roman physician of the second century CE, were core medical texts in the Middle Ages. Robertson believed that this quote was derived from Galen's *De simplicium medicamentorum*, XI.1: see K. G. Kühn (ed.), *Claudii Galeni Opera Omnia* (Leipzig, 1821-33), vol. 12, p. 313.

[39] This is almost certainly Richard Sunieve, whose cure was described by Benedict: see IV.76.

furlongs away from the great town that the common folk give the name of the confessor Omer.[40] We saw him leprous and we dismissed him from us cleansed, warning him to carry on his business without fraud (for he was a merchant), or to give up business entirely. For he had a suitable character for some other more honorable situation, and in strength of body he was not yet past the prime of life. He was cured in an easy manner, though he had a difficult disease, which should have been the more difficult since it was a year since it had broken out on his skin. He spent two nights in prayer with us, and left having had his face sprinkled with a moderate amount of the water. On departing, in a short time he felt its mighty and wonderful power. When he returned to give thanks, he made its effectiveness known to us, and we believed, since his cleansed face warranted faith.

What is the Lord doing, do you think, in healing so many lepers at the present time? Let no one find it tiresome if I say what I believe about this, for I do not presume to preempt a better judgment. To be sure, the Lord exalts the saint who suffered and acted for him in the causes of his people. Because secular power had condemned ecclesiastical liberty to a servitude it did not owe, and because the charity of many had cooled in the world's evening, it was necessary for the living sacrifice, pleasing to God, to be slaughtered. And so, he could cure leprosy, as well as other ailments, in order that the violence that had raged would be restrained through this, and the faith that had cooled would be rekindled. Thus, the high priest was sent by the decree of supernatural dispensation. He was chafed by a hairshirt, tested by exile, struck by affliction of his own and of his familiars, and fought invincibly for a long time in the battleline of trials. When the course of his combat was happily completed, what he was not able to do while living, he completed in death. In a wonderful way, after his death he rises again more powerfully against the enemy, as you say truly, *his weakness is stronger than men* [1 Cor 1:25]. And so, he cures all forms of leprosy, not only tyria and leonina, but also elephancia and alopecia, and any other forms of leprosy the physician contrives.[41] He also cures what is the greater: spiritual leprosy, namely the diversity of faults defiling the purity of the soul. For just as exterior leprosy defiles the body by making spots on it, so the beauty of souls is disfigured by its leprosy. For there are those with

---

[40] That is, the town Saint-Omer, named after the seventh-century bishop St. Omer (also known as St. Audomar).

[41] For a discussion of these four forms of leprosy, which were thought to correspond to the four humors of the body in medieval medical thinking, see Carole Rawcliffe, *Leprosy in Medieval England* (Woodbridge, 2006), 74–5.

the sternness of a lion, many the craftiness of a snake, not a few the deceit of a fox, and many have consciences cauterized and blackened, imitating in their customs the properties of the elephant.[42] And so, with benefits such as these, the good are invited to goodness, the bad are called back from evil, and by the grace of God, today's world sees such progress as has not been known since the time the apostles were upon the earth.

16. THE MIRACLE OF WILLIAM OF GLOUCESTER (BENEDICT ADDITION 7, SEE ABOVE PP. 299–301).

WILLIAM OF CANTERBURY III.1, PP. 253–6, Concerning a buried man

In a remarkable display of brotherly love and of peace within the church, the martyr Thomas warned his enemy, Roger, the bishop of York,[43] with a new wonder, a man extremely erudite in human and divine affairs if he had known according to knowledge. The bishop Roger was bringing water into his village of Churchdown from the top of a mountain about five hundred paces away. In the middle bulged a hill about twenty-four feet high, its steep top looking down on the surrounding plains and fields. When the work was at boiling point, the hill was dug through, such that it might take the course of the water in a straight direction through its opened side. A certain William, who had hired out his labours from the neighboring city of Gloucester, was hard at work. When he was laying the lead pipe in the depths of the opened hill, a heap of earth that had been dug out fell on top of him. His companions were flying here and there and wanted to dig him out, already all covered up, when behold, again from a steep cliff, an unstable, overhanging mound of earth suddenly rolled down and trapped the youth. They estimated what fell on him to be about a hundred cartloads. He himself was bent forward with his hands spread out before his face, and was wearing only a smock since he had been hard at work. When he saw that a means of escape was denied to him, he sighed for the Lord, the first and the last refuge for anyone in any need. He also invoked the blessed Virgin Mary, who, according to her name, is a star to the haven of eternal happiness for those tossed about in the turbulent sea of human misfortune. But because the Lord wished to glorify his martyr, he did

---

[42] William is playing here on the associations of the four types of leprosy with types of animals: *leonina* with the stern lion; *tyria* with the crafty serpent; *alopecia* with the deceitful fox; and *elephancia* with the blackened and wrinkly skin of an elephant.

[43] See Biographical Notes, Roger de Pont l'Évêque, archbishop of York.

not provide help at the invocation of his name. What should the miserable man do, cut off by the fall of such a great mound of earth? The blockage of air denied breath, the heaped-up mound separated him from all human help. The enclosed breath began to be stretched, and when he was tormented to the point of death, the name of the martyr Thomas came into his mouth. And he said, "Blessed Thomas, men say that you have power with your Lord, and what you are asked for, you can easily obtain. If you are so holy and are such a one as you are proclaimed by the mouth of the people, help me, I who have been placed at the point of death. Release me, caught in this most miserable way. Take me out of this prison, restoring me to my former place. You will be refuge to me, and I will seek the place consecrated by your precious blood, where living you strove for the freedom of the church and dead you conquered." Saying these things (for we do not concoct what he could have said, but rather we speak those things he did say, preferring to say less than to speak beyond the truth), the distended man breathed out the wind with which he was swollen with much belching, and, vomiting, he was relieved. From this point he regained the ability to breathe.

These things were happening in the heart of the earth. The cry was made, "Priest, priest, since he is dead!" Summoned, the priest performed the funeral rites, and when they were completed, he returned home. The buried man, left alone and by himself through the night, awaited the mercy of the martyr. Already fifty-one days had passed since the summer solstice,[44] and with Leo about to send the sun into Virgo, the nights had lengthened. And yet in such a length of nights, the Lord was to him a helper in tribulation. For a local woman had a vision, and in the morning said to her son, "I think, son, that the one who was buried still lives, for I saw in my sleep that he drank milk and rested in milk." And he, contrary to his usual custom, immediately got up from bed and went into the fields, not to work, but for whatever chance might bring. As if he were led by the Spirit, he came to the place, which was now not for water-bringing but for weeping. Putting his ear to the earth, he heard something like a groan. And he called to the man in charge of the fields, who had gone out early in the morning to care for the draught horse that he had turned out at night, saying, "See here! He still lives, for I hear something like a man's crying groan." He answered, "It is nothing, and if all of Gloucester said it was true, I would not believe it." "Come and listen," he replied, and when they had heard it, the other announced to the priest that he lived. Suspending the divine office, he came immediately to that place with the people. The same

---

[44] This indicates that the accident occurred on August 11, very likely in 1173.

thing was announced to Gloucester, that he still lived. There came many who were eager and devoted in mind to their neighbor – the old man, the young boy, the woman – and they applied themselves to remove the earth with scoops, platters, basins, and other homely utensils. The buried man, hearing the noisy activity and everyone working to find him first, called out to those standing above him, near and far, because he was worried either that they would hurt him with their iron tools or that they would fail to get to him. The day wore on to the third hour.[45] Then at last the buried man appeared, with battered cheeks and arms crushed almost to the breaking point, stiff and numb from the harsh subterranean cold. And so he was brought back to the surface so that sinners might be brought out of the depths. For we believe that the martyr saved the innocent soul for the purpose of reformation, such that the wicked might save their souls. You might think this, since with time passing he delayed openly showing himself at Canterbury, and it was said to some woman in her dreams that he was foolhardy to delay to exhibit the manifestation of divine compassion at the tomb of the martyr, and he would not escape punishment if he presumed to delay further. The same man who suffered these things told them to us, and he brought a letter saying the following:

"Greetings from Geoffrey, dean of Gloucester, to his venerable lord and father, prior of the Holy Trinity [of Canterbury], and all the convent.

Know that the bearer of these letters, William, was buried in a certain deep pit, twenty-three feet deep,[46] his co-workers having fled, and he was buried there for one night and up to the third hour of the next day. The funeral rites were conducted for him as if he were dead. He, however, feeling the approach of death, invoked God and prayed that he might be liberated from this great danger by the merits of his most glorious martyr Thomas. Crying aloud, he made a vow that he would go to the place where saint Thomas had been killed. After this was heard by some people who were passing that place, they announced to the entire village that they had heard a human voice in the pit. The priest and more than a hundred men hastened there and drew him out. But also many other miracles are done among us every day through Thomas, the most glorious martyr of Christ, which I will relate to you when I come to you in a short time, God willing."

---

[45] That is, mid-morning.
[46] In the copy of Dean Geoffrey's letter found in Benedict's collection, the pit is said to be twenty-four rather than twenty-three feet deep. Both collectors, too, have the number twenty-four. Something seems to have gone wrong either in the manuscript transmission of Geoffrey's letter or in Robertson's edition.

17. THE MIRACLE OF SALERNA OF IFELD (BENEDICT ADDITION 8, SEE ABOVE, PP. 301–3).

William of Canterbury III.3, pp. 258–61, Concerning a girl who threw herself into a well

In a certain estate of the church of Canterbury, there is a village called Ifeld in the English tongue.[47] A marvelous thing occurred there that is worthy to be told. In the house of a certain Thomas, a man far from humble according to earthly judgment, the mother of the family was absent, and the household servants, eating breakfast as they do, asked two daughters of the family to give them cheese to savor alongside their bread.[48] In this way they took advantage of the poor judgment of the younger daughter, named Salerna, who, having received the keys, went freely in and out of the larder. When the mother returned home, she did not find the right number of cheeses and summoned her daughters. Accusing both of an act of theft, she suspected the younger one. She gave her a whipping and threatened worse to come.

In the morning, the mother went to a chapel about three furlongs from her home. By the dispensation of the Lord who foresees what is to come, a servant had arrived from the mill sooner than was usual. Lying down on the straw, he had sought sleep. The girl had spent a troubled night premeditating her death, the whole night sleepless on account of her fears. She went into an inner room as if she were going to her little brother, who had been placed in her charge. Closing the door after her, she went out into the orchard. Crossing through the hedge, she walked back and forth, shrinking back from the wrongdoing she had planned. On the one side, the fear of death held her back. On the other, the enemy of the human race, transformed into the shape of one of the female servants, urged and propelled her on. At last, passing quickly through the hedge, she uncovered the well's mouth. Putting her legs inside, she hung by her arms. When a swineherd saw her from the field and shouted, she worried she would be stopped, and sent herself into the well, saying, "May the Lord and blessed Thomas provide for me."

---

[47] Ifield, Kent, now usually termed Singlewell, was a peculiar of the archbishop of Canterbury until 1846. See F. R. H. Du Boulay, *The Lordship of Canterbury: An Essay on Medieval Society* (London, 1966), pp. 350–1.

[48] For medieval Europeans, breakfast was not a common meal (the main meal of the day was usually eaten about 11am). For those who did it eat it, breakfast usually was nothing more than some bread. The household servants were asking for a treat.

O how vigilant and loving is the shepherd who snatches the lost sheep from the jaws of present and eternal death, lest the flock lose part of its body![49] O how benevolent and well-disposed is the father, who saves the unwilling soul hostile to him, lest the enemy exult over the damnation of one of his household! The prudence of the good shepherd watched over his successors and the shepherds of posterity, lest the envy of their detractors mock them as idlers not performing their pastoral duties. It watched over the diocese of church of Canterbury, lest it be marked with infamy.

And so, the virgin, having turned around many times, sunk to the bottom of the water three times. Emerging for the fourth time, she saw the blessed Thomas saying, "You will not die. You will come out of the well." I will speak of something wonderful and hardly to be believed, yet uncontaminated by falsehood. The depth of the well was twenty-five large cubits[50] to the top of the water, and eight more to the bottom of the water, and yet despite the well's depth, she who threw herself into it was preserved unharmed. For the divine hand had placed a plank across the well, put the shipwrecked girl upon it, and placed a staff in her hands, with which she propped herself up along the side of the well. This is the hand that is placed under the just man when he falls lest he be bruised, just as is said, *He will help him, and his arm will make his fast, so that the enemy may not prevail over him, and the son of iniquity may not add hurt to him* [Ps 88:22–3]. For this was the hand that led the sons of Israel out of slavery in Egypt, Jonah from the belly of the whale, Daniel from the lion's den, Peter from prison, and Paul from the depths of the sea.[51] It created the ivy that gave noontime shade to the prophet,[52] and it also created the plank for the assistance of shipwrecked girl. Do not be deceived lest you think that the plank had been put in the well deliberately for the support of those going into it, because they had this custom, that if something fell into it, as sometimes happens, it had to be pulled out and the bottom searched with a hook. From the time the well was dug, neither the lord nor any of the servants had noticed such a plank. Let one say what he pleases, and argue that it had been put there a long time before, and, long after it was forgotten, it was sometimes underneath the water, sometimes just at the surface, according to

---

[49] William is evoking the parable of the Good Shepherd seeking the lost sheep: see John 10:1–21.

[50] A cubit, a measure of the forearm from the elbow to the end of the middle finger, was understood to be one and a half times the size of a foot. In our terms, this would make the well about fifteen meters deep, filled with about three and a half meters of water.

[51] These are all well-known biblical stories: see the books of Exodus, Jonah, and Daniel, and for the stories of Peter and Paul, Acts 12:3–19 and Acts 27:27–28:5.

[52] For ivy giving shade to the prophet, see Jonah 4:6.

the increase or decrease of the well's water. And let him explain how this girl, just thirteen years old, for that was her age, who threw herself down from such a height, could get up on the plank and press down on it with her feet. What besides divine mercy, which does not wish anyone's death, sent the support into her hands?

The swineherd, seeing the virgin throw herself down, ran with shouts, calling the sleeping servant, who was seeing in his dream a man threatening him with a clenched fist, saying "Lie down: if you get up, you will immediately be stopped by this fist on your jaw. Sleep, lest you wake to your destruction." Speak, ungodly devil, what power your deceit now has. The multiplicity of your machinations does not prevail against the simple and innocent. Author of deceit, you deceived the young virgin, you thought of her as prey, but you did not keep her in possession, for your deceit was engulfed by the martyr's victory. You sent the servant to sleep and prohibited his assistance, but this and everything else you plotted was spoiled. You attack and are hostile to the shepherd's little sheep, but the provident shepherd fends off your deceits.

Woken by the servant's shouts, the servant heard about the wretched woman's fall. He quickly cast off his clothes, and, naked, he prepared to go down into the well and was lowered in. But seeing that this would not work, he seized a horse and notified the mother, along with those who were in the church, what had happened. Lamenting her guilt and the fear that she had struck in the very fearful virgin, she came to the well with a flood of villagers. Among them was a certain Ralph, a strong and agile young man, who, by divine will, had gone to that chapel on that day, contrary to his usual habit. Except for him, no-one there at that time dared to descend into the subterranean depths. Arriving there, they lowered a leather bag for holding liquid, which settled on the crossways plank next to the standing girl. This young man Ralph was let down by a rope, and he found the girl standing, as we have said, and he stood on the plank beside her. He tied the rope to her, and when she was pulled out she called out, "Get ready to measure my body, vowing to the blessed Thomas." And so the soul of the innocent and simple girl was saved. Having been misled by an evil spirit, she was drawn out without any harm to her limbs, blessed be God and the martyr forever! Let us say, "God, who reveals your mercy to the greatest extent when you generously give your grace to the unworthy, provide, we seek, that we who cannot be saved by our own merits, may always be helped by the intercession of your holy martyr Thomas, through the Lord, etc."[53]

---

[53] This would seem to be a well-known prayer for Thomas Becket's aid.

18. THE MIRACLE OF JOHN OF ROXBURGH (BENEDICT ADDITION 9, SEE ABOVE PP. 303–4).

WILLIAM OF CANTERBURY III.41, PP. 296–8, Concerning a man submerged through an entire night

There is a great village called Roxburgh at the borders of Loegria[54] which is washed by the Tweed, a deep river teeming with fish. A youth, John, was turning away from its channel with the horse he had been watering, when the fearful animal was frightened by a standing hurdle through which the sand was flowing.[55] Leaping into the depths, the horse cast off its rider and hurried back to its familiar stall. *Woe to him who is alone, for when he falls, he has no-one to lift him up* [Eccl 4:10]. The man thrown off began to sink, snatched by the strong current and dragged under the waves to the bottom of the riverbed. The shadows of night were falling and all human help was denied to him, and in this hopeless state he turned to prayer, saying, "Hurry to the rescue, Thomas, extraordinary martyr, and do not let your servant die, I who recently visited the holy threshold of your martyrdom. Help, champion of God, lest your pilgrim perish."

In each stage of life, it is right to strive for integrity.
Whether playing with a ball or carrying on in later years,
Worship is owed, a debt held by older and younger alike.[56]

If grace had not preceded the wretched one of whom we speak, that grace that freely justifies the ungodly, the grace of pilgrimage that preceded his peril, what good work could he have presented for the consideration of the one he called to his aid?

When he had said this brief prayer as well as the wave-tossed flood and his held breath would allow, he was engulfed and thrust underneath a certain stony concave. Either nature made it or the martyr hollowed it out for his shipwrecked one. There he was hidden in the deep, fixed in the mire, and in the middle of the night, behold, eight venerable personages were supported upon the waters, walking side by side in silence. On their approach, the submerged youth emerged, brought out at once from under the stone. By the

---

[54] Loegria is another term for England: see entry for *Loegria* in *DMLBS*.
[55] In other words, there was a fishing weir on the shore of the river that frightened the horse.
[56] The source of these verses is unknown. They may be William's own composition.

aid of an upward-flowing current, he was carried towards a bent willow tree licking the top of the water. When he grasped a small branch which hung down in his hands, it broke, either by the dispensation of the martyr, or by the heavy weight of the one grabbing it, or due to the weakness of the wood, or rather by the artifice of an evil spirit, and he was again hurled back into the water. In addition, a stone from the bank rolled onto him, throwing him well away from the shore. Then he was brought to a bridge which, with its arching arms, embraced the river channel. It was located more than a bowshot away from the spot where he had fallen from his horse. How wonderful is the love and zeal of the saints for the protection of mortals! Those who had first appeared to the shipwrecked one appeared again to him under the bridge. They rescued him, now at the point of death, and placed him upon the bridge, which stands three or four cubits[57] above the water. One of them, of handsome appearance and dressed like a priest, consoled him with common speech, saying, "Get up and go home. You were mindful of your own good yesterday when you remembered me. In the future, be intent on good deeds."

Once the vision of the saints slipped from his eyes, he vomited out the riverwater he had drunk. Having been given some strength for a time, he crept on hands and knees and knocked on the door of the tollkeeper whose house was attached to the bridge. Wondering who would knock at dawn, he asked who it was. He answered that he was John. "I still don't know you," he said, "for that name is given to many." The one who knocked added, "I am John, the nephew of Sweyn the merchant." "He will absolutely not come in," said the wife of the tollkeeper, "because he is dead." The news that he had been submerged and died had already spread widely.[58] Her husband replied, "Whether he is dead or alive, from what he has said, he will come in." And when the door was opened, he fell inside as if he were dead, deprived of strength, sight, and hearing, such that he was not able to get a word from him. He was carried to his own home, and as the day went on he opened his eyes and spoke.

On that day, William, the king of the Scots,[59] was in that village. Struck by the novelty of such a miracle, he wished to witness this thing beyond belief himself and with his own eyes. However, since the purple does not pass into

---

[57] A cubit was the measure of a forearm. In modern terms, this means that the bridge was about a meter and a half above the water.
[58] Compare with Acts 12:13-17 for the story of Peter, who escaped from prison and knocked on the door of a house of friends. Some of those inside could not believe it was Peter knocking, saying it had to be an angel.
[59] King William I "the Lion" (1165-1214).

the accommodations of the humble, he sent the bishop of Glasgow and his archdeacon to investigate the truth.[60] They summoned the shipwrecked one, and under pain of excommunication they forbade him to say anything that would deviate from the truth and mislead the people. He told his story as we have told it about him, which he also told to us after a short time.

---

[60] Ingram (also spelled Ingelram) was bishop of Glasgow from 1164 to 1174. He is known for opening the tomb of Waltheof, the second abbot of Melrose, in June 1171, in order to inspect the body for incorruption: see George Joseph McFadden, "An Edition and Translation of the Life of Waldef, Abbot of Melrose by Jocelin of Furness" (Columbia University, unpublished PhD thesis, 1952), pp. 341–4.

Select Bibliography

Manuscript Sources

Cambridge, Trinity College MS B.14.37
Florence, Biblioteca Medicea Laurenziana, Conv. soppr. 230
Heidelberg, Universitäts-Bibliotheck, cod. Salem IX.30
Heiligenkreuz, Stiftsbibliothek Cod. Sancrucensis 209
Heiligenkreuz, Stiftsbibliothek Cod. Sancrucensis 213
Lisbon, Bibl. Nacional, cod. Alcobaça CCLXXXIX/172
Lisbon, Bibl. Nacional, cod. Alcobaça CCXC/143
London, British Library Arundel MS 68
London, British Library Egerton MS 2818
London, Lambeth Palace Library MS 135
Paderborn, Erzbischöfliche Akademische Bibliothek Theodoriana Ba 2
Paris, Bibl. Nationale Lat. MS 5320
Porto, Bibl. Públ. Mun., Cod. Santa Cruz 60
St. Gallen, Stiftsbibliothek, Cod. Sang. MS 580
Tuy, Archivo de la Cathedral de Tuy MS 1

PRINTED PRIMARY SOURCES

Cartae Baronum, ed. Neil Stacy, PR n. s. vol. LXII (Woodbridge, 2019)
Caviness, Madeline, *The Windows of Christ Church Cathedral, Canterbury*, Corpus Vitrearum Medii Aevi: Great Britain, Volume II (London, 1981)
Charters of the Redvers Family and the Earldom of Devon, 1090–1217, ed. Robert Bearman, Devon and Cornwall Record Society 37 (Exeter, 1994)
The Chronicle of Battle Abbey, ed. and trans. Eleanor Searle, OMT (Oxford, 1980)
The Chronicles of Peterborough Abbey, Volume Two: Robert of Swaffham and Walter of Whittlesey, ed. and trans. Edmund King (Northampton, 2022)
Cornog, W. H., "The Poems of Robert Partes," *Speculum* 12 (1937): 215–50
The Correspondence of Thomas Becket, Archbishop of Canterbury 1162–1170, ed. and trans. Anne J. Duggan, OMT, 2 vols. (Oxford, 2000)
Decretales Ineditae Saeculi XII, ed. and revised Stanley Chodorow and Charles Duggan, Monumenta Iuris Canonici Series B: Corpus Collectionum 4 (Vatican City, 1982)
Documents Illustrative of the Social and Economic History of the Danelaw, from Various Collections, ed. F. M. Stenton (London, 1920)
English Benedictine Libraries: The Shorter Catalogues, ed. Richard Sharpe, Corpus of British Medieval Library Catalogues 4 (London, 1996)
Epistolae Cantuarienses, ed. William Stubbs, *Chronicles and Memorials of the Reign of Richard I*, RS vol. 38:2 (London, 1865)

Farmer, Hugh, "The Vision of Orm," *AB* 75 (1957): 72–82

The Foundation History of the Abbeys of Byland and Jervaulx, ed. and trans. Janet Burton, Borthwick Texts and Studies 35 (York, 2006)

Gervase of Canterbury, *The Historical Works of Gervase of Canterbury*, ed. W. Stubbs, RS 73, 2 vols. (London 1879–80)

Gregory the Great, *Homilies on the Book of the Prophet Ezekiel*, trans. Theodosia Tomkinson (Etna, CA, 2008)

Guernes de Pont-Sainte-Maxence, *La Vie de Saint Thomas Becket: A Life of Thomas Becket in Verse*, trans. Ian Short (Toronto, 2013)

John of Forde, *The Life of Wulfric of Haselbury, Anchorite*, trans. Pauline Matarasso, Cistercian Fathers Series 79 (Collegeville, MN, 2011)

The Letters and Charters of Gilbert Foliot, ed. A. Morey and C. N. L. Brooke (Cambridge, 1967)

The Letters and Charters of Henry II, King of England 1154–1189, ed. Nicholas Vincent, OMT, 7 vols. (Oxford, 2022)

The Letters of John of Salisbury Volume II: The Later Letters (1163–1180), ed. W. J. Millor and C. N. L. Brooke (Oxford, 1979)

The Letters of Peter of Celle, ed. and trans. Julian Haseldine, OMT (Oxford, 2001)

Liber Eliensis: A History of the Isle of Ely, trans. Janet Fairweather (Woodbridge, 2005)

The Library of Peterborough Abbey, ed. Karsten Friis-Jensen and James M. W. Willoughby, Corpus of British Medieval Library Catalogues 8 (London, 2001)

Liturgies in Honour of Thomas Becket, trans. Kay Brainerd Slocum (Toronto, 2004)

The Lives of Thomas Becket, trans. Michael Staunton (Manchester, 2001)

Materials for the History of Thomas Becket, Archbishop of Canterbury, ed. J. C. Robertson and J. B. Sheppard, RS 67, 7 vols. (London, 1875–85)

McFadden, George Joseph, "An Edition and Translation of the Life of Waldef, Abbot of Melrose by Jocelin of Furness" (Columbia University, unpublished PhD thesis, 1952)

The Miracles of Our Lady of Rocamadour: Analysis and Translation, trans. Marcus Bull (Woodbridge, 1999)

Pepin, Ronald E., trans., *Anselm and Becket: Two Canterbury Saints' Lives by John of Salisbury* (Toronto, 2009)

"Quaedam miracula gloriosi martyris Thomae archiepiscopi Cantuariae," *AB* 20 (1901): 427–9.

Ralph de Diceto, *Ymagines Historiarum, Historical Works*, ed. W. Stubbs, 2 vols, RS 86 (London, 1876)

RB 1980: The Rule of St Benedict in Latin and English with Notes, ed. Timothy Fry, OSB (Collegeville, 1981)

Reames, Sherry, ed. and trans., "Liturgical Offices for the Cult of St Thomas Becket," in Thomas Head (ed.), *Medieval Hagiography: An Anthology* (New York, 2001), pp. 561–94

Reginald of Durham, *The Life and Miracles of Saint Godric, Hermit of Finchale*, ed. and trans. Margaret Coombe, OMT (Oxford, 2022)

Sulpicius Severus: The Complete Works, trans. Richard Goodrich (New York, 2015)

Thomas of Monmouth, *The Life and Passion of William of Norwich*, ed. and trans. Miri Rubin (London, 2014)

Thómas Saga Erkibyskups: A Life of Archbishop Thomas Becket, in Icelandic, ed. and trans. Eiríkr Magnússon, RS 65 (London, 1883).

Ward, Jennifer C., ed. and trans., *Women of the English Nobility and Gentry, 1066–1500* (Manchester, 1995)

William Thorne's Chronicle of Saint Augustine's Abbey Canterbury, trans. A. H. Davis (Oxford, 1934)

Secondary Works

Abbott, E. A., *St Thomas of Canterbury: His Death and Miracles* (London, 1898)

Adams, Robert, "The Rokeles: An Index for a 'Langland' Family History," in Andrew Cole and Andrew Galloway (eds.), *The Cambridge Companion to Piers Plowman* (Cambridge, 2014), pp. 85–96

Adler, Michael, *The Jews of Medieval England* (London, 1939)

Bailey, Anne E. "Reconsidering the Medieval Experience at the Shrine in High Medieval England," *Journal of Medieval History* 47.2 (2021): 203–29

Barlow, Frank, *Thomas Becket* (London, 1986)

Barnaby, James, *Religious Conflict at Canterbury Cathedral in the Late Twelfth Century: The Dispute between the Monks and the Archbishops, 1184–1200* (Woodbridge, 2024)

Barrau, Julie, *Bible, lettres et politique: L'Écriture au service des hommes à l'époque de Thomas Becket* (Paris, 2013)

Bartlett, Robert, *Trial by Fire and Water: The Medieval Judicial Ordeal* (Oxford, 1986)

Bartlett, Robert, *Why Can the Dead Do Such Great Things: Saints and Worshippers from the Martyrs to the Reformation* (Princeton, 2013)

Bearman, Robert, "Baldwin de Redvers: Some Aspects of a Baronial Career in the Reign of King Stephen," *ANS* 28 (1995): 19–46

Blurton, Heather, *Inventing William of Norwich: Thomas of Monmouth, Antisemitism, and Literary Culture, 1150–1200* (Philadelphia, 2022)

Bollerman, Karen and Cary J. Nederman, "John of Salisbury and Thomas Becket," in Christophe Grellard and Frédérique Lachaud (eds.), *A Companion to John of Salisbury* (Leiden, 2015), pp. 63–104

Bollermann, Karen and Cary J. Nederman, "Dirty Laundry: Thomas Becket's Hair Shirt and the Making of a Saint," in Clare Frances Monagle (ed.), *The Intellectual Dynamism of the High Middle Ages* (Amsterdam, 2022), pp. 131–46

Brenner, Elma, "Thomas Becket and Leprosy in Normandy," in Paul Webster and Marie-Pierre Gelin (eds.), *The Cult of Thomas Becket in the Plantagenet World, c.1170–c.1220* (Woodbridge, 2016), pp. 81–94

Brett, Martin, "The Church at Rochester, 604–1185," in Nigel Yates with the assistance of Paul A. Welsby (eds.), *Faith and Fabric: A History of Rochester Cathedral, 604–1994* (Woodbridge, 1996), pp. 1–28

Bull, Marcus, "Criticism of Henry II's Expedition to Ireland in William of Canterbury's Miracles of St Thomas Becket," *Journal of Medieval History* 33 (2007): 107–29

Caviness, Madeline, "A Panel of Thirteenth Century Stained Glass from Canterbury in America," *Antiquaries Journal* 45 (1965): 192–9

Caviness, Madeline, *The Early Stained Glass of Canterbury Cathedral* (Princeton, 1977)

Consolino, Franca Ela, "Gli spazi del meraviglioso nei miracoli di Tommaso Becket," in Franca Ela Consolino, Francesco Marzella, and Lucilla Spetia (eds.), *Aspetti del meraviglioso nelle letterature medievali* (Turnhout, 2016), pp. 47–58

Constable, Giles, *The Reformation of the Twelfth Century* (Cambridge, 1998)

Cragoe, Carol Davidson, "Reading and Rereading Gervase of Canterbury," *Journal of British Archaeology* 154 (2001): 40–53

Crouch, David, *The English Aristocracy 1070–1272: A Social Transformation* (New Haven, 2011)

de Beer, Lloyd and Naomi Speakman, *Thomas Becket: Murder and the Making of a Saint* (London, 2021)

Doherty, H. F., "The Murder of Gilbert the Forester," *Haskins Society Journal* 23 (2011): 155–204

Draper, Peter, "Recent Interpretations of the Late-12th-Century Rebuilding of the East End of Canterbury Cathedral and Its Historical Context," in A. Bovey (ed.), *Medieval Art, Architecture and Archaeology at Canterbury Cathedral*, British Archaeological Association Conference Transactions 35 (London, 2013), pp. 106–15

Du Boulay, F. R. H., *The Lordship of Canterbury: An Essay on Medieval Society* (London, 1966)

Duggan, Anne, "The Cult of St. Thomas Becket in the Thirteenth Century," in Meryl Jancey (ed.), *St. Thomas Cantilupe: Essays in His Honour* (Hereford, 1982), pp. 21–44

Duggan, Anne, "The Lyell Version of the *Quadrilogus* Life of St Thomas of Canterbury," *AB* 112 (1994): 105–38

Duggan, Anne, "The Lorvão Transcription of Benedict of Peterborough's *Liber Miraculorum Beati Thome*: Lisbon, Cod. Alcobaça CCXC/143," *Scriptorium* 51 (1997): 51–68

Duggan, Anne, "Aspects of Anglo-Portuguese Relations in the Twelfth Century. Manuscripts, Relics, Decretals and the Cult of St. Thomas Becket at Lorvão, Alcobaça and Tomar," *Portuguese Studies* 14 (1998): 1–19

Duggan, Anne, "Diplomacy, Status, and Conscience: Henry II's Penance for Becket's Murder," in Peter Herde, Karl Borchardt, and Enno Bünz (eds.), *Forschungen zur Reichs-, Papst- und Landesgeschichte: Peter Herde zum 65. Geburtstag von Freunden, Schülern und Kollegen dargebracht* (Stuttgart, 1998), vol. 1, 265–90

Duggan, Anne, "The Santa Cruz Transcription of Benedict of Peterborough's

Liber Miraculorum Beati Thome: Porto, BPM, Cod. Santa Cruz 60," *Mediaevalia. Textos e estudos* 20 (2001): 27–55

Duggan, Anne, *Thomas Becket* (London, 2004)

Duggan, Anne, "A Becket Office at Stavelot: London, British Library, Additional Ms 16964," in Anne J. Duggan, Joan Greatrex, and Brenda Bolton (eds.), *Omnia Disce: Medieval Studies in Memory of Leonard Boyle, O.P.* (Aldershot, 2005), pp. 161–82

Duggan, Anne, "*Alexander ille meus*: The Papacy of Alexander III," in Peter D. Clarke and Anne J. Duggan (eds.), *Pope Alexander III (1159–1181): The Art of Survival* (Farnham, 2012), pp. 13–49

Duggan, Anne, "Religious Networks in Action: The European Expansion of the Cult of St Thomas of Canterbury," in Jeremy Gregory and Hugh McLeod (eds.), *International Religious Networks* (Woodbridge, 2012), pp. 20–43

Duggan, Anne, "Becket is Dead! Long Live St Thomas," in Paul Webster and Marie-Pierre Gelin (eds.), *The Cult of Thomas Becket in the Plantagenet World, c.1170–c.1220* (Woodbridge, 2016), pp. 25–51

Dunning, Andrew N. J., "St Frideswide's Priory as a Centre of Learning in Early Oxford," *Mediaeval Studies* 80 (2018): 253–96

Fabiny, Tibor, *Figura and Fulfillment: Typology in the Bible, Art and Literature* (Eugene, OR, 2016)

Fergusson, Peter, "Architecture during the Rule of Abbot Benedict," in Ron Baxter, Jackie Hall, and Claudia Marx (eds.), *Peterborough and the Soke: Art, Architecture, and Archaeology*, British Archaeological Association Conference Transactions XLI (London, 2019), pp. 179–99

Finucane, Ronald, *Miracles and Pilgrims: Popular Beliefs in Medieval England* (London, 1977)

Foreville, Raymonde, "Les *Miracula S. Thomae Cantuariensis*," in *Actes du 97e Congrès National des Sociétés Savants, Nantes 1972* (Paris, 1979), 443–63

Gaposchkin, Cecilia M., *Invisible Weapons: Liturgy and the Making of Crusade Ideology* (Ithaca, 2017)

Gelin, Marie-Pierre, *"Lumen ad revelationem genium": Iconographie et liturgie à Christ Church, Canterbury, 1175–1220* (Turnhout, 2006)

Gordon, Stephen, "Medical Condition, Demon or Undead Corpse? Sleep Paralysis and the Nightmare in Medieval Europe," *Journal of the Social History of Medicine* 28:3 (2015): 425–44

Guy, John, *Thomas Becket: Warrior, Priest, Rebel: A Nine-Hundred-Year-Old Story Retold* (New York, 2012)

Harper-Bill, Christopher, "Bishop William Turbe and the Diocese of Norwich, 1146–1174," *ANS* 7 (1985): 142–60

Hayes, Dawn Marie, "Body as Champion of Church Authority and Sacred Place: The Murder of Thomas Becket," in Mark D. Meyerson, Daniel Tiery, and Oren Falk (eds.), *A Great Effusion of Blood? Interpreting Medieval Violence* (Toronto, 2004), pp. 190–215

Holden, Brock, *Lords of the Central Marches: English Aristocracy and Frontier Society, 1087–1265* (Oxford, 2008)

Hudson, John, *The Formation of English Common Law: Law and Society in*

England from the Norman Conquest to Magna Carta, 2nd edition (New York, 2018)

Hughes, Andrew, "The Story of O: A Variant in the Becket Office," in Maureen Epp and Brian E. Power (eds.), *The Sounds and Sights of Performance in Early Music: Essays in Honour of Timothy J. McGee* (Farnham, 2009), pp. 27–59

Hughes, Andrew, ed. by Kate Helson, *The Becket Offices: Paradigms for Liturgical Research* (Lions Bay, 2014)

Hughes, Christopher G., "Art and Exegesis," in Conrad Rudolph (ed.), *A Companion to Medieval Art: Romanesque and Gothic in Northern Europe* (Oxford, 2006), pp. 173–92

Hurlock, Kathryn, *Medieval Welsh Pilgrimage c.1100–1500* (New York, 2018)

Jenkins, John, "St Thomas Becket and Medieval London," *History* 105 (2020): 652–72

Jenkins, John, "Who Put the 'a' in 'Thomas a Becket'? The History of a Name from the Angevins to the 18th Century," *Open Library of Humanities* 9:1 (2023), doi: https://doi.org/10.16995/olh.9353

Johns, Susan M., *Noblewomen, Aristocracy and Power in the Twelfth-Century Anglo-Norman Realm* (Manchester, 2003)

Jordan, Alyce A., "The 'Water of Thomas Becket': Water as Medium, Metaphor, and Relic," in Cynthia Kosso and Anne Scott (eds.), *The Nature and Function of Water, Baths, Bathing, and Hygiene from Antiquity through the Renaissance* (Leiden, 2009), pp. 479–500

Joubert, Estelle, "New Music in the Office of Thomas Becket from the Diocese of Trier," *Plainsong and Medieval Music* 18:1 (2009): 33–60

Keats-Rohan, K. S. B., *Domesday People: A Prosopography of Persons Occurring in English Documents 1066–1166, I. Domesday Book* (Woodbridge, 1999)

Keats-Rohan, K. S. B., *Domesday Descendants: A Prosopography of Persons Occurring in English Documents 1066–1166, II: Pipe Rolls to* Cartae Baronum (Woodbridge, 2002)

Keenan, Hugh T. (ed.), *Typology and English Medieval Literature* (New York, 1992)

Kidson, Peter, "Gervase, Becket, and William of Sens," *Speculum* 68 (1993): 969–91

King, Edmund, "Benedict of Peterborough and the Cult of Thomas Becket," *Northamptonshire Past and Present* 9 (1996): 213–20

Koopmans, Rachel, *Wonderful to Relate: Miracle Stories and Miracle Collecting in High Medieval England* (Philadelphia, 2011)

Koopmans, Rachel, "Testimonial Letters in the Late-Twelfth Century Collections of Thomas Becket's Miracles," in David C. Mengel and Lisa Wolverton (eds.), *Christianity and Culture in the Middle Ages: Essays to Honor John Van Engen* (Notre Dame, 2014), pp. 168–201

Koopmans, Rachel, "Visions, Reliquaries, and the Image of 'Becket's Shrine' in the Miracle Windows of Canterbury Cathedral," *Gesta* 54:1 (2015): 37–57

Koopmans, Rachel, "Thomas Becket and the Royal Abbey of Reading," *The English Historical Review* 131:1 (2016): 1–30

Koopmans, Rachel, "Water Mixed with the Blood of Thomas: Contact Relic

Manufacture Pictured in Canterbury Cathedral's Stained Glass," *Journal of Medieval History* 42:5 (2016): 535–58

Koopmans, Rachel, "Pilgrimage Scenes in Newly Identified Medieval Glass at Canterbury Cathedral," *Burlington Magazine* 161 (issue no. 1398, September 2019): 708–15

Koopmans, Rachel, "Gifts of Becket's Clothing Made by the Monks of Christ Church, Canterbury," in Tom Nickson (ed.), *The Cult of Thomas Becket: Art, Relics, and Liturgy in Britain and Europe*, special issue of the *Journal of the British Archaeological Association* 173:1 (2020): 39–60

Koopmans, Rachel, "Benedict of Peterborough's Compositions for Thomas Becket: Passion, Miracles, Office," *Medium Ævum* 90:2 (2021): 247–74

Koopmans, Rachel, "The Smallest Matters: Vanishing Water, Missing Birds, Revived Animals, Recovered Coins, and Other Trifling Miracles in the Thomas Becket Collections," *Journal of Medieval History* 48:5 (2022): 587–606

Koopmans, Rachel, "Pilgrims at Becket's Tomb and Shrine: Stained Glass Portrayals at Canterbury Cathedral and St Mary's Church, Nettlestead, Kent," in Alyce A. Jordan and Kay Brainerd Slocum (eds.), *Images of Thomas Becket in the Middle Ages and Beyond: The Uses and Reception of a Celebrity Saint* (Woodbridge, 2025)

Krötzl, Christian and Sari Katajala-Peltomaa (eds.), *Miracles in Medieval Canonization Processes: Structures, Functions, and Methodologies* (Turnhout, 2018)

Lee, Jennifer, "Searching for Signs: Pilgrims' Identity and Experience Made Visible in the *Miracula Sancti Thomae Cantuariensis*," in Sarah Blick and Rita W. Tekippe (eds.), *Art and Architecture of Late Medieval Pilgrimage in Northern Europe and the British Isles* (Leiden, 2004), pp. 473–91

Lenz, Philipp, "Construire un recueil de miracles: Les Miracula Sancti Thomae Cantuariensis de Benoît de Peterborough," unpublished PhD thesis, University of Geneva, 2003

Lett, Didier, "Deux hagiographes, un saint et un roi: conformisme et créativité dans les deux recueils de *Miracula* de Thomas Becket," in Michel Zimmermann (ed.), *Auctor et Auctoritas: Invention and conformisme dans l'écriture médiévale*, actes du colloque de Saint-Quentin-en-Yvelines (14–16 Juin 1999) (Paris, 2001), pp. 201–16

Licence, Tom, *Hermits and Recluses in English Society, 950–1200* (Oxford, 2011)

Lynch, Tom, *Making Miracles in Medieval England* (London, 2023)

MacLehose, William F., "Fear, Fantasy and Sleep in Medieval Medicine," in Elena Carrera (ed.), *Emotions and Health, 1200–1700* (Leiden, 2013), pp. 67–94

Mason, A. J., *What Became of the Bones of St Thomas?* (Cambridge, 1920)

Mesley, Matthew, "*De Judaea, muta et surda*: Jewish Conversion in Gerald of Wales's *Life of Saint Remigius*," in Sarah Rees Jones and Sethina Watson (eds.), *Christians and Jews in Angevin England: The York Massacre of 1190, Narratives and Contexts* (York, 2013), pp. 238–49

Miller, Andrew M., "'Tails' of Masculinity: Knights, Clerics, and the Mutilation of Horses in Medieval England," *Speculum* 88:4 (2013): 958–95

Morey, Adrian, *Bartholomew of Exeter, Bishop and Canonist* (Cambridge, 1937)

Morey, Adrian and C. N. L. Brooke, *Gilbert Foliot and His Letters* (Cambridge, 1965)

Mortimer, Richard, "The Beginnings of the Honour of Clare," *ANS* 3 (1980): 119–41

Myking, Synnøve Midtbø, "Thomas Becket, Clairvaux, and Ringsted: Saintly Diversity and European Influences in a Twelfth-Century Fragmentary Legendary from Denmark," *Classica et Mediaevalia: Danish Journal of Philology and History* 72 (2023): 255–88

Oppitz-Trotman, Gesine, "Birds, Beasts and Becket: Falconry and Hawking in the Lives and Miracles of St Thomas Becket," in Peter Clarke and Tony Claydon (eds.), *God's Bounty? The Churches and the Natural World* (Woodbridge, 2010), pp. 78–88

Oppitz-Trotman, Gesine, "Penance, Mercy, and Saintly Authority in the Miracles of St Thomas Becket," in Peter Clarke and Tony Claydon (eds.), *Saints and Sanctity* (Woodbridge, 2011), pp. 136–47

Oppitz-Trotman, Gesine, "The Emperor's Robe: Thomas Becket and Angevin Political Culture," *ANS* 37 (2014): 205–19

Orme, Margaret, "A Reconstruction of Robert of Cricklade's *Vita et Miracula S. Thomae Cantuariensis*," *AB* 84 (1966): 379–98

Partner, Nancy, *Serious Entertainments: The Writing of History in Twelfth-Century England* (Chicago, 1977)

Pfaff, Richard W., *The Liturgy in Medieval England: A History* (Cambridge, 2009)

Pinner, Rebecca, *The Cult of St Edmund in Medieval East Anglia* (Woodbridge, 2015)

Powell, Hilary, "The 'Miracle of Childbirth': The Portrayal of Parturient Women in Medieval Miracle Narratives," *Social History of Medicine* 25.4 (2012): 795–811

Power, Daniel, *The Norman Frontier in the Twelfth and Early Thirteenth Centuries* (Cambridge, 2004)

Prudlo, Donald S., *Certain Sainthood: Canonization and the Origins of Papal Infallibility in the Medieval Church* (Ithaca, 2015)

Rawcliffe, Carole, *Leprosy in Medieval England* (Woodbridge, 2006)

Reilly, Lisa, *An Architectural History of Peterborough Cathedral* (Oxford, 1997)

Richardson, H. G., "The Schools of Northampton in the Twelfth Century," *English Historical Review* 56 (1941): 595–605

Roberts, Phyllis, *Thomas Becket in the Medieval Latin Preaching Tradition: An Inventory of Sermons about St Thomas Becket, c.1170–c.1400*, Instrumenta Patristica 25 (The Hague, 1992)

Salter, Ruth J., *Saints, Cure-Seekers and Miraculous Healing in Twelfth-Century England* (York, 2021)

Scammell, G. V., *Hugh du Puiset: Bishop of Durham* (Cambridge, 1956)

Schofield, John, "Saxon and Medieval Parish Churches in the City of London: A Review," *Transactions of the London and Middlesex Archaeological Society* 45 (1994): 23–146

Shoham-Steiner, Ephraim, "Jews and Healing at Medieval Saints' Shrines:

Participation, Polemics, and Shared Cultures," *Harvard Theological Review* 103:1 (2010) 111–29

Sigal, Pierre-André, "Naissance et premier développement d'un vinage exceptionnel: L'eau de saint Thomas," *Cahiers de civilisation médiévale* 44 (2001): 35–44

Slocum, Kay, *The Cult of Thomas Becket: History and Historiography through Eight Centuries* (London, 2019)

Smalley, Beryl, *The Study of the Bible in the Middle Ages* (Notre Dame, 1964)

Southern, R. W., *The Monks of Canterbury and the Murder of Archbishop Becket* (Oxford, 1985)

Springer, Rebecca, "Bartholomew of Exeter's Sermons and the Cultivation of Charity in Twelfth-Century Exeter," *Historical Research* 92 (May 2019): 267–87

Staunton, Michael, "Thomas Becket's Conversion," *ANS 21* (1999): 193–211

Staunton, Michael, *Thomas Becket and His Biographers* (Woodbridge, 2006)

Staunton, Michael, "The *Lives* of Thomas Becket and the Church of Canterbury," in Paul Dalton, Charles Insley, and Louise J. Wilkinson (eds.), *Cathedrals, Communities and Conflict in the Anglo-Norman World* (Woodbridge, 2011), pp. 169–86

Staunton, Michael, "John of Salisbury and the Church of Canterbury," in Christophe Grellard and Frédérique Lachaud (eds.), *Jean de Salisbury, nouvelles lectures, nouveaux enjeux* (Florence, 2018), pp. 185–207

Strickland, Matthew, *Henry the Young King, 1155–1183* (New Haven, 2016)

Thomas, Hugh M., *Vassals, Heiresses, Crusaders, and Thugs: The Gentry of Angevin Yorkshire, 1154–1216* (Philadelphia, 2003)

Thomas, Hugh M., "Miracle Stories and the Violence of King Stephen's Reign," *Haskins Society Journal* 13 (2004 for 1999): 111–24

Thomas, Hugh M., "Shame, Masculinity, and the Death of Thomas Becket," *Speculum* 87:4 (October 2012): 1050–88

Thomson, R. M., *Catalogue of the Manuscripts of Lincoln Cathedral Library* (Cambridge, 1989)

Trenery, Claire, "Insane Innocents: Mad Children in Benedict of Peterborough's *Miracula Sancti Thomae Cantuariensis*," *Family & Community History* 18:2 (2015): 139–55

Trenery, Claire, *Madness, Medicine and Miracle in Twelfth-Century England* (New York, 2019)

Urry, William, *Canterbury under the Angevin Kings* (London, 1967)

Urry, William, "Some Notes on the Two Resting Places of St Thomas Becket at Canterbury," in Raymonde Foreville (ed.), *Thomas Becket: Actes du colloque international de Sédières 19–24 août 1973* (Paris, 1975), pp. 195–209

Uruszczak, Waclaw, "Répercussions de la mort de Thomas Becket en Pologne (XIIe–XIIIe siècles)," in Raymonde Foreville (ed.), *Thomas Becket: Actes du colloque international de Sédières 19–24 août 1973* (Paris, 1975), pp. 115–25

van Eickels, Klaus, "Gendered Violence: Castration and Blinding as Punishment for Treason in Normandy and Anglo-Norman England," *Gender & History* 16.3 (2004): 588–602 van Liere, Frans, "The Bible in Worship and Preaching," in Frans van Liere (ed.), *An Introduction to the Medieval Bible* (Cambridge, 2014), pp. 208–36

Vincent, Nicholas, "The Murderers of Thomas Becket," in N. Fryde and D. Reitz (eds.), *Bischofsmord im Mittelalter: Murder of Bishops* (Göttingen, 2003), pp. 211–72

Vincent, Nicholas, "William of Canterbury and Benedict of Peterborough: The Manuscripts, Date and Context of the Becket Miracle Collections," in Edina Bozóky (ed.), *Hagiographie, idéologie et politique au Moyen Âge en Occident: Actes du colloque international du Centre d'Études supérieures de Civilisatione médiévale de Poitiers 11–14 septembre 2008* (Turnhout, 2012), pp. 347–88

Vollrath, Hanna, "Was Thomas Becket Chaste?" *ANS* 27 (2004): 198–209

Walberg, Emmanuel, "Date de la composition des recueils de *Miracula Sancti Thomae Cantuariensis*," *Le Moyen Âge* 22 (1920): 259–74

Waltke, Bruce K., and James M. Houston with Erika Moore, "Psalm 51: 'The Psalm of All Psalms' in Penitential Devotion," in idem, *The Psalms as Christian Worship: An Historical Commentary* (Grand Rapids, MI, 2010), pp. 446–83

Ward, Benedicta, *Miracles and the Medieval Mind: Theory, Record, and Event* (Philadelphia, revised edition 1987)

Ward, Jennifer, "Fashions in Monastic Endowment: The Foundations of the Clare Family, 1066–1314," *Journal of Ecclesiastical History* 32:4 (1981): 427–51

Ward, Jennifer, "Royal Service and Reward: The Clare Family and the Crown," *ANS* 9 (1989): 261–78

Wardrop, Joan, *Fountains Abbey and Its Benefactors: 1132–1300* (Kalamazoo, 1987)

Watkins, Carl, "Sin, Penance and Purgatory in the Anglo-Norman Realm: The Evidence of Visions and Ghost Stories," *Past and Present* 175 (2002): 3–33

Watson, Sethina, "City as Charter: Charity and the Lordship of English Towns, 1170–1250," in Caroline Goodson, Anne Elisabeth Lester, and Carol Symes (eds.), *Cities, Texts and Social Networks, 400–1500: Experiences and Perceptions of Medieval Urban Space* (Farnham, 2010), pp. 235–62

Waugh, Scott L., *The Lordship of England: Royal Wardships and Marriages in English Society and Politics, 1217–1327* (Princeton, 1988)

Webb, Diana, "The Saint of Newington: Who Was Robert le Bouser?" *Archaeologia Cantiana* 119 (1999): 173–87

Wilkinson, Louise, *Women in Thirteenth-Century Lincolnshire* (Woodbridge, 2013)

Wilkinson, Louise, "'Is Still Not the Blood of the Blessed Martyr Thomas Fully Avenged?': Thomas Becket's Cult at Canterbury under Henry III and Edward I," *History* 105 (2020): 673–90

Williams-Jones, Keith, "Thomas Becket and Wales," *Welsh History Review* 5 (1971): 350–65

Wilson, Louise Elizabeth, "Writing Miracle Collections," in Sari Katajala-Peltomaa, Jenni Kuuliala, and Iona McCleery (eds.), *A Companion to Medieval Miracle Collections* (Leiden, 2021), 15–35

Winter, David, "Becket and the Wolves: Imagining the Lupine Welsh in a Thirteenth-Century Latin Preaching Exemplum from Llanthony Secunda Priory," in Tristan Sharp with Isabelle Cochelin, Greti Dinkova-Bruun, Abigail Firey, and Giulio Silano (eds.), *From Learning to Love: Schools, Law, and Pastoral Care in the Middle Ages, Essays in Honour of Joseph W. Goering* (Toronto, 2017), pp. 590–612

Yarrow, Simon, *Saints and Their Communities: Miracle Stories in Twelfth-Century England* (Oxford, 2005)

Index of Biblical Allusions

OLD TESTAMENT

Genesis [*Gn*]
1:4	Prologue, 78
1:9–10	IV.74, 283
4:1–16	I.2, 84
4:10	I.2, 84
18:27	IV.1, 221
25:25–34	Prologue, 79
27:38–9	III.77, 214
32:22–32	II.25, 128

Exodus [*Ex*]
34:14	Prologue, 79

Leviticus [*Lv*]
10:1–2	III.1, 169

Numbers [*Nm*]
11:1–3	III.1, 169
16:35	III.1, 169

Deuteronomy [*Dt*]
5:15	I.2, 84

Joshua [*Jo*]
15:14–19	II.6, 116

Judges [*Jgs*]
6:34	II.42, 140
7:16–22	Prologue, 78

1 Samuel [*1 Sm*]
2:6	IV.94, 295
2:10	Prologue, 77
5:6	II.66, 157
13:14	Prologue, 79
16:13	II.42, 140
45:4	Prologue, 79

1 Kings [*1 Kgs*]
17:13–16	II.6, 116

2 Kings [*2 Kgs*]
1:10–12	III.1, 169–70
4:1–7	I.21, 106; II.7, 117
5:1–14	IV.4, 232

Tobit [*Tb*]
4:12	I.1, 84
5:13	I.6, 90
5:23	Prologue, 79

Esther [*Est*]
13:17	Prologue, 76

Job [*Jb*]
2:7	Passion, 61
5:13	IV.2, 228
30:31	Prologue, 76
36:5	IV.94, 293; Will 14, 342–3

Psalms [*Ps*]
6:4	I.7, 92
6:10	III.37, 189
8:6	I.3, 86; II.25, 129
9:22	I.18, 103
20:3	I.19, 105
30:10	I.8, 93
31:5	Add 6, 299
33:16	III.2, 171
36:35	Add 9, 304
37:15	III.16, 177
38:11	II.25, 129
39:3	III.7, 173
39:4	III.7, 173
43:4	I.2, 84
44:3	I.4, 86
44:10	Prologue, 77
47:9	IV.4, 230
50	I.6, 89
50:11	III.59, 203
54:18	II.59, 152
58:12	II.26, 130
59:14	II.43, 141
60:4	I.7, 92
63:4	II.43, 141
68:16	II.68, 159; Add 8, 302
68:21	Prologue, 76
69:3	II.68, 159
71:18	II.6, 117
72:4	II.66, 157
72:9	Will 1, 324
72:28	II.23, 127

INDEX OF BIBLICAL ALLUSIONS

75:6	Passion, 65		5:25	IV.76, 284
75:12	II.62, 154		9:2	Prologue, 78
77:9	Prologue, 79		9:12	II.26, 130; II.42, 141
77:57	Prologue, 79		13:12	IV.38, 253
77:62	II.27, 131		31:9	III.2, 171
77:71	Prologue, 79		35:10	IV.94, 295
80:10	Prologue, 79		43:25	Passion, 74
80:11	Prologue, 80		46:8	Prologue, 79
85:9	I.2, 85		53:2	Add 6, 299
88:22–3	Will 17, 350		53:5	Will 10, 339
88:33–4	Add 6, 299		58:9	II.11, 120
99:3	Prologue, 79		60:14	III.64, 209
99:4	III.38, 190		61:1	II.42, 140
101:14	II.27, 132; II.53, 149		66:13	I.6, 89
105:2	IV.72, 281			
106:24	Add 8, 303			

Jeremiah [Jer]

17:5	II.66, 157
26:3	Prologue, 78
31:22	Add 7, 299
32:21	I.2, 84

106:29	III.20, 180
106:42	IV.72, 281
107:6	I.12, 97
107:13	II.23, 127
113:13	III.12, 176
115:18–19	II.62, 154
117:12	I.18, 103
117:24	II.1, 113–14
118:14	I.23, 108
120:4	II.26, 130
131:4	I.2, 84
134:6	Add 8, 303
134:7	II.69, 160
144:18	II.46, 143
146:5	II.28, 132

Lamentations [Lam]

1:1–2	Prologue, 76–7
1:2	IV.2, 225
1:4	Prologue, 77
1:12	IV.32, 249
2:6	Prologue, 77
3:41	II.33, 136
5:3	Prologue, 76
5:15	Prologue, 76
5:16	Prologue, 76

Proverbs [Prv]

1:17	Passion, 64
15:18	Passion, 64
23:14	Add 6, 299
24:16	III.20, 180
25:27	IV.1, 221

Ezekiel [Ez]

11:5	II.42, 140
18:20	II.17, 122
20:33	I.2, 84

Ecclesiastes [Eccl]

4:10	Will 18, 352

Daniel [Dn]

7:13	I.1, 83
14:27	Prologue, 79

Song of Solomon [Sg]

5:10	I.1, 83

Jonah [Jon]

4:6	Will 17, 350

Wisdom [Ws]

3:6	I.18, 103
4:14	I.4, 88
10:13	Add 8, 302
18:14	IV.6, 233

Micah [Mi]

4:2	IV.72, 281

Zechariah [Zec]

13:1	II.6, 116

Sirach (Ecclesiasticus) [Sir]

22:6	Prologue, 76
39:19–20	II.6, 117

Malachi [Mal]

3:3	I.18, 103

1 Maccabees [1 Mac]

3:6	Prologue, 77

Isaiah [Is]

2:3	IV.72, 281
3:14–15	II.27, 131

2 Maccabees [2 Mac]

10:38	Prologue, 77

NEW TESTAMENT

Matthew [Mt]

5:14	III.1, 170
5:15	Prologue, 78; III.1, 170
5:16	I.1, 83
5:46–7	III.17, 177
6:2	I.6, 90
6:33	III.53, 200
8:23–7	I.6, 90; I.15, 102
8:27	II.69, 160
9:6	IV.28, 247; IV.59, 267
10:27	I.6, 90
11:5	Prologue, 80; IV.4, 231
11:17	Prologue, 76
13:15	IV.14, 240
13:46	IV.73, 282
14:22–36	Add 9, 304; Will 4, 329
14:66–72	III.64, 207
15:22–8	II.46, 143
15:28	I.8, 93
16:24	Passion, 68
23:5	I.6, 90
25:14–30	II.6, 116
25:29	I.18, 105
26:6–13	I.7, 92
26:53	Passion, 75
26:55	Passion, 70
27:35	Passion, 71
27:38	III.64, 208
27:39	Passion, 71
27:43	Passion, 71
27:52–3	I.14, 100
27:66	II.29, 133

Mark [Mk]

2:11	IV.28, 147; IV.59, 267
4:21	III.1, 170
4:35–41	I.6, 90; I.15, 102
6:45–56	Add 9, 304; Will 4, 329
7:35	III.42, 193
14:3–9	I.7, 90
15:24	Passion, 71
15:27	III.64, 208
26:69–75	III.64, 207

Luke [Lk]

1:37	IV.68, 279
1:48–9	Prologue, 77
1:58	II.59, 152
1:63	Add 9, 303
1:66	Prologue, 79
1:68–9	III.26, 184; III.27, 184
1:78	Prologue, 77
1:79	I.7, 92
2:1	I.12, 97
2:5–6	IV.16, 241
2:48	IV.88, 291
4:18	II.42, 140
4:27	IV.4, 232
5:14	Add 6, 299
5:17	II.33, 135
5:24	IV.28, 247
5:26	I.6, 90; IV.88, 291
6:40	I.12, 97
7:22	IV.4, 231
7:36–50	I.7, 92
8:4–18	Prologue, 77
8:13	Passion, 68
8:16–18	III.1, 170
8:22–5	I.6, 90; I.15, 102
10:7	Will 15, 344
10:30	IV.2, 225
11:15	II.43, 141
11:33–6	III.1, 170
12:49	III.1, 170
13:16	II.8, 118
13:17	II.10, 119
14:16	IV.17, 242
15:8–9	IV.32, 249
15:24	IV.14, 240
16:8	III.1, 170
17:12–17	II.34, 137
17:17–18	III.46, 196
17:18	IV.73, 282
18:43	II.9, 119
19:6	IV.2, 225
19:12–28	II.6, 116
22:60–1	III.64, 207
23:32–43	III.64, 208
23:34	Passion
23:48	Prologue, 78
24:6	I.1, 83

John [Jn]

1:7	Add 7, 301
2:11	I.8, 93
2:24	Passion, 62
4:22	Prologue, 79
4:50	I.12, 96
4:53	IV.76, 285
5:1	II.33, 135
5:2–17	II.6, 116
5:3	II.33, 135
5:8	II.38, 138; IV.59, 267
5:14	IV.3, 230
5:15	II.55, 151
6:16–21	Add 9, 304; Will 4, 329
7:12–13	I.12, 97
9:3	II.25, 129
9:5	I.7, 92
9:21	IV.84, 288
9:32	II.76, 162
10:12–13	Prologue, 77

INDEX OF BIBLICAL ALLUSIONS 369

12:3	I.14, 100
12:18	II.59, 152; IV.14, 240
12:24–6	Prologue, 77
12:36	III.1, 170
13:30	Add 9, 304
14:7	III.1, 170
14:15	III.4, 172
14:26	III.4, 172
15:5	I.23, 107
15:26	III.4, 172
16:7	III.4, 172
16:21	I.16, 102
18:4	Passion, 69
18:5	Passion, 69
18:9	Passion, 69
18:16–27	III.64, 207
18:36	Passion, 74
19:23–4	Passion, 71
21:1	I.10, 94
21:14	I.10, 95
21:23	IV.2, 226
21:24	IV.11, 236

Acts of the Apostles [Acts]

1:11	I.3, 85
2:1–4	III.1, 1678
2:2	II.26, 131
3:9–10	II.7, 117
4:20	I.12, 97
5:29	I.12, 97
7:34	II.60, 153
7:54–60	I.4, 87
9:3	III.1, 169
10:34–5	Will 14, 342
10:41	I.8, 93
12:3–19	Will 17, 350
27:27–28:5	Will 17, 350

Romans [Rom]

3:23	III.20, 180
8:3–9	I.13, 98
8:11	III.1, 170
8:28	Will 7, 334
10:18	I.2, 85
11:4	Prologue, 79
11:33	IV.64, 274
12:20	III.64, 208
14:8	IV.54, 264

1 Corinthians [1 Cor]

1:25	Will 15, 345
3:16	III.1, 170
10:13	Prologue, 77
13:1	IV.1, 221

2 Corinthians [2 Cor]

2:17	Prologue, 77
6:7	III.11, 175

Galatians [Gal]

1:15	II.25, 129

Ephesians [Eph]

5:8	III.1, 170

Colossians [Col]

1:5	III.11, 175

1 Thessalonians [1 Thes]

5:5	III.1, 170

Hebrews [Heb]

2:10	IV.2, 227
3:3	I.3, 86
4:12	I.1, 84
9:12	I.12, 96
12:6	II.44, 142

James [Jas]

1:5	III.11, 175
1:18	III.11, 175
4:8	III.31, 186

1 Peter [1 Pt]

1:19	III.19, 179

1 John [1 Jn]

1:18	III.20, 180
5:9	Add 7, 301

Revelation (Apocalypse) [Rv]

1:18	I.1, 83
3:7	II.33, 136
4:1–11	I.4, 86
7:14	Prologue, 78; III.18, 179; IV.2, 226
12:1 1	Prologue, 78; III.18, 179
14:1 3	Prologue, 76

General Index

Abingdon, abbey of 283–4, 308–9, 339–40
abscesses 121, 147–9, 199–200, 238–9
accidents
    ear of rye ingested 251–2
    stone falls in ear 245
    wall falls on infant 290–1, 341–2
    worker buried 299–30, 346–8
    see also drowning; sea travel; suffocation
Ada, inhabitant of London 161
Adam *de Hadlega* 154–5
Aeliza, wife of Alan of Ratling 197, 304
Agnes, inhabitant of Canterbury 122–3
Agnes, inhabitant of Cornwall, widow of William 286
Ailmer, inhabitant of Canterbury 173
Ailred, sailor from Exeter 257
Ailwin, sailor from Bristol 256
Albert, papal legate 20–2, 51
Albinus, abbot of Darley 26, 235–6, 305
Albreda, wife of Eustace of Malling 172–3
alcohol and drunkenness 65, 114, 222, 275, 291–2, 336, 344
    acting as if drunk 285
Aldida, inhabitant of Staffordshire 211
Alditha, inhabitant of Worth 102
ale-making, miracle involving 291–2
Alelm, reveler at St. Omer 242
Alexander III, pope (1159-1181) 2, 20–2, 46, 50–1, 63–4, 78–80, 100
    canonization of Becket 2, 20–2, 47, 50–1, 227
    excommunications 60, 63–4, 100 n.52, 305, 314–16
    legates of 20–2, 47, 51
    papal schism 21, 51, 78–80
    relationship with Henry II 21, 47
Alexander, son of Hugh de Bodebi, knight 29, 287, 310
Aliza, wife of the fisherman Martin of Leicester 250
Aliza of Northampton, wife of the tanner Roger 213–14
alms, given to the poor 72, 102, 160, 178, 227, 251, 253–5
Alvida, daughter of Edith 188

Amalric, from region of Thérouanne and Ponthieu 245–6
ampullas 103–5, 105–6, 181–2, 182–3, 183, 233, 235–8, 280, 289, 291
    manufacture of 182
    string holding ampulla effects miracle 291
    see also Becket, blood of; water relic
anchors, miracles involving 257–8, 330
Anfrid of Ferring, knight 241–2, 305
animals
    barking dogs silenced 266
    hawk returned 202
    horse's eye healed 190–1
    worms expelled 122–3, 153
Anselm, monk of Reading 338–9
Anselm, priest of St. Swithuns, London 156–7, 338–40
Ansfreda, daughter of Hubert of Canterbury 152
Ansfrid, son of Edwin of Dover 135–6
aqueduct construction 299–301, 346
arm pain 94–5, 119, 127–8, 152, 160, 259
Augustine, monk of Reading 290, 340
Avisa of Goshall, daughter of Ordgar the skinner 176–7
Aziria, wife of knight William of Earley 149–50, 306

bakers, miracles concerning 114–15, 232–3, 248
Baldwin of Forde, archbishop of Canterbury 58
Baldwin, inhabitant of Parndon 234–5
Bartholomew, bishop of Exeter 84, 306
baths, at city of Bath 281–2, 339
Beatrice, daughter of William of Ramsholt 1, 198–9
Beatrice, pauper of Woodstock 24–5, 186–7
Becket, Gilbert, father of St. Thomas Becket 7–8, 258
Becket, Thomas, St., archbishop of Canterbury
    as archbishop of Canterbury 8–11
    as provost of Beverley 142, 324

blood of   12–13, 16–18, 49, 56–7, 70–3, 76, 78, 85, 96–7, 102–8, 114–15, 118, 120–1, 123, 135, 144, 162, 173, 179, 194, 235–8, 248, 250, 252, 262, 274, 280–2, 294, 297, 299, 332, 344, 347
  collected from martyrdom site   72
  cloth stained with   72, 96, 103, 114–15, 281
  miracles of multiplication or disappearance   102–6
  mixed with water (beginning of practice)   16–18, 96–7, 107
  pilgrims anointed with   108–9, 115, 118, 120, 144, 162, 194, 250, 281
  seen in visions   50, 178–9, 252, 262
  sent to St. John's Abbey, Colchester   104–5
  track of on face after martyrdom   12, 72, 252, 262
  see also water relic
body of   12–13, 70–3, 116, 130–4, 175, 234–5, 266
  hammer and axe found underneath   72
  temporary translation of   130–3
  threats to carry off or destroy   73, 130–1, 133
  track of blood on face   12, 72, 252, 262
brains of   56, 70, 85 n.8
burial of   13, 15, 73
canonization of   2, 20, 21–2, 47, 50–1, 227 n.9
clothing of   8, 57, 72–4, 85, 100, 105–6, 138, 152
  belt, worn during martyrdom   22, 138
  cloak, worn during martyrdom   70, 72–3, 100, 105–6
  given to the poor after martyrdom   13, 72, 105–6, 152
  glove   203
  hairshirt   13, 73–4, 191, 204, 208, 242–3, 294–5, 344–5
  outer garment, worn during martyrdom   72–3, 152
  shirt   57
  slipper   139
  stole   152
  surplice   57
  vestments   73, 83, 150, 191, 252
compared to Abel (biblical figure)   84–5
compared to the apostles   87–8, 168, 346
compared to Christ   11–12, 17, 37–40, 45–6, 48–9, 59, 70–2, 93, 97, 168–70, 238, 274, 280
compared to St Martin of Tours   170, 266
confrontation with knights in archbishop's palace   60–7
cult of
  Becket as doctor of the sick   153, 154, 182, 201, 248
  Becket better than other saints and martyrs   80, 87–8, 232
  Becket seen walking on water   256–7, 329
  period of persecution   14–18, 83–4, 92, 97, 100, 102, 141, 169–70
  slow beginning, "first days of miracles"   14–18, 46, 90, 179, 181, 208
  see also ampullas; Becket, blood of; Becket, clothing of; Becket, tomb of; glass vessels; candles; coins; confession of sins; crosses; invocation of Becket's name; measurement; miracles; pilgrimage to Canterbury; pyxes; offerings; water relic
death of   10–13, 67–71, 74–5, 169
dispute with Henry II   8–9, 14, 37, 61–7, 224 n.6
dust of bed, in London, drunk with water   151
early life   7–8
enemies of   25, 61, 69–70, 97, 100, 104, 130–1, 133, 141, 169, 177, 208–9, 228
exile of   9, 10, 13, 69, 98, 105, 159, 208, 345
foreknowledge of death   69, 74
ill in Kent at house of Turstan of Croydon   275, 336
liturgical Office of   4, 51–5, 85 n.8, 89 n.21, 91 n.26, 172 n.14, 222 n.3, 237 n.32
murder of, *see* death of
relationship with Christ Church monks   8–9
tomb of   15–16, 90, 95, 130, 133–5
  altar next to   180
  candles on   168–9
  confession before approaching   175; *see* confession of sins
  construction of   15–16, 130, 133–5
  crack in   282
  monks sitting or observing at   101, 169, 174–5, 180–1, 256, 267
  night-time vigils at   96, 121, 130, 143, 185–7

372 GENERAL INDEX

openings in   133–5
pilgrims allowed access to   15–16, 90, 116–17
pilgrims sleeping or resting head on   121–2, 249
Bedford, Augustinian priory of   224, 261
Bedford, burgesses of   228, 325
Belet, William, knight of Enborne, Berkshire   48–9, 94–5, 320
bells, ringing to announce a miracle   214, 227
Benedict of Peterborough, hagiographer
  background and entry into Christ Church   6–7
  career as prior of Christ Church and abbot of Peterborough, 54–8
  composition of the liturgical Office for Becket   4, 51–4
  composition of the *Miracles*   18–20, 22–54, 221, 323–4
  composition of the *Passion*   10–13, 49–50, 54
  methods of collecting miracles   2, 5, 18–20, 22–8
  and Henry II, king of England   55–6
  and Richard I, king of England   7
  prejudice against Jews   59, 97, 125, 162
  present in Canterbury on day Becket killed   1, 11
  silences barking dogs in Becket's name   266
  vision of Becket   15, 83–4
  writing style and ability   3–4, 5, 37–8, 59
Bertha of Gloucester (Bertha of Hereford)   91, 306
Bertha, widow of Elias Giffard   211, 306–7
blacksmiths, miracles involving   120, 279
blinding as judicial punishment   80, 224–7, 288–9, 327
blinding as miraculous punishment   249–50, 250, 250–1, 251
blindness and eye problems   92–3, 95–6, 115, 118–19, 120, 122, 134–5, 135–6, 136–7, 137, 138, 152, 162, 174, 176, 186–7, 188, 193, 194–5, 195–6, 196, 205–6, 209, 210, 211, 213, 224–7, 232, 248, 249, 249–50, 250, 250–1, 251, 260, 265, 272, 288–9, 298, 327
  blind from birth   162, 195–6, 196, 210, 265
  testing vision   135, 162, 176, 195–6, 196, 226–7, 248, 265, 327
  "the blind of St. Thomas"   251
blisters, miracles concerning   147, 149–50, 162, 195, 206, 261
blood, *see* Becket, blood of; flux; menstrual flow

breathing, *see* suffocation and breathing problems
Brian de Insula, provost   138, 307
Brithiva, inhabitant of Canterbury   48, 95–6
Byland, abbey of   204

cancer   192, 274–7, 335–7
candles
  lit candles seen in spot Becket confirmed children   215
  measuring for   120, 143–4, 153–4, 198, 223, 241, 268–9, 269–70, 298, 303, 326, 351
  miracles of relighting in Canterbury Cathedral at Pentecost   168–72
  miraculously relit candles preserved, parts given to petitioners   171
  see also offerings, candles
Canterbury Cathedral   22–3, 57–8
  altar of Virgin Mary   16, 130, 132
  marble pavement of   173
  martyrdom site   57, 70–2, 135, 137, 139, 172, 173, 347
  opening of crypt to pilgrims   15–16, 96 n.43, 116–17
  pilgrims seeing from afar   184, 273
  stained glass windows portraying Becket's miracles   37 n.88, 57, 58 n.129, 61 n.5, 72–3 n.29, 91 n.29, 96 n.41, 99 n.50, 107 n.71, 108 n.75, 117 n.14, 127 nn.27–8, 133 n.36, 182 n.26, 204 n.65, 210 n.81, 214 n.89, 244 n.44, 268 n.83, 277 n.99, 281 n.106, 285 n.119, 290 n.129, 293 n.136, 303 n.16
  suspension of services due to desecration by Becket's murder   14, 47, 76–7, 93 n.32, 113, 116, 306
  sweet smell emanating from   121, 190
  visions regarding   85–6, 88–9, 130–1
  see also Becket, Thomas, St., tomb of
Canterbury, city of
  Flemish citizens of   133
  hearths lit with fire from miraculously relit candles   171
  inns and lodging in   96, 102–3, 126, 141, 148, 172, 178, 189
  Jewish citizen of   125–6
  prayer facing towards   234
  prophecies about   90–1
  western suburb of   161
castration, judicial punishment   80, 221–9, 325–7
Cecilia, daughter of Jordan of Plumstock   26 n.75, 274–7, 324, 334–7

cheese and dairy products, miracles involving 120, 145–6, 198–9, 237 n.32, 301, 347, 349
children, at play 106, 114, 198, 222, 245, 252, 268–9, 269, 297–8, 326, 353
children, confirmation of by Becket and miracles where he stood 208–9, 215
children, miracles concerning 29, 107–8, 121–2, 139–40, 144, 151, 153, 161–3, 171–2, 175, 187, 198–9, 201, 210, 213–14, 234, 242–3, 245, 249, 251, 265, 268–70, 277–8, 283–4, 287, 293–5, 297–8, 337–8, 341–4
children, resurrections of 270–4, 277–8, 293–5, 333–4, 334–7, 337–8, 342–4
Christ Church, Canterbury, Benedictine monks 6–7
  accused of using diabolical arts 16, 141
  grief at Becket's death 14, 73–4, 76–7, 89–90, 113
  petitions for Becket's canonization 20–2, 50–1
  relationship with Becket 6–11, 13, 68–9, 73–4, 76–7
  servants of 114–15, 169, 303–4
  visions of 83–4, 88–90, 130–1
  witnessing miracles at Becket's tomb 22, 90, 118–19, 127, 133–4, 174, 188, 249, 279
  see also Benedict of Peterborough; Gervase of Canterbury; Odo, prior of Christ Church; Ralph, monk of Christ Church; Richard, cellarer of Christ Church; Richard of Dover, archbishop of Canterbury; Robert, sacrist of Christ Church; Roger, monk of Christ Church; William, cellarer of Christ Church; William of Canterbury
coins, miracles involving 34, 36, 196, 200–1, 201, 202, 253, 253–4, 254–5, 256, 271
coin-bending, cultic practice of 196, 271
confession of sins 124, 143, 154, 156, 175, 194, 203, 207, 223, 225, 227–8, 249–50, 250, 292, 325–6, 341
Constance, nun of Stixwould 29, 202–3, 316
constipation 146, 159, 280
contraction
  of body/general 171–2
  of feet, legs, and/or toes 131–2, 136–7, 163, 213–14, 247
  of hands, arms, and/or fingers 136, 205, 175, 247, 279, 280

  of nerves or sinews 115, 117, 123, 131–2, 135, 175, 176–7, 185, 245, 275
  of viscera 292
Corbie, abbey of 288–9
crosses
  branding arm with 223, 326
  carried before Becket 68
  commemorating Becket's footsteps, miracles at 207–15
  Invention of the Cross (feast day) 38, 47, 135–6
  making sign of the 148, 160, 204, 206, 225, 327
  offerings at tomb of (intended for St. James) 159
  praying in shape of 282
Curbaran, shoemaker of Dover 200–1
cures, see miracles
curses, illness resulting from 131, 212, 251, 325
de Broc family 9–10, 15, 46, 65, 67–8, 100, 103, 177–8, 314–16
deafness and hearing problems 29, 80, 121, 135–6, 177, 189, 287, 331
  stone stuck inside ear 245
  testing hearing 189, 287
death and dying, miracles concerning
  good death as a miracle 156–7, 157–8
  near-death recoveries 114, 119, 143, 196, 197, 199–200, 204, 239–41, 241–2, 242–3, 244, 251–2, 259–60, 263–4, 280, 286–7, 289–90, 297, 340–1
  recoveries or rescue of people thought dead 234, 268–70, 274–7, 299–301, 303–4, 346–8, 352, 352–4
  resurrection of people who had died 270–4, 277–8, 293–5, 333–4, 334–7, 337–8, 342–4
  spirit (supposed) of a dead man 304, 353
  womb as sepulchre for dead fetus 241
  see also, Becket - death of
death and dying, ritual practices concerning 119, 140, 143, 156–8, 199–200, 204, 234, 239–40, 270–1, 275–7, 278, 280, 294, 300–1, 333, 335, 337, 341, 343–4, 347–8
demons and evil spirits, miracles involving 98–9, 113, 123, 125 n.22, 134, 181, 252, 289–90, 301–2, 340–1, 349–51
diarrhea 146, 245, 297–8, see also flux
dining 96, 145–6, 189, 205, 242, 297–8, 331
doctors 96, 98, 101, 127, 128–9, 145, 153, 155, 157, 184, 202, 204, 241–3, 246, 248, 262, 263–4, 267, 281, 332, 339–40, 343–5

Becket as a doctor   153, 154, 182, 201, 248
saints as doctors   264
see also medicine (of human doctors); surgery
dreams, see visions
dropsy   153–4, 210, 248, 252, 265, 280, 290
drowning   268–9, 269–70, 277–8, 301–4, 337–8, 349–51, 352–3
folk belief that a person baptized on Whitsun eve could not drown   326
see also sea travel
Durand, son of Osborn of Eu   245
dysentery   128–30; see also diarrhea; flux

Eda, venerable woman from Scotland   267
Edilda, inhabitant of Canterbury   117–18
Edmund, archdeacon of Coventry   230, 307
Edmund, inhabitant of Canterbury   35, 118–19
Edric, inhabitant of Worcester   202
Edric, priest of Ramsholt   198–9
Edward Grim, hagiographer   3, 50, 55–6, 70, 208 n.77
Edwin, inhabitant of Dover   135–6
Eilgar, inhabitant of Calne   247
Eilward, inhabitant of Tenham   121
Eilward of Westoning   1, 24, 41, 44, 50, 80, 222–9, 325–7
Eilwecher, sailor of Dover   258
Eilwin, inhabitant of Berkhamsted   173–4
Eleanor of Aquitaine, queen of England   283, 307, 339–40
Elias, knight and reeve of Froyle   237, 307
Elias, monk of Reading   281, 339
Elias, nephew of Richard, dean *de Siburna*   292
Elias of Evesham, compiler of the *Quadrilogus II*   1, 11, 70
Eliza, inhabitant of Dunton   210
Eliza, inhabitant of Middleton   264–5
Elvida, inhabitant of Beckenham   137
Elward, inhabitant of Selling   134
Emelina, inhabitant of Canterbury   115–16
Emelina, with excessive menstrual flow   190–1
Emma, inhabitant of Thanington   137–8
Emma, wife of knight Robert de Sancto Andrea   39–40, 48, 92–3, 316
epilepsy   80, 189–90, 244, 247, 292–1; see also fits
Eremburga, inhabitant of London   1, 140–1
Ernald, baker of earl Simon de Senlis   248

Ernald from region of Thérouanne and Ponthieu   245–6
Ernulf from region of Thérouanne and Ponthieu   245–6
Ethelburga, matron known to Christ Church monks   119–20
Etheldreda, inhabitant of Canterbury   107
Everard, chaplain of St. Marys, Winchester   239–40

facial disfigurement, miracles involving   122–3, 129, 187, 198, 260, 268; see also leprosy
fasting, voluntary and involuntary   114, 136, 154–6, 200, 229, 237, 239, 241, 263, 275, 332, 335
fevers   101, 107, 115, 142, 151, 177–8, 201, 204–5, 255, 297, 341–2
fires
averted miraculously   232–3, 234
folk belief that person baptized on Whitsun eve could not be burned   326
lit to warm the drowned   277, 304, 338
miraculous relighting of candles   168–72
fistula   144–5, 245–6, 267–8
fits   150, 153, 292–3
Fitz-Eisulf, Jordan, see Jordan, son of Eisulf
Flanders and the Flemish, miracles concerning   133–4, 201–2, 279, 282
flux, miracles involving   128–30, 146, 183–5, 245–6, 280, 283, 297–8; see also diarrhea
foreign objects in body, vomiting, nausea   197
fruit pits   119, 155–6
"seeds" or "material" of disease or illness   129–30, 155, 178, 280
polyp   155
water (from drowning)   269, 353
worms   123, 153
see also accidents; nosebleeds; kidney stones; pregnancy and childbirth
France and French pilgrims, miracles concerning   27 n.79, 84–5, 187, 229(?), 242–6, 247, 257, 263–4, 267–8, 283(?), 288–9, 290
Frodo, from Bury St. Edmunds   138–9

Galen, ancient writer and physician   344
Geldewin, son of Godefrid the baker   114
genitals (male), miracles involving   80, 153, 174, 221–9, 246, 325–7
Geoffrey, blacksmith of Linby   279

Geoffrey, dean of Gloucester 300, 348
Geoffrey Malaeartes, knight 249–50
Geoffrey, monk of Mont-Dieu 290
Geoffrey of Wallingford, monk of Reading 289–90, 308, 340–1
Geoffrey, son of Liviva of Chalgrave 162
Geoffrey, son of Robert and Leticia of Winchester 290–1, 341–2
Gerard of Lille, youth of Flanders 282
Gerard of Samford, knight of Flanders 279
Germany and German pilgrim, miracle concerning 252
Gervase of Canterbury, historian and monk of Christ Church 7, 10, 14, 17, 55
Gilbert, baker of Rochester 232–3
Gilbert Foliot, bishop of London 9, 46, 195, 308, 311, 320, 322
Gilbert Foliot, steward and relative of Gilbert Foliot, bishop of London 195–6, 308
Gilbert, inhabitant of the Isle of Thanet 163
Gilbert of St. Valery, leper 283
Gilbert, shoemaker of London 144
Gilbert, son of Wulviva and Ralph of Sarre 269–70
Gilbert, son of William of Brun 297
Girard, sailor of Dover 330
glass vessels, containing blood or water relic 104–5, 193–4, 289
Godbold, inhabitant of Boxley, daughters of 214–15
Godefrid, baker of Christ Church 114–15, 308
Godeliva, inhabitant of Canterbury 125
Godfrey, bishop of St. Asaph and abbot of Abingdon 25, 283, 308–9, 339–40
Godfrey, son of Adam of Lillingston 186, 309
Goditha, daughter of Baldwin of Wye 170–1
Goditha, inhabitant of Canterbury 108
Goditha, inhabitant of Hayes 210
Godiva, inhabitant of Chelmsford 162
Godiva, inhabitant of Stratford 177
Godwin, inhabitant of Braithwell 188–9
gout, in arm 120
Griffin, inhabitant of Wales 192–3
Guncelin, monk of Norwich 152
Gunnilda *de Elfiestun* 172
Gunnilda *de Hameldene* 183–4
Gunnilda, inhabitant of Luton 190

Hadewisa, servant of Richard, dean 292
Haimo, inhabitant of Essex 126
hairshirt for the dying 275, 335
hairshirt of Becket, *see* Becket, clothing of
Hamelin de Warenne, earl 272, 309, 333
headache and brain 121, 137, 154, 154–5, 155–6, 246
heart problems 172–3, 210, 280
Hedewic, tanner of Gloucester 211
hemorrhoids 278
Henry I, king of England 131
Henry II, king of England 8–9, 37, 47, 61–7, 72, 84 n.7, 285, 331
  agreement with Becket at Fréteval 64–5
  and Alexander III, pope 21, 47
  and Benedict of Peterborough 55–6
  dispute with Becket 8–9, 14, 37, 61–7, 224 n.6
  penance for Becket's murder 21, 54
Henry de Longavilla, knight 189, 229 n.11, 309
Henry *de Topindenne* 215
Henry, inhabitant of Fordwich 120–1
Henry of Houghton, master and clerk of Becket 35, 205–8, 309
Henry, sailor of London 255
Henry, son of Aliza of Northampton 213–14
Henry, son of Eilmer and Edilda *de Beche* 139
Henry, son of Elias, of the marshes 176
Henry, son of William, knight of Kelvedon 153
Henry the Younger, son of King Henry II 60, 62, 64–6, 86 n.10, 306, 308–9, 311, 317
  coronation of 60, 62, 63 n.8, 64
  Becket's affection for 64
hepatic, *see* liver problems
Herbert of Bosham, clerk and hagiographer 13, 69 n.22
Hermer, son of Tetion 243
hernia 212–13, 287–8, 293–5, 343; *see also* prolapsed rectum
Hingan, neighbor of Robert *de Beveruno* 292–3
hospitals 57, 102, 161 n.83, 229, 247
Huelina, daughter of Aaliza of London 93–4
Hugh, cellarer of Jervaulx Abbey 204
Hugh de Beauchamp, baron of Eaton Soton 153–4, 310
Hugh de Puiset, bishop of Durham 26, 63 n.8, 227–8, 310–11, 323

Hugh, inhabitant of Ebblingham   299, 344–6
Hugh Morville, murderer of Becket   67, 310, 323, 331
Hugh, son of William of Bourne   145
Hugo de Tukin, knight of Provins   267–8
humor and laughter, miracles involving   145–6, 180–1, 198–9;
   derisive humor, 180–1, 181, 182, 183, 250
Humphrey, of the diocese of Chesterton   230–2

incantations and charms   125, 141, 143, 198
Ingelram, son of Stephen de Meinil (of Goulton), knight   261–3, 331–2
Ingram, bishop of Glasgow   354
injuries
   arm/hand injuries   202, 223, 242, 326
   eye injury   249
   head injury   223, 326
   leg/foot injuries   147, 187, 213, 201
   inflicted on Becket and the church   63–6
   on side of body, leading to miscarriage   172
   prolapsed rectum described as injury   243–4
   see also blinding, judicial punishment; castration; wounds
insanity and mental disorder   114, 116, 120–1, 134, 140–1, 150, 243, 252, 253, 265, 266
   acting as if insane   66, 197, 213, 226, 243, 245, 263, 271, 294, 344
   weary of life due to illness   128
   see also suicide (attempted)
invocation of Becket's name   102, 146, 148, 160, 191, 211, 234, 253, 254, 257, 266, 267, 279, 285, 290, 291, 347
Iselda, daughter of Henry de Longavilla, knight   189
Ivo, sailor of Lynn   258

James, son of Roger de Clare and Matilda de St. Hilary   41–2, 44, 52, 293–5, 312–13, 342–4
Jervaulx, abbey of   204–5
Jewish woman of Canterbury, miracle involving   125
Jocelin de Bohun, bishop of Salisbury   25, 63 n.8, 283–4, 311, 323
John, inhabitant of Bennington   199–200
John, inhabitant of Valenciennes   288–9
John Kinstan, abbot of Jervaulx   35, 204–5, 311

John of Salisbury, clerk of Becket and hagiographer   9, 15, 19, 50, 67, 79 n.13, 105 n.67, 306, 311–12, 320, 322
   censure of Becket's argument with the knights   67
John of the Chapel, clerk of Roger, archdeacon of Shrewsbury   155–6
John, servant of Sweyn of Roxburgh   303–4, 352–4
John, son of Vivian, borough reeve   185, 311
Jordan, son of Eisulf   41, 44, 270–4, 312, 324, 333–4
judicial trials, miracles concerning   221–9, 285, 286, 326–7
Juliana, daughter of Gerard of Rochester   248
Juliana, inhabitant of Godmersham   280
Juliana, wife of Robert Puintel, knight   142–3

kidney problems   139–40, 173–4, 205
kidney stones   161, 279, 292

Laetitia, born of noble father and humble mother   249
Lambert, inhabitant of St. Omer   242
lameness and mobility problems   23, 35, 38–9, 80, 108, 115–16, 117–18, 119, 131–2, 132, 135–6, 136–7, 137–8, 138–9, 139, 139–40, 147–9, 149–50, 163, 172, 173–4, 176–7, 185, 187, 188–9, 192–3, 201, 213–14, 214–15, 245–6, 267
   lame since birth   139, 176–7, 213–14, 214–15
   recovery tested   177
Lefseda, of the marshes   162
leprosy   229–30, 230–2, 247, 271–2, 281–2, 282, 283, 283–4, 284–5, 299, 333–4, 338–9, 339–40, 344–6
   Becket cures more lepers than any other saint   232
   relapses of   230, 283
   spiritual leprosy, cure of   345–6
Leuric, inhabitant of Barking in Suffolk   211
lientery   128–30; see also dysentery
light, miraculous   170, 215; see also candles; fires
liturgy and liturgical celebration
   biblical allusions and   38–9
   celebration of the Mass   97, 148, 158, 194, 232, 244, 294, 335, 347
   English going to taverns on feast days   222

Office for Becket by Benedict of
Peterborough   4, 51–5, 85 n.8, 89
n.21, 91 n.26, 172 n.14, 222 n.3, 237
n.32
priest celebrates Becket as martyr before
canonization   227
priests unable to conduct services due to
illness   148, 207
stress on events in Lent 1171 and at
Easter and Pentecost 1171 in the
Miracles   40–9
suspension of services due to
desecration of Canterbury
Cathedral   14, 47, 76–7, 93 n.32,
113, 116, 306
text of collect for Becket's aid   351
visions involving   83–4, 88–9, 89–90,
107
see also death and dying, ritual practices;
confession of sins; invocation of
Becket's name; prayer
liver problems   101–2, 248
Liveva, inhabitant of Darenth   179–80
Liveva, wife of Godric *de
Lefstanestun*   176
London, city of   96–7, 134–5, 140–1, 144,
151, 176, 255, 321
Luciana, daughter of Walter Torel   212

Mabel, daughter of Stephan *de
Aglandre*   263–4
madness, *see* insanity
Manwin, inhabitant of Canterbury   115
martyrdom, *see* Becket, death of
Mary, inhabitant of Rouen   244, 247 n.45
Matilda and Roger, inhabitants of London,
son of   144
Matilda de Percy, countess of
Warwick   294, 312
Matilda de St. Hilary, wife of earl Roger de
Clare   41–2, 44, 52, 293–5, 312–13,
343–4
Matilda, inhabitant of Canterbury, wife of
Ertin of Flanders   133–4
Matilda, inhabitant of Cologne   252
Matilda, widow of Robert, son of
Gilbert   29, 202–3, 316
Matilda, wife of Geoffrey Paris of
Ipswich   138
Matilda, wife of Silewin of Thornbury   197
Matilda, wife of William, son of
Robert   29, 202–3, 316
Melania, wife of William of Fontenay   268
measurement, of length of body, body
parts, and/or items to make
candles   120, 143, 144, 153–4,
198, 223, 241, 269, 298, 303, 326,
351; to make offering of silver
thread   268–9
medicine (of human doctors)   94, 115, 128,
143, 147, 198, 204, 264
menstrual flow, miracles concerning   190,
190–1
mental illness, *see* insanity
miracles
concerning accident and injury, *see*
accidents; drowning; foreign
objects; injuries; sea travel;
suffocation and breathing
problems; wounds
concerning animals, *see* animals
concerning demons, *see* demons and
evil spirits; epilepsy; fits; insanity
and mental disorder; suicide
(attempted)
concerning illness and disability, *see*
abscesses; arm pain; blindness
and eye problems; blisters;
cancer; constipation; contraction;
deafness and hearing problems;
death and dying; diarrhea; dropsy;
dysentery; epilepsy; fevers; fits;
fistula; flux; foreign objects;
genitals; gout; headache and brain;
heart problems; hemorrhoids;
hernia; kidney problems; kidney
stones; lameness and mobility
problems; leprosy; lientery;
liver problems; menstrual flow;
muteness and speech problems;
nosebleeds; paralysis; pestilence;
phthisis; pregnancy and childbirth;
prolapsed rectum; pustules;
quinsy; sclerosis (of liver); smell
(sense of); stomach problems;
swelling; suffocation and breathing
problems; toothache; ulcers; uterus;
viscera
concerning mental illness, *see* demons
and evil spirits; epilepsy; fits;
insanity and mental disorder;
suicide (attempted)
concerning natural forces, *see* ale-
making; ampullas; candles; fires;
glass vessels; light; rain; pyxes; sea
travel
concerning justice and behavior, *see*
blinding; castration; judicial trials;
punishments
concerning lost and found, multiplying
or disappearing items, *see* anchors;
ampullas; Becket, blood of; cheese

and dairy products; coins; glass vessels; humor and laughter; pyxes; water relic
concerning or involving visions, *see* visions and dreams
cure of the soul through confession more glorious than cure of body   175
denied to boys sleeping on tomb   121–2, 122
greatest, the thronging of the people   91
of good deaths   156–7, 157–8
termed delightful, sport, and/or joke miracles   123–6, 145–6, 181–2; *see also* humor and laughter
written account of miracles cures swelling   290
Miracles of St. Thomas Becket by Benedict of Peterborough   76–304
additions made after circulation begins   xi–xii, 53–4
biblical allusions and biblical parallelism in   xii, 37–49
captions not written by Benedict   xii
connective organization and miracle matching   30–7
dating of composition to 1171–3   20–1, 40–9, 50, 54
liturgical calendar, chronology, and dated miracles in   40–9
letters utilized in   25–6, 324
manuscript circulation of   xi–xii, 2–3
notetaking for   27–9
Prologue of   18, 21, 39, 50–2, 54
read aloud in chapterhouse   36
reconstruction of Becket's "first five" miracles   47–9, 92–7
three main categories of miracles in   22–7, 92
money, *see* alms; coins; offerings
Muriel, vomited fruit pits   35, 119
murderers of Becket   11–13, 60–74, 100, 310, 331; *see also* Hugh Morville; Reginald Fitz-Urse; Richard de Brito; William de Tracy
muteness and speech problems   96–7, 113–14, 135–6, 193, 212, 243, 289, 340–1

Newington, Kent, miracles at cross   208–15
Nicholas, son of Aileva   236, 313
Nicholas, son of Hugh de Beauchamp   153–4
nosebleeds   143–4, 204, 289
nuns and religious women, miracles involving   25, 102–3, 202–3, 235

oblations, *see* offerings
Odilda, inhabitant of Southwell   209
Odo of Falaise, knight   232
Odo, prior of Christ Church, Canterbury   9, 55, 57, 236, 288, 313, 340–1
offerings   93, 135, 143–4, 150, 154, 159–60, 174, 187, 202, 232, 241, 245, 243, 255–6, 258, 271
annual payment   197, 201, 229
belt   235
bent coins   196, 271
candles   120, 128, 168–9, 223, 298, 303
crosses (intended for St. James)   159
crutches   173, 174, 185, 189, 245
farthing   201
gold   256
hair   189
litter/bed   278
pennies   201, 202, 271, 229
silver thread   268–9
staff   116, 118, 127
stone removed from ear   245
vows of   93, 143, 196, 202, 241, 256, 271, 330
wax   160
wax in shape of anchor   258, 330
wax in shape of body part   150, 160, 187, 190–1
see also measurement for candles
Osbern, inhabitant of Lisieux   287–8

paralysis
of arm and/or hand   187–8, 207, 211, 262, 279, 280, 331–2
of body/general   80, 151, 155–6, 191–2, 239–40
of feet and legs   126–7
of tongue   96–7, 212
Passion of St. Thomas Becket by Benedict of Peterborough   1, 10–13, 60–75
comparison of Becket's death to Christ's   11–13
dating of to 1172, one of earliest accounts of Becket's death   49–50, 52, 54
surviving extracts found in *Quadrilogus II*   x–xi, 1, 11
peasants, miracles concerning   131, 145, 185 (villein), 250–1, 325
pestilence   198, 270–3
Peter de Arches, knight, healing of wife   278, 314
Peter *de Denintona*   286–7
Peter de Melida, master and clerk of Lincoln   151, 314
Peter, inhabitant of Essex   126
Peter of Celle, abbot of St.-Rémi   19, 290, 311, 313–14

GENERAL INDEX 379

Peterborough, Benedictine monastery of 56–7
Philip, cleric of Alnwick 246–7
Philip, son of Hugh Scot 277–8, 324, 337–8
phthisis 157–8
physicians, *see* doctors
pilgrimage to Canterbury
  barefoot 127, 263, 273, 286, 294–5, 344
  by boat or ship (within Britain) 140, 169, 205
  by cart 126, 129, 185, 250–1, 263
  by litter or carried 117, 127, 138, 139, 140, 172, 172–3, 173, 205, 267, 278
  delayed or put off 93, 102, 129, 244, 272–3, 333–4
  dispensing alms while on 227, 251, 253–4
  miracles occurring at different moments during 186
  predictions of Canterbury as a site for 90–1
  secret or unknown to the monks 97, 108, 116, 185, 230–1, 281, 283–4, 284–5, 339
  sites for Becket outside of Canterbury, *see* crosses; Newington, Kent; Whitchurch
  vows of 93, 94, 149–50, 150, 154, 159, 186, 188, 190, 197, 202, 241, 244, 245, 246, 256, 262, 263–4, 266, 271, 273, 286, 287–8, 292, 295, 298, 300, 301, 330, 333, 344, 348
  see also Flanders and Flemish pilgrims; France and French pilgrims; Germany and German pilgrim; sea travel; Scotland and Scottish pilgrims; Wales and Welsh pilgrims
pilgrimage to Compostela 91, 159, 252
pilgrimage to Jerusalem 90–1, 119, 223, 229–30, 252, 269
pilgrimage to Rome 91
pilgrimage to Saint-Gilles 91
Pontigny, abbot of 69
pope, *see* Alexander III
prayer
  at tomb or in cathedral 96, 101, 118, 121, 135, 172, 173, 174, 185, 188, 345
  facing in the direction of Canterbury 234
  lying prostate in 118, 120, 127, 129, 132, 139, 174, 229, 174, 259, 282, 284
  keeping vigil 96, 130, 143, 185, 187, 192, 224–6, 270, 327
  "presumptuous" 140
  recitation of the Lord's Prayer 199, 200, 256, 258, 259

text of collect (?) for Becket's aid 351
pregnancy and childbirth 102, 142–3, 172, 183–4, 241–2, 264–5; *see also* menstrual flow; swelling, breast; uterus
prolapsed rectum 242–3
punishments, miracles involving 123–5, 125, 126, 133–4, 141, 142, 144, 145–6, 179–80, 180–1, 181, 182, 182–3, 244, 249–50, 250, 250–1, 251, 270–4, 279, 324–5, 331–2
pustules 132, 198, 229, 246–7, 283
pyxes, wooden 102–3, 106, 123–5, 125, 126, 145–6, 179–80, 180–1, 181, 181–2, 236
  hung on the wall near Becket's tomb 181
  switch to metal ampullas 181–2
  water relic boiling in 123–5, 180–1

Quadrilogus II (Elias of Evesham) 1, 11, 60, 70
quinsy 142, 152, 199–200, 324–5

Radulf, monk of Byland Abbey 204
Ralph *de Hathfeld* 291–2
Ralph *de Tangis* 132
Ralph, fowler of Flanders, daughter of 201–2
Ralph, inhabitant of Bourne, daughter of 106
Ralph, inhabitant of Essex 160
Ralph, inhabitant of Sheppey 123–5
Ralph, monk of Christ Church 103–5
Ralph of Longueville, leper 229–30
Ralph, son of Ralph of Lincoln 143–4
Ralph, subprior of St. Augustine's, Canterbury 254–5
rain, miracle involving 235
Ranulf de Broc, king's official 9–10, 15, 46, 65, 68, 72, 100, 103, 314
Ranulph, priest of Froyle 237–41
Reading, abbey of 281–2, 289–90, 308, 322, 324, 338–9, 340–1
Reginald Fitz-Urse, murderer of Becket 60–71, 314
Reinard, burgess of Stafford 236
relics of Becket, *see* ampullas; Becket, blood of; Becket, body of; Becket, clothing of; Becket, dust of bed; Becket, tomb of; candles, miraculously relit preserved; pyxes; reliquary; water relic
relics, swearing on 62, 253, 257
reliquary, containing Becket's blood and hairshirt 294
resurrection miracles, *see* death and dying
Richard I, king of England 7

380 GENERAL INDEX

Richard, abbot of Sulby   193-4, 314-15
Richard de Brito, murderer of Becket   60 n.2
Richard de Lucy, royal justiciar   208 n.75, 208 n.77, 315
Richard *de Rokeleia*, knight   154
Richard, cellarer of Christ Church   12, 68, 74
Richard, cleric of the sheriff of Devon   253-4
Richard, knight of Stanley   205
Richard, master and monk of Ely   292, 315
Richard of Dover, archbishop of Canterbury   7, 50, 53, 80 n.16
Richard, scholar of Northampton   128-30
Richard, son of Roger of Salisbury   178-9
Richard, son of Eilnold of Bearsted   131-2
Richard Sunieve, shepherd   284-5
Richard Wise, member of Rohese de Vere's household   184-5
Robert, blacksmith on Isle of Thanet   120
Robert, canon of Croxton Abbey, Leicestershire   260
Robert, canon of St. Frideswide's, Oxford   146
Robert, clerk of Lincoln   258
Robert *de Baalim*   213
Robert *de Beveruno*   292
Robert de Broc, king's official   9-10, 15, 46, 65, 67-8, 103-4, 177, 315-16
Robert de Broi, prior of Lenton   236, 316
Robert de Sancto Andrea, knight   92-3, 316
Robert, inhabitant of London   176
Robert, knight, son of Jocelin of Springfield   156-7
Robert of Cricklade, prior of St Frideswide's, Oxford   146-9, 222 n.3, 225 n.5, 316
Robert of Swaffham, chronicler of Peterborough Abbey   7, 56-7, 59
Robert, sacrist of Christ Church   24, 138, 183, 287, 315
Robert, son of Asketil   287
Robert, son of Gilbert   29, 202, 316
Robert, son of Liviva of Rochester   268-9
Rochester, city of   114, 148, 184, 193-5, 206, 213, 232-3, 248, 251, 254, 268
Roger, archdeacon of Shrewsbury   317
Roger, clerk of London   151
Roger de Clare, earl of Hertford   41-2, 44, 52, 293-5, 317, 342-4
Roger de Pont L'Évêque, archbishop of York   37, 63 n.8, 311, 317, 346
Roger, knight, son of Herbert of Bisley   157-9

Roger, monk of Christ Church, abbot of St Augustine's   22, 56, 266-7, 317-18
Roger, son of Savaric de Vallibus, knight   297-8, 318
Rohese de Vere, countess   25, 184, 261, 318
rupture, *see* hernia

Saffrid, dean of Chesterton   230, 307
sailors, miracles involving   255-8, 328-30
St. Alban   205
St. Augustine's, abbey of   6, 56, 254-5
St. Catherine of Alexandria   275
St. Cecilia   212
St. Edith of Wilton   212
St. Edmund, martyr   138, 231, 264, 281
St. Etheldreda   211
St. Frideswide's, Oxford, priory of   146-9
St. Godric of Finchale   88 n.19
St. Giles   91
St. Ithamar of Rochester   194
St. James of Compestela   91, 159, 252
St. John's Abbey, Colchester   104
St. Lawrence   87
St. Leonard   264
St. Margaret of Antioch   264
St. Martin of Tours   170, 266
St. Omer   345
St. Peter (apostle)   279
St. Stephen (protomartyr)   87, 96
St. Thomas Becket, *see* Becket, Thomas, St.
St. Vincent   87
Salerna, daughter of Thomas of Ifield   301-3, 349-51
Samson, mute man cured on Easter   113-14
Samuel, cleric   215
Sandwich, port of   159, 282
Saxeva, inhabitant of Dover   127-8
sclerosis (of liver)   101
scourging   223, 326
Scotland and Scottish pilgrims, miracles concerning   267, 303-4, 352-4
sea travel, miracles involving   159, 160, 255, 256, 256-7, 257, 258, 328, 329, 330; *see also* sailors
Segiva, daughter of Richard of Essex   251-2
Seileva, inhabitant of Froyle   238-9
servants, miracles concerning
  female   133-4, 226, 237-8, 292
  male   99-101, 114-15, 201, 205-6, 284-5, 303-4
shepherds   145-6, 205-6, 284-5
ships, *see* sea travel
shoemakers   144, 200-1
Sibilla, matron   253
Silvester, treasurer and canon of

Lisieux 287–8, 318
Simeon, enemy of the martyr 25, 183
Simon de Senlis III, earl 25, 248, 318
skin problems, *see* abscesses; blisters; cancer; fistula; leprosy; ulcers
sleep, *see* visions and dreams
sleep disturbance, miracle concerning 98–9
sleeping on Becket's tomb 121–2, 122
sleeping outdoors resulting in illness 113, 132, 206
smell (sense of), miracle involving 121
Solomon, inhabitant of London 152
Stephen, canon of Bedford 261
Stephen de Meinil (of Goulton), knight 261–3, 318–19, 331–2
Stephen, knight of Holland 98–9, 319
stole
    Becket's 152
    priest's, blessed by Becket 102
stomach problems 119, 127–30, 144, 177, 183–4, 251–2, 280, 292; *see also* dropsy; flux; foreign objects; swelling; viscera
surgery, for hernia 293, 343
swelling
    arms/hands 94–5, 152, 160, 176, 259–60
    breast 238–9
    face/jaw 99–101, 122–3, 199–200, 229, 238, 245–6, 284
    eyes 162, 194–5, 206, 260, 298; horse's eye 190
    general/unspecified 142–3, 347
    genitals 174, 246
    head 93–4, 196, 260, 286–7
    kidneys 139–40
    legs/feet 108, 147–9, 188–9, 192–3
    neck 152
    stomach 107–8, 129–30, 177–8, 183–4, 261, 268, 278, 292, 304, 338
    uterus 203, 263–5
    see also dropsy; quinsy
suffocation and breathing problems 98–9, 157, 210, 286, 290–1, 292, 300, 324–5, 347; *see also* drowning
suicide (attempted) 301–3, 349–51

tanners 211, 213
tavern and wineseller's shop 144, 222, 326, 344
Tetion, son of Hertran 242–4
Theobald, archbishop of Canterbury 7–8, 336
Theodwin, papal legate 20–2, 51
Thomas of Etton, knight of region of York 142, 319, 324–5

Thomas of St. Valery, adolescent with foot injury 187
Thomas, son of Adam of the marshes 161
Thomas, venerable clerk 158–9
thread, *see* measurement; offering
toothache, miracle concerning 18, 99–101
clenched teeth 271, 277–8, 338, 341
Turstan of Croydon, clerk 275, 319–20, 336

ulcers 137–8, 150, 149–50, 229, 231, 246, 247, 274–7, 281, 284, 339–40; *see also* cancer; leprosy
uterus 184, 203, 241, 263–5

Vauluisant, abbot of 69
Vidoch *de Anoch* 244
Virgin Mary 86, 140, 170, 195, 226, 261, 279, 326, 343, 346
    altar of, in Canterbury Cathedral 16, 130, 132
    altar and image of, in St Mary's, Bedford 226, 327
viscera 151, 292; *see also* stomach
visions and dreams 72, 81–92, 96, 100, 107–8, 120, 127–8, 128–9, 130–1, 136, 139, 149–50, 155, 157, 161, 178–9, 188–9, 192–3, 199, 200–1, 205, 206, 214, 225–6, 228, 246, 250, 252, 255, 256–7, 258, 259, 262–3, 271–2, 282, 286, 229, 302, 304, 332, 302–3, 327, 332, 333–4, 348, 350, 352–3
    foretelling Canterbury's future 90–1
    liturgical visions 83–4, 88–9, 89–90, 107
    regarding Becket's blood 50, 178–9, 252, 262
    regarding Becket's position in heaven 86–8, 157
    regarding papal excommunication of murderers 100
    regarding rewards and punishments for the dead 275
    vision of Bartholomew, bishop of Exeter 84
    vision of Becket coming out of a shrine 246
    vision of Benedict of Peterborough 15, 42, 83–4
    vision of monk of Lewes, visited by dead monk 86–7
    vision of Orm 87–8
vomiting, *see* foreign objects
vows, *see* pilgrimage to Canterbury, vows of; measurement; offerings, vows of

382   GENERAL INDEX

Wales and Welsh pilgrims, miracles concerning   26, 59, 191–3, 265, 280
Walter, clerk of Hatcliffe   266
Walter de Walensis, abbot of Colchester   104, 320
Walter, inhabitant of Berkhamsted   174
Walter, knight of Lisors   247
wandering preacher   106
Warin Grosso, knight of Norfolk   259–60
water relic ("water of St Thomas" "water of Canterbury")   16–18, 35, 96–7, 107, 107–8, 115, 118, 119, 121, 122–3, 146, 148, 155–6, 156–7, 157–8, 159, 162, 177–8, 178–9, 179–80, 180–1, 181, 181–2, 182–3, 183, 183–4, 185, 193–4, 203, 204, 205, 210, 229–30, 230–2, 232–3, 235, 235–6, 237–8, 238–9, 242, 243, 244, 249–50, 250, 251–2, 259, 259–60, 260, 261, 263–4, 265, 270–4, 277–8, 280, 282, 286, 287, 289, 290, 292, 293, 297, 298, 333–4, 338, 339, 341, 343
  beginning of monks' practice of mixing blood and water   16–18, 96–7, 107–8
  changing into blood   235, 235–6
  containers kept hidden by pilgrims at first   182
  distribution of by monks to pilgrims   96–7, 107, 179–80
  importance of for spread of Becket's cult   17–18, 179, 182
  mocking of   183
  ordinary water presented as cures ill man   259
  similarities to Eucharist   17, 49, 97, 107
  stealing of, by women   179–80, 273–4
  termed "medicine"   108, 121, 134, 145, 156, 178, 194, 237, 259, 344
  see also Becket - blood of
wax, see candles, offerings
Wedeman, inhabitant of Folkestone, daughter of   175
Wekerilda, inhabitant of Horton   40, 136–7
Weremund, son of Wielard of Béthune   242–3
Whitchurch, relics and cures at   191–3
widows   202, 211, 269, 286
  five widows praying for recovery of drowned boy   269
  miracle concerning dowry   286
William I, king of Scotland   353–4
William, abbot of Croxton Abbey, Leicestershire   260, 315, 320
William Brito, son of Jordan son of Eisulf   270–4, 312, 333–4
William, cellarer of Christ Church   12, 68
William Crispin, youth of St. David's   280
William *de Benewella*, son of   251
William de Broc, brother of Robert de Broc   177–8
William de Tracy, murderer of Becket   60 n.2, 70
William de Vernon   263, 321
William de Warenne, knight   236
William FitzStephen, clerk and hagiographer   15, 27, 48, 70
William, inhabitant of Baldock, daughter of   298
William, inhabitant of Gloucester   299–301, 346–8
William, inhabitant of Horsepool   265
William, inhabitant of London   134–5
William, knight of Chester   160
William of Canterbury, monk of Christ Church and hagiographer   3–5, 7, 10, 13, 27–8, 50–1, 55
  begins composition of his *Miracles of St Thomas Becket* in 1172   27
  his accounts of the "parallel miracles" (miracles also described in Benedict's *Miracles*)   4–5, 323–54
William of Dene, knight of region of Canterbury   38, 126–7
William of Earley, knight   149–50, 306, 320–1
William of Monkton, cleric   50–1
William, owner of houses of Yarmouth   234
William Patrick, servant of William of Warbleton   99–101
William, priest of Bourne   105–6, 321
William, priest of London   17–18, 48–9, 96–7, 321
William, son of citizen of Canterbury   107–8
William, son of Eudes of Parndon   234
William, son of Payne *de Pech*   187–8
William, son of Ranulf, lord of Whitchurch   26, 191–2, 236 n.28, 321
William, son of wife of William of Lincoln   139–40
William the Templar, abbot of Reading Abbey   281–2, 322, 339
William Turbe, bishop of Norwich   26, 276–7, 322, 336–7
William, villein of Higham Ferrers   185
Wissant, church of St. Nicholas, relics held at   243
Wivelina, inhabitant of Littlebourne   196

Wlviva, inhabitant of Canterbury   35, 118
Wlviva, religious woman   52, 102–3
wounds
   Becket's from knights' swords   70
   from lance on jaw   267
   swearing by God's wounds   65
   thumb cut with knife   242
   "wound of disbelief"   146
   "wounds of the soul"   116
   see also accidents; blinding; cancer; castration; fistula; injuries

Other volumes in
Studies in the History of Medieval Religion

Details of volumes I–XLIX can be found on the Boydell & Brewer website.

L: St Stephen's College, Westminster: A Royal Chapel and English Kingship, 1348–1548
Elizabeth Biggs

LI: The Social World of the Abbey of Cava, c. 1020–1300
G. A. Loud

LII: Medieval Women Religious, c. 800–c. 1500: New Perspectives
Edited by Kimm Curran and Janet Burton

LIII: The Papacy and Ecclesiology of Honorius II (1124–1130): Church Governance after the Concordat of Worms
Enrico Veneziani

LIV: Women and Monastic Reform in the Medieval West, c. 1000–1500: Debating Identities, Creating Communities
Edited by Julie Hotchin and Jirki Thibaut

LV: Thomas of Eccleston's *De adventu Fratrum Minorum in Angliam* "The Arrival of the Franciscans in England", 1224–c.1257/8: Commentary and Analysis
Michael J. P. Robson

LVI: Religious Conflict at Canterbury Cathedral in the Late Twelfth Century: The Dispute between the Monks and the Archbishops, 1184–1200
James Barnaby

LVII: The Reception of Papal Legates in England, 1170–1250: Narrating the *Adventus* Ceremony
Emil Lauge Christensen

www.ingramcontent.com/pod-product-compliance
Lightning Source LLC
Chambersburg PA
CBHW052055300426
44117CB00013B/2131